Angélique Herzberg

Sustainability of External Imbalances

A Critical Appraisal

With a Preface by Prof. Dr. Heinz-Dieter Smeets

Springer Gabler

Angélique Herzberg
Düsseldorf, Germany

Dissertation Heinrich-Heine-Universität Düsseldorf, 2013

ISBN 978-3-658-07090-8 ISBN 978-3-658-07091-5 (eBook)
DOI 10.1007/978-3-658-07091-5

The Deutsche Nationalbibliothek lists this publication in the Deutsche Nationalbibliografie; detailed bibliographic data are available in the Internet at http://dnb.d-nb.de.

Library of Congress Control Number: 2014948137

Springer Gabler

Printed on acid-free paper

Springer Gabler is a brand of Springer DE.
Springer DE is part of Springer Science+Business Media.
www.springer-gabler.de

Preface

The term "global imbalances" denotes large and persisting current account surpluses and deficits between countries and country groups. The question of whether economies may have—or even should have—large surpluses and deficits in the current account ranks among the most controversial issues in international economics. Imbalances between the United States (as the largest deficit country) on the one hand and China, Germany, Japan, and the OPEC countries (as the largest surplus countries) on the other hand came to a head since the late 1990s. Many observers hold those imbalances to be one of the major causes of the global financial and economic crisis of 2008/2009. Although global imbalances had been somewhat reduced both during and after this financial crisis, most forecasts expect a renewed increase in the course of the coming years. These considerations lead to the question of how the limits of imbalances should be specified and, in particular, which imbalances should be regarded as excessive or unsustainable.

Against this background, Angélique Herzberg's dissertation deals with sustainability of external imbalances. The focus of this work lies, on the one hand, in a critical discussion of different methods available for assessing external sustainability and, on the other hand, in a discussion of the empirical studies on sustainability which are usually based on time series or panel tests. However, the large number of both theoretical concepts and empirical methods makes it difficult to arrive at a uniform conclusion regarding external sustainability of a country or group of countries.

Angèlique Herzberg also discusses the indicator-based scoreboard of the procedure for preventing and correcting macroeconomic imbalances in the European Union. However, the scoreboard's indicators are intended only to identify that an imbalance exists; to determine whether it is sustainable or not, requires further analysis. Nevertheless, the relevant empirical studies find some (although not unanimous) evidence that those indicators could have sent early warning signals of an upcoming sovereign debt and financial crisis.

Her thesis provides a comprehensive and most competent overview of the literature on external imbalances. Both the theoretical approaches and methods as well as the results of a large number of empirical studies on sustainability are presented and assessed. A comparable systematic survey has been lacking so far, although the theoretical and empirical literature on sustainability is large and heterogeneous. For all those who deal with the issue of global imbalances, both in academia and in practice, the present work gives valuable ideas and considerations.

Düsseldorf, June 2014 *Professor Dr. Heinz-Dieter Smeets*

Acknowledgments

This work is a doctoral thesis, written while I was a research assistant at Heinrich Heine University, Düsseldorf, briefly interrupted by visits to the University of California, Berkeley, and Princeton University.

It is a great pleasure to acknowledge the support of many people who have in one way or another contributed to the successful completion of this dissertation. First and foremost, I would like to express my deepest gratitude to my supervisor, Professor Dr. Heinz-Dieter Smeets, for his very valuable and helpful guidance at all stages of this thesis. I am also truly indebted to him for always supporting me in my efforts to balance work and family. Then I would like to thank my second advisor, Professor Dr. Albrecht F. Michler, not least for agreeing to review such a long thesis.

Our department provides an amazing social environment in a cordial atmosphere. It has been an invaluable source of support, and I would like to thank all my present and former colleagues, many of whom have become good friends over the years. In particular, I am grateful to Dipl.-Kff. Laura Cüppers, Dr. Christian Fürtjes, Dr. Lucas Kramer, Dipl.-Oec. Anita Schmid, and Marco Zimmermann, M.A., for all the lively discussions and helpful comments, for reading through parts of my thesis, for relieving my work burden during the last stage of my thesis, as well as for joyful conversations over coffee. Special and heartfelt thanks go to Birgit Knoke und Dipl.-Soz. Dagmar Neumann for strongly supporting and encouraging me even since I was an undergraduate. I also thank Dr. Monika Bucher and Dr. Achim Hauck who have helped me overcome several difficulties in writing the introduction. Many thanks go to Tim Böker, M.Sc., for thorough and detailed discussions of my econometric results. I am also very grateful to Markus Penatzer, M.Sc., for being always at help with technical problems (whether it was my computer or a dish washer). Further I am indebted to Inna Kurennoy and Rebecca Rothe, M.Sc., for their outstanding research assistance (which even included working on weekends to bring certain tricky tables of mine into final form). Not least, I am obliged to Dr. Kathrin Berensmann of the German Development Institute who helped me gain a better understanding of how the IMF's debt sustainability analyses and debt sustainability framework relate. Needless to say, I take sole responsibility for all remaining inadequacies of this work.

On a personal note, I would like to thank my family and friends for their continual support. It was a privilege to be surrounded by caring and loving people during the—sometimes quite difficult—time of thesis writing. A tremendous "thank you" goes to my husband who invested much time and patience in proofreading my thesis, was always ready to help fixing various mathematical and LaTeX problems and who endured an irritable and stressed me for quite a long time. I also thank my wonderful son for his sweet smile which always cheered me up. To my parents, I am infinitely grateful for taking care of my son and being always generous with their time and resources in a way I can never repay. Finally, the last word of acknowledgement is to God. He has been my major source of strength and without Him none of this would have been possible.

Düsseldorf, July 2014 *Angélique Herzberg*

Contents

1
Introduction

If something cannot go on forever, it will stop (Stein, 1997).

1.1 Motivation and aim of the study

In particular since the mid-1990s, sustainability of large and persistent current account positions—a deficit in the United States matched by surpluses run notably by Japan, China, Germany, and oil-exporting countries[1]—have been attracting much attention from policy makers and economists alike. The emergence of so-called "global imbalances" has been accompanied by two other developments: the "uphill" flow of financial capital from emerging markets to industrial countries and a large accumulation of international currency reserves.

For the United States and selected surplus countries, figures 1.1 and 1.2 show the evolution of the current account balances in proportion to gross domestic product (GDP) and in billions of US dollar (USD), respectively. Following Belke and Schnabl (2013), one can distinguish four generations of global imbalances. The first generation is given by the imbalance between the United States and Japan which emerged in the early 1980s after the liberalization of capital flows in Japan and a monetary tightening in the United States. After the Plaza agreement of 1987, the imbalance of the first generation experienced a decline which lasted until 1991. The second generation arose in the early/mid-1990s when the imbalance between the United States and Japan resumed its increase and Asian economies, in particular China, started running large current account surpluses. In 2002, oil-exporting economies joined the group of the surplus countries (see figures 1.1 and 1.2); this is the third generation. Finally, the fourth generation of imbalances originated in the euro area since 2002. Figure 1.3 plots the current account surpluses in selected "northern" countries and current account deficits in the main "southern" countries in the euro area. Global imbalances reached their climax between 2006 and 2008: For instance, the US current account deficit rose to 6.4 percent of GDP (800.6 billions USD) in 2006 and the Chinese current account surplus amounted to almost 10 percent of GDP (420.6 billions USD) in

[1] Oil-exporting countries include Algeria, Angola, Azerbaijan, Bahrain, Colombia, Republic of Congo, Ecuador, Equatorial Guinea, Gabon, Indonesia, Iran, Kazakhstan, Kuwait, Libya, Mexico, Nigeria, Norway, Oman, Qatar, Russia, Saudi Arabia, Sudan, Syria, Trinidad and Tobago, Turkmenistan, United Arab Emirates, Venezuela, and Yemen.

Fig. 1.1: Current account balances for selected countries (in percent of GDP)

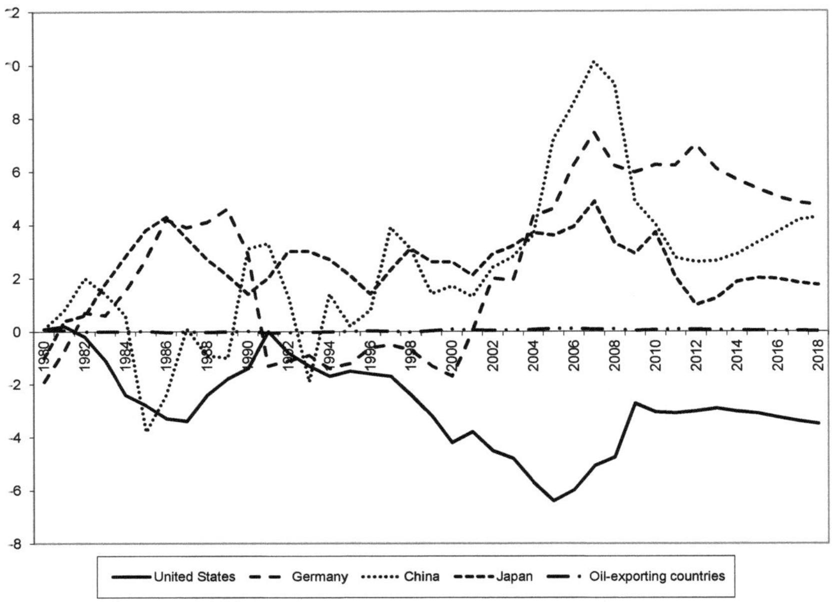

Source: International Monetary Fund, World Economic Outlook Database, April 2013.
Notes: Estimates start after 2011 for the United States and after 2012 for the remaining countries. For the definition of oil-exporting countries see footnote 1 on page 1.

2008. After a temporary reduction over the course of the world financial crisis, the US current account deficit has been widening again since 2009 (see figure 1.2).

A number of explanations have been put forward to account for the current pattern of global imbalances:[2] During the second half of the 1990s, the expectations of higher productivity growth in the United States relative to other countries have triggered both capital inflows and an increase in the US investment and consumption (Mann, 2002; Blanchard and Milesi-Ferretti, 2010). In the early 2000s, loose monetary policy in the United States and in many other countries—combined with a fall of interest rates due to the collapse of the "dot-com" bubble—have contributed to the "global liquidity glut" which boosted private credit-financed consumption, decreased saving, and worsened current account positions (Bernanke, 2005; Bracke and Fidora, 2008; Obstfeld and Rogoff, 2009; Taylor, 2010; Eickmeier et al., 2013). A large deterioration in the US fiscal balance from the early 2000s on, which further pushed down US

[2] A survey of explanations for global imbalances is provided by Backus et al. (2009) and Servén and Nguyen (2010).

Fig. 1.2: Current account balances for selected countries (in billions of USD)

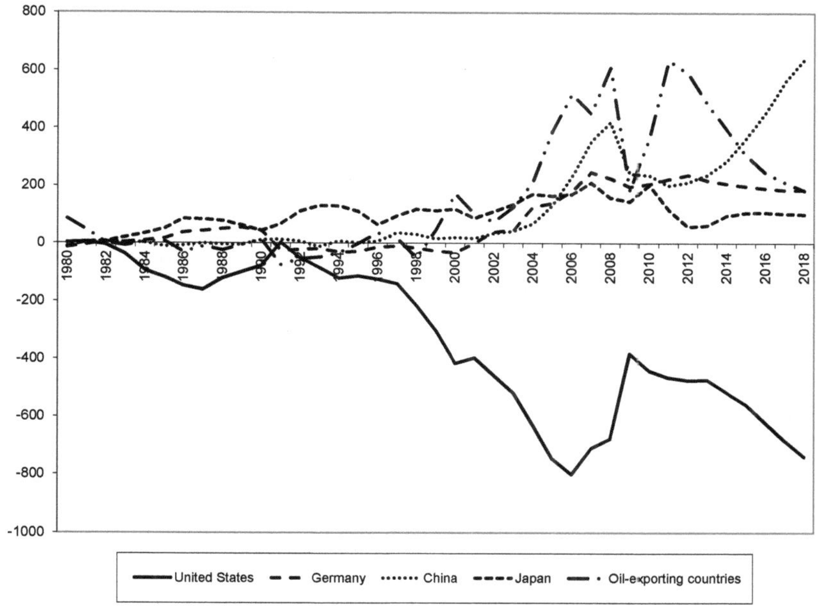

Source: International Monetary Fund, World Economic Outlook Database, April 2013.
Notes: Estimates start after 2011 for the United States and after 2012 for the remaining countries. For the definition of oil-exporting countries see footnote 1 on page 1.

saving, also have fueled the US current account deficit—thus leading to "twin deficits" (Kraay and Ventura, 2005; Bartolini and Lahiri, 2006; Bussiére et al., 2010). Further, the drop in the US national saving rate has resulted from the emergence of a "global savings glut" mainly arising from the accumulation of foreign reserves on the part of developing and emerging market countries with the purpose of building up a buffer stock against future financial crises or preventing currency appreciation by foreign exchange interventions (Bernanke, 2005; Chinn and Ito, 2007; Caballero et al., 2008a). In addition, windfall gains in oil-exporting countries due to a rise in oil prices have significantly contributed to the global savings glut (Higgins et al., 2006; IMF, 2006b; Arezki and Hasanov, 2013). Moreover, global imbalances have been attributed to demographic differences between countries (Feroli, 2003; Ferrero, 2010) as well as differences in financial development (Mendoza et al., 2009; Forbes, 2010). On a different note, Hausmann and Sturzenegger (2006, 2007) argue that the US current account deficit has been largely overestimated due to the mismeasurement of the income flows, in particular on foreign direct investment—the so called "dark matter". Gourinchas and Rey (2007a) point out that the

United States benefit from the "exorbitant privilege" by issuing short-term, low-return liabilities and mainly investing in higher-yield equity and direct investment abroad.

The recent pattern of global imbalances has also been compared to the Bretton-Woods System (BWS) which came to an end in 1973. According to Dooley et al. (2003, 2004a,b), the "revived BWS" (or BWS II) consists of three pillars: (i) the center or intermediary country (the United States) with deep and liquid financial markets, (ii) the trade account region (i.e., Asian countries, most notably China) which pursues an export-led development strategy and manages its exchange rates against the currency of the center country by buying the center's securities and preventing capital inflows via capital controls and taxes, and (iii) the capital account region (comprised of Europe, Canada, Australia, and most of Latin America) which has floating exchange rates and private investors who care about the risk/return characteristics of the assets (as opposed to official investors in the trade account countries). The center country's current account deficit was primarily financed by the capital account region in the second half of the 1990s and by the trade account region from the 2000s on.

Alongside global imbalances, imbalances within the euro area started widening shortly after the introduction of the euro, while the aggregated euro-area current account remained roughly balanced.[3] "Core" or "northern" countries such as Germany, Austria, Finland, and the Netherlands have been displaying current account surpluses, and "peripheral" or "southern" countries such as Greece, Ireland, Italy, Portugal, and Spain (labelled as GIIPS or, less favorably, as PIIGS) have been running current account deficits. Figure 1.3 shows the diverging current account balances for selected countries in the euro area. Thus in the euro area, capital has been flowing "downhill" from high-income countries to low-income countries (Blanchard and Giavazzi, 2002; Abiad et al., 2007; Ahearne et al., 2007; Waysand et al., 2010). Intra-euro imbalances have been boosted by the elimination of the exchange rate risk in a monetary union, the European Central Bank's anti-inflationary credibility, and the weak credibility of the no-bailout clause in the Maastricht Treaty—which all allowed southern countries to borrow at interest rates much lower than those before the introduction of the euro, thus creating incentives to larger public and private spending and stimulating credit, consumption, and housing investment booms (Lane and Milesi-Ferretti, 2007; Bonatti and Fracasso, 2013; Körner and Zemanek, 2013). Although nominal exchange rates have remained fixed in the European Monetary Union, high inflation rates in peripheral countries led to a large real exchange rate appreciation in those countries (Coudert et al., 2013). As a consequence, an increase in relative prices and unit labor costs have worsened the competitiveness of the southern countries and fostered the current account deficits (Gaulier and Vicard, 2012; Belke and Dreger, 2013). While the GIIPS' borrowing was first mainly financed by private lenders, central bank credit more and more replaced private financing since the temporary breakdown of the interbank market in August 2007, thus leading to a large accumulation of Target liabilities, i.e., liabilities of the national central banks in the euro area towards the Eurosystem (Sinn and Wollmershäuser, 2012).

Global imbalances are often held to be one of the major causes of the current financial crisis: Firstly, the global savings glut have depressed long-term real interest rates, thus encouraging investors' hunt for yield and fueling asset price bubbles in the housing markets (Bernanke, 2009). Secondly, inflows of easy foreign borrowing have allowed the deficit countries (notably the United States and the euro-area periphery) to postpone necessary macroeconomic policy

[3] An overview of intra-euro imbalances can be found in Bonatti and Fracasso (2013) and Bertola et al. (2013).

Fig. 1.3: Current account balances in the euro area (in billions of USD)

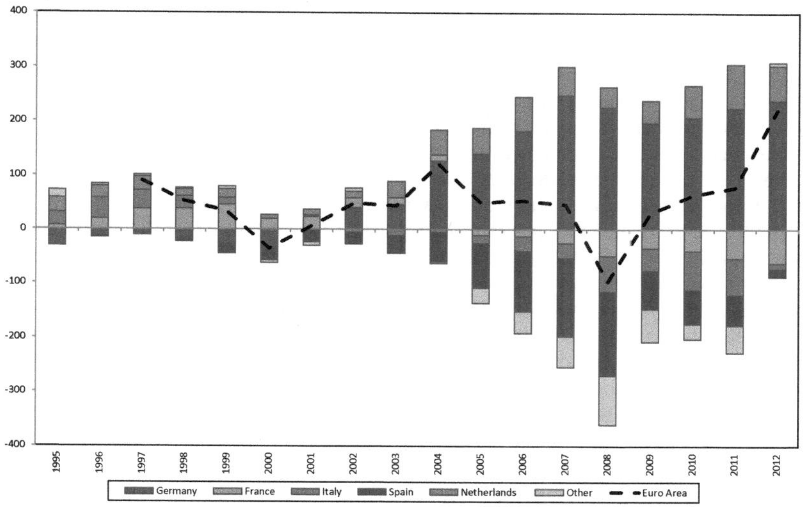

Source: International Monetary Fund, World Economic Outlook Database, April 2013.

measures such as fiscal consolidation (Obstfeld and Rogoff, 2009). Another view is that both global imbalances and the financial crisis are only the symptoms caused by the same disease: the excess supply of savings in combination with financial market distortions (Caballero et al., 2008b; Obstfeld and Rogoff, 2009; Acharya and Schnabl, 2010).

A decline in asset prices, the outbreak of the subprime and financial crisis as well as the decline in the oil prices and the worldwide recession contributed to the contraction of global imbalances starting in 2007 after they reached a peak around 2005/2006. The spillover of the US subprime crisis to Europe and the structural weaknesses in the euro-area periphery—such as high indebtedness of the public sector (e.g., Greece, Italy, Portugal) or of the private sector (e.g., Spain, Ireland) and the lack of competitiveness—precipitated a confidence crisis which led to a sudden stop in capital flows and ultimately to a reduction of the current account deficits in these countries.

However, the shrinkage of the US current account deficit was only a temporary phenomenon: Due to investors' "flight to safety" during the financial crisis, capital inflows into the United States were renewed through 2009/2010 and the US current account deficit widened again. By now, global imbalances and intra-euro imbalances still persist, albeit at a smaller magnitude than prior to the financial crisis. Before the financial crisis, one of the most controversial issues was how long global imbalances are going to continue. Now, after the recent "revival" of global imbalances, this issue is on the agenda again. Moreover, whenever large current account positions have emerged in the past, they have always triggered a debate on their sustainability.

The present dissertation extends the existing literature in at least two ways. Firstly, it provides a comprehensive investigation of both the methods and empirical studies available for assessing sustainability of external imbalances. Though the theoretical and empirical literature on external sustainability is large and heterogeneous, a systematic survey has been lacking so far. When evaluating the sustainability measures (empirical tests and indicators), we focus primarily on the question of how accurately these measures can judge whether a path of external imbalances is sustainable and whether they provide information on the size, the manner, and the timing of the adjustment required to maintain or restore external sustainability. This study also takes the research in areas related to the issue of external sustainability, such as the literature on fiscal sustainability and on current account reversals, into consideration.

Secondly, we examine for each sustainability measure whether, and if so, how it can be used to assess sustainability of actually observed global imbalances. In particular, as a part of this investigation, we apply time series techniques to analyze sustainability in the United States—an economy which plays a pivotal role in the recent global imbalances. For this purpose, we employ a methodology suggested by Bohn (2007)—which is the most general by now—to test an economy's sustainability based on the intertemporal budget constraint. So far, this methodology has only been used in the panel study by Durdu et al. (2010), which, however, sheds little light specifically on sustainability in the United States. In addition, we exploit the data on the US net international investment position measured at market value that was constructed by Gourinchas and Rey (2007b) and is the longest available data set on market value estimates. Relying on market values (rather than on historical cost) permits the inclusion of valuation effects arising from changes in asset prices and exchange rates. The recent research on international macrofinance stresses the significant impact of valuation effects on the external adjustment (Tille, 2003; Gourinchas and Rey, 2007a,b; Pavlova and Rigobon, 2010a,b). Tille (2003) estimates that nearly one third of the deterioration in the US net international investment position since the end of 1999 results from valuation effects.

1.2 Preliminaries: defining the main concepts

1.2.1 External imbalances

Global imbalances are usually associated with large and diverging current account positions. However, focusing solely on the current account ignores the financial dimension of imbalances (Bracke et al., 2008, p. 12). Therefore, alongside with the current account balances, we also analyze flow concepts (the capital and financial accounts) and the net international investment position which is a stock concept. Another possibility to arrive at a broader notion of global imbalances is to use the concept of the external imbalance which is defined as the imbalance in the "overall account", that is, the balance of payments net of changes in reserve assets (Gandolfo, 2001, pp. 64-66; Salvatore, 2007, pp. 461, 644). A deficit (surplus) in the overall account corresponds to an increase (decrease) in reserve assets, and the external balance is restored when the economy records no changes of reserve assets. In a floating exchange rate regime in which monetary authorities typically do not intervene in exchange markets, the stock of reserve assets does not significantly change so that the external balance is approximately zero. In this case, it is more insightful to examine the imbalances in the current, financial, and capital accounts separately rather than the total external balance.

Although the word "imbalance" does have a negative connotation by indicating that whatever is literally out of balance requires a correction, an external imbalance by itself is not necessarily a worrisome development; whether it is to be judged as "bad" or "good" depends on the factors which caused it to occur. The current account of open economies, for example, typically does not need to be balanced. According to the intertemporal approach to the current account, current account deficits or surpluses allow open economies to gain from intertemporal trade and to smooth consumption (Obstfeld and Rogoff, 1996, p. 8). Proponents of the twin-deficit theory, for example, would typically judge a current account deficit which is accompanied by a fiscal deficit as bad. In contrast, a current account deficit which reflects a surge in investment resulting from a relatively high growth of a country's productivity might be referred to as good. We again take a broad stance and use the term "external imbalance" both in a positive and in a negative sense.

Regarding the term "global imbalances", there have been only few attempts (e.g., ECB, 2007; Bracke et al., 2008; Dunaway, 2009) at defining them rigorously. We mainly follow the definition suggested by the ECB (2007, p. 62) and Bracke et al. (2008, p. 12) and denote by global imbalances external imbalances of (presumably) systemically important economies that potentially reflect economic distortions or are a source of risks for the global economy. However, a drawback of this definition is that there are no standard criteria by which to judge the systemic importance of an economy nor does there exist a commonly accepted list of systemically important countries. Large economies might be regarded as systemically important, yet small economies can also jeopardize global economic stability; the two prominent examples are Thailand during the 1997-98 Asian financial crisis (ECB, 2007, p. 63) and Greece during the recent European sovereign debt crisis. Further, since large external imbalances are likely to send negative repercussions to the world economy, a related question is whether there is a critical size when external imbalances become global imbalances. However, so far the term "global imbalances" has not been linked to a particular size or a dispersion of external imbalances.

Finally, it bears emphasizing that while the present study is motivated by and deals with recent global and intra-euro imbalances, it does not confine to these phenomena. This broader avenue allows us to evaluate a greater number of empirical studies on sustainability since large external imbalances are not a new phenomenon.

1.2.2 Sustainability concepts

Just as with global imbalances, there exists no single universally accepted notion of sustainability of external imbalances (or, briefly, external sustainability). Instead, a number of concepts emerged which capture different dimensions of complexity involved in defining sustainability. In a general sense, the term "sustainability" (derived from the Latin verb *sustinēre*) may refer to a situation in which a certain state or process can be kept up, maintained, or prolonged (Pitchford, 1995, p. 123; Burnside, 2005, p. 11). In this spirit, external sustainability can be defined as a situation in which a path of external imbalances generates no economic forces of its own to change its trajectory (Mann, 1999, p. 151; Mann, 2002, p. 143; Holman, 2001, p. 15). Conversely, an unsustainable path of external imbalances exerts forces which induce a change in macroeconomic variables affecting the external imbalance (such as domestic saving and investment, economic growth, interest rates, or exchange rates), thereby precipitating a change in its own trajectory.

Consider, for example, an economy which runs trade deficits and accumulates net foreign debts, thus generating a series of growing current account deficits. At some point, international investors might question whether the economy will be able to repay them and refuse to buy domestic assets at current prices. Currency depreciation (or a decline in unit labor cost in a monetary union) and an increase in interest rates would reduce domestic consumption and investment, thus *ceteris paribus* bringing about a return of the current account to its sustainable trajectory (Mann, 2002, pp. 144-145). Even in the unlikely scenario in which global investors continued lending to the economy in question and the terms of finance remained unchanged, financial payments on economy's net foreign liabilities could become so large at some point that they exceeded an economy's ability to generate trade surpluses. This results in another definition of sustainability: The unsustainable path of external imbalances is one whose continuation (without policy and exogenous changes) would lead to the boundary of feasible values[4] of economic variables (Pitchford, 1995, p. 124).

Hence, one source for unsustainability arises from excessive foreign borrowing or, to put it differently, from insolvency. Insolvency is defined as the inability of an economy (as a whole and each economic unit within it) to service its net foreign liabilities without explicitly defaulting on them (Milesi-Ferretti and Razin, 1996a, p. 1). A formal criterion for (*ex ante*) solvency is the intertemporal budget constraint which requires the initial value of country's net foreign assets (liabilities) to be no larger than the present discounted value of expected future trade balances. Thus, one approach defines sustainability in terms of solvency: The path of external imbalances is sustainable if its continuation into the indefinite future satisfies the economy's intertemporal budget constraint. This notion is motivated by the literature on fiscal sustainability. Testing the validity of the intertemporal budget constraint in the data has been one of the predominant ways of assessing external sustainability so far.

In spite of its popularity, this approach has serious limitations. The intertemporal budget constraint imposes only weak restrictions on the trajectory of external imbalances: An economy which is a net debtor towards the rest of the world can run large trade and current account deficits for a prolonged period of time and still meet the intertemporal budget constraint as long as it is expected to generate sufficiently large trade surpluses in the (even very distant) future (Corsetti and Roubini, 1991, p. 355; Corsetti et al., 1999, p. 312). Further, the intertemporal budget constraint is silent on how a reversal in the trade account required to maintain solvency will occur: whether it will take place smoothly or be accompanied by a financial crisis.

Therefore, Milesi-Ferretti and Razin (1996a,b) suggest a stricter definition, according to which external imbalances are regarded as sustainable only if a reversal from trade deficits to trade surpluses does not require an abrupt shift in monetary and financial policies nor does it lead to a financial crisis. A similar notion of sustainability is used in the International Monetary Fund's debt sustainability framework: An economy is sustainable if it satisfies the intertemporal budget constraint without a major correction in the balance of income and expenditure given the costs of financing (IMF, 2002, p. 6). However, this definition leaves rather vague what constitutes a "major" retrenchment.

The intertemporal budget constraint also does not take into account that an economy's repayment ability (as measured, e.g., by GDP) is in practice bounded. Although an indefinitely

[4] Infeasible values of variables are those which either cannot be achieved because it is not possible (e.g., negative capital stock) or because it would incur prohibitive costs (Pitchford, 1995, p. 124).

increasing ratio of net foreign debts in proportion to GDP is perfectly consistent with solvency as long as net foreign debts grow at a slower pace than the respective discount rate, net interest payments may become so large that they outstrip an economy's GDP (as already mentioned above). Thus, another sustainability concept amplifies the notion of solvency by requiring that the economy's net foreign debts are non-increasing in proportion to GDP (Roubini and Wachtel, 1998; Pitchford, 1995; Roubini, 2001). An implication of this criterion is that virtually any level of the net foreign debt-to-GDP ratio is sustainable as long as it is non-increasing and solvency is not violated. However, the higher an economy's net foreign debts in percent of GDP, the higher is, other things being equal, an economy's vulnerability towards unfavorable exogenous shocks (Goldstein, 2003, p. 14).

An alternative approach to external sustainability is based on the idea that external imbalances are sustainable when they are the outcome of agents' optimal decisions (e.g., Edwards, 2007; Blanchard and Milesi-Ferretti, 2009, 2011). So far, two approaches have been used to determine whether a path of external imbalances is on its optimal or equilibrium trajectory: the intertemporal approach to the current account (Sachs, 1982; Obstfeld and Rogoff, 1994) and the portfolio or stock equilibrium approach to the current account (Kraay and Ventura, 2000, 2002; Calderon et al., 2000). The intertemporal approach to the current account imposes stronger restrictions on the path of external imbalances than the intertemporal budget constraint as the latter is a necessary condition for the former. However, possible deviations from the optimal trajectory do not necessarily point to unsustainability as they might also result from the poor performance of the underlying model.

Finally, concepts of solvency and sustainability are closely linked to a concept of liquidity, that is, the ability to meet or roll-over maturing liabilities via liquid assets and available financing (IMF, 2002, p. 6). A liquidity crisis—reflected in a sharp and large increase in the cost of financing—might ultimately jeopardize economy's solvency since higher trade surpluses are required to finance net interest payments falling due. And vice versa, a liquidity crisis can result from investors' lack of confidence in an economy's solvency (Krugman, 1988, p. 258). Although the distinction between solvency and liquidity is blurred, in practice, it is often important to decide whether an economy is subject to a "solvency" or "liquidity" problem. In the former case, a debt reduction might be required to restore solvency, in the latter case, a debt rescheduling/restructuring might be a more promising strategy (Roubini, 2001, p. 3).

1.3 Outline of the study

The remainder of the present study is organized as follows. Chapter 2 provides a digression on the accounting concepts of the current account, the trade account, and the net international investment position as well as on the balance of payments accounting identities which will be used in the whole subsequent analysis.

Chapter 3 derives the intertemporal budget constraint imposed by the lenders on an economy. It starts with the stylized model of a small open economy with riskless bonds as the only asset; this model falls into the intertemporal approach to the current account. The thus obtained intertemporal budget constraint requires the economy's initial stock of net foreign debts (surpluses) to be matched by future expected trade surpluses (deficits) discounted by the interest rate. Transferring the argument provided by Bohn (1995b) for government deficits in a closed-economy general-equilibrium Lucas (1978) model to an open-economy setting, we show that the discounting by the interest rate is appropriate only in some special cases (such as the absence of uncertainty) and that the proper discount factor is the stochastic discount factor (which is determined by the marginal rate of substitution between present and future consumption and agents' subjective time-preference rate). Chapter 3 concludes by pointing to the limitations of the intertemporal budget constraint as a solvency criterion.

Chapter 4 identifies the testing conditions that imply the validity of the intertemporal budget constraint in the data. Herein, it differentiates between the notions of strong sustainability (which counts only the stationary current account as sustainable) and weak sustainability (which is consistent with the current account drifting arbitrarily far away from its mean over time). The empirical implications of the intertemporal budget constraint provide the basis for the empirical assessment of sustainability in the next chapter.

Chapter 5 evaluates the test methods and the results of the relevant empirical studies. All studies are summarized in the appendix to this chapter. The test methods are divided into three groups: (i) unit root tests applied to the net international investment position and the current account; (ii) tests for cointegration between the components of the current account; (iii) tests for the responsiveness of the trade account to changes in the net international investment position. Since the tests on the intertemporal budget constraint constitute the most widely used method to assess external sustainability, this work devotes to the intertemporal budget constraint significantly more space than to other measures of sustainability.

Chapter 6 determines the optimal or equilibrium current account path both within the intertemporal approach to the current account and the portfolio approach to the current account. We discuss the testing methodology and evaluate the relevant empirical studies (the studies are summarized in the appendix to chapter 6).

Chapter 7 explores the most widely used indicators of external sustainability. It starts with the resource gap (which indicates the adjustment in the trade balance required to prevent net foreign debts from rising in proportion to an economy's repayment ability) and discusses the relevant empirical literature. Next, it addresses the sustainability concept suggested by Milesi-Ferretti and Razin (1996a). By examining the experiences of countries with persistent external imbalances, Milesi-Ferretti and Razin (1996a) identify indicators that help to differentiate between sustainable episodes (which display no sharp policy reversal or an external crisis) and unsustainable episodes (which are characterized either by a drastic policy shift only or both by a drastic policy reversal and an external crisis). Further, we exploit the empirical literature on current account reversals for the sustainability analysis. Finally, indicators applied in the International Monetary Fund's debt sustainability analysis and in the Macroeconomic Imbalances Procedure in the European Union are reviewed. Chapter 8 concludes the present dissertation.

2

Digression on balance of payments accounting identities

2.1 Accounting identity based on trade balance and income balances

The balance of payments records all economic transactions between residents and non-residents during a specific period of time. In the balance of payments statistics,[1] an economy's current account is decomposed into international flows associated with transactions in goods and services, net factor income—also called primary income—and unilateral current transfers—also called secondary income (IMF, 2008, p. 13). The (nominal) current account balance over period t (CAB_t^n) can thus be written as the sum of balances on trade in goods and services (TB_t^n), primary income (PIB_t^n), and secondary income (SIB_t^n):

$$CAB_t^n = TB_t^n + PIB_t^n + SIB_t^n.$$

The superscript n indicates that the variables are measured in nominal terms. The trade balance equals the difference between exports (X_t^n) and imports (M_t^n) of goods and services: $TB_t^n = X_t^n - M_t^n$. The secondary income account records current transfers between residents and nonresidents, such as social benefits and contribution or current international cooperation (IMF, 2008, p. 307). The primary income account shows amounts payable and receivable in return for providing to another entity a temporary use of labor such as compensation of employees, investment income such as interest and dividends, and nonproduced nonfinancial assets such as rents (IMF, 2008, pp. 271-2). Investment income in the current period can be expressed as the return on the beginning of period's net international investment position (also called net foreign asset position or net external position). The net international investment position (NIIP) is the difference between the economy's external financial assets and liabilities at a point in time (IMF, 2008, p. 173). A positive NIIP indicates net foreign assets, and a negative NIIP net foreign liabilities. Countries with a positive NIIP are called "net creditors," and countries with a negative NIIP are often labeled as "net borrowers" or "net debtors"—although, strictly speaking, only nonequity components of the negative NIIP can be described as (external) debt. In sum, the current account balance can be rewritten as follows:

$$CAB_t^n = TB_t^n + i_t B_{t-1}^n + PIB_t^{rest,n} + SIB_t^n \tag{2.1}$$

[1] The accounting concepts used in this work are based on the Sixth Edition of the IMF's Balance of Payments Manual (IMF, 2008).

where B_{t-1}^n denotes the (nominal) NIIP at the end of period $t-1$, i.e., at the beginning of period t, the rate of return on the NIIP is approximated by the (nominal) interest rate that prevailed on date t (i_t), and $PIB_t^{rest,n}$ denotes all components of the NIIP except investment income. Equation (2.1) shows that a surplus in the current account arises from net exports of goods and services, from the return on economy's net foreign assets, or from compensation received by employees. Linking the current account to national income and product accounts leads to two further identities.

2.2 Accounting identity based on income and absorption

In the national account statistics, gross domestic product (GDP) measures the total market value of all goods and services produced domestically in one year and can be expressed as

$$Y_t^n = C_t^n + G_t^n + I_t^n + TB_t^n \tag{2.2}$$

where Y_t^n denotes (nominal) GDP, C_t^n denotes (nominal) private consumption, G_t^n is (nominal) public consumption, and I_t^n denotes (nominal) gross private and public investment (Carranza, 2002, p. 99). The sum of (private and public) consumption and investment equals the total expenditures on goods and services by domestic residents, also called domestic absorption (A_t^n): $A_t^n = C_t^n + G_t^n + I_t^n$. Consequently, the trade balance can be expressed as the difference between GDP and domestic absorption: $TB_t^n = Y_t^n - A_t^n$. Thus, identity (2.1) can be rewritten as

$$CAB_t^n = Y_t^n - C_t^n - G_t^n - I_t^n + i_t B_{t-1}^n + PIB_t^{rest,n} + SIB_t^n. \tag{2.3}$$

The sum of GDP and primary income equals gross national income (GNI). Adding the secondary income balance to GNI leads to gross national disposable income (GNDI) which is the most comprehensive income measure in an open economy:

$$GNDI_t^n = Y_t^n + i_t B_{t-1}^n + PIB_t^{rest,n} + SIB_t^n. \tag{2.4}$$

Combining identities (2.3) and (2.4) shows that the current account deficit equals the excess of domestic absorption over GNDI: $CAB_t^n = GNDI_t^n - A_t^n$. However, in practice, it should be taken into account that the national account and the balance of payments statistics may apply different definitions of certain accounting concepts, for example, concerning the treatment of net factor income payments and transfers (Isard et al., 2001, p. 6; IMF, 2008, pp. 122-3).

2.3 Accounting identity based on saving and investment

Subtracting private and public consumption from gross national disposable income yields gross domestic saving (S_t^n), that is, the share of GNDI which is not used for consumption: $S_t^n = GNDI_t^n - C_t^n - G_t^n$. Using this definition to rearrange the terms in identity (2.3), the current account can be expressed as the gap between gross domestic saving and gross domestic investment:

$$CAB_t^n = S_t^n - I_t^n. \tag{2.5}$$

Equation (2.5) implies first that an open economy can save either by acquiring foreign wealth (i.e., generating a current account surplus) or by building its capital stock (Krugman and Obstfeld, 2003, p. 304). Second, identity (2.5) indicates that investment can be financed with either external saving (i.e., running a current account deficit) or domestic saving (Carranza, 2002, p. 100).

The relationship between the public and private sectors can be seen more clearly by distinguishing between government saving and private saving. Private saving ($S_t^{p,n}$) can be defined as that part of GNDI less net taxes (i.e., net taxes minus all government transfer payments) which is not used for private consumption: $S_t^{p,n} = GNDI_t^n - T_t^n - C_t^n$ where T_t^n denotes net taxes. Government saving ($S_t^{g,n}$) can be expressed as the excess of government's net tax revenues over government spending: $S_t^{g,n} = T_t^n - G_t^n$ (Krugman and Obstfeld, 2003, p. 305). Trivially, government and private savings add up to total domestic saving. Using the definitions of public and government savings, equation (2.5) can be rewritten as

$$CAB_t^n = \left(S_t^{p,n} - I_t^n\right) + \left(T_t^n - G_t^n\right). \tag{2.6}$$

Identity (2.6) shows that the current account balance equals the gap between private saving and investment plus the fiscal balance.[2] In other words, a government budget deficit can be financed either with external saving (i.e., current account deficit) or with the excess of private saving over private investment (Carranza, 2002, p. 100).

2.4 Combining accounting identities

Ignoring net errors and omissions, the balance of payments is offset if the current account balance, the capital account balance (KAB^n), and the financial account balance (FAB^n) sum up to zero:

$$CAB_t^n + KAB^n + FAB_t^n = 0. \tag{2.7}$$

The capital account records all transactions involving the receipt or payment of capital transfers and the acquisition or disposal of nonproduced, nonfinancial assets (IMF, 2008, p. 321). The financial account pertains to transactions associated with the net acquisition and disposal of foreign financial assets and liabilities of an economy (IMF, 2008, p. 194). A surplus in the financial account ($FAB^n > 0$) corresponds to the net acquisition of financial assets, and a financial account deficit ($FAB^n < 0$) to the net purchase of assets. Rewriting identity (2.7) as $CAB_t^n + KAB^n = -FAB_t^n$ implies that a surplus (deficit) in the current and capital accounts must be matched by a deficit (surplus) in the financial account. In other words, the net provision of resources to the rest of the world (i.e., a surplus in the current and capital accounts) must equal an increase in net claims on the rest of the world (i.e., a financial account deficit) or, to put it differently, net lending (borrowing) on the current and capital accounts equals net borrowing (lending) on the financial account. Since a surplus in the financial account corresponds to an increase in

[2] More precisely, investment should be split up into private and public investment. In this case, equation (2.6) becomes $CAB_t^n = \left(S_t^{p,n} - I_t^{p,n}\right) + \left(S_t^{g,n} - I_t^{g,n}\right)$ where the superscripts p and g denote the private and the public sector, respectively. If net dissaving of the government sector is not offset by net saving of the private sector, the current account is in deficit (IMF, 2008, p. 159).

economy's net foreign liabilities or a reduction in net foreign assets, i.e., $FAB_t^n = -(B_t^n - B_{t-1}^n)$,[3] the current and capital accounts equal the change in the net international investment position:

$$CAB_t^n + KAB_t^n = \Delta B_t^n$$

where the (first) difference operator Δ denotes the change of a variable between two subsequent points, e.g., $\Delta B_t^n \equiv B_t^n - B_{t-1}^n$. Abstracting, for simplicity, from the capital account shows that the current account deficit (surplus) equals a decrease (an increase) in the NIIP:

$$CAB_t^n = \Delta B_t^n. \tag{2.8}$$

Equation (2.8) also implies that the NIIP corresponds to the accumulation of current account balances from period t back to period zero (Holmes, 2006, p. 17):[4]

$$B_t^n = CAB_t^n + CAB_{t-1}^n + CAB_{t-2}^n + \cdots + CAB_0^n. \tag{2.11}$$

Following the so called "analytic" presentation of the balance of payments which distinguishes between net reserve asset transactions (FX_t^n) and other items (IMF, 2008, p. 334), identity (2.8) can be rewritten as

$$CAB_t^n = \Delta B_t^{NR,n} - KAB_t^n + \Delta FX_t^n \tag{2.12}$$

where the superscript NR denotes financial account transactions excluding net reserve assets.[5] Equation (2.12) shows that a current account deficit can be financed through private funds—viz. financial inflows, i.e., a reduction in the NIIP net of reserves ($\Delta B_t^{NR,n} < 0$) and capital inflows ($KAB_t^n > 0$)—as well as through official funds via liquidating international reserves ($\Delta FX_t^n < 0$). A current account surplus is reflected in a net purchase of international reserves on the part of monetary authorities ($\Delta FX_t^n > 0$) or an increase in other net claims towards the rest of the world ($\Delta B_t^{NR,n} - KAB_t^n > 0$). In an independently floating exchange rate arrangement in which monetary authorities do not intervene in exchange markets, the stock of international reserves does

[3] More precisely, the financial account corresponds to the difference between the closing value (at the end of the period) and the opening value (at the beginning of the period) in the integrated statement of the NIIP if other changes in financial assets and liabilities (e.g., due to changes in volume or exchange rates) are neglected (IMF, 2008, pp. 11, 174).

[4] This can be shown by solving equation (2.8) for B_t^n and adding at first B_{t-2}^n on both sides of equation (2.8). This yields

$$B_t^n = CAB_t^n + B_{t-1}^n + B_{t-2}^n - B_{t-2}^n. \tag{2.9}$$

Substituting $CAB_{t-1}^n = B_{t-1}^n - B_{t-2}^n$ and adding B_{t-3}^n on both sides of equation (2.9) results in

$$B_t^n = CAB_t^n + CAB_{t-1}^n + B_{t-2}^n + B_{t-3}^n + B_{t-3}^n. \tag{2.10}$$

Substituting $CAB_{t-2}^n = B_{t-2}^n - B_{t-3}^n$ in equation (2.10) one obtains

$$B_t^n = CAB_t^n + CAB_{t-1}^n + CAB_{t-2}^n + B_{t-3}^n.$$

Repeated substitution finally leads to equation (2.11).

[5] In addition, in the "analytic" presentation of the balance of payments, exceptional financing items (e.g., debt forgiveness, debt for equity swaps, debt rescheduling/refinancing) are taken out from the current, capital, and financial accounts and are moved to the reserves and related items heading (see IMF, 2008, pp. 334, 352-375 for details). For simplicity, exceptional financing items are ignored here.

not change ($\Delta FX_t^n = 0$) so that $CAB_t^n = \Delta B_t^{NR,n} - KAB_t^n$. In a fixed peg arrangement, transactions in reserve assets are determined by the net demand or supply of foreign exchange at the particular exchange rate. Finally, in the intermediate exchange rate arrangement (such as crawling bands or managed floating), monetary authorities typically undertake purchases and sales of reserve assets aimed at influencing the exchange rate (IMF, 2008).[6] However, financing a current account deficit through a recourse to official reserves is limited as the stock of reserve assets is finite. Moreover, foreign private investors' willingness to lend might diminish when the monetary authorities are expected to shortly deplete an economy's reserves since a possible depreciation might *ceteris paribus* reduce the rate of return expected by investors (IMF, 2008). This situation can result in a currency crisis in which a speculative attack precipitates a devaluation or a sharp depreciation of the currency, or leads to a rapid exhaustion of international reserves or a sharp increase in interest rates (IMF, 1998). In contrast, purchases of international reserves are, at least theoretically, unlimited. Thus, there is an asymmetry between countries running current account deficits and those with current account surpluses. However, a large accumulation of reserve assets—if not sterilized through a matching reduction in net domestic assets—might increase a money supply and, thus, create inflationary pressures.[7]

Rearranging the terms in identity (2.12) one obtains

$$CAB_t^n + KAB_t^n - \Delta B_t^{NR,n} = \Delta FX_t^n \tag{2.13}$$

where the left-hand side of identity (2.13) represents the overall or external account, that is, the balance of payments net of reserve assets (which is sometimes simply referred to as the "balance of payments"). A deficit (surplus) in the external balance can be financed by a decrease (increase) in reserve assets. Finally, the external balance is achieved when the economy records no changes of reserve assets. From the global perspective, the sum of all balance of payments balances in the world must add up to zero (apart from statistical discrepancies) or, to put it differently, the sum of external imbalances of all countries in the world must equal the change in net world reserves (Gandolfo, 2001, pp. 64-68).

As already mentioned in chapter 1, the analysis of external sustainability should not rely exclusively on the current account balance, instead, it should consider all dimensions of the balance of payments. Specifically, this can be accomplished either by analyzing identity (2.12) or by combining identity (2.8) with identities (2.1), (2.3), or (2.5). This yields the following three balance of payments identities which represent different perspectives on the economy's transactions with the rest of the world:

$$B_t^n - B_{t-1}^n = TB_t^n + i_t B_{t-1}^n + PIB_t^{rest,n} + SIB_t^n + KAB_t^n \tag{2.14}$$

$$B_t^n - B_{t-1}^n = Y_t^n - C_t^n - G_t^n - I_t^n + i_t B_{t-1}^n + PIB_t^{rest,n} + SIB_t^n + KAB_t^n \tag{2.15}$$

$$B_t^n - B_{t-1}^n = S_t^n - I_t^n + PIB_t^n + SIB_t^n + KAB_t^n. \tag{2.16}$$

[6] The classification system of *de facto* exchange rate arrangements as identified by the IMF staff can be found in Ishii and Habermeier (2003).

[7] For costs and risks of the reserve accumulation see Higgins and Klitgaard (2004). The analysis of motives for accumulation of international reserves is provided by Aizenman and Lee (2007). Jeanne (2007); Aizenman (2008); Barnichon (2009). The general discussion of the effectiveness of foreign exchange interventions and sterilization can be found in Caballero and Krishnamurthy (2001); Taylor and Sarno (2001); Weber (1994); Reitz and Taylor (2008).

The left-hand side of each of the three identities represents trade in foreign assets. This international perspective is combined with the perspective based on international trade in goods and services (identity (2.14)) or with the domestic perspective based on national income and product accounts (identities (2.15) and (2.16), respectively) (Mann, 2002). By definition, each identity holds *ex post* in the particular period. Since identities are not based on any theory about the behavior of economic agents, no causal relationships can be deduced.

3

Intertemporal budget constraint as a sustainability criterion

This chapter is devoted to a widespread concept of external sustainability which is originally motivated by the notion of fiscal sustainability used in the literature on public finance. Fiscal sustainability is typically defined as the government's ability to indefinitely continue the same set of fiscal and/or monetary policies while remaining solvent (Burnside, 2005, p. 11). This notion encompasses two central aspects: It builds upon the concept of solvency, i.e., an entity's ability to repay its debt without explicitly defaulting on it. Beyond that, it imposes a "baseline" on future policy actions (Milesi-Ferretti and Razin, 1996a, p. 4) by requiring the policy stance to be unchanged.

The application of the first aspect to an open economy is straightforward: An economy is solvent if it is able (as a whole and each economic unit within it) to service its net foreign liabilities without explicitly defaulting on them. In contrast, the specification of a baseline for the policy stance regarding external imbalances is more difficult than the corresponding specification regarding government deficits: While government deficits are (at least partly) associated with direct policy decisions on taxation and public expenditures, external imbalances reflect the interactions between saving and investment decisions of domestic public and private agents, as well as lending decisions of foreign investors (Milesi-Ferretti and Razin, 1996a, p. 4; Milesi-Ferretti and Razin, 1996b, p. 9).

It is probably for this reason that a large strand of literature defines external sustainability in terms of solvency only—indeed, equates sustainability and solvency. According to this view, external sustainability can be defined as a situation in which the paths of the current account imbalances, the net international investment position, and the trade balances do not violate solvency. Solvency is typically formalized by the long-run budget constraint which confines the economy's initial net international investment position to the present value of (expected) future trade balances. Thus, the above definition of external sustainability can be stated more precisely as follows: The sustainable path of external imbalances is the one whose continuation into the indefinite future satisfies the economy's intertemporal budget constraint.

There are two widespread methods of deriving the intertemporal budget constraint: The first method simply iterates the balance of payments accounting identity forward, without (explicitly) relying on an economic model, while assuming that the economy does not engage in Ponzi games (i.e., does not pay interest on its net foreign liabilities out of new foreign borrowing).[1]

The second method embeds the balance of payments accounting identity into a stylized intertemporal model of the current account, thus bringing an economic/behavioral content to a mere accounting identity (which is a single-period budget constraint in the model). The intertemporal approach to the current account mainly developed by Sachs (1982) and Obstfeld and Rogoff (1994) is the natural theoretical framework since it represents the current account as the outcome of an intertemporal optimization over saving and investment by rational agents, subject to the agents' budget constraints. The intertemporal budget constraint is again obtained via the forward iteration of the single-period budget constraint, combined with a condition which precludes Ponzi games. However, in contrast to the first method, this framework is sufficiently rich to accommodate a proper justification for why and when an economy should refrain from Ponzi finance: Such a justification is provided by the argument in O'Connell and Zeldes (1988), according to which Ponzi games are not feasible in equilibrium when the number of optimizing lenders is finite.

Both methods yield an intertemporal budget constraint in which discounting occurs at the market interest rate. However, following Bohn (1991), it can be shown that the appropriate discount factor is a stochastic discount factor determined by the marginal rate of substitution between present and future consumption and the subjective time-preference rate; the stochastic discount factor equals the market discount factor only in special cases such as the absence of uncertainty or risk neutrality. For this reason, the intertemporal budget constraint with the market interest rate as the discounting rate will be referred to as the "specific" intertemporal budget constraint and the intertemporal budget constraint which multiplies the future trade balances with the stochastic discount factor as the "general" intertemporal budget constraint. In order to derive the "general" intertemporal budget constraint, we transfer Bohn's (1991) closed-economy general equilibrium Lucas (1978)-style model to an open economy (thus extending the stylized intertemporal model of the current account to incorporate complete markets).[2] This setting combines the intertemporal approach to the current account with asset pricing theory.[3] The "general" intertemporal budget constraint is determined by combining the single-period budget constraint with the first-order conditions for optimality in the first step, iterating the resulting equation in the second step, and imposing the "no-Ponzi finance" condition in the third step.

Section 3.1 in this chapter shows the second method of deriving the intertemporal budget constraint by setting up a stylized intertemporal model of the current account with riskless bonds as the only asset. It starts with the description of the model economy (subsection 3.1.1) and of the agents' single-period budget constraint (subsection 3.1.2). Subsection 3.1.3 first derives the

[1] Ponzi games (also known as rollover or pyramid schemes) take their name from Boston swindler Charles Ponzi who offered high returns to investors out of the money borrowed from subsequent investors (Feenstra and Taylor, 2008, p. 222).

[2] Typically, the term "intertemporal approach to the current account" is reserved for models with riskless bonds as the only asset—and the present work follows this convention. However, since models with complete markets can be viewed as extensions of models with bonds only, one can also apply the term "intertemporal approach to the current account" when referring to such models (Obstfeld and Rogoff, 1994, p. 3).

[3] A survey of the literature on asset pricing can be found in Duffie (2003) and Çelik (2012).

long-run budget constraint from the single-period budget constraint in the deterministic setting; after introducing uncertainty, one arrives at the "specific" long-run budget constraint.

Section 3.2 extends the theoretical framework of section 3.1 to a complete markets setting. After describing the stylized model and the economy's optimization problem in subsection 3.2.1, the "general" intertemporal budget constraint is determined in subsection 3.2.2 and compared to the "specific" intertemporal budget constraint in subsection 3.2.3.

Section 3.3 points to possible extensions of the theoretical framework employed in this chapter. Section 3.4 concludes this chapter with a discussion of the intertemporal budget constraint as a sustainability criterion.

3.1 Long-run budget constraint in the intertemporal approach to the current account

3.1.1 Description of the model economy

The intertemporal approach to the current account mainly put forward by Sachs (1982) and Obstfeld and Rogoff (1994, 1996) views the current account as the optimal outcome of agents' intertemporal saving and investment decisions. The stylized model of a small open economy presented in this section is the "workhorse" model in the literature on the intertemporal approach to the current account and is mainly based on Obstfeld and Rogoff (1994, 1996) and Wickens (2008).

The world consists of a large (finite) number of identical small open economies. The representative economy is inhabited by a large number of identical individuals which are represented by a single representative consumer (RC). Time is discrete, and the index t denotes time periods.[4] The population size is constant and normalized to one so that national aggregate quantities equal per-capita quantity variables. The RC is assumed to form rational expectations about the future, that is, the representative individual's forecasting errors and the information available at the time of the forecast are uncorrelated.[5]

An economy is small in the sense that it takes the world prices as given. We assume that every such small economy in our model is open and produces, consumes, and trades a single non-durable composite good with the rest of the world. International trade includes the exchange of assets. The only traded asset is a consumption-indexed bond with fixed face value which pays net real interest at rate r_t between $t-1$ and t and has a maturity of one-period. Hence, the economy's net international investment position consists only of riskless bonds. The world real interest rate is the same for borrowing and lending and is the only (and exogenously given) price in the model. Capital mobility is perfect, thus implying that the supply of bonds is infinitely elastic at the world interest rate (Milesi-Ferretti and Razin, 1996b, p. 6). Further, all

[4] The assumption of discrete time means that time is viewed as a series of distinct periods that are identified with integer values. During any single period, any variable takes only one value (Klein, 2001, p. 407).

[5] In particular, the rational expectations hypothesis is based on three assumptions: (i) the economy does not waste scarce information, (ii) expectations depend on the structure of the relevant system describing the economy, and (iii) "public predictions" have no substantial effect on the operation of the economic system (Muth, 1961, p. 316; Hamilton, 1994, p. 422).

contracts are perfectly enforceable so that promised payments coincide with actual payments and opportunistic defaults are not possible (O'Connell and Zeldes, 1988, p. 433).

Every economy has a government whose consumption (G_t) is exogenously given and is financed solely through lump-sum taxes, thus implying a balanced government budget. Further, government spending is assumed to enter the RC's utility function additively, so that the marginal utility of consumption is not affected by the level of government consumption.

Output is determined by the production function $Y_t = A_{t-1}F(K_{t-1}, L_{t-1})$ where K_{t-1} denotes the capital stock at the end of period $t-1$ which is carried over to the beginning of period t, L_{t-1} is labor supply at the beginning of period t, and A_{t-1} measures the (exogenously varying) state of technology, also called total factor or multi-factor productivity. Labor is internationally immobile and is supplied inelastically by the RC. Normalizing total labor quantity to unity, the production function reduces to $Y_{t-1} = A_{t-1}F(K_{t-1})$. $F(\cdot)$ is strictly increasing in capital and strictly concave ($F'(K) > 0$ and $F''(K) < 0$), and output can only be produced using capital ($F(0) = 0$). The production function is assumed to satisfy Inada (1964) conditions which state that (i) the marginal product of capital approaches infinity as the capital stock vanishes ($\lim_{K\to 0} F'(K) = \infty$), thus implying that the capital stock is strictly positive, and that (ii) it tends to zero as the capital stock becomes infinitely large ($\lim_{K\to\infty} F'(K) = 0$). The capital stock can be used to produce output and can be consumed afterwards (i.e., investment can become negative). It is assumed that the capital stock is accumulated without cost, that is, the relative price of capital in terms of consumption is assumed to be one.[6] Further, in each period a constant fraction δ ($\delta \in [0;1]$) of the capital stock is assumed to depreciate. Accordingly, an increase in the capital stock during period t corresponds to new investment minus depreciated capital:

$$K_t - K_{t-1} = I_t - \delta K_{t-1} \tag{3.1}$$

where K_t denotes the capital stock at the end of period t and I_t is new investment during period t.

Output (in terms of consumption goods) is either consumed (by domestic private agents, by domestic government, and by foreigners) or invested (increasing thereby the capital stock) so that one can write:

$$Y_t = C_t + G_t + I_t + X_t - M_t \tag{3.2}$$

where imports are subtracted because they are contained in I_t, C_t, and G_t. Equation (3.2) is exactly the same as the national income identity (2.2), the only difference being that the trade balance is explicitly written out as the gap between exports and imports ($TB_t = X_t - M_t$).

The RC's preferences are represented by

$$U_t = u(C_t) + v(G_t) + \sum_{n=t+1}^{\infty} \beta^{n-t} E_t \left[u(C_n) + v(G_n) \right]. \tag{3.3}$$

[6] An alternative approach suggested, e.g., by Hayashi (1982) allows for adjustment costs incurred by capital accumulation so that only a fraction of output can be embodied in capital (see, e.g., Khan and Thomas (2008) for a survey on adjustment costs). This approach is related to Tobin's "q theory", according to which the rate of investment is a function of the ratio of capital market value to its replacement cost (Brainard and Tobin, 1968; Tobin, 1969). This ratio is known as the "average" q; a survey of results on the "marginal" q can be found, e.g., in Abel (1979).

$E_t[\cdot]$ (or $E[\cdot|I_t]$) denotes the mathematical conditional expectation operator which is defined as the mean of the probability distribution where probabilities are conditioned on the public information set I_t in period t (Hamilton, 1994, pp. 741-742). According to the "strong" form of the rational-expectations hypothesis, the information set is assumed to contain all information available to the RC, including the information about the "true" model of the economy's structure and all current economic variables (Obstfeld and Rogoff, 1996, p. 79).[7] $\beta \in (0;1)$ is the constant subjective discount factor which measures the representative agent's time preference for current consumption over future consumption: The higher β, the more patient is the representative consumer. The assumption of constant subjective time-preferences implies in particular that an agent's intertemporal choices are time-consistent (Frederick et al., 2002, p. 358). The time-separable instantaneous utility function $u(\cdot)$ is strictly increasing in consumption, strictly concave ($u'(C) > 0$ and $u''(C) < 0$), and satisfies the Inada (1964) conditions $\lim_{C\to 0} u'(C) = \infty$ and $\lim_{C\to\infty} u'(C) = 0$. The strictly positive marginal utility of consumption implies non-satiation, that is, more consumption is always preferred to less consumption. Under uncertainty, the concavity of the utility function implies that $u(E[c]) \geq E[u(c)]$, that is, agents are risk-averse and strictly prefer the expected value of any consumption plan to the consumption plan itself (LeRoy and Werner, 2001, p. 88). The period utility function $v(\cdot)$ has the same properties as the period utility function $u(\cdot)$.

3.1.2 Single-period budget constraint

Each period, the representative agent faces the following budget constraint:

$$B_t = NO_t - C_t + (1+r_t)B_{t-1}. \tag{3.4}$$

Equation (3.4) restricts the net international investment position at the end of period t to the difference between net output in period t (defined as $NO_t = Y_t - G_t - I_t$) and t-period's consumption in period t plus the interest and principal to be paid (received) on the NIIP at the beginning of t. Equation (3.4) is known as single-period budget constraint. Alternative denominations of equation (3.4) are: 'period-by-period budget constraint,' 'static budget constraint' (because it refers only to one-period), and even 'dynamic budget constraint' (because it covers the time period between two dates: the beginning and the end of period t).

Substituting the economy's trade balance for the difference between net output and consumption, equation (3.4) can also be written as

$$B_t = TB_t + (1+r_t)B_{t-1}. \tag{3.5}$$

If the representative consumer is initially a net debtor towards the rest of the world ($B_{t-1} < 0$), the single-period budget constraint (3.5) implies that the RC can repay net foreign liabilities either by generating a trade surplus ($TB_t > 0$) and/or by borrowing abroad ($B_t < 0$).

All variables in the single-period budget constraint (3.5) are measured in real terms because the typical intertemporal model of the current account is real and assumes, among other things,

[7] In contrast, in its weak form, the rational-expectations hypothesis merely implies that agents optimally exploit information available to them for forming their expectations (Fisher, 1980, p. 212). Weakly rational expectations are consistent with the hypothesis of economically rational expectations, according to which expectations are based on the cost-benefit considerations of added information (Feige and Pearce, 1976, p. 500).

consumption-indexed bonds. Multiplying real variables in equation (3.4) with the price level (P_t), equation (3.5) can be equally converted into nominal terms:

$$B_t P_t = NO_t P_t - C_t P_t + (1+r_t) B_{t-1} P_{t-1} (1+\pi_t) \tag{3.6}$$

where π denotes the inflation rate with $P_{t-1}(1+\pi_t) = P_t$. The notation in equation (3.6) can be simplified by using the superscript n to denote nominal variables (e.g., $B_t P_t \equiv B_t^n$). This yields

$$B_t^n = NO_t^n - C_t^n + (1+i_t) B_{t-1}^n \tag{3.7}$$

where i_t is the t-period's nominal interest rate with $(1+r_t)(1+\pi_t) = (1+i_t)$. Provided that compensation of employees, secondary income, and the capital account are zero, equation (3.7) is exactly the balance of payments identity (2.14) discussed in chapter 2.

It is also insightful to normalize the variables in the single-period budget constraint by some measure of the country's ability to service its net foreign liabilities, for example, by GDP or GNP. Dividing each term in the budget constraint (3.5) by real GDP (Y_t) and rearranging the terms yields

$$\frac{B_t - B_{t-1}}{Y_t} = \frac{TB_t + r_t B_{t-1}}{Y_t}.$$

Defining the real growth rate as $\gamma_t = (Y_t - Y_{t-1})/Y_{t-1}$, one obtains:

$$\frac{B_t}{Y_t} - \frac{B_{t-1}}{Y_{t-1}(1+\gamma_t)} = \frac{TB_t}{Y_t} + \frac{r_t B_{t-1}}{Y_{t-1}(1+\gamma_t)}. \tag{3.8}$$

Subtracting B_{t-1}/Y_{t-1} on both sides of equation (3.8) and rearranging the terms yields[8]

$$\frac{B_t}{Y_t} - \frac{B_{t-1}}{Y_{t-1}} = \frac{TB_t}{Y_t} + \frac{B_{t-1}}{Y_{t-1}} \left(\frac{r_t - \gamma_t}{1+\gamma_t} \right). \tag{3.9}$$

Defining $b_t \equiv B_t/Y_t$, $b_{t-1} \equiv B_{t-1}/Y_{t-1}$, and $tb_t \equiv TB_t/Y_t$, one can express equation (3.9) as

$$b_t - b_{t-1} = tb_t + \left(\frac{r_t - \gamma_t}{1+\gamma_t} \right) b_{t-1}. \tag{3.10}$$

The single-period budget constraint in terms of real GDP (3.10) shows that the change in the NIIP-to-GDP ratio equals the trade balance-to-GDP ratio and a NIIP "dynamics" term which is positively correlated with the real interest rate and negatively correlated with the real GDP growth rate. For ease of interpretation, the NIIP "dynamics" term can be linearly approximated by $(r_t - \gamma_t) b_{t-1}$ for small values of the real interest rate r_t and the real growth rate γ_t.[9] Thus, equation (3.10) simplifies to

[8] Another way to arrive at equation (3.8) is to divide equation (3.5) by the GDP of the previous period (Y_{t-1}):

$$\frac{B_t(1+\gamma_t)}{Y_t} - \frac{B_{t-1}}{Y_{t-1}} = \frac{TB_t(1+\gamma_t)}{Y_t} + \frac{r_t B_{t-1}}{Y_{t-1}}.$$

Dividing both sides by $(1+\gamma_t)$ and rearranging the terms finally leads to equation (3.9).

[9] This can be shown by calculating the difference between $(r_t - \gamma_t)/(1+\gamma_t)$ and $r_t - \gamma_t$ which is $(-r_t\gamma_t + \gamma_t^2)/(1+\gamma_t)$. For small r_t and γ_t, the product of two rates is negligible so that the difference between $(r_t - \gamma_t)/(1+\gamma_t)$ and $r_t - \gamma_t$ is approximately zero.

$$b_t - b_{t-1} = tb_t + (r_t - \gamma_t)\, b_{t-1}. \tag{3.11}$$

The approximate single-period budget constraint (3.11) reduces the change in the NIIP-to-GDP ratio to the sum of the trade balance-to-GDP ratio and the real interest payments corrected for real GDP growth.

The nominal equivalent to the budget constraint (3.10) can be obtained by rearranging the terms and dividing all variables in equation (3.6) by the t-period's nominal GDP, i.e., the product between the real GDP (Y_t) and the price level (P_t):

$$\frac{B_t^n}{Y_t P_t} - \frac{B_{t-1}^n}{Y_{t-1}P_{t-1}(1+\pi_t)(1+\gamma_t)} = \frac{TB_t^n}{Y_t P_t} + \frac{i_t B_{t-1}^n}{Y_{t-1}P_{t-1}(1+\pi_t)(1+\gamma_t)}. \tag{3.12}$$

Using the lower-case notation and rearranging the terms, equation (3.12) can be rewritten as

$$b_t^n - b_{t-1}^n = tb_t^n + b_{t-1}^n \left(\frac{(1+i_t) - (1+\gamma_t)(1+\pi_t)}{(1+\gamma_t)(1+\pi_t)} \right). \tag{3.13}$$

The budget constraint (3.13) states that the change in the nominal NIIP-to-GDP ratio equals the nominal trade balance-to-GDP ratio and the NIIP "dynamics" term which increases with the nominal interest rate and decreases with the nominal GDP growth rate. Writing the nominal interest rate in terms of the real interest rate, i.e., $i_t = (r_t + 1)(\pi_t + 1) - 1$, the term $(\pi_t + 1)$ cancels out in the the NIIP "dynamics" term on the right-hand side of equation (3.13). Thus, equation (3.13) simplifies to

$$b_t^n - b_{t-1}^n = tb_t^n + b_{t-1}^n \left(\frac{r_t - \gamma_t}{1+\gamma_t} \right). \tag{3.14}$$

Consequently, the NIIP dynamics term is the same as in the single-period budget constraint in real terms (3.10); the only difference between equations (3.14) and (3.10) is that the trade balance and the NIIP are measured in nominal terms.

The economy faces the single-period budget constraint in each period. Extending the planning horizon of the representative agent to multiple or even infinitely many periods allows to derive the intertemporal budget constraint which restricts the RC's behavior in the long-run.

3.1.3 Intertemporal budget constraint in the deterministic setting

This section describes the prevailing way of arriving at the intertemporal budget constraint: first iterating the single-period budget constraint (3.5) forward and then imposing the appropriate terminal condition. Under certainty, the "specific" intertemporal budget constraint thus obtained coincides with the "general" intertemporal budget constraint. For this reason, this section begins within a deterministic setting and introduces uncertainty later.

Finite planning horizon

The economy is assumed to start in period t with both the predetermined stock of net foreign assets (liabilities) B_{t-1} (which can be zero) and the predetermined capital stock (K_{t-1}). Adopting the preliminary assumption that the RC has a finite planning horizon, the economy ends in the terminal period $t+N$, $N>0$. In the deterministic setting, the assumption of rational expectations implies that the RC's decisions are based on perfect foresight of the future, that is, changes in economic variables expected by the RC and actual changes are equal (Gandolfo, 2001, p. 198).

The single-period budget constraint (3.5) is a first-order difference equation[10] which can be solved forward. Appendix 3.A presents two methods to solve equation (3.5): the forward-iteration method and the telescoping-sum method. The two methods yield the following equation:

$$B_{t-1} = -\sum_{n=t}^{t+N} R_{t,n}TB_n + R_{t,t+N}B_{t+N} \tag{3.15}$$

where the discount factor $R_{t,n}$ from time n back to period t with $n=t,t+1,t+2,\ldots$ is defined as

$$R_{t,n} = \prod_{v=t}^{n}\left(\frac{1}{1+r_v}\right), \quad R_{t,t}=1, \quad R_{t,n}<1.$$

Equation (3.15) states that the economy's NIIP at the beginning of t is tantamount to the present value of future trade balances plus the discounted outstanding NIIP.

Solvency requires a net debtor economy to pay all debt obligations before the economy ends so that B_{t+N} in equation (3.15) cannot be negative. In fact, under perfect foresight, foreign investors would not allow the RC to "die" with unpaid debts. The requirement $B_{t+N}\geq 0$ is also called "supersolvency" (Buiter and Patel, 1992, p. 183). Likewise, a rational representative agent would not waste resources by leaving uncollected claims on foreign investors since there are no descendants to inherit it. Thus, B_{t+N} cannot be positive either (Obstfeld and Rogoff, 1996, pp. 61-62).

Hence, the NIIP at the end of the terminal period $t+N$ must be zero:

$$B_{t+N} = 0. \tag{3.16}$$

Equation (3.16) is the terminal condition that permits the solution of the first-order difference equation (3.5). It both ensures the economy's solvency and rules out a suboptimal situation of 'supersolvency." If the terminal condition (3.16) holds, the last term in equation (3.15) is zero and equation (3.15) reduces to

$$B_{t-1} = -\sum_{n=t}^{t+N} R_{t,n}TB_n. \tag{3.17}$$

Equation (3.17) is the economy's intertemporal budget constraint—also known as long-run or consolidated budget constraint—which restricts the value of the economy's initial NIIP to the (negative) present value of the future trade balances.

The intertemporal budget constraint (3.17) implies that permanent trade deficits (i.e., the right-hand side of equation (3.17) is positive) are feasible only if the economy starts out as a net creditor towards the rest of the world ($B_{t-1}>0$). If the initial NIIP is negative, the economy must run trade surpluses (at least in one period) which are sufficiently large to satisfy the long-run budget constraint (3.17). Similar considerations apply to current account balances in a

[10] A difference equation relates the value of a dependent variable to one or more of its lagged values (or to its differences), as well as to the value of one or more independent variables (Klein, 2001, p. 408).

finitely-lived economy. As follows from identity (2.8) of chapter 2, the current account balance equals the change in the NIIP:

$$CAB_t = B_t - B_{t-1}. \tag{3.18}$$

Iterating equation (3.18) by N periods forward[11] and imposing the terminal condition (3.16) yields

$$B_{t-1} = -\sum_{n=t}^{t+N} CAB_n. \tag{3.19}$$

An economy can run perpetual current account deficits (i.e., the right-hand side of equation (3.19) is positive) only if it is initially a net creditor; otherwise, it must generate sufficiently large current account surpluses at some point in the future (before the economy ends).

The main drawback of a finite horizon economy is the (in most cases) unrealistic assumption of a terminal date known with certainty and that the model solution might depend on the particular choice of the final date N. The usual way to bypass this problem is to extend the individual's planning horizon to infinity (which does not necessarily require the assumption of an infinitely-lived representative agent). The "perpetual youth" approach and the "intergenerational altruism" approach are the two most prominent ways of stipulating assumptions under which finitely-lived individuals have an infinite planning horizon.

The "perpetual youth" model developed by Blanchard (1985) and Yaari (1965) is an overlapping generations model[12] where individuals face uncertainty about the time of death and where the probability of an individual's death in a particular period is constant in time and independent of age (i.e., a young person is as likely to die as an old person). Given that there is no possibility of life insurance and that agents care only about themselves (i.e., have no bequest motives), finitely-lived individuals will leave some unintentional bequests due to uncertainty arising from the unknown lifespan (even a hundred years old person will not consume all of his assets since there is a chance that he might continue to live for some time). Thus, at the individual level (yet not at the aggregate level), the optimization problem of finitely-lived individuals does not differ from that of infinitely-lived individuals (Blanchard and Fischer, 1989, p. 116; Acemoglu, 2008, pp. 156-157; Wickens, 2008, pp. 67-68).

Barro (1974) constructs an overlapping generations model in which finitely-lived agents are motivated by intergenerational altruism and undertake operative intergenerational transfers.[13] Because parents care about the utility of their children who in turn care about the utility of their own children and so on, an infinite sequence of generations of altruistic individuals acts as if they were to live forever. In this case, Barro (1974)'s overlapping generations model coincides with an infinitely-lived agent model.[14]

[11] This can be done, e.g., using repeated substitution: Inserting the current account identity of period $t+1$, $CAB_{t+1} = B_{t+1} - B_t$, into $B_{t-1} = B_t - CAB_t$ permits the elimination of B_t and yields $B_{t-1} = B_{t+1} - CAB_{t+1} - CAB_t$. Substituting $B_{t+2} - CAB_{t+2}$ for B_{t+1}, one obtains $B_{t-1} = B_{t+2} - CAB_{t+2} - CAB_{t+1} - CAB_t$, and so on.

[12] At the heart of overlapping generations (OLG) models is the assumption of an infinite number of generations of finitely-lived agents, where agents are heterogeneous in terms of age (old and young), not necessarily in terms of preferences. OLG models were first introduced by Allais (1947), Samuelson (1958), and Diamond (1965).

[13] A detailed discussion of the assumption of intergenerational altruism in neoclassical growth models is provided by Michel et al. (2006).

[14] The basic infinitely-lived agent model is a Ramsey (1928) - Cass (1965) - Koopmans (1963) (RCK) model. In contrast to overlapping generations models, models of the RCK type usually presuppose a finite number

In addition, when the economy's end date is very distant, a finite horizon economy behaves similarly to an infinite horizon economy (Obstfeld and Rogoff, 1996, p. 59). Finally, the solutions in infinite horizon models are usually simpler than in finite horizon models because the former are stationary (since the time-horizon does not change as time proceeds). For these reasons, in what follows, it is assumed that the representative agent has an infinite planning horizon.

Infinite planning horizon

When the planning horizon is infinite, agents might forever postpone debt repayment by resorting to new borrowing, in other words, they might forever play Ponzi games. The first step in obtaining the infinite horizon budget constraint is letting N go to infinity in equation (3.15):

$$B_{t-1} = -\sum_{n=t}^{\infty} R_{t,n} TB_n + \lim_{N \to \infty} R_{t,t+N} B_{t+N}, \tag{3.20}$$

provided that the limit exists. Equation (3.20) states that the stock of net foreign assets (liabilities) at the beginning of period t is equal to the present value of future trade balances plus the limit of the discounted outstanding NIIP.

The infinite horizon counterpart of the terminal condition (3.16) is that the last term in equation (3.20) is zero:

$$\lim_{N \to \infty} R_{t,t+N} B_{t+N} = 0. \tag{3.21}$$

Equation (3.21)—which is also called transversality condition (TC)—is satisfied when the growth rate of the NIIP is below the interest rate. As the end of time is indefinite, condition (3.21) does not require the net borrower economy to pay off the principal—in contrast to the finite horizon terminal condition (3.16). As long as the economy generates trade surpluses which are sufficiently large to cover (at least) a part of the debt obligations, the growth rate of net foreign debts is below the interest rate and the economy remains solvent. In other words, permanently increasing net foreign debts (assets) are perfectly sustainable as long as they grow at a slower pace than the interest rate!

A heuristic rationale for the TC (3.21) is similar to the finite horizon case. The present value of net foreign debts cannot be positive because international investors would not allow the RC to pay interest on the old (foreign) debt out of the new debt, that is, to play Ponzi games. Thus, the no-Ponzi game condition must hold: $\lim_{N \to \infty} R_{t,t+N} B_{t+N} \geq 0$. The limit term cannot be positive either since in this case the economy would make an "unrequited gift" to foreigners instead of raising its lifetime utility by consuming and investing more. Hence, the optimality condition must hold: $\lim_{N \to \infty} R_{t,t+N} B_{t+N} \leq 0$. It follows that the transversality condition (3.21) is a combination of two conditions: the no-Ponzi game condition and the optimality condition (Obstfeld and Rogoff, 1996, p. 65).

Based on the work of Cass (1972) and Tirole (1982, 1985), O'Connell and Zeldes (1988) provide a rigorous justification of the transversality condition (3.21). They show under perfect

of identical infinitely-lived agents (Ginsburgh and Keyzer, 2002, p. 267). Gaspard (2004) argues that "there is no need to wait for Barro's (1974) justification of the consideration of economic agents with infinite life expectancy" because Ramsey's (1928) text already contains a justification for infinite lives by using the notion of families or dynasties (Gaspard, 2004, p. 11).

foresight that Ponzi games are not feasible when (i) the number of (finitely- or infinitely-lived) lenders is finite and (ii) agents consume under non-satiation, that is, prefer more consumption to less in each period. Both assumptions are satisfied in our stylized model. The idea behind this result is as follows: When a domestic borrower engages in a Ponzi scheme, the total lending of a group of foreign lenders grows (at least) at the same rate as the interest rate in equilibrium. At the individual level, no single lender would allow the growth rate of her net foreign assets to equal the interest rate as this would be a consumption-inefficient plan. Adding the plans of all agents implies that the growth of all net foreign assets possessed by a finite group of foreign lenders is below the interest rate. This means that the limit inferior[15] of the present value of the combined net foreign assets of all lenders must be non-positive, i.e.,

$$\liminf_{N\to\infty} R_{t,t+N} B^{f}_{t+N} \leq 0 \tag{3.22}$$

wherein B^{f}_{t+N} denotes the combined net foreign assets of all lenders at time $t+N$. In a sense, equation (3.22) is the optimality condition of the group of lenders. It implies that the (domestic) RC is constrained by the no-Ponzi game condition, i.e.,

$$\limsup_{N\to\infty} R_{t,t+N} B_{t+N} \geq 0. \tag{3.23}$$

The no-Ponzi game condition (3.23) requires the limit superior of the RC's discounted net foreign debts to be non-negative.[16]

Analogously, when the RC is a net creditor towards the rest of the world, he would not choose to be on the lending side of the Ponzi game as this plan would be consumption-inefficient. Thus, the RC's optimality condition must be satisfied:

$$\liminf_{N\to\infty} R_{t,t+N} B_{t+N} \leq 0. \tag{3.24}$$

Conditions (3.23) and (3.24) imply that

$$\liminf_{N\to\infty} R_{t,t+N} B_{t+N} \leq 0 \leq \limsup_{N\to\infty} R_{t,t+N} B_{t+N}. \tag{3.25}$$

Because the limit superior must at least equal the limit inferior, inequality (3.25) is satisfied if $\liminf_{N\to\infty} R_{t,t+N} B_{t+N} = \limsup_{N\to\infty} R_{t,t+N} B_{t+N} = 0$.[17] In this case, the sequence $R_{t,t+N} B_{t+N}$

[15] For a sequence of real numbers a_n, the limit superior of a_n is defined as $\limsup_{n\to\infty} a_n := \lim_{n\to\infty} (\sup_{m\geq n} a_m)$. $\sup_{m\geq n} a_m$ denotes the supremum of a_m for $m \geq n$, i.e., the lowest possible upper bound which is a number b such that $a_m \leq b$ for all $m \geq n$, and for every arbitrary small positive number ε there exists a finite index m such that $a_m > b - \varepsilon$ (so that $-\varepsilon < a_m \leq b$). The limit inferior of a_n is defined as $\liminf_{n\to\infty} a_n := \lim_{n\to\infty} (\inf_{m\geq n} a_m)$ where $\inf_{m\geq n} a_m$ denotes the infimum of a_m for $m \geq n$, i.e., the greatest possible lower bound with $\inf_{m\geq n} a_m = -\sup_{m\geq n} a_m$ (Bierens, 2005, pp. 285-287).

[16] Under the assumption that the domestic economy is the only net borrower in the world, the combined net foreign assets B^{f}_{t+N} of all lenders are equal to the borrower's net foreign indebtedness B_{t+N}. This assumption simplifies the notation, but is not crucial for the derivation of equation (3.21). When there are (finitely) many net borrower economies, each country faces the no-Ponzi game condition (3.23) where the sum of net foreign debts possessed by all borrower economies (B) sums up to the sum of net foreign assets held by net creditor economies (B^{f}).

[17] The superior limit is at least as large as the inferior limit, i.e. $\liminf_{n\to\infty} a_n \leq \limsup_{n\to\infty} a_n$ because $\inf_{m\geq n} a_m \leq \sup_{m\geq n} a_m$ for all $m \geq n$. If the limit inferior and the limit superior coincide, the sequence is convergent, i.e., there exists a single limit: $\lim_{n\to\infty} a_n = \liminf_{n\to\infty} a_n = \limsup_{n\to\infty} a_n$ (Bierens, 2005, pp. 285-287).

converges to zero, that is, the limit in the transversality condition (3.21) exists and equals zero so that the transversality condition (3.21) is satisfied.

Under perfect foresight, the crucial assumption for infeasibility of Ponzi games is that the number of lenders is finite. If the number of agents (who care only about themselves) were infinite, there would always be new agents to trade with. Although each agent would behave optimally at the individual level, the aggregate optimality condition (3.22) would not be satisfied and Ponzi games would be possible. Besides, when the interest rate were allowed to be different in different economies, the interesting implication of the argument by O'Connell and Zeldes (1988) would be that whether an economy can play Ponzi games depends on the characteristics of the lenders' economy (such as the interest rate in lenders' economies), and not on those of the borrower's economy (O'Connell and Zeldes, 1988, p. 446).

If the transversality condition (3.21) is satisfied, equation (3.20) simplifies to the intertemporal budget constraint (IBC)

$$B_{t-1} = -\sum_{n=t}^{\infty} R_{t,n} TB_n. \tag{3.26}$$

The infinite horizon budget constraint (3.26) restricts at any point of time the initial value of the economy's NIIP to the (negative) present value of the economy's future trade balances. The IBC requires a net debtor economy to have a positive present value of future trade balances. When the present value of trade balances is negative, an economy must be initially a net creditor in order to meet the IBC.

The above analysis relies on the assumption of the strictly positive interest rate (i.e., of the discount factor being less than one). If the interest rate is zero (i.e., if the discount factor is unity), the transversality condition will be violated unless the undiscounted B_{t+N} happens to converge to zero. A famous example of a model with a zero interest rate is the model developed by Ramsey (1928) where the "enjoyments" of the future generations are not discounted for ethical reasons (Ramsey, 1928, p. 543).[18] In an economy with negative interest rates, the IBC is no proper constraint because the NIIP diminishes over time even if no payments on the NIIP have been made. Historically, however, negative real interest rates have not been observed very frequently; the rare examples include Asian economies in the late 1990s and the United States during the Great Depression or more recently in 2003 (Fleming and Garbade, 2004, p. 1; Weber, 2007, p. 6).

If the interest rate happens to be constant at r, the one-period discount factor simplifies to $R = 1/(1+r)$ with $r > 0$. In this case, the transversality condition (3.21) can be written as

$$\lim_{N \to \infty} R^{N+1} B_{t+N} = 0 \tag{3.27}$$

and the corresponding IBC as

$$B_{t-1} = -\sum_{n=t}^{\infty} R^{n-t+1} TB_n. \tag{3.28}$$

The special case of constant interest rates is widely used in the empirical literature on the intertemporal budget constraint.

[18] A survey of the debate on whether the well-being of future generations (also known as the "pure" discount rate debate) should be discounted can be found in Ponthière (2003).

It is also insightful to formulate the intertemporal budget constraint in proportion to output. Typically, it is done by solving the single-period budget constraint in terms of real GDP (3.10) forward by N periods and letting $N \to \infty$. This yields

$$d_{t,n} = -\sum_{n=t}^{\infty} d_{t,n} tb_n + \lim_{N\to\infty} d_{t+N,n} b_{t+N} = 0. \tag{3.29}$$

The real discount factor (adjusted for the real GDP growth rate) from time n back to period t ($d_{t,n}$) is defined as

$$d_{t,n} = \prod_{v=t}^{n} \left(\frac{1}{1+\phi_v}\right), \quad \phi_v = \frac{r_v - \gamma_v}{1+\gamma_v}, \quad d_{t,t} = 1. \tag{3.30}$$

If the transversality condition

$$\lim_{N\to\infty} d_{t,t+N} b_{t+N} = 0 \tag{3.31}$$

is satisfied, the economy obeys the intertemporal budget constraint of the form

$$b_{t-1} = -\sum_{n=t}^{\infty} d_{t,n} tb_n. \tag{3.32}$$

The sufficient requirement for both the TC (3.31) and the IBC (3.32) being well-defined at least for all bounded b and tb is that $d_{t,n}$ decays at an exponential rate, which means that the real interest rate exceeds the real GDP growth rate in all but finitely many periods (i.e., if $r_n > \gamma_n > 0$ for all but finitely many $n \geq t$). Under certainty, this situation implies dynamic efficiency in which the capital stock is equal to or less than the golden-rule level (Phelps, 1961). The idea is that market forces tend to prevent the real interest rate from falling behind the real GDP growth rate permanently in a dynamically efficient economy. If the economy accumulates net foreign debts in proportion to GDP, the pressure on capital markets raises the interest rate so that GDP growth declines. If the economy continues borrowing, the GDP growth rate keeps declining till it falls behind the real interest rate (Fischer and Easterly, 1990, p. 136). In contrast, if the real interest rate equals the real GDP growth rate, the discount factor takes the value one so that the limit term in the transversality condition (3.31) does not converge to zero. When the real GDP growth rate is higher than the real interest rate, the discount factor is larger than one. In this case, the NIIP-to-GDP ratio decreases over time even if no debt servicing has taken place, and the IBC (3.32) is meaningless because the present value of future trade balances in proportion to GDP is unbounded. Consequently, sustainability is not possible in a deterministic dynamically inefficient economy.

The requirement that the real interest rate should exceed the real GDP growth rate has the notable—and possibly counterintuitive—implication that a constant NIIP-to-output ratio is not sustainable regardless of the size (unless it is zero) because this would mean that the real interest rate were equal to the NIIP growth rate and the transversality condition would be violated! At the same time, an ever increasing ratio of net foreign debts (assets) to GDP is sustainable as long as the NIIP growth rate is smaller than the real interest rate! Yet a continually rising ratio of net foreign debts to GDP implies that the net interest payments increase as well and might eventually outstrip output in case that the NIIP and the real interest rate grow far more rapidly than GDP (see subsection 7.1.1 of chapter 7 for a detailed discussion). Should this happen, the economy would not be able to service neither the principal nor the interest payments and would become insolvent. This shows that the IBC does not take into account the boundedness of the economy's capacity to generate exports! Under perfect foresight, rational investors will foresee the debt crisis so that the economy will have difficulties to sell its debt even before net investment payments are higher than output (see Fischer and Easterly (1990, p. 135) and Romer (2006, pp. 563-564) for the analogous case of government debts).

3.1.4 Specific intertemporal budget constraint in the stochastic setting

Endowed with perfect foresight, the representative consumer is able to correctly anticipate future events. The situation changes when a more realistic assumption is adopted, viz. that the decisions of the agents are subject to uncertainty. In this case, the relevant macroeconomic variables are random and sustainability is ensured when both Ponzi games and the situation of supersolvency are ruled out with probability one.

One approach is to require that the transversality condition

$$\lim_{N\to\infty} R_{t,t+N}B_{t+N} = 0 \tag{3.33}$$

must be satisfied "almost surely", i.e., with probability one. The "almost sure" transversality condition (3.33) then implies the "almost sure" intertemporal budget constraint

$$B_{t-1} = -\sum_{n=t}^{\infty} R_{t,n}TB_n. \tag{3.34}$$

All variables in equations (3.33) and (3.34) are random, in contrast to their perfect-foresight counterparts (3.21) and (3.26) (Obstfeld and Rogoff, 1996, p. 80).

The empirical literature on the intertemporal budget constraint typically examines two "weaker" versions of the "almost sure" IBC (3.26) which will be referred to here as (i) the IBC in conditional expectation and (ii) the IBC of the conditional means. When the transversality condition (3.33) is satisfied almost surely, it is also satisfied in (conditional) expectation, that is:

$$E_t\left[\lim_{N\to\infty} R_{t,t+N}B_{t+N}\right] = 0 \tag{3.35}$$

where E_t is, as above, the rational expectations operator in the sense of the "strong form" of the rational-expectations hypothesis. Equation (3.35) states that agents—on the basis of the information set I_t—rationally expect the economy's discounted net foreign assets (liabilities) to vanish over time. The transversality condition (3.35) implies the intertemporal budget constraint in expectation:

$$B_{t-1} = -E_t\left[\sum_{n=t}^{\infty} R_{t,n}TB_n\right]. \tag{3.36}$$

The IBC (3.36) shows that agents rationally expect the economy's initial NIIP to equal the negative present value of future trade balances.

Under additional purely technical assumptions, the almost sure transversality condition (3.33) also implies the transversality condition of the (conditional) means.[19] The latter is obtained by shifting the expectation operator behind the limit term in the transversality condition in expectation (3.35):

$$\lim_{N\to\infty} E_t\left[R_{t,t+N}B_{t+N}\right] = 0. \tag{3.37}$$

The transversality condition of the means has a slightly different interpretation: The limit of the expected discounted value of the NIIP (and not the expected limit of the discounted NIIP as it is the case in the TC in expectation (3.35)) has to be zero. The TC of the means (3.37) implies the intertemporal budget constraint of the means:

$$B_{t-1} = -\sum_{n=t}^{\infty} E_t\left[R_{t,n}TB_n\right]. \tag{3.38}$$

The IBC of the means (3.38) restricts the initial NIIP to the negative sum of expected discounted future trade balances.

Tests of the IBC of the means (3.38) are weaker than tests of the IBC in expectation (3.36) because the IBC of the means (3.38) is (in contrast to the IBC in expectation (3.36)) strictly speaking not the consequence of the almost sure IBC (3.34). In other words, empirical evidence in favor of the validity of the IBC of the means (3.38) does not always indicate that the almost sure IBC (3.34) is satisfied in the data. However, when the discounted NIIP has a Gaussian distribution and the variances of the discounted NIIP decay at a fractional-polynomial speed, the TC (IBC) of the means is sufficient for the almost sure TC (IBC) (Herzberg and Herzberg, 2013).

The main problem with this approach is the underlying assumption that the outstanding NIIP and future trade balances can be discounted by the expected interest rate (which is a risk-free interest rate because riskless bonds are the only asset in our stylized model). Yet as Bohn (1995b) points out, the proper discount factor under uncertainty depends on the probability distribution of the relevant variables across different states of nature and is identical with the market discount factor only in special cases (such as risk neutrality or when the subjective time-preference rate equals the interest rate). To put it differently, the TC (3.33) and the IBC (3.34) ensure external sustainability with probability one only in cases in which the stochastic discount factor equals the market discount factor. For this reason, the intertemporal budget constraint which uses the expected interest rate for discounting is called "specific" in this work. However, with the only exception of the study by Durdu et al. (2010), the large empirical literature on the economy's intertemporal budget constraint tests the "specific" intertemporal budget constraint!

Discounting by the interest rate poses also another problem: The "specific" intertemporal budget constraint expressed in proportion to GDP requires the real interest rate to exceed the real GDP growth rate. Under uncertainty, the violation of this requirement does not necessarily imply dynamic inefficiency. In a stochastic environment, dynamic efficiency depends on the relationship between the real output growth rate and the return on the "risky capital" rather than the risk-free interest rate (Abel et al., 1989; Zilcha, 1992). So if, for example, the GDP

[19] This is a consequence of Lebesgue's Dominated Convergence Theorem: If a sequence of random variables converges to zero almost surely and is uniformly bounded by an integrable random variable, then the (conditional) means of these random variables converge to zero as well (Bierens, 2005, pp. 143-144).

growth rate equals the real interest rate and the economy is dynamically efficient, the "specific" intertemporal budget constraint is not satisfied. At the same time, dynamic efficiency indicates that Ponzi games are not feasible (Bohn, 1995b, p. 258). This contradiction is resolved when the stochastic discount factor is used instead of the risk-free market discount factor. The "general" intertemporal budget constraint which uses the stochastic discount factor is determined in the next section.

3.2 Intertemporal budget constraint in a general-equilibrium model

Examining fiscal sustainability, Bohn (1991, 1995b) derives the "general" (or what he calls "model-based") intertemporal budget constraint of a government in a stochastic Lucas (1978) exchange model which has been modified to incorporate both government and complete markets in the sense of Arrow (1964) and Debreu (1959). We transfer Bohn's (1991, 1995b) analysis to external sustainability by assuming a large number of identical economies and focusing on the economy's net foreign assets (debts) and trade balances. The resulting model can be viewed as a combination of the intertemporal approach to the current account and asset pricing theory.[20]

3.2.1 Characteristics of the model economy and the representative agent's maximization problem

The world consists of a large number of identical small open economies. A representative country is inhabited by identical infinitely-lived agents which are represented by a single representative consumer. The population size is normalized to unity so that aggregate and per-capita variables are equal.

Following Arrow (1964) and Debreu (1959), uncertainty is modelled by assuming that there are different possible states of nature and that asset returns depend on what state of nature will occur in the future. The representative agent behaves according to subjective probabilities she assigns to different states of nature. The set of possible states of nature on date t is determined by the history of the world through date $t-1$ and is denoted by S_t. A state of nature which finally realizes on date t is indicated by s_t with $s_t \in S_t$. The world-wide state of nature follows a stochastic process with the Markov transition density function (s_{t+1}, s_t). The history of the world economy up to and including the date t is denoted by h_t where $h_t = (s_t, s_{t-1}, \dots, s_0)$ and h_t takes values in a set H_t. The (subjective) unconditional probability of the economy's history h_t is indicated by $\pi(h_t)$, and the (subjective) conditional probability of observing h_t given the history of economy on some date n is denoted by $\pi(h_t|h_n)$.

In contrast to the stylized model described in the previous section, Lucas (1978) "fruit tree" model is a pure exchange model. An economy is endowed with a large number of identical everlasting productive units ("firms") which are often thought of as "fruit trees." Trees produce, at zero cost, a stochastic exogenous output ("seedless fruits") $Y_t(h_t)$. The notation $Y_t(h_t)$ means that output is a function of the history h_t. It is assumed that fruits cannot be stored and consumed

20 This model mainly draws on Lucas (1978, 1982), Bohn (1991, 1995b), Arrow (1964), Blanchard and Fischer (1989, pp. 510-512), Obstfeld and Rogoff (1996, pp. 269-286, 340-342), Mark (2001, pp. 81-88), Ljungqvist and Sargent (2004, pp. 208-217, 420), Bertola et al. (2005, pp. 181-186), Durdu et al. (2010, pp. 12-14), and Nyberg (2010, pp. 203-206).

in future periods so that feasible consumption C_t (which is also contingent on the history h_t) cannot exceed production in any period: $0 \leq C_t(h_t) \leq Y_t(h_t)$. Each tree issues one perfectly divisible share. Lucas (1978, p. 1430) defines a share as a claim to all of the tree's fruit in period t. In our context, a share is a one-period-ahead Arrow-Debreu security—also known as Arrow security or primitive security—which pays one unit of the consumption good (fruit) to its owner if and only if in period $t+1$ the state of nature s_{t+1} occurs and pays nothing if any other state realizes. Trading of Arrow-Debreu securities takes place at each date $n \geq t$ (sequential trading).[21] The asset market is perfectly competitive and complete, i.e., the number of unique (linearly independent) Arrow-Debreu securities equals the number of future states of the world (Copeland et al., 2005, p. 77). Fruits—which can also be thought of as dividends—form the sole source of income for individuals and can be "eaten" or exchanged for trees, that is, for claims to future consumption. Each consumer is endowed at birth with one share so that the number of people equals the amount of trees and shares and is (as mentioned above) assumed to be one.

The representative agent's single-period budget constraint is given by

$$\sum_{s_{t+1} \in S_{t+1}} p(s_{t+1}|h_t) B_t(s_{t+1}, h_t) + C_t(h_t) = Y_t(h_t) + B_{t-1}(h_t) \tag{3.39}$$

where $p(s_{t+1}|h_t)$ denotes the period-t world price of one consumption unit in period $t+1$ if the state s_{t+1} occurs given the history h_t. $B_t(s_{t+1}|h_t)$ are claims to period-$t+1$ consumption the RC holds at the end of period t and carries over to period $t+1$ which are contingent on the realization of the state s_{t+1}. Similarly, $B_{t-1}(h_t)$ indicates contingent claims to period-t consumption owned by the RC at the end of period $t-1$, i.e., at the beginning of period t. The right-hand side of the budget constraint (3.39) represents the total resources available to the consumer in period t: the dividends from the assets he owns ($Y_t(h_t)$) and the assets themselves. The left-hand side of the budget constraint (3.39) shows that the RC can use his resources to purchase new shares and a history-dependent consumption plan.

The representative consumer's preferences over his present consumption and his future consumption in different states of nature are ordered by

$$U = u(C_t(h_t)) + \sum_{n=t}^{\infty} \sum_{h_n \in H_n} \pi(h_n) \beta^{n-t} u(C_n(h_n)) \tag{3.40}$$

where U denotes the agent's lifetime utility and the discount factor $\beta \in (0;1)$. The period utility function $u(\cdot)$ is strictly increasing in consumption, strictly concave, and satisfies Inada (1964) conditions $\lim_{C \to 0} u'(C) = \infty$ and $\lim_{C \to \infty} u'(C) = 0$.

The representative agent maximizes the utility function (3.40) subject to the budget constraint (3.39). The Lagrangian for (nonnegative) Lagrange multipliers $\lambda(h_n)$ is given by

[21] The assumption of the arrangement of sequential trading is not crucial for the results of the model because the Arrow-Debreu economy with sequential trading attains the same equilibrium allocation as the economy in which agents trade claims to consumption for all future dates only at the initial date (Ljungqvist and Sargent, 2004, pp. 226-227).

$$\mathcal{L} = \sum_{n=0}^{\infty} \sum_{h_n \in H_n} \pi(h_n)\beta^{n-t}u(C_n(h_n)) + \lambda(h_n)\Bigg((Y_n(h_n) - C_n(h_n) \\ + B_{n-1}(h_n) - \sum_{s_{n+1} \in S_{n+1}} p(s_{n+1}|h_n)B_n(s_{n+1}, h_n)\Bigg).$$

The first-order conditions for maximizing $\mathcal{L}$ with respect to $C_n(h_n)$ and $B_{n-1}(h_n)$ are

$$\pi(h_n)\beta^{n-t}u'(C_n(h_n)) - \lambda(h_n) = 0 \tag{3.41}$$

$$-\lambda(h_{n-1})p(s_n|h_{n-1}) + \lambda(h_n) = 0 \tag{3.42}$$

where the world's history h_n is defined as $h_n = (s_n, h_{n-1})$. The first-order conditions (3.41) and (3.42) together imply for $n = t+1$ the following Euler equation:

$$\pi(h_{t+1}|h_t)\beta\frac{u'(C_{t+1}(h_{t+1}))}{u'(C_t(h_t))} = p(s_{t+1}|h_t) \tag{3.43}$$

where it has been used that $\pi(h_{t+1})/\pi(h_t) = \pi(h_{t+1}|h_t)$. The left-hand side of equation (3.43) represents the one-period pricing kernel or one-period stochastic discount factor defined as the product of the state probability, the representative agent's time-preference factor, and the marginal rate of substitution between present and future consumption (Ljungqvist and Sargent, 2004, pp. 222-223). The Euler equation (3.43) thus shows that in equilibrium the stochastic discount factor equals the price for state-contingent claims.

3.2.2 General intertemporal budget constraint

Following Bohn (1991, 1995b), the intertemporal budget constraint is obtained by combining the Euler equation (3.43) with the single-period budget constraint (3.39) in the first step, iterating the resulting equation forward in the second step, and imposing the no-Ponzi game and optimality conditions in the third and final step. Substituting the Euler equation (3.43) into the budget constraint (3.39) results in

$$B_{t-1}(h_t) = \sum_{s_{t+1} \in S_{t+1}} \pi(h_{t+1}|h_t)\beta\frac{u'(C_{t+1}(h_{t+1}))}{u'(C_t(h_t))}B_t(s_{t+1}, h_t) + C_t(h_t) - Y_t(h_t). \tag{3.44}$$

Solving equation (3.44) forward by ∞ periods (see Appendix 3.B for details) leads to

$$B_{t-1}(h_t) = -\sum_{n=t}^{\infty}\sum_{h_n|h_t} \pi(h_n|h_t)\beta^{n-t}\frac{u'(C_n(h_n))}{u'(C_t(h_t))}\Big(Y_n(h_n) - C_n(h_n)\Big) \\ + \lim_{N\to\infty} \sum_{h_{t+N+1}|h_t} \pi(h_{t+N+1}|h_t)\beta^{N+1}\frac{u'(C_{t+N+1}(h_{t+N+1}))}{u'(C_t(h_t))}B_{t+N}(h_{t+N+1}) \tag{3.45}$$

where the history h_{t+N} is defined as $h_{t+N+1} = (s_{t+N+1}, s_{t+N}, \ldots, s_t, \ldots, s_0)$. Equation (3.45) shows that the RC's initial stock of contingent claims equals the (negative) present value of future output less consumption plus the limit of the outstanding stock of contingent claims weighted by the stochastic discount factor.

The proper transversality condition in a stochastic environment with complete markets is then given by

$$\lim_{N\to\infty} \sum_{h_{t+N+1}|h_t} \pi(h_{t+N+1}|h_t)\,\beta^{N+1}\frac{u'(C_{t+N+1}(h_{t+N+1}))}{u'(C_t(h_t))}B_{t+N}(h_{t+N+1}) = 0. \tag{3.46}$$

The justification for the transversality condition (3.46) follows closely the argument given by O'Connell and Zeldes (1988) for perfect foresight (see subsubsection 3.1.3). The idea is that an optimizing agent would not participate in another agent's Ponzi schemes. Applying Bohn's (1991, 1995b) proof to external sustainability, the optimality condition for all lenders is given by

$$\liminf_{N\to\infty} \sum_{h_{t+N+1}|h_t} \pi(h_{t+N+1}|h_t)\,\beta^{N+1}\frac{u'(C_{t+N+1}(h_{t+N+1}))}{u'(C_t(h_t))}B^f_{t+N}(h_{t+N+1}) \leq 0 \tag{3.47}$$

where $B^f_{t+N}(h_{t+N+1})$ are contingent claims owned by foreign lenders and the number of international lenders is finite. The lenders' optimality condition implies that the home country cannot engage in Ponzi finance, that is, the no-Ponzi game condition must be satisfied:

$$\limsup_{N\to\infty} \sum_{h_{t+N+1}|h_t} \pi(h_{t+N+1}|h_t)\,\beta^{N+1}\frac{u'(C_{t+N+1}(h_{t+N+1}))}{u'(C_t(h_t))}B_{t+N}(h_{t+N+1}) \geq 0. \tag{3.48}$$

Analogously, the representative agent's optimality condition is

$$\liminf_{N\to\infty} \sum_{h_{t+N+1}|h_t} \pi(h_{t+N+1}|h_t)\,\beta^{N+1}\frac{u'(C_{t+N+1}(h_{t+N+1}))}{u'(C_t(h_t))}B_{t+N}(h_{t+N+1}) \leq 0 \tag{3.49}$$

in case that the RC is a net creditor towards the rest of the world. The RC's optimality condition (3.49) and the no-Ponzi game condition (3.48) jointly imply the transversality condition (3.46).

The transversality condition (3.46) can also be put into the expectational form. Taking the expectation operator E_t with respect to information known in period t, i.e., to the world's history h_t and using the national-income identity (2.2) to substitute $C_{t+N+1}(h_{t+N+1}) = Y_{t+N+1}(h_{t+N+1}) - TB_{t+N+1}(h_{t+N+1})$, the transversality condition (3.46) can be rewritten as

$$\lim_{N\to\infty} E_t\left[\beta^{N+1}\frac{u'(Y_{t+N+1}(h_{t+N+1}) - TB_{t+N+1}(h_{t+N+1}))}{u'(Y_t(h_t) - TB_t(h_t))}B_{t+N}(h_{t+N+1})\right] = 0. \tag{3.50}$$

The transversality condition (3.50) is satisfied if the stochastic discount factor is absolutely higher than the NIIP growth rate.

The transversality condition (3.50) implies the intertemporal budget constraint given by

$$B_{t-1}(h_t) = -\sum_{n=t}^{\infty} E_t\left[\beta^{n-t}\frac{u'(Y_n(h_n) - TB_n(h_n))}{u'(Y_t(h_t) - TB_t(h_t))}TB_n(h_n)\right]. \tag{3.51}$$

The IBC (3.51) follows from equation (3.45) when the expectation operator is used and $TB_n(h_n) = Y_n(h_n) - C_n(h_n)$ for all $n \geq t$.

3.2.3 Comparison of the general intertemporal budget constraint to the specific intertemporal budget constraint

The crucial difference between the general and the specific intertemporal budget constraint is the choice of discounting: the general IBC uses an endogenously given stochastic discount factor, and the specific IBC uses the market discount factor. In other words, the general IBC is valid in equilibrium in which the agents have determined their optimal plan whereas the specific IBC is valid only for a certain level of the interest rate.

The difference between the two forms of discounting is illustrated best by rewriting the conditional expectation in the general intertemporal budget constraint (3.51) using the definition of (conditional) covariance[22]:

$$\begin{aligned}
&E_t\left[\beta^{n-t}\frac{u'(Y_n(h_n)-TB_n(h_n))}{u'(Y_t(h_t)-TB_t(h_t))}TB_n(h_n)\right]\\
=&E_t\left[\beta^{n-t}\frac{u'(Y_n(h_n)-TB_n(h_n))}{u'(Y_t(h_t)-TB_t(h_t))}\right]E_t\left[TB_n(h_n)\right]\\
&+\mathrm{Cov}_t\left(\beta^{n-t}\frac{u'(Y_n(h_n)-TB_n(h_n))}{u'(Y_t(h_t)-TB_t(h_t))},TB_n(h_n)\right)
\end{aligned}\tag{3.52}$$

where $n \geq t$ and Cov_t denotes the covariance conditioned on information available up to date t. The conditional expectation on the right-hand side of equation (3.52) can be further rewritten exploiting the Euler equation

$$\beta E_t\left[\frac{u'(Y_n(h_n)-TB_n(h_n))}{u'(Y_{n-1}(h_{n-1})-TB_{n-1}(h_{n-1}))}\right]=E_t\left[\frac{1}{1+r(s_n|h_{n-1})}\right]\tag{3.53}$$

which has to be satisfied in equilibrium by the rate of return $r(s_n|h_{n-1})$ on any security (Ljungqvist and Sargent, 2004, p. 223). Combining equations (3.53) and (3.52) with the IBC (3.51) yields

$$\begin{aligned}
B_{t-1}(h_t)=&-\sum_{n=t}^{\infty}E_t\left[\prod_{v=t}^{n}\left(\frac{1}{1+r(s_v|h_{v-1})}\right)TB_n(h_n)\right]\\
&-\sum_{n=t}^{\infty}\mathrm{Cov}_t\left(\beta^{n-t}\frac{u'\left(Y_n\left(h_n\right)-TB_n\left(h_n\right)\right)}{u'\left(Y_t\left(h_t\right)-TB_t\left(h_t\right)\right)},TB_n\left(h_n\right)\right)
\end{aligned}\tag{3.54}$$

where $\prod_{v=t}^{t}\left(1/\left(1+r(s_t|h_{t-1})\right)\right)=1$.

Similar considerations apply to the transversality condition (3.50) which can be rewritten as

$$\begin{aligned}
&\lim_{N\to\infty}\left(\prod_{v=t}^{t+N+1}\frac{1}{1+r(s_v|h_{v-1})}E_t[B_{t+N}(h_{t+N+1})]\right.\\
&\left.+\mathrm{Cov}_t\left(\beta^{N+1}\frac{u'\left(Y_{t+N+1}\left(h_{t+N+1}\right)-TB_{t+N+1}\left(h_{t+N+1}\right)\right)}{u'\left(Y_t\left(h_t\right)-TB_t\left(h_t\right)\right)},B_{t+N}(h_{t+N+1})\right)\right)\\
&=0.
\end{aligned}\tag{3.55}$$

[22] The conditional covariance between two random variables X and Y can be expressed as $\mathrm{Cov}_t(X,Y)=E_t[XY]-E_t[X]E_t[Y]$ (e.g., Pestman and Alberink, 1998, p. 4). Solving for $E_t[XY]$ yields $E_t[XY]=E_t[X]E_t[Y]+\mathrm{Cov}_t(X,Y)$.

It follows from equations (3.54) and (3.55) that sustainability does not necessarily require the interest rate to be always strictly positive. With zero interest rates, the IBC (3.54) and the TC (3.55) are satisfied if the covariance term is large enough and has the right sign. Similarly, sustainability does not necessarily depend on the relationship between the real interest rate and the real GDP growth rate. Expressing the TC (3.55) in proportion to real GDP yields

$$\begin{aligned}&\lim_{N\to\infty}\left(\prod_{v=t}^{t+N+1}\frac{1}{1+\phi(s_v|h_{v-1})}E_t\left[b_{t+N}(h_{t+N+1})\right]\right.\\&\left.+\mathrm{Cov}_t\left(\beta^{N+1}\frac{u'\left(1-tb_{t+N+1}\left(h_{t+N+1}\right)\right)}{u'\left(1-tb_t\left(h_t\right)\right)},b_{t+N}(h_{t+N+1})\right)\right)\\&=0\end{aligned} \tag{3.56}$$

where

$$\phi(s_v|h_{v-1})=\frac{r(s_v|h_{v-1})-\gamma(s_v|h_{v-1})}{1+\gamma(s_v|h_{v-1})}, \tag{3.57}$$

$$tb_{t+N+1}\left(h_{t+N+1}\right)\equiv\frac{TB_{t+N+1}\left(h_{t+N+1}\right)}{Y_{t+N+1}\left(h_{t+N+1}\right)},\quad N\geq 0. \tag{3.58}$$

Even if the real interest rate equals the real GDP growth rate, the IBC (3.56) is satisfied as long as the covariance term equals the expected outstanding NIIP with the opposite sign. This in particular implies that a constant NIIP/GDP ratio might be consistent with the general TC (3.56)—in contrast to the specific TC!

The general IBC (3.54) and the general TC (3.55) are equivalent to their specific counterparts—those that discount by interest rates—only when the covariance term is zero. The covariance term drops out trivially in the deterministic setting (because the expected values of non-random variables always equal the observed values). Under the more realistic assumption of uncertainty, the covariance term is zero if (i) the stochastic discount factor and/or the trade balance is constant (because covariance between a constant and a random variable or between two constants is zero) or (ii) when the stochastic discount factor and the trade balance vary over time and are uncorrelated.

A series of constant trade balances (in levels or relative to output) might occur when a country aims at achieving a target trade balance, for example, via exchange rate policy, capital controls, or taxes. However, the policy of trade balance targeting is not likely to be successful indefinitely and might in addition reduce welfare by preventing consumers from consumption smoothing in the face of income shocks (Kimbrough, 1988, p. 318).

The stochastic discount factor is constant if both the time-preference rate and the marginal rate of substitution (MRS) are constant or if both compensate each other so that the product remains constant over time. The marginal rate of substitution is constant when individuals are risk-neutral, i.e., are indifferent between the expected value of any consumption plan and the consumption plan itself (Obstfeld and Rogoff, 1996, p. 279). In this case, the period utility function is linear (and not concave, as assumed above) so that the marginal utility of consumption $u'(Y_n(h_n)-TB_n(h_n))$ remains constant for all $n\geq t$. However, empirical studies have predominantly found (decreasing) risk aversion, not risk neutrality (Levy, 1994; Hartog et al., 2002; Lee, 2008; Paravisini et al., 2010).

The MRS is also constant when the (constant) subjective time-preference factor equals the (constant) market discount factor (i.e., $\beta = (1+r)^{-1}$). In this case, the Euler equation (3.53) simplifies to

$$E_t[u'(Y_n(h_n) - TB_n(h_n))] = E_t[u'(Y_{n-1}(h_{n-1}) - TB_{n-1}(h_{n-1}))]. \qquad (3.59)$$

Due to the monotonicity of the expectation operator, it follows from equation (3.59) that

$$u'(Y_n(h_n) - TB_n(h_n)) = u'(Y_{n-1}(h_{n-1}) - TB_{n-1}(h_{n-1})). \qquad (3.60)$$

Equation (3.60) implies that $u'(Y_{t+N+1}(h_{t+N+1}) - TB_{t+N+1}(h_{t+N+1})) = u'(Y_t(h_t) - TB_t(h_t))$ in the transversality condition (3.55) and that $u'(Y_n(h_n) - TB_n(h_n)) = u'(Y_t(h_t) - TB_t(h_t))$ in the intertemporal budget constraint (3.54) so that the MRS is unity in both cases. However, the empirical evidence suggests that the time-preference rate is declining over time and that it does not converge to the market interest rate (Frederick et al., 2002, pp. 380-381, 389, 391).[23]

When the marginal rate of substitution and the trade balance (and possibly also the time-preference rate) are time-varying and non-zero in at least one period, the covariance term will disappear only when the stochastic discount factor from period n (from period $t+N+1$) to period t is uncorrelated with the n-period's trade balance (the $t+N+1$-period's NIIP). To the best of our knowledge, there are no empirical studies exploring the correlation relationship between the stochastic discount factor and the trade balance or the NIIP. Therefore, it is difficult to rate how likely a non-zero correlation between the trade balance and the stochastic discount factor is. Yet one can approach this question by exploiting the empirical literature on the correlation between output and the trade balance. Since consumption equals the difference between output and the trade balance ($C_n = Y_n - TB_n$), an improvement in the trade balance of period n reduces consumption in that period unless an increase in the trade balance is offset by an increase of the same magnitude in the period-n output. A one-to-one positive correlation between the trade balance and output lacks, however, empirical support: In most countries, the trade balance is countercyclical (Backus and Kehoe, 1992; Neumeyer and Perri, 2005; Aguiar and Gopinath, 2007). With countercyclical trade balance, an increase in n-period's net exports reduces n-period's consumption and—under the above assumption of strictly concave utility function—increases the marginal utility of consumption in period n. In the (admittedly unrealistic) case that the time-preference rate is constant, this implies a positive correlation between the stochastic discount factor and the trade balance.

In view of the above considerations, the covariance term in the general intertemporal budget constraint (3.54) is likely to be non-zero. Thus, the specific intertemporal budget constraint will in most cases deviate from the general intertemporal budget constraint, which is the proper sustainability criterion.

3.3 Discussion of the theoretical framework

The stylized models used to derive both the specific and the general intertemporal budget constraints are, by construction, subject to several limitations. The first of those limitations concerns

[23] An alternative utility model which is consistent with the empirical finding of decreasing time-preference rate is, for example, the model with hyperbolic discounting (e.g., Laibson, 1997), see also Rubinstein (2003) for the critique of the experimental results on hyperbolic discounting.

the structure of asset markets. The traditional intertemporal approach to the current account (section 3.1) assumes an extreme form of incomplete markets by considering a riskless bond as the only asset in the economy and ignoring many other types of assets such as stocks or insurances. Replacing it with the assumption of complete markets in the Lucas (1978)-style model (section 3.2) also comes at a cost: This assumption requires an unrealistically large number of assets in order to allow the agents to insure against all possible contingencies (Flood, 1991, p. 44). In practice, however, some of the required assets might not exist when agents have asymmetric information or not enough money to trade at the appropriate point of time (Geanakoplos, 1990, p. 2). A less extreme, and more realistic, assumption is that of incomplete markets where agents are also able to trade other assets than bonds and in which the number of future states of the world exceeds the number of unique (linearly independent) Arrow-Debreu securities.[24] This significantly less stylized but—accordingly—analytically less tractable class of models will be briefly discussed now.

Magill and Quinzii (1994, 1996) derive the agents' transversality condition and the intertemporal budget constraint in the continuous time general-equilibrium model with incomplete markets and heterogeneous agents. The argument for the validity of the transversality condition in equilibrium goes along the lines of O'Connell and Zeldes (1988): Rational agents would not choose an optimal consumption plan which places them onto the lending side of a Ponzi scheme. When the number of lenders is finite, no agent could find a lender which permits her to play Ponzi games. The main difference to the complete markets setting is that on incomplete markets marginal rates of substitution and, therefore, discount factors are different for agents on different sides of the transaction. At the same time, when agents are heterogeneous and markets are large, no agent can be expected to have full knowledge about the discount factors of all other agents—and thus apparently lacks the ability to detect Ponzi schemes. This represents a nontrivial difficulty for ensuring the absence of Ponzi schemes, i.e., establishing the transversality condition. The difficulty can be resolved by exploiting the notion of competitive perceptions introduced by Grossman and Hart (1979): An agent uses his own discount factor when no information on the valuations of other agents can be deduced from observed or anticipated prices. In order to arrive at an equilibrium with the transversality condition, further assumptions are needed. The first assumption (suggested by Bewley, 1972) states that agent's preferences are continuous in the Mackey (1946) topology. In other words, agents are impatient in the sense that they prefer present consumption to future consumption. Because consumption becomes unimportant in the very distant future, this assumption also permits the approximation of the infinite horizon economy by a finite horizon economy. The second assumption ascertains that the degree of impatience is bounded away from zero uniformly across the nodes (of the tree of possible future paths of the economy), that is, the agent is willing to give up at least some positive fraction of future consumption to obtain an additional unit of commodity at each node. Finally, the information available at time t is assumed to be the same for all agents in the economy (symmetric information). These considerations lead to the following transversality condition:

$$\lim_{N\to\infty} \sum_{\xi' \in \mathbf{D_{t+N}}(\xi)} \pi^i(\xi')q^i(\xi')z^i(\xi') = 0 \quad \xi \in \mathbf{D} \tag{3.61}$$

[24] A survey of the literature on the general equilibrium theory with incomplete markets is provided by Geanakoplos (1990).

where $\mathbf{D}$ is the event-tree which consists of all nodes ξ and $\mathbf{D_N}(\xi)$ denotes the subset of nodes at date $t+N$. The vector π^i describes how agent i discounts a stream of income in the future back to date t and is chosen by the agent i such that the marginal cost of each security equals the marginal benefit of its return at the following nodes. The portfolio owned by agent i at node ξ' is denoted by $z^i(\xi')$, and $q^i(\xi')$ is the row vector of prices of the securities issued at node ξ'. The transversality condition (3.61) is then the analogue of the general transversality condition in our continuous time, complete markets setting.

Further, Pavlova and Rigobon (2010a) construct a general-equilibrium, two country, continuous time, Lucas (1978) exchange model with multiple risky assets and incomplete markets. After taking into account the endogenous responses of asset prices to underlying shocks, Pavlova and Rigobon (2010a) show that in equilibrium the NIIP equals the (negative) present value of the expected future trade balances multiplied with the stochastic discount factor—which corresponds to the general intertemporal budget constraint.

In addition to the assumptions on the structure of asset markets, there is also a second limitation of the stylized models studied in this chapter: The analysis of a small economy which faces exogenously given world prices might not be applicable to large economies such as the United States. Further limitations are as follows. The Lucas (1978) exchange model (section 2) treats production as exogenous. The model from section 1 assumes a simple Cobb-Douglas production function with fixed, perfectly inelastic labor and no adjustment costs of investment. These are not negligible limitations, because incorporating installment costs and modeling labor explicitly might well change the form of the intertemporal budget constraint. Besides, the assumption of internationally immobile labor means that emigration of workers and the resulting remittances are ignored (Obstfeld and Rogoff, 1996, p. 45). This again need not be an innocuous limitation, since remittances from developed to developing countries constitute a considerable share of total international inflows, e.g., 31 percent for low-income countries[25] during 1994-1999 (Gammeltoft, 2003, p. 104).

Government spending is also exogenous in the stylized models above. The model in section 1 assumes balanced government budgets in each period which—coupled with the assumption of intertemporal separability of the utility function—imply that government consumption affects the current account only to the extent that it tilts the private component of net output (Obstfeld and Rogoff, 1996, p. 12). Allowing for fiscal deficits or surpluses does not change this result if taxes are lump-sum in nature. The reason is that, in this case, the timing of lump-sum taxes does not affect the RC's decisions and fiscal imbalances are irrelevant to resource allocation and to the current account. The hypothesis that whether government spending is financed by lump-sum taxes or borrowing does not matter for private consumption is known as Ricardian equivalence (Obstfeld and Rogoff, 1996, pp. 130-131; Harms, 2008, pp. 129-134). However, Ricardian equivalence fails, for example, when government spending is financed via proportional income taxes or when the government's time horizon exceeds the private agents' time horizon

[25] According to the World Bank classification, low-income countries are countries with gross national income (GNI) per capita of 1,035 USD or less in 2012; middle-income countries are countries with GNI per capita ranging from 1,036 USD to 12,615 USD, and high-income countries have GNI per capita of 12,616 USD or more in 2012 (World Bank, 2013).

(Harms, 2008, pp. 134-136).[26] This could mean that the findings of the stylized sustainability analysis of section 1 cannot be maintained in the presence of, e.g., proportional income taxes.

Although external sustainability refers to both the public and private sectors, examining fiscal (external) sustainability separately could point to causes of external sustainability. Such a separate examination of fiscal sustainability would, by the way, be in line with the twin-deficits hypothesis which states that fiscal deficits caused by a fiscal shock generate current account deficits. The twin-deficits hypothesis has been suggested as an explanation for recently observed global imbalances, yet the empirical support for the twin deficits hypothesis seems to be rather weak (see, e.g., surveys by Bartolini and Lahiri, 2006 and Abbas et al., 2011).

Further, both models used in this chapter are real models with effectively no monetary sector so that the interest rate is treated as exogenous. There is also no scope for the impact of exchange rates on the trade balance. However, in case of the validity of the Marshall-Lerner condition, a real depreciation improves an economy's trade balance in the long-run.[27] In the short run, the trade balance may temporarily deteriorate before improving—which yields the pattern of a J, known as the J-curve effect, when rendered graphically. However, the recent review of the empirical literature (combined with a re-evaluation of the results of previous studies) conducted by Hegerty et al. (2013) provides only weak support for the validation of the Marshall-Lerner condition. Similarly, the review by Bahmani-Oskooee and Ratha (2004) finds merely ambiguous or inconclusive evidence in favor of the J-curve phenomenon.

The rational expectations hypothesis, though being a standard modelling assumption in economics, has been challenged on theoretical and empirical grounds by Simon (1955, 1957), Kahneman and Tversky (1973, 1979) and others (see also surveys by Lovell, 1986, Sargent, 1993, and Conlisk, 1996).[28] Bounded rationality may arise from adaptive learning when agents modify their choices on the basis of past performance because they do not know the underlying "law of motion" of the economy (Honkapohja, 1993, p. 587). Chow (1988, 2011) shows that the adaptive expectations hypothesis dominates the rational expectations in present value. Therefore, it could prove fruitful to incorporate adaptive expectations into the above setting. The assumption of the representative consumer is popular in the macroeconomic literature, yet not without controversy (e.g., Kirman, 1992, 2006). However, in a complete markets environment and when agents face the same prices, prices and per-capita consumption behave as if there existed a single representative consumer who owns the economy's average endowment (Obstfeld and Rogoff, 1996, pp. 292-293). Besides, Magill and Quinzii (1994, 1996) show the existence of the equilibrium with the transversality condition when agents are heterogeneous.

Furthermore, difficulties in enforcing contracts might create incentives for sovereign borrowers to default opportunistically on the liabilities towards international lenders and limit the range of contracts international investors are willing to conclude *ex ante* (Obstfeld and Rogoff,

---

[26] A survey of the arguments in favor and against the Ricardian equivalence can be found in Ricciuti (2003).

[27] The Marshall-Lerner condition was first introduced by Bickerdike (1920) and Marshall (1923) and further developed by Lerner (1944) and Robinson (1949). Provided that the initial trade balance is zero and the price elasticities of the export and import supply are infinite, the Marshall-Lerner condition states, in its simplest form, that a real depreciation of an economy's currency improves the economy's trade balance if the sum of price elasticities of the export and import demand is greater than one in absolute.

[28] See, e.g., Rubinstein (2001), Plott and Zeiler (2005), Fudenberg (2006), and Binmore and Shaked (2010) for a critical discussion of the implications of experimental economics for economic theory.

1996, p. 349).[29] Perfect international capital mobility might be in practice hampered by capital controls (e.g., Obstfeld, 1996; Frankel, 1992) which in turn might limit the availability of funds.

Finally, chapter 6 examines several modifications of the canonical intertemporal approach to the current account: habit formation, the existence of durable goods (i.e., long-lived goods) and of non-traded goods which do not enter international trade, e.g., due to prohibitively high transport costs or tariffs.

3.4 Conclusion

The informational content of the intertemporal budget constraint is limited in the sense that it can only lead to dichotomous results: sustainability or no sustainability. If, for example, a reversal from a trade deficit to a trade surplus is required to maintain sustainability, the IBC does not provide information on the timing or the manner (smoothly or abruptly) of the necessary adjustment.

Although the intertemporal budget constraint has been widely used in the theoretical and empirical literature on external sustainability, this criterion is subject to several limitations. Firstly, both the specific and general intertemporal budget constraints impose only weak restrictions on the paths of the current account, the NIIP, and the trade account. A net debtor economy can run large and persistent trade and current account deficits and still satisfy the IBC as long as it is expected to generate sufficiently large trade surpluses in the—even very distant—future (Corsetti and Roubini, 1991, p. 355; Corsetti et al., 1999, p. 312). Similarly, the accumulation of net foreign assets (debts) is sustainable forever as long as the growth rate of the NIIP is smaller than the stochastic discount factor. Besides, the specific intertemporal budget constraint has the puzzling implication that the constant ratio of the NIIP to output is *per se* unsustainable—disregarding of its size—because it implies that the growth rate of the NIIP exceeds the interest rate (assuming the output growth rate to be higher than the interest rate).

Secondly, both the specific and the general intertemporal budget constraints ignore that the economy's capacity to generate trade surpluses might be bounded: Continually increasing net interest payments arising from the—even sustainable—accumulation of net foreign debts might at some point become larger than output and precipitate a debt crisis. This shows that sustainability requires both solvency and economic feasibility of external imbalances (Pitchford, 1995, p. 124; IMF, 2002, p. 5). Moreover, solvency must be accompanied by political and social feasibility: An economy should be both able and willing to divert output from internal use to external use (Milesi-Ferretti and Razin, 1996a, p. 1; IMF, 2002, p. 5).

Further, the intertemporal budget constraint does not take into account the maturity structure of the NIIP. Even if the overall level of the NIIP is consistent with the IBC, a certain combination of short-run liabilities and long-run assets might lead to illiquidity[30]. Illiquidity problems can also arise if investors have a finite planning horizon and refuse to postpone the repayment of the principal forever (Harms, 2008, p. 229). If no further financing is available, interest rates might rise and eventually jeopardize economy's solvency. This also shows that the distinction

[29] An overview of debt problems arising in the sovereign context can be found in Kolb (2011).

[30] An economy is said to be illiquid if its liquid assets and available financing are insufficient to meet or prolong its liabilities falling due (IMF, 2002, p. 5).

between solvency and liquidity is not always sharp (IMF, 2002, p. 5). In sum, relying merely on the intertemporal budget constraint does not fully capture sustainability.

It is often argued that the intertemporal budget constraint considers only the net borrower economy's ability to pay and neglects investors' willingness to lend (see, e.g., Milesi-Ferretti and Razin, 1996a; Önel and Utkulu, 2006). However, this critique applies only to those cases in which the intertemporal budget constraint is understood as the "specific" one and the market discount factor is different from the stochastic discount factor. In contrast, the "general" intertemporal budget constraint takes into account both willingness to lend and ability to pay. Moreover, the argument for the validity of the ("general") intertemporal budget constraint even collapses when the lenders' optimization problem is ignored. However, aside from the IBC, investors might well impose additional constraints on an economy, such as bounds on the NIIP-to-GDP ratio (Bohn, 2007, p. 1845).

Finally, Bagnai (2004, pp. 5-6) argues, in the context of fiscal sustainability, that the inherent problem of the intertemporal budget constraint as a sustainability criterion is that it *must* be satisfied in equilibrium in economies with certain characteristics such as that the number of optimizing agents is finite: Ponzi games are not feasible in equilibrium if the number of optimizing agents is finite.[31] The reason is that in those economies no agent is allowed to play Ponzi games because no other agent will consent to be on the lending side of a Ponzi game. Hence, insolvency or supersolvency cannot occur in equilibrium at all—whence there is no need for the sustainability analysis in the sense of the IBC, so Bagnai (2004). In contrast, if the structure of an economy is such that it permits Ponzi games (e.g., because a number of agents is infinite), the economy is not constrained (at least at the aggregate level) by the intertemporal budget constraint in equilibrium. In this case, there is no need to investigate sustainability either, simply because this economy is never solvent in equilibrium.

However, this point does not imply that the sustainability assessment based on the intertemporal budget constraint is totally meaningless. Testing empirically for the IBC always makes sense when the information on the relevant characteristics of the economy is insufficient for a theoretical judgment about feasibility of Ponzi finance. Further, even if we know that the number of optimizing lenders is finite (or infinite) over the course of history, the argument of O'Connell and Zeldes (1988) only shows that Ponzi games are not feasible (or are feasible) *in expectation*. Thus, there still might be states of the world in which Ponzi games are feasible (or are not feasible). In this case, the empirical analysis can reveal whether the economy in question is in fact constrained by the IBC. Besides, transferring the conclusions derived in a model with no scope for money, bounded rationality, information asymmetries, etc. directly to the "real" world might be misleading. Finally, even if Ponzi games are theoretically feasible, in practice, investors might well question a net debtor economy's repayment ability (in particular if net foreign debt is high and increasing), for example, if lenders are not aware of the fact that their number is infinite or if their planning horizon is finite. In this case, policy intervention (for instance, with the aim of improving the trade balance) would be appropriate in order to impose the IBC on the economy.

[31] As discussed above, this result holds in great generality: It was first established under perfect foresight (O'Connell and Zeldes, 1988), then proved under uncertainty with complete markets (Bohn, 1991) and finally even incomplete markets (Magill and Quinzii, 1994, 1996).

These considerations lead to the following interpretation of the empirical results: If the empirical analysis supports the validity of the IBC in the data, we conclude that a given path of external imbalances is consistent with solvency and that there is no need to worry. If the empirical tests detect the violation of the IBC in the data, we conclude that the external imbalances violate solvency and, on normative terms, policy measures imposing the IBC will be prudent. The next two chapters will illustrate the econometric methodology for testing the validity of the intertemporal budget constraint.

Appendix to Chapter 3

3.A Appendix to subsection 3.1.3

3.A.1 Recursive substitution method

The difference equation (3.5), i.e.,

$$B_t = TB_t + (1+r_t)B_{t-1} \tag{3.62}$$

can be solved forward using the recursive substitution method.[32]

Forwarding equation (3.62) by one period yields

$$B_{t+1} = TB_{t+1} + (1+r_{t+1})B_t. \tag{3.63}$$

Combining equations (3.62) and (3.63) so that B_t can be eliminated one arrives at

$$B_{t+1} = TB_{t+1} + (1+r_{t+1})TB_t + (1+r_{t+1})(1+r_t)B_{t-1}. \tag{3.64}$$

Analogously, forwarding equation (3.62) by two periods one obtains

$$B_{t+2} = TB_{t+2} + (1+r_{t+2})B_{t+1}. \tag{3.65}$$

Substituting equation (3.64) into equation (3.65) results in

$$\begin{aligned} B_{t+2} =& TB_{t+2} + (1+r_{t+2})TB_{t+1} + (1+r_{t+2})(1+r_{t+1})TB_t \\ &+ (1+r_{t+2})(1+r_{t+1})(1+r_t)B_{t-1}. \end{aligned} \tag{3.66}$$

Repeating in the same way for $B_{t+3}, B_{t+4}, \ldots, B_{t+N}$ one obtains for $N \geq 0$

$$\begin{aligned} B_{t+N} =& TB_{t+N} + (1+r_{t+N})TB_{t+N-1} + \ldots \\ &+ (1+r_{t+N})(1+r_{t+N-1}) \cdot \ldots \cdot (1+r_{t+1})TB_t \qquad (3.67) \\ &+ (1+r_{t+N})(1+r_{t+N-1}) \cdot \ldots \cdot (1+r_t)B_{t-1}. \qquad (3.68) \end{aligned}$$

Solving equation (3.68) for B_{t-1} yields

[32] This subsection is based on Obstfeld and Rogoff (1996, pp. 60-61, 64) and Enders (2004, pp. 10-11).

$$\begin{aligned} B_{t-1} = &((1+r_{t+N})(1+r_{t+N-1})\cdot\dots\cdot(1+r_t))^{-1}B_{t+N} \\ &-((1+r_{t+N})(1+r_{t+N-1})\cdot\dots\cdot(1+r_t))^{-1}TB_{t+N} \\ &-(1+r_{t+N-1})(1+r_{t+N-2})\cdot\dots\cdot(1+r_t))^{-1}TB_{t+N-1} \\ &-((1+r_t))^{-1}TB_t. \end{aligned} \tag{3.69}$$

Writing equation (3.69) more succinctly one finally arrives at equation (3.15) in the text:

$$B_{t-1} = -\sum_{n=t}^{t+N} R_{t,n}TB_n + R_{t,t+N}B_{t+N} \quad \text{where} \quad R_{t,n} = \prod_{v=t}^{n-1}\left(\frac{1}{1+r_v}\right). \tag{3.70}$$

3.A.2 Telescoping Argument

In general, the forward iteration of an equation of the form

$$TB_n = B_n - (1+r_n)B_{n-1} \text{ for all } n \geq t \tag{3.71}$$

(for arbitrary B, TB and $r \neq -1$) is defined as the following equation:

$$B_{t-1} = -\sum_{n=t}^{t+N} R_{t,n}TB_n + R_{t,t+N}B_{t+N} \text{ for all } N \geq 0 \tag{3.72}$$

where

$$R_{t,n} = \prod_{v=t}^{n-1}\left(\frac{1}{1+r_v}\right).$$

In order to prove equation (3.72) from equation (3.71), one can utilize the method of differences (also known as telescoping sum argument). For this purpose, the general identity $\sum_{n=t}^{t+N}(X_n - X_{n-1}) = X_{t+N} - X_{t-1}$ is applied to the sequence X defined via $X_n \equiv B_n R_{t,n}$.

Multiplying both sides of equation (3.71) by $\sum_{n=t}^{t+N} R_{t,n}$ leads to

$$\begin{aligned} \sum_{n=t}^{t+N} R_{t,n}TB_n &= \sum_{n=t}^{t+N} R_{t,n}(B_n - (1+r_n)B_{n-1}) \\ &= \sum_{n=t}^{t+N}(B_n R_{t,n} - B_{n-1}(1+r_n)R_{t,n}) \end{aligned} \tag{3.73}$$

Using that $(1+r_n)R_{t,n} = R_{t,n-1}$, equation (3.73) can be rewritten as

$$\sum_{n=t}^{t+N} R_{t,n}TB_n = \sum_{n=t}^{t+N}(B_n R_{t,n} - B_{n-1}R_{t,n-1}) \tag{3.74}$$

Applying the method of differences to equation (3.74), one obtains

$$\sum_{n=t}^{t+N} R_{t,n}TB_n = B_{t+N}R_{t,t+N} - B_{t-1}R_{t,t-1}. \tag{3.75}$$

Because $R_{t,t-1} = 1$ by definition of R, equation (3.75) simplifies to

$$\sum_{n=t}^{t+N} R_{t,n}TB_n = B_{t+N}R_{t,t+N} - B_{t-1}. \tag{3.76}$$

Solving equation (3.76) for B_{t-1} yields finally equation (3.20) in the text.

3.B Appendix to subsection 3.2.2

The single-period budget constraint (3.44), i.e.,

$$B_{t-1}(h_t) = \sum_{s_{t+1}\in S_{t+1}} \pi(h_{t+1}|h_t)\,\beta\frac{u'(C_{t+1}(h_{t+1}))}{u'(C_t(h_t))}B_t(s_{t+1},h_t) + C_t(h_t) - Y_t(h_t), \tag{3.77}$$

can be solved forward by using, e.g., the recursive substitution method. Iterating equation (3.77) forward by one period yields

$$B_t(h_{t+1}) = \sum_{s_{t+2}\in S_{t+2}} \pi(h_{t+2}|h_{t+1})\,\beta\frac{u'(C_{t+2}(h_{t+2}))}{u'(C_{t+1}(h_{t+1}))}B_{t+1}(s_{t+2},h_{t+1}) + C_{t+1}(h_{t+1}) - Y_{t+1}(h_{t+1}) \tag{3.78}$$

where $h_{t+1} = (s_{t+1},h_t)$. Eliminating $B_t(s_{t+1},h_t)$ in equation (3.77) by substituting equation (3.78) into equation (3.77) leads to

$$\begin{aligned} B_{t-1}(h_t) = &\sum_{s_{t+1}\in S_{t+1}} \pi(h_{t+1}|h_t)\,\beta\frac{u'(C_{t+1}(h_{t+1}))}{u'(C_t(h_t))} \\ &\left(\sum_{s_{t+2}\in S_{t+2}} \pi(h_{t+2}|h_{t+1})\,\beta\frac{u'(C_{t+2}(h_{t+2}))}{u'(C_{t+1}(h_{t+1}))}B_{t+1}(s_{t+2},h_{t+1})\right) \\ &-\sum_{s_{t+1}\in S_{t+1}} \pi(h_{t+1}|h_t)\,\beta\frac{u'(C_{t+1}(h_{t+1}))}{u'(C_t(h_t))}\left(Y_{t+1}(h_{t+1}) - C_{t+1}(h_{t+1})\right) \\ &-Y_t(h_t) + C_t(h_t). \end{aligned} \tag{3.79}$$

Using the definition of conditional probability, one can write

$$\pi(h_{t+1}|h_t)\,\pi(h_{t+2}|h_{t+1}) = \frac{\pi(h_{t+1},h_t)}{\pi(h_t)}\frac{\pi(h_{t+2},h_{t+1})}{\pi(h_{t+1})} \tag{3.80}$$

Because the joint probabilities $\pi(h_{t+1},h_t)$ and $\pi(h_{t+2},h_{t+1})$ equal $\pi(h_{t+1})$ and $\pi(h_{t+2})$, respectively, the right-hand side of equation (3.80) equals $\pi(h_{t+2})/\pi(h_t)$ or simply $\pi(h_{t+2}|h_t)$. Thus, equation (3.79) can be rewritten as

$$\begin{aligned} &B_{t-1}(h_t) \\ &= \sum_{h_{t+2}|h_t} \pi(h_{t+2}|h_t)\,\beta^2\frac{u'(C_{t+2}(h_{t+2}))}{u'(C_t(h_t))}B_{t+1}(s_{t+2},h_{t+1}) \\ &\quad + \sum_{s_{t+1}\in S_{t+1}} \pi(h_{t+1}|h_t)\,\beta\frac{u'(C_{t+1}(h_{t+1}))}{u'(C_t(h_t))}\left(C_{t+1}(h_{t+1}) - Y_{t+1}(h_{t+1})\right) \\ &\quad + C_t(h_t) - Y_t(h_t) \end{aligned}$$

where following Ljungqvist and Sargent (2004, p. 421) the summation over $h_{t+2}|h_t$ means that one sums over all possible histories $\tilde{h}_{t+2}$ such that $\tilde{h}_t = h_t$.

Continued substitutions by N periods yield

$$\begin{aligned} B_{t-1}(h_t) = & \sum_{h_{t+N+1}|h_t} \pi(h_{t+N+1}|h_t)\beta^{N+1}\frac{u'(C_{t+N+1}(h_{t+N+1}))}{u'(C_t(h_t))}B_{t+N}(h_{t+N+1}) \\ & + \sum_{n=t}^{t+N}\sum_{h_n|h_t}\pi(h_n|h_t)\beta^{n-t}\frac{u'(C_n(h_n))}{u'(C_t(h_t))}(C_n(h_n)-Y_n(h_n)) \end{aligned} \tag{3.81}$$

where the history $h_{t+N+1} = (s_{t+N+1}, s_{t+N}, \ldots, s_t, \ldots, s_0)$. Letting $N \to \infty$ results in

$$\begin{aligned} B_{t-1}(h_t) = & \lim_{N\to\infty}\sum_{h_{t+N+1}|h_t} \pi(h_{t+N+1}|h_t)\beta^{N+1}\frac{u'(C_{t+N+1}(h_{t+N+1}))}{u'(C_t(h_t))}B_{t+N}(h_{t+N+1}) \\ & + \sum_{n=t}^{\infty}\sum_{h_n|h_t}\pi(h_n|h_t)\beta^{n-t}\frac{u'(C_n(h_n))}{u'(C_t(h_t))}(C_n(h_n)-Y_n(h_n)). \end{aligned} \tag{3.82}$$

Requiring that the limit term on the right-hand side of equation (3.83) is zero, one finally obtains the intertemporal budget constraint

$$B_{t-1}(h_t) = -\sum_{n=t}^{\infty}\sum_{h_n|h_t}\pi(h_n|h_t)\beta^{n-t}\frac{u'(C_n(h_n))}{u'(C_t(h_t))}(Y_n(h_n)-C_n(h_n)).$$

4

Empirical implications of the intertemporal budget constraint

The main task of this chapter is to identify testing conditions that imply the validity of the intertemporal budget constraint and, equivalently, the transversality condition in the data. Empirical tests, by their nature, examine the question whether the IBC is satisfied *provided that* there will be no major changes in the relevant features of the macroeconomic environment and no changes in the fiscal or monetary policies (Corsetti and Roubini, 1991, p. 355). Further, as sections 4.1 and 4.2 in this chapter will show, it has been so far only possible to find *sufficient* conditions for the respect of the IBC in the data. In other words, empirical tests can provide evidence in favor of sustainability, yet they cannot verify the lack of sustainability. Different sufficient conditions for the validity of the IBC in the data have different implications for the path of the current account balance. Following the terminology coined by Quintos (1995, p. 411) for the area of fiscal sustainability, we divide them into two categories: those which imply a stationary current account series and those which entail a nonstationary current account series.

The first category implies that the current account follows a (weakly) stationary process,[1] possibly with mean zero.[2] This means that the current account series exhibits a tendency of reverting to a long-run equilibrium path over time. Thus, shocks have only a temporary effect on the current account dynamics, and continually growing current account deficits or surpluses are not possible (Baharumshah et al., 2003, p. 91). This type of sustainability is referred to as *strong sustainability* since a current account which fluctuates around its mean is considered to be sustainable in the sense that it can be maintained indefinitely. Section 4.1 derives sufficient conditions for the strong notion of sustainability.

---

[1] A *stochastic process* $\{X_t : t \in T\}$, indexed by some linearly ordered set T, is a collection of random variables X_t defined on a common probability space $(\Omega, \mathfrak{F}, P)$, where Ω denotes the sample space, $\mathfrak{F}$ a σ-algebra on Ω (whose elements are called *events*) and P the probability measure (Bhattacharya and Waymire, 2009, p. 1); for definitions of the concepts of σ-algebra and probability measure, see, e.g., Bierens (2005, pp. 3-5). The elements of an observed time series $X_0, X_1, \ldots, X_t$ are (partial) realizations of a stochastic process $\{X_t : t \in T\}$. For simplicity, the time series and the underlying stochastic process will be denoted by the same symbol X_t. The underlying stochastic process is said to have generated the observed time series and is therefore called *data generating process* (DGP) (Lütkepohl, 2007, pp. 2-3).

[2] A stochastic process X_t is said to be (*covariance-* or *weakly*) *stationary* if, for all integers t and h, the mean μ_t and autocovariances $\gamma_{t,h}$ are finite and independent of time index t: $E[X_t] = \mu$ and $E[(X_t - \mu)(X_{t-h} - \mu)] = \gamma_h$ for some μ and γ_h such that $|\mu|, |\gamma_h| < \infty$. Hence, the variances γ_0 are also finite and time-invariant: $E\left[(X_t - \mu)^2\right] = \gamma_0 < \infty$ (e.g. Hendry, 1995, p. 42; Lütkepohl, 2004, p. 11)

The second category includes sufficient conditions for the validity of the IBC which imply a nonstationary current account series. The current account series which is integrated of order one[3] has the property that its variance increases over time and that shocks have permanent effects which do not decay, but cumulate. Thus, the current account may deviate from its mean for long periods of time, implying persistently growing current account deficits (surpluses). When the current account series is stationary in first differences, the NIIP is, by definition, stationary in second differences. Though it might be not intuitively evident, a prolonged rise of net foreign debts and current account deficits is fully consistent with the intertemporal budget constraint as long as the growth rate of net foreign debts is below the discount rate (thus making discounted net foreign debts to converge to zero over time). However, a nonstationary increase of net foreign debts might undermine the willingness of foreign investors to continue lending or to prolong existing credit lines to the economy in question, thus potentially leading to a liquidity or debt crisis. For this reason, a sustainability notion which implies that the current account is stationary in first differences and the NIIP is stationary in second differences is called a weak one. Finally, the intertemporal budget constraint is satisfied even if the current account is stationary in second differences or higher. Following Bohn (2007, p. 1841), we refer to this type of sustainability as "absurdly weak." However, the absurdly weak notion of sustainability is likely to occur rarely since most time series are stationary in levels or first differences. Section 4.2 shows sufficient conditions which imply the weak and absurdly weak notions of sustainability, and section 4.3 concludes.

4.1 Sufficient conditions for the strong notion of sustainability

4.1.1 Stationarity of the NIIP and the trade balance

The pioneering study by Hamilton and Flavin (1986) first provided a direct way to test the intertemporal budget constraint. Since then, a large empirical literature on the IBC both in the fiscal and the external context emerged which further generalized the approach taken by Hamilton and Flavin (1986). We start this section with carrying Hamilton and Flavin's (1986) methodology over to external sustainability.

Hamilton and Flavin (1986) examine the null hypothesis that the IBC is satisfied against the class of alternative hypotheses given by

$$B_{t-1} = -E_t\left[\sum_{n=t}^{\infty} R^{n-t+1} TB_n\right] + A_0 R^{-t} + \varepsilon_t \tag{4.1}$$

where ε_t is a regression disturbance term (reflecting, among other influences, changes in real short-term interest rates and a measurement error) and $A_0 \neq 0$. Note that this is equivalent to

$$E_t\left[\lim_{N\to\infty} R^{N+1} B_{t+N}\right] = A_0. \tag{4.2}$$

[3] A stochastic process X_t is said to be *integrated* of order d or difference-stationary of order d, denoted by $I(d)$, where the integration order d is an integer with $d \geq 1$ if d differences are necessary to make this stochastic process stationary, i.e., if $\Delta^d x_t$ is stationary. (Lütkepohl, 2004, pp. 21-22). If a series is stationary in levels (and not necessarily invertible), we refer to it as $I(0)$. Further, we use the denominations "integrated of order d" and "difference-stationary of order d" synonymously.

Equation (4.1) is a general solution to the difference equation $B_t = TB_t + (1+r)B_{t-1}$. Both the IBC and the TC are satisfied if A_0 in equations (4.1) and (4.2) is zero.

Hamilton and Flavin (1986) introduce two methods for testing whether $A_0 = 0$. The first one is based on the idea that for any stationary process for $\left(E_t\left[\sum_{n=t}^{\infty} R^{n-t+1} TB_n\right], \varepsilon_t,\right)$, B_{t-1} is stationary when $A_0 = 0$ and B_{t-1} is nonstationary when $A_0 \neq 0$. Thus, testing for sustainability basically amounts to testing for stationarity in the trade account and the NIIP using unit root tests (which are described below in chapter 5). The current account balance equals the change in the NIIP when the capital account balance is ignored: $CAB_t = \Delta B_t$. Thus, stationarity of the NIIP implies that the current account is stationary in levels and, therefore, sustainable in the strong sense.[4] Thus, the validity of the IBC can also be examined by testing for stationarity of the current account series.

The second way is to estimate the coefficient A_0 directly by putting equation (4.1) in a regression form. Hamilton and Flavin (1986) apply two regression tests: the restricted Flood-Garber test for self-fulfilling price bubbles (Flood and Garber, 1980) and a generalization of the Flood-Garber test due to Diba and Grossman (1984) and Hamilton and Whiteman (1985). The information set in the generalized Flood-Garber test contains the lagged values of both the trade balance and the NIIP series so that one can estimate the following regression, e.g., by ordinary least squares (OLS):

$$B_{t-1} = c_0 + A_0 R^{-t} + c_1 B_{t-2} + c_2 B_{t-3} + \cdots + c_p B_{t-p-1} \tag{4.3}$$

$$+ b_0 TB_{t-1} + b_1 TB_{t-2} + \cdots + b_{p-1} TB_{t-p} + u_t \tag{4.4}$$

where the error term u_t is a residual obtained from projecting $\left(\varepsilon_t + E_t\left[\sum_{n=t}^{\infty} R^{n-t+1} TB_n\right]\right)$ onto $B_{t-2}, B_{t-3}, \ldots, B_{t-p-1}, TB_{t-1}, TB_{t-2}, \ldots, TB_{t-p}$ and where the lags of the NIIP are included in order to eliminate the serial correlation of u_t (Hamilton and Flavin, 1986, p. 816).

In contrast, the restricted Flood-Garber test assumes that investors form their expectations solely on the basis of the lagged trade account values, so that the information set consists only of $TB_{t-1}, TB_{t-2}, \ldots$. This is a quite restrictive assumption, as agents' expectations might also be based on additional information such as on exogenous shocks to which the trade account reacts (Hamilton and Flavin, 1986, p. 817). The restricted Flood-Garber test can be performed by jointly estimating the following pair of equations using nonlinear least squares (NLS):

$$TB_{t-1} = k_2 + a_1 TB_{t-2} + a_2 TB_{t-3} + a_3 TB_{t-4} + u_{2t-1} \tag{4.5}$$

$$\begin{aligned} B_{t-1} = {} & A_0 R^{-t} + k_1 + \frac{R}{(1-R)(1-a_1R-a_2R^2-a_3R^3)} k_2 \\ & + \frac{a_1R+a_2R^2+a_3R^3}{1-a_1R-a_2R^2-a_3R^3} TB_{t-1} + \frac{a_2R+a_3R^2}{1-a_1R-a_2R^2-a_3R^3} TB_{t-2} \\ & + \frac{a_3R}{1-a_1R-a_2R^2-a_3R^3} TB_{t-3} + u_{1t} \end{aligned} \tag{4.6}$$

[4] However, while the current account series is stationary in this case, it is overdifferenced and thus not invertible since it cannot be represented as an autoregressive process of order zero, i.e., $AR(0)$. Note that, for convenience, we use the notation $I(0)$ for stationary series, disregarding of whether they are invertible or not.

The first equation represents the trade account as a function of its own past values and the error term u_{2t-1}, and the second equation shows that the NIIP is a function of the current and past values of the trade account and of the error term u_{1t}. Equation (4.6) assumes that the error term in equation (4.1) follows a white noise process given by[5]

$$\varepsilon_t = k_1 + u_{1t}. \tag{4.7}$$

Further, equation (4.6) exploits the formula in Hansen and Sargent (1980, p. 16) which has been adapted by Hamilton and Flavin (1986, p. 817) as follows:

$$\begin{aligned} & E\left[\sum_{n=t}^{\infty} R^{n-t+1} TB_n | TB_{t-1}, TB_{t-2}, \ldots\right] \\ & = \frac{R}{(1-R)(1-a_1R-a_2R^2-a_3R^3)} k_2 + \frac{a_1R+a_2R^2+a_3R^3}{1-a_1R-a_2R^2-a_3R^3} TB_{t-1} \\ & + \frac{a_2R+a_3R^2}{1-a_1R-a_2R^2-a_3R^3} TB_{t-2} + \frac{a_3R}{1-a_1R-a_2R^2-a_3R^3} TB_{t-3}. \end{aligned} \tag{4.8}$$

Inserting equations (4.8) and (4.7) into equation (4.1) yields equation (4.6). Hamilton and Flavin (1986) test whether the coefficient A_0 is significantly different from zero in regressions (4.4) or (4.6) using the conventional t-test and interpret a failure to reject the null hypothesis of $A_0 = 0$ as evidence for $A_0 = 0$. However, A_0 might still be (slightly) different from zero with the uncontrolled probability of the type II error (i.e. the error to accept the wrong null hypothesis as true).

Hamilton and Flavin's (1986) approach is subject to two important limitations. Firstly, it cannot be applied to the nonstationary trade account and NIIP series. Yet many economic variables are stationary in first differences. Besides, A_0 can be zero even if the trade account is nonstationary (Wilcox, 1989, pp. 297-298). Secondly, real interest rates—which are by assumption constant—in practice rarely remain unchanged for long periods of time.

Wilcox (1989) extends Hamilton and Flavin's (1986) analysis by considering stochastic violations of the IBC and the TC (i.e., A_0 is time-varying). In addition, the relevant variables are discounted back to a fixed reference date by using *ex post* real interest rates. This allows introducing variations in real interest rates without the need to make particular assumptions about the process which governs real interest rates. Wilcox (1989) shows that the sufficient condition for the IBC to be met is that the discounted NIIP series is stationary with unconditional mean zero. In case that the discounted NIIP is $I(0)$ and the IBC is met, the trade balance process must also be $I(0)$.

Uctum and Wickens (2000) confirm this result for the case in which the trade balance is weakly exogenous in the sense that it experiences feedback effects from the NIIP that might arise from wealth and income due to net foreign earnings. Rising net foreign debts (i.e., decreasing net wealth) might decrease domestic expenditures, thereby lowering imports and improving the trade balance (Wickens and Uctum, 1993, pp. 428, 432). Uctum and Wickens (2000) show that the sufficient condition for sustainability is zero mean stationarity of the discounted NIIP-to-GDP ratio and the discounted trade balance-to-GDP ratio (provided that both processes are

[5] In general, a white noise process, denoted by ε_t, is a process with a constant mean ($E[\varepsilon_t] = \mu$), a constant variance ($E[\varepsilon_t^2] = \sigma^2$), and zero autocovariances except at lag zero (Brooks, 2008, p. 209).

stable)—disregarding whether the discounted trade balance-to-GDP ratio is strongly exogenous (i.e., not affected by the NIIP) or weakly exogenous.

4.1.2 First-difference-stationarity of the NIIP

Stationarity of the NIIP series (combined with stationarity of the trade balance series) is only sufficient for the validity of the IBC in the data. Analyzing fiscal and external sustainability, Trehan and Walsh (1991) show that the IBC is also met when the NIIP is $I(1)$ and the real discount factor series is uniformly bounded from above by a positive constant *in expected value* and the NIIP is independent from the real discount factor. We show that the IBC is also satisfied when the NIIP is $I(1)$ and the real discount factor series is uniformly bounded from above *almost surely*—disregarding of whether the NIIP is correlated with the real discount factor or not.

Following Trehan and Walsh (1991, pp. 209, 213-215), the conditional expectation of the discounted NIIP in the transversality condition (3.37) can be expressed as a product of conditional expectations provided that $R_{t,t+N}$ and B_{t+N} are uncorrelated for all sufficiently large N (i.e., that $\text{cov}_t(R_{t,t+N}, B_{t+N}) = 0$):

$$\lim_{N\to\infty} E_t\left[R_{t,t+N}B_{t+N}\right] = \lim_{N\to\infty}\left(E_t\left[R_{t,t+N}\right]E_t\left[B_{t+N}\right]\right) = 0.$$

Further, it is assumed that the NIIP is $I(1)$ and is given by

$$\Delta B_t = (1-\beta L)\,\varepsilon_t + k \tag{4.9}$$

where ε_t is a zero-mean white noise and L is the lag operator.[6] Making use of the method of differences and of equation (4.9), one can express $E_t\left[B_{t+N}\right]$ as

$$\begin{aligned} E_t\left[B_{t+N}\right] &= E_t\left[B_t + \sum_{n=t+1}^{t+N}(B_n - B_{n-1})\right] \\ &= B_t + \sum_{n=t}^{t+N} E_t\left[(1-\beta L)\,\varepsilon_n + k\right]. \end{aligned} \tag{4.10}$$

Because $E_t\left[\varepsilon_n\right] = 0$ for all $n > t$ by assumption, equation (4.10) simplifies to

$$E_t\left[B_{t+N}\right] = B_t - \beta\varepsilon_t + Nk, \tag{4.11}$$

thus implying that the growth of the NIIP is, in expectation, at most linear in N.

Under the assumption that the real discount factor series is a sequence of independent random variables[7], $E_t\left[R_{t,t+N}\right]$ can be written as

[6] For any integer i and a sequence $(X_t)_{t=-\infty}^{\infty}$, the lag operator is defined as $L^iX_t \equiv X_{t-i}$ and $L^{-i}X_t \equiv X_{t+i}$ (Hamilton, 1994, pp. 26-27).

[7] A collection of random variables $X_1, X_2, ..., X_N$ is *independent* if and only if the joint distribution function $F_{X_1,X_2,...,X_N}(x_1, x_2, ..., x_N)$ can be written as the product of the distribution functions F_{X_t}, $t = 1, 2, \ldots, N$, that is: $F_{X_1,X_2,...,X_N}(x_1, x_2, ..., x_N) = F_{X_1}(x_1)\,F_{X_2}(x_2)\cdots F_{X_T}(x_N)$ (e.g., Amemiya, 1994, p. 46; Bierens, 2005, p. 30). An example for such a series is a Gaussian white-noise process, a sequence of independent, serially uncorrelated random variables with $N\left(0, \sigma^2\right)$.

$$E_t\left[R_{t,t+N}\right] = E_t\left[\prod_{v=t}^{t+N} \frac{1}{1+r_v}\right] = \prod_{v=t}^{t+N} E_t\left[\frac{1}{1+r_v}\right].$$

If the real discount factor series is uniformly bounded from above by a constant $c > 0$ in expected value, i.e., $E_t\left[(1+r_v)^{-1}\right] \leq c$ for all $v \geq t$, the real discount rate series has a property that

$$E_t\left[R_{t,t+N}\right] \leq c^{N+1}.$$

That is, the discount factor series decays at least exponentially in expected value.

Hence, since (at least) exponential decay of the real discount factor series dominates (at most) linear growth of the NIIP, the limit in the transversality condition (3.37) decays exponentially due to de l'Hospital's rule[8]. Thus, the intertemporal budget constraint is satisfied if the NIIP is $I(1)$ and the real discount factor series is uniformly bounded from above in expected value—provided that (i) $R_{t,t+N}$ and B_{t+N} are not correlated for sufficiently large N and (ii) $R_t, R_{t+1}, \ldots, R_{t+N}$ are independent.

Although assumptions (i) and (ii) are not mentioned by Trehan and Walsh (1991), they are implicitly contained in their analysis. Assumption (i) of zero correlation between $R_{t,t+N}$ and B_{t+N} is not problematic as long as data are available for a sufficiently long time span (which, however, might be difficult to obtain in practice). However, the question still remains whether a large sample of, say, 50 years is sufficiently large in this case. Otherwise, it is likely that B_{t+N} and $R_{t,t+N}$ are negatively correlated since a rise in the real interest rate (i.e., a decrease in the real discount factor) might *ceteris paribus* increase the net interest payments and contribute to the increase in the NIIP in subsequent periods. Assumption (ii) seems to be quite restrictive because the empirical evidence does not support the hypothesis that (ex ante) real interest rates are independent (see, e.g., Neely and Rapach (2008) who provide a detailed survey of studies on long-run properties of real interest rates).

However, we show that relaxing assumptions (i) and (ii) does not substantially alter the result achieved by Trehan and Walsh (1991). Instead of assumption (ii), we allow the real discount factor series to be dependent. More specifically, the real discount factor series is uniformly bounded from above by $c' > 0$ *in probability one* (and not in expected value, as in Trehan and Walsh (1991)). Thus, $(1+r_v)^{-1} \leq c'$ for all $v \geq t$. This leads to

$$E_t\left[R_{t,t+N}\right] = E_t\left[\prod_{v=t}^{t+N} \frac{1}{1+r_v}\right] \leq E_t\left[\prod_{v=t}^{t+N} c'\right] \leq c'^{N+1}. \tag{4.12}$$

Inequality (4.12) shows that the decay of the expected real discount factor is at least exponential. Hence, equations (4.12) and (4.11) together imply that the TC and, thus, the IBC are satisfied.

In addition, we abandon assumption (i) and allow for correlation between B_{t+N} and $R_{t,t+N}$. However, in this case, the conditional expectation of the discounted NIIP cannot be decomposed

[8] Application of de l'Hospital's rule shows that for any affine linear function f with $f(x) = ax + b$ (for some $a, b \in \mathbb{R}$ with $a \neq 0$) and the exponential function g with $g(x) = \exp(x)$ and $\lim_{x\to\infty} g(x) = \infty$, the limit is

$$\lim_{x\to\infty} \frac{f(x)}{g(x)} = \frac{ax+b}{\exp(x)} = \lim_{x\to\infty} \frac{f'(x)}{g'(x)} = \lim_{x\to\infty} \frac{a}{\exp(x)} = 0$$

(Riedel and Wichardt, 2007, p. 95).

in $E_t[R_{t,t+N}]$ and $E_t[B_{t+N}]$. Yet under the above assumption that the real discount factor series is uniformly bounded from above by $c' > 0$ with probability one, one obtains (using Jensen's inequality together with the nonnegativity of the discount factor)

$$0 \leq |E_t[R_{t,t+N}B_{t+N}]| \leq E_t[R_{t,t+N}|B_{t+N}|] \leq c'^{N+1}E_t|B_{t+N}|. \tag{4.13}$$

To show that the NIIP grows linearly, we first exploit the generalized triangle inequality[9], equation (4.9), and the method of differences so that $E_t|B_{t+N}|$ can be estimated as follows:

$$\begin{aligned} E_t|B_{t+N}| &\leq E_t|B_t| + \sum_{n=t+1}^{t+N} E_t|B_n - B_{n-1}| \\ &\leq E_t|B_t| + \sum_{n=t+1}^{t+N} E_t|(1-\beta L)\varepsilon_n + k|. \end{aligned} \tag{4.14}$$

The last term on the right-hand side of inequality (4.14) can be estimated by using the generalized triangle inequality again:

$$E_t|\varepsilon_n - \beta\varepsilon_{n-1} + k| \leq E_t[|\varepsilon_n| + \beta|\varepsilon_{n-1}|] + k.$$

Assuming that ε_n is (not just uncorrelated with, but) independent of $\varepsilon_1, \ldots, \varepsilon_t$ whenever $n > t$, the term $E_t[|\varepsilon_n| + \beta|\varepsilon_{n-1}|] + k$ can be further simplified as $E|\varepsilon_n| + \beta E|\varepsilon_{n-1}| + k$ for $n > t+1$ which is in turn equal to $(1+\beta)E|\varepsilon_t| + k$ because, by assumption, the random variables ε_n all have the same distribution. Combining this with the observation that (for similar reasons) $E_t[|\varepsilon_{t+1}| + \beta|\varepsilon_t| + k] = E|\varepsilon_t| + \beta|\varepsilon_t| + k$, inequality (4.14) can now be written as

$$\begin{aligned} E_t|B_{t+N}| &\leq |B_t| + E|\varepsilon_t| + \beta|\varepsilon_t| + k + \sum_{n=t+2}^{t+N} ((1+\beta)E|\varepsilon_t + k) \\ &\leq |B_t| + E|\varepsilon_t| + \beta|\varepsilon_t| + k + ((1+\beta)E|\varepsilon_t| + k)(N-1) \\ &\leq |B_t| + \beta|\varepsilon_t| + ((1+\beta)E|\varepsilon_t| + k)N. \end{aligned} \tag{4.15}$$

Inequality (4.15) finally implies that the NIIP grows, in expectation, at most linearly in N. Since the real discount factor series decays in expectation at least exponentially, the TC and thus the IBC are satisfied due to de l'Hospital's rule, provided that the real discount factor series is bounded *almost surely* from above by a positive constant. In sum, the validity of the IBC can be basically examined by testing whether the NIIP is $I(1)$ using unit root tests. A finding of the NIIP being $I(1)$ in the data implies sustainability in the strong sense because in this case the current account is stationary.

4.1.3 Cointegration between current account components

An alternative way to test the intertemporal budget constraint is to test for cointegration of the components of the current account (such as the trade balance and the NIIP).[10] When the components of the current account are each $I(1)$ and cointegrated, there exists a long-run relationship

[9] The generalized triangle inequality for any real numbers $x_1, x_2, \ldots, x_k$ is as follows: $|x_1 + x_2 + \ldots + x_k| \leq |x_1| + |x_2| + \ldots + |x_k|$.

[10] The components of a vector $\mathbf{x}_t$ are said to be *cointegrated* of order (d, b) if (i) all components of $\mathbf{x}_t$ are integrated of order d and (ii) there exists a vector $\alpha\,(\neq 0)$ such that the linear combination $\alpha'\mathbf{x}_t$ is integrated of order

between those components and deviations from the long-run economic equilibrium are only temporary. Thus, sustainability can also be tested using cointegration tests (which are discussed in chapter 5). For the appropriate cointegrating vector, the current account series itself will be stationary. This methodology was first suggested by Haug (1991), Hakkio and Rush (1991b), Smith and Zin (1991), and Trehan and Walsh (1991) in the context of fiscal sustainability and by Trehan and Walsh (1991) for external sustainability. Subsection 4.1.3 focuses on the cointegrating relationship between the trade account and the NIIP using the approach suggested by Trehan and Walsh (1991). Transferring the approach developed by Hakkio and Rush (1991b) to the setting of external sustainability, subsection 4.1.3 deals with cointegration between exports and imports inclusive of net interest payments.

Cointegration between the NIIP and the trade balance

Following Trehan and Walsh (1991), it is assumed that the trade balance is (quasi) difference-stationary with mean zero:

$$(1-\rho L)\,TB_{t+1} = A(L)\,\varepsilon_{t+1} \sim I(0)$$

where ρ satisfies the restriction $\rho \in \left[0, R^{-1}\right)$. The stochastic disturbance term ε_t is a martingale difference sequence which generates the information set of private agents at the beginning of period t.[11] The information set at the beginning of period t includes only current and lagged values of ε: $I_t = \{\varepsilon_t, \varepsilon_{t-1}, \varepsilon_{t-2}, \ldots\}$. $A(L)$ denotes the power series in the lag operator such that $A(L) = \sum_{i=0}^{\infty} \alpha_i L^i$ and $\sum_{i=0}^{\infty} |\alpha_i|^2 < \infty$ so that the variance of $(1-\rho L)\,TB_{t+1}$ is finite. The real interest rate series is assumed to be uncorrelated over time with a positive and constant conditional expectation: $E_t[r_n] = r$ for all $n \geq t$.

Inserting $(1-\rho L)\,TB_{t+1} = A(L)\,\varepsilon_{t+1}$ into the IBC (4.1) and ignoring, for simplicity, the measurement error yields

$$\begin{aligned} B_{t-1} = {} & -E_t\left[RTB_t + R^2\left(\rho\, TB_t + A(L)\,\varepsilon_{t+1}\right) + R^3\left(\rho^2 TB_t + \rho A(L)\,\varepsilon_{t+1}\right.\right. \\ & \left.\left. + A(L)\,\varepsilon_{t+2}\right)\ldots\right] + A_0 R^{-t}. \end{aligned}$$

Rearranging the terms one obtains

$$\begin{aligned} B_{t-1} = {} & \left\{1 + R\rho + (R\rho)^2 + \ldots\right\} R\left(-TB_t - E_t\left[\sum_{n=t+1}^{\infty} R^{n-t} A(L)\varepsilon_n\right]\right) \\ & + A_0 R^{-t}. \end{aligned} \tag{4.16}$$

The sum in curly brackets on the right-hand side of equation (4.16) reduces to $(1-R\rho)^{-1}$ when the formula for an infinite geometric series[12] is applied. The expected value of the discounted

$(d-b)$, $b > 0$. The vector α is called the cointegrating vector (Engle and Granger, 1987, p. 253). Most of the literature concentrates on the case $d = b$ so that $\alpha'\mathbf{x}_t$ is $I(0)$. If a process is cointegrated of order (d, b), we will refer to it more briefly as being $CI(d,b)$. If a process is cointegrated of order $(1, 0)$, it is said to be *cointegrated of order one*.

[11] A real-valued martingale difference sequence ε_t is defined as a sequence of real-valued random variables which satisfies $E\left[\varepsilon_n | \varepsilon_{n-1}, \varepsilon_{s-2}, \ldots\right] = 0$ for $n = 1, \ldots, t+1$ (Hamilton, 1994, p. 189).

[12] The formula for an infinite geometric series can be applied because $\rho R \in [0,1)$ for $\rho \in [0; R^{-1})$.

disturbance terms can be simplified by shifting the expectation operator behind the infinite sum and using the formula in Hansen and Sargent (1980, p. 14):

$$E_t\left[\sum_{n=t+1}^{\infty} R^{n-t}A(L)\varepsilon_n\right] = \frac{A(L)-RL^{-1}A(R)}{1-RL^{-1}}\varepsilon_t - A(L)\varepsilon_t = \frac{A(L)-A(R)}{R^{-1}L-1}\varepsilon_t.$$

Thus, equation (4.16) can be rewritten as

$$B_{t-1} = -\frac{1}{R^{-1}-\rho}TB_t - \frac{1}{R^{-1}-\rho}\left(\frac{A(L)-A(R)}{R^{-1}L-1}\right)\varepsilon_t + A_0R^{-t}. \quad (4.17)$$

If B_{t-1} and TB_t are each $I(1)$ and together cointegrated with cointegrating vector $\left(1,(R^{-1}-\rho)^{-1}\right)$, A_0 must be zero, thus implying that the IBC holds. Setting consequently $A_0 = 0$, multiplying equation (4.17) by $(R^{-1}-\rho)$, and simplifying the notation results in

$$\mu B_{t-1} + TB_t = B(L)\varepsilon_t \sim I(0) \quad (4.18)$$

where $\mu \equiv 1+r-\rho$ and $B(L) \equiv -\left(A(L)-A(R)\right)\left(R^{-1}L-1\right)^{-1}$. Because $B(L)\varepsilon_t \sim I(0)$, equation (4.18) implies that B_{t-1} and TB_t are cointegrated with cointegrating vector $(\mu,1)$. Further, inserting equation (4.18) into the single-period budget constraint $\Delta B_t = rB_{t-1} + TB_t$ and rearranging the terms also shows that the NIIP is (quasi) difference-stationary with $(1-\rho L)B_t = B(L)\varepsilon_t \sim I(0)$.

Now, three cases—which all imply the validity of the IBC—can be distinguished:

(1) For $\mu \in (r, 1+r]$, i.e., $\rho \in [0,1)$, both TB_t and B_{t-1} are stationary so that the current account is also stationary. This case has been analyzed in subsection 4.1.1.
(2) For $\mu = r$, e.g., $\rho = 1$, equation (4.18) simplifies to $rB_{t-1} + TB_t = B(L)\varepsilon_t$. In this case, the trade account and the NIIP are both $I(1)$ and cointegrated with vector $(r,1)$. This also implies that the current account is stationary.
(3) For $\mu \in (0,r)$, e.g., $\rho \in (1,1+r)$, TB_t and B_{t-1} are mildly explosive, not difference-stationary and thus not cointegrated.[13] The current account is neither stationary nor difference-stationary of any (integer) order in this case.[14]

Cases (1) and (2) imply that the current account is stationary in levels and sustainable in the strong sense. Case (3) requires neither cointegration between TB_t and B_{t-1} nor stationarity of the current account in order to ensure the validity of the IBC. This shows that cointegration is only sufficient for sustainability. The testing method in case (3) will be discussed in more detail in subsubsection 4.2.2.

[13] If $B_t(1-\rho L) \sim I(0)$ for some $\rho \in (1;1+r)$, but not for any $\rho \in [0,1]$, B_t and TB_t each exhibit exponential growth and are not integrated of any (integer) order. To show this, B_{t-1} is first subtracted from each side of $B_t - \rho B_{t-1} = e_t^B$ where $\rho \in (1;1+r)$. This allows to write: $\Delta B_t - (\rho-1)B_{t-1} = e_t^B \sim I(0)$. Taking $d-1$ differences yields $\Delta^d B_t - (\rho-1)L\Delta^{d-1}B_t = \Delta^{d-1}e_t^B \sim I(0)$ for all $d \geq 1$. If $\Delta^d B_t$ were $I(0)$ for any $d \geq 1$, $\Delta^{d-1}B_t$ would also be $I(0)$ because $e_t^B \sim I(0)$. Analogously, $\Delta B_t \sim I(0)$ would imply $B_t \sim I(0)$. Yet B_t is not $I(0)$ for any $\rho \in [0;1]$ (Bohn, 2007, p. 1844).

[14] Footnote 13 implies that the current account can be written as $CAB_t = \Delta B_t = e_t^B + (\rho-1)B_{t-1}$ where $e_t \sim I(0)$, $\rho \in (1;1+r)$, and $(1-\rho L)B_t \sim I(0)$. Thus, the current account series is neither $I(0)$ nor integrated of any (integer) order.

Cointegration between exports and imports inclusive of interest

This subsubsection is based on Hakkio and Rush (1991b) who show that the government's IBC is satisfied if revenues inclusive of interest and expenditures are each $I(1)$ and jointly $CI(1,1)$ with an appropriate cointegrating vector. Applying this approach to external sustainability implies that the long-run relationship between exports and imports, inclusive of net interest payments is sufficient for sustainability. In the literature on external sustainability, a large number of empirical studies builds on Hakkio and Rush's (1991) approach, among others Husted (1992), Liu and Tanner (1996), Fountas and Wu (1999), Kalyoncu (2006), and more recently Önel and Utkulu (2006) and Tang (2006).

Following Hakkio and Rush (1991b), the interest rate r is assumed to be stationary around mean r, $r > 0$. Writing out the trade balance as the difference between exports of goods and services (X) and imports of goods and services (M), the single-period budget constraint can be written as

$$\Delta B_t = X_t - M_t + r_t B_{t-1}. \tag{4.19}$$

Adding rB_{t-1} on both sides of equation (4.19), one can introduce an auxiliary variable F which captures deviations of real interest rates from their unconditional mean:

$$B_t - (1+r) B_{t-1} = X_t - F_t \tag{4.20}$$

where $F_t \equiv M_t - (r_t - r) B_{t-1}$. Both X_t and F_t are assumed to follow a random walk with drift, i.e., $\Delta X_{t+1} = \eta_1 + \varepsilon_{1,t+1}$ and $\Delta F_{t+1} = \eta_2 + \varepsilon_{2,t+1}$ where $\varepsilon_{1,t+1}$ and $\varepsilon_{2,t+1}$ are white-noise processes. Taking the first difference of equation (4.20) one obtains:

$$\Delta B_{t+1} - (1+r)\Delta B_t = \Delta X_{t+1} - \Delta F_{t+1}. \tag{4.21}$$

Iterating equation (4.21) forward by ∞ periods results in

$$\Delta B_t = E_t \left[\sum_{n=t+1}^{\infty} R^{n-t} \left(\Delta F_n - \Delta X_n \right) \right] + E_t \left[\lim_{N \to \infty} R^N \Delta B_{t+N} \right]. \tag{4.22}$$

Imposing the transversality condition which requires the limit term on the right-hand side of equation (4.22) to be zero, one arrives at the intertemporal budget constraint expressed in first differences. Since X_t and F_t are each a random walk with drift, equation (4.22) can be written as

$$\Delta B_t = E_t \left[R(\eta_2 + \varepsilon_{2,t+1} - \eta_1 - \varepsilon_{1,t+1}) + R^2(\eta_2 + \varepsilon_{2,t+2} - \eta_1 - \varepsilon_{1,t+2} + \ldots) \right]$$

or more succinctly as

$$\Delta B_t = (\eta_2 - \eta_1) \sum_{n=t+1}^{\infty} R^{n-t} + E_t \left[\sum_{n=t+1}^{\infty} R^{n-t} \left(\varepsilon_{2,n} - \varepsilon_{1,n} \right) \right]. \tag{4.23}$$

Because R is less than one in absolute value by definition, the infinite sum $\sum_{n=t+1}^{\infty} R^{n-t}$ reduces to r^{-1}. Simplifying the notation in equation (4.23), one obtains the IBC of the form

$$\Delta B_t = a + e_t \tag{4.24}$$

where $a \equiv (\eta_2 - \eta_1) r^{-1}$ and $e_t \equiv E_t \left[\sum_{n=t+1}^{\infty} R^{n-t} (\varepsilon_{2,n} - \varepsilon_{1,n}) \right]$. Since e_t is $I(0)$ (because e_t is the sum of the discounted white-noise processes), the IBC (4.24) implies that ΔB_t must also be $I(0)$. In other words, sustainability can be tested by examining whether the current account is stationary around a constant mean a.

Substituting the right-hand side of the single-period budget constraint (4.19) for ΔB_t in (4.24) and rearranging the terms yields

$$X_t - MM_t = a + e_t \tag{4.25}$$

where MM_t denotes $M_t - r_t B_{t-1}$, that is, imports inclusive of net interest payments on the NIIP. Since e_t is $I(0)$ and X_t is $I(1)$, the IBC (4.25) is satisfied if the processes X_t and MM_t are jointly $CI(1,1)$ with cointegrating vector $(1,-1)$. Equation (4.25) can be written as a cointegration regression of the form

$$X_t - \beta MM_t = a + e_t. \tag{4.26}$$

Based on equation (4.26), sustainability can be assessed by testing whether (i) X_t and MM_t are $CI(1,1)$ and (ii) $\beta = 1$. If conditions (i) and (ii) are satisfied, the current account is stationary and sustainable in the strong sense.

Analogously, one can substitute $TB_t + rB_{t-1}$ for ΔB_t in equation (4.24); this yields $TB_t + r_t B_{t-1} = a + e_t$. It follows that the IBC is satisfied if TB_t and rB_{t-1} are each $I(1)$ and jointly $CI(1,1)$ with cointegrating vector $(1,-1)$ or TB_t and B_{t-1} are each $I(1)$ and cointegrated with cointegrating vector $(1,-r)$. Thus, Hakkio and Rush's (1991) approach corresponds to case (2) in the approach taken by Trehan and Walsh (1991).

Further, representing the current account as the difference between savings and investment, one can rewrite equation (4.24) as

$$S_t - I_t = a + e_t. \tag{4.27}$$

Thus, if savings and investment are each stationary in first differences and jointly cointegrated with cointegrating vector $(1,-1)$, the IBC (4.27) is also satisfied.

4.1.4 Conclusion

Summing up this section, we arrive at the following sufficient conditions for the validity of the IBC:

1. The NIIP is $I(0)$ provided that the interest rate is constant.
2. The NIIP is $I(1)$ provided that
   (a) the discount factor series is uniformly bounded from above by a positive constant *in expected value* and the NIIP is uncorrelated with the trade balance or
   (b) the discount factor series is uniformly bounded from above *almost surely*.
3. The trade balance and the NIIP are each $I(1)$ and together $CI(1,1)$ with cointegrating vector $(1,r)$ or the trade balance and the net interest payments are each $I(1)$ and together $CI(1,1)$ with cointegrating vector $(1,1)$, provided that the interest rate is constant.
4. Exports and imports inclusive of net interest payments are each $I(1)$ and together $CI(1,1)$ with cointegrating vector $(1,-1)$, provided that the interest rate is constant.
5. Savings and investment are each $I(1)$ and together $CI(1,1)$ with cointegrating vector $(1,-1)$, provided that the interest rate is constant. .

6. The relationship

$$\mu B_{t-1} + TB_t = B(L)\varepsilon_t \sim I(0)$$

holds for $\mu \in (0, r)$ and the constant interest rate.

Conditions (1) and (5) all imply that the current account is stationary around a constant mean (which is not necessarily zero) so that continually growing current account deficits and surpluses are precluded. Following the terminology used by Quintos (1995) for fiscal sustainability, the notion of sustainability which implies a stationary current account series is considered to be strong in the literature on external sustainability.

In contrast, condition (6) implies that the NIIP and the trade balance are mildly explosive and the current account is not integrated of any (integer) order. However, as will be in more detail discussed in the next section, a mildly explosive path of net foreign debts might at some point undermine the investors' willingness to lend. For this reason, the sustainability notion implied by condition (6) is weaker than the one implied by conditions (1)-(5). Further sufficient conditions for weak sustainability will be derived in the next section.

4.2 Sufficient conditions for the strong and weak notions of sustainability

This section derives sufficient conditions for the validity of the IBC which imply a nonstationary growth of the NIIP and, thus, a nonstationary current account series. A nonstationary growth of net foreign debts (rather than assets) might be problematic for several reasons. Firstly, it can lead to a situation in which net interest payments become so large that they cut into current private consumption and investment, thus lowering GDP growth and making it more difficult to service the debt (Mann, 2002, p. 143). Net interest payments may even outstrip GDP and thus an economy's ability to service its debts (see also chapter 7 for a detailed discussion). Finally, a nonstationary increase of net foreign debts (in particular in proportion to GDP) makes an economy more vulnerable to unfavorable shocks: In case of an exogenous decline in an economy's GDP growth, for example, investors are more likely to question the repayment ability of the economy with a high and increasing ratio of net foreign debt to output than in the case where net foreign debts are low and non-increasing relative to GDP (Hakkio and Rush, 1991b, p. 433, see also Barro, 1976, p. 343, Barro, 1979, p. 942, McCallum, 1984, pp. 133-135, Kremers, 1988, p. 260, Kremers, 1989, pp. 221-222, Roubini and Wachtel, 1998, p. 4). For this reason, following Quintos (1995, p. 411), we consider a nonstationary increase in an economy's net foreign debts to be a weak notion of sustainability.

In contrast to net foreign debts, a nonstationary increase in net foreign assets is technically feasible and in general not worrisome unless it implies a nonstationary increase in net foreign debts of another economy. Further, it might be desirable for an economy to reduce lending to foreigners and instead increase consumption and investment (Kool, 2010, p. 78). Thus, we consider a nonstationary increase in net foreign assets also as weakly sustainable—although with a less compelling justification than in case of net foreign debts.

Subsection 4.2.1 shows that cointegration between the current account components is not necessary for sustainability. The IBC is also satisfied if the NIIP is difference-stationary of any order, disregarding whether the current account components are cointegrated or not. Finally, subsection 4.2.2 derives testing conditions which are based on the responsiveness of the trade balance towards the NIIP.

4.2.1 Difference-stationarity of the NIIP of any order

Following Hakkio and Rush (1991b, p. 33), it can be shown that (i) cointegration of order one between exports and imports inclusive of net interest payments and (ii) $\beta = 1$ are only sufficient conditions for the validity of the IBC in the data. The IBC is also satisfied if condition (i) is satisfied and $0 < \beta < 1$. However, even condition (i) is not necessary for sustainability. Following the analysis by Quintos (1995) in the area of fiscal sustainability, the economy obeys the IBC as long as the NIIP is at most $I(2)$ and $0 < \beta \leq 1$, regardless of whether X_t and MM_t are cointegrated.

Bohn (2007) generalizes these results by showing that difference-stationarity of the NIIP of *any* order alone is sufficient to ensure the validity of the IBC. Bergman (2001) arrives at the similar result, yet his argument additionally requires the individual's rate of time preference to be bounded from below by a positive number (Bergman, 2001, p. 28). This subsection focuses on the proof presented by Bohn (2007) as it does not rely on the additional restriction on time-preference rate.

More specifically, the transversality condition of the means given by

$$\lim_{N \to \infty} R^{N+1} E_t \left[B_{t+N} \right] = 0 \tag{4.28}$$

is satisfied if the NIIP is integrated of any finite order $d \geq 0$, provided that the interest rate is either (i) positive and constant ($r_t = r > 0$) or (ii) uncorrelated over time with a positive and constant conditional expectation $E_t \left[r_t \right] = r > 0$, or (iii) stationary with mean $r > 0$. The idea behind this result can be explained as follows: The real interest rate grows exponentially (i.e., the discount factor decays exponentially). If $B_t \sim I(d)$, $E_t \left[B_{t+N} \right]$ is at most a polynomial of order d. Due to de l'Hospital's rule (applied d times), the exponential decay of the discount factor dominates the polynomial growth of the NIIP so that the limit in the TC goes to zero as $N \to \infty$.

This proof can first be illustrated for the case of $d = 0$. For $d = 0$, $E_t[B_{t+N}]$ converges in mean square to $E[B_t]$ for given t, which, in combination with the polynomial growth of the interest rate, implies that the TC (4.28) is met.

For $d \geq 1$, B_{t+N} can be written (using the method of differences) as

$$B_{t+N} = B_t + \sum_{i=1}^{N} \Delta B_{t+i} = B_t + \sum_{i=1}^{N} \left(\Delta B_t + \sum_{j=1}^{j} \left(\Delta^2 B_{t+j} \right) \right). \tag{4.29}$$

The double sum in equation (4.29) can be simplified as follows:

$$\begin{aligned}\sum_{i=1}^{N}\sum_{j=1}^{j}(\Delta^2 B_{t+j}) =&\Delta^2 B_{t+1}+(\Delta^2 B_{t+1}+\Delta^2 B_{t+2})\\ &+\cdots+(\Delta^2 B_{t+1}+\Delta^2 B_{t+2}+\cdots+\Delta^2 B_{t+N})\\ =&N\Delta^2 B_{t+1}+(N-1)B_{t+2}+\cdots+\Delta^2 B_{t+N}\\ =&\sum_{i=1}^{N} i\Delta^2 B_{t+(N+1-i)}.\end{aligned} \tag{4.30}$$

Combining equations (4.29) and (4.30) results in

$$\begin{aligned}B_{t+N} &= B_t + i\Delta B_t + \sum_{i=1}^{N} i\Delta^2 B_{t+(N+1-i)} = \cdots\\ &= \sum_{k=0}^{d-1} p_k(N)\Delta^k B_t + \sum_{i=1}^{N} p_{d-1}(i)\Delta^d B_{t+(N+1-i)}\end{aligned} \tag{4.31}$$

where $p_k(N)$ are k^{th}-order polynomial functions of N ($p_k(N) \geq 0$ for all N and k) with $p_0(N) = 1$, $p_1(N) = 1$ and $p_k(N) = \sum_{j=1}^{N} p_{k-1}(j)$ for $k \geq 2$. Thus, the dth-order integration of B_{t+N} implies an at most polynomial growth.

Equation (4.31) allows to rewrite the term $R^{N+1}E_t[B_{t+N}]$ in the TC (4.28) as

$$\begin{aligned}R^{N+1}E_t[B_{t+N}] =&E_t\left[R^{N+1}\sum_{k=0}^{d-1} p_k(N)\Delta^k B_t\right]\\ &+R^{N+1}N^d E_t\left[\frac{1}{N^d}\sum_{i=1}^{N} p_{d-1}(i)\right]E_t\left[\Delta^d B_{t+(N+1-i)}\right].\end{aligned} \tag{4.32}$$

Because $\Delta^k B_t$ are constants for a given t and $p_k(N)$ is a polynomial, $R^{N+1}\sum_{k=0}^{d-1} p_k(N)$ and therefore the whole first term on the right-hand side of the TC (4.32) goes to zero as $N \to \infty$. The second term on the right-hand side of equation (4.32), i.e. $q(N) \equiv \frac{1}{N^d}\sum_{i=1}^{N} p_{d-1}(i)$, has a finite limit $q(N) \to q$ due to the scale factor $1/N^d$. Because $\Delta^d B_t \sim I(0)$, $E_t[\Delta^d B_{t+(N+1-i)}]$ converges in mean square to $E[\Delta^d B_t]$ as $N \to \infty$. Therefore $E_t\left[\frac{1}{N^d}\sum_{i=1}^{N} p_{d-1}(i)\Delta^d B_{t+(N+1-i)}\right]$ converges in mean square to $qE[\Delta^d B_t]$. Since $R^{N+1}N^d$ goes to zero over time, the whole second term on the right-hand side of (4.32) vanishes over time. As the two terms on the right-hand side of (4.32) tend to zero as $N \to \infty$, the transversality condition (4.28) is satisfied.

The requirement that the NIIP be $I(d)$ is equivalent to the requirement that the current account is integrated of any order d_{CA} with $d_{CA} = d-1 \geq 0$ because $CA_t = \Delta B_t$. The requirement of difference-stationarity of the NIIP also corresponds to the requirement that the components of the current account are difference-stationary (possibly of different orders of integration). If $X_t \sim (d_X)$ and $MM_t \sim I(d_{MM})$, then $B_t \sim I(d)$ with $d \leq \max(d_X, d_{MM}) + 1$.[15] Analogously, if

[15] To see this, assume that $\Delta^{d_{MM}}MM_t = u_t \sim I(0)$ and $\Delta^{d_X}X_t = v_t \sim I(0)$ where $\Delta B_t = MM_t + X_t$. Consider first the case where MM_t and X_t are integrated of different orders. If $d_X < d_{MM}$, $\Delta^{d_X}(\Delta B_t) = \Delta^{d_X - d_{MM}}u_t + v_t \sim I(0)$. Hence, $B_t \sim I(d_X + 1)$. If $d_X > d_{MM}$, then $\Delta^{d_{MM}}(\Delta B_t) = u_t + \Delta^{d_{MM}-d_X}v_t \sim I(0)$. Thus, $B_t \sim I(d_{MM}+1)$. In both

savings and investment are difference-stationary with $S_t \sim (d_S)$ and $I_t \sim I(d_I)$, then B_t will be $I(d)$ with $d \leq \max(d_S, d_I) + 1$, the same result analogously applies to the relationship between the trade balance and the NIIP.

Viewed in this light, sustainability conditions which require the NIIP or the current account to be difference-stationary of at most second order are simply special cases of Bohn's (2007) proposition. Further, cointegration conditions or restrictions on β such as $0 < \beta \leq 1$ turn out to be merely sufficient conditions for sustainability. Thus, if these conditions are not satisfied in the data, one cannot conclude that the IBC is violated because sufficient conditions, by their nature, can only produce evidence in favour of sustainability and never against sustainability.

In sum, testing for sustainability amounts to testing for the integration order in the current account series, and/or in the NIIP series, and/or in the current account components (such as trade account and NIIP, savings and investment) using unit root tests. Although most economic series are stationary in levels or in first differences, it is (at least theoretically) possible that the current account series is, say, $I(2)$. However, the higher the integration order of the NIIP series, the faster the undiscounted NIIP (in levels or in proportion to GDP) goes to infinity, implying serious policy implications for an economy. For this reason, Bohn (2007, p. 1841) ironically labels the NIIP being integrated of at least third order (the current account being integrated of at least second order) as "absurdly weakly" sustainable. Finally, the failure to provide evidence for a particular integration order in the current account, the NIIP, or the components of the current account does not imply unsustainability. As Trehan and Walsh (1991) show, sustainability is also consistent with the mildly explosive NIIP (see case (3) on page 4.28). Thus, stationarity and difference-stationarity are merely sufficient conditions for sustainability.

4.2.2 Responsiveness of the trade account to the NIIP

This subsection presents two approaches which are based on the idea that sustainability implies a negative responsiveness of the trade account to the NIIP. A sustainable current account path is such that an economy responds to growing (decreasing) net foreign debts by improving (deteriorating) the trade account.

Wickens and Uctum's (1993) approach

Wickens and Uctum (1993) analyze current account sustainability under the assumption that the trade account as a fraction of GDP is weakly exogenous and stationary in first differences. This approach is related to that of Uctum and Wickens (2000) already mentioned in subsection 4.1.1.

Wickens and Uctum (1993) start with a complete linear model of economy where the balance of payments identity is one equation and all endogenous and exogenous variables except for tb_t and b_t are eliminated. Under the assumption of fixed real interest rates adjusted for real GDP growth, the system can be reduced to the two following equations:

---

cases, $B_t \sim I(d)$ where $d = \max(d_{MM}, d_X) + 1$. Consider finally the case where MM_t and X_t are integrated of the same order, that is: $d_X = d_{MM}$. If MM_t and X_t are not cointegrated, $B_t \sim I(d)$ with $d = d_X + 1 = d_{MM} + 1$. If MM_t and X_t are cointegrated, $B_t \sim I(d)$ with $d = (d_X - d_{MM}) + 1$. In both cases, $B_t \sim I(d)$ where $d \leq \max(d_{MM}, d_X) + 1$. Hence, in all cases, $B_t \sim I(d)$ with $d \leq \max(d_X, d_{MM}) + 1$ if $X_t \sim (d_X)$ and $MM_t \sim I(d_{MM})$ (Bohn, 2007, p. 842).

$$\Delta b_t = tb_t + (r-\gamma)b_{t-1} \tag{4.33}$$
$$\Delta tb_t = \eta - \alpha b_{t-1} + \beta tb_{t-1} + e_t. \tag{4.34}$$

The first equation is the balance of payments identity (3.10), and the second equation permits feedback effects from the NIIP to the trade account (with a lag). If $\alpha \neq 0$, the trade balance is weakly exogenous. In other words, a net debtor (net creditor) economy experiences an increase (a decrease) in the trade balance if $\alpha > 0$ and a decline (a rise) in the trade balance if $\alpha < 0$. The higher α, the higher, everything else being equal, is the change in the trade balance. If $\alpha = 0$, the trade balance is strictly exogenous and does not respond to changes in the NIIP at all. The error term e_t summarizes the effects of all eliminated variables and is, therefore, likely to be nonstationary.

Equations (4.33) and (4.34) can be put in a matrix form after adding tb_{t-1} on both sides of equation (4.33) (which yields $\Delta b_t - \Delta tb_t = tb_{t-1} + (r-\gamma)b_{t-1}$):

$$\begin{pmatrix} 1 & -1 \\ 0 & 1 \end{pmatrix} \begin{pmatrix} \Delta b_t \\ \Delta tb_t \end{pmatrix} = \begin{pmatrix} 0 \\ \eta \end{pmatrix} + \begin{pmatrix} (r-\gamma) & 1 \\ -\alpha & \beta \end{pmatrix} \begin{pmatrix} b_{t-1} \\ tb_{t-1} \end{pmatrix} + \begin{pmatrix} 0 \\ e_t \end{pmatrix}. \tag{4.35}$$

Equation system (4.35) can be transformed into the VAR by multiplying both sides of (4.35) by $\begin{pmatrix} 1 & 1 \\ 0 & 1 \end{pmatrix}$ (which is the inverse of the first matrix on the left-hand side of (4.35)):

$$\begin{pmatrix} \Delta b_t \\ \Delta tb_t \end{pmatrix} = \begin{pmatrix} 1 \\ 1 \end{pmatrix} \eta + \begin{pmatrix} (r-\gamma)-\alpha & 1+\beta \\ -\alpha & \beta \end{pmatrix} \begin{pmatrix} b_{t-1} \\ tb_{t-1} \end{pmatrix} + \begin{pmatrix} 1 \\ 1 \end{pmatrix} e_t. \tag{4.36}$$

Writing the VAR (4.36) more succinctly one obtains

$$\Delta \mathbf{x_t} = \mathbf{m} + \Theta \mathbf{x_{t-1}} + \mathbf{u_t} \tag{4.37}$$

where all variables can be stationary or nonstationary. If tb_t is stationary, the balance of payments identity (4.33) implies that b_t is stationary for $(r-\gamma) < 0$ and nonstationary for $(r-\gamma) > 0$.[16] If tb_t is nonstationary, tb_t and b_t may be cointegrated implying that u_t is stationary.

Solvency requires the economy to respect the transversality condition. In order to arrive at the transversality condition, equation (4.37) can be first rewritten in terms of b_t. Multiplying both sides of the VAR (4.37) from the left by $\mathbf{e_1}' \equiv \begin{pmatrix} 1 & 0 \end{pmatrix}$, one obtains

$$\Delta \mathbf{e_1}'\mathbf{x_t} = \mathbf{e_1}'\mathbf{m} + \mathbf{e_1}'\Theta \mathbf{x_{t-1}} + \mathbf{e_1}'\mathbf{u_t} \tag{4.38}$$

where $b_t = \mathbf{e_1}'\mathbf{x_t}$. Following Wickens and Uctum (1993), the transversality condition is derived by the repeated backwards iteration. Transferring equation (4.38) into period $t+N$ and rearranging the terms yields

$$\mathbf{e_1}'\mathbf{x_{t+N}} = \mathbf{e_1}'\mathbf{m} + \mathbf{e_1}'(\mathbf{I}+\Theta)\mathbf{e_1}'\mathbf{x_{t+N-1}} + \mathbf{e_1}'\mathbf{u_{t+N}}. \tag{4.39}$$

16 Using the lag operator, the balance of payments identity (4.33) can be written as $(1-L-(r-\gamma)L)b_t = tb_t$ which is stationary for $tb_t \sim I(0)$. The characteristic root, $1/(1+r-\gamma)$, is greater than one in absolute value for $(r-\gamma) < 0$ and less than one for $(r-\gamma) > 0$.

Substituting $\mathbf{e_1}'\mathbf{m}+\mathbf{e_1}'(\mathbf{I}+\Theta)\,\mathbf{x_{t+N-2}}+\mathbf{e_1}'\mathbf{u_{t+N-1}}$ for $\mathbf{e_1}'\mathbf{x_{t+N-1}}$ in (4.39), one obtains

$$\mathbf{e_1}'\mathbf{x_{t+N}}=\mathbf{e_1}'\mathbf{m}+\mathbf{e_1}'(\mathbf{I}+\Theta)\,\mathbf{m}+\mathbf{e_1}'(\mathbf{I}+\Theta)^2\,\mathbf{x_{t+N-2}}+\mathbf{e_1}'(\mathbf{I}+\Theta)\,\mathbf{u_{t+N-1}}+\mathbf{e_1}'\mathbf{u_{t+N}}.$$

Iterating repeatedly and taking the limit as $N\rightarrow\infty$ finally yields the transversality condition:

$$\lim_{N\rightarrow\infty}\mathbf{e_1}'d^N E_t\left[b_{t+N}\right]=\lim_{N\rightarrow\infty}\left[\mathbf{e_1}'\sum_{v=0}^{N-1}d^N(\mathbf{I}+\Theta)^v\,\mathbf{m}+\mathbf{e_1}'d^N(\mathbf{I}+\Theta)^N\,\mathbf{x_t}\right.$$
$$\left.+\sum_{v=0}^{N-1}\mathbf{e_1}'d^N(\mathbf{I}+\Theta)^v E_t\left[u_{t+N-v}\right]\right]=0. \qquad (4.40)$$

The TC (4.40) is met if the roots λ_i of the matrix $\mathbf{I}+\Theta$ are less than $1+r-\gamma$ in absolute value, that is: $|\lambda_i|<1+r-\gamma$, $i=1,2$, and if $r-\gamma>0$. The latter condition implies that the difference equation (4.33) is unstable and that $1+r-\gamma>0$. Appendix 4.A shows that each term on the right-hand side of (4.40) vanishes over time if (i) $|\lambda_i|<1+r-\gamma$ and (ii) $1+r-\gamma>0$; restrictions (i) and (ii) on the roots of $\mathbf{I}+\Theta$ will be hereafter simply referred to as “the root condition.”

The root condition is not satisfied for the strongly exogenous trade account (i.e., for $\alpha=0$) because in this case one of the roots equals $1+r-\gamma$.[17] If, however, the trade balance is weakly exogenous and the root condition is satisfied, $\beta-(r-\gamma)>0$ implies $\alpha>0$.[18] In other words,

[17] The eigenvalues are calculated by solving $\det((\mathbf{I}+\Theta)-\lambda\mathbf{I})=\mathbf{0}$. One obtains

$$|(\mathbf{I}+\Theta)-\lambda\mathbf{I}|=\left|\begin{pmatrix}r-\gamma-\alpha+1-\lambda & 1+\beta\\ -\alpha & 1+\beta-\lambda\end{pmatrix}\right|$$
$$=(r-\gamma-\alpha+1-\lambda)(1+\beta-\lambda)+(1+\beta)\alpha=0.$$

Rearranging the terms leads to the characteristic equation

$$\lambda^2-\lambda\,(2+\beta+r-\gamma-\alpha)+(1+r-\gamma)\,(1+\beta)=0.$$

This yields the roots

$$\lambda_i=1/2\,(2+\beta-\alpha+r-\gamma)\pm\sqrt{1/4\,(2+\beta-\alpha+r-\gamma)^2-(1+r-\gamma)\,(1+\beta)}. \qquad (4.41)$$

For $\alpha=0$, equation (4.41) simplifies to

$$\lambda_i=1/2\,(2+\beta+r-\gamma)\pm\sqrt{1/4\,(2+\beta+r-\gamma)^2-(1+r-\gamma)\,(1+\beta)}.$$

Expanding the brackets yields

$$\lambda_i=1+r/2-\gamma/2+\beta/2\pm(r/2-\gamma/2-\beta/2).$$

Thus, one obtains $\lambda_1=1+r-\gamma$ and $\lambda_1=1+\beta$.

[18] For $\alpha\neq0$ and very small α, β and r, one can neglect the discriminant on the right-hand side of equation (4.41) and approximate equation (4.41) by $\lambda=1+\beta/2-\alpha/2+r/2-\gamma/2$. The root condition requires $|\lambda|<1+r-\gamma$, i.e. $|1+\beta/2-\alpha/2+r/2-\gamma/2|<1+r-\gamma$. For $(1+\beta/2-\alpha/2+r/2-\gamma/2)>0$, $|1+\beta/2-\alpha/2+r/2-\gamma/2|<1+r-\gamma$ implies that $\beta-(r-\gamma)<\alpha$. When $(\beta-(r-\gamma))>0$, α must be strictly positive. The inequality $\beta-(r-\gamma)<\alpha$ is also satisfied for $\alpha<0$ and $\beta<(r-\gamma)$.

when $\beta - (r-\gamma) > 0$, negative feedback from the NIIP to the trade account is sufficient to satisfy the root condition and to meet the transversality condition. This result is intuitive as negative feedback from the NIIP implies that the trade account improves when economy has net foreign debts. Thus, instead of testing the root condition, one can test for negative feedback from the NIIP to the trade account because the root condition is likely to be satisfied if $\alpha > 0$. Strictly speaking, when testing for $\alpha > 0$, one should in addition test whether $\beta > r-\gamma$ because otherwise the root condition is violated. It bears emphasizing that $\alpha < 0$ does not necessarily imply the lack of sustainability. If $\alpha < 0$ and $\beta < (r-\gamma)$, the root condition is met, thus implying sustainability. If the trade account is $I(1)$ and weakly exogenous and the root condition is satisfied, the current account can be nonstationary and still sustainable. From equation (4.34) follows that, for $\alpha \neq 0$, the NIIP may be $I(1)$, either cointegrated with the trade account or not, or integrated of higher order, provided that the error term is difference-stationary of the appropriate order. For example, both the NIIP and the error term may be $I(2)$ implying weak sustainability if the root condition is satisfied.

In order to derive sufficient conditions for sustainability in case of strictly exogenous trade account, Wickens and Uctum (1993) examine which (additional) properties the trade account must display so as to satisfy the transversality condition. When the trade account is strictly exogenous (i.e. $\mu = 0$) and $I(1)$, equation (4.34) becomes

$$\Delta tb_t = \eta + e_t. \tag{4.42}$$

It is in addition assumed that $\Delta e_t = \sum_{i=0}^{m} \psi_i \varepsilon_{t-v} = \Psi(L)\varepsilon_t$ where $\psi_0 = 1$, $\sum_{i=0}^{m} \psi_i^2$ is finite, the roots of the polynomial $\Psi(L)$ lie outside the unity circle, and ε_t is a zero-mean white noise. Substituting equation (4.42) into the balance of payments identity (3.10) yields

$$\Delta b_t = \eta + (1+r-\gamma)\Delta b_{t-1} + e_t. \tag{4.43}$$

The aim is now to derive conditions under which the IBC,

$$b_{t-1} = -E_t\left[\sum_{n=t}^{\infty} d^{n-t+1} tb_n\right], \tag{4.44}$$

and therefore the appropriate TC are satisfied. Writing equation (4.42) in terms of period $t+N$ and iterating the resulting equation back to period $t+1$ results in

$$\begin{aligned} tb_n &= \eta + tb_{n-1} + e_n = \eta + \eta + tb_{n-2} + e_{n-1} + e_n = \cdots \\ &= (n-t+1)\eta + tb_{t-1} + \sum_{j=t}^{n} e_j \end{aligned} \tag{4.45}$$

for $n = t, t+1, \cdots, t+N$. Inserting equation (4.45) into the IBC one obtains

$$\begin{aligned} b_{t-1} &= -E_t\left[\sum_{n=t}^{\infty} d^{n-t+1}\left((n-t+1)\eta + tb_{t-1} + \sum_{j=t}^{n} e_j\right)\right] \\ &= -\frac{d}{(1-d)^2}\eta - \frac{d}{1-d} tb_{t-1} - E_t\left[\sum_{n=t}^{\infty} d^{n-t+1} \sum_{j=t}^{n} e_j\right]. \end{aligned} \tag{4.46}$$

The last term on the right-hand side of equation (4.46) can be rewritten as

$$\begin{aligned}
&E_t\left[\sum_{n=t}^{\infty} d^{n-t+1}\sum_{j=t}^{n} e_j\right]\\
=&E_t\left[de_t+d^2(e_t+e_{t+1})+d^3(e_t+e_{t+1}+e_{t+2})+\cdots\right]\\
=&E_t\left[d(e_t+e_{t+1}+e_{t+2}+\cdots)+d^2(e_t+e_{t+1}+\cdots)+d^3(e_t+e_{t+1}+\cdots)+\cdots\right]\\
=&E_t\left[\left(\sum_{n=t}^{\infty} d^{n-t+1}\right)\left(\sum_{n=t}^{\infty} d^{n-t}e_n\right)\right]. \qquad (4.47)
\end{aligned}$$

Using the formula for the sum of a geometric series, the first sum in equation (4.47) reduces to

$$E_t\left[\sum_{n=t}^{\infty} d^{n-t+1}\right]=\frac{1}{1-d}-1=\frac{d}{1-d}=\frac{(1+r-\gamma)^{-1}}{1-(1+r-\gamma)^{-1}}=\frac{1}{r-\gamma}. \qquad (4.48)$$

Shifting the expectation operator behind the infinite sum and exploiting the formula in Hansen and Sargent (1980, p. 14), the second sum in equation (4.47) can be rewritten as

$$E_t\left[\sum_{n=t}^{\infty} d^{n-t}e_n\right]=(1-L)^{-1}\frac{\Psi(L)-L^{-1}d\Psi(d)}{1-dL^{-1}}\varepsilon_t \qquad (4.49)$$

with $e_t=(1-L)^{-1}\Psi(L)\varepsilon_t$. Combining equations (4.46), (4.48), and (4.49), the IBC becomes

$$b_{t-1}=-\frac{d}{(1-d)^2}\eta-\frac{d}{1-d}tb_{t-1}-\frac{d\left(\Psi(L)-L^{-1}d\Psi(d)\right)}{(1-d)(1-L)(1-dL^{-1})}\varepsilon_t. \qquad (4.50)$$

Multiplying each side of equation (4.50) by $(1-L)((L^{-1}-d^{-1})$ results in

$$\begin{aligned}
\Delta b_t-d^{-1}\Delta b_{t-1}=&-\frac{d}{1-d}\Delta tb_t+\frac{1}{1-d}\Delta tb_{t-1}\\
&-\frac{(L^{-1}-d^{-1})(d\Psi(L)-d^2L^{-1}\Psi(d))}{(1-d)(1-dL^{-1})}\varepsilon_t.
\end{aligned}$$

Using $tb_t=\eta+e_t$ and rearranging the terms one obtains

$$\Delta b_t-d^{-1}\Delta b_{t-1}=\eta-\frac{d}{1-d}e_t+\frac{1}{1-d}e_{t-1}-\frac{L^{-1}d\Psi(d)-\Psi(L)}{1-d}\varepsilon_t. \qquad (4.51)$$

Substituting $e_{t-1}=e_t+\Psi(L)\varepsilon_t$ into equation (4.51) and rearranging the terms again, the IBC can finally be written as

$$\begin{aligned}
\Delta b_t&=\eta+d^{-1}\Delta b_{t-1}+e_t-\frac{L^{-1}d\Psi(d)}{1-d}\varepsilon_t \qquad (4.52)\\
&=\eta+(1+r-\gamma)\Delta b_{t-1}+e_t-\frac{\Psi(d)}{r-\gamma}\varepsilon_{t+1}. \qquad (4.53)
\end{aligned}$$

Equations (4.53) and (4.43) are the same for $\Psi(d) = 0$. Multiplying both sides of equation (4.43) by $(1-d-1L)^{-1}$ reveals that $\Delta b_t = \eta(1-d-1L)^{-1})^{-1} + (1-d-1L)^{-1}(1-L)^{-1}\Psi(L)\varepsilon_t$ is $I(0)$ because $\varepsilon_t \sim I(0)$. This implies that the current account must also be stationary.

Hence, if the trade balance-to-GDP ratio is strictly exogenous and $I(1)$, a sufficient condition for sustainability is that Δtb_t has a root at $|1+r-\gamma|$. In this case, the NIIP will also be $I(1)$, the NIIP and the trade balance will be cointegrated, and the current account will be stationary and thus sustainable in the strong sense. Note that cointegration between the NIIP and the trade balance ratios alone is neither necessary nor sufficient for sustainability, it becomes sufficient only when Δtb_t has a root at $|1+r-\gamma|$.

In sum, the testing procedure suggested by Wickens and Uctum (1993) consists mainly of the following two steps. The first step consists of testing for difference-stationarity of the NIIP, the trade account, and the current account. The second step involves testing either whether the roots of the matrix $\mathbf{I}+\Theta$ are equal to or less than $1+r-\gamma$ in absolute value (where $r-\gamma > 0$) and/or whether the coefficient α is larger than zero.

If the NIIP and the trade account are each found to be either (a) $I(0)$ or (b) $I(1)$ in the fist step and one of the roots is estimated to be at $|1+r-\gamma|$ in the second step, the current account is sustainable in the strong sense because in case (a) stationarity of the NIIP implies stationarity of the current account and in case (b) the trade account and the NIIP will be cointegrated with cointegrating vector $(1,-r)$ so that the current account is stationary.

If unit root tests, applied in the first step, indicate that the NIIP and the trade account are difference-stationary and if in the second step the roots are estimated to be less than $1+r-\gamma$ in absolute value (where $r-\gamma > 0$) and/or there is negative feedback from the NIIP to the trade account (i.e. $\alpha > 0$), then the current account is sustainable. Testing for the order of integration of the current account reveals then whether it is sustainable in the weak or in the strong sense.

This approach appears to be quite complicated as it relies on a number of conditions (difference-stationarity of the variables involved plus the restrictions on the roots of the economy's dynamic structure). Further, these conditions are merely sufficient for sustainability. This means that, for example, the finding of a negative feedback from the NIIP to the trade account ($\alpha > 0$) implies sustainability, but the finding of a positive feedback ($\alpha < 0$) cannot be interpreted as unsustainability. Bohn (2007) suggests a testing approach which is also based on the idea that negative feedback from the NIIP to the trade account must be sufficient for sustainability. Bohn's (2007) approach is, however, more general, as it applies to difference-stationary processes of any order, and is more simple, as it relies only on few conditions.

Bohn's (2007) approach

Bohn (2007) relies on the framework developed by Trehan and Walsh (1991) and already discussed in subsubsection 4.1.3. It is assumed that (i) the interest rate is constant at $r_t = r$; (ii) the trade account follows a quasi difference-stationary mean zero process $TB_t\,(1-\rho L) \sim I(0)$ with $\rho \in [0;1+r)$, and (iii) $\mu B_{t-1} + TB_t = e_t \sim I(0)$ is a linear stationary combination of TB_t and B_{t-1} with $\mu = 1+r-\rho$. The last two assumptions imply that the NIIP is also quasi difference-stationary:

$$\begin{aligned} B_t - \rho B_{t-1} &= \mu^{-1}(-TB_{t+1} + e_{t+1} + \rho\, TB_t + -\rho\, e_t) \\ &= -\mu^{-1}(1-\rho L)\, TB_{t+1} + \mu^{-1}(1-\rho L)\, e_{t+1}. \end{aligned} \tag{4.54}$$

Because both addends on the right-hand side of (4.54) are $I(0)$, $B_t - \rho B_{t-1} \sim I(0)$. The order of integration of B_t and TB_t depends on the root ρ (see three cases described on page 57). As a reminder, the three cases are summarized in table 4.1.

Table 4.1: Relationship between the quasi difference-stationary trade account, the quasi difference-stationary NIIP, and the current account

	$\mu \in (r; 1+r]$; $\rho \in [0,1)$	$\mu = r$; $\rho = 1$	$\mu \in (0; r)$; $\rho \in (1; 1+r)$
B_t	$I(0)$	$I(1)$	mildly explosive
TB_t	$I(0)$	$I(1)$	mildly explosive
CA_t	$I(0)$	$I(0)$	not difference-stationary
	Strong sustainability	Strong sustainability	Weak sustainability

Based on these considerations, Bohn (2007) suggests to test a quasi error correction type specification of the form

$$TB_t = -\mu B_{t-1} + e_t \sim I(0), \qquad \mu \in (0; 1+r]. \tag{4.55}$$

Equation (4.55) is expressed in real terms; it can also be defined in nominal terms (in this case, all variables are nominal and $\mu \in (0; 1+i]$ where i denotes, as before, the nominal interest rate). The variables in equation (4.55) can also be set in proportion to GDP, GNP, or population; in the case of nominal GDP, all variables are nominal in proportion to nominal GDP and $\mu \in \left(0; \frac{1+i}{1+\gamma^n}\right]$; in the case of real GDP, all variables are real relative to real GDP and $\mu \in \left(0; \frac{1+r}{1+\gamma}\right]$.

Equation (4.55) can be interpreted as a reaction function which describes the response of the trade account to changes in the NIIP. In this case, if the IBC holds, sustainability requires the economy under consideration to respond to growing net foreign debts (assets) by increasing (at least) linearly the trade surplus (deficit). In other words, the economy's agents (households, firms, and the government) adjust their saving and investment plans over time in such a way that they satisfy the financing requirements implied by changes in the economy's NIIP (Durdu et al., 2010, p. 8). The higher μ, i.e., the stronger the response of the trade balance, the "stronger" the notion of sustainability (as follows from table 4.1). The condition that μ be strictly positive ensures that this "reaction mechanism" exists (the rather technical condition that $\mu \leq (1+r)$ is not affected in case of unit roots (Bohn, 2007, p. 1845)). In case that $\mu \leq 0$, a net debtor economy would be oblivious to the accumulation of net foreign debts and could run a Ponzi scheme, thus violating the intertemporal budget constraint (Bohn, 1995a, p. 2). The quasi error correction specification can also be adapted to savings and investment, as well as to exports and imports inclusive of net interest payments:

$$S_t = \frac{\mu}{r} I_t + e_t \sim I(0), \qquad \frac{\mu}{r} \in (0; \frac{1+r}{r}] \tag{4.56}$$

$$X_t = \frac{\mu}{r} MM_t + e_t \sim I(0), \qquad \frac{\mu}{r} \in (0; \frac{1+r}{r}]. \tag{4.57}$$

Equation (4.57) can also be rewritten as

$$X_t = \mu M_t + e_t \sim I(0), \qquad \mu \in (0; 1+r] \tag{4.58}$$

However, the economic interpretation of equations (4.56) and (4.57) is less intuitive than in case of the trade balance and the NIIP: Sustainability requires an economy to increase savings in response to growing investment (equation (4.56)) and to raise exports in case of growing imports inclusive of net interest payments (equation (4.57)).

The model in (4.55) can be generalized for any (finite) integration order d so that

$$TB_t = -\mu B_{t-1} + \varepsilon_t \sim I(d), \quad \mu \in (0; 1+r] \tag{4.59}$$

implies sustainability (Bohn, 2007, pp. 1843-1845).[19] However, as already mentioned above, the sustainability notion which implies a current account series being, say, $I(3)$ and the NIIP series being $I(4)$ is absurdly weak. Since most time series are at most $I(1)$, it is, however, unlikely that the estimation of equation (4.59) will be needed. Yet equation (4.59) illustrates once again that the intertemporal budget constraint imposes only weak restrictions on the trade balance, the NIIP, and thus, on the current account!

A major advantage of the sufficient conditions (4.55) and (4.59) is that they imply the validity of the general intertemporal budget constraint (3.51) (the proof is given in Appendix 4.B). In contrast, all other sufficient conditions derived previously in this chapter imply only the specific IBC which is valid in special, and not very probable, cases (such as the absence of uncertainty).

In sum, the validity of the general IBC in the data can be tested by estimating the reaction function (4.59): A finding of μ being statistically significant and positive implies sustainability. The value of μ shows whether the trade balance and the NIIP are stationary in levels or difference-stationary or not difference-stationary at all—thus indicating whether external imbalances are strongly or weakly sustainable. An important aspect involves determining the appropriate discount rate. However, because the discount rate is typically a relatively small figure,

[19] The proof is similar to the case of $\varepsilon_t \sim I(0)$. For $\mu \in (r; 1+r]$, i.e., $\rho \in [0;1)$, $B_t \sim I(d)$ because all characteristic roots are less than one in absolute value. For $\mu = r$, i.e., $\rho = 1$, $B_t \sim I(d+1)$ because $\Delta B_t \sim I(d)$. In both cases, the NIIP is difference-stationary, which implies sustainability. For $\mu \in (0; r)$, i.e., $\rho \in (1; 1+r)$, one can show that $R^{N+1} E_t[B_{t+N}]$ tends to zero so that the TC is satisfied. Because of $B_{t+1} = \rho B_t + e_{t+1}$, $R^{N+1} E_t[B_{t+N}]$ can be written as

$$R^{N+1} E_t[B_{t+N}] = R^{N+1} \rho^N B_t + R^{N+1} \sum_{i=1}^{N} \rho^{N-i} e_{t+i}$$

$$= R(R\rho)^N + B_t + R(R\rho)^N \sum_{i=1}^{N} \rho^{N-i} e_{t+i}$$

Similar to equations (4.32) and (4.31), the method of differences allows to represent the sum $\sum_{i=1}^{N} \rho^{N-i} e_{t+i}$ as a linear combination of $\Delta^k e_t$ and $\Delta^d e_{t+i}$ (which are stationary due to $e_t \sim I(d)$) for $0 \leq k < d$ and $1 \leq i \leq N$. Since $\rho^{-1} < 1$, the weights in the linear combination are bounded from above by polynomials. Because of $(R\rho) < 1$, $(R\rho)^N$ tends to zero as $N \to \infty$. Thus, $R^{N+1} E_t[B_{t+N}]$ vanishes over time (Bohn, 2007, pp. 1844-1845).

it might be difficult to distinguish between a unit root and a $1+r$-root in the NIIP and between μ-values which are near zero (Bohn, 2007, p. 1845).

4.3 Conclusion

This chapter has demonstrated that there is a large number of testing conditions that imply the validity of the intertemporal budget constraint in the data (summarized in table 4.2). We distinguish strong, weak, and even "absurdly" weak notions of sustainability, mainly depending on the characteristics of the current account series.

The current account which is stationary in levels displays mean-reverting behavior so that persistently growing deficits and surpluses are not possible—this is the strong notion of sustainability. Aside from the current account series being $I(0)$, strong sustainability is ensured when the NIIP is at most $I(1)$, the components of the current account (savings and investment, exports and imports inclusive of net interest payments as well as the trade balance and the NIIP) are stationary in levels or stationary in first differences and together cointegrated of order one with the appropriate cointegrating vector (see table 4.2 for details).

The intertemporal budget constraint is also satisfied if the current account series is integrated of order one. Since an $I(1)$-series has a tendency to wander from its mean, growing current account deficits and surpluses are feasible for prolonged periods of time. Similarly, a net international investment series that is $I(2)$ is also consistent with the IBC. The rationale is that the polynomial growth of the NIIP dominates the exponential growth of the discount rate so that the discounted NIIP vanishes over time. However, a non-stationary increase in the (undiscounted) net foreign debt might increase an economy's vulnerability to adverse shocks and even finally lead to an unsustainable situation in which net interest payments exceed an economy's repayment ability, resulting in at least a partial debt default/restructuring and thus a violation of solvency. For this reason, any notion of sustainability which does not imply that the current account series is stationary in levels is considered to be weak. Although a non-stationary increase in (undiscounted) net foreign assets is, in principle, problematic only when it is reflected in a non-stationary increase in (undiscounted) net foreign debts of other economies, it might be desirable for an economy to cut its foreign lending and instead to increase consumption and investment. Therefore, we refer to a situation where both net foreign assets and debts are $I(2)$ as "weakly sustainable."

Further conditions for weak sustainability are: stationarity of the components of the current account in first differences, without cointegration; stationarity in second differences and cointegration with the appropriate cointegrating vector (see table 4.2 for details). The current account components might even be mildly explosive, with the roots not greater than one plus the market interest rate, and still consistent with weak sustainability. Note that in the latter case the current account series is not difference-stationary at all.[20]

Finally, "absurdly" weak sustainability refers to one of the following three situations: either the current account series is integrated of order two or higher, or the NIIP is integrated of order three or higher, or both series are not difference-stationary at all (see table 4.2 for details).

[20] More specifically, the current account series is given by $CAB_t = e_t^B + (\rho - 1)B_{t-1}$ with $e_t^B \sim I(0)$, $\rho \in (1;1+r)$, and $(1-\rho L)B_t \sim I(0)$.

However, since most time series are at most $I(1)$, this type of sustainability is not likely to occur often.

Because the weak and "absurdly" weak notions of sustainability impose only weak restrictions on the paths of external imbalances, it might be appropriate to strengthen the IBC through the use of additional criteria: for instance, using only the strong notion of sustainability or, even stricter, requiring stationarity of the NIIP in levels for sustainability. Finally, it bears emphasizing that the testable conditions derived in this chapter are only sufficient for sustainability. In other words, so far, it is only possible to verify sustainability, and not its violation.

The last row of table 4.2 points to tests which can be conducted to examine the validity of the sufficient conditions for sustainability in the data: tests for unit roots in the NIIP and the current account series, tests for cointegration between the components of the current account, and estimations of the (quasi) error-correction relationship between the current account components. These tests and the relevant studies will be discussed in the next chapter.

Table 4.2: Sufficient conditions for strong, weak, and "absurdly" weak sustainability

	Current account balance	**NIIP**	**Saving and investment**	**Exports and imports incl. of net interest payments**	**Trade balance and NIIP**
Strong sustainability	$I(0)$	$I(0)$ or $I(1)$	(i) both $I(0)$; (ii) both $I(1)$, jointly $CI(1,1)$ with vector $(1,-1)$	(i) both $I(0)$; (ii) both $I(1)$, jointly $CI(1,1)$ with vector $(1,-1)$	(i) both $I(0)$; (ii) both $I(1)$, jointly $CI(1,1)$ with vector $(1,r)$
Weak sustainability	$I(1)$	$I(2)$	(i) $S_t = -\mu/rI_t + e_t \sim I(0)$ with $\mu/r \in (0;1)$; (ii) both $I(1)$, jointly $CI(1,1)$ with other vector than $(1,-1)$ or not cointegrated at all; (iii) $S_t \sim I(0)$ and $I_t \sim I(1)$ or vice versa; (iv) both $I(2)$, jointly $CI(1,1)$ with vector $(1,-1)$	(i) $X_t = -\mu/rMM_t + e_t \sim I(1)$ with $\mu/r \in (0;1)$; (ii) both $I(1)$, jointly $CI(1,1)$ with a vector other than $(1,-1)$ or not cointegrated at all; (iii) $X_t \sim I(0)$ and $MM_t \sim I(1)$ or vice versa; (iv) both $I(2)$, jointly $CI(1,1)$ with vector $(1,-1)$	(i) $TB_t = -\mu B_{t-1} + e_t \sim I(1)$ with $\mu \in (0;r)$; (ii) both $I(1)$, jointly $CI(1,1)$ with other vector than $(1,r)$ or not cointegrated at all; (iii) $TB_t \sim I(0)$ and $B_{t-1} \sim I(1)$ or vice versa; (iv) both $I(2)$, jointly $CI(1,1)$ with vector $(1,r)$
"Absurdly" weak sustainability	$I(d), d \geq 2$	$I(d), d \geq 3$	(i) $S_t = -\mu/rI_t + e_t \sim I(1)$ with $\mu/r \in (0;1)$; (ii) $I(d)$ of different orders, at least one component with $d \geq 2$; (iii) $S_t = -\mu/rI_t + e_t \sim I(d)$ with $d \geq 2$ and $\mu/r \subset [0;(1+r)/r)$	(i) $X_t = -\mu/rMM_t + e_t \sim I(1)$ with $\rho \in (0;1)$; (ii) $I(d)$ of different orders, at least one component with $d \geq 2$; (iii) $X_t = -\mu/rMM_t + e_t \sim I(d)$ with $d \geq 2$ and $\mu/r \in [0;(1+r)/r)$	(i) $TB_t = -\mu B_{t-1} + e_t \sim I(1)$ with $\mu \in (0;r)$; (ii) $I(d)$ of different orders, at least one component with $d \geq 2$; (iii) $TB_t = -\mu B_{t-1} + e_t \sim I(d)$ with $d \geq 2$ and $\mu \in (0;1+r]$
	Unit root tests		**Tests for unit roots, cointegration, and (quasi) error-correction relationship**		

Abbreviations: B_{t-1}: net international investment position at the beginning of period t, I_t: investment in period t, MM_t: imports inclusive of net interest payments; r_t: real interest rate; S_t: savings in period t, TB_t: trade balance in period t; X_t: exports.

Appendix to Chapter 4

4.A Appendix to subsubsection 4.2.2.1

This section shows that the transversality condition given by

$$\lim_{N\to\infty} d^N E_t\left[b_{t+N}\right]$$

$$\lim_{N\to\infty}\left[\mathbf{e_1}'\sum_{v=0}^{N-1} d^N\left(\mathbf{I}+\Theta\right)^v\mathbf{m}+\mathbf{e_1}'d^N\left(\mathbf{I}+\Theta\right)^N\mathbf{x_t}\right.$$
$$\left.+\sum_{v=0}^{N-1}\mathbf{e_1}'d^N\left(\mathbf{I}+\Theta\right)^v E_t\left[u_{t+N-v}\right]\right]=0 \tag{4.60}$$

is satisfied if the roots of the matrix $d(\mathbf{I}+\Theta)$ are less than $1+r-\gamma$ in absolute value. In this case, each term on the right-hand side of the transversality condition goes to zero. However, each term being zero is only the sufficient condition for the transversality condition to be satisfied as the limit in equation (4.60) can also be zero if the terms which are different from zero add up to zero. For simplicity, this section specifies conditions under which each term in the transversality condition is zero.

It is more convenient to start with the second term on the right-hand side of equation (4.60). The matrix $\mathbf{A}\equiv\mathbf{d}\left(\mathbf{I}+\Theta\right)$ is a square (2×2) matrix given by

$$\mathbf{A}=\frac{1}{1+r-\gamma}\begin{pmatrix} r-\gamma-\alpha+1 & 1+\beta \\ -\alpha & 1+\beta \end{pmatrix}.$$

Provided that $\mathbf{A}$ has two linearly independent eigenvalues ($\lambda_1^{'}\neq\lambda_2^{'}$), the Spectral (or Eigen) Decomposition Theorem allows to rewrite $\mathbf{A}$ as an eigen decomposition $\mathbf{A}=\mathbf{Q}\Lambda\mathbf{Q^{-1}}$ where $\mathbf{Q}$ denotes the eigenvector matrix of $\mathbf{A}$ and Λ is the diagonal matrix with corresponding eigenvalues on the diagonal (see e.g. Tsay (2005, pp. 396-397) for details regarding the Spectral (or Eigen) Decomposition Theorem). From $\mathbf{A}=\mathbf{Q}\Lambda\mathbf{Q^{-1}}$, it follows that $\mathbf{A}^N=\mathbf{Q}\Lambda^N\mathbf{Q}^{-1}$. The matrix $\mathbf{A}^N=d^N\left(\mathbf{I}+\Theta\right)^N$ tends to zero as $N\to\infty$ if both eigenvalues are smaller than one in absolute value, that is: $|\lambda_i^{'}|<1$ for $i=1,2$. This implies that the matrix $\mathbf{A}^N d^{-N}=\left(\mathbf{I}+\Theta\right)^N$ goes to zero as time tends to infinity if $|\lambda_i|<d^{-1}$ where λ_i are the roots of the matrix $\mathbf{A}^N d^{-N}$ with $d\lambda_i^{'}=d^{-1}\lambda_i$ and $d^{-1}=1+r-\gamma$ for $i=1,2$. Therefore, the limit of the second term on

the right-hand side of equation (4.60) is zero if the roots of the matrix $(\mathbf{I}+\Theta)$ are absolutely smaller than $1+r-\gamma$.

The first term on the right-hand side of equation (4.60) can be rewritten as

$$\mathbf{e_1}'\sum_{v=0}^{N-1} d^N (\mathbf{I}+\Theta)^v \mathbf{m} = \mathbf{e_1}'\sum_{v=1}^{N} d^N (\mathbf{I}+\Theta)^{N-v} \mathbf{m} = d^N (\mathbf{I}+\Theta)^N \sum_{v=1}^{N} (\mathbf{I}+\Theta)^{-v} \mathbf{m}.$$

Using the formula for the sum of a geometric series[21] one obtains

$$d^N (\mathbf{I}+\Theta)^N (\mathbf{I}-(\mathbf{I}+\Theta)^{-\mathbf{N}})\Theta^{-\mathbf{1}}\mathbf{m}$$

or rearranging the terms

$$d^N (\mathbf{I}+\Theta)^N \Theta^{-1}\mathbf{m} - \mathbf{d}^{\mathbf{N}}\Theta^{-\mathbf{1}}\mathbf{m} \tag{4.62}$$

provided that Θ^{-1} exists. The first term in equation (4.62) tends to zero as $N \to \infty$ for $|\lambda_i| < (1+r-\gamma)$ and the second one for $1 < 1+r-\gamma$, i.e. for $r > \gamma$ (implying that $(1+r-\gamma) > 0$).

The third term on the right-hand side of (4.60) can be analogously rewritten as

$$\begin{aligned}&\sum_{v=0}^{N-1} \mathbf{e_1}' d^N (\mathbf{I}+\Theta)^v E_t\left[u_{t+N-v}\right] = \sum_{v=1}^{N} \mathbf{e_1}' d^N (\mathbf{I}+\Theta)^{N-v} E_t\left[u_{t+N-v}\right]\\ &= \mathbf{e_1}' d^N (\mathbf{I}+\Theta)^N \sum_{v=1}^{N} (\mathbf{I}+\Theta)^{-v} \begin{pmatrix}1\\1\end{pmatrix} E_t\left[e_{t+v}\right]\end{aligned} \tag{4.63}$$

To show that the expression (4.63) tends to zero over time, one needs to describe the process ruling the (possibly nonstationary) term. Wickens and Uctum (1993) assume that e_t is difference-stationary with mean zero and distinguish between three cases: (1) $e_t \sim I(0)$, (2) $e_t \sim I(1)$, and (3) e_t is at least $I(2)$.

In case (1), it is assumed that e_t is stationary with $e_t = \sum_{i=0}^{m} \psi_i \varepsilon_{t-v} = \Psi(L)\varepsilon_t$ where $\psi_0 = 1$, $\sum_{i=0}^{m} \psi_i^2$ is finite, the roots of the polynomial $\Psi(L)$ lie outside the unity circle, and ε_t is zero mean white-noise process. To illustrate that the limit of the term (4.63) goes to zero for stationary e_t, it is sufficient to focus on two special cases: (a) $\Psi(L) = 1+\psi L$ and (b) $\Psi(L) = (1+\psi L)^{-1}$ with $|\psi| < 1$.

In case (a), $\sum_{v=1}^{N} E_t\left[e_{t+v}\right] = E_t\left[\varepsilon_{t+1} + \psi\varepsilon_t + \varepsilon_{t+2} + \psi\varepsilon_{t+1} + \cdots + \varepsilon_{t+N} + \psi\varepsilon_{t+N-1}\right]$. Because ε_t has mean zero, the conditional expectation of all terms except for $\psi\varepsilon_t$ is zero. This means

[21] Calculating the difference between $\sum_{v=0}^{N-1} (\mathbf{I}+\Theta)^{-v} (\mathbf{I}+\Theta)$ and $\sum_{v=0}^{N-1} (\mathbf{I}+\Theta)^{-v}$ one obtains

$$\sum_{v=0}^{N-1} (\mathbf{I}+\Theta)^{-v} (\mathbf{I}+\Theta) - \sum_{v=0}^{N-1} (\mathbf{I}+\Theta)^{-v} = \mathbf{I} - (\mathbf{I}+\Theta)^{\mathbf{N}}.$$

Solving for $\sum_{v=0}^{N-1} (\mathbf{I}+\Theta)^{v}$ yields the formula for the sum of the geometric series generated by $(\mathbf{I}+\Theta)^{-1}$:

$$\sum_{v=0}^{N-1} (\mathbf{I}+\Theta)^{-v} = \left(\mathbf{I} - (\mathbf{I}+\Theta)^{-\mathbf{N}}\right)\left((\mathbf{I}+\Theta)-\mathbf{I}\right)^{-1} \tag{4.61}$$

provided that the matrix Θ is invertible. This is the case if the determinant of Θ, denoted by $\det\Theta$ is different from zero: $\det\Theta = (r-\gamma-\alpha)\beta + \alpha(1+\beta) \neq 0$ for $r-\gamma = -\alpha/\beta$.

that $E_t[e_{t+1}] = \psi\varepsilon_t$ and $E_t[e_{t+v}] = 0$ for $v > 1$. Consequently, $\sum_{v=1}^{N} E_t\left[e_{t+v}\right] = \psi\varepsilon_t$ and $\sum_{v=1}^{N}\left(\mathbf{I}+\Theta\right)^{-v} E_t\left[e_{t+v}\right] = \left(\mathbf{I}+\Theta\right)^{-1}\psi\varepsilon_t$ provided that $\left(\mathbf{I}+\Theta\right)^{-1}$ exists.[22]

Thus, the expression (4.63) becomes

$$\begin{aligned}
&\mathbf{e_1}' d^N \left(\mathbf{I}+\Theta\right)^N \sum_{v=1}^{N} \left(\mathbf{I}+\Theta\right)^{-v} \begin{pmatrix}1\\1\end{pmatrix} E_t\left[e_{t+v}\right] = \mathbf{e_1}' d^N \left(\mathbf{I}+\Theta\right)^N \begin{pmatrix}1\\1\end{pmatrix} \left(\mathbf{I}+\Theta\right)^{-1}\psi\varepsilon_t \\
&= \mathbf{e_1}' d^N \left(\mathbf{I}+\Theta\right)^{N-1} \begin{pmatrix}1\\1\end{pmatrix} \psi\varepsilon_t
\end{aligned}$$

This term tends to zero as $N \to \infty$ for $|\lambda_i| < (1+r-\gamma)$.

In case (b), $(1-\psi L)e_t = \varepsilon_t$ so that

$$\begin{aligned}
E_t\left[e_{t+1}\right] &= E_t\left[\varepsilon_{t+1} + \psi e_t\right] = \psi e_t \\
E_t\left[e_{t+2}\right] &= E_t\left[\varepsilon_{t+2} + \psi e_{t+1}\right] = \psi^2 e_t \\
&\dots \\
E_t\left[e_{t+N}\right] &= \psi^N e_t,
\end{aligned}$$

that is: $\sum_{v=1}^{N} E_t\left[e_{t+v}\right] = \sum_{v=1}^{N}\psi^v e_t$. Thus, the term (4.63) can be written as

$$\begin{aligned}
&\mathbf{e_1}' d^N \left(\mathbf{I}+\Theta\right)^N \sum_{v=1}^{N} \left(\mathbf{I}+\Theta\right)^{-v} \begin{pmatrix}1\\1\end{pmatrix} E_t\left[e_{t+v}\right] \\
&= \mathbf{e_1}' d^N \left(\mathbf{I}+\Theta\right)^N \sum_{v=1}^{N} \left(\mathbf{I}+\Theta\right)^{-v} \psi^v \begin{pmatrix}1\\1\end{pmatrix} e_t.
\end{aligned}$$

Provided that the matrix $\left(\psi^{-1}\left(\mathbf{I}+\Theta\right)-\mathbf{I}\right)$ is invertible,[23] one can exploit the formula for the sum of the geometric series generated by $\psi\left(\mathbf{I}+\Theta\right)^{-1}$. This yields

$$\begin{aligned}
&\mathbf{e_1}' d^N \left(\mathbf{I}+\Theta\right)^N \left(\mathbf{I} - \psi^{\mathbf{N}}\left(\mathbf{I}+\Theta\right)^{-\mathbf{N}}\right) \left(\psi^{-1}\left(\mathbf{I}+\Theta\right)-\mathbf{I}\right)^{-1} \begin{pmatrix}1\\1\end{pmatrix} e_t \\
&= \mathbf{e_1}' d^N \left(\mathbf{I}+\Theta\right)^N \left(\psi^{-1}\left(\mathbf{I}+\Theta\right)-\mathbf{I}\right)^{-1} \begin{pmatrix}1\\1\end{pmatrix} e_t \\
&-\mathbf{e_1}' d^N \psi^N \left(\psi^{-1}\left(\mathbf{I}+\Theta\right)-\mathbf{I}\right)^{-1} \begin{pmatrix}1\\1\end{pmatrix} e_t
\end{aligned} \tag{4.64}$$

The first term on the right-hand side of equation (4.64) vanishes over time if $|\lambda_i| < (1+r-\gamma)$, and the second term on the right-hand side of equation (4.64) goes to zero in the limit if $r > \gamma$ (as $|\psi| < 1$ by assumption).

In case (2), it is assumed that e_t is $I(1)$ with $\Delta e_t = \sum_{i=0}^{m}\psi_i\varepsilon_{t-v} = \Psi(L)\varepsilon_t = \xi_t$ where $\psi_0 = 1$, $\sum_{i=0}^{m}\psi_i^2$ is finite, the roots of the polynomial $\Psi(L)$ lie outside the unity circle, and ε_t is zero mean white noise process. Thus, $E_t[e_{t+v}] = e_t + \sum_{j=1}^{v} E_t[\xi_{t+j}]$ for $v > 0$.

[22] The matrix $(\mathbf{I}+\Theta)$ is invertible if $\det(\mathbf{I}+\Theta) = (r-\gamma-\alpha+1)(1+\beta)+\alpha(1+\beta) \neq 0$. This is the case if $r-\gamma \neq$ and $\beta \neq -1$.

[23] The inverse of $\left(\psi^{-1}\left(\mathbf{I}+\Theta\right)-\mathbf{I}\right)$ exists if $det\left(\psi^{-1}\left(\mathbf{I}+\Theta\right)-\mathbf{I}\right) = (r-\gamma-\alpha+1-\psi)(1+\beta-\psi)+\alpha(1+\beta) \neq 0$. This is the case if $r-\gamma = -((1+\beta)(1-\psi)+\psi(\psi+\alpha-1))(1+\beta-\psi)^{-1}$, $\psi \neq 0$ and $1+\beta \neq \psi$.

In the special case (a), $E_t[e_{t+v}] = e_t + E_t[\varepsilon_{t+1} + \psi\varepsilon_t + \varepsilon_{t+2} + \psi\varepsilon_{t+1} + \cdots + \varepsilon_{t+N} + \psi\varepsilon_{t+N-1}] = e_t + \psi\varepsilon_t$ for $v > 0$ because $E_t[\varepsilon_{t+v}] = 0$ for $v > 0$. Thus, equation (4.63) becomes

$$\begin{aligned}
&\mathbf{e_1}'d^N(\mathbf{I}+\Theta)^N \sum_{v=1}^{N} (\mathbf{I}+\Theta)^{-v} \begin{pmatrix}1\\1\end{pmatrix} E_t[e_{t+v}] \\
&= \mathbf{e_1}'d^N(\mathbf{I}+\Theta)^N \sum_{v=1}^{N} (\mathbf{I}+\Theta)^{-v} \begin{pmatrix}1\\1\end{pmatrix} (e_t + \psi\varepsilon_t) \\
&= \mathbf{e_1}'d^N(\mathbf{I}+\Theta)^N \left(\mathbf{I} - (\mathbf{I}+\Theta)^{-\mathbf{N}}\right) \Theta^{-1} \begin{pmatrix}1\\1\end{pmatrix} (e_t + \psi\varepsilon_t) \\
&= \mathbf{e_1}'d^N(\mathbf{I}+\Theta)^N \Theta^{-1} \begin{pmatrix}1\\1\end{pmatrix} (e_t + \psi\varepsilon_t) - \mathbf{e_1}'d^N\Theta^{-1} \begin{pmatrix}1\\1\end{pmatrix} (e_t + \psi\varepsilon_t)
\end{aligned} \tag{4.65}$$

where the formula for the sum of a geometric series was utilized. The first term on the right-hand side of equation (4.65) goes to zero over time if $|\lambda_i| < (1+r-\gamma)$, and the second term on the right-hand side of equation (4.65) vanishes if $r > \gamma$.

In case (b), one obtains $\xi_{t+v} = (1-\psi L)\varepsilon_{t+v}$ or, after rearranging the terms, $\xi_{t+v} = \varepsilon_{t+v} + \psi\xi_{t+v-1}$ for $v \geq 0$. Thus, $E_t[e_{t+v}] = e_t + \sum_{j=1}^{v} E_t[\varepsilon_{t+v} + \psi\xi_{t+v-1}] = e_t + \sum_{j=1}^{v} E_t\left[\psi^2\xi_{t+v-2}\right] = \cdots = e_t + \sum_{j=1}^{v} \psi^v\xi_t$ for $v > 0$. Thus,

$$\begin{aligned}
&\mathbf{e_1}'d^N(\mathbf{I}+\Theta)^N \sum_{v=1}^{N} (\mathbf{I}+\Theta)^{-v} \begin{pmatrix}1\\1\end{pmatrix} E_t[e_{t+v}] \\
&= \mathbf{e_1}'d^N(\mathbf{I}+\Theta)^N \sum_{v=1}^{N} (\mathbf{I}+\Theta)^{-v} \begin{pmatrix}1\\1\end{pmatrix} \left(e_t + \sum_{j=1}^{v} \psi^v\xi_t\right)
\end{aligned}$$

Applying the formula for $\sum_{j=1}^{v} \psi^v$ yields

$$\mathbf{e_1}'d^N(\mathbf{I}+\Theta)^N \sum_{v=1}^{N} (\mathbf{I}+\Theta)^{-v} \begin{pmatrix}1\\1\end{pmatrix} \left(e_t + \frac{1-\psi^v}{1-\psi}\psi\xi_t\right).$$

Rearranging the terms and using the formula for $\sum_{v=1}^{N} (\mathbf{I}+\Theta)^{-v}$ and $\sum_{v=1}^{N} (\mathbf{I}+\Theta)^{-v}\psi^v$ one obtains

$$\begin{aligned}
&\mathbf{e_1}'d^N(\mathbf{I}+\Theta)^N \left(\mathbf{I} - (\mathbf{I}+\Theta)^{-\mathbf{N}}\right) \Theta^{-1} \begin{pmatrix}1\\1\end{pmatrix} \left(e_t + \left(\frac{1}{1-\psi}\right)\psi\xi_t\right) \\
&-\mathbf{e_1}'d^N(\mathbf{I}+\Theta)^N \left(\mathbf{I} - \psi^{\mathbf{N}}(\mathbf{I}+\Theta)^{-\mathbf{N}}\right) \left(\psi^{-1}(\mathbf{I}+\Theta) - \mathbf{I}\right)^{-1} \begin{pmatrix}1\\1\end{pmatrix} \left(\frac{1}{1-\psi}\right)\psi\xi_t.
\end{aligned}$$

The previous expression tends to zero as $N \to \infty$ if $|\lambda_i| < (1+r-\gamma)$ and $r > \gamma$ (as $|\psi| < 1$ by assumption).

Finally, it can be assumed that e_t is integrated of at least second order. For example, $\Delta^2 e_t = (1+\psi L)\varepsilon_t$ or, rearranging the terms, $e_t = 2e_{t-1} - e_{t-2} + \varepsilon_t + \psi\varepsilon_{t-1}$. This implies that $E_t[e_{t+1}] = E_t[2e_t - e_{t-1} + \varepsilon_{t+1} + \psi\varepsilon_t] = e_t + \Delta e_t + \psi\varepsilon_t$, $E_t[e_{t+2}] = E_t[2e_{t+1} - e_t + \varepsilon_{t+2} + \psi\varepsilon_{t+1}] = E_t[2e_t + 2\Delta e_t + 2\psi\varepsilon_t - e_t + \varepsilon_{t+2} + \psi\varepsilon_{t+1}] = e_t + 2\Delta e_t + 2\psi\varepsilon_t, \ldots, E_t[e_{t+v}] = e_t + v\Delta e_t + v\psi\varepsilon_t$ for $v > 0$.

Thus, the expression (4.63) can be written as

$$\begin{aligned}
&\mathbf{e_1}'d^N(\mathbf{I}+\Theta)^N\sum_{v=1}^{N}(\mathbf{I}+\Theta)^{-v}\begin{pmatrix}1\\1\end{pmatrix}E_t\left[e_{t+v}\right]\\
&=\mathbf{e_1}'d^N(\mathbf{I}+\Theta)^N\sum_{v=1}^{N}(\mathbf{I}+\Theta)^{-v}\begin{pmatrix}1\\1\end{pmatrix}(e_t+v\Delta e_t+v\psi\varepsilon_t)\\
&=\mathbf{e_1}'d^N(\mathbf{I}+\Theta)^N\sum_{v=1}^{N}(\mathbf{I}+\Theta)^{-v}\begin{pmatrix}1\\1\end{pmatrix}e_t\\
&+d^N(\mathbf{I}+\Theta)^N\sum_{v=1}^{N}\mathbf{e_1}'(\mathbf{I}+\Theta)^{-v}\begin{pmatrix}1\\1\end{pmatrix}v(\Delta e_t+\psi\varepsilon_t)
\end{aligned}$$

Using the formula for the sum of a geometric series allows to write

$$\begin{aligned}
&\mathbf{e_1}'d^N(\mathbf{I}+\Theta)^N\left(\mathbf{I}-(\mathbf{I}+\Theta)^{-\mathbf{N}}\right)\Theta^{-1}\begin{pmatrix}1\\1\end{pmatrix}e_t\\
&+\mathbf{e_1}'d^N(\mathbf{I}+\Theta)^N\Theta^{-1}\left(\left(\mathbf{I}-(\mathbf{I}+\Theta)^{-\mathbf{N}}\right)\left(\mathbf{I}-(\mathbf{I}+\Theta)^{-\mathbf{1}}\right)^{-1}\right.\\
&\left.-N\left(\mathbf{I}+\Theta\right)^{-\mathbf{N}}\right)(\Delta e_t+\psi\varepsilon_t)
\end{aligned}$$

provided that the matrices Θ, $(\mathbf{I}+\Theta)$, and $\left(\mathbf{I}-(\mathbf{I}+\Theta)^{-\mathbf{1}}\right)$ are invertible.[24] The previous expression vanishes over time if $|\lambda_i|<(1+r-\gamma)$ and $r>\gamma$ (where $|\psi|<1$). This result can be generalized to cases where e_t is integrated of higher order than two (Wickens and Uctum, 1993, p. 431).

[24] The formula for the sum of $S_N \equiv \sum_{v=1}^{N}\mathbf{e_1}'(\mathbf{I}+\Theta)^{-v}v$ can be derived as follows: Subtracting S_N from $(\mathbf{I}+\Theta)S_N$ yields

$$(\mathbf{I}+\Theta)S_N-S_N=\mathbf{I}+(\mathbf{I}+\Theta)^{-\mathbf{1}}+(\mathbf{I}+\Theta)^{-\mathbf{2}}+\cdots+(\mathbf{I}+\Theta)^{-\mathbf{N}+\mathbf{1}}-\mathbf{N}(\mathbf{I}+\Theta)^{-\mathbf{N}}. \tag{4.66}$$

Adding $-N(\mathbf{I}+\Theta)^{-N}$ on both sides of equation (4.66) and multiplying the resulting series by $(\mathbf{I}+\Theta)^{-1}$ one obtains

$$\left(\Theta S_N+N(\mathbf{I}+\Theta)^{-N}\right)(\mathbf{I}+\Theta)^{-1}=(\mathbf{I}+\Theta)^{-1}+(\mathbf{I}+\Theta)^{-2}+\cdots+(\mathbf{I}+\Theta)^{-N}. \tag{4.67}$$

Subtracting equation (4.67) from $\left(\Theta S_N+N(\mathbf{I}+\Theta)^{-N}\right)$ results in

$$\left(\Theta S_N+N(\mathbf{I}+\Theta)^{-N}\right)\left(\mathbf{I}-(\mathbf{I}+\Theta)^{-1}\right)=\mathbf{I}-(\mathbf{I}+\Theta)^{-N}. \tag{4.68}$$

Rearranging the terms in equation (4.68) one obtains finally

$$S_N=\Theta^{-1}\left(\left(\mathbf{I}-(\mathbf{I}+\Theta)^{-N}\right)\left(\mathbf{I}-(\mathbf{I}+\Theta)^{-1}\right)^{-1}-N(\mathbf{I}+\Theta)^{-N}\right).$$

The matrix $\left(\mathbf{I}-(\mathbf{I}+\Theta)^{-1}\right)$ is invertible if $\det\left(\mathbf{I}-(\mathbf{I}+\Theta)^{-1}\right)=(r-\gamma)(r-\gamma+1)\beta(1+\beta)^{-1}+\alpha(r-\gamma)(r-\gamma+1)^{-1}(1+\beta)^{-1}+\alpha(r-\gamma+1)^{-2}\neq 0,\ \beta\neq -1,\ r-\gamma\neq -1.$

4.B Appendix to subsubsection 4.2.2.2

Slightly modifying the proof made by Bohn (1998), we show that the general transversality condition (3.50), that is,

$$\lim_{N\to\infty} E_t\left[\beta^{N+1}\frac{u'\left(Y_{t+N+1}\left(h_{t+N+1}\right)-TB_{t+N+1}\left(h_{t+N+1}\right)\right)}{u'\left(Y_t\left(h_t\right)-TB_t\left(h_t\right)\right)}B_{t+N}(h_{t+N+1})\right]=0 \tag{4.69}$$

implies the error-correction type specification (4.55)

$$TB_t = -\mu B_{t-1} + e_t \sim I(0), \qquad \mu \in (0;1+r]. \tag{4.70}$$

Inserting equation (4.70) into the balance-of-payments identity $\Delta B_t = TB_t + rB_{t-1}$ yields $B_t = (1+r-\mu)B_{t-1}+\varepsilon_t$ which can be approximated, for small μ and r, by

$$B_t = (1+r)(1-\mu)B_{t-1}+\varepsilon_t. \tag{4.71}$$

In contrast to Bohn (1998), the interest rate is assumed to be constant, in line with equation (4.70), but the proof can be easily generalized for time-varying interest rates. Iterating equation (4.71) by N periods and taking expectations leads to

$$B_{t-1} = \frac{E_t\left[B_{t+N}\right]}{\left((1+r)(1-\mu)\right)^{N+1}} - \sum_{v=t}^{t+N}\frac{1}{\left((1+r)(1-\mu)\right)^{v-t+1}}E_t\left[\varepsilon_v\right]. \tag{4.72}$$

Solving equation (4.72) for B_{t+N} one obtains

$$\begin{aligned} E_t\left[B_{t+N}\right] =& B_{t-1}\left((1+r)(1-\mu)\right)^{N+1} \\ &+\left((1+r)(1-\mu)\right)^{N+1}\sum_{v=t}^{t+N}\frac{1}{\left((1+r)(1-\mu)\right)^{v-t+1}}E_t\left[\varepsilon_v\right]. \end{aligned} \tag{4.73}$$

Inserting equation (4.73) into the transversality condition (4.69) yields

$$\begin{aligned} &\lim_{N\to\infty} E_t\Big[u_{t,N+1}B_{t-1}\left((1+r)(1-\mu)\right)^{N+1} \\ &+ u_{t,N+1}\left((1+r)(1-\mu)\right)^{N+1}\frac{1}{\left((1+r)(1-\mu)\right)^{v-t+1}}E_t\left[\varepsilon_v\right]\Big]=0 \end{aligned} \tag{4.74}$$

where $u_{t,N+1} \equiv \beta^{N+1}u'(Y_{t+N+1}(h_{t+N+1})-TB_{t+N+1}(h_{t+N+1}))/u'(Y_t(h_t)-TB_t(h_t))$. In equilibrium, $E_t[u_{t,1}(1+r)]=1$ and $E_t[u_{t,N+1}(1+r)^{N+1}]=1$ so that equation (4.74) reduces to

$$\lim_{N\to\infty}\left(B_{t-1}(1-\mu)^{N+1}+(1-\mu)^{N+1}\sum_{v=t}^{t+N}\frac{1}{\left((1+r)(1-\mu)\right)^{v-t}}E_t\left[\varepsilon_v\right]\right)=0 \tag{4.75}$$

Using the assumption made by Trehan and Walsh (1991) that ε_t is zero-mean white noise with $E_t[\varepsilon_v]=0$ for $v\geq t+1$, equation (4.75) can be further simplified to

$$\lim_{N\to\infty}\left(B_{t-1}(1-\mu)^{N+1}+(1-\mu)^{N}(1+r)^{-1}\varepsilon_t\right)=0 \tag{4.76}$$

Because $(1-\mu)^{N+1}$ converges to zero as $N\to\infty$ for $|1-\mu|<1$, i.e., for $0<\mu<2$, so does the whole limit term in (4.76), entailing that the transversality condition (4.69) is satisfied.

5

Empirical studies on the validity of the intertemporal budget constraint

This chapter gives an overview of the empirical studies on the intertemporal budget constraint (IBC). Based on the sufficient conditions for the validity of the IBC derived in the previous chapter, the relevant empirical literature can be mainly divided into three groups. The first group seeks to determine the order of integration in the net international investment position (NIIP) and the current account series because difference-stationarity of the NIIP and the current account (of any order) is sufficient to satisfy the IBC. When the NIIP is stationary in levels or first differences, the current account is stationary in levels and sustainable in the strong sense; when the NIIP is stationary in (at least) second differences, the current account is stationary in first differences and sustainable in the weak sense. The first group of the studies on the validity of the IBC is examined in section 5.1.

The second group investigates whether there is a cointegrating relationship between the components of the current account: between exports and imports inclusive of net interest payments, between savings and investment, or between the trade balance and the NIIP. Cointegration combined with the appropriate cointegrating vector ($(1,r)$ in the latter case or $(1,-1)$ in the two former cases) implies that the current account is stationary in levels and sustainable in the strong sense. Studies on cointegration between the current account components are discussed in section 5.2.

Finally, the third group tests whether the trade balance responds negatively to changes in the NIIP (section 5.3). The present chapter is concluded by section 5.4 which also leads on to the next chapter.

5.1 Testing for stationarity of the NIIP and the current account

5.1.1 Overview

The empirical studies which test for stationarity of the NIIP and/or current account series are summarized in table 5.10 in Appendix 5.A. Differences in sample periods and variable measurement, however, hamper the comparability of the empirical studies. Some studies use real values (because real values are more easily comparable over time), others rely on nominal values; some studies put the NIIP and the current account into a proportion of GDP (because scaling by GDP might help to remove heteroscedasticity in the time series), others do not. Three studies (Dülger and Özdemir, 2005, Holmes, 2006, and Clarida et al., 2006) use seasonally adjusted data to remove (at least partly) seasonal correlation. Further, the majority of the studies focuses on the current account series; only five studies (Trehan and Walsh, 1991, Wickens and Uctum, 1993, Sawada, 1994, Chortareas et al., 2004, and Durdu et al., 2010) investigate the properties of the NIIP series. In practice, however, the current account and the NIIP may differ by the capital account. Trehan and Walsh (1991, p. 221), for example, report different results depending on whether the same tests are applied to the NIIP or the current account during the same sample period.

Regarding the geographical focus, most studies cover the OECD countries. Holmes (2003) and Chu et al. (2007) examine African countries. Yan (1999) investigates whether the IBC was satisfied prior to the East Asian financial crisis in 1997/1998; Asian countries are also studied by Lau and Baharumshah (2005) and Lau et al. (2006). The focus of Sawada (1994) is in particular on heavily indebted countries (HICs). Chortareas et al. (2004) evaluate sustainability in Latin American countries. Only the studies by Durdu et al. (2010) and Cuestas (2013) cover transition economies. Due to space limitations, we are not able to discuss the test results for each country in detail. Therefore, we mainly focus on the United States, firstly because this country has been studied most extensively in the relevant empirical literature and secondly because it plays an important role in the recent global imbalances. However, we also address other countries which are involved in global imbalances.

The appropriate statistical tools for determining the integration order in the time series are unit root tests (which test the null hypothesis of a unit root in the series) and stationarity tests (which have stationarity as the null hypothesis). In the following, unit root and stationarity tests are briefly referred to as "unit root tests." Unit root tests might be classified according to whether they are based on a linear model (as opposed to being nonlinear) and according to whether they use time series data only (as opposed to using both time series and cross-sectional data, i.e., panel data). Studies which use linear univariate tests are presented in the next subsection; studies with panel-based tests (both linear and nonlinear) can be found in subsection 5.1.3, and studies applying nonlinear univariate unit root tests are discussed in subsection 5.1.4. The last subsection provides a short conclusion.

5.1.2 Linear univariate unit root tests

Dickey-Fuller test

As follows from table 5.10 in Appendix 5.A, the most widely used tests are unit root tests of the "first generation": the Dickey-Fuller test (Dickey and Fuller, 1979), the augmented Dickey-Fuller test (Said and Dickey, 1984), and the Phillips-Perron test (Phillips, 1987; Phillips and Perron, 1988).[1]

The Dickey-Fuller (DF) test examines an AR(1) model given by

$$y_t = \rho y_{t-1} + e_t \tag{5.1}$$

where y_t is the time series under investigation, ρ is a real number, and e_t is a white-noise sequence with mean zero and variance σ^2. For $|\rho| < 1$, y_t converges to a stationary time series

[1] A survey on testing procedures for unit roots is provided, e.g., by Dickey et al. (1986).

over time; for $\rho = 1$, y_t is a random walk with variance $t\sigma^2$, and for $|\rho| > 1$, y_t is nonstationary and explosive with the exponentially growing variance. Consequently, testing the null hypothesis of a unit root against the stationarity of a time series amounts to testing the null hypothesis that $\rho = 1$ against the one-sided alternative $|\rho| < 1$. In practice, however, it is more convenient to estimate the regression given by

$$\Delta y_t = \alpha y_{t-1} + e_t \tag{5.2}$$

where $\alpha = \rho - 1$. Equation (5.2) is obtained by subtracting y_{t-1} from each side of equation (5.1). Testing the null hypothesis that $\rho = 1$ against the alternative that $|\rho| < 1$ in equation (5.1) is equivalent to testing for $\alpha = 0$ against $-2 < \alpha < 0$ in equation (5.2). Following the common practice in the literature on unit root testing, in the following only the alternative hypothesis that $\rho < 1$ in equation (5.1), i.e., $\alpha < 0$ in equation (5.2) is considered. Rejecting the null of a random walk in equations (5.2) or (5.1) provides evidence for a zero-mean stationary process. In case that a time series is suspected to contain a drift or/and a time trend, the regression (5.2) can be adjusted to include a constant or both a constant and a linear deterministic time trend. Under the null hypothesis of a unit root, the DF test statistics do not follow the standard normal t-distribution, the critical values for the test statistics are tabulated in Fuller (1976).

For the United States, Trehan and Walsh (1991) report that the DF test rejects the null hypothesis of a unit root in the NIIP series, thus implying sustainability in the strong sense during 1946-1987. However, applied to the US current account series from the late 1940s to the late 1980s, the Dickey-Fuller tests (with or without a drift, no trend) fail to reject the null hypothesis of a unit root (Trehan and Walsh, 1991; Gundlach and Sinn, 1992; Wickens and Uctum, 1993). Moreover, Wickens and Uctum (1993) are not able to reject the null of a unit root even in the current account-to-GDP series in first differences. They interpret their finding as evidence for the current account-to-GDP being $I(2)$. This interpretation is in line with the common practice in the unit root testing: The failure to reject the null hypothesis at the conventional significance levels 1%, 5%, or 10% is typically regarded as evidence in favour of the null hypothesis. However, the root of the time series in question might be slightly less than one with an unknown probability of a type II error (i.e., the probability of accepting the wrong null hypothesis as true). For this reason, table 5.10 in Appendix 5.A always differentiates between the cases in which the null hypothesis is rejected (saying, e.g., that the NIIP is $I(1)$) and those in which the null cannot be rejected (saying, e.g., that the null hypothesis of unit root in the NIIP cannot be rejected).[2]

Augmented Dickey-Fuller test

The Dickey-Fuller tests are not applicable when the error term is autocorrelated because in this case the true size of the test (that is, the proportion of times the correct null hypothesis is wrongly rejected) is larger than the nominal size (Brooks, 2008, pp. 379-380). To eliminate autocorrelation in the error term, the DF tests can be "augmented" by introducing lagged values of the dependent variable Δy_t into the DF regresssion (5.2):[3]

[2] For space reasons, we do not report the significance levels at which the null hypothesis is rejected or not rejected. All studies rely on the "standard" significance levels 1%, 5%, and 10%.

[3] In greater detail, the AR(p) model is given by:

$$\Delta y_t = \alpha y_{t-1} + \sum_{l=1}^{p} \gamma_l \Delta y_{t-l} + e_t \tag{5.4}$$

where $\alpha = \left(\sum_{l=1}^{p} \rho_l\right) - 1$ and $\gamma_l = \sum_{j=l}^{p} \rho_j$. The augmented Dickey-Fuller (ADF) test constructed by Said and Dickey (1984) examines the null that $\alpha = 0$ against $\alpha < 0$ in equation (5.4). Analogously to the DF test, allowing for an intercept or including both an intercept and a linear time trend leads to two further ADF regressions. Test statistics and the critical values are the same as in the DF tests.

In practice, the performance of the ADF tests depends crucially on the correct number of lags. Using too few lags does not eliminate the autocorrelation of the error term and using too many lags reduces the power of the ADF test to reject the null hypothesis, as more lags increase the number of parameters to be estimated and therefore lead to a loss in degrees of freedom (Enders, 2004, p. 216). The correct number of lags can be chosen using rules of thumb (e.g., the one suggested by Schwert (1989)) or data-dependent rules which use sample information. Data-dependent rules are, for example, the general-to-specific (Gets) approach or information-based selection rules.[4] Ng and Perron (1995) find that data-dependent rules are superior to rules of thumb and that the use of Akaike's (1974) or Schwarz's (1978) Bayesian information criteria leads to larger size distortions than the Gets methodology.

Overall, the ADF tests provide mixed evidence for different countries. For the United States, Jansen (1996) reports that the current account-to-GDP series is zero mean stationary using the ADF test with one lag during 1952-1991. Analyzing the current account-to-GDP series during 1950-1988, Gundlach and Sinn (1992) find that the ADF test (without a drift) with one lag rejects the null of a unit root and the ADF test with two lags "accepts" it. From the 1970s on, several studies are not able to reject the null of a unit root using the ADF tests (Wickens and Uctum, 1993; Liu and Tanner, 1996; Wu, 2000; Raybaudi et al., 2004; Holmes, 2006; Kalyoncu, 2006), thus implying weak sustainability during this time period. Christopoulos and León-Ledesma (2010) are not even able to reject the null hypothesis of a unit root from the 1960s.

$$y_t = \rho_1 y_{t-1} + \rho_2 y_{t-2} + \cdots + \rho_{p-1} y_{t-p+1} + \rho_p y_{t-p} + e_t \tag{5.3}$$

(which is an extension of the AR(1) model (5.1)). Adding and subtracting $\rho_p y_{t-p+1}$ and rearranging terms allows to rewrite equation (5.3) as

$$y_t = \rho_1 y_{t-1} + \rho_2 y_{t-2} + \cdots + (\rho_{p-1} + \rho_p) y_{t-p+1} - \rho_p \Delta y_{t-p}.$$

Adding and subtracting $(\rho_{p-1} + \rho_p) y_{t-p+2}$, then $(\rho_{p-2} + \rho_{p-1} + \rho_p) y_{t-p+3}$ etc. and finally $(\rho_1 + \rho_2 + \cdots + \rho_{p-2} + \rho_{p-1} + \rho_p - 1) y_{t-1}$ yields equation (5.4).

[4] The Gets approach (Hall, 1994; Campbell and Perron, 1991; Ng and Perron, 1995) consists of starting with a relatively high lag order, testing the ADF regression(s) for the significance of the coefficients on the additional lags (using t-tests and/or F-tests), and reducing the lag number iteratively until the test statistic is significant or the number of zero lags is reached. Using the information criteria, the correct order of lags is the one which minimizes the value of the information criteria. The most common information criteria are Akaike's (1974) information criterion (AIC), Schwarz's (1978) Bayesian information criterion (SBIC), the Hannan-Quinn infomation criterion (HQIC,) or the modified standard criteria such as the modified Akaike's information criterion (MAIC) constructed by Ng and Perron (2001). A comparison of different information criteria is provided, e.g., by Tsay (1984), Lütkepohl (1985), Mills and Prasad (1992), Raffalovich et al. (2008), and Shittu and Asemota (2009).

The failure to find stationarity from the 1970s on might also result from the presence of structural changes. In fact, Liu and Tanner (1996) detect a (discrete) structural break in 1983 using a procedure similar to Christiano (1992). They then conduct the ADF test modified by Perron (1989) as to allow for a known one-time jump in the intercept (the "crash" model) and are able to prove the null hypothesis of a unit root false.

In response to the limitations of the Perron (1989) test which assumes a known break date, a variety of tests which endogenize the break point have been developed. One of them is the sequential unit root test suggested by Zivot and Andrews (2002). This test uses the full sample, sequentially increasing the date of the possible break and using different dummy variables (Maddala and Kim, 1999, p. 401). The break date is then the date which corresponds to the minimum t-statistics. If the t-statistic exceeds in absolute value the critical values tabulated in Zivot and Andrews (2002), the null hypothesis of a unit root can be rejected. Perron (1997) modifies the Perron (1989) test for an unknown structural break. An advantage of the Perron (1997) test over the ZA test is that it allows for structural breaks both under the null and the alternative hypothesis. The Lumsdaine-Papell (LP) test suggested by Ben-David et al. (1996) and Lumsdaine and Papell (1997) extends the Zivot-Andrews (ZA) test to allow for two breaks with unknown break points. Saikkonen and Lütkepohl (2002) and Lanne et al. (2002) propose a unit root test with a level shift at unknown time. The Lanne-Lütkepohl-Saikkonen (LLS) test is based on the idea that the deterministic term is estimated in the first step (via generalized least squares) and subtracted from the original time series in the second step so that the limiting distribution of the subsequent ADF-type test applied to the adjusted series does not depend on the estimator of the break date. Under the null hypothesis of a unit root, the test statistic does not have a standard normal limiting distribution; the critical values are tabulated in Lanne et al. (2002).

Phillips-Perron test

In order to shed light on the conflicting results yielded by DF and ADF tests, some studies use the non-parametric test developed by Phillips (1987) and Phillips and Perron (1988) which allows both for autocorrelation and heteroscedasticity in the error terms. The Phillips-Perron Z statistics are the Dickey-Fuller statistics adjusted non-parametrically such that they follow the asymptotic DF distribution under the null hypothesis of a unit root. Since the Phillips-Perron (PP) tests tend to have large size distortions in finite samples when the moving average errors are negatively correlated, one can use the modified PP tests based on the autoregressive spectral density estimator which has been constructed by Perron and Ng (1996) and Ng and Perron (2001) (simply denoted as NP tests hereafter).

The PP tests performed by Gundlach and Sinn (1992) for the period 1950-1988 and by Liu and Tanner (1996) for the quarterly data from 1970 to 1990 fail to reject the null of a unit root. The modified PP test conducted by Christopoulos and León-Ledesma (2010) also does not reject the null of a unit root for the United States during 1960.Q1-2004.Q1. However, allowing for a structural break, PP tests performed by Liu and Tanner (1996) indicate stationarity for the US current account during 1970-1990.

Data frequency and unit root tests of the first generation

The failure to reject the null hypothesis of a unit root might also be explained by the poor performance of unit root tests in short time periods (Shiller and Perron, 1985; Perron, 1989). An increase in the time span increases the power of the DF, ADF, and PP tests (Shiller and Perron, 1985; Perron, 1989; Ng, 1995). Indeed, Coakley and Kulasi (1997), Taylor (2002), and Durdu et al. (2010) who use long time spans of annual data are able to provide evidence for stationarity.

Because long-term annual data are not always available, the question is whether increasing the data frequency makes the tests more powerful. For point-sampled data (such as the data on the NIIP), Shiller and Perron (1985) and Perron (1989) show that the power of unit root tests is affected more by the time span than by the data frequency. Choi and Chung (1995) reexamine this finding by using a more general simulation format and show that the use of highly frequent data significantly improves the power of the ADF test, yet does not significantly change the power of the PP test. They also find that the PP test proves to be more powerful than the ADF test for low-frequency data.

For flow data (such as the data on the current account) which are often obtained by aggregation of subinterval data, the overall evidence also indicates that an increase in the sample frequency leads to a gain in the power of the ADF and PP tests (when the time span remains unchanged). Choi (1992) shows that the use of subinterval data leads to higher power of the ADF and PP tests than the use of annual data obtained by time aggregation and that the PP test is more powerful in finite samples with aggregated flow data than the ADF test. These results are supported by Ng (1995) who finds for flow data that (i) increasing the number of the data frequency improves the test power (but at a diminishing rate) when the time span remains the same and decreases the test power when the time span decreases, and (ii) increasing the time span for the same data frequency increases the test power.

However, the issue of data frequency does not strongly affect the test results for the United States. Among the studies which fail to reject the null hypothesis of a unit root using the ADF test, the increase in the sample frequency for small samples (covering not more than 50 years) does not change the test results. Kalyoncu (2006) is not able to reject the null hypothesis for the data set which contains 42 annual observations from the 1960s on, as well as Christopoulos and León-Ledesma (2010) who use the quarterly data set for the similar sample period (1960.Q1-2004.Q1). Other studies (Wickens and Uctum, 1993, Wu, 2000, Raybaudi et al., 2004, and Holmes (2006)) also use quarterly observations (though for approximately 20 years) and are not able to prove the null hypothesis of a unit root false. However, the use of seasonally adjusted data in the study by Holmes (2006) might explain why the ADF test rejects the null of a unit root only in two cases out of eleven: Seasonal adjustment reduces at the same time the power of the ADF and the PP tests by inducing the bias towards the "acceptance" of the null hypothesis of a unit root (Ghysels and Perron, 1993; Olekalns, 1994).

Apart from low-power problems in short time spans, unit root tests fail to reject the null of a unit root when the true data generating process is a near-unit root process, i.e., a stationary process with a root close to, but below unity (Cochrane, 1991). Further, the DF, ADF, and PP tests have low power in distinguishing between trend-stationary processes and random walks with drift (Nankervis et al., 1992).

Stationarity tests

One possibility to deal with the low-power problem of conventional unit root tests is to conduct confirmatory data analysis, that is, to use unit root tests in conjunction with stationarity tests (which have stationarity as their null hypothesis). The confirmatory analysis leads to consistent results if unit root tests fail to reject the null hypothesis of a unit root and stationarity tests reject the null of stationarity in favour of the alternative hypothesis, or vice versa. However, in case that unit root and stationarity tests either both reject or both fail to reject the particular null hypothesis, the results of the confirmatory analysis are inconclusive.

The two most widely used stationarity tests are the non-parametric test developed by Kwiatkowski et al. (1992) which is an analogue of the PP test and the test by Leybourne and McCabe (1994) which is an analogue of the ADF test. Because these two tests deal differently with autocorrelation under the null, they might lead to different results (Leybourne and McCabe, 1994, p. 157). The Kwiatkowski-Phillips-Schmidt-Shin test (KPSS) is, besides, more sensitive to the choice of the lag order (Leybourne and McCabe, 1994).

Amano and van Norden (1995) find that the joint use of the KPSS and PP tests or of the KPSS and ADF tests is superior to the use of either of these tests, in particular when the DGP is stationary and samples are small (less than 50 observations) with a large truncation lag. Schlitzer (1995) also advocates the joint use of the ADF and KPSS tests as it reduces the number of erroneous conclusions (in particular when the moving average parameter is negative), although at the same time the confirmatory analysis produces a large number of inconclusive answers.

Among the relevant studies on the IBC, only Raybaudi et al. (2004) perform confirmatory analysis. For the quarterly data on the current account between 1970s and early 2000s, the ADF test fails to reject the null hypothesis of a unit root for all five countries and the KPSS test rejects the null hypothesis of stationarity for three countries in the sample. In this case, the confirmatory analysis provides evidence for first-difference stationarity (and thus sustainability in the weak sense) for three countries in the sample (Japan, the United Kingdom, and the United States).

However, stationarity tests described above suffer from the similar lack of power and similar size distortions as the conventional unit root tests (Lee et al., 1997; Caner and Kilian, 2001; Müller, 2005). For this reason, Maddala and Kim (1999, pp. 46, 145) even argue that “such a confirmatory analysis is an illusion” and instead recommend the use of more powerful unit root tests.

Dickey-Fuller generalized least squares test

Only five studies reported in table 5.10 in Appendix 5.A (Dülger and Özdemir, 2005; Lau et al., 2006; Herwartz and Xu, 2008; Christopoulos and León-Ledesma, 2010; Cuestas, 2013) employ more powerful unit root tests of the second generation: the Dickey-Fuller generalized least squares test, tests for fractional integration, and tests for bounded unit roots.

In the Dickey-Fuller generalized least squares (DF-GLS) test developed by Elliott et al. (1996), the variable y_t is detrended in the DF regression (5.2) or in the ADF regression (5.4). If the DGP is trend-stationary, detrending is conducted by regressing y_t on a deterministic polynomial time trend and saving the residuals. Suppose that the DGP is given by

$$y_t = a_0 + a_1 t + B(L)\varepsilon_t$$

where $B(L)\varepsilon_t$ is a polynomial in the error term. Elliott et al. (1996) suggest to perform near-differencing by subtracting by_{t-1} from y_t where the constant b is close to unity and selected such that $B(L)\varepsilon_t - b\varepsilon_{t-1} \equiv e_t$ is stationary. Thus, one obtains

$$y_t - by_{t-1} = (1-b)a_0 + a_1\left((1-b)t + b\right) + e_t$$

where $t = 2, 3, \ldots, T$. The initial value of the series $y_t - by_{t-1}$ for $t = 1$ is assumed to equal y_1; this is the same as assuming that $b = 0$ and $\varepsilon_0 = 0$. Estimates of a_0 and a_1 can then be used to obtain the detrended time series y_t^d: $y_t^d = y_t - \hat{a}_0 - \hat{a}_1 t$. Elliott et al. (1996) recommend to choose the lag length for the ADF regression using the Schwarz's information criterion. If the DF-GLS regression contains a constant and no trend, one can use the DF critical values. If there is a trend, the critical values depend on the value of the chosen constant b and are tabulated in Elliott et al. (1996). The DF-GLS test has been criticized for being based on the quite restrictive assumption that the initial value of the series $(y_t - by_{t-1})$ is equal to y_1, implying that the first value of the error term is zero (Enders, 2004, pp. 241-242).

Lau et al. (2006) conduct both the ADF test and the DF-GLS test analyzing the current account-to-GDP series in five Asian countries. Both tests cannot reject the null of a unit root for their sample. Christopoulos and León-Ledesma (2010) are also not able to reject the null of a unit root in the US current account-to-GDP ratio during 1960.Q1-2004.Q1 via the DF-GLS test.

Tests for fractional integration

Conventional unit root tests also perform poorly when the DGP is a fractionally integrated process (Sowell, 1990; Hassler and Wolters, 1994). For fractionally integrated processes, the differencing parameter d does not need to be an integer and can take any real value.[5] When $d > 1$, a process is nonstationary and persistent, implying that a shock causes the process to deviate from its starting point. When $d \in [0.5; 1)$, a process is nonstationary, yet mean-reverting, that is, shocks have no permanent effects on the time series. When $d \in (0.0, 5)$, the process is stationary and displays long-memory behavior (or long-range positive dependence) in the sense that its autocorrelations are positive and decay hyperbolically. When $d = 0$, a process is stationary and exhibits short memory (or short-range dependence) with an exponentially decaying autocorrelation function. When $d \in (-0.5; 0)$, it has antipersistent/intermediate memory (or long-range negative dependence) in the sense that its autocorrelations are negative and decay at a hyperbolic rate to zero (Baillie, 1996, pp. 10-14; Chambers, 1996, p. 20; Maddala and Kim, 1999, pp. 297-298; Dülger and Özdemir, 2005, p. 54). Allowing for fractional integration requires a clarification of the definitions of strong and weak sustainability used previously. For the sake of consistency with integer integration orders, we interpret stationarity and/or mean-reverting behavior of the current account, that is, $d \in [0; 1)$ as strong sustainability, and a fractional integration order of at least unity as weak sustainability.

Dülger and Özdemir (2005) test for fractional order of integration in the current account-to-GDP series first using the modified rescaled range (MRR) statistic suggested by Lo (1991). The

[5] Fractionally integrated processes and autoregressive fractionally integrated moving average (ARFIMA or FARIMA) models were first studied by Granger and Joyeux (1980) and Hosking (1981). A survey can be found in Baillie (1996) and Lima and Xiao (2010).

rescaled R/S range statistic developed by Hurst (1951) and Mandelbrot (1972) is the range of the partial sums of deviations of a time series from its mean rescaled by its standard deviation (Mills, 1999, p. 117). Because the R/S statistic is sensitive to short-range dependence, Lo (1991) incorporates the short-run dependence into the denominator of the R/S statistic (Mills, 1999, p. 117). The selection of the optimal value of the truncation lag is important for Lo's MRR test.[6] Lo (1991) examines the null hypothesis of short memory against the alternative hypothesis of $d > 0$. Under the null hypothesis, the modified R/S statistic follows the distribution function contained in Kennedy (1976), with critical values tabulated in Lo (1991). One of the major limitations of the Lo's MRR test is that it tends to "accept" the null hypothesis of short memory (Teverovsky et al., 1999). However, for the data used by Dülger and Özdemir (2005), Lo's MRR test rejects the null hypothesis of short memory in favour of $d > 0$ for all G7 countries in the sample.

Further, Dülger and Özdemir (2005) perform the frequency-domain score test developed by Robinson (1994). Under the null hypothesis that the differencing parameter equals some value d_0, Robinson's score statistics converges to standard normal distribution. Dülger and Özdemir (2005) consider values of the differencing parameter between 0 and 1.30 in 0.05 percentage point steps (i.e., $d_0 = 0.00; 0.05; 0.10; \ldots; 1.25; 1.30$). The null hypothesis that $d = d_0$ is rejected in favour of the alternative hypothesis that $d > d_0$ when the significantly positive score test statistic is larger than the critical value for the significance level of 5 percent (i.e., 1.645) and in favour of the alternative hypothesis that $d < d_0$ if the significantly negative score test statistic is less than -1.645. Robinson's score test results show that the integration order of the current account in all countries in the sample is larger than 0.70, thus implying nonstationarity for the whole sample. The current account in the United States is found to be persistent (i.e., $d > 1$).

In addition, using the Whittle's approximate maximum likelihood (WML) estimator[7], Dülger and Özdemir (2005) estimate the autoregressive fractionally integrated moving average model (ARFIMA or FARIMA) for each country in the sample. The results for ARFIMA models indicate that the current account is nonstationary in all countries and mean-reverting in three countries (Canada, France, and Italy). Because the WML results partly contradict the results obtained through Robinson's score test regarding the mean-reversion property, Dülger and Özdemir (2005) analyze the impulse response coefficients calculated on the basis of the estimated ARFIMA. The impulse responses show zero long-run persistence for Canada, France, and Italy and non-zero long-run persistence for the remaining countries. This finding is fully consistent with the WML estimation results.

In sum, all tests performed by Dülger and Özdemir (2005) indicate fractional nonstationarity for the current account of each of the G7 countries during 1974.Q1-2001.Q3 and persistence for the current account series in the United States and Japan.[8] This in particular implies weak sustainability for the United States. Robinson's score test finds mean-reverting behavior for

[6] A data-dependent rule for choosing the truncation lag can be found, e.g., in Andrews (1991). Giraitis et al. (2003) recommend to conduct several tests and consider a range of values for the truncation lag taking into account the length of the time series.

[7] A discussion of the Whittle's approximate maximum likelihood estimator can be found in Whittle (1953), Fox and Taqqu (1986), and Lopes et al. (2004).

[8] Dülger and Özdemir (2005) use seasonally adjusted data. However, to our knowledge, there are no relevant empirical studies on how seasonal adjustment affects the power of tests for fractional integration. The same applies to panel tests performed by Holmes (2006), and tests for TAR models used by Clarida et al. (2006).

France and the United Kingdom (provided that the error term is an autoregressive process of order one). Both the Whittle's approximate maximum likelihood estimator and the impulse responses point to mean-reverting behavior in Canada, France, and Italy.

Cuestas (2013) applies the pooled regression test constructed by Robinson (1995) and are not able to reject the null hypothesis of $d = 0$ for any country in the sample consisting of ten Central and Eastern European countries during 1999.Q1-2011.Q3. The estimation of an ARFIMA model by the Whittle's approximate maximum likelihood estimator suggests persistent behavior of the current account-to-GDP series only in Romania, stationarity only in Estonia and Slovenia, and nonstationary, yet mean-reverting behavior for the remaining seven countries in the sample.

Tests for bounded integration

When the time series is limited by certain bounds, conventional unit root tests tend to overreject the null hypothesis of a unit root (Cavaliere, 2005). This could explain why some studies find evidence in favor of stationarity in the United States. In order to tackle this problem, Cavaliere (2005) introduces a two-stage procedure which first involves estimations of the nuisance parameters related to the position of the bounds and then uses these estimates to derive bound-robust (asymptotic) critical values which can be applied to the standard Phillips-Perron tests.

The current account and the NIIP series might be in particular limited by fixed bounds when they are constructed as a proportion of GDP. Using the bounded PP test suggested by Cavaliere (2005), Herwartz and Xu (2008) are able to reject the null hypothesis of (unbounded) nonstationarity (i.e., ∞ bounds) for 12 out of 26 OECD countries and the null hypothesis of bounded nonstationarity (bounds up to 10 percent) only for six countries (notably not for the Unites States). Thus, the rejection of the null hypothesis of a unit root for the other six countries might result from the boundedness of the current account series rather than from stationarity of the underlying DGP. For the United States, these results rather point to weak sustainability.

However, the bounded Phillips-Perron tests have the same finite sample size problems as the standard PP unit root tests. More robust tests have been developed by Cavaliere and Xu (2012), but not yet applied to the sustainability analysis.

5.1.3 Linear panel-based unit root tests

In order to address the problematic limitations of the unit root tests, several studies increase the sample size by exploiting both time series and cross-sectional information. The most popular panel tests is the Im-Pesaran-Shin test (Im et al., 2003); many studies also use the Levin-Lin-Chu test (Levin et al., 2002), the Harris-Tzavalis test (Harris and Tzavalis, 1999), the Breitung test (Breitung, 2000), and the common correlated effects mean-group estimator test (Pesaran, 2006).[9]

Levin et al. (2002) test the regression given by

$$\Delta y_{i,t} = \alpha y_{i,t-1} + \sum_{l=1}^{p_i} \gamma_i \Delta y_{i,t-l} + \delta_i d_t + e_{i,t} \tag{5.5}$$

[9] An overview of panel unit root tests is provided, e.g., by Banerjee (1999) and Maddala and Wu (1999).

where $i = 1,2,\ldots,N$ is the index variable of the panel members and each of them contains $t = 1,2,\ldots,T$ time series observations, d_t is the deterministic component (e.g., intercept and/or time trend), and $e_{i,t}$ is the identically independently distributed error process with mean zero and variance σ^2. The LLC test consists of three steps. The first step is to perform the ADF regression for each country where the lag order varies across countries and can be chosen, e.g., using the general-to-specific approach by Campbell and Perron (1991). Having selected the appropriate lag order, two auxiliary regressions are implemented in order to generate orthogonalized residuals. Step two is the estimation of the ratio of long-run to short-run deviations for each country. Step three is the pooling of all cross-sectional and time series observations in order to compute the panel test statistic which has a limiting normal distribution under the assumption that N and T go to infinity and that N/T goes to zero (implying that T grows at a faster space than N). The null hypothesis is that all panel members have a unit root $\alpha = 0$ against the homogeneous alternative of stationarity for all panel members ($\alpha < 0$).

Harris and Tzavalis (1999) modify the LLC test under the assumption that the number of time series observations is fixed and N goes to infinity. Thus, the Harris-Tzavalis (HT) test is appropriate for micro-panel data in which the number of cross-sectional observations is large compared to the number of time series observations for each panel member.[10] Under the null hypothesis, the test statistic converges over time to a standard normal distribution and the convergence rate is $\sqrt{N}$. Further, the HT test allows for fixed effects and individual deterministic effects. One of the drawbacks is, however, that the HT test is applicable only when errors are serially uncorrelated.

Breitung (2000) finds that the LLC and IPC tests lose power when individual specific trends are included and that they are therefore sensitive to the specification of the deterministic component. Breitung (2000) constructs a test statistics which does not require a bias correction and has a standard limiting normal distribution (assuming that N and T go to infinity). The Breitung test (UB test) uses, like the LLC and HT tests, the homogeneous alternative hypothesis.

Im et al. (2003) construct tests which allow the autoregressive parameter α to vary across panel members under the alternative hypothesis (simply substituting α_i for α in equation (5.5)). Under the null hypothesis of $\alpha_i = 0$, the IPS t-bar statistic converges to a standard normal distribution; under the heterogeneous alternative that $\alpha_i < 0$, the t-bar statistic converges to negative infinity. Like the LLC test, the IPS test is based on the assumption that N and T go to infinity, yet with the weaker additional requirement that $\sqrt{N}/T$ goes to zero. Instead of pooling the data, they use N separate ADF test statistics for N panel members and average them across panel members. Hence, the IPS test is based on the assumption that each panel member has the same number of time series observations and the same mean, thus requiring balanced panel data (Maddala and Kim, 1999, p. 137; Bergheim, 2008, p. 130).

Maddala and Wu (1999) propose the use of the Fisher (1932) test which combines evidence from N unit root tests and has the same null and alternative hypotheses as the IPS test. If the test statistics are continuous and the observed significance levels from i different tests ($\pi_{i,t}$) are independent and uniform $(0,1)$ variables, then the test statistics has a χ^2 distribution with

[10] However, this aspect is ignored by Lau and Baharumshah (2005) and Lau et al. (2006) as they apply the HT test although the number of countries ($N = 12$ and $N = 5$, respectively) in their data sets is small relative to the number of time series observations ($T = 32$ and $T = 120$, respectively).

$2N$ degrees of freedom. The advantage of the Maddala-Wu (MW) panel test is that it does not require the balanced panel data set (T can be different for different panel members) and can be implemented for any unit root test (thus allowing for different unit root tests for different panel members). The disadvantage is that the test statistics have to be derived by Monte Carlo methods (Maddala and Kim, 1999, p. 137).

Maddala and Wu (1999) find that the MW test is a better test than the LLC and IPS tests. In contrast, the large-scale simulations performed by Hlouskova and Wagner (2006) show that the LLC and UB tests have the smallest size distortions. However, Hlouskova and Wagner (2006) admit that the tests with the heterogeneous alternative hypothesis are disadvantaged in their study because under both the null and the alternative only homogeneous panels are considered.

Table 5.10 in apppendix 5.A shows that panel-based unit root tests are in many cases able to reject the null hypothesis of joint nonstationarity where the univariate unit root tests fail to reject the null hypothesis of a unit root. For example, Coakley and Kulasi (1997) find that the ADF test does not reject the null hypothesis of unit root for neither of the G7 countries, whereas the IPS test provides evidence for joint stationarity for the whole group of the G7 countries. Notably, all panel tests when applied to the same sample yield the same results.

The panel unit root tests discussed above assume cross-section independence. However, in the presence of cross-unit cointegration, the null hypothesis of a unit root in the panel is rejected too often (Banerjee et al., 2005). In practice, current account balances of some countries might be dependent on each other, e.g., due to contagion effects between countries (as was the case during the Asian financial crisis in the late 1990s).[11] For the panel of 27 advanced countries during the period from 1980 to 2008, Lanzafame (2012) applies the diagnostic test of cross-section dependence suggested by Pesaran (2004) and rejects the null hypothesis of cross-section independence. Conducting two panel unit root tests which are robust to cross-section dependence—the BD test developed by Breitung and Das (2005) and the cross-sectionally augmented IPS test suggested by Pesaran (2007)—Lanzafame (2012) is not able to reject the null hypothesis of panel unit root. This finding contradicts the results of the standard panel unit root tests: the MW, IPS, and LLC tests all provide evidence in favor of panel stationarity (see table 5.10 of Appendix 5.A).

In case that the current account series is bounded, Herwartz and Xu (2008) combine the p-values of the PP statistics to an aggregate measure using both the MW panel test and the modified inverse normal method (Hartung, 1999; Demetrescu et al., 2006) which allows for cross-sectional correlation in the errors. In both cases, they are not able to reject the null hypothesis of joint bounded nonstationarity for the sample of 26 OECD countries. Taking into account that the bounded univariate PP test indicates stationarity only for six countries in their sample, they interpret this finding as evidence against strong sustainability in the OECD countries.

Finally, panel-based unit root tests can only provide evidence for joint stationarity in the sample, which cannot be interpreted as evidence for stationarity of each country in the panel. The rejection of the null hypothesis of joint nonstationarity only means that a statistically significant proportion of panel members is stationary (Pesaran, 2011). Thus, it still remains unclear which

[11] A survey on cross-sectional dependence in panel data analysis can be found, e.g., in Sarafidis and Wansbeek (2012).

panel members are stationary and which are nonstationary. Yet the focus of a sustainability analysis often lies on a particular country and on whether this country should undertake some corrective measures to achieve sustainability. The evidence of joint stationarity might be interesting only for some particular research questions, for example, current account sustainability in the euro area or sustainability of global imbalances. However, the composition of countries in panel data sets is often motivated by other criteria, such as the membership in the OECD.

One solution to this problem is the test constructed by Breuer et al. (2002) which applies seemingly unrelated regressions to the ADF tests.[12] The seemingly unrelated regressions augmented Dickey-Fuller (SURADF) tests examine the null hypothesis of a unit root for each member of a panel—thus allowing to identify which series in the panel is stationary.

Holmes (2006) finds joint stationarity for the sample of eleven OECD countries using the LLC, IPS, and MW panel tests while the SURADF test rejects the null hypothesis of a unit root both for the current account-to-GDP ratio only in four countries. Similarly, Holmes (2003) applies the SURADF test to a sample of 26 African countries for which the LLC and IPS test reject the null of a unit root. The SURADF test, however, indicates stationarity of the current account-to-GDP series only for 21 countries in the sample. The results of the SURADF test conducted by Chu et al. (2007) for the sample of 48 African countries—which was found to be jointly stationary by the LLC, IPS, and MW panel tests—indicates stationarity for 37 countries in the sample. Notably, the SURADF test results by Holmes (2003) and Chu et al. (2007) contradict each other in five cases (Algeria, Congo, Morocco, Uganda and Zambia). One possible explanation is that the results of the SURADF test are sensitive to the selection of panel members (Ford et al., 2006). Thus, arbitrary selection rules of the panel members might for some countries lead to unreliable conclusions.

Another possibility to identify which panel members have a unit root and which are stationary is to apply the sequential panel selection method (SPSM) introduced by Chortareas and Kapetanios (2009). The SPSM starts with testing the null hypothesis of unit root for the whole panel (using, e.g., the IPS test). In case of the rejection of the null hypothesis, those time series which display the strongest evidence of stationarity (e.g., those with the minimum individual DF t-test statistic) are removed, and the second step involves testing the unit root for the reduced panel. This procedure is repeated until the null hypothesis of (panel) unit root cannot be rejected or all series have been removed from the panel. Applying the sequential panel selection method, Lanzafame (2012) finds that 13 out of 27 countries in the sample exhibit stationary behavior.

5.1.4 Nonlinear unit root tests

Conventional unit root tests are biased towards the "acceptance" of the null hypothesis of a unit root when the DGP is nonlinear (Enders and Granger, 1998; Shin and Lee, 2001; Kilian and Taylor, 2003). Changes in the agent's perceptions about risk, portfolio allocation decisions, future policy changes etc. can lead to a nonlinear behavior of the current account (Christopoulos and León-Ledesma, 2004, pp. 4-5). The presence of (non-)linearity in the data can be detected using diagnostic tests: Applying the Lagrange multiplier (LM) or score test developed by Luukkonen et al. (1988) and Teräsvirta (1994), Clarida et al. (2006) reject the null hypothesis of linearity

[12] A review of the literature on seemingly unrelated regressions is provided by Srivastava and Dwivedi (1979), Srivastava and Giles (1987), Fiebig (2003), and Moon and Perron (2008).

for four countries in the sample (France, Germany, Japan, and the United States) during the period 1979.Q1-2003.Q3. Christopoulos and León-Ledesma (2010) perform four tests for the presence of (non-)linearity: the regression specification error test (RESET) introduced by Ramsey (1969), the generalized RESET suggested by Arai (2004), Granger and Teräsvirta (1993) test, and Ludlow and Enders (2000) test. For the quarterly data of the US current account series between 1960.Q1-2004.Q1, all tests except Ramsey's RESET indicate nonlinearity (Granger and Teräsvirta (1993) test suggests an exponential smooth transition regression model). The failure to reject the null hypothesis of no nonlinearity by the RESET might be explained by its lack of robustness in the presence of unit root or near-unit root processes (Christopoulos and León-Ledesma, 2010, p. 449).

When there is evidence for nonlinear behavior in the data, the next step is to select the nonlinear model under the alternative hypothesis. In general, nonlinear econometric models can be divided into two categories: those that do not have a linear model as a special case (such as disequilibrium models by Fair and Jaffee (1972)) and those that nest a linear model as a special case (Teräsvirta, 2004, p. 222). The latter category includes regime switching models which allow the behavior of the stochastic process to depend on the state of the system (Enders, 2004, p. 393). To the family of the regime switching models belong models with thresholds which assume that the particular variable adjusts to its long-run equilibrium at different speeds, depending on whether the previous state of this variable is above or below a certain threshold. The regime switches are endogenous in these models since the adjustment process depends on the current state of the system. The adjustment to the equilibrium can take place radically as in the threshold autoregressive models (TAR) or smoothly as in the more general smooth transition regression models (STAR). In contrast, Markov switching models assume exogenous regime switches.[13]

Threshold autoregressive models

Chortareas et al. (2004), Fattouh (2005), and Clarida et al. (2006) estimate the threshold autoregressive (TAR) models first introduced by Tong (1978) and Tong and Lim (1980). The TAR process is given by

$$\Delta y_t = \alpha_1' \mathbf{x}_{t-1} \mathbf{I}_{\{y_{t-k} \leq \delta_1\}} + \alpha_2' \mathbf{x}_{t-1} \mathbf{I}_{\{y_{t-k} > \delta_2\}} \mathbf{x_{t-1}} + e_t$$

where y_t is the time series under investigation, $\mathbf{x}_{t-1} = (\mu, y_{t-1}, \Delta y_{t-1}, \ldots, \Delta y_{t-p})'$ with μ being the intercept, y_{t-k} is the threshold variable with the delay order $k \geq 1$, δ is the threshold value which takes values in the interval $[\delta_1, \delta_2]$, α_1 and α_2 are autoregressive coefficients with $-2 < \alpha_1, \alpha_2 < 0$, and e_t is i.i.d. with mean zero and variance σ^2. The indicator function $\mathbf{I}_{\{\mathbf{y_{t-k}} < \delta\}}$ takes the value one when $y_{t-k} < \delta$ and zero otherwise; the indicator function $\mathbf{I}_{\{\mathbf{y_{t-k}} \geq \delta\}}$ takes the value one when $y_{t-k} \geq \delta$ and zero otherwise. Under the null hypothesis that $\alpha_1 = \alpha_2 = 0$, y_t is a linear unit root process; under the alternative hypothesis, y_t follows a nonlinear stationary TAR process.

The null hypothesis of a linear unit root can be tested via the Wald statistic which is, however, not identified under the null hypothesis and whose asymptotic distribution depends on

[13] An overview of the regime switching models can be found in Tong (2011).

the data structure (Davies, 1987; Hansen, 1996; Caner and Hansen, 2001). Therefore, Fattouh (2005) implements two bootstrap procedures suggested by Caner and Hansen (2001) to approximate the asymptotic distribution of the Wald statistic, whereas Chortareas et al. (2004) use the exponential average of the Wald statistic whose asymptotic critical values are tabulated in Kapetanios and Shin (2002).

Further, a TAR model requires a correct choice of the delay parameter k and the lag order p. Fattouh (2005) selects k and p such that they minimize both the residual variance and the value of the Akaike information criterion and arrives at $p = 4$ and $k = 2$ (that is, it takes two periods for a regime switch to occur). Besides, Fattouh (2005) selects *a priori* one threshold model (i.e., $\delta_1 = \delta_2$) which implies two regimes. The null hypothesis of linearity is consecutively tested against all four hypotheses (i)-(iv). For the long-span data from 1869-2002 for the United States, Fattouh (2005) is able to reject the null hypothesis of a linear unit root in the current account-to-GDP series in favour of nonlinear stationarity of the TAR form. He also finds that the US account-to-GDP series is mean-reverting above the threshold of 0.12 percent (the upper regime) and follows a random walk below this threshold (the lower regime). His analysis shows that the current account is in the lower, nonstationary regime between 1977 and 2001, thus indicating weak sustainability in this period.

Clarida et al. (2006) choose $p = 1$ (because the second-lag terms are statistically insignificant) and k of two quarters. They demean the current account-to-net output ratio in order to allow for the existence of long-run deficit or surplus means for each country rather than a zero current account balance (in their sample only Italy's current account has mean zero). In order to determine the number of thresholds, Clarida et al. (2006) apply the sequential procedure suggested by Hansen (1999) and test sequentially for zero, one, and two thresholds. For the sample of G7 countries during 1979.Q1-2003.Q3, they obtain evidence for two asymmetric thresholds which can then be estimated jointly by minimizing the overall sum of squared errors via the double grid search recommended by Hansen (1997). Thus, the current account-to-GDP series is a nonlinear stationary TAR process with three regimes. In the upper and the lower regime, the current account-to-GDP series is mean-reverting. Because the null hypothesis that the current account follows a random walk in the middle regime cannot be rejected in favour of the mean-reverting behavior, Clarida et al. (2006) conclude—despite of possibly large type II error probabilities arising from the "acceptance" of the false null hypothesis—that the middle regime is characterized by the absence of adjustment ("inertia regime"). For the United States, Clarida et al. (2006) estimate the lower threshold of -2.15 percent which implies together with the mean of -2.011 percent that current account adjustment begins when the current account deficit exceeds -4.19 percent of net output. This finding is at odds with Fattouh (2005) who finds that the adjustment begins when the current account exceeds 0.12 percent of GDP. The deficit threshold of -4.19 percent, however, is mainly consistent with the empirical literature on current account reversals according to which reversals of current account deficits in the industrial countries typically begin at four to five percent of GDP (see section 7.3 of chapter 7 for details).

Smooth transition regression models

Christopoulos and León-Ledesma (2010) apply the exponential smooth transition regression model (ESTAR) of order one which is based on Kapetanios et al. (2003) and Kilic (2003). The sample comprises the quarterly data of the US current account relative to GDP over the period 1960.Q1-2004.Q1. The univariate ESTAR(1) model is given by

$$y_t = \rho y_{t-1} + \rho^* \Phi(\gamma, \theta, \Delta y_{t-k}) + e_t \tag{5.6}$$

where y_t is stationary ergodic (for the mean)[14] and e_t is identically and independent distributed with the mean zero and the variance σ^2. The exponential smooth transition function is defined by

$$\Phi(\psi, \theta, z_t) = 1 - \exp\left(-\chi\left(\Delta y_{t-k} - \theta\right)^2\right) \tag{5.7}$$

where ψ is the slope parameter which determines the speed of transition between the extreme regimes, θ is the threshold value which controls the location of the transition function, and Δy_{t-k} is the transition variable with the delay parameter $k \geq 1$. For $\Delta y_{t-k} = \theta$, the exponential function on the right-hand side of equation (5.7) is unity so that the transition function takes the value zero; this is the middle regime. For $(\Delta y_{t-k} - \theta) \to \pm\infty$, the exponential function converges to zero and the transition function converges to one; these are the outer regimes. Thus, the transition function (5.7) is bounded and symmetrically U-shaped around zero. In the middle regime, the model becomes a linear AR(1) model with $y_t = \rho y_{t-1} + e_t$. In the outer regimes, the behavior of y_t is given by a different AR(1) model: $y_t = (\rho + \rho^*) y_{t-1} + e_t$ (provided that $\rho^* \neq 0$). Rearranging the terms (similar to the procedure in footnote 3 on page 83), equation (5.6) can be rewritten as

$$\Delta y_t = \alpha y_{t-1} + \rho^* \Phi(\gamma, \theta, \Delta y_{t-k}) + \sum_{l=1}^{p} \gamma_l \Delta y_{t-l} + e_t \tag{5.8}$$

where $\alpha = \left(\sum_{l=1}^{p} \rho_l\right) - 1$ and $\gamma_l = \sum_{j=l}^{p} \rho_j$. When $\alpha = 0$ and $\rho^* < 0$, equation (5.8) describes a process which is locally nonstationary, but globally stationary. In other words, when Δy_{t-k} equals θ, y_t follows a random walk; when Δy_{t-k} takes large values, y_t is approximately an AR(1) process with the stable root ρ^* with $-2 < \rho^* < 0$. Christopoulos and León-Ledesma (2004) use the supremum-type t-statistic developed by Kilic (2003) to test the null hypothesis of a unit root (i.e., $\rho^* = 0$). Kilic (2003) shows that this t-statistic is superior to the ADF and PP tests under the alternative of the ESTAR model. Contrary to the linear unit root tests applied by Christopoulos and León-Ledesma (2010) (see table 5.10 in Appendix 5.A), the supremum-type t-statistic rejects the null hypothesis of a unit root, implying stationarity of the US current account. Further, the speed of mean reversion is faster when the current account changes above the estimated threshold value of 0.011 percent of GDP. Following Taylor and Peel (2000), Christopoulos and León-Ledesma (2010) also construct indicators of the degree of deviation from the mean and the degree of mean reversion. They find that the US current account is characterized by frequent fluctuations showing no persistent dynamics and identify three periods (1960-1974, 1975-1991, 1992-2003) of the current account history since 1960. The first period and the last one show both small mean deviation and rapid mean reversion whereas the second one exhibits both large deviation from the mean and slower mean reversion. This finding might also explain why the unit roots of the "first generation" fail to reject the null hypothesis of unit root between the 1970s and 1990s.

[14] A covariance-stationary process y_t is called *ergodic for the mean* if the sample mean $\bar{y} = \frac{1}{T}\sum_{t=1}^{T} y_t$ converges in probability to $E[y_t]$ as $T \to \infty$ (Hamilton, 1994, pp. 46-47).

The ESTAR model based on Kapetanios et al. (2003) and Kilic (2003) is a symmetric model which assumes that the speed of mean reversion is not affected by the sign of the shocks. An asymmetric ESTAR model which takes into account that the speed of mean reversion depends both on the size and the sign of the shocks has been suggested by Sollis (2009), however not yet applied to the external sustainability.

Lanzafame (2012) tests the nonlinear heterogeneous ESTAR model using the nonlinear cross-sectionally augmented panel IPS test constructed by Cerrato et al. (2011). Analogously to the univariate equation (5.6), Lanzafame (2012) examines the panel model given by

$$y_{i,t} = \rho_i y_{i,t-1} + \rho_i^* y_{i,t-1} \Phi\left(\theta_i, \Delta y_{i,t-k}\right) + e_{i,t} \quad t = 1,2,\cdots T \quad i = 1,2,\cdots N \tag{5.9}$$

where the error term $e_{i,t}$ has a one-factor structure. The null hypothesis of a unit root (i.e., $\theta_i = 0$ for all i) is tested against the possibly heterogeneous alternatives that some time series in the set follow a stationary ESTAR model (i.e., that $\theta_i > 0$ for $i = 1,2,\cdots,N_1$) and that some time series are unit root processes (i.e., that $\theta_i = 0$ for $i = N_1+1, N_1+2,\cdots,N$). Lanzafame (2012) finds that the nonlinear cross-sectionally augmented panel IPS test strongly rejects the null hypothesis of a unit root in favor of the alternative hypothesis for the panel set of 27 advanced countries.

Markov switching model

In contrast to the TAR and STAR models in which adjustment depends on the current state of the system, the regime switches in the Markov switching models developed by Hamilton (1989) are exogenous and driven by a Markov chain (Enders, 2004, p. 464). Raybaudi et al. (2004) use a Markov switching model to identify the periods in which the current account is a random walk ("unstable" regime) and the periods in which the current account is stationary ("stable" regime). The idea is that the periods associated with the unstable regime might serve as a "red signal": The longer the current account stays in the unstable regime (compared to the time spent in the stable regime), the more likely is that short-run imbalances might lead to future violations of the intertemporal budget constraint. Raybaudi et al. (2004) study the Markov switching model suggested by Hall et al. (1999):

$$\Delta y_t = \mu_0(1-s_t) + \mu_1 s_t + \alpha(1-s_t)y_{t-1} + e_t \tag{5.10}$$

where $-2 < \alpha < 0$, e_t is a white-noise process, and s_t denotes the state or regime in which the system is in period t. The state variable s_t takes values in $\{0,1\}$ and is a first-order Markov chain with transition probabilities $p_{ij} = \Pr(s_t = j|s_{t-1} = i)$, $i,, j \in \{0,1\}$, which are independent of e_t. Thus, when $s_t = 0$, y_t follows a stationary process given by $\Delta y_t = \mu_0 + \alpha y_{t-1} + e_t$, and when $s_t = 1$, y_t is a random walk with drift given by $\Delta y_t = \mu_1 + e_t$. Raybaudi et al. (2004) estimate the parameters of the Markov switching model in equation (5.10) via the maximum likelihood method under the assumption of a Gaussian probability density function of Δy_t. For the United States, Raybaudi et al. (2004) find that the expected time of remaining in the unstable regime is relatively high. As the unstable regimes are persistent in the US, the current account is likely to evolve as a random walk, thus implying weak sustainability. This result is not consistent with the results of the STAR model used by Christopoulos and León-Ledesma (2010) or the TAR model tested by Fattouh (2005). Raybaudi et al. (2004) find the unstable regime in the United States to be associated with two periods: 1983-1987 and 1993-2002. The first period might have been caused by persistent trade deficits due to the strong US dollar appreciation, and the second period might be attributed to the strong US economic growth relative to the growth in the US trading countries (Liu and Tanner, 1996, p. 743; Raybaudi et al., 2004, p. 223). The first period is in line with Liu and Tanner (1996) who find a structural break in the US current account in 1983.

One of the drawbacks of the nonlinear models used in the studies described above, except for Clarida et al. (2006), is that they fix the number of regimes *a priori*. Further, the question still remains whether the current account in the United States follows a TAR process as assumed by Fattouh (2005), an ESTAR process as found by Clarida et al. (2006), a Markov switching model as described by Raybaudi et al. (2004), or some other process.

5.2 Testing for cointegration between the components of the current account

5.2.1 Overview

This section examines studies on cointegration between the current account components: (i) savings and investment; (ii) exports and imports inclusive of imports. No study tests for cointegration between the trade balance and the NIIP. The relevant studies are summarized in tables 5.11 and 5.12 in Appendix 5.B.

A sufficient condition for the strong form of sustainability is a cointegrating relationship between savings and investment or between imports inclusive of net interest payments and exports, in each case with cointegrating vector $(1,-1)$. A finding of cointegration with the cointegrating vector $(1,-\beta)$, $0<\beta<1$ points to the weak form of sustainability. Thus, provided that the variables in question are $CI(1,1)$, the knowledge of cointegrating vector helps to distinguish between strong or weak sustainability. However, as already discussed in the previous chapter, the absence of cointegration does not necessarily imply the lack of sustainability: If the current account components are stationary in first differences and not cointegrated, the current account series is also stationary in first differences and sustainable in the weak sense. Note that, in a similar vein as table 5.10 in Appendix 5.A, we do not report evidence in favor of the null hypothesis in case that the null hypothesis cannot be rejected.

Most studies which examine the validity of the IBC via cointegration tests analyze the relationship between imports of goods and services inclusive of net interest payments and exports of goods and services (rather than savings and investment). Some studies add net current international transfers to net interest payments. Two studies (Sawada, 1994 and Önel and Utkulu, 2006) subtract reserve assets to obtain a current account measure which excludes the actions of the central bank. Only two studies (Corbin, 2004; Matsubayashi, 2005) assess sustainability by testing for cointegration between savings and investment. However, we in addition consider the results of the empirical literature on the Feldstein-Horioka puzzle and exploit their results for the assessment of external sustainability.

For the sample of 16 OECD countries between 1960 and 1974, Feldstein and Horioka (1980) estimate the cross-sectional regression

$$\frac{I}{Y}_j = \eta + \beta \frac{S}{Y}_j + u_j$$

where I/Y and S/Y are gross domestic investment and gross domestic saving as a share of GDP, respectively, j is the country index, and β is known as the savings-retention coefficient. Feldstein and Horioka (1980) argue that, in case of perfect international capital mobility, the savings-retention coefficient should be close to zero because domestic savings search highest returns in the world capital market while the world capital market serves domestic investment needs so that the domestic savings rate is independent of the domestic investment rate. Imperfect international capital mobility in contrast implies that the savings-retention coefficient is close to unity because domestic savings remain mainly in the home country. For the entire 15-year sample and for the five-year-subperiods, Feldstein and Horioka (1980) find that the estimates of β are close to unity. Yet because capital mobility within the OECD is commonly regarded as high and growing, Feldstein and Horioka's (1980) result is known as the "Feldstein-Horioka puzzle."[15] The Feldstein-Horioka result was confirmed by a series of studies which applied cross-sectional, time series, or panel-based tests.

In the time series and panel-based estimations, the regression of I/Y on S/Y might be spurious when both investment and savings rates are not stationary (as shown by Yule (1926) and Granger and Newbold (1974)) unless the two variables in question are cointegrated. Differencing of the variables prior to a regression would avoid spurious regression, but would at the same time neglect the long-run properties of the variables. In contrast, cointegration tests allow to evaluate the long-run relationship between variables in levels while saving the long-run information contained in the data. Therefore, the time series or panel studies on the Feldstein-Horioka puzzle examine cointegration between saving and investment (rates) and estimate the cointegrating coefficient β. This is exactly the information we require for the analysis of external sustainability: When saving and investment are $CI(1,1)$ and $\beta = 1$, external imbalances are strongly sustainable.

When evaluating studies on capital mobility, the measurement of saving and investment is important, as not every measure of saving and investment corresponds to the current account balance. The current account can be measured as the gap between gross saving and gross investment or between net saving and net investment.[16] Some studies use "basic saving" (Baxter and Crucini, 1993, p. 420) which is defined as the difference between GDP and private and public consumption. Thus, basic saving corresponds to gross saving if one neglects primary income and net current transfers. However, this measure is less appropriate for the sustainability analysis because net interest payments might be quite large in some countries and do play an important role in the IBC. Thus, the results obtained by studies which rely on basic saving should therefore be viewed with a "grain of salt." Further, some studies use gross capital fixed formation as a measure of investment (i.e., gross formation exclusive of inventory investment and valuables). Although gross capital fixed formation is a narrower and thus less appropriate measure for the sustainability analysis than gross investment, it has the advantage of being less prone to procyclical behavior, as pointed out by Bayoumi (1990).

[15] A survey of the empirical literature on the Feldstein-Horioka puzzle can be found in Tesar (1991), Frankel (1992, pp. 197-199), Coakley et al. (1998), and Apergis and Tsoumas (2009)).

[16] Gross saving is typically calculated by subtracting private and public consumption from gross national disposable income: $GS = GNDI - C - G$. Gross investment (also called gross capital formation) includes fixed capital, inventory investment, and valuables. Net saving and net investment are obtained by subtracting fixed capital from gross saving and gross investment, respectively (IMF, 2008, p. 330).

Saving and investment as well as exports and imports are analyzed both in levels and in rates, in nominal and in real values. For the same sample, Holmes (2006) obtains evidence for strong sustainability when the real current account-to-GDP ratio is analyzed and evidence for weak sustainability when the nominal current account-to-GDP ratio is examined. Five studies (Miller, 1988, Bodman, 1995, Moreno, 1997, Papapetrou, 2006, and Polat, 2011) use seasonally adjusted data. Bodman (1995) points out that seasonal adjustment might bias cointegration tests towards the non-rejection of the null hypothesis of no cointegration.

A large number of studies uses quarterly data, and two studies use even monthly data. Hakkio and Rush (1991a) and Lahiri and Mamingi (1995) find that time disaggregation (i.e., using monthly or quarterly data instead of annual data) yields no increase in power of cointegration tests. However, Zhou (2001) generalizes the approach taken by Hakkio and Rush (1991a) and finds that a higher sample frequency increases the power of cointegration tests and reduces size distortions for a fixed time span; Zhou's (2001) results are consistent with Hooker (1993), Hu (1996), and Haug (2002). However, one can achieve even higher power gains and smaller size distortions when the time span is increased for a given sample frequency (Hu, 1996; Zhou, 2001). Zhou (2001) shows that using data with high frequency is in particular important when the sample period comprises less than 30 to 50 years—which is, due to problems with data availability, most often the case (see tables 5.11 and 5.12 in Appendix 5.B).

The regional focuses of the studies in tables 5.11 and 5.12 in Appendix 5.B are quite diverse, although the majority concentrates on OECD countries. Arize (2002) analyzes a large sample of 50 countries which includes Asian, Middle Eastern, African, European, Latin American and Caribbean, and Pacific countries, as well as Canada and the United States. Asian countries are also covered by Bahmani-Oskooee and Rhee (1997), Anoruo (2001), Sinha (2002), Baharumshah et al. (2003), Lau and Baharumshah (2003), Narayan (2005), Ang (2007), Holmes et al. (2007), Singh (2008), and Tang and Lean (2011). Sinha and Sinha (1998) focus on Latin American countries; Özmen (2007) chooses 10 countries in the Middle East and Nord Africa (MENA) region. Further, Mamingi (1997) investigates 58 developing countries, Sawada (1994) picks out 13 highly indebted countries, and Narayan and Narayan (2005) study 13 of the least developed countries (LDCs). No study focuses on transition economies. As in the previous section, cointegration tests are compared using primarily the example of the best-studied country, the United States.

Following Maddala and Kim (1999), time series cointegration tests can be divided into those which have the null hypothesis of no cointegration and those which test the null hypothesis of cointegration.[17] Cointegration tests can be based on a single equation (subsections 5.2.2-5.2.5) or use multi-equation system methods (subsection 5.2.6). Cointegration tests can rely on time series data (subsections 5.2.2-5.2.6) or use panel data (subsection 5.2.7).

5.2.2 Two-step Engle-Granger methodology

The Engle-Granger (EG) methodology is a residual-based test which consists of two steps. Before performing the first step, the EG approach requires pretesting of the variables in order to determine their integration order. If the variables have different integration orders, one might

[17] An overview of tests for cointegration can be found, e.g., in Banerjee and Hendry (1992).

test for multicointegration as there might exist several cointegration relationships. This "deeper form of cointegration" was first introduced by Granger and Lee (1989).

If the variables are difference-stationary of the same order, the first step in the EG approach involves estimating (by ordinary least squares) the long-run equilibrium relationship of the simplest form:

$$y_{1t} = \beta y_{2t} + e_t \tag{5.11}$$

where e_t is the disturbance term. In the second step, one tests for stationarity of the residual sequence from equation (5.11) because stationarity of $\hat{e}_t$ implies that y_{1t} and y_{2t} are cointegrated. For this purpose, it is most common to use the ADF test. The critical values depend on the number of regressors in regression (5.11) and whether a drift and/or a time trend is included (Maddala and Kim, 1999, p. 199); they are tabulated in Engle and Yoo (1987) and Phillips and Ouliaris (1990). The rejection of the null hypothesis of a unit root, i.e., of $\alpha = 0$ in the ADF regression

$$\Delta \hat{e}_t = \alpha \hat{e}_{t-1} + \sum_{l=1}^{p} \gamma_l \hat{e}_{t-l} + \varepsilon_t \tag{5.12}$$

indicates stationarity of the residual sequence which—together with the finding of y_{1t} and y_{2t} being integrated of the same order—implies cointegration between y_{1t} and y_{2t}. If the null hypothesis of a unit root cannot be rejected, the null hypothesis of no cointegration cannot be rejected either.

If y_{1t} and y_{2t} are cointegrated, Stock (1987) shows that the OLS estimator of β is "superconsistent", i.e., $\hat{\beta}$ converges to its true value β at the rate T. However, Ng and Perron (1997) point out that the least-squares estimator can have poor sample properties when normalized in one direction and good sample properties when normalized in another direction.[18] As this "asymmetry" is more likely to occur when one of the variables has a root which is slightly larger or less than unity, Ng and Perron (1997) recommend to test the variables for fractional integration and to use the less integrated variable as a regressand.

Applying the Engle-Granger two-step methodology, Miller (1988) rejects the null hypothesis of no cointegration between savings and investment for the sample period over 1946.Q1-1987.Q3 in the United States. Miller (1988) normalizes both with respect to saving and to investment. In both cases, OLS estimates of β and $1/\beta$ are significantly different from unity, thus implying weak sustainability. Introducing intercepts in the appropriate regressions, Gulley (1992) cannot confirm Miller's (1988) results. For the period 1960-1993, the analysis by Hussein (1998) indicates weak sustainability using the EG approach together with the ADF test and the PP test. However, the majority of studies is not able to provide evidence for cointegration for different sample periods and different data frequency (Gulley (1992), Leachman (1991), Barkoulas et al. (1996), Jansen (1996), Coakley and Kulasi (1997), Kejriwal (2008), Husted (1992), Fountas and Wu (1999), and Wu et al. (2001)). One explanation of the failure to reject the null hypothesis are low power and size distortions which the EG methodology shares with the unit roots of the first generation. Husted (1992), for example, is not able to reject the null of no cointegration using the common ADF test for the EG approach, yet rejects the null of cointegration using the Perron test which allows for structural breaks. Therefore, Maddala and

[18] Equation (5.11) is normalized with respect to y_{1t}; normalizing with respect to y_{2t} would yield $y_{2t} = 1/\beta y_{2t} + v_t$.

Kim (1999) suggest to use more powerful unit root tests such as the DF-GLS test in conjunction with the EG procedure.

Kremers et al. (1992) argue that low power of the two-step EG procedure might be due to its neglect of the equation dynamics (i.e., imposing a common factor restriction) in a static regression (5.11). They suggest using the error-correction mechanism (ECM) tests which are more powerful than the residual-based tests if the common factor restriction is violated.

5.2.3 Error-correction model tests

According to the Granger representation theorem (Engle and Granger, 1987), there exists an error correction representation for every cointegrating relationship. The error correction representation for two cointegrated variables y_{1t} and y_{2t} can be of the form

$$\Delta y_{1t} = \alpha_1 (y_{1t-1} - \beta y_{2t-1}) + \gamma_1 \Delta y_{2t} + \varepsilon_{1t} \tag{5.13}$$

$$\Delta y_{2t} = \alpha_2 (y_{1t-1} - \beta y_{2t-1}) + \gamma_2 \Delta y_{1t} + \varepsilon_{2t} \tag{5.14}$$

where ε_{1t} and ε_{2t} are (possibly correlated) white-noise error terms and the restriction $\alpha_1 = \alpha_2 \neq 0$ ensures that y_{1t} and y_{2t} are cointegrated with cointegrating vector $(1, -\beta)$. If y_{1t} and y_{2t} are $I(1)$, both sides of equations (5.13) and (5.14) are stationary (so that there is no spurious regression problem). The error-correction term $(y_{1t-1} - \beta y_{2t-1})$ describes the past period's deviation from the long-run equilibrium and is therefore called "equilibrium error"; it can be estimated by the residual $\hat{e}_{t-1}$ from the regression (5.11) in the first step of the EG procedure. Thus, the ECM allows to estimate both the long-run dynamics (represented by the error-correction term with the long-run parameter β) and the short-run dynamics (captured by the short-run parameters α_1 and α_2 which measure the speed of adjustment to the long-run equilibrium) as well as γ_1 and γ_2. Because all variables in equations (5.13) and (5.14) are stationary, the test statistics used in the standard vector autoregressive (VAR) analysis can also be applied to the ECM. For example, the restriction that all short-run parameters are zero can be tested via an F-test (Enders, 2004, p. 375).

Provided that the residuals from equations (5.13) and (5.14) are serially uncorrelated and/or the cross-correlations are zero, the asymptotic distribution of $\hat{\beta}$ is normal, and the OLS estimate of β can be tested using t-tests and F-tests. However, if this is not the case, the asymptotic distribution of $\hat{\beta}$ depends on nuisance parameters due to possible endogeneity of the regressor(s) and serial correlation in errors (Maddala and Kim, 1999, p. 158; Enders, 2004, p. 376). In order to eliminate the nuisance parameters, one can use alternative estimation methods: the fully modified ordinary least squares (FMOLS) procedure (Phillips and Hansen, 1990) which corrects non-parametrically the OLS $\hat{\beta}$-estimator; the dynamic ordinary least squares (DOLS) introduced by Saikkonen (1991) and further developed by Stock and Watson (1993) which are obtained by adding leads and lags of $\Delta y_{2,t}$ into equation (5.11); the nonlinear least squares (NNLS) suggested by Phillips and Loretan (1991) which augment equation (5.11) not only by adding lags of $\Delta y_{2,t}$, but also by introducing the deviations from the long-run equilibrium $(y_{1,t} - \beta y_{2,t})$.

In order to circumvent the estimation of the long-run parameter β, equations (5.13) and (5.14) can be rearranged as follows:

$$\Delta y_{1t} = \alpha_1 (y_{1t-1} - y_{2t-1}) + \gamma_1 \Delta y_{2t} + \delta_1 y_{2t-1} + \varepsilon_{1t} \quad (5.15)$$

$$\Delta y_{2t} = \alpha_2 (y_{2t-1} - y_{2t-1}) + \gamma_2 \Delta y_{1t} + \delta_2 y_{2t-1} + \varepsilon_{2t} \quad (5.16)$$

where $\delta_1 = \alpha_1(1-\beta)$ and $\delta_2 = \alpha_2(1-\beta)$, thus implying that y_{1t} and y_{2t} are cointegrated with cointegrating vector $(1,-1)$. In the long-run equilibrium ($\Delta y_1 = \Delta y_{2t} = 0$), equations (5.15) and (5.16) reduce to

$$\alpha(y_1 - y_2) + \delta y_2 = 0 \quad (5.17)$$

where the absence of the time index indicates that the variables are in the long-run equilibrium. When $\alpha \neq 0$, y_1 and y_2 are cointegrated with cointegrating vector $\big(1,(\delta/\alpha - 1)\big)$ which is the same as the cointegrating vector $(1,-\beta)$. When in addition $\delta = 0$, the cointegrating vector becomes $(1,-1)$, thus implying that the current account is stationary with mean zero. When $\delta \neq 0$, savings and investment being each $I(1)$ implies that the current account is also $I(1)$.

Kremers et al. (1992) suggest to test the conditional (single-equation) ECM where the speed-of-adjustment parameter α_2 is assumed to be zero (meaning that y_{2t} is weakly exogenous) and the short-run parameters δ_1, γ_2, and δ_2 are also zero. They show that under the assumption that errors are Gaussian white noise, the t_{ECM}-statistic is approximately normally distributed under the null hypothesis of no cointegration (i.e., $H_0 : \alpha_1 = 0$) in large samples. If y_{1t-1} and y_{2t-1} are each $I(1)$, but not cointegrated, the ECM is not the correct specification to estimate because the error-correction term is $I(1)$ and the other variables are $I(0)$. Instead, one should estimate equation (5.11) in first differences:

$$\Delta y_{1t} = \Delta \beta y_{2t} + u_t. \quad (5.18)$$

For the United States, the conditional ECM test suggested by Kremers et al. (1992) leads to conflicting results. Both Jansen (1996) who analyzes annual data during 1952-1991 and Coakley and Kulasi (1997) who use the long sample during 1870-1989 find that the conditional ECM test—like the EG test—provides no evidence for cointegration. In contrast, the study by Taylor (1996) which also uses a long sample period (1850-1992) indicates evidence for cointegration in the US during the subperiod 1914-1971 where the long-run coefficient is estimated to be unity during 1946-1971, thus indicating strong sustainability.

5.2.4 Autoregressive distributed lag bounds test

Cointegrated relationships with at least one (but not all) weakly exogenous variables can also be tested in the autoregressive distributed lag (ARDL) framework. Pesaran and Shin (1995) and Pesaran et al. (2001) suggest the ARDL bounds testing procedure which has an advantage that it can be implemented disregarding whether the variables involved are stationary in levels, in first differences, or are mutually cointegrated (which is in particular useful when unit root tests provide ambiguous evidence on whether the variables are $I(0)$ or $I(1)$).

The test statistic in the ARDL bounds procedure is the Wald or F-statistic, used to test the significance of lagged values of the variables in the unrestricted conditional ECM:

$$\Delta y_{1t} = \theta_1 + \theta_2 y_{1t-1} + \theta_3 y_{2t-1} + \sum_{j=1}^{p-1} \theta_{4j} \Delta y_{1t-j} + \sum_{l=0}^{q-1} \theta_{5j} \Delta y_{2t-j} + \varepsilon_{1t} \quad (5.19)$$

where ε_{1t} is a white-noise disturbance. Under the null hypothesis that there is no relationship in levels between the variables involved, both test statistics have nonstandard asymptotic distributions. The joint F-test can be used to test the null hypothesis that $\theta_2 = \theta_3 = 0$ against the alternative that, e.g., $\theta_2 \neq \theta_3 \neq 0$, and the Wald test can be used to test the null hypothesis that $\theta_1 = 0$ against the alternative of $\theta_1 \neq 0$. For the two extreme cases (the variables are either purely $I(1)$ or purely $I(0)$), two sets of critical values are calculated and used to derive critical value bounds for all classifications of the regressors into purely $I(1)$, purely $I(0)$, or mutually cointegrated (the upper bound assumes that the regressors are purely $I(1)$, and the lower bound assumes that the regressors are purely $I(0)$). If the computed Wald or F-statistic exceeds the upper critical value bound, the null hypothesis of no relationship in levels can be rejected in favour of the alternative of a cointegrated relationship. If the computed Wald or F-statistic is below the lower critical value bound, the null hypothesis cannot be rejected. Finally, if the computed Wald or F-statistic falls inside the critical value bounds, inference is inconclusive and knowledge of the integration order of the underlying variables is required.

Provided that $\theta_1 \neq \theta_2 \neq 0$, there exists a stable long-run relationship between y_1 and y_2 (i.e., $\Delta y_1 = \Delta y_2 = 0$ and $\varepsilon = 0$) of the form

$$y_1 = a + \beta y_2 \tag{5.20}$$

where $a = -\theta_1/\theta_2$ and $\beta = -\theta_3/\theta_2$. If $\theta_3 = -\theta_2$, y_1 and y_2 are cointegrated with cointegrating vector $(1, -1)$. Thus, testing the restriction that $\theta_3 = -\theta_2$ amounts to testing sustainability in the strong sense. The long-run coefficient in equation (5.20) can be estimated via OLS only if there is no serial correlation in the residuals and no problems of endogenous regressors; otherwise, the test statistics should be appropriately modified. Corbin (2004) estimates β using the Δ-method suggested by Pesaran and Shin (1997), as it yields consistent estimates disregarding whether the variables are $I(1)$ or $I(0)$. For the United States, she finds weak sustainability during 1881-1913 and strong sustainability during 1918-1971. This result is consistent with the ECM test by Taylor (1996) which suggests strong sustainability for the period 1946-1971. The ARDL bounds test applied by De Vita and Abbott (2002) indicates weak sustainability for the period 1971.Q3-2001.Q2 and is in line with the results of the EG test by Hussein (1998).

5.2.5 Gregory-Hansen test with structural breaks

As in the case of unit root tests, the power of cointegration tests might be affected by the presence of structural breaks. Gregory and Hansen (1996) and Gregory et al. (1996) find that the power of the ADF test applied in the second step of the EG methodology tends to underreject the null hypothesis of no cointegration when the cointegrating relationship is subject to an unknown structural break. Gregory and Hansen (1996) suggest the ADF and PP-type tests for the null hypothesis of no cointegration against the alternative of cointegration with a possible regime shift (a break in the intercept and/or in the slope coefficient). For all possible break dates, Gregory and Hansen (1996) estimate three models (a model with a level shift; with a level shift and a time trend; with a regime shift) by OLS and calculate, from the residuals thus obtained, the ADF and PP-type test statistics. The smallest values of these statistics are then used to test the null hypothesis of no cointegration. The critical values are tabulated in Gregory and Hansen (1996).

For the United States, the Gregory-Hansen tests unanimously indicate no evidence for cointegration between exports and imports (Wu et al., 1996 and Fountas and Wu, 1999) or between saving and investment (Kejriwal, 2008). Because the GH test may suffer from loss of power when the DGP is subject to multiple structural breaks, Kejriwal (2008) extends the residual-based test for a single unknown break (constructed by Arai and Kurozumi, 2007), so as to allow for multiple structural breaks. In contrast to the GH test, the Arai-Kurozumi test has cointegration with a structural break as its null hypothesis and no cointegration as its alternative hypothesis. Kejriwal (2008) derives the limiting distribution and calculates critical values only for the model with a regime shift because his data do not indicate the presence of a trend. The Arai-Kurozumi-Kejriwal (AKK) test confirms the results of the GH test for the Unites States as it rejects the null hypothesis of cointegration with (in this case) three breaks—thus providing evidence for the absence of the long-run relationship between saving and investment.

The cointegration tests described above are single-equation methods which do not allow to determine the number of cointegrating relationships. This problem is solved, for example, by Johansen (1988) and Johansen and Juselius (1990) who take a multi-equation approach.

5.2.6 Johansen methodology

The Johansen methodology is basically a multivariate generalization of the DF regression (5.1) (Enders, 2004, p. 386):

$$\mathbf{y_t} = \mathbf{A}\mathbf{y_{t-1}} + \mathbf{e_t} \tag{5.21}$$

where $\mathbf{y_t} = (y_{1t}, y_{2t}, \ldots, y_{nt})'$, $\mathbf{e_t} = (e_{1t}, e_{2t}, \ldots, e_{nt})'$, and $\mathbf{A}$ is the $(n \cdot n)$ matrix of parameters. Subtracting $\mathbf{y_{t-1}}$ from each side of equation (5.25), one obtains

$$\Delta\mathbf{y_t} = \pi\mathbf{y_{t-1}} + \mathbf{e_t} \tag{5.22}$$

where $\pi = \mathbf{A} - \mathbf{I}$ is the $(n \cdot n)$ matrix of parameters. The rank of the matrix π equals the number of independent cointegrating vectors. If π is zero, all components of $\mathbf{y_t}$ are unit root processes; if π has full rank n, the vector process is stationary; if π is of rank one, there is one single cointegrating vector, and if rank of π is larger than one and less than n, there are multiple cointegrating vectors. The regression (5.25) can be generalized to include lags of $\mathbf{y_t}$ (analogously to the univariate ADF regression (5.4)), a drift and/or a time trend (see Johansen (1992) and Perron and Campbell (1993)).

Johansen (1988) suggests two likelihood ratio (LR) test statistics: the trace statistic and the maximum eigenvalue statistic. The trace statistic tests the null hypothesis that there are at most r distinct cointegrating vectors against a general alternative hypothesis. The trace statistics is given by

$$\lambda_{trace}(r) = -T \sum_{j=r+1}^{n} \ln(1 - \hat{\lambda}_j) \tag{5.23}$$

where the $\hat{\lambda}_j$ are the estimated values of the characteristic roots obtained from the estimated π matrix (in increasing order according to their distance from zero). When π is zero and all characteristic roots are zero, the trace statistic is zero, too. The further the estimated characteristic roots are from zero, the more negative is $\ln(1 - \hat{\lambda}_j)$ and the larger is the trace statistic.

The maximum eigenvalue (ME) statistic tests the null hypothesis that the number of distinct cointegrating vectors equals $r+1$ against the specific alternative hypothesis that there are r cointegrating vectors. The maximum eigenvalue statistic has the form

$$\lambda_{\max}(r,,r+1) = -T\ln(1-\hat{\lambda}_{r+1}). \tag{5.24}$$

In analogy to the trace statistic, the value of the maximum eigenvalue statistic is small if the estimated eigenvalues are close to zero. The critical values for $\lambda_{trace}(r)$ and $\lambda_{\max}(r,,r+1)$ are obtained via Monte Carlo simulations and are tabulated in Johansen (1988), Johansen and Juselius (1990), and Osterwald-Lenum (1992). To obtain estimates of the cointegrating vector, the standard t- or F-statistics are not appropriate because the coefficients are super-consistent, but the standard errors typically are not (which makes it impossible to judge whether the estimates are statistically significant or not). If the errors are correlated with each other, one can use, for example, the DOLS estimator (Enders, 2004, pp. 425-427).

Johansen and Juselius (1990) argue that the maximum eigenvalue statistic might perform better than the trace statistic. However, Cheung and Lai (1993) find that the trace statistic is more robust than the ME statistic when the innovations display skewness (i.e., are not symmetric about the mean value) and excess kurtosis (i.e., their distribution has fat tails). As shown by Cheung and Lai (1993), both the ME and the trace statistics tend to overreject the null hypothesis of no cointegration, in particular when the lag length increases—this makes a proper selection of the lag order an important issue. Cheung and Lai (1993) find that the AIC and the SIC perform well for AR processes, yet badly in the presence of moving average components.

Gregory (1994) investigates the finite-sample performance of several single- and multi-equation tests in the class of linear quadratic models and shows that the ADF and PP tests used in the second step of the EG procedure appear to be more reliable in terms of size and power than the Johansen ME and trace tests. Elliott (1998) shows that both the EG procedure and Johansen ME and trace tests have low power when the variables are nearly unit root processes.

As tables 5.11 and 5.12 in Appendix 5.B show, Johansen trace and maximum eigenvalue tests typically yield the same results. For the United States, the exception is the study by Bodman (1995) which finds evidence for cointegration via the trace test, but not via the ME test. Johansen ME and trace tests do not indicate cointegration for the majority of studies on the United States (Bodman, 1995, Barkoulas et al., 1996, Jansen, 1996, Wu et al., 1996, Coakley and Kulasi, 1997, Tsoukis and Alyousha, 2001, and Wu et al., 2001). However, some results are inconclusive. Levy (2004) reports strong sustainability for quarterly data on savings and investment, but not for annual data for the same sample period. In contrast to the results obtained by Levy (2004), Wu et al. (1996) and Wu et al. (2001) obtain no evidence for cointegration analyzing exports and imports although they also use quarterly data during the similar period and apply similar Johansen test specifications. Hoffmann (1999) finds strong sustainability during the long period 1874-1992 conducting ME and trace tests (both with two lags, no trend) on national saving and national investment in levels. In contrast, for gross domestic saving/GDP and gross domestic investment/GDP during the period 1870-1989, Coakley and Kulasi (1997) find no evidence for cointegration using ME and trace tests (both with two lags, no trend) either.

As Johansen and Juselius (1990) point out, the limiting distribution of Johansen LR tests depends on whether there is a deterministic trend or not. One possibility to tackle this problem is a multiple-equation two-step testing procedure suggested by Saikkonen and Lütkepohl (2000a,b) (hereafter denoted by SL) which excludes the linear trend from the cointegration relationship. The first step involves estimating the mean term by generalized least squares. Substituting the estimated mean in

$$\Delta \mathbf{y_t} = \pi (\mathbf{y_{t-1}} - \mu) + \sum_{j=1}^{p} \Gamma_j \Delta \mathbf{y_{t-j}} + \mathbf{e_t} \tag{5.25}$$

for μ, one can in the second step apply the LR-type test based on a reduced rank regression. Saikkonen and Lütkepohl (2000a,b) show that the LR test based on a prior trend adjustment has asymptotically more power in small samples than the standard LR test used in the Johansen procedure. The SL cointegration test is applied by Holmes et al. (2007). Because both the Johansen trace test and the SL test necessitate estimating various structural and nuisance parameters, Holmes et al. (2007) also perform the nonparametric Breitung test (Breitung, 2002; Breitung and Taylor, 2003) which does not require estimations of the lag structure or deterministic terms. The Breitung test is robust against misspecification and structural breaks in the short-run components and can be applied to test nonlinear or fractionally integrated models. For the data set used by Holmes et al. (2007), the SL and Breitung tests yield the same results as the Johansen trace test.

5.2.7 Panel cointegration tests

Panel-based cointegration tests help to increase the sample size by using both time series and cross-sectional information. Among the studies which assess sustainability by testing for cointegration between exports and imports, only two studies (Wu et al., 2001 and Holmes, 2006) resort to panel tests. One explanation is that the sustainability analysis is typically interested in the sustainability of an individual country, rather than a group of countries. In contrast, panel tests are useful in the analysis of the Feldstein-Horioka puzzle since they might shed light on the degree of capital mobility among, say, industrialized countries and developing countries. However, the composition of panels in the studies on capital mobility is not very insightful for examining sustainability: The sustainability analysis would focus on, e.g., countries which are involved in global imbalances rather than all industrialized countries. For this reason and due to space limitations, we do not exploit panel studies on capital mobility for the sustainability assessment.

Analyzing quarterly data for eleven OECD countries during 1980.Q1-2002.Q4, Holmes (2006) applies the panel fully modified OLS test suggested by Pedroni (1999, 2000, 2001) for cointegration in heterogeneous panels. The test statistics can be computed by estimating the regression given by

$$\mathbf{y_{1,it}} = \mathbf{a_i} + \beta_i \mathbf{y_{2,it}} + \mathbf{e_{it}} \tag{5.26}$$

where the error process is assumed to be stationary and uncorrelated across countries and the residuals are used to estimate the cointegrating slope coefficient β_i. The null hypothesis to be tested is that $\beta_i = \beta_{i0}$ for all i. The within-dimension statistic tests the alternative hypothesis that the long-run parameter β_i is identical in all countries ($H_A : \beta_i = \beta_A \neq \beta_{i0}$) where β_A is the same for all i. In contrast, the between-dimension statistic allows β_i to vary across countries under the alternative hypothesis ($H_A : \beta_i \neq \beta_{i0}$). Both statistics are standard normally distributed as T and N tend to infinity. For his data set, Holmes (2006) obtains evidence in favour of strong (joint) sustainability of the real current account/GDP ratio and weak (joint) sustainability of the nominal current account/GDP ratio.

Wu et al. (2001) use the panel cointegration test proposed by Kao (1999) and Kao and Chiang (1999) for homogeneous panels. Assuming either endogenous or strictly exogenous regressors in homogeneous panels, Kao (1999) derives DF- and ADF-type statistics for cointegration which are standard normally distributed. Kao and Chiang (1999) derive the within-dimension OLS, DOLS, and FMOLS estimators and show that they have asymptotically normal limiting distributions in cointegrated panel regressions. For G7 countries (excluding the United Kingdom) during 1973.Q2-1998.Q4, Kao-Chiang (KC) test indicates joint cointegration between exports and imports, inclusive of net interest payments and unilateral transfers. The within-dimension DOLS and FMOLS estimators suggest that the cointegrating coefficient is unity (thus pointing to strong sustainability) whereas the within-dimension OLS estimator yields that the long-run parameter is different from unity (thus implying weak sustainability). Yet because Kao and Chiang (1999) show that the within-dimension DOLS estimator outperforms both the within-dimension FMOLS and the OLS estimators, strong sustainability is more likely in this case. However, as with unit root panel tests, a drawback of most studies which apply cointegration panel tests is that they typically do not indicate how many and which countries in the panel are cointegrated.

5.3 Testing for the responsiveness of the trade account to the NIIP

This section presents four studies which depart from the above literature by putting to the fore the existence of the negative feedback from the NIIP to the trade account (see table 5.13 in Appendix 5.C). According to this criterion, an economy is on a sustainable path if it responds to rising net foreign debts (assets) by improving (decreasing) the trade balance. The studies by Wickens and Uctum (1993) and Bodman (1997) investigate sustainability in the United States and Australia, respectively, using the approach suggested by Wickens and Uctum (1993). The study by Durdu et al. (2010) applies the testing approach suggested by Bohn (2007) to a large panel data set which covers 21 industrial countries and 29 emerging markets. The more recent study by Camarero et al. (2013) uses the multicointegration approach for a group of 23 OECD countries over the period from 1970 to 2012.

5.3.1 Wickens and Uctum's (1993) approach

Wickens and Uctum (1993) examine sustainability in the United States during the period 1970.Q1-1988.Q4. Using the ADF and PP tests, they find in the first step that both the trade account-to-GDP series and the current account-to-GDP series are $I(1)$ and the NIIP-to-GDP series is $I(2)$.[19] If the trade account is strongly exogenous, the sufficient condition for sustainability derived by Wickens and Uctum (1993) requires both the trade account-to-GDP series and the NIIP-to-GDP series to be either $I(0)$ or $I(1)$—which is not satisfied for this data set. Hence, the next step is to check whether the sufficient sustainability condition in case of the

[19] Strictly speaking, the finding of $tb \sim I(1)$ and $\Delta b_t \sim I(1)$ contradicts the balance-of-payments identity $tb_t = \Delta b_t - (r-\gamma)b_{t-1}$ because the left-hand side is $I(1)$ and the right-hand side is $I(2)$. However, Wickens and Uctum (1993, p. 438) argue that $(r-\gamma)b_{t-1}$ can be neglected for small $r-\gamma$ so that $tb_t \approx \Delta b_t$.

weakly exogenous trade account is satisfied, that is, whether the roots λ_i of the matrix $\mathbf{I}+\Theta$ are less than $1+r-\gamma$ in absolute value and $r-\gamma>0$.

This root condition can be examined directly or indirectly by testing whether there is negative feedback from the NIIP to the trade account (i.e., whether $\alpha > 0$) because the root condition is likely to be satisfied for $\alpha > 0$. Both possibilities involve estimating equation (4.34) on page 64, that is:

$$\Delta tb_t = \eta - \alpha b_{t-1} + \beta tb_{t-1} + e_t.$$

When $b_{t-1} \sim I(2)$ and $tb_{t-1} \sim I(1)$, the error term must also be $I(2)$; otherwise equation (4.34) is not well specified. In order to avoid estimation of an equation with an $I(2)$ error term, Wickens and Uctum (1993) estimate the second difference of equation (4.34) via maximum likelihood and obtain statistically significant $\alpha = 0.264$ and $\beta = -0.825$. The finding of $\alpha > 0$ consequently implies sustainability. In order to test the root condition directly, Wickens and Uctum (1993) approximate $r-\gamma$ by the difference between the real ex post rates of return on eurodollar assets and the real GDP growth rate.[20] Assuming for simplicity the variable $r-\gamma$ to be constant over time, the average value of $r-\gamma$ for the whole sample period is 0.64 percent. Using the formula (4.41) in footnote 17 on page 65, the roots of the matrix are calculated as $\lambda_1 = 0.64$ and $\lambda_2 = 0.27$. As $0.0064 > 0$ and both roots are in absolute value less than 1.0064, the root condition is satisfied. Because the current account-to-GDP series is $I(1)$, one obtains sustainability in a weak sense for the United States during 1970.Q1-1988.Q4.

However, as already mentioned above, the approach suggested by Wickens and Uctum (1993) is unnecessarily complicated because it requires both testing for the presence of unit roots in all variables involved and for the roots of the dynamic economic system and/or for the existence of the negative feedback from the NIIP to the trade account. Yet the finding of (difference-)stationarity of the current account alone is sufficient for sustainability. Likewise, as shown by Bohn (2007), the existence of the negative feedback from the NIIP to the trade account alone is also sufficient for sustainability.

5.3.2 Multicointegration approach

Camarero et al. (2013) test for the presence of multicointegration between exports in proportion to GDP (x_t) and imports in proportion to GDP (m_t) for a group of 23 OECD countries during the period 1970-2012. Following Engsted et al. (1997), two $I(1)$ variables x_t and m_t are multicointegrated if (i) they are $CI(1,1)$ such that

$$m_t - \beta x_t = e_t \sim I(0) \tag{5.27}$$

and (ii) the cumulated cointegration error $\sum_{j=1}^{t} e_j$, which is, by definition, $I(1)$, cointegrates with x_t (or alternatively with m_t) such that

$$\sum_{j=1}^{t} e_j - \delta x_t = u_t \sim I(0). \tag{5.28}$$

[20] As Wickens and Uctum (1993, p. 437) point out, the choice of the eurodollar rate appears somewhat arbitrary, yet might be viewed as an acceptable approximation if uncovered interest parity holds to a first approximation and the yield curve is not steeply sloped.

Exploiting equation (5.30) to substitute for $\sum_{j=1}^{t} e_j$, equation (5.28) can be rewritten as

$$\sum_{j=1}^{t} m_j - \beta \sum_{j=1}^{t} x_j - \delta x_t = u_t \sim I(0). \tag{5.29}$$

Because the cumulated stocks of imports and exports over GDP are, by definition, each $I(2)$, equation (5.29) implies that they must be together $CI(2,1)$ with vector $(1, -\beta)$. Thus, equation (5.29) shows two levels of cointegration: The first level refers to the relationship between the stocks of imports and exports over GDP, and the second level relates the linear combination between the stocks of imports-to-GDP and exports-to-GDP ratios and the level of exports.

Including the intercept and a linear trend, equation (5.29) leads to the following model

$$\sum_{j=1}^{t} m_j = \alpha + \alpha_2 t + \beta \sum_{j=1}^{t} x_j + \delta x_t + u_t. \tag{5.30}$$

Berenguer-Rico and Carrion-i-Silvestre (2011) modify equation (5.30) to allow for structural breaks:

$$\begin{aligned}\sum_{j=1}^{t} m_j =& \alpha_1 + \alpha_2 t + \sum_{i=1}^{l} \theta_i DU_{i,t} + \sum_{i=1}^{l} \gamma_i DT_{i,t} + \beta_0 \sum_{j=1}^{t} x_j \\ &+ \sum_{i=1}^{l} \beta_i DU_{i,t} \sum_{j=1}^{t} x_j + \delta_0 x_t + \sum_{i=1}^{l} \delta_i DU_{i,t} x_t + u_t\end{aligned} \tag{5.31}$$

where l is the number of structural breaks, $DU_{i,t}$ takes the value one and $DT_{i,t}$ takes the value $(t - T_i)$ if $t > T_i$ and are zero otherwise, $T_i = [\delta_i T]$ denotes the i-th break point, and $i = 1, 2, \ldots, l - \delta_i$ is the break function parameter.

Testing for the presence of multicointegration boils down to testing for stationarity of the error u_t: $u_t \sim I(0)$ implies multicointegration, $u_t \sim I(1)$ provides evidence for cointegration between the cumulated stocks of imports and exports over GDP, but no cointegration between the flow and stock variables, and $u_t \sim I(2)$ indicates that there is no cointegration relationships at all. Applying the t-ratio ADF test statistics, Camarero et al. (2013) can reject the null hypothesis of a unit root in u_t in favor of stationarity in levels only for six out of 23 countries in the sample: Austria (with no breaks), Japan (with two breaks), the Netherlands (with one break), New Zealand (with two breaks), Portugal (with zero, one, and two breaks), and Spain (with two breaks). Thus, these results point rather to weak than strong sustainability in the United States.

For these countries, Camarero et al. (2013) in addition determine the "degree" of sustainability by performing the DOLS estimation of the parameters in equation (5.31). When $\sum_{j=0}^{l} \beta_j > 1$ with $i = 0, 1, \ldots, l$, trade deficits have been predominant whereas $\sum_{j=0}^{l} \beta_j < 1$ implies that an economy has been on average running more trade surpluses. In the former case, the trade balance is improved when exports increase due to $\sum_{j=0}^{l} \delta_j > 0$, and in the latter case, a reduction in exports due to $\sum_{j=0}^{l} \delta_j < 0$ accommodates the trade surpluses.

Because trade deficits (surpluses) are reflected in an increase in net foreign debts (assets), provided that primary and secondary income is zero, multicointegration combined with

$\sum_{j=0}^{l}\beta_j > 1$ and $\sum_{j=0}^{l}\delta_j > 0$ or $\sum_{j=0}^{l}\beta_j < 1$ and $\sum_{j=0}^{l}\delta_j < 0$ implies that exports increase (diminish) when the level of net foreign debts (assets) rises. Thus, the responsiveness of exports towards the change in the respective economy's NIIP resembles the "reaction rule" suggested by Bohn (2007).

However, the multicointegration approach suffers from mainly two drawbacks. Firstly, the interpretation of the parameters is difficult. The first layer of cointegration with the cointegrating coefficient being in $(0;1+r]$ implies the validity of the intertemporal budget constraint, as shown by Trehan and Walsh (1991) and Bohn (2007). However, when $\sum_{j=0}^{l}\delta_j$ and $\sum_{j=0}^{l}\beta_j$ do not move in the same direction, Camarero et al. (2013) conclude—despite of the validity of the IBC—that the external position is not sustainable. Thus, Camarero et al. (2013) must be relying on some other concept of sustainability, whose theoretical foundations, however, are not explicitly laid out. Secondly, completely ignoring primary and secondary income might be problematic for some countries.

5.3.3 Bohn's (2007) approach

Panel analysis

Durdu et al. (2010) take the approach suggested by Bohn (2007) and test for sustainability of global imbalances using the data set constructed by Milesi-Ferretti and Lane (2006) for net international investment positions during the period 1970-2004. Because the data set covers only 34 annual observations, Durdu et al. (2010) increase the sample size by exploiting cross-country information. For 50 countries, they estimate the panel error-correction reaction function of the form

$$tb^n_{i,,t} = -\mu_i b^n_{i,t-1} + e_{i,,t} \qquad \mu_i \in \left(0;\frac{1+i}{1+\gamma^n}\right] \tag{5.32}$$

where $e_{i,,t}$ is $I(0)$, tb^n_i denotes the nominal trade balance relative to GDP, b^n_i is the nominal NIIP as a fraction of GDP, i and γ^n are nominal interest rates. Following Pesaran et al. (1999), the error-correction reaction function (5.32) can be nested into an autoregressive distributed lag model so that one obtains

$$\Delta b_{it} = \theta_{i1} + \theta_{i2} tb_{it-1} + \theta_{i3} b_{it-1} + \sum_{j=1}^{p-1}\theta_{ij,4}\Delta tb_{it-j} + \sum_{l=0}^{q-1}\theta_{ij,5}\Delta b_{it-j} + \varepsilon_{it}. \tag{5.33}$$

Equation (5.33) can be rearranged to become

$$\Delta b_{it} = \theta_{i1} + \theta_{i2}\left(tb_{it-1} - \mu_i b_{it-1}\right) + \sum_{j=1}^{p-1}\theta_{ij,4}\Delta tb_{it-j} + \sum_{l=0}^{q-1}\theta_{ij,5}\Delta b_{it-j} + \varepsilon_{it} \tag{5.34}$$

where $\mu_i = -\theta_{i3}/\theta_{i2}$ describes the long-run relationship between the trade account and the NIIP and θ_{i2} denotes the speed at which the trade balance converges towards its long-run value after a change in the NIIP. A negative and statistically significant μ_i ensures that a negative feedback exists from the NIIP to the trade balance and that, therefore, the intertemporal budget constraint is satisfied. Durdu et al. (2010) estimate equation (5.34) using mean-group and pooled mean-group estimators. The mean-group (MG) estimator is obtained by estimating separate error-correction equations for each country and calculating the coefficient means; it is consistent for large N and T (Pesaran and Smith, 1995). Because the MG estimator does not take into account that the long-run coefficient might be the same for all groups, Pesaran et al. (1999) suggest a pooled mean group (PMG) estimator which requires the long-run coefficients to be the same, but allows the intercepts, short-run coefficients, and error variances to differ across countries (Pesaran et al., 1999). The MG or PMG estimates can then be used to derive estimates of the long-run average values of the NIIP ($E[b_i]$). It follows from equation (5.34) that the long-run relationship between the trade balance and the NIIP (where $\Delta b_i = \Delta tb_i = 0$ and $\varepsilon = 0$) is given by

$$\theta_{i1} + \theta_{i2}\left(tb_i - \mu_i b_i\right) = 0.$$

Substituting $tb_i = -rb_i$ (which follows from the balance of payments identity), solving for b_i, and forming the expected value yields the long-run value of the NIIP:

$$E[b_i] = \frac{\theta_{i1}}{\theta_{i2}(r+\mu_i)}. \tag{5.35}$$

The long-run average value of the NIIP $E[b_i]$ exists if the NIIP is stationary—which is the case if (i) $\theta_{i2} < 0$ (otherwise, the error-correction specification (5.34) is not well defined), (ii) $\mu_i < 0$, and (iii) $|\mu| > r$. These conditions imply that the denominator of the right-hand side of equation (5.35) is strictly positive (because both θ_{i2} and $(r+\mu_i)$ are strictly negative) and that therefore the signs of $E[b_i]$ and θ_{i2} must be equal. Hence, the higher the response coefficient μ_i in absolute value, the lower is in absolute value the long-run average NIIP, if everything remains the same. This result indicates that countries which have higher response coefficients might have limited access to international capital markets as they borrow and lend less than countries with lower response coefficients (Durdu et al., 2010, p. 11).

Durdu et al. (2010) reject the null hypothesis of no error-correction relationship between the trade balance and the NIIP under both the MG and the PMG estimators using the t-statistic for the full sample and for the subsamples (industrial countries and emerging markets, debtor economies and creditor countries). The Hausman (1978) test cannot reject the homogeneity restriction that the long-run coefficient is the same for all countries. Durdu et al. (2010) take this result as evidence that the PMG estimator should be preferred to the MG estimator. The PMG estimates of μ_i are negative and statistically significant, thus pointing to sustainability. For the full sample, the estimated μ is about -0.07 (meaning that an increase (decrease) of one percentage point in the NIIP decreases (increases) the trade balance by 0.07 percentage points). When the real interest rate is below 7 percent, the trade balance, the NIIP, and the current account are stationary in levels. In this case, external imbalance are sustainable in the strong sense. When the real interest rate equals 7 percent, the trade balance and the NIIP are $CI(1,1)$ with cointegrating vector $(1,r)$ so that the current account is also stationary in levels and sustainable in the strong sense.

The estimate of the error-coefficient θ_{i2} is 0.31 and can be used to calculate the half-life as follows: $\log(0.5)/\log(1-0.31) = 1.87$, thus implying that the adjustment of the trade balance to a change in the NIIP has an average half-life of approximately 1.87 years. The response coefficients are found to be higher and the error-coefficients lower in emerging markets than in industrial countries. In other words, the adjustment in the trade balance in response to changes in the NIIP is larger and takes place at a slower pace in emerging markets than in industrial countries. Possible reasons might be underdeveloped financial markets or large financial frictions in emerging markets (Durdu et al., 2010, p. 16). Further, Durdu et al. (2010) report the long-run NIIP values for countries in which θ_{i2} and θ_{i1} are statistically significant (the United States are not among those). As expected, the calculated long-run NIIP values are on average lower for net borrowing emerging markets than for net borrowing industrial countries.

Durdu et al. (2010) also calculate the impulse response functions of b and tb using the PMG estimates, setting the initial b and tb to their long-run values, and exposing them to a one-standard-deviation noise shock. They find that the trade balance converges faster to its long-run equilibrium than the NIIP since the latter needs 10 to 50 years to respond to a shock.

The testing approach suggested by Bohn (2007) and implemented by Durdu et al. (2010) allows to avoid low power problems and size distortions associated with unit root tests as well as with some cointegration tests. This approach could be generalized to allow for a time-varying response coefficient μ (e.g., similar to the approach taken by Canzoneri et al. (2001) for fiscal deficits) and nonlinearity in the response of the trade account to the NIIP (similar to Bohn (1998) for fiscal sustainability).

Time series analysis

The panel ARDL approach used by Durdu et al. (2010) provides little information on external sustainability specifically in the United States. Therefore, we apply time series methods in order to test for the negative feedback from the NIIP to the trade balance in the United States. For this purpose, we exploit the quarterly data set constructed by Gourinchas and Rey (2007a) which measures the NIIP at market value and is the longest available market-value data set so far for the United States. Estimates for the NIIP at market value are also provided by the U.S. Bureau of Economic Analysis which, however, start in 1982.[21] Measurement at market value (rather than at historical cost) allows to capture "valuation effects" arising from changes in exchange rates and asset prices. The recent research on international macro-finance stresses the important role of valuation effects for the adjustment of external imbalances (Tille, 2003; Gourinchas and Rey, 2007a,b; Pavlova and Rigobon, 2010a,b). Tille (2003) estimates that nearly one third of the deterioration in the US net international investment position since the end of 1999 results from valuation effects (see also Gourinchas and Rey (2007b) for the similar result).

Figure 5.1 shows the (nominal) cumulated current account measured at historical cost and the (nominal) net international investment position measured at market value. Both series are put in proportion to GDP in order to account for the fact that an economy's repayment capacity (approximated by the GDP) is typically bounded. The difference between the both series corresponds to the net valuation component. The cumulated current account measure overestimates the NIIP at market value before 1980 and underestimates it from 1980 to approximately 2000. Figure 5.1 also reveals that the valuation effects are mostly negative while the United States is a net creditor towards the rest of the world and are mostly positive when the US NIIP is negative. This indicates that the valuation component has a stabilizing effect on the US external position over almost the whole sample period (Gourinchas and Rey, 2007a). For this reason, we expect

[21] As Gourinchas and Rey (2007a) and the Bureau of Economic Analysis do not employ the same estimates, we cannot extend the data set in Gourinchas and Rey (2007a) by a mere inclusion of data provided by the Bureau of Economic Analysis.

Fig. 5.1: Net international investment position at market value and cumulated current account in proportion to GDP in the United States

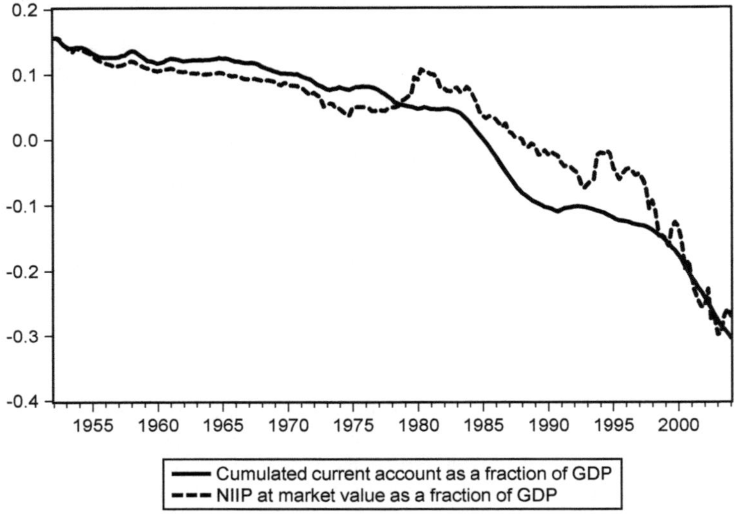

Source: Gourinchas and Rey (2007a)

more evidence in favor of external sustainability based on the NIIP at market value than when the NIIP is measured at historical cost.

Following Bohn (2007), we examine whether the relationship

$$tb_t^n = -\mu b_{t-1}^n + e_t \sim I(0), \qquad \mu \in \left(0; \frac{1+i}{1+\gamma^n}\right] \tag{5.36}$$

exists. As before, tb_t^n and b_{t-1}^n denote the nominal trade balance-to-GDP ratio and the nominal NIIP-to-GDP ratio, respectively, i is the nominal interest rate, and γ^n is the nominal GDP growth rate.

We shortly review the empirical implications of equation (5.36) which are in detail discussed in subsubsection 4.2.2 of chapter 4. When $\mu \in \left(i/(1+\gamma^n);(1+i)/(1+\gamma^n)\right]$ and $e_t \sim I(0)$, both the trade balance and the NIIP over GDP must be stationary in levels. In this case, the current account is also stationary in levels and sustainable in the strong sense. Simply regressing tb_t^n on b_{t-1}^n (possibly also on further potential determinants of the trade balance) and finding the regression coefficient μ to lie in $\left(i/(1+\gamma^n);(1+i)/(1+\gamma^n)\right]$ is sufficient to show strong sustainability. In addition, unit root tests on the NIIP and the trade current account can be performed to verify the implication of stationarity.

When $\mu = i/(1+\gamma^n)$ and $e_t \sim I(0)$, both series must be stationary in first differences and together $CI(1,1)$ with cointegrating vector $(1, i/(1+\gamma^n))$. The current account is stationary in levels and sustainable in the strong sense in this case. As a confirmatory analysis, unit root and cointegration tests can be used to show the existence of the cointegrating relationship with the said cointegrating vector.

When $\mu \in (0; i/(1+\gamma^n))$ and $e_t \sim I(0)$, the trade balance and the NIIP over GDP are mildly explosive, with a root lying in $(1/(1+\gamma^n); (1+i)/(1+\gamma^n))$. The current account is weakly sustainable in this case. Finally, $\mu < 0$ implies that the relationship (5.36) does not exist and that both time series are highly explosive with a root exceeding $(1+i)/(1+\gamma^n)$. In this case, the intertemporal budget constraint is not likely to be satisfied.

In practice, many estimation techniques require the knowledge of the integration order of the time series involved. Therefore, for convenience, we first pretest the variables for the presence of unit roots and then estimate the coefficient μ. However, we keep in mind that we cannot always infer the range in which μ lies from the knowledge of the integration order of the variables involved. For example, a finding of the trade balance and the NIIP being both $I(1)$ and together $CI(1,1)$ does not imply that μ must equal $i/(1+\gamma^n)$. Further, a finding of first-difference stationarity and no cointegration does not necessarily mean the absence of sustainability; $\mu \in \left(i/(1+\gamma^n); (1+i)/(1+\gamma^n)\right]$ and $e_t \sim I(1)$ also imply sustainability (in the weak sense).[22] Since the finding of stationarity or difference-stationarity of the NIIP alone is sufficient for sustainability, this procedure allows us to compare the results of two approaches to test for sustainability: unit root tests on the NIIP-to-GDP series and estimation of equation (5.36).

Thus, our first step is to test for stationarity of the NIIP-to-GDP series at market value. The NIIP series being stationary in levels or in first differences is sufficient for sustainability in the strong sense, and the NIIP series being integrated of order two or higher implies sustainability in the weak sense. The visual observation of figure 5.1 suggests that the NIIP series at market value is either trend-stationary or a random walk with drift (see figure 5.1).

In order to reduce seasonal effects for quarterly data, we adjust the NIIP-to-GDP series using the X12 seasonal adjustment program provided by the US Census Bureau. The seasonally adjusted series is depicted in figure 5.2. We first use the augmented Dickey-Fuller (ADF) test (see subsubsection 5.1.2 for the explanation) to test the null hypothesis of a unit root with drift against the alternative hypothesis of a trend-stationary process. For quarterly data, we choose a maximum number of five lags. As the power of the ADF test largely depends on the correct choice of lags, we rely on several information criteria when determining the optimal lag structure. Alongside with the "standard" information criteria such as the Akaike information criterion (AIC), the Schwarz information criterion (SIC), and the Hannan-Quinn information criterion (HQ), we also use the modified AIC, SIC, and HIC criteria which improve the size of the unit root tests in comparison to the standard information criteria (Ng and Perron, 2001). Table 5.1 summarizes the results of the augmented Dickey-Fuller test. When both an intercept

[22] In this case, the relationship of the form

$$tb_t^n = -\mu b_{t-1}^n + e_t \sim I(1), \qquad \mu \in \left(0; \frac{1+i}{1+\gamma^n}\right]$$

exists (see subsubsection 4.2.2 of chapter 4 for details).

and a linear trend are included, neither of them is statistically significant. However, in the regressions with a constant only, the constant is statistically significant at the 5% level. The ADF test cannot reject the null hypothesis of a unit root with drift and/or trend in favor of the alternative hypothesis of a stationary process with drift and/or trend. However, the ADF test rejects the null hypothesis of a unit root in the first-differenced series in favor of no unit roots in the first-differenced series at the 1% significance level. This indicates that the NIIP-to-GDP series is stationary in first differences.

Table 5.1: Augmented Dickey-Fuller tests on the NIIP and the trade balance in the United States

Variable (Sample)	**Statistics**	**Constant**	**Trend**	**Lags**	**Criteria for the lag selection**
NIIP/GDP(s)	0.563227	yes	yes	4	AIC, SIC, HQ, MHQ
(1952.Q1-2004.Q1)	0.166623	yes	yes	5	MAIC
	0.166573	yes	yes	0	MSIC
	2.434959	yes*	no	4	AIC, SIC, HQ
	1.994121	yes*	no	5	MAIC, MHQ
	1.105854	yes*	no	3	MSIC
ΔNIIP/GDP(s)	−4.864515**	yes*	no	5	AIC
(1952.Q1-2004.Q1)	−7.713634**	yes*	no	3	SIC
	−5.898305**	yes*	no	4	HQ
	−6.467228**	yes*	no	2	MAIC, MSIC, MHQ
TB/GDP(s)	−1.941688	yes	yes†	4	AIC, MAIC
(1960.Q1-2004.Q1)	−2.004675	yes	yes*	0	SIC, MSIC
	−2.337157	yes†	yes*	1	HQ, MHQ
ΔTB/GDP(s)	−4.586678**	no	no	5	AIC, MAIC
(1960.Q1-2004.Q1)	−11.29168**	no	no	0	SIC, HQ
	−6.638371**	no	no	2	MSIC, MHQ
	−4.884222**	yes	yes	5	AIC
	−11.44165**	yes	yes	0	SIC, HQ
	−6.840477**	yes	yes	2	MAIC, MSIC, MHQ

Notes: All variables are measured in nominal values. **, *, and † denote the rejection of the null hypothesis at the 1%, 5%, and 10% level, respectively. Critical values are tabulated in Fuller (1976). The maximum lag number is five.

Abbreviations: AIC: Akaike Information Criterion, GDP: Gross Domestic Product, HQ: Hannan-Quinn Information Criterion, MAIC: Modified Akaike Information Criterion, MHQ: Modified Hannan-Quinn Information Criterion, MSIC: Modified Schwarz Information Criterion, NIIP: Net International Investment Position, (s): seasonal adjustment (X12 Census method), SIC: Schwarz Information Criterion, TB: Trade Balance.

We also perform the non-parametric Phillips-Perron (PP) test (see subsubsection 5.1.2 of this chapter). To compute the PP statistic, we rely on the widely used Bartlett kernel which ensures the non-negativity of the estimated variance of the regression residuals. As Kim and Schmidt (1990) and Cheung and Lai (1997) show, the choice of the kernel does not significantly affect the power of the PP test. We use data-based bandwidth selection methods since they lead to a higher test power than the data-independent selection methods do (Cheung and Lai, 1997). Table 5.2 reports the results of the Phillips-Perron test both for the bandwidth selection procedure suggested by Newey and West (1987) and the one proposed by Andrews (1991). The PP test confirms the results of the ADF test: The null hypothesis of a random walk with a drift and/or trend cannot be rejected whereas the null hypothesis of a unit root in the first-differenced series can be rejected at the 1% level in favor of a random walk.

Table 5.2: Phillips-Perron tests on the NIIP and the trade balance in the United States

Variable (Sample)	**Statistics**	**Constant**	**Trend**	**Bandwidth**	**Bandwidth selection method**
NIIP/GDP(s)	0.011365	yes	yes	7	Newey-West aut.
(1952.Q1-2004.Q1)	−4.002786	yes	yes	1.93	Andrews aut.
	1.969099	yes**	no	8	Newey-West aut.
	1.897927	yes**	no	1.83	Andrews aut.
ΔNIIP/GDP(s)	−13.06729**	yes**	no	6	Newey-West aut.
(1952.Q1-2004.Q1)	−12.96026**	yes**	no	0.426	Andrews aut.
TB/GDP(s)	−2.361083	yes	yes*	3	Newey-West aut.
(1960.Q1-2004.Q1)	−2.362776	yes	yes*	3.03	Andrews aut.
ΔTB/GDP(s)	−11.28784**	no	no	7	Newey-West aut.
(1960.Q1-2004.Q1)	−11.29168**	no	no	0.477	Andrews aut.
	−11.37563**	yes	yes	9	Newey-West aut.
	−11.44165**	yes	yes	0.404	Andrews aut.

Notes: All variables are measured in nominal values. **, *, and † denote the rejection of the null hypothesis at the 1%, 5%, and 10% level, respectively. Critical values are tabulated in Fuller (1976). The Bartlett kernel is used as the spectral estimation method.
Abbreviations: aut.: automatic, GDP: Gross Domestic Product, NIIP: Net International Investment Position, (s): seasonal adjustment (X12 Census method), TB: Trade Balance.

As a confirmatory analysis, we also conduct the Kwiatkowski-Phillips-Schmidt-Shin (KPSS) test (see subsubsection 5.1.2 of this chapter) based on the Bartlett window and the Newey-West or Andrews bandwidth selection methods. Table 5.3 shows that the KPSS test rejects the null hypothesis of trend-stationarity in favor of the alternative hypothesis of a random walk with drift and trend at the 1% level.

Table 5.3: Kwiatkowski-Phillips-Schmidt-Shin tests on the NIIP and the trade balance in the United States

Variable (Sample)	**Statistics**	**Constant**	**Trend**	**Bandwidth**	**Bandwidth selection method**
NIIP/GDP(s)	0.324380**	yes*	yes*	11	Newey-West aut.
(1952.Q1-2004.Q1)	1.382368**	yes*	yes*	577	Andrews aut.
TB/GDP(s)	0.106111	yes*	yes*	10	Newey-West aut.

(1960.Q1-2004.Q1)	0.090821	yes*	yes*	349	Andrews aut.

Notes: All variables are measured in nominal values. **, *, and † denote the rejection of the null hypothesis at the 1%, 5%, and 10% level, respectively. Critical values are tabulated in Fuller (1976). The Bartlett kernel is used as the spectral estimation method.
Abbreviations: aut.: automatic, GDP: Gross Domestic Product, NIIP: Net International Investment Position, (s): seasonal adjustment (X12 Census method), TB: Trade Balance.

As already discussed above, unit root tests of the first generation are subject to low power and size distortion problems. Because the PP test tends to overreject the null hypothesis of a unit root when the root is close to minus one, we also apply the Ng-Perron test already mentioned in subsubsection 5.1.2. From table 5.4 follows that all four statistics (modified Za and Zt statistics as well as MSB and MPT statistics) do not reject the null hypothesis of a random walk and strongly reject the null hypothesis of $I(2)$ in favor of $I(1)$.

Table 5.4: Ng-Perron tests on the NIIP and the trade balance in the United States

Variable (Sample)	**MZa**	**MZt**	**MSB**	**MPT**	**Constant**	**Trend**	**Band-width**	**Bandwidth selection method**
NIIP/GDP(s)	−0.66368	−0.26386	0.39758	40.2108	yes	yes	7	Newey-West aut.
(1952.Q1-2004.Q1)	−0.59947	−0.24079	0.40168	41.0439	yes	yes	1.93	Andrews aut.
	3.49626	3.72149	1.06442	117.675	yes	no	8	Newey-West aut.
	3.47626	3.61908	1.04109	112.572	yes	no	1.83	Andrews aut.
ΔNIIP/GDP(s)	−98.4626**	−7.01515**	0.07125**	0.93069**	yes	yes	9	Newey-West
(1952.Q1-2004.Q1)	−102.748**	−7.16625**	0.06975**	0.89188**	yes	yes	0.296	Andrews
	−110.129**	−7.42014**	0.06738**	0.22323**	yes	no	6	Newey-West aut.
	−97.4508**	−6.97991**	0.07162**	0.25227**	yes	no	0.426	Andrews aut.
TB/GDP(s)	−10.7407	−2.23853	0.20842	8.88115	yes	yes	3	Newey-West aut.
(1960.Q1-2004.Q1)	−10.7556	−2.24019	0.20828	8.86964	yes	yes	3.03	Andrews aut.
	1.36731	0.86080	0.62956	33.9254	yes	no	6	Newey-West aut.
	1.28250	0.78156	0.60941	31.7882	yes	no	2.78	Andrews aut.
ΔTB/GDP(s)	−70.3134**	−5.92724**	0.08430**	1.30512**	yes	yes	9	Newey-West aut.
(1960.Q1-2004.Q1)	−77.3379**	−6.21647**	0.08038**	1.18666**	yes	yes	0.404	Andrews aut.
	−54.2746**	−5.17282**	0.09531**	0.54237**	yes	no	9	Newey-West aut.
	−59.3426**	−5.41217**	0.09120**	0.49664**	yes	no	0.439	Andrews aut.

Notes: All variables are measured in nominal values. **, *, and † denote the rejection of the null hypothesis at the 1%, 5%, and 10% level, respectively. Critical values are tabulated in Ng and Perron (2001). The Bartlett kernel is used as the spectral estimation method. The significance of the deterministic regressors is not tested here anymore.

Abbreviations: aut.: automatic, GDP: Gross Domestic Product, NIIP: Net International Investment Position, (s): seasonal adjustment (X12 Census method), TB: Trade Balance.

We also perform the Dickey-Fuller Generalized Least Squares (DF-GLS) test of Elliott, Rothenberg and Stock, which is based on the detrending of the variable in the ADF regression (see subsubsection 5.1.2 of this chapter). Since Elliott et al. (1996) recommend the use of the Schwarz information criterion to determine the optimal lag number, we only rely on the Schwarz and modified Schwarz information criteria. Table 5.5 shows that the results of the DF-GLS test are consistent with the ADF and PP tests: The null hypothesis cannot be rejected at levels and is strongly rejected in first differences.

Table 5.5: Elliott-Rothenberg-Stock DF-GLS tests on the NIIP and the trade balance in the United States

Variable (Sample)	Statistics	Constant	Intercept	Lags	Criteria for the lag selection
NIIP/GDP(s)	−0.207565	yes	yes	4	SIC, MSIC
(1952.Q1-2004.Q1)	3.693494	yes	no	4	SIC
	2.198147	yes	no	3	MSIC
Δ NIIP/GDP(s)	−8.205937**	yes	yes	3	SIC
(1952.Q1-2004.Q1)	−6.739148**	yes	yes	2	MSIC
	−5.329198**	yes	no	4	SIC
	−4.351807**	yes	no	5	MSIC
TB/GDP(s)	−1.936966	yes	yes	0	SIC, MSIC
(1960.Q1-2004.Q1)	1.010911	yes	no	0	SIC
	0.651962	yes	no	1	MSIC
ΔTB/GDP(s)	−10.52923**	yes	yes	0	SIC
(1960.Q1-2004.Q1)	−3.858373**	yes	yes	5	MSIC
	−2.452972*	yes	no	5	SIC, MSIC

Notes: All variables are measured in nominal values. **, *, and † denote the rejection of the null hypothesis at the 1%, 5%, and 10% level, respectively. Critical values are tabulated in Fuller (1976) in the constant-only case and in Elliott et al. (1996) and Ng and Perron (2001) when both a constant and a trend are included. The maximum lag number is five. The significance of the deterministic regressors is not tested here anymore.
Abbreviations: GDP: Gross Domestic Product, MSIC: Modified Schwarz Information Criterion, NIIP: Net International Investment Position, (s): seasonal adjustment (X12 Census method), SIC: Schwarz Information Criterion, TB: Trade Balance.

However, unit root tests tend to underreject the null hypothesis of a unit root when there are structural breaks. For this reason, we also perform the Perron (1997) test which was already mentioned in subsubsection 5.1.2 of this chapter. [23] Perron (1997) constructs a unit root test which allows for endogenous structural breaks both under the null and alternative hypothesis. Depending on the location of a break, the Perron (1997) test considers three models: (i) the model with a change in the intercept, (ii) the model with a change in the slope coefficient, and (iii) the model with both a shift in mean and a trend. Table 5.6 shows that the Perron (1997) test identifies a structural break in the early/mid-1990s which was a start for the large deterioration of both the current account balance and the NIIP in the United States. The Perron (1997) test does not reject the null hypothesis of a random walk with a structural break in favor

[23] The source code for the EViews econometric package for the Perron (1997) test is provided by Ibarra (2009).

of stationarity with a structural break under any of the three specifications. Thus, the Perron (1997) does not provide evidence in favor of trend-stationarity of the NIIP series.

Table 5.6: Perron (1997) tests on the NIIP and the trade balance relative to GDP in the United States

Variable (Sample)	**Statistics**	**Break in the intercept**	**Break in the trend**	**Lags**	**Breakpoint**
NIIP/GDP(s)	−1.91165	yes	no	4	1996.Q2
(1952.Q1-2004.Q1)	−2.55849	no	yes	4	1992.Q4
	−2.81258	yes	yes	4	1992.Q4
TB/GDP(s)	−3.59077	yes	no	4	1987.Q3
(1960.Q1-2004.Q1)	−2.21879	no	yes	4	1997.Q3
	−3.95405	yes	yes	4	1988.Q4

Notes: All variables are measured in nominal values. **, *, and † denote the rejection of the null hypothesis at the 1%, 5%, and 10% level, respectively. Critical values are tabulated in Perron (1997). The optimal lag length is selected using the Akaike information criterion; the maximum lag number is five. The significance of the deterministic regressors is not tested here anymore.
Abbreviations: GDP: Gross Domestic Product, NIIP: Net International Investment Position, (s): seasonal adjustment (X12 Census method), TB: Trade Balance.

Overall, we obtain clear evidence that the NIIP-to-GDP series under investigation is stationary in first differences. Because the change in the NIIP including the valuation component approximately equals the current account, the NIIP relative to GDP being $I(1)$ implies that the current account balance as a fraction of GDP is stationary in levels. Thus, the performed unit root tests on the NIIP series measured at the market value suggest strong sustainability in the United States over the period from 1952.Q1 to 2004.Q1.

In addition, we want to complement this finding by testing for the negative feedback from the NIIP to the trade balance. If the NIIP and the trade balance over GDP are $CI(1,1)$ with cointegrating vector $(1,\mu)$ where $\mu = i/(1+\gamma^n)$, then the current account balance is stationary in levels and strongly sustainable.

We begin with pretesting for the presence of unit roots in the US trade balance series. The quarterly data on the nominal trade balance are obtained from the OECD database; the data on nominal GDP are provided by Gourinchas and Rey (2007a). As with the NIIP series, we seasonally adjust the trade balance relative to GDP via the X12 Census method. The series thus obtained is shown in the lower part of figure 5.2. The visual observation of the trade balance relative to GDP series suggests either trend-stationarity or a random walk with drift and/or trend.

We apply the same unit root tests to the trade balance relative to GDP as to the NIIP-to-GDP series. The ADF, PP, DG-GLS, and NP tests fail to reject the null hypothesis of a unit root in levels, and they reject the null hypothesis of a unit root in first differences (see tables 5.1, 5.2, 5.5, and 5.4). The KPSS test supports these results by rejecting the null hypothesis of stationarity in favor of a random walk (see table 5.3). In addition, when possible structural breaks are taken into account, the Perron (1997) test cannot reject the null hypothesis of a random walk with drift and/or trend, thus providing no evidence for trend-stationarity (see table 5.6). In sum,

Fig. 5.2: NIIP and trade balance at market value relative to GDP in the United States

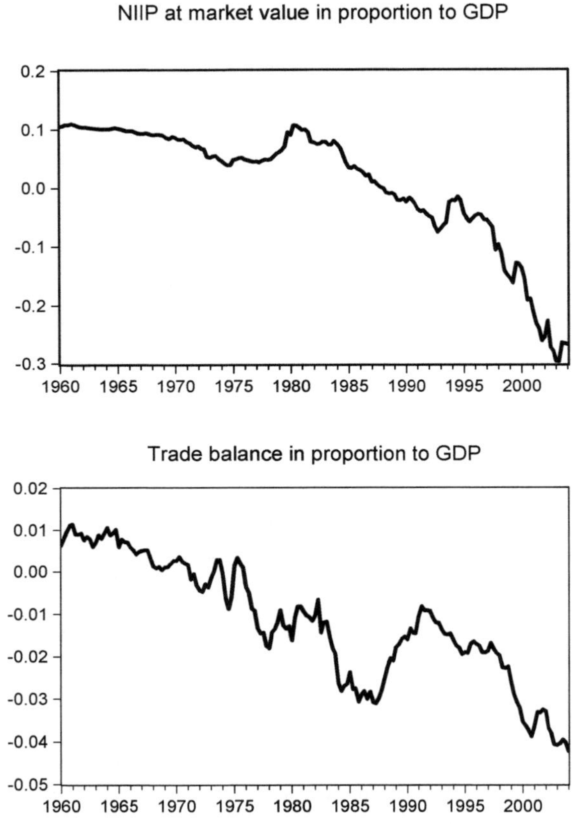

Notes: The data on the nominal NIIP at market value and on nominal GDP are from Gourinchas and Rey (2007a); the data on the nominal trade balance are from the OECD database. Both series are seasonally adjusted using the X12 Census method.

Unit root tests unanimously indicate that the trade balance relative to GDP is stationary in first differences.

Having found both the NIIP and the trade balance over GDP to be $I(1)$, the next step is to test for the cointegrating relationship between the two series. Figure 5.2 could indeed indicate that both variables share a common stochastic trend.

We perform the multi-equation Johansen cointegration test described in subsection 5.2.6. The sequential modified likelihood ratio (LR) test statistic and the Akaike information criterion select five lags for an undifferenced vector autoregressive model whereas the Schwarz and Hannan-Quinn information criteria indicate two lags (see table 5.14 of Appendix 5.C). We choose the larger number of five lags in order to ensure the absence of autocorrelation in the residuals. At lag five, the LM test statistics does not reject the null hypothesis of serial correlation in the residuals (see table 5.15 of Appendix 5.C). However, due to the excess kurtosis in the residuals, the Jarque-Bera statistics rejects the null hypothesis that residuals are multivariate normal (see table 5.16 of Appendix 5.C); this problem remains even at lag lengths which are larger than five.

Table 5.7 shows the results of the Johansen cointegration test. Since the trace statistic is more robust than the ME statistic when the residuals display excess kurtosis (Cheung and Lai, 1993), we rely more on the trace statistic. We include an intercept and a trend into the cointegrating equation. However, the trace statistic (as well as the ME statistic) fails to reject both the null hypothesis of at most one cointegrating vector and the null hypothesis of no cointegration.

Table 5.7: Johansen cointegration test on the NIIP and the trade balance in the United States

Number of cointegrating equations	**Trace statistic**	**Maximum eigenvalue statistic**
None	9.720952	5.374867
At most one	4.346084	4.346084
Slope coefficient μ	**Constant**	**Trend**
-0.01220	0.004558	-0.000636
(0.1983)		(0.00036)**

Notes: All variables are measured in nominal values. Critical values are tabulated in Johansen and Juselius (1990). The maximum lag length is 5. The cointegrating equation contains an intercept and a linear trend, the VAR contains neither a constant nor a trend. The normalized cointegrating vector is obtained by setting the coefficient on the trade balance as a fraction of GDP to one. ** denotes significance at the 1% level; the values in parentheses are standard errors. The sample comprises seasonally adjusted data for the NIIP at market value and the trade balance in proportion to GDP over the period 1960.Q4-2001.Q1 in the United States.

When the cointegrating coefficient on the trade balance as a fraction to GDP is normalized to one, the estimate of the slope coefficient μ is negative, thus indicating a reduction in the trade balance due to a deterioration of the NIIP. The finding of both no cointegration and a positive feedback from the NIIP to the trade balance does not support the finding of sustainability obtained by the unit root tests on the NIIP. A possible reason for this result is the low power of the Johansen cointegration test in the presence of structural breaks. Johansen et al. (2000) augment the Johansen cointegration test by allowing for up to two known structural breaks and compute the respective critical values. However, in our case, the timing of the structural breaks is not known *a priori*. The Perron (1997) test identifies different breaks for the both series so that it is difficult to judge which breakpoint is the correct one. For this reason, we apply the Gregory-

Hansen test which is applicable in the presence of unknown structural breaks (see subsection 5.2.5 for the explanation).

The Gregory-Hansen test examines three models: a model with a level shift (model C), a model with a level shift and a linear time trend (model C/T), and a model with both a level shift and a shift in the slope coefficient (model C/S).[24] When computing the ADF test statistics, we choose, as above, a maximum length of five lags and determine the optimal lag length using six information criteria (AIC, SIC, HQ, and their modified counterparts). For the Phillips-Perron test statistics, we follow Gregory and Hansen (1996) and use the quadratic spectral (QS) kernel in combination with the Andrews bandwidth selection methods (see table 5.8).

Applying the ADF statistics, the GH test rejects the null hypothesis of no cointegration at the 5% level in most cases only for the level shift model with a time trend. Depending on the optimal lag length, the structural break in the intercept is estimated to occur in 1988.Q3, 1988.Q4, 1989.Q1, or 1989.Q2. The PP test statistics, Za and Zt, also indicate cointegration only for the C/T formulation; a level shift is found to be in 1889.Q2 (see table 5.8). The structural break at the end of the 1980s reflects the recession in the United States which started after the stock market crash in 1987 as well as the subsequent savings and loans crisis. Overall, we conclude that the trade balance and the NIIP, relative to GDP, are cointegrated of order one where the cointegrating regression contains a shift in the intercept at the end of the 1980s and a linear time trend.[25]

Table 5.8: Gregory-Hansen cointegration test on the NIIP and the trade balance in the United States

Model	ADF statistics	Lags	Criteria for the lag selection	Breakpoint
Level shift	−3.386266	2	AIC	1978.Q2
	−3.532504	3	SIC, HQ	1974.Q1
	−2.948854	4	MAIC	1974.Q1
	−2.784801	0	MSIC	1976.Q3
	−2.773128	0	MHQ	1974.Q4
Level shift with time trend	−5.091759*	3	AIC	1989.Q2
	−4.820586*	1	SIC	1988.Q4
	−5.004869*	2	HQ	1989.Q1
	−4.484051†	0	MAIC, MSIC, MHQ	1988.Q3
Regime shift	−3.278546	2	AIC	1978.Q2
	−3.026750	1	SIC	1974.Q4
	−3.156972	2	HQ	1980.Q4
	−2.724330	0	MAIC, MSIC, MHQ	1980.Q1

[24] The EViews source code for the Gregory-Hansen test can be found in Ocakverdi and Tang (2009).

[25] We also apply the single-equation Engle-Granger (EG) procedure discussed in subsection 5.2.2. The ADF test does not reject the null hypothesis of no cointegration for any of the examined specifications (without a constant and a trend; with a constant only; both with an intercept and a trend) when the maximum lag length is five and the Schwarz and the modified Schwarz information criteria are used. Because the ADF statistics in the EG procedure does not reject the null hypothesis of no cointegration and the ADF statistics in the GH procedure does reject the null hypothesis of no cointegration in the C/T model, following Gregory and Hansen (1996), we conclude that structural breaks are important for the cointegrating relationship under investigation.

Model	Za-statistics	Zt-statistics	Bandwidth selection	Breakpoint
Level shift	−20.55129	−3.216377	QK, Andrews	1974.Q4
Level shift with time trend	−40.46130†	−4.753144*	QK, Andrews	1989.Q2
Regime shift	−19.09962	−3.081569	QK, Andrews	1980.Q2

Notes: All variables are measured in nominal values. * and † denote the rejection of the null hypothesis at the 5% and 10% level, respectively. Critical values are tabulated in Gregory and Hansen (1996). For the ADF statistics, the maximum lag length is five.
Abbreviations: (s): seasonal adjustment (X12 Census method), AIC: Akaike Information Criterion, HQ: Hannan-Quinn Information Criterion, SIC: Schwarz Information Criterion, MAIC: Modified Akaike Information Criterion, MSIC: Modified Schwarz Information Criterion, MHQ: Modified Hannan-Quinn Information Criterion, QK: Quadratic Kernel.

The final step involves estimating the cointegrating vector. The C/T model is given by

$$tb_t^n = \alpha_1 + \alpha_2 \phi_{t\tau} + \alpha_3 t + \alpha_4 b_{t-1}^n + \varepsilon_t \tag{5.37}$$

where, as above, tb_t^n and b_{t-1}^n denote the (nominal) trade balance and the (nominal) NIIP in proportion to GDP, respectively, α_1 is the intercept before the break, α_1 is the constant due to the break, and t is the time trend with $t = 1, 2, \ldots, n$. The slope coefficient α_4 equals $-\mu$ in equation (5.36). The dummy variable $\phi_{t\tau}$ is defined as follows

$$\phi_{t\tau} = \begin{cases} 0, \text{if} & t \leq [n\tau] \\ 1, \text{if} & t > [n\tau] \end{cases} \tag{5.38}$$

where τ is the relative timing of the breakpoint, n is the total number of observations, and $[\cdot]$ denotes the integer part.

The cointegrating vector is estimated using the fully modified OLS (FMOLS) and the dynamic OLS (DOLS) estimators already mentioned in subsection 5.2.3. We choose the breakpoint in 1989.Q2 because it has been identified both by the ADF statistics and the PP statistics (see table 5.8). The FMOLS estimates are computed based on the Bartlett kernel and the Newey-West fixed or Andrews automatic bandwidth selection methods. The DOLS estimates are calculated using the Akaike, Schwarz, and Hannan-Quinn information criteria and the maximum lag length of five. Table 5.9 summarizes the results.

Table 5.9: FMOLS and DOLS estimates of the cointegrating equation between the NIIP and the trade balance in the United States

	Slope coefficient μ	**Constant**	**Dummy**	**Trend**	**Bandwidth selection**	
FMOLS	−0.053671 (0.012478)**	0.008476 (0.002218)**	0.021239 (0.002353)**	−0.000315 (0.0000249)**	Newey-West fix.	
	−0.049998 (0.008738)**	0.008692 (0.001554)**	0.020090 (0.001648)**	−0.000313 (0.0000175)**	Andrews aut.	
	Estimate	**Constant**	**Dummy**	**Trend**	**Information criterion**	**Leads (lags)**
DOLS	−0.055535 (0.015371)**	0.008923 (0.002402)**	0.022850 (0.002559)**	−0.000325 (0.0000257)**	AIC	4(2)
	−0.049108 (0.012892)**	0.008881 (0.002233)**	0.020266 (0.002400)**	−0.000315 (0.0000250)**	SIC	1/0
	−0.049607 (0.013056)**	0.008937 (0.002229)**	0.020803 (0.002409)**	−0.000318 (0.0000250)**	HQ	2/0

All variables are measured in nominal values. ** denotes significance at the 1% level. The values in parentheses are standard errors. The dummy variable takes the value zero before and in 1989.Q2 (i.e., at the estimated breakpoint) and the value one otherwise.
Abbreviations: AIC: Akaike information criterion, aut.: automatic, DOLS: Dynamic Least Squares, fix: fixed, FMOLS: Fully Modified Ordinary Least Squares, SIC: Schwarz Information Criterion, HQ: Hannan-Quinn information criterion.

All estimates of equation (5.38) are statistically significant at the 1% level. However, all FMOLS and DOLS estimates of the scope coefficient μ are negative (i.e., estimates of α_4 are positive) and range from -0.055535 to -0.049108. The value of -0.055535, for example, implies that a reduction in the NIIP-to-GDP ratio by one percentage point reduces the trade balance by 0.055535 percentage points. Although the cointegrating coefficient μ is relatively small, the estimates imply a positive feedback between the NIIP and the trade balance. The Wald test rejects the null hypothesis that the slope coefficient is zero for each of the estimates.

When the cointegrating coefficient μ is indeed negative, the current account over GDP must be nonstationary. Besides, when $\mu < 0$, equation (5.36) implies that both the trade balance and the NIIP are highly explosive. In this case, shocks have permanent and ever-increasing effect on these variables and the intertemporal budget constraint is not likely to be satisfied. In contrast, unit root tests suggest that both the trade balance and the NIIP are unit root processes and the current account is stationary and strongly sustainable.

One explanation for this disagreement is that unit root test falsely indicate the presence of one unit root whereas the true data generating process has a root which is larger than one. There is, however, not much research on the performance of unit root tests when the DGP is explosive. Evans (1991) finds that standard unit root and cointegration tests erroneously provide evidence either for stationarity in levels or the property of a random walk in the presence of periodically collapsing rational bubbles.

Another explanation for this disagreement is that accounting for only one structural break yields biased estimates of the slope coefficient μ when the DGP is subject to multiple structural breaks. However, the trade balance and NIIP graphs in figure 5.2 move in the same direction so that a positive feedback seems to be consistent with the data. Thus, further research would be needed to identify whether there is an explosive behavior in the NIIP and the trade balance; possible techniques include tests for fractional integration, nonlinear time series analysis, and right-sided unit root tests. If further research verified explosive behavior in the both series, we could conclude that testing for feedback effects from the NIIP to the trade balance exhibits greater precision as a method of assessing sustainability than unit root tests.

5.4 Conclusion

Overall, the evidence on (difference-)stationarity of the current account and the NIIP series in the United States is mixed. A large majority of unit root tests (including most of the tests of the first generation as well as tests of the second generation such as the DF-GLS test, tests for fractional integration, and tests for bounded integration) do not reject the null hypothesis of a unit root in favor of the alternative hypothesis of stationarity in levels. In contrast, allowing for structural breaks as well as for nonlinearity provides evidence in favor of stationarity of the US current account series and, therefore, strong sustainability. Further, the use of long-span data also allows to identify strong sustainability.

The majority of cointegration tests does not indicate the existence of a long-run relationship between savings and investment as well as between imports inclusive of net interest payments and exports in the United States. In contrast to unit root tests, accounting for structural breaks (using Gregory-Hansen tests for one structural break and the Arai-Kurozumi-Kejriwal test for multiple breaks) does not suggest cointegration either. However, most studies which exploit long-span data find support for cointegration. The studies which find evidence in favor of cointegration and which report the cointegrating vector often suggest weak sustainability from the late 1940s on. Finally, studies which test for the presence of unit roots in the components of the current account typically find that the current account components are stationary in first differences—which alone indicates sustainability. In sum, the use of both criteria—cointegration between the current account components and/or (difference-)stationarity of the current account components—provides considerable support for sustainability in the United States.

Further, the results obtained by Wickens and Uctum (1993) point to the existence of a negative feedback effect between the NIIP and the change in the trade account. However, their approach does not allow to distinguish between weak and strong sustainability directly. For the panel data set comprising 50 countries, Durdu et al. (2010) find that an increase of one percentage point in net foreign debt increases the trade balance by 0.07 percentage points, thus implying strong sustainability as long as the interest rate does not exceed seven percent. Our test results unanimously yield that the NIIP-to-GDP series measured at market value is stationary in first differences, thus implying weak sustainability in the United States over the period from 1952.Q1 to 2004.Q1. However, we find a positive feedback from the NIIP to the GDP which indicates that the NIIP and trade series are highly explosive. Thus, we cannot confirm the finding of sustainability in the United States. Nonlinear unit root and cointegration techniques could be fruitful to shed more light on the feedback effects from the NIIP to the trade balance.

Further, there is also evidence for sustainability of other countries which experience large external imbalances. Taylor (2002), Clarida et al. (2006), and Durdu et al. (2010) find strong sustainability and Dülger and Özdemir (2005), Corbin (2004), and Onafowara et al. (2011) report weak sustainability in Germany in the period till the mid or late 2000s. In case of Japan, Taylor (2002), Raybaudi et al. (2004), Clarida et al. (2006), Holmes (2006), and Durdu et al. (2010) report strong sustainability as well as Dülger and Özdemir (2005) and Camarero et al. (2013) find weak sustainability in the period till the early and mid 2000s. For Saudi Arabia, Durdu et al. (2010) and Özmen (2007) report strong sustainability. However, Durdu et al. (2010) cannot reject the null of unit root in the NIIP during 1970-2004 in China, thus possibly pointing to weak sustainability.

Overall, these findings rather suggest that the recently observed global imbalances have been sustainable. However, one should keep in mind that global imbalances—being a systemic phenomenon (Eichengreen, 2004)—are not confined to countries with the largest current account positions such as the US, Japan, Germany, China, and Saudi Arabia. Durdu et al. (2010) examine the large panel data set consisting of 21 industrial and 29 emerging markets during 1970-2004 and come to the conclusion that the recent global imbalances are sustainable.

As for the recent imbalances in the euro area, Taylor (2002), Dülger and Özdemir (2005), Herwartz and Xu (2008), and Durdu et al. (2010) indicate strong sustainability and Onafowara et al. (2011) weak sustainability in France. Similarly, there is evidence for strong sustainability in the period till the mid 2000s in Italy (Taylor, 2002; Dülger and Özdemir, 2005; Clarida et al., 2006; Kalyoncu, 2006; Herwartz and Xu, 2008; Durdu et al., 2010), Spain (Taylor, 2002; Kalyoncu, 2006; Durdu et al., 2010; Lanzafame, 2012), the Netherlands (Taylor, 2002; Durdu et al., 2010; Camarero et al., 2013), Portugal (Durdu et al., 2010; Camarero et al., 2013), Greece (Kalyoncu, 2006; Papapetrou, 2006; Mastroyiannis, 2007; Durdu et al., 2010; Camarero et al.,

2013), and Ireland (Durdu et al., 2010; Lanzafame, 2012; Camarero et al., 2013). Thus, the tests on the intertemporal budget constraint also indicate sustainability of the intra-eurozone imbalances.

However, the tests on the validity of the IBC failed to predict the occurrence of the European debt crisis. Even if the root of the European debt crisis had not been primarily in external imbalances, external debt played an important role at least in Portugal and Greece (Gros, 2011).[26] One explanation is that statistical tests, by their nature, are based on historical data and are inherently backward-looking (Burnside, 2005, p. 47). They are only capable to predict future developments by projecting past information into the future. Even if the IBC is found to be satisfied for a particular historical data set, sudden changes in the economic environment might undermine investors' confidence in an economy's solvency, leading to a sudden stop in capital flows, and possibly resulting in an external debt crisis. For example, tests which examine the data sets ending in the mid 2000s are unable to capture an increase in the net external debts of Greece by almost double in the period from 2003 to 2009 and an increase in the Greek trade deficit by one fourth in the same period (ELSTAT, 2013) as well as the investors' crisis of confidence in late 2009/early 2010.

Finally, the IBC imposes rather weak restrictions on the paths of external imbalances: Even a current account series which is mildly explosive or stationary in many differences is sufficient to satisfy the IBC. However, even if the data support the validity of the IBC, foreign investors may well base their lending decisions on additional criteria such as upper bounds on net foreign debts in percent of GDP (Bohn, 2007, p. 1845). In order to construct a stronger sustainability criterion one can bolster the intertemporal budget constraint with additional criteria which will be discussed in the next two chapters.

[26] The tests of the government's budget constraint also indicate fiscal sustainability in the European countries which experienced a debt crisis later on. Trachanas and Katrakilidis (2013) find weak fiscal sustainability in Italy, Greece, and Spain during the period from 1970 to 2010. This result is consistent with Afonso and Rault (2010) who find joint strong sustainability of public finances in the EU-15 over the period 1970-2006.

Appendix to Chapter 5

5.A Appendix to section 5.1

Table 5.10: Overview of unit root tests on the NIIP and current account

Studies	Sample	Test Results	Sustainability?
Trehan and Walsh (1991)	The US/1946-1987	$NIIP^r$ is $I(1)$ (DF and PP tests)	Strong sustainability
Gundlach and Sinn (1992)	23 OECD c. (Australia, Austria, Belgium, Canada, Denmark, Finland, France, Germany, Greece, Iceland, Ireland, Italy, Japan, the Netherlands, New Zealand, Norway, Portugal, Spain, Sweden, Switzerland, Turkey, the UK, and the US)/1950-1988	CAB/GDP is $I(0)$ in all countries except Germany, Greece, Ireland, Japan, Portugal, the US, and possibly Turkey (DF, ADF, and PP tests);	Strong sustainability in Australia, Austria, Belgium, Canada, Denmark, Finland, France, Iceland, Italy, the Netherlands, New Zealand, Norway, Spain, Sweden, Switzerland, and the UK
Wickens and Uctum (1993)	The US/1970.Q1-1988.Q4	H_0 that (i) CAB/GDP is $I(0)$; (ii) CAB/GDP is $I(1)$; (iii) NIIP/GDP is $I(1)$; (iv) NIIP/GDP is $I(2)$ cannot be rejected (DF and ADF tests)	No evidence for strong and weak sustainability
Argimón and Roldán (1994)	Belgium, Denmark, France, Germany, Ireland, Italy, the the Netherlands, and the UK/1960-1980, Spain/1964-1989	CAB^r is $I(0)$ in all countries except Italy and Belgium (in Denmark with mean different from 0) (ADF test)	Strong sustainability in all countries except Italy and Belgium
Sawada (1994)	13 HICs (Argentina, Brazil, Chile, Colombia, Ecuador, Indonesia, Korea, Malaysia, Mexico, Peru, the Philippines, Thailand, and Venezuela)/ 1955-1990	NIIP is $I(1)$ in Indonesia, Malaysia, South Korea, and Thailand (ADF test)	Strong sustainability for Indonesia, Malaysia, South Korea, and Thailand

Table 5.10: Overview of unit root tests on the NIIP and current account

Studies	Sample	Test Results	Sustainability?
Jansen (1996)	23 OECD c. (Canada, Denmark, France, Greece, and Sweden/1951-1991; Finland, Germany, Ireland, the Netherlands, New Zealand, Norway, Switzerland, and the US/1952-1991; Australia, Austria, Italy, Japan, and the UK /1953-1991; Belgium/1954-1991; Portugal/1955-1991; Spain/1956-1991; Turkey/1961-1991; Iceland/1962-1991)	CAB/GDP is $I(0)$ in all countries except for Canada (ADF test), with mean 0 only in Austria, Belgium, Denmark, Ireland, Italy, Japan, Norway, Portugal, Turkey, the US, with a trend in Australia, France, Greece, Japan, New Zealand, Sweden	Strong sustainability in all countries except Canada
Liu and Tanner (1996)	G7 (Canada, France, the former West Germany, Japan, Italy, the UK, and the US) / 1970-1990 (quarterly data)	CAB is $I(0)$ in France and Italy (ADF and PP tests), in Germany, Japan and the US (only with breaks), in Canada and the UK (according to PP tests, not to ADF tests, both with and without breaks),	Strong sustainability in France, Germany, Japan, Italy, the US, and possibly for Canada and the UK
Coakley and Kulasi (1997)	11 OECD c. (Australia/1900-1988, Canada/1927-1988, France/1950-1988, Germany/1950-1988, India/1900-1988, Japan/1885-1988, Korea/1953-1989, the Netherlands/1950-1988, Taiwan/1951-1989, the UK/1870-1989, and the US/1870-1989)	CAB/GDP is $I(0)$ in Australia, Canada, France, India, Japan, the Netherlands, and the US (ADF test); CAB/GDP is jointly $I(0)$ in Australia, Canada, India, Japan, the UK, and the US during the 1927-1988 (IPS panel test for 1927-1988)	Strong sustainability in Australia, Canada, France, India, Japan, the Netherlands, the US, and possibly in the UK

Table 5.10. Overview of unit root tests on the NIIP and current account

Studies	Sample	Test Results	Sustainability?
Yan (1999)	6 East Asian c. (Indonesia/1992.Q4-1996.Q1, Korea/1993.Q4-1997.Q1, Malaysia/1991-1995, the Philippines/1993.Q2-1996.Q3, Singapore/1983-1996, Taiwan/1994.Q1-1997.Q2, and Thailand/1993.Q3-1996.Q4)	CAB^r is $I(0)$ only in Taiwan during 1994.Q1-1996.Q2 (rolling ADF test)	Strong sustainability in Taiwan during 1994.Q1-1996.Q2
Wu (2000)	10 OECD c. (Australia, Canada, Japan, France, Germany, Italy, the Netherlands, Spain, the UK, and the US)/1977.Q1-1997.Q4	CAB/GDP is $I(0)$ only in Spain (ADF test) and jointly $I(0)$ in the whole sample (except Spain) and in G7 countries (IPS panel test)	Strong joint sustainability
Taylor (2002)	Argentina, Australia, Canada, Denmark, Finland, France, Germany, Italy, Japan, the Netherlands, Norway, Spain, Sweden, the UK, and the US/1870-2002	CAB/GNP is $I(0)$ for all countries in the sample (ADF test)	Strong sustainability
Holmes (2003)	26 African c. (Algeria, Benin, Botswana, Burkina Faso, Burundi, CAR, Chad, Congo, Egypt, Ghana, Ivory Coast, Kenya, Lesotho, Madagascar, Malawi, Mauritania, Mauritius, Morocco, Niger, Nigeria, Rwanda, Senegal, South Africa, Togo, Uganda, and Zambia) /1960-2000	CAB/GDP is $I(0)$ only for 13 countries (Algeria, CAR, Congo, Ivory Coast, Kenya, Madagascar, Malawi, Mauritius, Niger, Nigeria, Rwanda, South Africa, and Togo) (ADF test); CAB/GDP is jointly $I(0)$ (LLC and IPS panel tests), CAB/GDP is $I(0)$ in further 8 countries (Benin, Botswana, Burundi, Chad, Egypt, Morocco, Uganda, and Zambia) (SURADF panel test)	Strong sustainability in 21 countries (Algeria, Benin, Botswana, Burundi, CAR, Chad, Congo, Egypt, Ivory Coast, Kenya, Madagascar, Malawi, Mauritius, Morocco, Niger, Nigeria, Rwanda, South Africa, Togo, Uganda, and Zambia)

Table 5.10: Overview of unit root tests on the NIIP and current account

Studies	Sample	Test Results	Sustainability?
Chortareas et al. (2004)	12 Latin American c. (Argentina, Bolivia, Brazil, Chile, Colombia, El Salvador, Guatemala, Mexico, Nicaragua, Panama, Peru, and Venezuela)/ 1970.Q4-2000.Q4	external debt^r (dem., det.) and external debt/GDP(dem., det.) are each $I(0)$ in Panama, discounted external debt^r (dem., det.) is $I(0)$ in Bolivia, Panama and Peru, discounted external debt/GDP(dem., det.) is $I(0)$ in Bolivia (DF and ADF tests); external debt^r (dem., det.) is $I(0)$ SETAR in Argentina, Brazil, Colombia, El Salvador, Nicaragua, Venezuela, and Panama; external debt/GDP(dem., det.) is $I(0)$ SETAR in Panama, Guatemala, and Venezuela; discounted external debt^r (dem., det.) is $I(0)$ SETAR in Argentina, Bolivia, El Salvador, Panama, and Peru; discounted external debt/GDP(dem., det.) is $I(0)$ SETAR in Argentina, Bolivia, Colombia, Mexico, and Peru (SETAR)	Strong sustainability in all countries except from Chile
Raybaudi et al. (2004)	Argentina/1992.Q1-2001.Q3, Brazil/1995.Q1-2002.Q2, Japan/1970.1-2002.Q4, the UK/1970.1-2002.Q4, and the US/1970.Q1-2002.Q4	CAB^r is $I(1)$ in Japan, the UK, the US (KPSS test); H_0 unit root cannot be rejected for neither country in the sample (ADF test); the (unstable) regimes in which CAB^r is $I(1)$ are associated with 1993.Q3-1994.Q1, the end of 1996 and the whole 1997 for Argentina, 1996 for Brazil, 1973 and 1979 in Japan, 1973-1974 and 1987-1989 in the UK, 1983-1987 and 1993-2002 in the US (Markov switching ADF test); the expected time of CAB^r remaining in $I(1)$ regime is relatively low for Brazil, Japan, the UK and relatively high for Argentina and the US	Strong sustainability in Brazil, Japan, and the UK; weak sustainability in Argentina and the US

Table 5.10: Overview of unit root tests on the NIIP and current account

Studies	Sample	Test Results	Sustainability?
Dülger and Özdemir (2005)	G7 c. (Canada, France, Germany, Italy, Japan, the UK, and the US)/1974.Q1-2001.Q3	CAB/GDP(s) is $I(d)$ with $d > 0.5$ in all countries in the sample (Lo's MRR test; Robinson's score test; WML estimator; impulse responses); CAB/GDP(s) is mean reverting in France, the UK (Robinson's score test) and in Canada, France, Italy (WML estimator; impulse responses)	Strong sustainability in France and possibly in Canada and Italy; at least weak sustainability in the UK; weak sustainability in Germany, Japan, and the US
Fattouh (2005)	The US/1869-2001	CAB/GDP is TAR $I(0)$ above 0.12% and is $I(1)$ below this threshold, during 1881-1896 and since 1977 (Wald test)	Weak sustainability during 1881-1896 and since 1977; strong sustainability for the rest of the sample period
Lau and Baharumshah (2005)	12 Asian c. (Bangladesh, India, Indonesia, Japan, Korea, Malaysia, Nepal, Pakistan, the Philippines, Singapore, Sri Lanka, and Thailand)/1970-2002	CAB/GDP is jointly $I(0)$ for the whole sample (HT, IPS, and UB panel tests); CAB/GDP is $I(0)$ only in Bangladesh, Korea, and Singapore (SURADF panel test)	Strong sustainability in Bangladesh, Korea, and Singapore
Matsubayashi (2005)	The US/1965.Q1-1998.Q2	CAB^r/GDP^r (s) is $I(0)$ (PP test, with and without structural breaks, ADF test)	Strong sustainability
Clarida et al. (2006)	G7 (Canada, France, Germany, Italy, Japan, the UK, and the US)/1979.Q1-2003.Q3	CAB/NO(s, dem.) is TAR $I(0)$ in all countries	Strong sustainability

Table 5.10: Overview of unit root tests on the NIIP and current account

Studies	Sample	Test Results	Sustainability?
Holmes (2006)	11 OECD c. (Australia, Belgium, Canada, France, Germany, Italy, Japan, Norway, Spain, the UK, and the US)/1980.Q1-2002.Q4	CAB/GDP(s) and CAB(s) are both $I(0)$ only in Australia and Japan (ADF test), jointly $I(0)$ for the whole sample (LLC, IPS, and CCEMG panel tests); CAB/GDP(s) is $I(0)$ in Australia, Belgium, Japan, and the UK, and CAB is $I(0)$ in Australia, Japan, and the UK (SURADF panel test)	Strong sustainability in Australia, Japan, the UK and possibly in Belgium
Kalyoncu (2006)	22 OECD c. (Australia, Austria, Belgium, Canada, Denmark, Finland, France, Germany, Greece, Iceland, Ireland, Italy, Japan, Korea, Luxembourg, the Netherlands, New Zealand, Norway, Spain, Sweden, the UK, and the US)/1960-2002	CAB/GDP is $I(0)$ in Austria, Greece, Iceland, Italy, Korea, New Zealand, Norway, Spain, the UK (ADF test) and is jointly $I(0)$ for the remaining countries in the sample (IPS panel test)	Strong sustainability at least in Austria, Greece, Iceland, Italy, Korea, New Zealand, Norway, Spain, and the UK
Lau et al. (2006)	ASEAN-5 (Indonesia, Korea, Malaysia, the Philippines, and Thailand)/1976.Q1-2001.Q4	CAB/GDP is $I(1)$ (ADF and DF-GLS tests); CAB/GDP is jointly $I(0)$ (IPS, HT and UB panel tests)	Weak, possibly strong, sustainability

Table 5.10: Overview of unit root tests on the NIIP and current account

Studies	Sample	Test Results	Sustainability?
Chu et al. (2007)	48 African c. (Algeria, Angola, Benin, Botswana, Burkina Faso, Burundi, Cameroon, Cape Verde, CAR, Chad, Comoros, Congo, DR Congo, Côte d'Ivoire, Djibouti, Equatorial Guinea, Ethiopia, Gabon, Gambia, Ghana, Guinea, Guinea-Bissau, Kenya, Lesotho, Madagascar, Malawi, Mali, Mauritania, Mauritius, Morocco, Mozambique, Namibia, Niger, Nigeria, Rwanda, São Tomé and Príncipe, Senegal, Seychelles, Sierra Leone, South Africa, Sudan, Swaziland, Tanzania, Togo, Tunisia, Uganda, Zambia, Zimbabwe)/1980-2004	CAB/GDP is jointly $I(0)$ (IPS, LLC and MW panel tests); CAB/GDP is $I(0)$ in all countries except Algeria, Congo, Côte d'Ivoire, Guinea, Guinea-Bissau, Mauritania, Morocco, Swaziland, Tanzania, Uganda, Zambia (SURADF panel test)	Strong sustainability in all countries in the sample except Algeria, Congo, Côte d'Ivoire, Guinea, Guinea-Bissau, Mauritania, Morocco, Swaziland, Tanzania, Uganda, and Zambia
Mastroyiannis (2007)	Greece/1960-2003	CAB/GDP is $I(0)$ during 1960-2003 and the first subperiod 1960-1992 (DF, ADF, PP tests)	Strong sustainability (possibly only during 1960-1992)

Table 5.10: Overview of unit root tests on the NIIP and current account

Studies	Sample	Test Results	Sustainability?
Herwartz and Xu (2008)	26 OECD c. (Australia, Austria, Belgium, Canada, Denmark, Finland, France, Germany, Greece, Hungary, Iceland, Ireland, Italy, Japan, Korea, Mexico, the Netherlands, Norway, New Zealand, Portugal, Spain, Sweden, Switzerland, Turkey, the UK, and the US)/ 1971-2004	CAB/GDP is $I(0)$ only in Australia, France, Hungary, Iceland, Italy, Japan, Korea, Mexico, New Zealand, Spain, Turkey, and the UK and CAB/GDP is $BI(0)$ only in France, Hungary, Iceland, Italy, Korea, New Zealand (bounded PP test); H_0 of joint $BI(1)$ cannot be rejected for the whole sample (bounded PP test combined with MW panel test or with the modified inverse normal method)	Strong sustainability in France, Hungary, Iceland, Italy, Korea, and New Zealand
Christopoulos and León-Ledesma (2010)	The US/1960.Q1-2004.Q1	H_0 of unit root cannot be rejected for CAB/GDP(ADF, modified PP, and DF-GLS tests); CAB/GDP is $I(0)$ (ESTAR(1) Kilic (2003) test)	Strong sustainability

Table 5.10: Overview of unit root tests on the NIIP and current account

Studies	Sample	Test Results	Sustainability?
Durdu et al. (2010)	21 industrial c. (Australia, Austria, Belgium, Canada, Denmark, Finland, France, Germany, Greece, Ireland, Italy, Japan, the Netherlands, New Zealand, Norway, Portugal, Spain, Sweden, Switzerland, the UK, and the US) and 29 emerging markets (Argentina, Brazil, Chile, China, Colombia, Costa Rica, Ecuador, Egypt, El Salvador, Hong Kong, Hungary, India, Indonesia, Israel, Jordan, Korea, Malaysia, Mexico, Morocco, Pakistan, Peru, the Philippines, Saudi Arabia, Singapore, South Africa, Thailand, Turkey, Uruguay, Venezuela)/1970-2004	NIIP/GDP is $I(1)$ in all countries except Belgium, China, Colombia, and Norway; H_0 of unit root in Δ NIIP/GDP cannot be rejected for Belgium, China, Colombia, and Norway (ADF, PP, and KPSS tests)	Strong sustainability in all countries except Belgium, China, Colombia, and Norway
Lanzafame (2012)	27 advanced c. (Australia, Belgium, Canada, Cyprus, Czech Rep., Denmark, Finland, France, Germany, Greece, Hong Kong, Iceland, Ireland, Israel, Italy, Japan, Korea, New Zealand, Norway, Portugal, Singapore, Spain, Sweden, Switzerland, Taiwan, the UK, the US)/1980-2008	CAB is jointly $I(0)$ (Choi (2001), MW, IPS, LLC, and NCIPS panel tests), H_0 of joint unit root cannot be rejected (BD and CIPS panel tests), CAB is $I(0)$ only in Australia, Belgium, Canada, Czech Rep., Finland, Korea, Ireland, Israel, Norway, Spain, Switzerland, Taiwan, and the UK (SPSS/NCIPS panel tests)	Strong joint sustainability for the whole sample, strong individual sustainability in Australia, Belgium, Canada, Czech Rep., Finland, Korea, Ireland, Israel, Norway, Spain, Switzerland, Taiwan, and the UK

Table 5.10: Overview of unit root tests on the NIIP and current account

Studies	Sample	Test Results	Sustainability?
Cuestas (2013)	10 CEECs (Bulgaria, the Czech Republic, Estonia, Hungary, Latvia, Lithuania, Poland, Romania, Slovakia, Slovenia)/1999.Q1-2011.Q3	H_0 of joint unit root in CAB/GDP (s) cannot be rejected (LLC, IPS, and MW/ADF panel tests; panel KPSS test due to Hadri (2000)); CAB/GDP (s) is jointly $I(0)$ (MW/PP panel test; panel KPSS test due to Hadri (2000)); CAB/GDP (s) is $I(0)$ only in the Czech Rep., Estonia, and Lithuania (NP, Kapetanios et al. (2003) for dem. data, and Sollis (2009) tests) and in Latvia (NP test); H_0 of asymmetry is rejected only for the Czech Rep. and Lithuania (Sollis (2009) test); H_0 of stationarity ($d = 0$) cannot be rejected for any country in the sample (Robinson (1995) test); $d \in (0;0.5)$ in Estonia and Slovenia, $d > 1$ in Romania, $d \in [0.5;1)$ for the rest of the sample (ARFIMA estimation with Fox and Taqqu (1986) approach)	Weak sustainability in Romania, strong sustainability for the rest of the sample

Table 5.10: Overview of unit root tests on the NIIP and current account

Studies	Sample	Test Results	Sustainability?

Abbreviations:

- Data:
  ASEAN: Association of Southeast Asian Nations, CAB: Current-Account Balance, c.: countries, CEEC: Central and Eastern European Countries, dem.: demeaning, det.: detrending, GDP: Gross Domestic Product, GNP: Gross National Product, HIC: Highly Indebted Countries, NIIP: Net International Investment Position, NO: Net Output, OECD: Organisation for Economic Co-operation and Development, s: seasonal adjustment, the UK: United Kindgdom, the US: United States. The superscript ^{r} denotes a real variable, the absence of the superscript indicates that a variable is measured in nominal terms.
- Tests and models:
  ADF test: Augmented Dickey-Fuller test (Said and Dickey, 1984), BD panel test: Breitung-Das panel test (Breitung and Das, 2005), bounded PP test: bounded Phillips-Perron test (Cavaliere, 2005), CCEMG panel test: Common Correlated Effects Mean Group panel test (Pesaran, 2006), CIPS panel test: Cross-Sectionally Augmented Im-Pesaran-Shin panel test (Pesaran, 2007), DF test: Dickey-Fuller test (Dickey and Fuller, 1979), DFGLS test: Dickey-Fuller Generalized Least Squares test (Elliott et al., 1996), ESTAR: Exponential Smooth Transition Regression model, H_0: the null hypothesis, HT panel test (Harris and Tzavalis, 1999), IPS panel test: Im-Pesaran-Shin panel test (Im et al., 2003), KPSS test: Kwiatkowski-Phillips-Schmidt-Shin test (Kwiatkowski et al., 1992), LLC panel test (Levin et al., 2002), Lo's MRR test: Lo's modified Rescaled Range statistic test (Lo, 1991), MW panel test: Maddala-Wu panel (Maddala and Wu, 1999), Markov switching ADF test: Markov switching Augmented Dickey-Fuller test (Hall et al., 1999), NCIPS: Nonlinear Cross-Sectionally Augmented Im-Pesaran-Shin panel test (Cerrato et al., 2011), NP test: Ng-Perron test (Ng and Perron, 2001); PP test: Phillips-Perron test (Phillips, 1987; Phillips and Perron, 1988), Robinson's score test: Robinson's score test (Robinson, 1994), SETAR: Self-Exciting Threshold Autoregressive model, SPSM: Sequential Panel Selection Method (Chortareas and Kapetanios, 2009), SURADF panel test: Seemingly Unrelated Regression Augmented Dickey-Fuller panel test (Breuer et al., 2002), TAR: Threshold Autoregressive model, UB panel test: Breitung panel test (Breitung, 2000), WML estimator: Whittle's maximum likelihood estimator (Whittle, 1953).

5.B Appendix to section 5.2

Table 5.11: Overview of studies on cointegration between savings and investment

Studies	Sample	Test Results	Sustainability?
Miller (1988)	The US/1946.Q1-1987.Q3	GNS/GNP(s) and GPDI/GNP(s) are each $I(1)$ (ADF test) and together $CI(1,1)$ with coefficient $\in (0;1)$ only during 1946.Q1-1971.Q2 (ADF/EG tests)	Weak sustainability during 1946.Q1-1971.Q2
Leachman (1991)	24 OECD c. (Australia, Austria, Belgium, Canada, Denmark, Finland, France, Germany, Greece, Iceland, Ireland, Italy, Japan, Luxembourg, the Netherlands, New Zealand, Norway, Portugal, Spain, Sweden, Switzerland, Turkey, the UK, and the US)/1960-1984	H_0 of unit root cannot be rejected in NetS/GDP and NetI/GDP except for German NetI/GDP (ADF test); H_0 of no cointegration cannot be rejected for any country in the sample (EG/ADF test)	No evidence of sustainability
Gulley (1992)	The US/1946.Q1-1987.Q3	GNS/GNP and GPDI/GNP are each $I(0)$ during 1946.Q1-1971.Q2 and 1946.Q2-1987.Q3, GNS/GNP is $I(1)$ and GPDI/GNP is $I(0)$ during 1971.Q3-1987.Q3 (ADF test); GNS and GDI are each $I(1)$ during 1946.Q1-1987.Q3, 1946.Q1-1971.Q2, and 1946.Q1-1987.Q3, H_0 of no cointegration cannot be rejected (EG/ADF test)	Strong sustainability of CAB/GNP; weak sustainability of CAB

Table 5.11: Overview of studies on cointegration between savings and investment

Studies	Sample	Test Results	Sustainability?
Argimón and Roldán (1994)	Belgium, Denmark, France, Germany, Ireland, Italy, the Netherlands, the UK/1960-1980, and Spain/1964-1989	NS and NI are each $I(1)$ and $CI(1,1)$ in Belgium, Denmark, France, Italy, and Spain, with cointegrating vector $(1,1)$ only in Denmark (Johansen ME and trace tests);	Strong sustainability in Denmark; weak sustainability in Belgium, Denmark, France, Italy, Spain
Haan and Siermann (1994)	Australia/1900-1988, Canada/1927-1988, France/1950-1989, Germany/1950-1989, India/1900-1988, Japan/1948-1988, Korea/1960-1989, the Netherlands/1950-1988, Taiwan/1951-1980, and the UK/1920-1989	GDS/GDP and GDI/GDP ratios are each $I(1)$ and together $CI(1,1)$, with unity coefficient in India and coefficient $\in (0;1)$ in Australia, France, Japan, Taiwan, Korea, and the UK (EG /ADF test)	Strong sustainability in India, weak sustainability in Australia, France, Japan, Korea, Taiwan, and the UK
Bodman (1995)	Australia, Canada, France, Germany, Japan, Italy, the UK, and the US/1960.Q1-1993.Q1	NS/GDP(s) and PDI/GDP(s) are $I(1)$ in all countries (ADF and PP tests) and $CI(1,1)$ in Canada, Germany, France, Japan and Australia; H_0 of no cointegration cannot be rejected for Italy, the UK, and the US (Johansen ME test); NS/GDP(s) and PDI/GDP(s) are $CI(1,1)$ in all countries (Johansen trace test); cointegrating coefficients are $\in (0;1)$ in all countries	Weak sustainability in all countries

Table 5.11: Overview of studies on cointegration between savings and investment

Studies	Sample	Test Results	Sustainability?
Barkoulas et al. (1996)	24 OECD c. (Australia, Austria, Belgium, Canada, Denmark, Finland, France, Germany, Greece, Iceland, Ireland, Italy, Japan, Luxembourg, the Netherlands, New Zealand, Norway, Portugal, Spain, Sweden, Switzerland, Turkey the UK, and the US)/1960-1988	H_0 of unit root in GDS/GDP and GDI/GDP cannot be rejected except for GDI/GDP in Luxembourg and New Zealand (ADF test); GDS/GDP and GDI/GDP are each $I(0)$ in Canada, Finland, Ireland, Norway, Portugal, the UK (Johansen trace test); GDS/GDP and GDI/GDP are $CI(1,1)$ only in Belgium, Denmark, France and Iceland, with coefficient $\in (0;1)$ with coefficient > 1 in Iceland and < 1 in Belgium, Denmark, and France (Johansen ME test)	Strong sustainability in Canada, Finland, Ireland, Norway, Portugal, and the UK; weak sustainability in Belgium, Denmark, France, and Iceland
Jansen (1996)	23 OECD c. (Canada, Denmark, France, Greece, and Sweden/1951-1991; Finland, Germany, Ireland, the Netherlands, New Zealand, Norway, Switzerland, and the US/1952-1991; Australia, Austria, Italy, Japan, and the UK /1953-1991; Belgium/1954-1991; Portugal/1955-1991; Spain/1956-1991; Turkey/1961-1991; Iceland/1962-1991)	GDS/GDP is $I(0)$ in Italy, New Zealand, Norway, and GDI/GDP is $I(0)$ in Australia, Finland, New Zealand, and the US (ADF test); GDS/GDP and GDI/GDP are $CI(1,1)$ in all countries except Belgium, Canada, Norway, Portugal, Switzerland, Turkey, and the US (ECM test with DF critical values), in all countries except Belgium, Canada, Germany, Ireland, Japan, Norway, Portugal, Switzerland, the UK, and the US (EG/ADF test), in all countries except Canada, Germany, Norway, Portugal, Switzerland, Turkey, and the US (Johansen trace and ME tests) and in addition except for Italy and Japan (Johansen trace test); the coefficient is $\in (0;1)$ in Australia and 1 in other countries except Belgium, Canada, Norway, Portugal, Switzerland, Turkey, and the US	Strong sustainability in Austria, Denmark, Finland, France, Greece, Iceland, the Netherlands, New Zealand, Spain, and Sweden, weak sustainability in Australia

Table 5.11: Overview of studies on cointegration between savings and investment

Studies	Sample	Test Results	Sustainability?
Taylor (1996)	12 OECD c. (Argentina, Australia, Canada, Denmark, France, Germany, Italy, Japan, Norway, Sweden, the UK, and the US)/1850-1992	GDI/GNI and GDS/GNI are $I(1)$ (DF test) and $CI(1,1)$ with coefficient $\in (0,1)$ in Argentina (1914-1945), Australia (1946-1971), Denmark (1946-1971), France (1880-1913), Germany (1914-1945), Italy (1914-1945), Japan (1980-1913, 1972-1992), the UK (1880-1913), the US (1914-1945), the long-run parameter is close to 1 in Argentina (1946-1992), Australia (1914-1945, 1972-1992), Canada (1914-1971), Denmark (1880-1945), France (1946-1992), Germany (1880-1913, 1946-1971), Italy (1946-1992), Japan (1946-1971), Norway (1914-1971), Sweden (1880-1945), the UK (1914-1945, 1972-1992), the US (1946-1971) (ECM test)	Weak sustainability in Argentina (1914-1945), Australia (1946-1971), Denmark (1946-1971), France (1880-1913), Germany (1914-1945), Italy (1914-1945), Japan (1980-1913, 1972-1992), the UK (1880-1913), and the US (1914-1945), possibly strong sustainability in Argentina (1946-1992), Australia (1914-1945, 1972-1992), Canada (1914-1971), Denmark (1880-1945), France (1946-1992), Germany (1880-1913, 1946-1971), Italy (1946-1992), Japan (1946-1971), Norway (1914-1971), Sweden (1880-1945), the UK (1914-1945, 1972-1992), and the US (1946-1971)

Table 5.11: Overview of studies on cointegration between savings and investment

Studies	Sample	Test Results	Sustainability?
Coakley and Kulasi (1997)	11 OECD c. (Australia/1900-1988, Canada/1927-1988, France/1950-1988, Germany/1950-1988, India/1900-1988, Japan/1885-1988, Korea/1953-1989, the Netherlands/1950-1988, Taiwan/1951-1989, the UK/1870-1989, and the US/1870-1989)	GDS/GDP is $I(0)$ in the US, GDI/GDP is $I(0)$ in Australia, the Netherlands, the US, H_0 of unit root cannot be rejected for the rest of the sample (ADF test); GDS/GDP and GDI/GDP are $CI(1,1)$ in Australia, France, India, Japan, the Netherlands (EG/ADF test), in Australia, Canada, France, India, Japan, the Netherlands, the UK (ECM test), in France, India, the Netherlands (Johansen ME and trace tests); the coefficient is not reported	Strong sustainability in the US, weak sustainability in Australia, Canada, France, India, Japan, the Netherlands, and the UK

Table 5.11: Overview of studies on cointegration between savings and investment

Studies	Sample	Test Results	Sustainability?
Mamingi (1997)	58 developing c. (Algeria, Benin, Brazil, Burkina Faso, Burundi, Cameroon, Central African Republic, Chile, Colombia, Congo, Côte d'Ivoire, Costa Rica, Dominican Republic, Ecuador, Egypt, El Salvador, Fiji, Gabon, Gambia, Ghana, Guatemala, Haiti, Honduras, India, Israel, Jamaica, Kenya Korea Republic, Lesotho, Madagascar, Malawi, Malaysia, Mali, Malta, Mauritania, Mauritius, Mexico, Morocco, Nepal, Niger, Nigeria, Pakistan, Paraguay, Peru, the Philippines, Rwanda, Senegal, Sierra Leone, Sri Lanka, Thailand, Togo, Trinidad & Tobago, Tunisia, Turkey, Uganda, Venezuela, Zambia, Zimbabwe)/1970-1990	GNS/GDP and GDI/GDP are each $I(0)$ for Kenya and Benin and $I(1)$ for the remaining 56 countries; GNS/GDP and GDI/GDP are $CI(1,1)$ in all countries except for Kenya and Benin (ECM test); coefficient is close to 1 in Jamaica, Malawi, Nepal, Niger, Tunisia, Burundi, Guatemala, $\in (0;1)$ in Algeria, Cameroon, Congo, Ecuador, Gabon, Haiti, Mauritania, Paraguay, Senegal, Togo, Brazil, Central African Republic, Egypt, Honduras, Korea, Mauritius, Trinidad, Venezuela, Burkina, Chile, Côte d'Ivoire, El Salvador, Ghana, India, Mexico, Nigeria, Sri Lanka, Zambia, Dominican Republic, Israel, Madagaskar, Malta, Pakistan, Rwanda, Thailand, Turkey, Zimbabwe (FMOLS estimator)	Strong sustainability in Benin, Kenia, Jamaica, Malawi, Nepal, Niger, Tunisia, Burundi, Guatemala, weak sustainability in the remaining countries

Table 5.11: Overview of studies on cointegration between savings and investment

Studies	Sample	Test Results	Sustainability?
Moreno (1997)	The US and Japan/1965.Q1-1991.Q4	NS and NI are each $I(1)$ (ADF, PP, KPSS tests) NS^r and NI^r are each $I(0)$ (ADF and PP tests) and each $I(1)$ (KPSS test) in the US and Japan; NS and NI, and NS^r and NI^r are $CI(1,1)$ in the US only during 1965.Q1-1980.Q4, resp.; NS(s) and NI(s) are $CI(1,1)$ in Japan during 1965.Q1-1991.Q4 only at the 20% level; NS/I^r(s) and NI/G^r(s) are $CI(1,1)$ in Japan during 1965.Q1-1991.Q4 at the 5% level (Johansen ME and trace tests); the coefficient is $\in (0;1)$ in the US (1965.Q1-1980.Q) and close to 1 for nominal values and larger than 1 for real values in Japan (1965.Q1-1991.Q4)	Weak sustainability of CAB and CAB^r in the US, strong sustainability of CAB in Japan, weak sustainability of CAB^r in Japan
Bajo-Rubio (1998)	Spain/1960-1994	GNS/GDP and GDI/GDP are each $I(1)$ (ADF test) and $CI(1,1)$ with a coefficient close to 1 (ECM test, EG/ADF test, FMOLS estimator)	Strong sustainability
Hussein (1998)	23 OECD c. (Australia, Austria, Belgium, Canada, Denmark, Finland, France, Germany, Greece, Iceland, Ireland, Italy, Japan, Luxembourg, the Netherlands, New Zealand, Norway, Portugal, Spain, Sweden, Switzerland, the UK, and the US)/1960-1993	NS/GDP and GDI/GDP are each $I(1)$ and $CI(1,1)$ in all countries in the sample (EG/ADF and EG/PP tests); the coefficient is 1 in Austria, France, Iceland, Spain, the UK and is $\in (0;1)$ in Belgium, Canada, Denmark, Finland, Iceland, Luxembourg, the Netherlands, Norway, Sweden, Switzerland, and the US (DOLS estimator, Wald test)	Strong sustainability in Austria, France, Iceland, Spain, and the UK, weak sustainability in the remaining countries

Table 5.11: Overview of studies on cointegration between savings and investment

Studies	Sample	Test Results	Sustainability?
Sinha and Sinha (1998)	10 Latin American c. (Colombia/1957-1994, Dominican Republic, Ecuador, Honduras and Venezuela/1950-1995, El Salvador/1951-1995, Guatemala, Mexico and Panama/1950-1994, and Jamaica/1950-1993)	GDS/GDP and GFCF/GDP are each $I(0)$ in Dominican Republic, H_0 of unit root cannot be rejected for the rest of the sample (ADF and PP tests); GDS/GDP and GFCF/GDP are $CI(1,1)$ in Ecuador, Honduras, Jamaica and Panama (Johansen ME and trace tests); coefficient is close to 1 in Ecuador, Jamaica and $\in (0;1)$ in Honduras and Panama (normalized cointegrating vector)	Strong sustainability in Dominican Republic, Ecuador, Jamaica, weak sustainability in Honduras and Panama
Sarno and Taylor (1998)	The UK/1955.Q1-1994.Q4	H_0 of unit root in GS/PDI and GFCF/GDP cannot be rejected (ADF test); GS/PDI and GFCF/GDP are $CI(1,1)$ (EG/ADF); coefficient is $\in (0;1)$ during 1955.Q1-1979.Q4 and < 0 during 1980.Q1-1994.Q4 (OLS estimators)	Weak sustainability
Taylor (1998)	Argentina/1880-1992	GNS/GDP and GNI/GDP are $CI(1,1)$ in Argentina (1880-1992) with coefficient $\in (0,1)$ during 1914-1945, 1972-1992 and possibly close to 1 for the rest of the sample period (ECM test)	Weak sustainability during 1914-1945 and 1972-1992, possibly strong sustainability during 1880-1813 and 1946-1971
Hoffmann (1999)	The UK/1850-1992 and the US/1874-1992	NS and NI are $CI(1,1)$ with unity coefficient in both countries for the whole sample, allowing for structural breaks (Johansen trace and ME tests)	Strong sustainability
Anoruo (2001)	ASEAN-5 (Indonesia, Malaysia, the Philippines, Singapore, Thailand)/1960-1996	GDS/GDP and GDI/GDP are $I(1)$ (ADF test) and $CI(1,1)$ (Johansen ME and trace tests) in all countries; no information on the coefficient	At least weak sustainability

Table 5.11: Overview of studies on cointegration between savings and investment

Studies	Sample	Test Results	Sustainability?
Schmidt (2001)	Canada/1961.Q2-1999.Q1, France/1970.Q2-1998.Q3, Japan/1959.Q2-1998.Q4, UK/1970.Q2-1999.Q1, and the US/1959.Q2-1991.Q1	GPS and GPDI are $CI(1,1)$ with coefficient $\in (0;1)$ in Japan and close to 1 in the rest of the sample (Johansen ME and trace tests)	Strong sustainability in Canada, France, the UK, the US, weak sustainability in Japan
Tsoukis and Alyousha (2001)	7 OECD c. (Australia/1959.Q3-1997.Q2, Canada/1957.Q4-1998.Q1, Germany/1978.Q2-1994.Q2, Japan/1957.Q4-1997.Q4, Netherlands/197.Q1-1998.Q1, the UK/1957.Q4-1998.Q1, the US/1957.Q4-1998.Q1)	GDS/GDP is $I(0)$ in the Netherlands; H_0 of unit root in GDS/GDP and GDI/GDP cannot be rejected for the rest of the sample (ADF test); the GDS/GDP and GDI/GDP are $CI(1,1)$ in Australia and the UK for the complete sample and during the 1980.Q1-1994.Q2 only in Germany (Johansen trace test); the coefficient is not reported	At least weak sustainability in Australia and the UK for the whole sample and in Germany during 1980.Q1-1994.Q2
De Vita and Abbott (2002)	The US/1946.Q1-2001.Q2	GNS/GDP and GDI/GDP are each $I(0)$ during 1946.Q1-1971.Q2 and for the whole sample and each $I(1)$ during 1971.Q3-1987.Q3 (ADF and PP tests); GNS/GDP is $I(1)$ (PP test) and $I(0)$ (ADF test) during 1971.Q3-2001.Q2; GDI/GDP is $I(1)$ (ADF and PP tests) during 1971.Q3-2001.Q2; GNS/GDP and GDI/GDP are $CI(1,1)$ during 1971.Q3 1987.Q3 and 1971.Q3-2001.Q2 with coefficients being both $\in (0;1)$ (ARDL bounds test)	Strong sustainability during 1946.Q1-1971.Q2; weak sustainability during 1971.Q3-2001.Q2

Table 5.11. Overview of studies on cointegration between savings and investment

Studies	Sample	Test Results	Sustainability?
Sinha (2002)	Hong Kong/1961-1999, India/1960-1998, Japan/1955-1998, Malaysia/1955-1999, Myanmar/1961-1998, Pakistan/1960-1999, the Philippines/1948-1999, Singapore/1957-1999, South Korea/1953-1998, Sri Lanka/1950-1999), and Thailand/1950-1999	GDS/GDP and GFCF/GDP are each $I(1)$ in Japan, India, Pakistan, the Philippines, Singapore, South Korea, and Thailand (ADF and PP tests); GDS/GDP and GFCF/GDP $CI(1,1)$ with coefficient close to 1 in Thailand and > 1 in Japan (Johansen ME and trace tests without structural breaks); GDS/GDP and GFCF/GDP $CI(1,1)$ with unity coefficient in Thailand and coefficient $\in (0;1)$ in Myanmar (Johansen ME and trace tests with structural breaks)	Strong sustainability in Thailand, weak sustainability in the rest of the sample
Özmen and Parmaksiz (2003)	The UK/1948-1998	GDS/GNP and GDI/GNP are $I(1)$ (ADF and KPSS tests) and $CI(1,1)$ with coefficient $\in (0;1)$ (Johansen ME and trace tests; EG/ADF test); the coefficient is lower after 1979 (FMOLS estimators; Johansen ME and trace tests)	Weak sustainability
Pelagidis and Mastroyiannis (2003)	Greece/1960-1997	GNS/GDP and GDI/GDP are each $I(1)$ (ADF test) and $CI(1,1)$ with long-run coefficient $\in (0,1)$ (ECM test)	Weak sustainability

Table 5.11: Overview of studies on cointegration between savings and investment

Studies	Sample	Test Results	Sustainability?
Corbin (2004)	12 industrialized c. (Argentina, Australia, Canada, Denmark, France, Germany, Italy, Japan, Norway, Sweden, the UK, and the US)/1880-2001 (divided into 4 subperiods)	GDS/GDP and GDI/GDP are $CI(1,1)$ with a long-run coefficient close to unity in Argentina (1891-1913), in Australia (1922-2001), in Canada (1891-1945), in Denmark (1876-1945), in France (1951-1971), in Germany (1870-1971), in Italy (1865-1913 and 1947-2001), in Japan (1918-1971), in Norway (1915-1970), in Sweden (1875-1971), in the UK (1852-2001), in the US (1918-1971), with coefficient $\in (0;1)$ in Argentina (1919-1971), in Denmark (1950-1971), in France (1883-1913), in Germany (1974-2001), on Italy (1918-1945), in Norway (1977-2001), in the US (1881-1913) (ARDL bounds test, Δ-method with 95% asymptotic confidence bands from the estimated standard errors)	Strong sustainability in Argentina (1891-1913), Australia (1922-2001), Canada (1891-1945), Denmark (1876-1945), France (1951-1971), Germany (1870-1973), Italy (1865-1913 and 1947-2001), Japan (1918-1971), Norway (1915-1970), Sweden (1875-1971), the UK (1852-2001), the US (1918-1971); weak sustainability in Argentina (1919-1971), Denmark (1950-1971), France (1883-1913), Germany (1974-2001), Italy (1918-1945), Norway (1977-2001), the US (1881-1913)

Table 5.11: Overview of studies on cointegration between savings and investment

Studies	Sample	Test Results	Sustainability?
Levy (2004)	The US/1947.Q1-1987.Q3 (quarterly and annual)	GDI is $I(1)$ during 1947.Q1-1987.Q3, H_0 of unit root cannot be rejected for GDS (neither in levels nor in differences) 1947.Q1-1987.Q3, GNS/GDP and GDI/GDP are each $I(0)$ during 1947.Q1-1987.Q3 (ADF test for annual data); GNS and GDI are each $I(1)$ for the whole period and all subperiods, GNS/GDP and GDI/GDP are each $I(0)$ only during 1947.Q1-1987.Q3 and 1947.Q1-1971.Q2 (ADF test for quarterly data); GNS and GDI are $CI(1,1)$ with unity coefficient during 1947.Q1-1987.Q3 and 1947.Q1-1971.Q2; GNS/GDP and GDI/GDP are $CI(1,1)$ with unity coefficient during 1971.Q3-1987.Q3 and 1980.Q1-1987.Q3; the H_0 of no cointegration cannot be rejected for annual data (Johansen ME and trace tests)	Strong sustainability of CAB and of CAB/GDP
Matsubayashi (2005)	The US/1975.Q1-1998.Q2	PS/GDP, PI/GDP; FGR/GDP, FGE/GDP are each $I(1)$ (ADF test); PS/GDP and PI/GDP are $CI(1,1)$; FGR/GDP, FGE/GDP are $CI(1,1)$; NIIP/GDP and (PI-PS+FGR-FGE)/GDP are $CI(1,1)$ (ADF tests; Johansen ME and trace tests); the cointegrating vector is not reported	At least weak sustainability

Table 5.11: Overview of studies on cointegration between savings and investment

Studies	Sample	Test Results	Sustainability?
Narayan (2005)	China/1952-1998	H_0 of unit root in S and I cannot be rejected (ADF, PP, LP and ZA tests); S and I are $CI(1)$ (ARDL bounds and GH tests); coefficient is close to 1 in 1952-1994 and > 1 in 1952-1998 (ARDL bounds test, FMOLS and DOLS estimators, ECM test)	Strong sustainability during 1952-1994
Papapetrou (2006)	Greece/1980.Q1-2003.Q4	TS/GDP(s) and TGCI/GDP(s) are each $I(1)$ (ADF, PP, KPSS, and ZA tests) and are $CI(1)$ with coefficient in $(0;1)$ (FMOLS estimator); coefficient is $\in (0;1)$ (recursive OLS, rolling OLS, Markov switching regime regression)	Weak sustainability
Ang (2007)	Malaysia/1965-2003	GDS/GDP and GDI/GDP are either $I(0)$ or $I(1)$ (ADF, PP, and KPSS tests); GDS/GDP and GDI/GDP are $CI(1)$ with coefficient $\in (0;1)$ (ARDL bounds test)	Weak sustainability
Özmen (2007)	10 MENA c. (Algeria, Egypt, Iran, Israel, Jordan, Morocco, Saudi Arabia, Syria, Tunisia, Turkey)/1976-2001	GNS/GDP and GFCF/GDP are $CI(1)$ in all countries in the sample; coefficient is close to 1 in Saudi Arabia, is $\in (0;1)$ in Egypt, Israel, Jordan, Syria and is either < 0 or > 1 in the remaining countries (ARDL bounds test)	Strong sustainability in Saudi Arabia, weak sustainability in the rest of the sample

Table 5.11: Overview of studies on cointegration between savings and investment

Studies	Sample	Test Results	Sustainability?
Kejriwal (2008)	21 OECD c. (Australia/1959.Q3-2005.Q4, Austria/1964.Q1-1999.Q1, Canada, the UK and the US/1957.Q1-2006.Q1, Finland, France, Italy, Spain/1970.Q1-1998.Q4, Germany/1960.Q1-1998.Q4, the Netherlands/1977.Q1-1999.Q1, Norway/1961.Q1-2006.Q1, Turkey/1987.Q1-2005.Q4, Denmark/1977.Q1-2005.Q4, Mexico/1981.Q1-2005.Q4, Portugal/1977.Q1-1998.Q4, Japan/1957.Q1-2005.Q4, Sweden/1980.Q1-2006.Q1, Switzerland/1970.Q1-2005.Q4, Belgium/1980.Q1-1998.Q4, Korea/1960.Q1-2006.Q3)	BS is $I(0)$ in Canada, Finland, Norway, Switzerland, GFCF is $I(0)$ in Denmark, Portugal, Sweden, Turkey (NP tests); BS and GFCF are $CI(1)$ in Australia, Belgium, Denmark, Japan, Mexico (EG/ADF and EG/PP tests), additionally in Finland, the Netherlands, Norway, Turkey, Switzerland, Korea (GH test); BS and GFCF are not $CI(1)$ in Australia, Finland, Italy, Portugal (AKK test); coefficient is $\in (0;1)$ in Australia, Belgium (1983.Q2-1993.Q2), Denmark (1987.Q4-2005.Q4), Japan, the Netherlands (1981.Q1-1999.Q1), Turkey, Korea (1960.Q1-2006.Q3), 1981.Q2 and 1990.Q1-2006.Q3), with a coefficient close to unity in Belgium (1980.Q1-1983.Q2), the Netherlands (1977.Q1-1981.Q1), Norway (1961.Q1-1973.Q4), Switzerland (1970.Q1-1992.Q3), Korea (1981.Q2-1990.Q1), for Mexico not reported,	Strong sustainability in Belgium (1980.Q1-1983.Q2), the Netherlands (1977.Q1-1981.Q1), Norway (1961.Q1-1973.Q4), Switzerland (1970.Q1-1992.Q3), Korea (1981.Q2-1990.Q1), weak sustainability in Australia, Belgium (1983.Q2-1998.Q4), Denmark , Finland, Italy, Japan, Korea (1990.Q2-2006.Q3), Mexico, the Netherlands (1981.Q2-1999.Q1), Norway (1974.Q1-2006.Q1), Portugal, Turkey, Switzerland (1992.Q4-2005.Q4)

Table 5.11: Overview of studies on cointegration between savings and investment

Studies	Sample	Test Results	Sustainability?
Singh (2008)	India/1950-2002	GDS/GDP and GDI/GDP are either $I(0)$ or $I(1)$ (ADF, PP, and KPSS tests); H_0 of no cointegration cannot be rejected (EG/ADF test); H_0 of cointegration cannot be rejected (EG/KPSS test); GDS/GDP and GDI/GDP are $CI(1)$ (EG/PP test; DOLS, FMOLS, NLLS esimators); H_0 of unity coefficient cannot be rejected (DOLS, FMOLS, NLLS estimators); GDS/GDP and GDI/GDP are $CI(1)$ with coefficient close to 1 (ARDL bounds test; Johansen ME and trace tests)	Strong sustainability
Onafowara et al. (2011)	8 EU c. (Belgium, Denmark, France, Germany, Italy, Luxembourg, the Netherlands, and the UK)/1970-2008	GDS/GDP and GDI /GDP are either $I(0)$ and $I(1)$ (ZA test); GDS/GDP and GDI /GDP are $CI(1,1)$ in Belgium, Denmark; H_0 of no cointegration cannot be rejected in France and Italy, inconclusive results for the rest of the sample (ARDL bounds test); coefficient is not reported	At least weak sustainability in Belgium, Denmark; weak sustainability in the rest of the sample
Tang and Lean (2011)	Malaysia/1960-2007	GDS/GDP and GDI/GDP are either $I(0)$ or $I(1)$ (ADF and PP tests; ZA and LP tests with structural breaks); H_0 of no cointegration cannot be rejected (ARDL bounds test without a rolling window); GDS/GDP and GDI/GDP are $CI(1,1)$ during 1960-1997 (rolling windows ARDL bounds test); coefficient is not reported	At least weak sustainability during 1960-1997

Table 5.11: Overview of studies on cointegration between savings and investment

Studies	Sample	Test Results	Sustainability?

Abbreviations:

- Data:
  ASEAN: Association of Southeast Asian Nations, BS: Basic Saving, c.: countries,EU: European Union, FGE: Federal Government Expenditures minus Interest Income, FGR: Federal Government Revenues, GFCF: Gross Fixed Capital Formation, GDI: Gross Domestic Investment, GDI: Gross Domestic Investment, GDS: Gross Domestic Saving, GDP: Gross Domestic Product, GNP: Gross National Product, GNS: Gross National Saving, GPDI: Gross Private Domestic Investment, I: Investment, MENA: Middle East and North Africa, NetI: Net Investment, NetS: Net Saving, NI: National Investment, NS: National Saving, OECD: Organisation for Economic Co-operation and Development, PDI: Personal Disposable Income, PI: Private Equipment Investment+ Private Residential Investment + Private Inventory Investment, PS: Private Saving minus Interest Income, S: Saving, s: seasonal adjustment, TGCI: Total Gross Capital Investment, TI: Total Investment, TS: Total Savings, the UK: United Kindgdom, the US: United States. The superscript ^{r} denotes a real variable, the absence of the superscript indicates that a variable is measured in nominal terms.
- Tests and models:
  ADF: Augmented Dickey-Fuller test (Said and Dickey, 1984), AKK test: Arai-Kurozumi-Kejriwal test (Arai and Kurozumi, 2007; Kejriwal, 2008), ARDL bounds test: Autoregressive Distributed Lag bounds test (Pesaran et al., 2001), DOLS estimator: Dynamic Ordinary Least Squares (Saikkonen, 1991; Stock and Watson, 1993), ECM test: Error Correction Model test (Engle and Granger, 1987; Kremers et al., 1992), EG test: Engle-Granger procedure (Engle and Granger, 1987), FMOLS estimator: Fully Modified Ordinary Least Squares estimator (Phillips and Hansen, 1990), GH test: Gregory-Hansen test (Gregory and Hansen, 1996), H_0: the null hypothesis, Johansen ME and trace tests: Johansen Maximum Eigenvalue and trace tests (Johansen, 1988; Johansen and Juselius, 1990), KPSS test: Kwiatkowski-Phillips-Schmidt-Shin test (Kwiatkowski et al., 1992), LP test: Lumsdaine-Papell test (Lumsdaine and Papell, 1997), NNLS estimator: Nonlinear Least Squares estimator (Phillips and Loretan, 1991), OLS estimator: Ordinary Least Squares estimator, PP test: Phillips-Perron test (Phillips and Perron, 1988), NP test: Ng-Perron test (Ng and Perron, 2001) , ZA test: Zivot-Andrews test (Zivot and Andrews, 2002). “Coefficient” refers to the coefficient β in the regression $y_{1t} = \beta y_{2t} + e_t$ where y_{1t} denotes savings, y_{2t} denotes investment, and e_t is the error term.

Table 5.12: Overview of studies on cointegration between exports and imports inclusive of primary and secondary income

Studies	Sample	Test Results	Sustainability?
Husted (1992)	The US/1967.Q1-1989.Q4	X and MM, and X/GNP and MM/GNP, also in real terms, are each $I(1)$ (ADF and PP tests) and $CI(1,1)$ with cointegrating vector $(1,-1)$ only when a break is included (EG/ADF test, EG/Perron test)	Strong sustainability

Table 5.12: Overview of studies on cointegration between exports and imports inclusive of primary and secondary income

Studies	Sample	Test Results	Sustainability?
Wu et al. (1996)	Canada and the US/1973.Q4-1994.Q4	X^r/GNP^r and MMT^r/GNP^r are each $I(1)$ (ADF and normalized bias tests); no evidence of cointegration in both countries (Johansen ME and trace tests, ZA test) and in the US (GH test); cointegration with coefficient $\in (0;1)$ in Canada (GH test, DOLS estimator);	Weak sustainability
Sawada (1994)	13 HICs (Argentina, Brazil, Chile, Colombia, Ecuador, Indonesia, Korea, Malaysia, Mexico, Peru, the Philippines, Thailand, and Venezuela)/ 1955-1990	H_0 of unit root cannot be rejected in X and MMTFX (ADF test); X and MMTFX are $CI(1,1)$ with unity coefficient in Indonesia, Malaysia, South Korea, Thailand (EG/ADF test)	Strong sustainability in Indonesia, Malaysia, South Korea, Thailand
Bahmani-Oskooee and Rhee (1997)	Korea/1963-1991 (quarterly data)	X and M, both in USD and in KRW, in nominal and real terms, resp., are each $I(1)$ (ADF test) and are $CI(1,1)$ resp. (Johansen ME and trace tests), coefficient is $\in (0;1)$ only for X and M in KRW and are near 0 or >1 for other X and M measures	Weak sustainability
Bodman (1997)	Australia/1965.Q1-1993.Q3	Xg and Mg, and X and MM are each $I(1)$ (ADF test) and $CI(1,1)$ (Johansen ME and ECM tests); coefficient is not reported	Weak sustainability
Fountas and Wu (1999)	The US/1967.Q1-1994.Q4	X and MMT, X/GNP and MMT/GNP, both nominal and real, are each $I(1)$ (PP test); no evidence for cointegration (EG/ADF, ZA and GH tests)	Weak sustainability

Table 5.12: Overview of studies on cointegration between exports and imports inclusive of primary and secondary income

Studies	Sample	Test Results	Sustainability?
Apergis et al. (2000)	Greece/1960-1994	X^r/GDP^r and MMT^r/GDP^r are each $I(1)$ (DF test); no evidence of cointegration (Johansen ME and trace tests); X^r/GDP^r and MMT^r/GDP^r are $CI(1,1)$ (GH test) with unity coefficient (DOLS estimator)	Strong sustainability
Wu et al. (2001)	G7 (Canada, France, Germany, Italy, Japan, the UK, and the US)/1973.Q2-1998.Q4	X/GDP and MMT/GDP are each $I(1)$, except MMT/GDP in the UK which are $I(0)$; no evidence of cointegration (EG/ADF test, Johansen ME and trace tests); X/GDP and MMT/GDP are jointly $CI(1,1)$ in the sample, excl. the UK (KC panel test); coefficient is close to 1 (panel DOLS and FMOLS estimators) and is $\in (0;1)$ (panel OLS estimator)	At least weak sustainability in all countries; joint and strong sustainability for G7 countries, excluding the UK

Table 5.12: Overview of studies on cointegration between exports and imports inclusive of primary and secondary income

Studies	Sample	Test Results	Sustainability?
Arize (2002)	50 c. (Bolivia, Canada, Chile, Costa Rica, Dominican Rep., Ecuador, El Salvador, Guatemala, Hong Kong, Kenya, Malaysia, Morocco, Tunisia, the US/1973.Q2-1998.Q1; Cyprus, India, Israel, Japan, Korea, Myanmar, the Netherlands, Pakistan, Singapore, Sri Lanka/1973.Q2-1997.Q4; Austria, Fiji, Indonesia, Jordan, Kuwait, Portugal, South Africa, Thailand, Venezuela/1973.Q2-1997.Q3; Australia, Mexico/1973.Q2-1997.Q2; Burundi, Colombia, Egypt, Haiti, Hungary, Mauritius, New Zealand, Sweden/1973.Q2-1997.Q1; Zambia/1973.Q2-1996.Q3; Greece/1973.Q2-1994.Q1; Iran/1973.Q2-1985.Q4; Paraguay/1973.Q2-1996.Q2; Ethiopia/1973.Q2-1996.Q1; Nigeria/1973.Q2-1995.Q1; Papua New Guinea/1973.Q2-1994.Q1)	X/GDP and M/GDP are each $I(1)$ in all countries (ADF and Johansen (1995) tests) and are $CI(1,1)$ in all countries except Ethiopia, Burundi, Cyprus, Dominican Republic, Guatemala, Haiti, Hong Kong, Hungary, Jordan, Morocco, the Netherlands, Papua New Guinea, Paraguay, Portugal, Sri Lanka (Johansen ME and trace tests); coefficient is close to 1 only in Canada, Japan, Iran, Kenya, Mauritius, Tunisia, Singapore, Pakistan (normalized vector, score test), in New Zealand, Mexico, South Africa, Tunisia (DOLS and FMOLS estimators), in South Africa and Tunisia (FMOLS), in Mauritius (DOLS)	Strong sustainability in New Zealand, Mexico, South Africa, Tunisia; at least weak sustainability in Canada, Chile, Egypt, Indonesia, Mauritius; weak sustainability in the remaining countries

Table 5.12: Overview of studies on cointegration between exports and imports inclusive of primary and secondary income

Studies	Sample	Test Results	Sustainability?
Baharumshah et al. (2003)	ASEAN-4 (Indonesia, Malaysia, the Philippines, Thailand)/1961-1999	X^r and MMT^r are each $I(1)$ (ADF, PP, and KPSS tests) and are $CI(1,1)$ only in Thailand and Indonesia for the whole sample period and only in Malaysia during 1961-1997 (Johansen ME and trace tests); X^r and MMT^r are $CI(1,1)$ in Indonesia, the Philippines and Thailand for the whole sample period and only in Malaysia during 1961-1997 (GH test); coefficient is close to 1 in Malaysia and is $\in (0;1)$ in Indonesia, the Philippines, and Thailand (DOLS estimator)	Strong sustainability in Malaysia (1961-1997); weak sustainability in the remaining countries
Lau and Baharumshah (2003)	Malaysia/1961-2001	X^r/GDP^r and MMT^r/GDP^r are each $I(1)$ (ADF, PP, and KPSS tests) and are $CI(1,1)$ only during 1961-1997 (Johansen ME and trace tests, GH test); coefficient is 1 (DOLS estimator)	Strong sustainability during 1961-1997, weak sustainabilty during 1997-2001
Irandoust and Ericsson (2004)	France, Italy, the UK, and the US/1971.Q1-1997.Q4, Germany/1971.Q1-1994.Q4, Sweden/1971.Q1-1994.Q2	$\ln X^r$(s) and $\ln M^r$(s) are each $I(1)$ in Germany, Sweden, the UK, the US, are each $I(0)$ in France, $\ln X^r$(s) is $I(1)$ and $\ln M^r$(s) is $I(0)$ in Italy (ADF test); $\ln X^r$(s) and $\ln M^r$(s) are $CI(1,1)$ in Germany, Sweden, and the US with coefficient close to 1 (Johansen ME and trace tests)	Strong sustainability in France, Germany, Sweden, and the US

Table 5.12: Overview of studies on cointegration between exports and imports inclusive of primary and secondary income

Studies	Sample	Test Results	Sustainability?
Narayan and Narayan (2005)	22 LDCs (Bangladesh, Burkina, Burundi, Chad, CAR, Gambia, Haiti, Lesotho, Madagascar, Malawi, Mauritania, Niger, Rwanda, Togo, Uganda, Zambia/1960-2000, Guinea-Bissau, Sao Tome, Sierra Leone/1970-2000, Mali/1967-2000, Nepal/1965-2000, Senegal/1968-2000)	X/GDP and M/GDP are $CI(1,1)$ in Burundi, Chad, Guinea-Bissau, Madagascar, Uganda and Zambia (ECM test), coefficient is significant (being $\in (0;1)$) only in Chad, Guinea-Bissau, Madagascar, Uganda (ARDL, DOLS, FMOLS, OLS estimators)	Weak sustainability in Chad, Guinea-Bissau, Madagascar, Uganda and possibly in Burundi and Zambia
Naqvi and Morimune (2005)	Pakistan/1972-2003	X and M, both in PKR and in USD, nominal and real, resp., are each $I(1)$ (ADF test) and are $CI(1,1)$, resp. (Johansen ME and trace tests); coefficient is close to 1 (normalized vector, LR test)	Strong sustainability
Herzer and Nowak-Lehmann (2006)	Chile/1975-2004	$\ln X^r$ and $\ln M^r$ are $I(1)$ (Perron (1997) test with structural breaks), H_0 of no cointegration in $\ln X^r$ and $\ln M^r$ cannot be rejected (EG/ADF and EG/DW tests), $\ln X^r$ and $\ln M^r$ are $CI(1,1)$ (GH test); coefficient is not statistically different from 1 (DOLS and F-test)	Strong sustainability
Holmes (2006)	11 OECD c. (Australia, Belgium, Canada, France, Germany, Italy, Japan, Norway, Spain, the UK, the US)/1980.Q1-2002.Q4	X/GDP and MM/GDP, and X^r/GDP^r and MM^r/GDP^r are jointly $CI(1,1)$, resp. (Pedroni group test); coefficient is close to 1 for X^r/GDP^r and MM^r/GDP^r and is $\in (0;1)$ for X/GDP and MM/GDP (FMOLS panel estimator)	Strong (joint) sustainability of CAB^r/GDP^r and weak (joint) sustianability of CAB/GDP

Table 5.12. Overview of studies on cointegration between exports and imports inclusive of primary and secondary income

Studies	Sample	Test Results	Sustainability?
Önel and Utkulu (2006)	Turkey/1970-2002	X^r and $MMTFX^r$ are each $I(1)$ (ADF and PP tests) and are $CI(1,1)$ (EG/ADF test, GH test); coefficient is in $(0;1)$ (FMOLS and DOLS estimators)	Weak sustainability
Tang (2006)	Japan/1975.M1-2004.M11	H_0 of unit root in TB^r (s) and X^r/M^r (s) cannot be rejected (LLS test)	No evidence of sustainability
Holmes et al. (2007)	India/1950-2003	X/GDP and MM/GDP are each $I(1)$ (ADF, PP, Breitung and LLS tests) and are $CI(1,1)$ (Johansen trace, SL and Breitung tests); coefficient is close to unity (Wald test); X/GDP and MM/GDP are each $CI(1,1)$ after 2001 (Johansen trace test with expanding window), after 1995 (SL test with expanding window), after 1999 (Breitung test with expanding window); in 1997, 2000 and 2003 (Johansen trace test with rolling window), in 1995 and after 1999 (SL test with rolling window); no evidence of cointegration (Breitung test with rolling window)	Strong sustainability for the late 1990s, weak sustainability for the rest of the sample
Hamori (2009)	G7 c. (Canada, France, Germany, Italy, Japan, the UK, the US)/1960-2005	X and M are each jointly $I(1)$ (IPS, MW, and Choi (2001) panel unit root tests), H_0 of no joint panel cointegration cannot be rejected (IPS, MW, and Choi (2001) panel cointegration tests)	Weak sustainability for the panel of G7 countries

Table 5.12: Overview of studies on cointegration between exports and imports inclusive of primary and secondary income

Studies	Sample	Test Results	Sustainability?
Holmes and Panagiotidis (2009)	US/1960.Q4-2007.Q2	H_0 of unit root in X/NO, M/NO, and CAB/NO cannot be rejected (DFGLS, SL, and Breitung tests), H_0 of no unit root in X/NO, M/NO, and and CAB/NO cannot be rejected (KPSS test), X/NO and M/NO are $CI(1,1)$ (Johansen ML and trace tests), H_0 of no cointegration in X/NO and M/NO cannot be rejected (Breitung test), X/NO and M/NO are $CI(1,1)$ from the mid 1970s to the mid 1980s and from the late 1990s to 2003 (recursive Johansen and Breitung tests), H_0 of no cointegration in X/NO and M/NO cannot be rejected for the rest of the sample (recursive Johansen and Breitung tests), the coefficient is < 1 (Hansen and Johansen (1999) test)	Weak sustainability from the mid 1970s to the mid 1980s and from the late 1990s to 2003
Polat (2011)	Turkey/2000.M1-2010.M6	X^r(s) and MMT^r(s) are each $I(1)$ (ZA test) and are $CI(1,1)$ with coefficient $\in (0;1)$ (ARDL bounds test)	Weak sustainability

Table 5.12: Overview of studies on cointegration between exports and imports inclusive of primary and secondary income

Studies	Sample	Test Results	Sustainability?
Camarero et al. (2013)	23 OECD c. (Australia, Austria, Belgium, Canada, Denmark, Finland, France, Germany, Greece, Iceland, Ireland, Italy, Japan, Malta, the Netherlands, New Zealand, Norway, Portugal, Spain, Sweden, Switzerland, the UK, and the US)/1870-2012	X/GDP and M/GDP are $CI(1,1)$ in Austria, Japan, Malta, the Netherlands, Norway, Portugal, Spain, Sweden (EG/the pseudo t-ratio ADF and EG/the normalized bias ADF) and in Australia, Switzerland, the US (EG/the normalized bias ADF), in Australia, Denmark, Greece, Ireland, New Zealand, Sweden (GH test); H_0 of cointegration between X/GDP and M/GDP is rejected in Finland, Greece, New Zealand when coefficient is unity and in Finland when the cointegrating coefficient is not constrained (Carrion-i-Silvestre and Sansoò test); coefficient is 1.58 in Australia, 1.15 in Spain, 1.17 in the US, -1.22 in Norway, coefficient is < 1 in Austria, Denmark, Greece, Ireland, Japan, Malta, the Netherlands, New Zealand, Portugal, Sweden, Switzerland (DOLS)	Weak sustainability in Austria, Denmark, Greece, Ireland, Japan, Malta, the Netherlands, New Zealand, Portugal, Sweden, Switzerland

Table 5.12: Overview of studies on cointegration between exports and imports inclusive of primary and secondary income

Studies	Sample	Test Results	Sustainability?

Abbreviations:

- Data:
  ASEAN: Association of Southeast Asian Nations, c.: countries, HIC: Highly Indebted Countries, KRW: Korean Won, M: Imports of goods and services, LCD: Least Developed Countries Mg: Imports of goods, MM: Imports of goods and services, inclusive of net interest payments on the net international investment position, MMT: Imports of goods and services, inclusive of net interest payments and unilateral transfers, MMTFX: Imports of goods and services, inclusive of net interest payments and unilateral transfers and exclusive foreign exchange reserves, NO: Net Output, OECD: Organisation for Economic Co-operation and Development, PKR: Pakistani Rupee, TB: trade balance, the UK: United Kindgdom, the US: United States, USD: the US Dollar, X: Exports of goods and services, Xg: Exports of goods. The superscript ^{r} denotes a real variable; the absence of the superscript ^{r} indicates that a variable is measured in nominal terms.

- Tests and models:
  ADF: Augmented Dickey-Fuller test (Said and Dickey, 1984), ARDL bounds test: Autoregressive Distributed Lag bounds test (Pesaran et al., 2001), Breitung test: Breitung test (Breitung, 2002; Breitung and Taylor, 2003), Carrion-i-Silvestre and Sansoò test: (Carrion-i-Silvestre and Sansó, 2006) test; Dynamic Ordinary Least Squares (Saikkonen, 1991; Stock and Watson, 1993), ECM test: Error Correction Model test (Engle and Granger, 1987; Kremers et al., 1992), EG test: Engle-Granger test (Engle and Granger, 1987), Fully Modified Ordinary Least Squares estimator (Phillips and Hansen, 1990), GH test: Gregory-Hansen test (Gregory and Hansen, 1996), Johansen ME and trace tests: Johansen Maximum Eigenvalue and trace tests (Johansen, 1988; Johansen and Juselius, 1990), H_0: the null hypothesis, KC panel test: Kao-Chiang panel test (Kao, 1999; Kao and Chiang, 1999), LLS test: Lanne-Lütkepohl-Saikkonen test (Saikkonen and Lütkepohl, 2002; Lanne et al., 2002), OLS estimator: Ordinary Least Squares estimator, PP test: Phillips-Perron test (Phillips and Perron, 1988), Perron test: Perron test (Perron, 1989), s: seasonal adjustment, ZA test: Zivot-Andrews test (Zivot and Andrews, 2002).

5.C Appendix to section 5.3

Studies	Sample	Test results	Sustainability?
Wickens and Uctum (1993)	The US/1970.Q1-1988.Q4	Existence of the negative feedback from $NIIP^r/GDP^r$ to TB^r/GDP^r, and the root condition is satisfied (ML estimation); CAB^r/GDP^r is $I(1)$ (ADF and PP tests)	Weak sustainability
Bodman (1997)	Australia/1965.Q1-1993.Q3	Existence of the negative feedback from $NIIP^r/GDP^r$ to TB/GDP (ML estimation); CAB^r/GDP^r, $NIIP^r/GDP^r$, and TB^r/GDP^r are each $I(1)$ (Johansen, ADF, and PP tests)	Strong stationarity
Durdu et al. (2010)	21 industrial c. (Australia, Austria, Belgium, Canada, Denmark, Finland, France, Germany, Greece, Ireland, Italy, Japan, the Netherlands, New Zealand, Norway, Portugal, Spain, Sweden, Switzerland, the UK, the US) and 29 emerging markets (Argentina, Brazil, Chile, China, Colombia, Costa Rica, Ecuador, Egypt, El Salvador, Hong Kong, Hungary, India, Indonesia, Israel, Jordan, Korea, Malaysia, Mexico, Morocco, Pakistan, Peru, the Philippines, Saudi Arabia, Singapore, South Africa, Thailand, Turkey, Uruguay, Venezuela)/1970-2004	Statistically significant and negative relationship between TB/GDP and NIIP/GDP for the full sample and the two subsamples (industrial and emerging countries; creditor and debtor countries) (panel ARDL test, MG and PMG estimators)	Joint sustainability (strong if interest rate is $< 7\%$)

Studies	Sample	Test results	Sustainability?
Camarero et al. (2013)	23 OECD c. (Australia, Austria, Belgium, Canada, Denmark, Finland, France, Germany, Greece, Iceland, Ireland, Italy, Japan, Malta, the Netherlands, New Zealand, Norway, Portugal, Spain, Sweden, Switzerland, the UK, and the US)/1870-2012	Multicointegration between X/GDP and M/GDP in Austria (without structural breaks), Portugal (with 0, 1, or 2 breaks), the Netherlands (with one break), and Japan, New Zealand, Spain (with two breaks) (BC ADF test); the first layer of cointegration: weak sustainability in Austria, Japan in 1982, the Netherlands after 1979, in New Zealand after 1991, Spain before 1987, strong sustainability in Spain in 1987-2004, Portugal in 1980-2012; the second layer of cointegration: negative relationship between the cumulated trade balance (i.e., the change in the NIIP) and exports in Japan in 1982-2000, the Netherlands after 1979 (DOLS estimator)	Weak sustainability in Austria, Japan before 2000, the Netherlands after 1979, in New Zealand after 1991, Spain before 1987, strong sustainability in Spain in 1987-2004, Portugal in 1980-2012

Table 5.13: Overview of studies on the responsiveness of the trade balance to the NIIP

Abbreviations

- Data:
  CAB: Current-Account Balance, c.: countries, GDP: Gross Domestic Product, M: Exports, NIIP: Net International Investment Position, TB: Trade Balance, the UK: United Kingdom, the US: United States, X: Exports. The superscript ^{r} denotes a real variable, the absence of the superscript indicates that a variable is measured in nominal terms.
- Tests and models:
  ADF: Augmented Dickey-Fuller test (Said and Dickey, 1984), BC ADF: Berenguer-Rico and Carrion-i-Silvestre (2011) Augmented Dickey-Fuller test statistics, Johansen test: Johansen test (Johansen, 1995), ML estimation: maximum likelihood estimation, MG estimator: mean group estimator (Pesaran and Smith, 1995), panel ARDL test: panel Autoregressive Distributed Lag test (Pesaran et al., 1999), PMG estimator: pooled mean group estimator (Pesaran et al., 1999), PP test: Phillips-Perron test (Phillips and Perron, 1988)

Table 5.14: VAR lag order selection criteria, trade balance and NIIP in the United States

Lag	LR	AIC	SC	HQ
0	not available	-12.93948	-12.90289	-12.92464
1	1289.225	-20.52153	-20.41173*	-20.47698*
2	6.211468	-20.51221	-20.32921	-20.43796
3	1.539522	-20.47503	-20.21884	-20.37108
4	2.604875	-20.44450	-20.11511	-20.31085
5	23.26074*	-20.54246*	-20.13987	-20.37912

Notes: * indicates the lag order selected by the criterion. VAR: vector autoregression, LR: sequential modified LR test statistic (each test at 5% level), AIC: Akaike information criterion, SC: Schwarz information criterion, HQ: Hannan-Quinn information criterion. The sample comprises seasonally adjusted data for the NIIP at market value and the trade balance in proportion to GDP over the period 1960.Q4-2001.Q1 in the United States.

Table 5.15: VAR residual serial correlation LM test, trade balance and NIIP in the United States

Lags	LM-statistics	p-value
1	2.469100	0.6502
2	8.903092	0.0636
3	13.61902	0.0086
4	8.494735	0.0750
5	1.964862	0.7422

Notes: P-values for the Lagrange Multiplier (LM) test are calculated from the χ^2-distribution with four degrees of freedom. The sample comprises seasonally adjusted data for the NIIP at market value and the trade balance in proportion to GDP over the period 1960.Q4-2001.Q1 in the United States.

Table 5.16: VAR residual normality test, trade balance and NIIP in the United States

Component	**Skewness**	χ^2	**Degrees of freedom**	**p-value**
TB/GDP(s)	-0.411922	4.864152	1	0.0274
NIIP/GDP(s)	-0.126203	0.456578	1	0.4992
Joint		5.320729	2	0.0699
Component	**Kurtosis**	χ^2	**Degrees of freedom**	**p-value**
TB/GDP(s)	5.250647	36.30212	1	0.0000
NIIP/GDP(s)	8.792327	240.4492	1	0.0000
Joint		276.7513	2	0.0000
Component		**Jarque-Bera**	**Degrees of freedom**	**p-value**

TB/GDP(s)	41.16627	2	0.0000
NIIP/GDP(s)	240.9058	2	0.0000
Joint	282.0721	4	0.0000

Notes: The orthogonalization is performed using a Cholesky split, as suggested in Lütkepohl (2007). The sample comprises seasonally adjusted data for the NIIP at market value and the trade balance in proportion to GDP over the period 1960.Q4-2001.Q1 in the United States.

6

Dynamic benchmarks of external sustainability

One approach to external sustainability is based on the idea that external imbalances are sustainable as long as they are the outcome of agents' optimal decisions (e.g., Edwards, 2007; Blanchard and Milesi-Ferretti, 2009, 2011). An example for external imbalances which are not worrisome are current account surpluses in countries in which the population ages faster than in other countries and which increase their savings in anticipation of the future dissaving once when the number of retirees increases (Blanchard and Milesi-Ferretti, 2009). Another example are current account deficits run by countries which have deeper and more advanced financial markets than other countries and which attract international investors and accumulate foreign liabilities (Mendoza et al., 2007; Caballero et al., 2008a). Thus, one approach to external sustainability envisions comparing the observed path of external imbalances with their optimal or equilibrium benchmark path which has been derived within an economic model (e.g., Milesi-Ferretti and Razin, 1996a).

Two models have been mainly used as a "dynamic benchmark" (Hudson and Stennett, 2003, p. 12): the intertemporal model of the current account and the stock equilibrium or portfolio model of the current account. The traditional intertemporal model of the current account which assumes a small open representative agent economy with perfect capital mobility and bonds as the only asset was already described in section 3.1 of chapter 3. Under additional assumptions on the representative agent's utility function, the optimal current account path implied by this model allows the agents to fully smooth their consumption. When the economy's current account is on its consumption-smoothing path, the intertemporal budget constraint is satisfied as well, however not vice versa. The portfolio- or stock-equilibrium approach to the current account explicitly takes into account the determinants of investors' portfolio decisions. In this context, the optimal current account path is the one which allows domestic and foreign investors to attain the desired portfolio allocation of assets across countries.

This chapter is organized as follows: Section 1 derives the dynamic sustainability benchmark in the intertemporal approach to the current account and discusses the appropriate testing methodology. It starts with the stylized model (subsection 6.1.1) and then sequentially generalizes the main assumptions (subsections 6.1.2-6.1.7). Section 2 shows the sustainability benchmark implied by the portfolio model of the current account which was constructed and tested by Calderon et al. (2000).

6.1 Dynamic benchmark in the intertemporal approach to the current account

6.1.1 Consumption-smoothing current account path under certainty equivalence

In this subsection, we pick up the traditional intertemporal model of the current account which was already discussed in section 3.1 of chapter 3, however, without deriving the solution to the representative agent's optimization problem. In addition, we adopt the typical assumption that the certainty equivalence principle which was formulated for the first time by Simon (1956) and Theil (1957) holds. The certainty equivalence principle says that agents act as if future random variables were sure to turn out to be their conditional means (Obstfeld and Rogoff, 1996, p. 81).

Theoretical foundations

The representative agent maximizes her expected lifetime utility, i.e.,

$$U_t = u(C_t) + v(G_t) + \sum_{n=t+1}^{\infty} \beta^{n-t} E_t \Big[u(C_n) + v(G_n) \Big]$$

subject to the single-period budget constraint (3.4) on page 21. The solution to the RC's maximization problem can be obtained using, for instance, the method of Lagrange multipliers. Substituting $A_{t-1}F(K_{t-1})$ for Y_t and $K_t - (1-\delta)K_{t-1}$ for I_t, the single-period budget constraint (3.4) may be rewritten as

$$B_t = A_{t-1}F(K_{t-1}) - K_t + (1-\delta)K_{t-1} - G_t - C_t + (1+r_t)B_{t-1}.$$

The Lagrangian can then be formed as

$$\begin{aligned} \mathscr{L} &= u(C_t) + v(G_t) + \sum_{n=t+1}^{\infty} \beta^{n-t} E_t \Big[u(C_n) + v(G_n) \Big] \\ &+ \sum_{n=t}^{\infty} \lambda_n \Big(A_{n-1}F(K_{n-1}) - K_n + (1-\delta)K_{n-1} - G_n - C_n - B_n + (1+r_n)B_{n-1} \Big) \end{aligned}$$

where λ_n is a (nonnegative) Lagrange multiplier n periods ahead.

In each period, the representative consumer chooses the optimal consumption level, the optimal stock of net foreign assets (liabilities), and the optimal capital stock (except for B_{t-1} and K_{t-1} which are by assumption predetermined). Differentiating the Lagrangian with respect to C_n, B_{n-1}, and K_{n-1} yields then the following first-order conditions:

$$\frac{\partial}{\partial C_n}\mathscr{L} = E_t\left[\beta^{n-t}u'(C_n)\right] - \lambda_n = 0 \tag{6.1}$$

$$\frac{\partial}{\partial B_{n-1}}\mathscr{L} = -\lambda_{n-1} + \lambda_n E_t\left[1+r_n\right] = 0 \tag{6.2}$$

$$\frac{\partial}{\partial K_{n-1}}\mathscr{L} = -\lambda_{n-1} + \lambda_n\Big(E_t\left[A_{n-1}F'(K_{n-1})\right] + 1 - \delta\Big) = 0 \tag{6.3}$$

where $\frac{\partial}{\partial C_n}\mathscr{L}$, $\frac{\partial}{\partial B_{n-1}}\mathscr{L}$, and $\frac{\partial}{\partial K_{n-1}}\mathscr{L}$ denote the first partial derivatives of the Lagrangian in the direction of C_n, B_{n-1}, and K_{n-1}, respectively. The first derivative of the utility function (with respect to C_n) is denoted by $u'(C_n)$, and $F'(K_{n-1})$ is the first derivative of the production function (with respect to K_{n-1}).

Eliminating the Lagrange multipliers by combining the first-order conditions (6.1) and (6.2), one obtains the Euler equation

$$\beta E_t\left[\frac{u'(C_n)}{u'(C_{n-1})}\right] = E_t\left[\frac{1}{1+r_n}\right]. \tag{6.4}$$

For $n = t+1$, the Euler equation (6.4) simplifies to

$$\beta E_t\left[\frac{u'(C_{t+1})}{u'(C_t)}\right] = E_t\left[\frac{1}{1+r_{t+1}}\right]. \tag{6.5}$$

The Euler condition (6.5) equates the expected marginal rate of substitution of present for future consumption (the left-hand side of equation (6.5)) to the expected relative price of future and present consumption (the right-hand side of equation (6.5)). Hence, a representative consumer cannot gain from consumption shifts over time.

In general, there are infinitely many paths satisfying the difference equation (6.5), and as the time horizon is infinite, there is no fixed terminal point that would entail a natural boundary condition. In order to find the optimal one among the paths satisfying the difference equation (6.5), additional information is required, such as suitable boundary (initial or terminal) conditions (Kamihigashi, 2006, p. 1). Following Wickens (2008, p. 57), one such terminal condition is given by

$$\lim_{N\to\infty} \beta^N E_t\left[u'(C_{t+N})B_{t+N}\right] = 0. \tag{6.6}$$

The terminal condition (6.6) requires the expected discounted marginal utility of $t+N$-period consumption multiplied by the expected outstanding NIIP stock to go to zero as $N \to \infty$. In case that $\beta^N u'(C_{t+N})$ is positive in the limit, it is optimal for an economy to consume all remaining net foreign assets, so that B_{t+N} is zero (with probability one). As a consequence, the terminal condition (6.6) will be satisfied. Thus, the terminal condition (6.6) rules out overaccumulation of financial wealth (Blanchard and Fischer, 1989, p. 43; Wickens, 2008, pp. 56-57).[1] In addition to the terminal condition (6.6), another terminal condition of the form

$$\lim_{N\to\infty} \beta^N E_t\left[u'(C_{t+N})K_{t+N}\right] = 0 \tag{6.7}$$

is required for the optimal solution (Wickens, 2008, p. 18).

Further, combining equations (6.2) and (6.3) yields

$$E_t\left[A_{n-1}F'(K_{n-1})\right] - \delta = E_t[r_n] \tag{6.8}$$

For $n = t+1$, equation (6.8) becomes

[1] Concerning necessity and/or sufficiency of the terminal condition (6.6) for the optimal solution, both in the deterministic setting and under uncertainty see, e.g., Stokey et al. (1989, pp. 97-99, 280-281), Kamihigashi (2000, 2005, 2006), and Buiter and Sibert (2004)).

$$A_tF'(K_t) - \delta = E_t[r_{t+1}]. \tag{6.9}$$

Equation (6.9) states that the marginal return on capital minus the depreciation rate equals the expected real interest rate. Thus, the optimal capital stock can be chosen independently of domestic consumption preferences—the result known as Fisherian separability (Fisher, 1930). In sum, the optimal solution to the RC's intertemporal maximization problem is determined by the Euler equation (6.5), equation (6.9), the single-period budget constraint (3.4), as well as the terminal conditions (6.6) and (6.7).

The optimal consumption-smoothing current account can be derived under the assumption that the time-preference rate is equal to the real interest rate in each period. In this case, the Euler equation (6.5) reduces to

$$E_t\left[u'(C_{t+1})\right] = u'(C_t). \tag{6.10}$$

Equation (6.10) says that the expected marginal utility of future consumption equals the marginal utility of present consumption.

Let us now further assume that the period utility function can be approximated by a linear-quadratic function given by

$$u(C) = C - \frac{\alpha}{2}C^2, \quad \alpha > 0.$$

In this case, the marginal utility of consumption is linear in consumption:

$$u'(C) = 1 - \alpha C \tag{6.11}$$

where $C < 1/\alpha$ ensures that $u'(C) > 0$.

Finally, the (expected) real interest rate is assumed to remain constant at r:

$$E_t[r_n] = r \quad n \geq t. \tag{6.12}$$

All three assumptions (i.e., equations (6.10), (6.11), and (6.12)) taken together yield a trendless long-run path for consumption:

$$E_t\left[C_{t+1}\right] = C_t. \tag{6.13}$$

Equation (6.13) states that the expected value of $t+1$-period consumption conditional on all information available in period t is equal to its t-period value. In other words, consumption follows a martingale, as was shown by Hall (1978).

Now, equation (6.13) can be combined with the "specific" intertemporal budget constraint (3.38). This leads to

$$\sum_{n=t}^{\infty} R^{n-t} C_t = \sum_{n=t}^{\infty} R^{n-t} E_t\left[NO_n\right] + (1+r) B_{t-1} \tag{6.14}$$

wherein the identity $TB_n = NO_n - C_n$ for $n \geq t$ has been used. Solving equation (6.14) for C_t and exploiting the formula for geometric series (i.e., $\sum_{n=t}^{\infty} R^{n-t} = (1+r)/r$ for $|R| < 1$) yields the optimal consumption path of the representative consumer:

$$C_t = \frac{r}{1+r}\left\{\sum_{n=t}^{\infty} R^{n-t} E_t\left[NO_n\right] + (1+r) B_{t-1}\right\}. \tag{6.15}$$

Equation (6.15) shows that the RC replaces unknown future variables with their conditional expectations, whence consumption follows the certainty equivalence principle.

Equation (6.15) also shows that consumption is determined by the t-period's interest payments (receipts) on the initial net foreign debts (assets) and the permanent level of net output, i.e., the annuity value of net output at the prevailing interest rate.[2] To put it differently, consumption equals the annuity value of the representative agent's wealth:

$$C_t = \frac{r}{1+r} W_t \tag{6.17}$$

where wealth W_t is defined as the term in the curly brackets on the right-hand side of equation (6.15). Hence, the optimal consumption path is consistent with the "permanent income hypothesis" put forward by Friedman (1957) according to which agents consume in each period a fraction of their permanent income.

Further, equation (6.15) implies that consumption smoothing (via the current account) is the representative agent's only saving motive. Substituting equation (6.15) for C_t in the single-period budget constraint (3.5) and using $CAB_t = B_t - B_{t-1}$ yields the consumption-smoothing current account path:

$$CAB_t = NO_t - \frac{r}{1+r} \sum_{n=t}^{\infty} R^{n-t} E_t \left[NO_n \right]. \tag{6.18}$$

Equation (6.18) shows that the current account is determined by deviations of current net output from permanent net output. A particularly succinct reformulation of equation (6.18) is the fundamental equation of the current account (Obstfeld and Rogoff, 1996, p. 74):

$$CAB_t = NO_t - NO^P = \left(Y_t - Y^P\right) - \left(G_t - G^P\right) - \left(I_t - I^P\right) \tag{6.19}$$

where the superscript P denotes the permanent level of a variable. Equation (6.19) shows that consumers can smooth their consumption by borrowing or lending towards the rest of the world whenever output, government spending, or investment temporarily deviate from their respective permanent level. A temporary increase in economy's net output beyond its permanent level—e.g., due to a temporary increase in its current output caused by a positive technology shock—can be cushioned by acquiring net foreign assets, thus leading to a surplus in the current account. In contrast to temporary country-specific shocks, global shocks cannot be smoothed away because in our stylized model with identical economies each economy responds symmetrically to a shock (Glick and Rogoff, 1995, p. 166; Kano, 2008, p. 758).

---

[2] The annuity value of a variable X at the prevailing interest rate is a hypothetical constant value with the same present value as the variable itself, i.e.,

$$\sum_{n=t}^{\infty} R^{n-t} X_t^P = \sum_{n=t}^{\infty} R^{n-t} X_n \tag{6.16}$$

where the superscript P denotes the permanent level of a variable. Solving equation (6.16) for X^P yields the permanent level of the variable X:

$$X_t^P = \frac{r}{1+r} \sum_{n=t}^{\infty} R^{n-t} X_n$$

(Obstfeld and Rogoff, 1996, p. 74).

Rearranging the terms in equation (6.18) one obtains[3]

$$CAB_t = -\sum_{n=t+1}^{\infty} R^{n-t} E_t [\Delta NO_n]. \tag{6.22}$$

Equation (6.22) states that the optimal consumption-smoothing current account is in deficit (surplus) when the present discounted value of expected future changes in the net output is positive (negative).

Our solution for the consumption-smoothing current account path can also be deduced from the (general) intertemporal budget constraint—provided that the number of optimizing lenders is finite—and thus satisfies the same: In analogy to the general intertemporal budget constraint (3.51) on page 35, the general IBC in our model is given by

$$B_{t-1} = -\sum_{n=t}^{\infty} E_t \left[\beta^{n-t+1} \frac{u'(C_n)}{u'(C_t)} (NO_n - C_n) \right]. \tag{6.23}$$

Assuming that the period utility function is approximated by a linear-quadratic function and the real interest rate equals the time-preference rate, equation (6.23) can be rewritten as

$$B_{t-1} = -\sum_{n=t}^{\infty} R^{n-t+1} \left(E_t [NO_n] - C_t \right). \tag{6.24}$$

Multiplying both sides of equation (6.24) by $(1+r)$ and solving for C_t yields exactly the optimal consumption path (6.15). The latter leads—after rearranging the terms as above—to the optimal current account path (6.18).

Since the optimal current account path is always sustainable in the sense of the IBC, empirical evidence that the current account path evolves according to its particular sustainability benchmark can be interpreted as evidence for solvency. Yet the converse implication need not hold. Solvency does not necessarily imply that the current account equals its particular benchmark path because the latter relies on specific assumptions about the utility function, the relationship between the time preference and the market discount factor etc. Similarly, the violation of the benchmark in the current account data does not necessarily imply that the data do not support the IBC.

Testing methodology

The methodologies for testing the empirical adequacy of the intertemporal approach to the current account can be divided into two classes (Milesi-Ferretti and Razin, 1996a, p. 6): On the

[3] The details are as follows. Once $NO_t - rNO_t/(1+r)$ has been simplified, equation (6.18) may be rewritten thus:

$$CAB_t = \frac{1}{1+r} NO_t - \frac{r}{(1+r)^2} E_t [NO_{t+1}] - \frac{r}{(1+r)^3} E_t [NO_{t+2}] - \ldots. \tag{6.20}$$

Adding and subtracting $\sum_{n=t+1}^{\infty} \left(\frac{1}{1+r}\right)^{n-t} NO_n$ on both sides of equation (6.20), one obtains

$$CAB_t = -\frac{1}{1+r} \Delta E_t [NO_{t+1}] - \frac{1}{(1+r)^2} \Delta E_t [NO_{t+2}] - \frac{1}{(1+r)^3} \Delta E_t [NO_{t+3}] - \ldots. \tag{6.21}$$

Using the sum notation, one arrives at equation (6.22).

one hand, one can assess the responses of the current account and other macroeconomic variables, such as consumption and net output, to different kinds of shocks—be it global shocks or country-specific shocks, which in turn can be either permanent or transitory (e.g., Leiderman and Razin, 1992; Razin, 1995; Glick and Rogoff, 1995; Hoffmann, 2001; Gruber, 2002; Bussiére et al., 2010). On the other hand, one can apply vector autoregressive analysis for the estimation of the equilibrium current account path. This section focuses on the latter approach because it permits the construction of a dynamic sustainability benchmark.

Campbell (1987) and Campbell and Shiller (1987) have developed a framework for testing stochastic present-value models with two variables, which they have applied to financial saving and stock prices, respectively.[4] The optimal current account path is constructed by estimating the present value of expected future net output changes conditional on the information set used by economic agents (denoted by $\mathbf{I}_t$), i.e., by estimating the right-hand side of equation (6.22):

$$CAB_t = -\sum_{n=t+1}^{\infty}\left(\frac{1}{1+r}\right)^{n-t} E\left[\Delta NO_n|\mathbf{I}_t\right]. \tag{6.25}$$

Because the public's information set $\mathbf{I}_t$ is usually smaller than the econometrician's information set (denoted by $\mathbf{H_t}$), Campbell (1987) and Campbell and Shiller (1987) suggest to capture additional information available to market participants by including current and lagged values of the current account into the information set $\mathbf{H_t}$. The idea is that the current account incorporates all information of market participants on future net output changes if the model given by equation (6.25) is true and is, therefore, the best predictor of expected changes in net output.

Following Campbell (1987) and Campbell and Shiller (1987), net output is assumed to be stationary in first differences. This implies that the current account is stationary in levels because CAB_t is a linear combination of stationary variables according to equation (6.25). The stationarity of CAB_t and ΔNO_t can be tested by means of unit root tests described in chapter 5. When net output is $I(1)$ and the current account is $I(0)$, the current account identity $CAB_t = NO_t + rB_{t-1} - C_t$ implies that net output (inclusive of net interest payments) and consumption must be $CI(1,1)$ with cointegrating vector $(1,-1)$ (or, alternatively, net output, the NIIP, and consumption must be cointegrated with vector $(1,r,-1)$). The existence of the cointegrating relationship can be tested using the cointegration tests also discussed in chapter 5.

The processes CAB_t and ΔNO_t are assumed to be stationary and to admit a vector autoregressive representation of order p:

$$\begin{bmatrix} \Delta NO_t \\ CAB_t \end{bmatrix} = \begin{bmatrix} a(L) & b(L) \\ c(L) & d(L) \end{bmatrix} \begin{bmatrix} \Delta NO_{t-1} \\ CAB_{t-1} \end{bmatrix} + \begin{bmatrix} \varepsilon_{1t} \\ \varepsilon_{2t} \end{bmatrix} \tag{6.26}$$

wherein $a(L)$, $b(L)$, $c(L)$, and $d(L)$ are polynomials in the lag operator of order p, and ε_{1t}, ε_{2t} are serially uncorrelated random vectors with mean zero and time-invariant, positive definite[5] covariance matrix $E[\varepsilon_{it}\varepsilon_{it}'] = \Sigma$ (for $i = 1,2$). The system of equations (6.26) can be stacked into a VAR model of order one as follows:

[4] This section is based on Campbell (1987), Campbell and Shiller (1987), Sheffrin and Woo (1990), Otto (1992), Obstfeld and Rogoff (1996, pp. 91-93), Cashin and McDermott (1998), Mercereau and Miniane (2004), and Nason and Rogers (2006).

[5] An $n \times n$ symmetric matrix $\mathbf{B}$ is positive definite if $\mathbf{x}'\mathbf{B}\mathbf{x} > 0$ for all non-zero n-dimensional vectors $\mathbf{x}$ where $\mathbf{x}'$ denotes the transpose of $\mathbf{x}$ (Schmidt and Trenkler, 2006, p. 96).

$$\begin{bmatrix} \Delta NO_t \\ \vdots \\ \Delta NO_{t-p+1} \\ CAB_t \\ \vdots \\ CAB_{t-p+1} \end{bmatrix} = \begin{bmatrix} a_1 \dots a_p \; b_1 \dots b_p \\ 1 \; \ddots & & \\ & 1 & \\ c_1 \dots c_p \; d_1 \dots d_p \\ & 1 \; \ddots & \\ & & 1 \end{bmatrix} \begin{bmatrix} \Delta NO_{t-1} \\ \vdots \\ \Delta NO_{t-p} \\ CAB_{t-1} \\ \vdots \\ CAB_{t-p} \end{bmatrix} + \begin{bmatrix} \varepsilon_{1t} \\ 0 \\ \vdots \\ \varepsilon_{2t} \\ 0 \\ \vdots \end{bmatrix}. \tag{6.27}$$

With the obvious choices for $\mathbf{A}$, $\mathbf{u}$, and $\mathbf{v}$, the equation system (6.27) can be written more succinctly:

$$\mathbf{u}_t = \mathbf{A}\mathbf{u}_{t-1} + \mathbf{v}_t. \tag{6.28}$$

The matrix $\mathbf{A}$ is called *companion matrix* of the VAR.

The unrestricted forecast of the right-hand side of equation (6.25) can be calculated by projecting equation (6.25) onto the econometrician's information set $\mathbf{H}_t$:

$$CAB_t = -\sum_{n=t+1}^{\infty} R^{n-t} E\left[E\left[\Delta NO_n|\mathbf{I}_t\right]|\mathbf{H}_t\right] = -\sum_{n=t+1}^{\infty} R^{n-t} E\left[\Delta NO_n|\mathbf{H}_t\right] \tag{6.29}$$

where the left-hand side remains unchanged after projection onto $\mathbf{H}_t$, because CAB_t is included in $\mathbf{H}_t$. Exploiting the VAR implication that $E\left[\mathbf{u}_n|\mathbf{H}_t\right] = \mathbf{A}^{n-t}\mathbf{u}_t$ (which follows from equation (6.28) via a straightforward mathematical induction in n) and noting that ΔNO_t is the first component of the vector $\mathbf{u}_t$, one obtains

$$E\left[\Delta NO_n|\mathbf{H}_t\right] = \mathbf{e}_1'\mathbf{A}^{n-t}\mathbf{u}_t \quad \forall n > t \tag{6.30}$$

where $\mathbf{e}_1$ is a first unit column vector[6] of length $2p$. Using equation (6.30), the right-hand side of equation (6.29) can be rewritten as

$$CAB_t = -\sum_{n=t+1}^{\infty} R^{n-t}\mathbf{e}_1'\mathbf{A}^{n-t}\mathbf{u}_t. \tag{6.31}$$

Because ΔNO_t and CAB_t are $I(0)$ by assumption, the eigenvalues of $R\mathbf{A}$ must be of norm < 1, whence the infinite sum on the right-hand side of equation (6.31) converges to $\mathbf{e}_1'R\mathbf{A}\left(\mathbf{I} - R\mathbf{A}\right)^{-1}$ where $\mathbf{I}$ is the $2p \times 2p$-dimensional identity matrix and $\left(\mathbf{I} - R\mathbf{A}\right)^{-1}$ is a nonsingular matrix (otherwise its determinant would be zero and the inverse $\left(\mathbf{I} - R\mathbf{A}\right)^{-1}$ would not exist). The VAR forecast of the optimal current account is thus given by

$$CAB_t = \mathbf{k}\,\mathbf{u}_t \tag{6.32}$$

where $\mathbf{k} \equiv -\mathbf{e}_1'R\mathbf{A}\left(\mathbf{I} - R\mathbf{A}\right)^{-1}$ is a $2p$-column vector.

There are several, both "formal" and "informal", avenues for assessing whether the current account evolves according to equation (6.32). Firstly, the vector $\mathbf{k}$ can be estimated and informally compared with its theoretical value, i.e., with a $p+1^{\text{st}}$ unit vector. Herein, the estimation

[6] A kth unit vector (denoted as $\mathbf{e}_k$) has all components being equal to zero except for the kth component which equals one.

of $\mathbf{k}$ requires pre-specifying the value of the real interest rate r. Another informal way to evaluate how well a given current account path tracks the predicted one is to plot both, using the estimate of $\mathbf{k}$, and to compare them visually.

A formal method would be to examine whether the ratio of the (intertemporal) variance of the estimated current account series to the (intertemporal) variance of the observed current account series is significantly different from one; if this is the case, then the sustainability benchmark is likely not to be satisfied. Further, one can assess whether the correlation between the estimated and the observed current account is high. One can also test for stationarity of the deviations of the observed current account path from the estimated one.

Finally, the Wald test can be used to test whether $\mathbf{k}$ is a $p+1^{st}$ unit vector of length $2p$. Equation (6.56) implies the following nonlinear restrictions:

$$\tilde{\mathbf{k}} \equiv \mathbf{e}_{p+1}' + \mathbf{e}_1' R\mathbf{A}\left(\mathbf{I} - R\mathbf{A}\right)^{-1} = 0 \tag{6.33}$$

where $\tilde{\mathbf{k}}$ is the vector of deviations of the actual value of $\mathbf{k}$ from its theoretical value. The null hypothesis that $\tilde{\mathbf{k}} = \mathbf{0}$ can be tested using the Wald test statistic of the form

$$W = \tilde{\mathbf{k}}\left(\mathbf{JVJ}'\right)^{-1}\tilde{\mathbf{k}}'. \tag{6.34}$$

Because $\tilde{\mathbf{k}}$ is a non-linear function of the VAR parameters, the variance-covariance matrix ($\mathbf{V}$) of the coefficient estimates in the VAR is typically linearly approximated according to the Delta method by $\mathbf{JVJ}'$ where $\mathbf{J}$ is the Jacobian matrix of partial derivatives of the $\tilde{\mathbf{k}}$ vector with respect to the VAR parameters.[7] Under the null hypothesis that $\tilde{\mathbf{k}} = \mathbf{0}$, the test statistic W is asymptotically χ^2 distributed with $2p$ degrees of freedom (since there are $2p$ parameter restrictions). The lag order p of the VAR can be selected using the Akaike information criterion (see, e.g., Lütkepohl, 1985 and Ozcicek and McMillin, 1999 for the comparison of different selection criteria). A rejection of the null hypothesis consequently provides evidence against sustainability. Typically, the failure to reject the null hypothesis is interpreted as evidence in favor of sustainability in the empirical literature. Yet because the null hypothesis of sustainability might be false with the unknown and possibly high probability of a type II error, we simply state in such cases that the null hypothesis cannot be rejected in favor of the particular alternative hypothesis.

However, Mercereau and Miniane (2004, 2008) show that estimating equation (6.56) is problematic in the near-singularity region, that is, when the matrix $\mathbf{I} - R\mathbf{A}$ has at least one eigenvalue close to zero (or the companion matrix $\mathbf{A}$ has at least one eigenvalue close to R^{-1}). In the case of near-singularity, small errors in the coefficients of the estimated companion matrix $\mathbf{A}$ lead to overproportionally large errors in $(\mathbf{I} - R\mathbf{A})^{-1}$ and, therefore, in the coefficients of the $\mathbf{k}$ vector. Consequently, the estimated current account path as well as its variances and covariances become very imprecise. Further, under near-singularity the Delta method yields a bad linear approximation of the variance-covariance matrix $\mathbf{V}$ and the Wald test which relies on the Delta method leads, therefore, to false rejections or acceptances of the null hypothesis (Mercereau and Miniane, 2008, p. 5). The problem of near-singularity arises when the current account series is persistent—which is the case for many countries (see, e.g., Chinn and Prasad, 2003; Mercereau and Miniane, 2004, 2008 and table 5.A of Appendix 5.4).

[7] The exception is the study by Makrydakis (1999) which obtains the nonlinear variance-covariance matrix from bootstrap simulations.

As suggested by Campbell and Shiller (1988, 1989), the problematic linear approximation can be avoided by postmultiplying both sides of equality (6.33) by $(\mathbf{I}-R\mathbf{A})$. This yields

$$\mathbf{e}'_{p+1}(\mathbf{I}-R\mathbf{A})+\mathbf{e}'_1 R\mathbf{A}=0 \tag{6.35}$$

After rearranging the terms, equation (6.35) simplifies to

$$\tilde{\ell} \equiv \mathbf{e}'_{p+1}-(\mathbf{e}_{p+1}-\mathbf{e}_1)' R\mathbf{A}=0 \tag{6.36}$$

where $\ell \equiv (\mathbf{e}_{p+1}-\mathbf{e}_1)' R\mathbf{A}$. The Wald test statistic W^ℓ can be constructed as

$$W^\ell = \tilde{\ell}\left(\mathbf{J}^\ell \mathbf{V} \mathbf{J}^{\ell'}\right)^{-1} \tilde{\ell}' \tag{6.37}$$

where $\mathbf{J}^\ell$ is the Jacobian matrix of partial derivatives of $\tilde{\ell}$ with respect to the VAR parameters. Under the null hypothesis that $\tilde{\ell}=\mathbf{0}$, the test statistic W^ℓ is asymptotically $\chi^2(2p)$ distributed (Bouakez and Kano, 2009, p. 1216). The linear restrictions (6.36) can also be tested using the likelihood ratio test statistics which is also $\chi^2(2p)$-distributed (Bouakez and Kano, 2009, p. 1217). Note that the Wald test on the linear restrictions (6.36) is not equivalent to the Wald test on the nonlinear restrictions (6.33) because the test statistic is not invariant to nonlinear transformations of the restrictions (Campbell and Shiller, 1988, pp. 209-210). However, despite the drawbacks of the "nonlinear" Wald test, the relevant empirical literature almost solely applies the nonlinear test statistics (6.37), with the single exception of Cashin and McDermott (2002) who perform the "linear" Wald test.

An alternative to testing equation (6.56) is testing whether the difference between the predicted and observed current account path is unpredictable given the information available up to period $t-1$ since only country-specific, transitory shocks should affect the dynamics of the sustainable current account. Substituting $\mathbf{e}'_{p+1}\mathbf{u}_t$ for CAB_t in the VAR (6.56) yields the following VAR restrictions:

$$\mathbf{e}'_{p+1} = -\mathbf{e}'_1 R\mathbf{A}(\mathbf{I}-R\mathbf{A})^{-1} \tag{6.38}$$

where $\mathbf{e}_{p+1}$ is a $(p+1)^{\text{st}}$ unit column vector of length $2p$. Postmultiplying both sides of equation (6.38) by $(\mathbf{I}-R\mathbf{A})$ one obtains

$$\mathbf{e}'_{p+1}(\mathbf{I}-R\mathbf{A}) = -\mathbf{e}'_1 R\mathbf{A}. \tag{6.39}$$

If the VAR restrictions (6.39) are satisfied, a country optimally smooths its consumption path.

The VAR restrictions given by equation (6.39) can be tested by running a linear regression. Writing out equation (6.39) leads to

$$[\underbrace{0\ldots0}_{p\text{ times}}\,1\ \underbrace{0\ldots0}_{(p-1)\text{ times}}\ ]\left(\begin{bmatrix}1 & \ldots\ldots\ldots & 0\\ 0\ 1 & \ldots\ldots & 0\\ 0\ 0 & \ddots & 0\\ 0\ 0 & \ldots\ldots & 1\ 0\\ 0\ 0 & \ldots\ldots & 0\ 1\end{bmatrix} - R\begin{bmatrix}a_1 \ldots a_p\, b_1 \ldots b_p\\ 1\ \ddots & \\ \quad 1 & \\ c_1 \ldots c_p\, d_1 \ldots d_p\\ \quad 1\ \ddots\\ \qquad 1\end{bmatrix}\right)$$

$$= -\begin{bmatrix}1\,0 \ldots\ 0\,0\end{bmatrix}\begin{bmatrix}a_1 \ldots a_p\, b_1 \ldots b_p\\ 1\ \ddots & \\ \quad 1 & \\ c_1 \ldots c_p\, d_1 \ldots d_p\\ \quad 1\ \ddots\\ \qquad 1\end{bmatrix}$$

which can be calculated as

$$\begin{bmatrix}-Rc_1\\ -Rc_2\\ \vdots\\ -Rc_p\\ (1-Rd_1)\\ -Rd_2\\ \vdots\\ -Rd_p\end{bmatrix}' = \begin{bmatrix}-Ra_1\\ -Ra_2\\ \vdots\\ -Ra_p\\ -Rb_1\\ -Rb_2\\ \vdots\\ -Rb_p\end{bmatrix}' . \tag{6.40}$$

The equality (6.40) shows that the linear restrictions imposed by equation (6.39) on individual coefficients are:

$$c_i = a_i \quad \text{for} \quad i = 1, 2, \cdots, p \tag{6.41}$$

$$R^{-1} = d_1 - b_1 \tag{6.42}$$

$$d_i = b_i \quad \text{for} \quad i = 2, \cdots, p. \tag{6.43}$$

Subtracting the ΔNO_t-equation of the VAR from the CAB_t-equation of the VAR (i.e., the first row from the $p+1^{\text{st}}$-row in equation system (6.27)) results in

$$\begin{aligned}CAB_t - \Delta NO_t = & (c_1 - a_1)\Delta NO_{t-1} + \ldots + (c_p - a_p)\Delta NO_{t-p}\\ & + (d_1 - b_1)\, CAB_{t-1} + \ldots + (d_p - b_p)\, CAB_{t-p}\\ & + \varepsilon_{2t} - \varepsilon_{1t}.\end{aligned} \tag{6.44}$$

Making use of restrictions (6.41), (6.42), and (6.43) reduces equation (6.44) to

$$CAB_t - \Delta NO_t - R^{-1} CAB_{t-1} = \varepsilon_{2t} - \varepsilon_{1t}. \tag{6.45}$$

Equation (6.45) implies that $CAB_t - \Delta NO_t - R^{-1}CAB_{t-1}$ should be orthogonal to information available up to $t-1$. In other words, $\Gamma_t \equiv CAB_t - \Delta NO_t - R^{-1}CAB_{t-1}$ cannot be predicted given the lagged values of ΔNO_t and CAB_t, i.e., $E[\Gamma_t|\mathbf{I_{t-1}}] = 0$. Thus, whether the current account follows its optimal path can be tested by regressing Γ_t on information available at time $t-1$ or alternatively $t-2$ and testing whether the coefficients of all regressors in the information set are zero—using, e.g., an F-test, t-test, or the Lagrange multiplier test. However, because Γ_t includes CAB_{t-1} which is also included in the information set $\mathbf{I}_{t-1}$, expectation errors might be correlated with $\mathbf{I}_{t-1}$. For this reason, using the information set $\mathbf{I}_{t-2}$ might be more appropriate (Işcan, 2002, p. 400). A rejection of the null hypothesis that the coefficients on the lagged ΔNO_t and CAB_t are zero indicates unsustainability. Despite potentially large errors of the second kind, the "acceptance" of the null hypothesis is mainly interpreted as evidence in favor of sustainability in the empirical literature.

The orthogonality of Γ is a weaker implication of the model than equation (6.56): Sustainability implies that $E[\Gamma_t|\mathbf{I}_{t-1}] = 0$, yet not vice versa because $E[\Gamma_t|\mathbf{I}_{t-1}] = 0$ is consistent with a more general form of equation (6.22) which contains a "bubble" term (i.e., which does not require the transversality condition to be satisfied). Besides, the parameters estimated by the F-test and the linear Wald test merely have an *asymptotic* justification (Mercereau and Miniane, 2008, p. 5, 11). Nevertheless, Mercereau and Miniane (2008) find that the F-test and the linear Wald test have much better coverage than the nonlinear Wald test both in small samples (under 30 years of annual or quarterly observations) and in samples which comprise 40 or 60 years. Their Monte-Carlo simulations show that the frequency to reject the false model at 95% confidence by the F-test and the linear Wald test is about 5% and 6%, respectively, whereas the rejection probability for the nonlinear Wald test ranges from nearly 12% to 28% in small samples. The Monte-Carlo simulations performed by Bouakez and Kano (2009) support this finding: The linear Wald test, the maximum likelihood test, and the likelihood ratio test have the correct size at the 5% and 1% critical values, whereas the nonlinear Wald test tends to overreject the null hypothesis in small and moderately sized samples.

Further, Kasa (2003) shows that the VAR representation (6.26) only exists when net output is trend-stationary or its permanent and transitory components are perfectly correlated. Yet the VAR representation is invalid when the net output process contains orthogonal permanent and transitory components which are observed by the agents in the model, but not by the econometrician. In this case, the model's moving average representation might be non-invertible, so that current and past values of the current account and net output do not reveal the innovations to agents' information sets. Thus, the model can lead to false inferences about current account dynamics (Kasa, 2003, p. 562). An alternative is to deal with the moving-average representation directly, as suggested by Hansen and Sargent (1991, p. 95). However, none of the studies that apply the above methodology to the current account implements this suggestion.

Finally, one can test the implication of the intertemporal model that the current account helps in the prediction of subsequent changes in net output, i.e., that CAB_t linearly Granger-causes future ΔNO_t.[8] If the current account is not Granger-causal with respect to ΔNO_t, the current

[8] In a bivariate model, CAB_t is said to Granger-cause future changes in NO_t if for all $n > t$ the mean squared error of a forecast of ΔNO_n based only on $(\Delta NO_t, \Delta NO_{t-1}, \dots)$ is higher than the the mean squared error of a forecast of ΔNO_n based on both $(\Delta NO_t, \Delta NO_{t-1}, \dots)$ and $(CAB_t, CAB_{t-1}, \dots)$ (Granger, 1969, pp. 428-9; Hamilton, 1994, p. 303).

account itself is an exact linear function of current and lagged values of ΔNO_t.[9] The null hypothesis that CAB_t does not Granger-cause ΔNO_t can be tested within the F-test framework as the joint hypothesis that the lags of CAB_t do not enter the ΔNO_t-equation of the VAR in equations (6.26) or (6.27). Rejecting the null hypothesis that $b_1 = b_2 = \cdots = b_p = 0$ in the VAR (6.27) consequently indicates sustainability. Granger-causality is, however, a weaker implication than the orthogonality of Γ to $\mathbf{I}_{t-1}$ (Milbourne and Otto, 1992, p. 378; Otto, 1992, p. 425).

In sum, the intertemporal model of a current account has the following main implications:

(i) the current account is $I(0)$ provided that net output is $I(1)$;
(ii) net output and consumption inclusive of net interest payments are $CI(1,1)$ provided that net output is $I(1)$;
(iii) the actual current account equals the predicted one, i.e., $CAB_t = \mathbf{k}'\mathbf{u}_t$ where $\mathbf{k} = -\mathbf{e}_1' R\mathbf{A}(\mathbf{I} - R\mathbf{A})^{-1}$ is a $p+1^{st}$ unit vector or $CAB_t = \mathbf{l}'\mathbf{u}_t$ where $\mathbf{l} = (\mathbf{e}_{p+1} - \mathbf{e}_1)' R\mathbf{A}$ is a $p+1^{st}$ unit vector;
(iv) the ratio of the variance of the predicted current account path to the variance of the observed current account path (z) is one;
(v) correlation between the actual and the predicted current account is high;
(vi) the deviation of the observed current account path from the estimated one is stationary;
(vii) the current account balance Granger-causes future changes in net output;
(viii) the cross-equation restrictions implied by the VAR are satisfied in the data, in particular, $\Gamma = CAB_t - \Delta NO_t - R^{-1}CAB_{t-1}$ is unpredictable given the lagged values of the current account and changes in net output.

The validity of the implications (i)-(viii) in the data admits two rival interpretations: as evidence for external sustainability or, alternatively, as evidence for empirical adequacy of the intertemporal approach to the current account. The former interpretation, which has been adopted for this section, takes a *normative* approach, in so far as it employs the intertemporal model of the current account as a benchmark. In contrast, the latter interpretation corresponds to a *positive* approach which makes no judgment on whether it is good or bad if the observed current account does not behave according to the intertemporal approach to the current account. Because the same testing methodology is used to examine both approaches, the positive approach can also be exploited for the sustainability analysis. Accordingly, table 6.1 in Appendix 6.B considers both empirical studies which primarily investigate external sustainability (Ostry, 1997; Cashin and McDermott, 1998; Callen and Cashin, 1999; Adedeji, 2001; Kim et al., 2002; Landeau, 2002; Hudson and Stennett, 2003; Belkar et al., 2008; Ismail and Baharumshah, 2008; Ogus and Sohrabji, 2008; Karunaratne, 2010) and those which assess the statistical performance of the intertemporal approach (the remaining studies in table 6.1).

Table 6.1 in Appendix 6.B summarizes all relevant empirical studies. The last column in table 6.1 makes a final "judgment" on whether the current account is sustainable according

[9] The reason is that when the current account does not Granger-cause ΔNO_t, the n-periods ahead expectation of ΔNO_n conditional on $\mathbf{H}_t$ is just the expectation conditional on current and lagged ΔNO, i.e.: $E[\Delta NO_n|\mathbf{H}_t] = E[\Delta NO_n|\Delta NO_t, \Delta NO_{t-1}, \ldots]$ for all $n > t$. Thus, the expectation of CAB_t conditional on $\mathbf{H}_t$ is the expectation conditional on current and lagged ΔNO: $E[CAB_t|\mathbf{H}_t] = E[CAB_t|\Delta NO_t, \Delta NO_{t-1}, \ldots]$ for all $n > t$. In other words, current account is a linear function of current and lagged values of ΔNO_t (Campbell, 1987, p. 1257; Campbell and Shiller, 1987, pp. 1066-1067).

to the respective benchmark or not.[10] In case that various tests yield contradictory results, a kind of "decision rule" is useful in order to ensure the consistent treatment of the test results. Due to the problems associated with estimating the vector **k** in equation (6.56) and with the nonlinear Wald test under near-singularity, i.e., with testing the implications (iii)-(vi), the F-test on the implications (vii) and (viii) appears to be more reliable and, therefore, is assigned more weight. Because the implication (vii) that the current account is Granger-causal to future changes ΔNO_t is weaker than the implication (viii) that the forecast innovation Γ is orthogonal to the information up to period $t-1$, it gets less weight than the implication (viii). Besides, the failure to reject the null hypothesis is not treated as evidence in favor of the null hypothesis in table 6.1 in Appendix 6.B as the unknown probability of the type II-error might be large. Given these considerations, the following "decision rules" are proposed:

1. The current account path is regarded as *unsustainable* only if the linear Wald test rejects the null hypothesis that the vector **l** is a $(p+1)^{st}$ unit vector and/or the F-test rejects the null hypothesis that Γ is unpredictable given the lagged values of the current account and changes in net output.
2. The current account path is said to be *sustainable* only if the F-test rejects the null hypothesis that the current account does not Granger-cause future changes in net output provided that the F-test does not reject the null hypothesis that Γ is orthogonal to past information.
3. The current account is said to be *possibly sustainable* if
   - the linear Wald test does not reject the null hypothesis that the vector **l** is a $(p+1)^{st}$ unit vector,
   - the F-test fails to reject the null hypothesis that Γ is unpredictable given the lagged values of the current account and changes in net output
   - and/or if the nonlinear Wald test fails to reject the null hypothesis that **k** is a $(p+1)^{st}$ unit vector.
4. The current account is said to be *possibly unsustainable* if
   - the F-test fails to reject the null hypothesis of no Granger-causality
   - and/or the nonlinear Wald test rejects the null hypothesis that **k** is a $(p+1)^{st}$ unit vector.

Certainly, these decision rules are stylized and should be taken, as it were, with a grain of salt. In particular, since we have no information about the relative reliability of the tests in comparison to each other, the decision rules inevitably contain an arbitrary component. For example, one could just as well interpret the evidence in favor of Granger-causality as merely "possibly sustainable." A further difficulty arises when the F-test indicates that Γ is unpredictable (given the information available up to period $t-1$) while the current account is found to be Granger-causal to subsequent changes in net output—as is the case for Australia in the study by Milbourne and Otto (1992), Turkey in the study by Ogus and Sohrabji (2008), and Ireland in the study by Campa and Gavilan (2011). As the final judgment, we propose "not sustainable" in those cases because Granger-causality is a weaker implication of the model. However, if the studies in question had not performed the F-test on the orthogonality of Γ to $\mathbf{I}_{t-1}$, the final judgment on sustainability would have been exactly the opposite, namely that the current account is in fact sustainable (even though with a lesser degree of confidence, in view of the weakness

[10] For space reasons, we do not report the significance levels at which the null hypothesis is rejected or not rejected. All studies rely on the "standard" significance levels 1%, 5%, and 10%.

of Granger causality). As a remedy, we suggest that studies with more or stronger tests should *ceteris paribus* trump those with less or weaker tests.

The methodology described above was first applied to the intertemporal model of the current account by Sheffrin and Woo (1990). For the annual data from 1957 to 1985 and the real interest rate of 4 or 14 percent, Sheffrin and Woo (1990) reject the null hypothesis that the vector $\mathbf{k}$ is a $(p+1)^{st}$ unit vector for the whole sample (Belgium, Canada, Denmark, and the United Kingdom) using the nonlinear Wald test. The F-test on the significance of coefficients of Γ also indicates unsustainability in the UK and Canada, as well as in Belgium only for the higher interest rate of 14 percent and the information set $\mathbf{I}_{t-1}$, and in Denmark only for the information set $\mathbf{I}_{t-2}$. Thus, at least in Canada and the United Kingdom, the current account does not evolve according to the sustainability benchmark under certainty equivalence. The test results for Canada are confirmed by Obstfeld and Rogoff (1996, pp. 90-94) and Nason and Rogers (2006).

However, the discrepancy between the observed and the benchmark current account path might not necessarily result from unsustainability. Under special circumstances (resulting from certain specific assumptions in particular countries), the consumption-smoothing current account under certainty equivalence might not be the appropriate benchmark. The "usual suspects" (Nason and Rogers, 2006, p. 160) include imperfect international capital mobility, the presence of consumption tilting and/or precautionary saving, non-separable preferences such as habit formation, and the existence of durable goods and non-traded goods. The rest of the section examines the extensions of the "baseline" model under certainty equivalence and perfect capital mobility.

6.1.2 Consumption-smoothing current account path under certainty equivalence and limited capital mobility

Perfect capital mobility is typically assumed to prevail within the OECD countries, whereas the capital flows between developed and developing countries are usually considered to be dominantly characterized by imperfect capital mobility (Razin, 1995, p. 3). Thus, the sustainability benchmark under perfect capital mobility might not be applicable to non-OECD countries even if the current account paths in those countries were sustainable in the sense that they are perfectly consistent with agents' optimal plans. When capital mobility is limited, consumers are not able to fully smooth consumption via the current account.

Huang (1993) suggests to incorporate constraints on capital mobility by differentiating between two types of consumers. Consumers of the first type have no access to international financial markets at all and have to consume in each period the whole fraction of the respective period's net output available to them. In contrast, consumers of the second type can cushion country-specific technology shocks by borrowing and lending in the international financial markets freely. Thus, consumption can be written as

$$C_t = \theta NO_t + (1-\theta)\frac{r}{1+r}\left(\sum_{n=t}^{\infty} R^{n-t} E_t\left[NO_n\right] + (1+r)B_{t-1}\right) \quad 0 \leq \theta \leq 1 \qquad (6.46)$$

where θ denotes the fraction of net output consumed by the consumers of the first type. The parameter θ reflects the degree of international capital mobility: capital is perfectly mobile for $\theta = 0$ and immobile for $\theta = 1$. Equation (6.46) leads to the following current account path:

$$CAB_t = -(1-\theta) \sum_{n=t+1}^{\infty} R^{n-t} E_t [\Delta NO_n] . \tag{6.47}$$

With no access to international financial markets ($\theta = 1$), the current account balance is zero. Whenever international lending or borrowing is possible ($0 \leq \theta < 1$), the current account is in deficit (surplus) in case that temporary country-specific shocks to net output are positive (negative). Equation (6.47) implies the following VAR estimate

$$CAB_t = \mathbf{k}^{\theta'} \mathbf{u}_t \tag{6.48}$$

where $\mathbf{k}^{\theta} \equiv -(1-\theta)\mathbf{e}_1' R\mathbf{A} (\mathbf{I} - R\mathbf{A})^{-1}$ is a $(p+1)^{st}$ unit column vector of length $2p$.

Although Taiwan had foreign-exchange controls in the postwar period till the mid-1980s, Huang (1993) finds θ being negligibly small over the whole sample period 1961-1990. The Wald test rejects the null hypothesis that $\mathbf{k}^{\theta}$ is a $(p+1)^{st}$ unit vector whereas the F-test cannot reject the null hypothesis that Γ is unpredictable given past information, thus pointing to the current account in Taiwan being possibly sustainable.

6.1.3 Adjusting for consumption tilting under linear-quadratic utility

The representative agent's consumption behavior is motivated both by the consumption-smoothing and consumption-tilting desire when the real interest rate deviates from the time-preference rate (Obstfeld and Rogoff, 1996, pp. 74-76). Frederick et al. (2002) find that the time-preference factor is likely to be different from the real market discount factor. For this reason, Milbourne and Otto (1992) and Otto (1992) suggest to purge the consumption-tilting component from the data and test only the consumption-smoothing current account.

When $\beta \neq R$, Hall's (1978) result formulated in equation (6.13) is no longer valid. Under the assumption of linear-quadratic utility (i.e., using equation (6.11)), the intertemporal Euler equation (6.5) becomes

$$E_t[C_{t+1}] = \frac{\beta(1+r)-1}{\alpha\beta(1+r)} + \frac{1}{\beta(1+r)} C_t . \tag{6.49}$$

Substituting equation (6.49) into the specific intertemporal budget constraint (3.38) one obtains

$$C_t + \frac{\beta(1+r)-1}{\alpha\beta(1+r)^2} + \frac{1}{\beta(1+r)^2} C_t = \sum_{n=t}^{\infty} R^{n-t} E_t [NO_n] + (1+r) B_{t-1} . \tag{6.50}$$

Exploiting the formula for geometric infinite series (since $|\beta(1+r)^2| < 1$) to rewrite the left-hand side of equation (6.50) and solving equation (6.50) for C_t yields

$$C_t = -\frac{\beta(1+r)-1}{\alpha\beta(1+r)^2} + \frac{(\beta(1+r)^2-1)}{\beta(1+r)^2} \left(\sum_{n=t}^{\infty} R^{n-t} E_t [NO_n] + (1+r) B_{t-1} \right) . \tag{6.51}$$

The studies by Ghosh (1995), Ghosh and Ostry (1995), Cashin and McDermott (1998), and Agénor et al. (1999) neglect the constant term on the right-hand side of equation (6.52) (without mentioning it, however). When the constant term is set to zero and the consumption-tilting factor is defined as $\nu \equiv (\beta(1+r)r) \left((\beta(1+r)^2 - 1) \right)^{-1}$, equation (6.51) becomes

$$C_t = \frac{1}{v}\frac{r}{1+r}\left\{\sum_{n=t}^{\infty} R^{n-t}E_t\left[NO_n\right] + (1+r)B_{t-1}\right\}. \tag{6.52}$$

Equation (6.52) shows that consumption is proportional to the representative agent's wealth (i.e., to the term in curly brackets on the right-hand side of equation (6.52)). For $v = 1$, consumption is solely determined by the consumption-smoothing motive; this is the case discussed in the last subsection. The consumption-tilting factor is less than one if $\beta > (1+r)^{-1}$, i.e., if the representative agent is relatively patient. In this case, the economy consumes more than the annuity value of its wealth so that the consumption path is tilted upward. If the representative agent is impatient so that $\beta < (1+r)^{-1}$, the consumption-tilting factor exceeds unity and the consumption path is tilted downward (Obstfeld and Rogoff, 1996, pp. 70-71).

Equation (6.52) shows that the current account contains a consumption-smoothing and a consumption-tilting component. Using the current account identity (3.4), the consumption-smoothing component of the current account can be defined as

$$CAB^{sm} = NO_t + rB_{t-1} - vC_t. \tag{6.53}$$

Using equation (6.52) to eliminate C_t in identity (6.53) yields

$$CAB_t^{sm} = NO_t - \frac{r}{1+r}\sum_{n=t}^{\infty} R^{n-t}E_t\left[NO_n\right]. \tag{6.54}$$

Rearranging the terms as in subsubsection 6.1.1, equation (6.54) reduces to

$$CAB_t^{sm} = -\sum_{n=t+1}^{\infty} R^{n-t}E_t\left[\Delta NO_n\right]. \tag{6.55}$$

The consumption-tilting parameter corresponds to the cointegrating parameter in equation (6.53). If net output inclusive of net interest payments and consumption are individually $I(1)$ and together $CI(1,1)$ with cointegrating vector $(1;-v)$, then both sides of equation (6.53) are $I(0)$. This is consistent with the implication (i) (page 185) that the consumption-smoothing current account follows a stationary process. As suggested by Otto (1992), the consumption-tilting parameter v can be estimated by regressing $NO_t + rB_{t-1}$ on C_t and using, e.g., the fully modified OLS estimator (Phillips and Hansen, 1990). The knowledge of the consumption-tilting parameter allows separating the consumption-smoothing and consumption-tilting components of the current account. Most studies find the consumption-tilting parameter to be different from one (see table 6.1 in Appendix 6.B for details). This suggests that consumption-tilting behavior does affect current account dynamics.

For a large sample of 45 developing countries, Ghosh and Ostry (1995) find that the consumption-tilting parameter equals unity only in South Korea and that the current account is "sustainable" or "possibly sustainable" in 34 countries. These results are largely consistent with Ostry (1997) who examines five ASEAN countries, Adedeji (2001) for Nigeria, and Hudson and Stennett (2003) for Jamaica.

The evidence against sustainability in Canada obtained by the three studies discussed in subsection 1.1 is confirmed by Otto (1992) for quarterly data during 1950.Q1-1987.Q4, yet not by Ghosh (1995). Ghosh (1995) uses a real interest rate which is about 2 percentage points smaller than the one used by Otto (1992). Although Sheffrin and Woo (1990) and Ogus and Sohrabji (2008) find that the "fit" of the model is better with the lower interest rates, the difference of 2 percentage points seems to be too small to account for the contradicting results. Moreover, Milbourne and Otto (1992) and Otto (1992) report that the results are not sensitive to the choice of the real interest rate.

For Australia, the results are mixed (see table 6.1 in Appendix 6.B). The null hypothesis that Γ is predictable given past values of the current account and net output changes can be rejected for the real interest rate of 4 percent and quarterly, seasonally adjusted data during 1961.Q1-1989.Q1 (Milbourne and Otto, 1992) and cannot be rejected for the annual data during 1954-1994 and almost the same real interest rate of 4.04 percent (Cashin and McDermott, 1998). In contrast, evidence for Granger causality is found by all studies on Australia (Milbourne and Otto, 1992; Cashin and McDermott, 1998, 2002; Karunaratne, 2010).

As already mentioned above, the assumption of perfect capital mobility might not be appropriate for developing countries. Callen and Cashin (1999) modify the above analysis to incorporate credit constraints. Agents' access to international funds might be limited due to capital controls imposed by the government or due to the respective country's political and economical instability—which cuts into agents' ability to repay debts and, therefore, reduces international investors' willingness to lend to the country in question (Adedeji, 2001). With credit constraints, agents cannot cushion an expected rise in country's net output by net foreign borrowing and running a current account deficit. In contrast, agents' behavior in case of temporary negative technology shocks remains unchanged through borrowing constraints. Thus, current account surpluses, if sustainable, should be Granger-causal to future declines in net output, yet no Granger-causality should exist between current account deficits and future increases in net output. For India from 1952 to 1999, Callen and Cashin (1999) are not able to reject the null hypothesis of no Granger-causality under perfect capital mobility. Yet when the asymmetric access to international capital markets is taken into account, the F-test indicates that current account surpluses do Granger-cause the subsequent decreases in net output. This asymmetry regarding Granger-causality is also found by Adedeji (2001) for Nigeria during 1960-1997.

Callen and Cashin (1999) also examine whether the current account is given by

$$CAB_t = \mathbf{k}' \mathbf{u}_t^{As} \tag{6.56}$$

where the $4p$-column vectors $\mathbf{k}$ and $\mathbf{u}_t^{As}$ are defined as follows: $\mathbf{k} \equiv -\mathbf{e}_1' R\mathbf{A}(\mathbf{I}-R\mathbf{A})^{-1}$ and $\mathbf{u}_t^{As} = \left(\Delta NO^h, \Delta NO^l, CAB^h, CAB^l\right)$. The variable CAB^h (CAB^l) takes the value one when the current account balance is positive (negative) and is zero otherwise. The variables ΔNO^h and ΔNO^l are defined analogously. The Wald test does not reject the null hypothesis that $\mathbf{k}$ is a $(p+1)^{st}$ unit vector for India from 1952 to 1999. Assuming perfect capital mobility, Ghosh and Ostry (1995) are also not able to reject the null hypothesis that the Indian current account equals the predicted current account during 1960-1990, yet find evidence for Granger-causality between the current account and the subsequent changes in future net output.

Many studies report that the observed current account path is more volatile than the optimal current account path, i.e., that consumption is too smooth (e.g., Sheffrin and Woo, 1990; Ghosh, 1995; Cashin and McDermott, 1998). The excess current account volatility can be attributed to the (aforementioned) "usual suspects." However, the question still remains why large excess volatility can be found for some periods and is not found for other (Mercereau and Miniane,

2008, p. 4). The statistical analysis performed by Mercereau and Miniane (2004, 2008) does not provide evidence for any excess current account volatility.

6.1.4 Adjusting for consumption tilting under power utility

The assumption of linear-quadratic utility can be misleading for several reasons. Firstly, linear-quadratic utility is an accurate approximation of the utility function (at best) only near the point of approximation because the performance of every linearized model deteriorates the more it deviates from the initial level. Yet at the same time, linear-quadratic utility implies that consumption is a martingale and will eventually move far away from its initial level (Obstfeld and Rogoff, 1996, p. 37).

Further, the Arrow (1970)-Pratt (1964) measure of absolute risk aversion which is defined as $-u''(C)/u'(C)$ equals $-\alpha(1-\alpha C)^{-1}$ in case of linear-quadratic utility. This means that the Arrow-Pratt measure is increasing in C (because $\alpha > 0$ by assumption). In other words, the absolute risk aversion is increasing, that is, the RC's propensity to reduce consumption in order to avoid risks increases with increasing wealth. However, the empirical evidence mainly points to decreasing absolute risk aversion (Levy, 1994; Hartog et al., 2002; Lee, 2008; Paravisini et al., 2010).[11]

Finally, linear-quadratic utility rules out the possibility of precautionary saving which is motivated by income uncertainty.[12] Under linear-quadratic utility, $u'''(C) = 0$ so that the Kimball (1990) coefficient of absolute prudence (which measures the strength of precautionary saving and is defined as $-u'''(C)/u''(C)$) is zero, thus implying no precautionary saving. In other words, an increase in consumption required to keep the same level of expected marginal utility due to a small increase in risk is independent of the initial level of consumption (Blanchard and Mankiw, 1989, p. 3). Hence, linear-quadratic utility implies risk aversion, but no prudence.

In contrast, a utility function with $u'''(C) > 0$ (and $u'(C)$ being a convex function of C) allows for precautionary saving. An increase in uncertainty about income in period $t+1$ raises the expected marginal utility $E_t[u'(C_{t+1})]$. The Euler equation (6.5) remains satisfied only if the marginal utility of current consumption $u'(C_t)$ increases which is *ceteris paribus* the case if the RC reduces current consumption and increases saving.

A standard example for a utility function with $u'''(C) > 0$ is a utility function with constant elasticity given, for example, by:

$$u(C) = \frac{C^{1-\sigma}}{1-\sigma}, \quad \sigma < 0, \quad \sigma \neq 1 \tag{6.57}$$

where σ is the intertemporal elasticity of substitution. Because the isoelastic function (6.57) implies that $u'(C) = C^{-\sigma}$ and $u''(C) = -\sigma C^{-\sigma-1}$, absolute and relative risk aversion[13] are both constant. However, empirical evidence rather points to decreasing absolute risk aversion (as mentioned above) and to decreasing relative risk aversion (e.g., studies by Friend and Blume

[11] An overview of empirical literature on absolute and relative risk aversion is provided, e.g., by Damodaran (2007).

[12] The theory on precautionary saving was first developed by Leland (1968) and continued by Sandmo (1970), Drèze and Modigliani (1972), Zeldes (1989), Caballero (1990), and more recently Gourinchas and Parker (2001).

[13] The Arrow-Pratt measure of relative risk aversion is defined as $-Cu''(C)/u'(C)$.

(1975) and Morin and Fernandez Suarez (1983) when wealth is defined exclusive the value of housing) although there is some support for constant relative risk aversion (e.g., Friend and Blume (1975) when wealth includes housing; Chiappori and Paiella (2011)). A further disadvantage of the isoelastic utility function of the form (6.57) is that it does not allow for a separation of the (representative) consumer's risk aversion from intertemporal substitution (Obstfeld and Rogoff, 1996, p. 279). Nevertheless, we assume the constant elasticity (CES) utility in this subsection as it facilitates the calculation of the optimal current account path and allows for precautionary saving.

Substituting the marginal utility $u'(C) = C^{-\sigma}$ which follows from the CES utility function (6.57) into the Euler equation (6.5), one obtains

$$E_t[C_{t+1}] = C_t \beta^{\sigma}(1+r)^{\sigma}. \tag{6.58}$$

Using equation (6.58) to eliminate $E_t[C_{t+1}]$, $E_t[C_{t+2}]$, etc. in the IBC of the means (3.38) yields

$$C_t\left(1+\frac{\beta^{\sigma}(1+r)^{\sigma}}{1+r}+\left(\frac{\beta^{\sigma}(1+r)^{\sigma}}{1+r}\right)^2+\dots\right) = \sum_{n=t}^{\infty} R^{n-t} E_t[NO_n] + (1+r)B_{t-1}. \tag{6.59}$$

Assuming that $|\beta^{\sigma}(1+r)^{\sigma-1}| < 1$, the infinite sum in in the brackets on the right-hand side of equation (6.59) can be reduced to the expression $(1 - R\beta^{\sigma}(1+r)^{\sigma})^{-1}$. Solving equation (6.59) for C_t and multiplying with $(1 - R\beta^{\sigma}(1+r)^{\sigma})$ results in

$$C_t = \frac{r+\nu^P}{1+r}\left(\sum_{n=t}^{\infty} R^{n-t} E_t[NO_n] + (1+r)B_{t-1}\right) \equiv \frac{r+\nu}{1+r} W_t \tag{6.60}$$

where $\nu^P \equiv 1 - \beta^{\sigma}(1+r)^{\sigma}$ denotes the consumption-tilting parameter under power utility. The desired consumption path is tilted upward if the representative agent is relatively patient so that $\nu^P < 0$, and it is tilted downward if the RC is relatively impatient so that $\nu^P > 0$. Only if $\nu^P = 0$, the optimal consumption equals its permanent level, and the desired consumption path corresponds to the steady-state consumption path (Obstfeld and Rogoff, 1996, pp. 70-71).

Substituting equation (6.60) into the single-period budget constraint (3.4) on page 21, the optimal current account path is given by

$$CAB_t = NO_t - NO^P - \nu^P R^{-1} W_t. \tag{6.61}$$

Equation (6.61) shows that the current account consists of the consumption-smoothing component $NO_t - NO^P$ and the consumption-tilting component $-\nu^P R^{-1} W_t$. When the consumption-tilting parameter ν^P is strictly positive (negative), the current account is smaller (larger) than the consumption-smoothing level. Finally, when the consumption-tilting parameter is zero, the current account equals its consumption-smoothing level.

Braeu (2010) reports that $\nu^P = 0.85$ for Canada during 1979.Q1 to 2007.Q1, thus implying that the consumption path is tilted downward. In contrast, Belkar et al. (2008) find that the estimated consumption-tilting parameter is significantly less than zero in Australia so that the consumption path is tilted upward. For Australia, Belkar et al. (2008) confirm the presence of Granger causality (mentioned before) both for the whole sample period 1949-2005 and for the second subperiod 1984-2005. However, the important question remains how sustainability of the consumption-tilting component of the current account can be appropriately tested.

6.1.5 Introducing habit formation under linear-quadratic utility

Hitherto it was assumed that the representative agent's preferences are intertemporally additive and are given by the discounted utility function (3.3) which was first introduced by Samuelson (1937). The utility function (3.3) has several implications. Because lifetime utility equals the discounted value of period utilities, it implies utility independence (Frederick et al., 2002, p. 357). It also implies consumption independence since the marginal rate of substitution between consumption in any two periods is independent of consumption in any third period (Obstfeld and Rogoff, 1996, p. 12). Finally, the instantaneous utility function is assumed to remain constant over time. However, agents' preferences may change over time. Further, utility arising from current consumption might be influenced by past consumption. In other words, the utility function may display habit formation which might raise the volatility of the current account.[14] A theoretical account of habit formation was first suggested by Duesenberry (1952) and further developed by Pollak (1970) and Ryder and Heal (1973). Empirical evidence on habit formation is, however, mixed: Whereas Heien and Durham (1991), Ferson and Constantinides (1991), Braun et al. (1993), Naik and Moore (1996), Guariglia and Rossi (2002), and Alessie and Teppa (2010) find that preferences exhibit habit formation, Dunn and Singleton (1986) (only on annual frequency) and Dynan (2000) obtain no support for habit formation.

Following Alessie and Lusardi (1997) and Gruber (2004), habit formation can be introduced as follows:

$$U_t = \sum_{n=t}^{\infty} E_t \left[\beta^{n-t} u(C_n - \delta C_{n-1})\right] \tag{6.62}$$

where government spending is, for simplicity, ignored. The depreciation rate of consumption δ with $\delta \in [0,1)$ can be interpreted as the strength of consumption habits. Equation (6.62) shows that utility is increasing in the current consumption level minus the depreciated value of past period's consumption. The stronger the habits of the representative consumer, i.e., the closer δ to unity, the lower is *ceteris paribus* utility.

Adding and subtracting δC_n within the argument of the period utility function in equation (6.62) shows that the representative consumer maximizes the weighted average of the current consumption level and the change in consumption:

$$U_t = \sum_{n=t}^{\infty} E_t \left[\beta^{n-t} u((1-\delta)C_n + \delta \Delta C_n)\right]. \tag{6.63}$$

When δ is close to unity, the RC has strong habits by assigning more weight to changes in consumption than to consumption levels. When δ is zero, the RC maximizes only the current consumption and the utility function (6.62) coincides with the utility function without habit formation (3.3).

[14] Frederick et al. (2002) provide a detailed discussion of the discounted utility function and its alternative specifications.

Denoting the argument of the utility function (6.62) by $C_n - \delta C_{n-1} \equiv C_n^h$, equation (6.62) is simplified thus:

$$U_t = E_t\left[\sum_{n=t}^{\infty} \beta^{n-t} u\left(C_n^h\right)\right]. \tag{6.64}$$

The representative agent maximizes the utility function (6.64) subject to the single-period budget constraint (3.4) on page 21. Under the assumption that $E_t[r_n] = r$ for all $n \geq t$, the intertemporal Euler equation[15] is given by

$$\beta E_t\left[\frac{u'\left(C_n^h\right)}{u'\left(C_{n-1}^h\right)}\right] = E_t\left[\frac{1}{1+r}\right]. \tag{6.65}$$

Following Gruber (2004), it is assumed that the period utility function $u(C^h)$ is linear-quadratic and $\beta = (1+r)^{-1}$. In this case, the Euler equation (6.65) implies the martingale property of consumption: $E_t\left[C_{t+1}^h\right] = C_t^h$ or $E_t\left[C_{t+1} - \delta C_t\right] = C_t - \delta C_{t-1}$.

The next step is deriving the optimal consumption path under habit formation. Adding $\sum_{n=t}^{\infty} R^{n-t} \delta E_t[C_{n-1}]$ on both sides of the intertemporal budget constraint (3.38) on page 31 and substituting $TB_n = NO_n - C_n$ for $n \geq t$, one obtains

$$\sum_{n=t}^{\infty} R^{n-t} E_t\left[C_n - \delta C_{n-1}\right] = \sum_{n=t}^{\infty} R^{n-t} \delta E_t[C_{n-1}] + \sum_{n=t}^{\infty} R^{n-t} E_t\left[NO_n\right] + (1+r)B_{t-1}. \tag{6.66}$$

Using the martingale property of consumption and applying the infinite formula for geometric series for $|R| < 1$, the left-hand side of equation (6.66) reduces to the expression $(C_t - \delta C_{t-1})r(1+r)^{-1}$. In addition, the first sum on the right-hand side of equation (6.66) can be rewritten as $-\delta C_{t-1} - \delta R \sum_{n=t}^{\infty}\left(\frac{1}{1+r}\right)^{n-t} E_t\left[C_n\right]$:

$$\frac{1+r}{r}(C_t - \delta C_{t-1}) = -\delta C_{t-1} - \delta R \sum_{n=t}^{\infty}\left(\frac{1}{1+r}\right)^{n-t} E_t\left[C_n\right] + \sum_{n=t}^{\infty} R^{n-t} E_t\left[NO_n\right] + (1+r)B_{t-1}. \tag{6.67}$$

Using the intertemporal budget constraint (3.38) again to eliminate $E_t\left[C_n\right]$, equation (6.75) becomes

$$\frac{1+r}{r}(C_t - \delta C_{t-1}) = -\delta C_{t-1} - \frac{\delta}{1+r}\left((1+r)B_{t-1} + \sum_{n=t}^{\infty} R^{n-t} E_t\left[NO_n\right]\right) + \sum_{n=t}^{\infty} R^{n-t} E_t\left[NO_n\right] + (1+r)B_{t-1}. \tag{6.68}$$

15 In addition to the Euler equation (6.65), the calculation of the optimal solution to the representative agent's optimization problem requires, as discussed in section 6.1.1, equation (6.9), the single-period budget constraint (3.4), as well as the terminal conditions (6.6) and (6.7). For reasons of space, the full characterization of the solution (described in the above section) will not be repeated in what follows.

Solving equation (6.68) for C_t finally yields the optimal consumption path:

$$C_t = \frac{\delta}{1+r}C_{t-1} + \left(1-\frac{\delta}{1+r}\right)\frac{r}{1+r}\left((1+r)B_{t-1} + \sum_{n=t}^{\infty} R^{n-t}E_t\left[NO_n\right]\right) \tag{6.69}$$

$$= \frac{\delta}{1+r}C_{t-1} + \left(1-\frac{\delta}{1+r}\right)\frac{r}{1+r}W_t. \tag{6.70}$$

Equation (6.70) shows that the optimal consumption equals a fraction of past period's consumption and a fraction of its permanent level for $\delta \in [0,1)$. The stronger the habits (i.e., the higher δ), the more the optimal consumption deviates from its permanent level. Thus, consumption is smoother and more sluggish with habit formation than without (Kano, 2008, p. 73).

The optimal current account path can be obtained by substituting equation (6.69) into the single-period budget constraint $CAB_t = NO_t - C_t + rB_{t-1}$. This yields

$$CAB_t = NO_t - \frac{\delta}{1+r}C_{t-1} - \left(1-\frac{\delta}{1+r}\right)\left(rB_{t-1} + \frac{r}{1+r}\sum_{n=t}^{\infty} R^{n-t}E_t\left[NO_n\right]\right) + rB_{t-1}. \tag{6.71}$$

Adding $\delta NO_t(1+r)^{-1}$ on both sides of equation (6.71) and rearranging the terms results in

$$CAB_t = \left(1-\frac{\delta}{1+r}\right)NO_t - \frac{\delta}{1+r}C_{t-1} - \left(1-\frac{\delta}{1+r}\right)\frac{r}{1+r}\sum_{n=t}^{\infty} R^{n-t}E_t\left[NO_n\right] + \frac{\delta}{1+r}NO_t + \frac{\delta}{1+r}rB_{t-1}. \tag{6.72}$$

Using the formula derived in footnote 3 on page 178, equation (6.72) reduces to

$$CAB_t = -\left(1-\frac{\delta}{1+r}\right)\sum_{n=t+1}^{\infty} R^{n-t}E_t\left[\Delta NO_n\right] - \frac{\delta}{1+r}C_{t-1} + \frac{\delta}{1+r}NO_t + \frac{\delta}{1+r}rB_{t-1}. \tag{6.73}$$

Adding $\delta NO_{t-1}(1+r)^{-1}$ on both sides of equation (6.73), using $CAB_{t-1} - rB_{t-2} = NO_{t-1} - C_{t-1}$, and rearranging the terms, one obtains

$$CAB_t = -\left(1-\frac{\delta}{1+r}\right)\sum_{n=t+1}^{\infty} R^{n-t}E_t\left[\Delta NO_n\right] + \frac{\delta}{1+r}CAB_{t-1} + \frac{\delta}{1+r}\Delta NO_t + \frac{\delta}{1+r}rB_{t-1} - \frac{\delta}{1+r}rB_{t-2}. \tag{6.74}$$

Substituting CAB_{t-1} for ΔB_{t-1} and rearranging the terms in equation (6.74) again finally yields

$$CAB_t = -\left(1-\frac{\delta}{1+r}\right)\sum_{n=t+1}^{\infty} R^{n-t}E_t\left[\Delta NO_n\right] + \delta CAB_{t-1} + \frac{\delta}{1+r}\Delta NO_t. \tag{6.75}$$

For $\delta = 0$, equation (6.75) coincides with the consumption-smoothing current account given by equation (6.22). When $\delta \in (0,1)$, the optimal current account (6.75) equals the δ-fraction of the last period's current account balance and the weighted average of current and future changes in net output. Hence, with habit formation, permanent shocks to net output affect the current account, and transitory shocks have greater impact on the current account than they would have without habits. For this reason, current account volatility increases when habit formation is introduced into the model (Gruber, 2004, p. 1499).

Equation (6.75) can be tested in analogy to the consumption-smoothing current account. Using identity (6.56), equation (6.75) can be rewritten in terms of VAR as

$$CAB_t = \delta CAB_{t-1} + \frac{\delta}{1+r}\Delta NO_t + \left(1 - \frac{\delta}{1+r}\right)\mathbf{k}'\mathbf{u_t} \tag{6.76}$$

where $\mathbf{k} \equiv -\mathbf{e_1}'R\mathbf{A}\left(\mathbf{I} - R\mathbf{A}\right)^{-1}$ is a $(p+1)^{st}$ unit vector. The habit parameter δ can be estimated using, for example, the fully modified OLS estimator or generalized method of moments (GMM) estimator. As in the "baseline" model without habits, the question whether the observed current account path is given by equation (6.76) can be tested by examining whether $\mathbf{k}$ is a $(p+1)^{st}$ unit vector.

As in the model without habits, subtracting the ΔNO_t-equation of the VAR from the CAB_t-equation of the VAR results in

$$\begin{aligned} &CAB_t - \Delta NO_t - R^{-1}\Delta NO_{t-1} \\ &\quad - \delta\left(CAB_{t-1} - \Delta NO_{t-1} - R^{-1}CAB_{t-2}\right) = \varepsilon_{2t} - \varepsilon_{1t}. \end{aligned} \tag{6.77}$$

If the present-value model is true, the left-hand side of equation (6.77) cannot be predicted conditional on information set $\mathbf{I}_{t-1}$ or $\mathbf{I}_{t-2}$. The current account path equals the sustainability benchmark (6.76) if

$$\Gamma^h \equiv CAB_t - \Delta NO_t - R^{-1}\Delta NO_{t-1} - \delta\left(CAB_{t-1} - \Delta NO_{t-1} - R^{-1}CAB_{t-2}\right)$$

is orthogonal to information available up to period $t-1$.

Gruber (2004) analyzes quarterly data for eight OECD countries and finds that the GMM estimate of δ varies from -0.281 to 0.920 being on average 0.873. The value of δ is significantly different from zero in six countries in the sample (Canada, Italy, Japan, the Netherlands, Spain, and the United States)—thus providing evidence for habit formation. Both the F-test and the Wald test indicate unsustainability only in Canada (see table 6.1, Appendix 6.B for details). Thus, evidence in favor of unsustainability for Canada is mainly consistent with the studies discussed above, in contrast to the result for the United Kingdom. The failure to reject sustainability in case of France is in line with the finding of sustainability in the study by Agénor et al. (1999).

The actual current account path has higher volatility than the predicted current account path in all countries with the exception of the United States and Japan. Overall, the empirical fit of the habit model is better than of the non-habit model for seven countries in the sample (with the exception of France).

However, Kano (2009) argues that Gruber's (2004) results do not necessarily provide evidence for the presence of habit formation in agents' consumption behavior. Kano (2008) shows that the above model with habit formation and the model without habit formation (section 6.1.1) modified with an arbitrary AR(1) transitory consumption component are observationally equivalent in the sense that they impose the same cross-equation restrictions on the unrestricted VAR. Such a transitory consumption component might be a stochastic slow-moving world real interest rate which follows an AR(1) process. Thus, there exists an identification problem since the better fit of the model with habit formation might result both from persistent world real interest rate shocks on the current account dynamics and from habit formation. On the example of the quarterly data for Canada (1973.Q1-2005.Q2) and the United Kingdom (1973.Q1-2003.Q4), Kano (2009) tests the real business-cycle model of a small open economy[16] with habit formation and/or the persistent real world interest rate. His results indicate that the shocks to the real interest rate rather than habit formation play a crucial role for the current account fluctuations.

6.1.6 Incorporating durable goods under linear-quadratic utility

So far, it has been assumed that the representative consumer produces and consumes one single nondurable good (such as perishable food). In practice, however, durable goods (i.e., long-lived goods such as clothing, furniture, or vehicles) may account for a large portion of households' consumption (Obstfeld and Rogoff, 1996, p. 96). Further, Baxter (2005, p. 1808) finds that durable goods raise the volatility of trade and current account balances (Baxter, 2005, p. 1808).

Following Işcan (2002, pp. 389-392),[17] consumption of both durables and nondurables can be incorporated into the RC's utility function (3.3) as follows:

$$U_t = u(C_{ND,t}, D_t) + \sum_{n=t+1}^{\infty} \beta^{n-t} E_t \left[u(C_{ND,n}, D_n) \right] \tag{6.78}$$

where $C_{ND,n}$ denotes RC's consumption of nondurable goods in period n and D_n is the stock of durable goods at the end of period n. Government spending is, for simplicity, ignored. Durable goods are assumed to yield service flows in the same period they are purchased. The period utility function $u(\cdot)$ is additive in C_{ND} and D and is linear-quadratic of the form:

$$u(C_{ND}, D) = \alpha_0 - \frac{\alpha}{2} C_{ND}^2 - \frac{1}{2} D^2. \tag{6.79}$$

RC's total consumption expenditure in terms of nondurables is given by

$$C_t = C_{ND,t} + P_{D,t} C_{D,t} \tag{6.80}$$

where $P_{D,t}$ is the relative price of durables in terms of nondurables which is determined in the world market and is taken as given by our small economy. The price of the numéraire nondurable good is normalized to unity. The consumption expenditure of durables is given by

$$C_{D,t} = D_t - (1-\delta) D_{t-1} \tag{6.81}$$

where δ is the depreciation rate with $0 < \delta \leq 1$. Using the definition of the total consumption expenditure (6.80) and of the durables' consumption expenditure (6.81), the single-period budget constraint (3.4) can be rewritten as

[16] The intertemporal model of the current account in a small open economy presented in section 6.1.1 is a closed-form solution of the standard real business-cycle model of a small open economy (Kano, 2009, p. 72).

[17] This subsubsection is mainly based on Işcan (2002, pp. 389-392) and Obstfeld and Rogoff (1996, pp. 96-99).

$$B_t = (1+r_t)B_{t-1} + NO_t - C_{ND,t} - P_{D,t}\left(D_t - (1-\delta)D_{t-1}\right). \tag{6.82}$$

where r_t is the rate on return on bonds which are indexed to consumption of nondurables.

The RC maximizes the utility function (6.78) subject to the budget constraint (6.82). Thus, the Lagrangian becomes

$$\begin{aligned}\mathscr{L} = &\sum_{n=t+1}^{\infty} \beta^{n-t} E_t\left[u(C_{ND,n}, D_n)\right] \\ &+ \lambda_n\left(NO_n - C_{ND,n} - P_{D,n}(D_n - (1-\delta)D_{n-1}) + (1+r_n)B_{n-1} - B_n\right).\end{aligned} \tag{6.83}$$

Differentiating the Lagrangian (6.83) with respect to $C_{ND,n}$, B_{n-1}, and D_{n-1} yields the following first-order conditions:

$$\frac{\partial}{\partial C_{ND,n}}\mathscr{L} = E_t\left[\beta^{n-t}\frac{\partial}{\partial C_{ND}}u(C_{ND,n}, D_n)\right] - \lambda_n = 0 \tag{6.84}$$

$$\frac{\partial}{\partial C_{B_{n-1}}}\mathscr{L} = -\lambda_{n-1} + \lambda_n E_t[1+r_n] = 0 \tag{6.85}$$

$$\begin{aligned}\frac{\partial}{\partial D_{n-1}}\mathscr{L} = &\beta^{n-t-1}E_t\left[\frac{\partial}{\partial D}u(C_{ND,n}, D_{n-1})\right] + \lambda_n(1-\delta)E_t[P_{D,n}] \\ &- \lambda_{n-1}E_t[P_{D,n-1}] = 0.\end{aligned} \tag{6.86}$$

Combining equations (6.84) and (6.85) yields for $n = t+1$ the “standard” Euler equation for nondurables consumption

$$\beta\frac{E_t\left[\frac{\partial}{\partial C_{ND}}u(C_{ND,t}, D_{t+1})\right]}{E_t\left[\frac{\partial}{\partial C_{ND}}u(C_{ND,t}, D_t)\right]} = \frac{1}{E_t\left[1+r_{t+1}\right]}. \tag{6.87}$$

Equations (6.84) and (6.86) together imply for $n = t+1$ the Euler equation

$$P_{D,t} - \beta(1-\delta)\frac{E_t\left[u'(C_{ND,t+1})\right]}{E_t\left[u'(C_{ND,t})\right]}E_t\left[P_{D,t+1}\right] = \frac{\frac{\partial}{\partial D}u(C_{ND,t+1}, D_t)}{u'(C_{ND,t})}. \tag{6.88}$$

The left-hand side of equation (6.88) reflects the net expense of buying a durable good in one period, using it in the same period, and selling it in the next period—provided there are no transaction costs. Thus, it can be interpreted as the user cost of durables in terms of nondurables consumption (Obstfeld and Rogoff, 1996, p. 97). The right-hand side of equation (6.88) shows the marginal rate of substitution of durables consumption for nondurables consumption.

Linear-quadratic utility given by (6.79) implies the following marginal utilities: $\frac{\partial}{\partial C_{ND}}u(C_{ND}, D) = -\alpha C_{ND}$ and $\frac{\partial}{\partial D}u(C_{ND}, D) = -D$. Hence, for linear-quadratic utility, the Euler equation (6.87) can be rewritten as

$$\beta E_t\left[\frac{C_{ND,t+1}}{C_{ND,t}}\right] = E_t\left[\frac{1}{1+r_{t+1}}\right] \tag{6.89}$$

and the Euler equation (6.88) becomes

$$P_{D,t}-\beta(1-\delta)E_t\left[\frac{C_{ND,t+1}P_{D,t+1}}{C_{ND,t}}\right]=\frac{D_t}{\alpha C_{ND,t}}. \tag{6.90}$$

Simplifying matters by assuming that $P_{D,n}=P_D$ and $r_n=r$ for $n\geq t$, the Euler equations (6.89) and (6.90) jointly imply

$$\left(\frac{r+\delta}{1+r}\right)\alpha P_D=\frac{D_t}{C_{ND,t}}. \tag{6.91}$$

Substituting $E_t[C_{ND,n}+P_D(D_n-(1-\delta)D_{n-1})]$ for $E_t[C_n]$ in the "specific" intertemporal budget constraint (3.38), one obtains:

$$B_{t-1}(1+r)+\sum_{n=t}^{\infty}R^{n-t}E_t[NO_n]=\sum_{n=t}^{\infty}R^{n-t}E_t[C_{ND,n}+P_D(D_n-(1-\delta)D_{n-1})]. \tag{6.92}$$

The sum $\sum_{n=t}^{\infty}R^{n-t}E_t[P_D(D_n-(1-\delta)D_{n-1})]$ on the right-hand side of the IBC (6.92) can be calculated as $-(1-\delta)P_DD_{t-1}+(r+\delta)/(1+r)\sum_{n=t}^{\infty}R^{n-t}E_t[D_n]$. Using equation (6.91) to eliminate D_n, equation (6.92) can be rewritten as

$$\begin{aligned}B_{t-1}(1+r)+\sum_{n=t}^{\infty}R^{n-t}E_t[NO_n]&=-(1-\delta)P_DD_{t-1}\\&+\left(\frac{(r+\delta)^2P_D^2\alpha}{(1+r)^2}+1\right)\sum_{n=t}^{\infty}R^{n-t}E_t[C_{ND,n}].\end{aligned} \tag{6.93}$$

Under the assumption that the time-preference factor equals the real discount factor ($\beta=(1+r)^{-1}$), the Euler equation (6.89) implies that consumption of nondurables is a martingale: $E_t[C_{ND,t+1}]=C_{ND,t}$. Exploiting the martingale property and using the formula for the infinite geometric series, the sum $\sum_{n=t}^{\infty}R^{n-t}E_t[C_{ND,n}]$ on the right-hand side of equation (6.93) simplifies to $C_{ND,t}(1+r)/r$. Thus, the IBC (6.93) can be rewritten as

$$\begin{aligned}B_{t-1}(1+r)+\sum_{n=t}^{\infty}R^{n-t}E_t[NO_n]&=-(1-\delta)P_DD_{t-1}\\&+\left(\frac{(1+r)^2+(r+\delta)^2P_D^2\alpha}{(1+r)^2}\right)\left(\frac{1+r}{r}\right)C_{ND,t}.\end{aligned} \tag{6.94}$$

Solving the IBC (6.94) for $C_{ND,t}$, one obtains the optimal level of nondurables consumption:

$$C_{ND,t}=\theta\frac{r}{1+r}\left(B_{t-1}(1+r)+\sum_{n=t}^{\infty}R^{n-t}E_t[NO_n]+(1-\delta)P_DD_{t-1}\right) \tag{6.95}$$

where $\theta=(1+r)^2/((1+r)^2+(r+\delta)^2P_D^2\alpha)$. Equation (6.95) can also be rewritten as

$$C_{ND,t}=\theta W_{t,ND}+\theta\left(\frac{r}{1+r}\right)(1-\delta)P_DD_{t-1} \tag{6.96}$$

where (as above) the superscript P denotes the permanent level of a variable. Equation (6.96) says that the optimal consumption of nondurables equals the representative agent's wealth from nondurables plus a term which (among other things) positively depends on the initial stock of durables.

The optimal current account path can be obtained by inserting equation (6.95) into the single-period budget constraint (6.82) and using the identity $CAB_t = B_t - B_{t-1}$. Following Obstfeld and Rogoff (1996, p. 98), the single-period budget constraint (6.82) can be rewritten as

$$CAB_t = rB_{t-1} + NO_t - \frac{1}{\theta} C_{ND,t} + \frac{1-\theta}{\theta} C_{ND,t} - P_D \left(D_t - (1-\delta) D_{t-1} \right) \tag{6.97}$$

where the identity $C_{ND,t} = (-1/\theta + (1-\theta)/\theta) C_{ND,t}$ has been exploited. Substituting equation (6.96) for the first occurrence of $C_{ND,t}$ and equation (6.91) for the second occurrence of $C_{ND,t}$ in equation (6.97) one obtains

$$\begin{aligned} CAB_t =& rB_{t-1} + NO_t - rB_{t-1} - \frac{r}{1+r} \sum_{n=t}^{\infty} R^{n-t} E_t[NO_n] \\ & - \frac{r(1-\delta)P_D}{1+r} D_{t-1} + \frac{(1-\theta)}{\theta} \frac{(1+r)}{(r+\delta)\alpha P_D} - P_D D_t + P_D (1-\delta) D_{t-1}. \end{aligned} \tag{6.98}$$

The fraction $(1-\theta)/\theta$ can be calculated as $(r+\delta)^2 P_D^2 \alpha/(1+r)^2$ using the definition of θ. Thus, equation (6.98) can be rewritten as

$$\begin{aligned} CAB_t =& NO_t - \frac{r}{1+r} \sum_{n=t}^{\infty} R^{n-t} E_t[NO_n] - \frac{r(1-\delta)P_D}{1+r} D_{t-1} \\ & + \frac{(r+\delta)P_D}{(1+r)} D_t - P_D D_t + P_D (1-\delta) D_{t-1}. \end{aligned} \tag{6.99}$$

Combining the last four additive terms on the right-hand side of equation (6.99), one arrives at

$$CAB_t = NO_t - \frac{r}{1+r} \sum_{n=t}^{\infty} R^{n-t} E_t[NO_n] - \frac{1-\delta}{1+r} P_D \Delta D_t \tag{6.100}$$

$$= NO_t - NO^P - \frac{1-\delta}{1+r} P_D \Delta D_t. \tag{6.101}$$

Equation (6.101) shows that the current account is determined by deviations of current net output from permanent net output minus a "stock adjustment term" (Işcan, 2002, p. 391) which is positively related to the t-period's change in the stock of durables, the price of durables, the real interest rate and negatively related to the depreciation rate. When the depreciation rate δ equals one, equation (6.101) coincides with the fundamental current account equation without durables (6.19).

The sum $NO_t - \frac{r}{1+r} \sum_{n=t}^{\infty} R^{n-t} E_t[NO_n]$ on the right-hand side of equation (6.100) can be calculated as $-\sum_{n=t+1}^{\infty} R^{n-t} E_t[\Delta NO_n]$ (see footnote 3 on page 178 for details) so that equation (6.100) can be rewritten as

$$CAB_t = - \sum_{n=t+1}^{\infty} R^{n-t} E_t[\Delta NO_n] - \frac{1-\delta}{1+r} P_D \Delta D_t. \tag{6.102}$$

Equation (6.102) states that the optimal current account level equals the present value of expected future changes in net output and the stock adjustment term. A decrease (increase) in the current stock of durables reduces (raises) *ceteris paribus* the current account beyond its consumption-smoothing level.

Işcan (2002) suggests to augment the VAR system by an additional variable $\alpha^D \Delta D_t$ where $\alpha^D = (1-\delta)R^{-1}P_D$. Thus, equation system (6.28) becomes

$$\mathbf{u}_t^D = \mathbf{A}^D \mathbf{u}_{t-1}^D + \mathbf{v}_t^D \tag{6.103}$$

where $\mathbf{u}_t^D = (\Delta NO_t, CAB_t, \alpha^D \Delta D_t)'$, $\mathbf{A}$ is a $3p \times 3p$-matrix, and $\mathbf{v}_t^D = (\varepsilon_{1t}, \varepsilon_{2t}, \varepsilon_{3t})'$. In analogy to equation (6.32), the VAR forecast of the optimal curent account is given by

$$CAB_t = \mathbf{k}^{D'} \mathbf{u}_t^D \tag{6.104}$$

where $\mathbf{k}^D \equiv -\left(\mathbf{e_1}' - \mathbf{e_{2p+1}}'\right) R\mathbf{A}\left(\mathbf{I} - R\mathbf{A}\right)^{-1}$. The observed current account path is sustainable when $\mathbf{k}^D$ is a $(p+1)^{st}$ unit vector of length $3p$. Equation (6.104) also implies that $\Gamma^D \equiv CAB_t - \Delta NO_t - R^{-1}CAB_{t-1} - \alpha^D \Delta D_t$ should be orthogonal to ΔNO_t, CAB_t, and $\alpha^D \Delta D_t$ with one or two lags, respectively.

For annual and quarterly data for Canada (1926-1995 and 1961.Q1-1997.Q2), Işcan (2002) reports that Γ^D is not orthogonal to the information contained in the information sets $\mathbf{I}_{t-1}$ or $\mathbf{I}_{t-2}$, neither for the "baseline" model without durable goods nor the model with durables. Işcan (2002) also incorporates non-traded goods into the model with durables. Non-traded goods do not enter international trade due to prohibitively high transport costs or tariffs (Obstfeld and Rogoff, 1996, p. 199). For annual data, Işcan (2002) does not find that $\Gamma^D \equiv CAB_t - \Delta NO_t^T - R^{-1}CAB_{t-1} - \alpha^D \Delta D_t$ (where NO^T denotes net output from traded goods) is correlated with expectation errors. Thus, differentiating between traded and non-traded goods changes the test results in the direction of "possible sustainability." The next subsection will provide a more rigorous illustration of how changes in the relative price of the non-traded goods affect the current account dynamics.

6.1.7 Differentiating between traded and non-traded goods under power utility

Following Bergin and Sheffrin (2000, pp. 537-540, 556-558),[18] it is assumed that the economy produces two types of a nondurable composite good: a non-traded good and an internationally traded good. Thus, the utility function (3.3) can be rewritten as

$$U_t = u(C_{Tt}, C_{Nt}) + \sum_{n=t+1}^{\infty} \beta^{n-t} E_t \left[u(C_{Tn}, C_{Nn})\right] \tag{6.105}$$

where the indices T and N denote the traded and the non-traded good, respectively. To simplify matters, the model abstracts from the existence of durable goods and government spending. The RC's total consumption expenditure in terms of the traded good (C_t) consists of consumption expenditure of the traded good (C_{Tt}) and consumption expenditure of the non-traded good (C_{Nt}) expressed in terms of the traded goods:

[18] This subsubsection mainly draws on Bergin and Sheffrin (2000, pp. 537-540, 556-558), Obstfeld and Rogoff (1994, pp. 18-21), and Obstfeld and Rogoff (1996, pp. 226-235).

$$C_t = C_{Tt} + P_t C_{Nt}. \tag{6.106}$$

P_t is the relative price of the domestic non-traded good in terms of the traded good, and the international price of the numéraire traded good is unity. The single-period budget constraint (3.4) on page (3.4) can thus be rewritten as

$$B_t = NO_t - C_{Tt} - P_t C_{Nt} + (1+r_t)B_{t-1} \tag{6.107}$$

where r_t is the real interest rate in terms of the traded good.

The representative consumer maximizes the utility function (6.105) subject to the single-period budget constraint (6.107). The corresponding Lagrangian is given by

$$\begin{aligned}\mathscr{L} =& u(C_{Tt}, C_{Nt}) + \sum_{n=t+1}^{\infty} \beta^{n-t} E_t \left[u(C_{Tn}, C_{Nn})\right] \\ &+ \lambda_n \left(NO_n - C_{Tn} - P_n C_{Nn} + (1+r_n)B_{n-1} - B_n\right).\end{aligned} \tag{6.108}$$

Differentiating the Lagrangian (6.108) with respect to C_{Tn} and C_{Nn} yields

$$\frac{\partial}{\partial C_{Tn}} \mathscr{L} = E_t \left[\beta^{n-t} \frac{\partial}{\partial C_{Tn}} u(C_{Tn}, C_{Nn})\right] - \lambda_n = 0 \tag{6.109}$$

$$\frac{\partial}{\partial C_{Nn}} \mathscr{L} = E_t \left[\beta^{n-t} \frac{\partial}{\partial C_{Nn}} u(C_{Tn}, C_{Nn})\right] - \lambda_n P_n = 0. \tag{6.110}$$

Combining equations (6.109) and (6.110) yields for $n = t$

$$P_t \frac{\partial}{\partial C_{Tt}} u(C_{Tt}, C_{Nt})) = \frac{\partial}{\partial C_{Nt}} u(C_{Tt}, C_{Nt}). \tag{6.111}$$

The instantaneous utility function is assumed to be isoelastic of the form

$$u(C_{Tt}, C_{Nt}) = \frac{\left(C_{Tt}^{\alpha} C_{Nt}^{1-\alpha}\right)^{1-\sigma}}{1-\sigma}, \quad 0 < \alpha < 1, \quad \sigma < 0, \tag{6.112}$$

where α denotes the weight of the traded good and σ is the intertemporal elasticity of substitution. Equation (6.112) assumes that the *intra*temporal elasticity of substitution between tradables and nondurables is unity.

The first partial derivatives of the utility function (6.112) in C_{Tt} and C_{Nt} direction, respectively, are

$$\frac{\partial}{\partial C_{Tt}} u(C_{Tt}, C_{Nt}) = \left(C_{Tt}^{\alpha} C_{Nt}^{1-\alpha}\right)^{-\sigma} \alpha C_{Tt}^{\alpha-1} C_{Nt}^{1-\alpha} \tag{6.113}$$

$$\frac{\partial}{\partial C_{Tt}} u(C_{Tt}, C_{Nt}) = \left(C_{Tt}^{\alpha} C_{Nt}^{1-\alpha}\right)^{-\sigma} \alpha C_{Tt}^{\alpha} C_{Nt}^{-\alpha}. \tag{6.114}$$

Inserting equations (6.113) and (6.114) into the period utility function (6.111) implies that

$$C_{Tt} = \alpha(1-\alpha)^{-1} P_t C_{Nt}. \tag{6.115}$$

Substituting equation (6.115) into the equation (6.106) yields the following optimal allocation of consumption expenditure between the traded good and the non-traded good:

$$C_{Tt} = \alpha C_t \tag{6.116}$$

$$C_{Nt} = (1-\alpha)\frac{C_t}{P_t}. \tag{6.117}$$

Further, the RC's consumption index of tradables and non-tradables is assumed to be a Cobb-Douglas function of the form

$$C_t^* = C_{Tt}^{\alpha} C_{Nt}^{1-\alpha}. \tag{6.118}$$

Using equations (6.116) and (6.117), the total consumption index (6.118) can be written as

$$C_t^* = (\alpha C_t)^{\alpha}\left((1-\alpha)\frac{C_t}{P_t}\right)^{1-\alpha}. \tag{6.119}$$

The consumption-based price index P_t^* is defined as the minimum amount of the consumption expenditure C_t (that is determined by equation (6.106)) such that the index of total consumption is unity given P_t^*. Using the definition of P_t^*, equation (6.119) can be rewritten as

$$(\alpha P_t^*)^{\alpha}\left((1-\alpha)\frac{P_t^*}{P_t}\right)^{1-\alpha} = 1. \tag{6.120}$$

Solving equation (6.120) for P_t^* yields

$$P_t^* = \alpha^{-\alpha}(1-\alpha)^{\alpha-1}P_t^{1-\alpha}. \tag{6.121}$$

Equation (6.121) shows that the consumption-based price index P_t^* is a function of the weight of the traded good α and the relative price of the non-traded good.

Now, the RC's maximization problem can be reformulated in terms of the total consumption index C^* and the consumption-based price index P^* so that the Lagrangian (6.108) becomes

$$\mathscr{L} = u(C_t^*) + E_t\sum_{n=t}^{\infty}\beta^{n-t}\left[u(C_n^*)\right] + \lambda_n\left(NO_n - P_n^* C_n^* + (1+r_n)B_{n-1} - B_n\right). \tag{6.122}$$

Differentiating the Lagrangian (6.122) with respect to C_n^* and B_{n-1} one obtains

$$E_t[u'(C_n^*)] = \beta^{n-t}E_t[u'(C_n^*)] - \lambda_n E_t[P_n^*] \tag{6.123}$$

$$E_t[u'(B_{n-1})] = -\lambda_{n-1} + \lambda_n E_t[1+r_n]. \tag{6.124}$$

Combining the first-order conditions (6.123) and (6.124) results in the Euler equation of the form

$$\beta E_t\left[(1+r_n)\left(\frac{u'(C_n^*)}{u'(C_{n-1}^*)}\right)\left(\frac{P_{n-1}^*}{P_n^*}\right)\right] = 1. \tag{6.125}$$

Assuming $n = t+1$ and inserting $u'(C_n) = C_n^{-\sigma}$, the Euler equation (6.125) becomes

$$\beta E_t\left[(1+r_{t+1})\left(\frac{C_{t+1}^*}{C_t^* t}\right)^{\sigma}\left(\frac{P_t^*}{P_{t+1}^*}\right)\right] = 1. \tag{6.126}$$

It is convenient to rewrite the Euler equation (6.126) in terms of the consumption expenditure and the relative price of the domestic non-traded good in terms of the traded good. Using the definition of P_t^* one obtains

$$\frac{P_t^*}{P_{t+1}^*} = \frac{P_t^{1-\alpha}\alpha^{-\alpha}(1-\alpha)^{\alpha-1}}{P_{t+1}^{1-\alpha}\alpha^{-\alpha}(1-\alpha)^{\alpha-1}} = \left(\frac{P_t}{P_{t+1}}\right)^{1-\alpha}. \tag{6.127}$$

Using the definition of C_t^* one obtains

$$\begin{aligned}\left(\frac{C_{t+1}^*}{C_t^*t}\right)^{\sigma} &= \left(\frac{\alpha^{\alpha}C_t^{\alpha}(1-\alpha)^{\alpha}C_t^{1-\alpha}P_t\alpha-1}{\alpha^{\alpha}C_{t+1}^{\alpha}(1-\alpha)^{\alpha}C_{t+1}^{1-\alpha}P_{t+1}\alpha-1}\right)^{\sigma}\\ &= \left(\frac{C_t}{C_{t+1}}\right)^{\sigma}\left(\frac{P_t}{P_{t+1}}\right)^{(\alpha-1)\sigma}.\end{aligned} \tag{6.128}$$

Substituting equations (6.127) and (6.128) into the Euler equation (6.126) results in

$$\beta E_t\left[(1+r_{t+1})\left(\frac{C_t}{C_{t+1}}\right)^{\sigma}\left(\frac{P_t}{P_{t+1}}\right)^{(1-\alpha)(1-\sigma)}\right] = 1. \tag{6.129}$$

The Euler equation (6.129) can be further simplified by log-linearizing. For this purpose, the Euler equation is first rewritten using the inverse of the intertemporal elasticity of substitution, i.e., $\gamma = \sigma^{-1}$, and raising both sides of equation (6.129) to the power γ:

$$E_t\left[\beta^{\gamma}(1+r_{t+1})\gamma\left(\frac{C_t}{C_{t+1}}\right)\left(\frac{P_t}{P_{t+1}}\right)^{(1-\alpha)(1-\gamma)}\right] = 1. \tag{6.130}$$

Joint (conditional) lognormality is assumed for the inverse of the real discount factor $(1+r_{t+1})$, the consumption growth rate ($\Delta c_{t+1} = \log C_{t+1} - \log C_t$), and the change in the relative price of the non-traded good ($\Delta p_{t+1} = \log P_{t+1} - \log P_t$). Further, it is assumed that conditional variances and covariances[19] between these variables do not change over time.

After taking logarithms on both sides of equation (6.130) and rearranging the terms, one arrives at

$$\begin{aligned}E_t\left[\Delta c_{t+1}\right] =& \gamma E_t\left[\log\beta + r_{t+1} + \frac{1-\gamma}{\gamma}(1-\alpha)\Delta p_{t+1}\right]\\ &+\frac{1}{2}E\left[\gamma\log\beta + r_{t+1} + \frac{1-\gamma}{\gamma}(1-\alpha)\Delta p_{t+1} - \Delta c_{t+1}\right.\\ &\left.-E\left[\left(\log\beta + r_{t+1} + \frac{1-\gamma}{\gamma}(1-\alpha)\Delta p_{t+1} - \Delta c_{t+1}\right)^2\right]\right].\end{aligned} \tag{6.131}$$

[19] A conditional variance of a random variable X (denoted by $\mathrm{Var}_t(X)$) is defined as $\mathrm{Var}_t(X) = E_t[(X - E_t[X])^2]$. An unconditional covariance between two random variables X and Y (denoted by $\mathrm{Cov}_t(X,Y)$) is defined as $\mathrm{Cov}_t(X,Y) = E_t[(X - E_t[X])]E_t[(Y - E_t[Y])]$.

Herein, the identities

$$\log E_t[X] = E_t[\log X] + \frac{1}{2}\text{Var}_t(\log X) \quad \text{and}$$
$$\text{Var}_t(\log X) = E\left[(\log X - E[\log X])^2\right]$$

for constant conditional variances and covariances have been exploited (Campbell et al., 1997, p. 306). Multiplying out the brackets on the right-hand side of equation (6.131) one obtains

$$\begin{aligned}
E_t[\Delta c_{t+1}] &= \gamma E_t\left[\log\beta + r_{t+1} + \frac{1-\gamma}{\gamma}(1-\alpha)\Delta p_{t+1}\right]\\
&+\frac{1}{2}\Big(\gamma^2 E\left[(r_{t+1}-E[r_{t+1}])^2\right] + (1-\gamma)^2(1-\alpha)^2 E\left[(\Delta p_{t+1}-E[\Delta p_{t+1}])^2\right]\\
&+\gamma^2 E\left[(\Delta c_{t+1}-E[\Delta c_{t+1}])^2\right] - 2\gamma E[(r_{t+1}-E[r_{t+1}])(\Delta c_{t+1}-E[\Delta c_{t+1}])]\\
&+2(1-\gamma)(1-\alpha)E[(r_{t+1}-E[r_{t+1}])(\Delta p_{t+1}-E[\Delta p_{t+1}])]\\
&-2(1-\gamma)(1-\alpha)E[(\Delta p_{t+1}-E[\Delta p_{t+1}])(\Delta c_{t+1}-E[\Delta c_{t+1}])]\Big).
\end{aligned} \tag{6.132}$$

Using the definition of unconditional variances and covariances, the notation in equation (6.132) can be simplified as follows:

$$\begin{aligned}
E_t[\Delta c_{t+1}] =& \gamma E_t\left[\log\beta + r_{t+1} + \frac{1-\gamma}{\gamma}(1-\alpha)\Delta p_{t+1}\right]\\
&+\frac{1}{2}\Big(\gamma^2\text{Var}(r_{t+1}) + (1-\gamma)^2(1-\alpha)^2\text{Var}(\Delta p_{t+1}) + \gamma^2\text{Var}(\Delta c_{t+1})\\
&-2\gamma\text{Cov}(r_{t+1},\Delta c_{t+1}) + 2(1-\gamma)(1-\alpha)\text{Cov}(r_{t+1},\Delta p_{t+1})\\
&-2(1-\gamma)(1-\alpha)\text{Cov}(\Delta p_{t+1},\Delta c_{t+1})\Big).
\end{aligned} \tag{6.133}$$

Based on equation (6.133), the expected consumption-based real interest rate r_t^* can be defined as

$$\begin{aligned}
E_t[r_{t+1}^*] =& E_t\left[r_{t+1} + \frac{1-\gamma}{\gamma}(1-\alpha)\Delta p_{t+1}\right]\\
&+\Big\{\log\beta + \frac{1}{2}\gamma^2\text{Var}(r_{t+1}) + \gamma^2\text{Var}(\Delta c_{t+1})\\
&+(1-\gamma)^2(1-\alpha)^2\text{Var}(\Delta p_{t+1}) - 2\gamma\text{Cov}(r_{t+1},\Delta c_{t+1})\\
&+2(1-\gamma)(1-\alpha)\text{Cov}(r_{t+1},\Delta p_{t+1})\\
&-2(1-\gamma)(1-\alpha)\text{Cov}(\Delta p_{t+1},\Delta c_{t+1})\Big\}
\end{aligned} \tag{6.134}$$

where the term in curly brackets on the right-hand side of equation (6.134) is a constant due to the assumption of joint homoscedasticity. Equation (6.134) shows that the expected consumption-based real interest rate is determined by the expected real interest rate, the expected change in the relative price of the non-traded good, and a constant term. Thus, the consumption-based real interest rate incorporates both changes in the conventional real interest rate and changes in the real exchange rate (since $\Delta p_{t+1} > 0$ reflects real exchange-rate appreciation).[20]

The definition of the consumption-based real interest rate (6.134) permits a reformulation of equation (6.133) as

$$E_t\left[\Delta c_{t+1}\right] = \gamma E_t\left[r^*_{t+1}\right]. \tag{6.138}$$

Equation (6.138) states that the expected change in optimal consumption equals the intertemporal elasticity of substitution γ multiplied by the expected consumption-based real interest rate.

The optimal current account path can be determined by combining the above considerations with the "specific" intertemporal budget constraint (3.38):

$$\sum_{n=t}^{\infty} E_t\left[R_{t+1,n}C_n\right] = \sum_{n=t}^{\infty} E_t\left[R_{t+1,n}NO_n\right] + (1+r_t)B_{t-1} \tag{6.139}$$

where the identity $TB_n = NO_n - C_n$ has been employed. Next, it is useful to linearize the IBC (6.139). For this purpose, the expectation operator is omitted temporarily (and will be inserted later) and the notation is changed as follows:

$$\Phi_t - \Psi_t = \mathscr{B}_t \tag{6.140}$$

where $\Phi_t \equiv \sum_{n=t}^{\infty} E_t\left[R_{t+1,n}C_n\right]$, $\Psi_t \equiv \sum_{n=t}^{\infty} E_t\left[R_{t+1,n}NO_n\right]$, and $\mathscr{B}_t = (1+r_t)B_{t-1}$.

Following Campbell and Mankiw (1990, pp. 204-205, 212-213), Huang and Lin (1993, pp. 321-322, 337), and Bergin and Sheffrin (2000, pp. 557-558), the IBC (6.140) can be linearized as follows:

---

[20] The real exchange rate (Q_t) can be defined as the ratio of national price indices times the nominal exchange rate in price quotation (S_t)

$$Q_t = S_t \frac{P_t^{*f}}{P_t^*}. \tag{6.135}$$

The nominal exchange rate in price (or direct) quotation is defined as the domestic currency price of one foreign-currency unit (Rivera-Batiz and Rivera-Batiz, 1994, p. 13). Assuming that both the national and the foreign price indices are given by equation (6.121) with the same weight α home and abroad, equation (6.135) can be rewritten as

$$Q_t = S_t \frac{\alpha^{-\alpha}(1-\alpha)^{\alpha-1}\left(P_t^f\right)^{1-\alpha}}{\alpha^{-\alpha}(1-\alpha)^{\alpha-1}P_t^{1-\alpha}} \tag{6.136}$$

where f denotes foreign variables. Assuming that the law of one price applies to the traded good, S_t equals the ratio of the domestic price of the traded good to the foreign price of the traded good and is unity because the foreign and domestic prices of tradables are unity. Normalizing in addition P_t^f to one, equation (6.136) finally simplifies to

$$Q_t = P_t^{\alpha-1}. \tag{6.137}$$

Thus, an increase (decrease) in the relative price of the domestic non-traded good *ceteris paribus* leads to a real exchange-rate appreciation (depreciation).

$$no_t - \left(1 - \frac{1}{\rho_2}\right) \lfloor_t - \frac{c_t}{\rho_2} = - \sum_{n=t+1}^{\infty} \beta^{n-t} E_t \left[\Delta no_n - \frac{\Delta c_n}{\rho_2} - \left(1 - \frac{1}{\rho_2}\right) r_n\right]$$
$$+ k_2 + \left(1 - \frac{1}{\rho_2}\right) \frac{\beta}{1-\beta} k \tag{6.141}$$

where $no_t \equiv \ln(NO_t)$, $\lfloor_t \equiv \ln(\mathscr{B}_t)$, and $c_t \equiv \ln(C_t)$. The parameter ρ_2, k_2, and k are defined as follows: $\rho_2 = 1 - \mathscr{B}/\Psi$, $k_2 \equiv \ln(\rho_2) - (1 - 1/\rho_2)\ln(1 - \rho_2)$, $k = \ln(\beta) - (1 - 1/\beta)\ln(1 - \beta)$. The derivation of equation (6.141) can be found in Appendix 6.A.

Inserting the log-linearized Euler equation (6.138) into equation (6.141) one obtains

$$no_t - \left(1 - \frac{1}{\rho_2}\right) \lfloor_t - \frac{c_t}{\rho_2} = - \sum_{n=t+1}^{\infty} \beta^{n-t} E_t \left[\Delta no_n - \frac{\gamma r_n^*}{\rho_2} - \left(1 - \frac{1}{\rho_2}\right) r_n\right]$$
$$+ k_2 + \left(1 - \frac{1}{\rho_2}\right) \frac{\beta}{1-\beta} k. \tag{6.142}$$

Linearizing equation (6.142) around the steady state in which net foreign assets are zero so that $\rho_2 = 1$ (and $k_2 = 0$) yields

$$cab_t = - \sum_{n=t+1}^{\infty} \beta^{n-t} E_t \left[\Delta no_n - \gamma r_n^*\right] \tag{6.143}$$

where $cab_t \equiv \ln(CAB_t)$ and $cab_t = no_t - c_t$. Equation (6.143) says that an expected increase (decrease) in future net output leads to a current account deficit (surplus) since the representative consumer seeks to smooth his consumption. The larger the expected increase (decline) in future net output, the higher is the current account deficit (surplus). At the same time, an increase (a decline) in the expected consumption-based interest rate—all other things being equal—raises (decreases) the optimal current account path beyond the consumption-smoothing path.

Following Bergin and Sheffrin (2000), equation (6.143) can be tested by extending the VAR(p) (6.26) to include the the consumption-based real interest rate r^*:

$$\mathbf{u}_t^T = \mathbf{A}\mathbf{u}_{t-1}^T + \mathbf{v}_t^T \tag{6.144}$$

where $\mathbf{u}^T = (\Delta NO_t, CAB_t, r_t^*)'$ is a $3p$ column vector, the companion matrix $\mathbf{A}$ is a $3p \times 3p$ dimensional matrix, and $\mathbf{v}^T = (\varepsilon_{1t}, \varepsilon_{2t}, \varepsilon_{3t})'$.

Analogously to equation (6.56), the VAR forecast of the optimal current account can be obtained by

$$CAB_t = \mathbf{k}^{T'} \mathbf{u}_t^T \tag{6.145}$$

where $\mathbf{k}^T \equiv -\left(\mathbf{e}_1' - \theta \mathbf{e}_{2p+1}'\right) \beta \mathbf{A} (\mathbf{I} - \beta \mathbf{A})^{-1}$ is a $3p$-column vector.

Bergin and Sheffrin (2000) investigate three model specifications: (i) the "baseline" model without changes in the consumption-based real interest rate, (ii) the model with changes in the real interest rates only, and (iii) the model with both changes in the real interest rate and the real exchange rate. The world real interest rate is computed following Barro and Sala-i-Martin (1990) using time-varying weights for each country based on its share of real GDP in the total GDP for G7 countries. The subjective time-preference factor is calculated as the sample mean for the data set which is $\beta = 0.94$. Regarding the share of tradables, Bergin and Sheffrin (2000) use the estimate of Stockman and Tesar (1995) which yields $\alpha = 0.5$ and the estimate obtained by Kravis et al. (1982) who find α being close to 0.75. Based on Mehra and Prescott (1985) and Campbell and Shiller (1988), Bergin and Sheffrin (2000) consider a range of values for the elasticity of intertemporal substitution γ, namely: $\gamma = 0.5$, $\gamma = 1.0$, or the level which minimizes χ^2, or the level which matches the variance.

Analyzing quarterly, seasonally adjusted data from 1961.Q4 to 1996.Q2 for Canada, Australia, and the United Kingdom, the nonlinear Wald test fails to reject the null hypothesis that $\mathbf{k}^T$ is a $(p+1)^{st}$ unit vector for Canada and Australia only when both changes in the real interest rate and the real exchange rate are taken into account. This result is mainly consistent with the rest of the empirical literature (Sheffrin and Woo, 1990; Obstfeld and Rogoff, 1996; Otto, 1992; Gruber, 2004 for Canada and Cashin and McDermott, 1998 for Australia). The better "fit" of the model specification (iii) suggests that exchange rates have an important effect on the current account path at least in Canada and Australia. For the United Kingdom, the Wald test strongly rejects the null hypothesis of sustainability disregarding of the model specification. This finding is in line with Sheffrin and Woo (1990), Gruber (2004), and Kano (2008).

Landeau (2002) estimates quarterly data during the period 1960.Q1-1999.Q4 for Chile and is not able to reject the null hypothesis that $\mathbf{k}^T$ is a $(p+1)^{st}$ unit vector disregarding whether the changes in the real interest rate and/or the exchange rate are considered. Landeau (2002), however, omits pretesting for the unit root in the time series although the VAR representation might not exist when cab_t, Δno_t, and r_t^* are not stationary in levels.

Moccero (2008) modifies the analysis suggested by Bergin and Sheffrin (2000) to take into account capital controls in Argentina. The appreciation of the real exchange rate (Δp_{t+1}) can be decomposed into the appreciation of the commercial, i.e., regulated exchange rate (Δp_{t+1}^S) and the appreciation of the unregulated exchange rate in the free or black market (Δp_{t+1}^M). Thus, equation (6.143) can be rewritten as

$$cab_t = -\sum_{n=t+1}^{\infty} \beta^{n-t} E_t \Big[\Delta no_n - \gamma r_n - (1-\gamma)(1-\alpha)\left(b\Delta p_{t+1}^S + (1-b)\Delta p_{t+1}^M\right)\Big]. \tag{6.146}$$

Equation (6.146) leads on to the following VAR equation:

$$\mathbf{u}_t^E = \mathbf{A}^E \mathbf{u}_{t-1}^E + \mathbf{v}_t^E \tag{6.147}$$

where $\mathbf{u}^{E'} = (\Delta no_t, cab_t, r_t, \Delta p_t^S, \Delta p_t^M)$ is a $5p$ column vector, the companion matrix $\mathbf{A}^E$ is a $5p \times 5p$ dimensional matrix, and $\mathbf{v}^{E'} = (\varepsilon_{1t}, \varepsilon_{2t}, \varepsilon_{3t}, \varepsilon_{4t}, \varepsilon_{5t})$. The VAR prediction of the current account is given by

$$CAB_t = \mathbf{k}^{E'} \mathbf{u}_t^E \tag{6.148}$$

where $\mathbf{k}^E \equiv -\left(\mathbf{e}_1' - \gamma \mathbf{e}_{2p+1}' - (1-\gamma)(1-\alpha)\mathbf{m}'\right) \beta \mathbf{A}^E \left(\mathbf{I} - \beta \mathbf{A}^E\right)^{-1}$ is a $5p$-column vector and $\mathbf{m}$ is a $5p$-column vector whose elements are zero except for the $(3p+1)^{st}$ element which is b and the $(4p+1)^{st}$ element which equals $(1-b)$.

Moccero (2008) tests the null hypothesis that $\mathbf{k}^E$ is a $(p+1)^{st}$ unit vector using the nonlinear Wald test. For the real interest rate, the method suggested by Barro and Sala-i-Martin (1990) is not appropriate because the cost of borrowing might be higher for Argentina than the G7-average. Therefore, Moccero (2008) takes the implicit yield of an internal government bond as a proxy for the real interest rate. The value of b is (*ad hoc*) chosen to be 0.2. The Wald test provides evidence against sustainability both for the full sample period from 1885 to 2002 and the subsample period during 1885-1930 which was characterized by relatively high capital mobility and the absence of financial crises disregarding of the model specification. This result is consistent with the result obtained by Ghosh and Ostry (1995) for the "baseline" model in Argentina during 1960-1990.

For Ghana, Darku (2010) also incorporates constraints on capital mobility. Sustainability is found for the sample period during 1960-2002 only when the asymmetric access to international financial markets is taken into account (as suggested by Callen and Cashin (1999)).

Saksonovs (2006) examines quarterly data between 1975 and 2004 for ten countries which experienced a currency crisis during the sample period and seven "non-crisis" countries. For the full sample period, the Wald test indicates the lack of sustainability in six non-crisis countries (Canada, Germany, Japan, Netherlands, Switzerland, and the United States) and in five crisis countries (Mexico, Norway, Philippines, South Korea, and Sweden). The fact that evidence against sustainability is obtained for only half of the "crisis" countries which have *ex post* unsustainable current accounts raises questions about the appropriateness of the sustainability benchmark. However, the failure to detect sustainability might be explained by the deficiencies of the Wald test in case that the current account series is persistent. For this reason, it would be fruitful to perform an F-test on the restrictions of the VAR and/or for Granger-causality between the current account and the future changes in net output.

Finally, Campa and Gavilan (2011) report that the test results largely depend on the value of the intertemporal elasticity of substitution. They find that the "fit" of the model in many European countries is better for small values of γ.

6.1.8 Conclusion

The sustainability notion used in this section defines the sustainable current account path as the equilibrium current account path predicted by the intertemporal approach to the current account. The testing methodology developed by Campbell (1987) and Campbell and Shiller (1987) provides several tests for assessing whether the observed current account coincides with the dynamic sustainability benchmark. It also allows for a quantitative estimation of the extent to which the actual current account path deviates from the sustainable path. However, only Hudson and Stennett (2003) address this issue by suggesting *ad-hoc* criteria in order to differentiate between "large" and "chronic" current account imbalances: They declare imbalances to be large (chronic) when the deviation of the observed current account path from the predicted path is less than or equal to the difference between the mean deviation and four (five) standard deviations. As with all *ad-hoc* criteria, the major drawback of this proposal is the lack of analytic justification for the terminology and a resulting inherent arbitrariness. On a different note, many studies purge the consumption-tilting component from the current account series and test the consumption-smoothing component only. In principle, a methodology for evaluating the sustainability of the consumption-tilting component of the current account series will be required.

The tests of the intertemporal approach to the current account also have the advantage that they can be used as tests of the intertemporal budget constraint. Empirical evidence in favor of the validity of the intertemporal approach to the current account in the data also indicates the validity of the intertemporal budget constraint. The opposite is, however, not necessarily true as the economy might be constrained by the IBC, yet specific assumptions of the intertemporal model concerning, for example, the relationship between the real interest rate and the time-preference rate might not be satisfied. Almost all studies in table 6.1, Appendix 6.B find that the current account is stationary in levels, thus indicating sustainability in the strong sense—even though most of them perform unit root tests of the first generation which are particularly prone to the low-power and size-distortion problems discussed in chapter 5.

As for the question whether the recently observed global imbalances and the intra-euro-zone imbalances are sustainable, the evidence is mixed. For the United States and Japan, the study by Gruber (2004) says "possibly yes" (when the habit formation has been taken into account), and the study by Saksonovs (2006) says "possibly no". The recent data for Asian economies or oil-exporting economies have not been examined so far. Saksonovs (2006) and Campa and Gavilan (2011) find no support for the intertemporal model of the current account in Germany, yet there is some (although weak) evidence for sustainability in Italy, Spain, and Portugal (Gruber, 2004; Saksonovs, 2006; Campa and Gavilan, 2011).

Further, in the same way as the tests on the intertemporal budget constraints, the tests on the validity of the intertemporal model of the current account are backward-looking and cannot capture future changes in the economic environment. This inherent limitation of the statistical tests can explain why Saksonovs (2006) finds support for the validity of the sustainability benchmark although five out of ten countries in his data set experienced a currency crisis. Similarly, the tests indicate that the intertemporal model of the current account is possibly satisfied in Portugal and Spain (Gruber, 2004; Saksonovs, 2006; Campa and Gavilan, 2011) prior 2005. However, these countries experienced a sovereign debt crisis, in which external debt played an important role (Gros, 2011), less than a decade later.

The main problem in defining sustainability in terms of the equilibrium current account path is that the sustainability benchmark relies heavily on additional assumptions such as linear-quadratic utility, inclusion or no inclusion of non-traded goods and/or durable goods. Thus, the violation of the sustainability benchmark can be interpreted either as evidence against sustainability or as evidence against some underlying assumptions used to derive the benchmark. Although the extensions of the "baseline" model under certainty equivalence presented in this section eliminate many of the "usual suspects", the identification problem still remains.

One drawback is that this methodology ignores the effect of government spending on the current account by assuming balanced government deficits. However, government spending may affect external sustainability. Suppose, for example, that the government has an external balance target and cuts its spending in case of expected current account deficits due to technology shocks. In this case, the current account position would not turn into a deficit although private agents fully smooth consumption (Ghosh, 1995, p. 126).

It would also be desirable to extend this approach to large countries which play an important role in the emergence of global imbalances. The studies by Otto (1992), Ghosh (1995), Gruber (2004), and Saksonovs (2006) apply this approach to the United States although this methodology is intended for the analysis of small countries. As expected, these studies provide little support for the validity of the intertemporal model of the current account in the United States. Further, when the current account balance is determined by both the consumption-smoothing and consumption-tilting components, only the sustainability of the former has been addressed so far. However, criteria for the sustainability of the consumption-tilting part of the current account are also needed.

Finally, the intertemporal model to the current account suffers from further theoretical limitations such as the rational-expectation hypothesis or exogenous labor supply; these issues have already been discussed in section 3.3 of chapter 3. The next section extends the intertemporal approach to the current account by incorporating investment risk and investment returns.

6.2 Dynamic benchmark in the portfolio approach to the current account

The portfolio- or stock-equilibrium approach to the current account was first introduced by Kraay and Ventura (2000, 2002) and Ventura (2001) and further developed by Devereux and Sutherland (2007, 2010), Didier and Lowenkron (2009), Guo and Jin (2009), Tille and van Wincoop (2010), and others. According to the mean-variance theory pioneered by Markowitz (1952) and Tobin (1958), the portfolio approach assumes that utility-maximizing risk-averse investors choose their optimal portfolios using two criteria: maximization of mean returns and minimization of risk.

Based on the portfolio approach to the current account, Calderon et al. (2000) suggest a dynamic sustainability benchmark against which the actual current account series can be compared. In this context, the path of external imbalances is sustainable if two conditions are satisfied. Firstly, in the long-run equilibrium, domestic and foreign investors attain the desired portfolio allocation of assets across countries. Secondly, as an immediate portfolio adjustment may be impossible due to imperfections in financial and factor markets, in the short run, external imbalances are driven by dynamic adjustment resulting from asset reallocation in order to achieve the desired stock position (Calderon et al., 2000, p. 26).

Following Calderon et al. (2000), the long-run portfolio equilibrium is characterized as follows:

$$\alpha\left(\overset{+}{RE},\overset{-}{RI}\right)W+\alpha^{f}\left(\overset{+}{RE},\overset{-}{RI}\right)W^{f}=A \tag{6.149}$$

where W and W^f denote domestic and foreign wealth, respectively, α is the share of domestic assets desired to be held by domestic investors, α^f is the share of domestic assets desired to be owned by foreign investors, and A denotes agents' total assets. Equation (6.149) shows that the desired holdings of a country's assets by both domestic and foreign residents equal its total existing assets in the long-run portfolio equilibrium. According to the mean-variance theory, the shares of a country's assets in investors' portfolios are increasing in the anticipated return of the country's assets relative to those in the rest of the world (denoted by RE) and decreasing in the perceived riskiness relative to the rest of the world (denoted by RI).

The net international investment position is defined as the difference between external financial assets of residents (i.e., claims on foreigners) and domestic assets held by foreign investors (i.e., liabilities of residents on nonresidents):

$$B=(1-\alpha)W-\alpha^{f}W^{f} \tag{6.150}$$

where the time indices are omitted in the long-run equilibrium. It is convenient to normalize the variables by dividing both sides of equation (7.1.4) by W:

$$\frac{B}{W} = 1 - \alpha - \alpha^f \left(\frac{W^f}{W}\right). \tag{6.151}$$

Because both α and α^f, by assumption, are increasing in RE and decreasing in RI, equation (6.151) can be more compactly rewritten as

$$\frac{B}{W} = f\left(\overset{-}{RE}, \overset{+}{RI}, \overset{-}{\frac{W^f}{W}}\right). \tag{6.152}$$

Equation (6.152) is the long-run sustainability condition which states that the long-run equilibrium ratio of the NIIP to a country's wealth is decreasing in investment returns in the country relative to the rest of the world and in the ratio of foreign-owned to domestic-owned wealth and is increasing in the investment risk in the country relative to the rest of the world.

Calderon et al. (2000) arrive at an econometric model by assuming that the country's ratio of net foreign assets to wealth (denoted by y_{1t}) follows an autoregressive distributed lag model of the form

$$y_{1t} = a + by_{1t-1} + cy_{2t} + dy_{2t-1} + \varepsilon_{1t} \tag{6.153}$$

where the country index is, for convenience, ignored. The set of explanatory variables RE, RI, and W^f/W is denoted by y_{2t}. For simplicity, y_{2t} is univariate and follows an AR(1) process:

$$y_{2t} = \rho y_{2t-1} + e_t. \tag{6.154}$$

Thus, there exists a single long-run relationship between y_{1t} and y_{2t}. The explanatory variable y_2 may be allowed to be endogenous in the sense that shocks in y_2 may be correlated with contemporaneous shocks in y_1. With sufficiently many lags in the autoregressive process in y_1 and y_2, ε_1 and e are serially uncorrelated. Further, shocks in y_{1t} and y_{2t} are assumed to be identically, independently and normally distributed. In sum:

$$\begin{pmatrix} \varepsilon_{1t} \\ e_t \end{pmatrix}, \qquad i.i.d\,(0,\Sigma) \quad \Sigma = \begin{pmatrix} \sigma_{\varepsilon_1 \varepsilon_1} & \sigma_{\varepsilon_1 e} \\ \sigma_{e \varepsilon_1} & \sigma_{ee} \end{pmatrix}.$$

Under the assumption that the disturbance terms ε_1 and e are jointly normal, one obtains

$$\varepsilon_{1t} = \left(\frac{\sigma_{\varepsilon_1 e}}{\sigma_{ee}}\right) e_t + \varepsilon_{2t} \tag{6.155}$$

where $\sigma_{\varepsilon_1 e}/\sigma_{ee}$ is the regression coefficient of the regression of ε_{1t} on e_t and ε_{2t} is distributed independently from e_t. Substituting equation (6.155) into equation (6.153) and using equation (6.154) to eliminate e_t results in

$$y_{1t} = a + by_{1t-1} + \left(c + \frac{\sigma_{\varepsilon_1 e}}{\sigma_{ee}}\right) y_{2t} + \left(d - \rho \frac{\sigma_{\varepsilon_1 e}}{\sigma_{ee}}\right) y_{2t-1} + \varepsilon_{2t}. \tag{6.156}$$

Subtracting y_{1t-1} and $\left(d - \rho\left(\sigma_{\varepsilon_1 e}/\sigma_{ee}\right)\right)y_{2t}$ on both sides of equation (6.156) and rearranging the terms allows rewriting equation (6.156) as an error-correction model:

$$\Delta y_{1t} = a - (1-b)\left\{ y_{1t-1} - \left[\frac{d + c(1-\rho)\frac{\sigma_{\varepsilon_1 e}}{\sigma_{ee}}}{1-b}\right] y_{2t} \right\} + \left(d - \rho\frac{\sigma_{\varepsilon_1 e}}{\sigma_{ee}}\right)\Delta y_{2t} + \varepsilon_{2t} \tag{6.157}$$

where $(1-b)$ is the speed of adjustment, the term in curly brackets in equation (6.157) is the error-correction term, and the term in square brackets in equation (6.157) is the long-run coefficient. The error-correction specification (6.157) has the advantage that it permits the estimation of both the short-run and the long-run dynamics of the model.

Calderon et al. (2000) proceed as follows: First, they examine whether the stock-equilibrium model is valid by estimating the error-correction model (6.157) on the basis of panel data. The data set contains time series and cross-sectional data in the period from 1965 to 1997 for 48 industrial and developing countries and was constructed by Kraay et al. (2000). For the countries in which the stock-equilibrium model "performs" best, external sustainability is assessed in the second step by constructing the long-run equilibrium series of the NIIP-to-wealth ratio and comparing it with the observed NIIP-to-wealth series.

The error-correction model (6.157) is estimated by means of the pooled mean group estimator suggested by Pesaran et al. (1999). The PMG estimator assumes that the long-run coefficient represents equilibrium conditions which are country-independent and is, therefore, the same for all countries whereas the intercept and other coefficients are country-specific. As the sample contains a large number of heterogeneous countries, equation (6.157) is also tested for four subsamples: (i) high and upper-income countries; (ii) low and lower middle-income countries; (iii) countries with low capital controls; (iv) countries with high capital controls.

For the whole sample, the long-run coefficients have the expected sign (positive for *RE* and negative for *RI* and W^f/W), yet the coefficient on *RE* is not statistically significant. When time effects are taken into account by using demeaned data, all coefficients have a correct sign and are statistically significant. The Hausman (1978) test statistic does not reject the null hypothesis of individual or joint homogeneity of the long-run coefficients. The speed-of-adjustment coefficient is negative, less than one in absolute value (so that the model is stable), and is statistically significant both with and without time effects. The average short-run parameters show statistically significant lagged effects of B/W and W^f/W with no time effects and in addition of *RE* when time effects are included. The average value of the country-specific adjusted R^2 is about 0.4 both with and without time effects, thus implying that the explanatory power of the model is satisfactory.

For the two (overlapping) subsamples of high and upper-income countries as well as countries with low capital controls, all long-run coefficients and the error-correction coefficient are correctly signed and statistically significant, both for raw and demeaned data. The Hausman (1978) test statistic fails to reject the PMG restrictions on the long-run coefficients. For high- and upper-income countries, the short-run coefficients reveal significant lagged effects of B/W and W^f/W. In addition, a significant lagged effect is also found for countries with low capital controls when time effects are omitted.

For low- and lower-middle income countries, all long-run coefficients have the anticipated sign, yet the coefficient on *RE* is not statistically significant when no time effects are included. Accounting for time effects, the coefficients on *RE* and *RI* have both the wrong sign and are not statistically significant. For countries with high capital controls, the long-run parameters are correctly signed. Absent time effects, the long-run coefficient on *RE* is not significant. Adding time effects, the long-run coefficient on *RI* is not statistically significant and its homogeneity is rejected by the (individual) Hausman statistics. Overall, the explanatory power of the model is best for countries with high- and upper-middle income and the worst for low-income countries.

Thus, the estimation results support the stock equilibrium model for countries with low capital controls and/or high and upper-middle income, but not in countries with high capital controls and/or low income. The reasons might be that capital controls lessen the importance of risk and return for portfolio decisions and that the NIIP positions in low-income countries are to a large extent determined by non-market forces (such as political interests or humanitarian reasons) rather than by investors' optimal diversification decisions (Calderon et al., 2000, pp. 4, 23).

For countries in which there is evidence for validity of the stock-equilibrium model, the sustainable long-run equilibrium series of the NIIP-to-wealth ratio can be constructed using the long-run PMG estimates. The degree of deviations from the long-run value represents the degree of unsustainability. Under the assumption that y_1, y_2, and ε_1 remain constant in the long-run equilibrium, equation (6.156) shows the steady-state relationship between the NIIP-to-wealth ratios and the explanatory variables:

$$y_1 = \frac{a}{1-b} + \left(\frac{c+d+(1-\rho)\frac{\sigma_{\varepsilon_1 e}}{\sigma_{ee}}}{1-b} \right) y_2 + \varepsilon_2. \tag{6.158}$$

Calderon et al. (2000) only visually compare the graphs of the observed and the long-run equilibrium NIIP-to-wealth ratios. The observed NIIP-to-wealth series closely tracks the long-run equilibrium series in Chile, Germany, Korea, and the United Kingdom whereas it largely deviates from the long-run sustainable series in Argentina and the United States. For the United States, for example, the long-run equilibrium NIIP-to-wealth series is positive and has a slightly rising trend due to an increase in the country's wealth since the beginning of 1980s (Calderon et al., 2000, pp. 25-27). The observed series remains below the benchmark series during the whole sample period 1970-1996 and is increasingly diverging from the second half of the 1980s on. Thus, the adjustment of the actual series towards the long-run equilibrium requires sufficiently large trade surpluses. Applying this method to more recent data (since 1997) could be insightful in assessing the sustainability of the recent global imbalances.

In sum, the portfolio approach to the current account has an advantage of accounting for both asset risks and returns. Because Calderon et al. (2000) first test the validity of the stock-equilibrium model and then assess sustainability in the countries in which the model appears to be justified, they avoid the identification problem encountered in the last section. However, in addition to the visual comparison of the benchmark and the observed plots, statistical tests could shed more light on how close the observed NIIP-to-wealth series tracks the equilibrium path. Further, although the portfolio approach does not rely on the assumption of a small economy, it focuses only on two regions (the domestic country and the rest of the world). Finally, the "practical" application of the long-run equilibrium appears to be at odds with the theoretical notion of the steady state. In order to construct the benchmark series, the long-run values are computed for every point of time and are found to be fluctuating over time. However, in accordance with the usual definition of the steady-state equilibrium, the derivation of the long-run value in equation (6.158) assumes that the NIIP-to-wealth ratio remains unchanged in the long run. The next chapter also discusses steady-state values (implied by a particular model) as a sustainability benchmark. However, the difference is that steady-state values serve only as "static benchmarks" which remain constant over some period of time.

Appendix to chapter 6

6.A Appendix to subsection 6.1.7

The log-linearization of the intertemporal budget constraint (6.139) in the text, i.e., of

$$\sum_{n=t}^{\infty} E_t\left[R_{t+1,n}C_n\right] = \sum_{n=t}^{\infty} E_t\left[R_{t+1,n}NO_n\right] + (1+r_t)B_{t-1}$$

is easier when the notation is simplified as follows:

$$\begin{aligned}
\Phi_t &\equiv \sum_{n=t}^{\infty} E_t\left[R_{t+1,n}C_n\right] \\
\Psi_t &\equiv \sum_{n=t}^{\infty} E_t\left[R_{t+1,n}NO_n\right] \\
\mathscr{B}_t &\equiv (1+r_t)B_{t-1}.
\end{aligned}$$

Thus, the IBC (6.139) in the text can be rewritten as

$$\Phi_t - \Psi_t = \mathscr{B}_t. \tag{6.159}$$

The definition of Φ_t implies the following law of motion:

$$\Phi_{t+1} = (\Phi_t - C_t)(1+r_{t+1}). \tag{6.160}$$

Dividing equation (6.160) by Φ_t yields

$$\frac{\Phi_{t+1}}{\Phi_t} = (1+r_{t+1})\left(1-\frac{C_t}{\Phi_t}\right). \tag{6.161}$$

Taking natural logarithm on both sides of equation (6.161) results in

$$\phi_{t+1} - \phi_t = r_{t+1} + \ln\left(1-\frac{C_t}{\Phi_t}\right) = r_{t+1} + \ln\left(1-\exp\left(c_t-\phi_t\right)\right) \tag{6.162}$$

where $\ln(\Phi_t) \equiv \phi_t$, $\ln(C_t) \equiv c_t$, and $\ln(1+r_{t+1}) \approx r_{t+1}$. A first-order Taylor expansion of $\ln\left(1-\exp\left(c_t-\phi_t\right)\right)$ around the steady-state level $c-\phi$ yields

$$\ln(1-\exp(c_t-\phi_t)) \approx \ln(1-\exp(c-\phi)) \\ -\frac{\exp(c-\phi)}{1-\exp(c-\phi)}((c_t-\phi_t)-(c-\phi)). \tag{6.163}$$

Equation (6.163) can be more succinctly written as

$$\ln(1-\exp(c_t-\phi_t)) \approx k+\left(1-\frac{1}{\rho}\right)(c_t-\phi_t) \tag{6.164}$$

where $\rho \equiv 1-\exp(c-\phi) = 1-C/\Phi$ and $k \equiv \ln(\rho)-(1-1/\rho)\ln(1-\rho)$. The parameter ρ can thus be interpreted as the average ratio of to $C-\Phi$ to Φ. Substituting equation (6.164) into equation (6.162) one obtains

$$\phi_{t+1}-\phi_t = r_{t+1}+k+\left(1-\frac{1}{\rho}\right)(c_t-\phi_t). \tag{6.165}$$

Adding and subtracting c_t+c_{t+1} on both sides of equation (6.165) and rearranging the terms yields

$$\Delta c_{t+1}+(c_t-\phi_t)-(c_{t+1}-\phi_{t+1}) = r_{t+1}+k+\left(1-\frac{1}{\rho}\right)(c_t-\phi_t). \tag{6.166}$$

Rearranging the terms again, equation (6.166) becomes

$$\frac{1}{\rho}(c_t-\phi_t)-(c_{t+1}-\phi_{t+1}) = r_{t+1}+k-\Delta c_{t+1}. \tag{6.167}$$

Equation (6.167) is a first-order equation which can be solved forward to obtain

$$c_t-\phi_t = \sum_{n=t+1}^{\infty} \rho^{n-t}(r_n-\Delta c_n)+\frac{\rho}{1-\rho}k \tag{6.168}$$

where the terminal condition

$$\lim_{N\to\infty} \rho^N(c_{t+N}-\phi_{t+N}) = 0$$

is assumed to hold. Analogously, one obtains

$$no_t-\psi_t = \sum_{n=t+1}^{\infty} \rho_1^{n-t}(r_n-\Delta no_n)+\frac{\rho_1}{1-\rho_1}k_1 \tag{6.169}$$

where $\ln(\Psi_t) \equiv \psi_t$, $\ln(NO_t) \equiv no_t$, $\ln(1+r_{t+1}) \approx r_{t+1}$, $\rho_1 \equiv 1-\exp(no-\psi) = 1-NO/\Psi$, and $k_1 \equiv \ln(\rho_1)-(1-1/\rho_1)\ln(1-\rho_1)$. Equation (6.169) is satisfied if the terminal condition

$$\lim_{N\to\infty} \rho_1^N(no_{t+N}-\psi_{t+N}) = 0$$

holds.

The next step is to linearize equation (6.159). Dividing equation (6.140) by Ψ_t and taking natural logarithm on both sides of equation (6.140) one obtains

$$\psi_t - \phi_t = k_2 + \left(1 - \frac{1}{\rho_2}\right)(\lfloor_t - \phi_t) \tag{6.170}$$

where $\lfloor_t \equiv \ln(\mathscr{B}_t)$, $\rho_2 \equiv 1 - \exp(\lfloor - \psi) = 1 - \mathscr{B}/\Psi$, and $k_2 \equiv \ln(\rho_2) - (1 - 1/\rho_2)\ln(1 - \rho_2)$. Solving equation (6.170) for $-\phi/\rho_2$ and combining it with equations (6.168) and (6.169) results in

$$\begin{aligned}\frac{1}{\rho_2}\left(\rho^{n-t}(r_n - \Delta c_n) - c_t + \frac{\rho}{1-\rho}k\right) &= k_2 + \left(1 - \frac{1}{\rho_2}\right)\lfloor_t \\ &+ \sum_{n=t+1}^{\infty} \rho^{n-t}(r_n - \Delta no_n) - no_t + \frac{\rho}{1-\rho}k \end{aligned} \tag{6.171}$$

where it has been assumed that $\rho \approx p_1$ and $k \approx k_1$. Rearranging the terms in equation (6.171) one obtains

$$\begin{aligned} no_t - \left(1 - \frac{1}{\rho_2}\right)\lfloor_t - \frac{c_t}{\rho_2} &= -\sum_{n=t+1}^{\infty} \rho^{n-t}\left(\Delta no_n - \frac{\Delta c_n}{\rho_2} - \left(1 - \frac{1}{\rho_2}\right) r_n\right) \\ &+ k_2 + \left(1 - \frac{1}{\rho_2}\right)\frac{\rho}{1-\rho}k. \end{aligned} \tag{6.172}$$

Taking conditional expectations on both sides of equation (6.172) and assuming that ρ approximately equals the time-preference factor β yields equation (6.141) in the text:

$$\begin{aligned} no_t - \left(1 - \frac{1}{\rho_2}\right)\lfloor_t - \frac{c_t}{\rho_2} &= -\sum_{n=t+1}^{\infty} \beta^{n-t} E_t\left[\Delta no_n - \frac{\Delta c_n}{\rho_2} - \left(1 - \frac{1}{\rho_2}\right) r_n\right] \\ &+ k_2 + \left(1 - \frac{1}{\rho_2}\right)\frac{\beta}{1-\beta}k. \end{aligned}$$

6.B Empirical studies to section 6.1

Table 6.1: Overview of studies on the intertemporal model of the current account

Studies	Data	Test results	Sustainable according to the benchmark?
		Current account path under certainty equivalence	
Sheffrin and Woo (1990)	Belgium, Canada, Denmark, the UK/1957-1985; r is 4% or 14%	H_0 of unit root in NO_t can be rejected only for the UK; H_0 of a unit root in CAB_t cannot be rejected for the rest of the sample (ADF test); **k** is not a $(p+1)^{st}$ unit vector in Canada, Denmark, and the UK (Wald test); Γ is not orthogonal to past information in the UK, Canada, Belgium (only for $r = 14\%$ and I_{t-1}), in Denmark (only for I_{t-2}) (F-test)	Possibly yes in Belgium and Denmark, no in Canada and the UK
Obstfeld and Rogoff (1996, pp. 90-94)	Belgium/ 1954-1990, Canada/1952-1990, Denmark and Sweden/1951-1990, the UK (1949-1990); $r = 4\%$	**k** is not a $(p+1)^{st}$ unit vector in Belgium (Wald-test); the Wald-test for the rest of the sample is not reported; the graphical comparison of the observed CAB_t with the predicted CAB_t indicates unsustainability	Possibly no for the whole sample
Nason and Rogers (2006)	Canada/1963.Q1-1997.Q4; r is 3.7%	**k** is not a $(p+1)^{st}$ unit vector (Wald-test)	Possibly no

Table 6.1: Overview of studies on the intertemporal model of the current account

Studies	Data	Test results	Sustainable according to the benchmark?
Current account path under certainty equivalence and with constraints on capital mobility			
Huang (1993)	Taiwan/1961-1990; $r = 4\%$	ΔNO_t is $I(0)$; H_0 that CAB_t is $I(0)$ cannot be rejected (ADF test); $\mathbf{k}^{\theta}$ is not a $(p+1)^{st}$ unit vector (LR-test); θ is negligibly small; H_0 that Γ is orthogonal to past information cannot be rejected (F-test)	Possibly yes
Consumption-smoothing and consumption-tilting components of the current account under linear-quadratic utility			
Milbourne and Otto (1992)	Australia/1961.Q1-1989.Q1 (s.); r is 4.04%	ΔNO_t and CAB_t are each $I(0)$ (ADF test); $v = 1.132$; CAB_t Granger-causes ΔNO_t (F-test); Γ is not orthogonal to past information (F-test)	No
Otto (1992)	Canada/1950.Q1-1987.Q4 (dem., s), the US/1950.Q1-1988.Q4 (dem., s); r is 4.04%	CAB_t is $I(0)$ and NO_t is $I(1)$ in both countries (ADF test); C_t and $NO_t + rB_{t-1}$ is $CI(1,1)$; $v = 0.98$ (FMOLS); CAB_t Granger-causes ΔNO_t only in the US (F-test); Γ is not orthogonal to past information in both countries (F-test); $z = 0.735$ and $corr = 0.735$ in Canada; $z = 0.876$ and $corr = 0.932$ in the US	No in both countries

Table 6.1: Overview of studies on the intertemporal model of the current account

Studies	Data	Test results	Sustainable according to the benchmark?
Ghosh (1995)	Canada, Japan, the UK, and the US/1960-1988, Germany/1962-1988; r is 2%	C_t and $(NO_t + rB_{t-1})$ are $CI(1,1)$ in Canada, Japan, the UK, the US, H_0 of no cointegration cannot be rejected for Germany (EG/ADF und EG/DW tests); v is less than 1 in Canada, the UK, and the US and higher than 1 in Japan and Germany for the full sample period (OLS); CAB_t Granger-causes NO_t in all countries (F-test); H_0 that $\mathbf{k}$ is a $(p+1)^{st}$ unit vector cannot be rejected in all countries (Wald test); z is sign. higher than 1 in all countries except the US; *corr* is close to 1 in Canada, Japan, and the US; *corr* is 0.81 in Germany and 0.70 in the UK	Possibly yes for the whole sample

Table 6.1: Overview of studies on the intertemporal model of the current account

Studies	**Data**	**Test results**	**Sustainable according to the benchmark?**
Ghosh and Ostry (1995)	Botswana/1960-88, Ethiopia/1963-91, Ghana/1955-90, Kenya/1964-89, Liberia/1965-88, Malawi/1964-91, Mauritius/1953-90, Morocco/1957-91, Argentina, Brazil, Colombia, India, Indonesia, Israel, Nigeria, Peru, and Senegal/1960-90, Tanzania/1965-90, Pakistan and Tunisia /1960-91, Zambia/1957-87, Hong Kong/1960-91, Korea/1953-91, Malaysia/1970-90, Papua New Guinea/1973-90, the Philippines/1948-91, Singapore/1968-91, Guatemala, Honduras, Sri Lanka, and Venezuela/1950-91, Thailand/1950-90, Egypt/1974-90, Iran/1964-90, Jordan/1969-91, Saudi Arabia/1968-89, Bolivia/1950-91, Chile/1955-91, Ecuador/1965-91, El Salvador/1951-91, Paraguay and Jamaica/1960-89, Mexico/1950-86, Panama/1950-90, Uruguay/1955-91	$CAB_t \sim I(0)$ in all countries except Botswana, Chile, Egypt, Ethiopia, Ghana, Jamaica, Panama, Singapore, Tanzania, Uruguay, $\Delta NO_t \sim I(0)$ in all countries except Brazil, Korea, Pakistan, Singapore, Thailand (ADF test); $v = 1$ in Korea, $v < 1$ in Ghana, Tunisia, India, ~~M~~alaysia, the Philippines, Thailand, Brazil, Colombia, Mexico, Peru, $v > 1$ in Pakistan, Panama, Venezuela (OLS); CAB_t Granger-causes ΔNO_t in all countries but Botswana, Ethiopia, Ghana, Indonesia, Israel, Jamaica, Liberia, Malaysia, Morocco, Peru, Singapore, Sri Lanka, Thailand, Tanzania (t-test); **k** is not a $(p+1)^{st}$ unit vector in Argentina, Botswana, Ghana, Guatemala, Hong Kong, Korea, Liberia, Pakistan, Paraguay, Senegal, Singapore, Sri Lanka, Thailand, Uruguay, Venezuela, Zambia (Wald test)	Possibly yes in Colombia, Ethiopia, Indonesia, Israel, Jamaica, Nigeria, Malaysia, Morocco, Peru, Tanzania; possibly no in Argentina, Botswana, Egypt, Ghana, Liberia, Pakistan, Saudi Arabia, Singapore, Sri Lanka, Thailand, Uruguay; yes for the rest
Ostry (1997)	Indonesia, Malaysia, the Philippines, Singapore, and Thailand/1975-1995	v is less than 1 in all countries except Singapore; k is not a $(p+1)^{st}$ unit vector only in Singapore and Thailand (Wald test); $corr$ is close to 1 in all countries except Thailand, $corr$ is 0.68 in Thailand	Possibly no in Singapore and Thailand, possibly yes in Indonesia, Malaysia, and the Philippines

Table 6.1: Overview of studies on the intertemporal model of the current account

Studies	**Data**	**Test results**	**Sustainable according to the benchmark?**
Cashin and McDermott (1998)	Australia/1954-1994; r is 4%	C_t and NO_t are $CI(1,1)$ (EG/PP test); v (FMOLS) is sign. less than 1 for the full sample 1954-1994 and the subperiods 1954-1974 and 1975-1994 (t-test); CAB_t Granger-causes ΔNO_t for the full sample and the subperiods 1954-1974 and 1975-1994 (F-test); H_0 that **k** is a $(p+1)^{st}$ unit vector can be rejected only for the subperiod 1954-1974 (Wald test); H_0 that Γ is orthogonal to past information cannot be rejected for most specifications (t-test); z is 2.277 (1954-1994), 2.277 (1954-1994), 3.499 (1954-1974), 2.965 (1975-1994); H_0 of unit root in deviations of the observed B_t from the predicted B_t cannot be rejected (ADF and PP tests)	Yes
Agénor et al. (1999)	France/1970.Q1-1996.Q4 (s.); r is 4%	H_0 of no cointegration between C_t, Y_t, I_t, and G_t cannot be rejected (L_c test); $v = 0.982$ (FMOLS); CAB_t Granger-causes ΔNO_t (F-test); H_0 that **k** is a $(p+1)^{st}$ unit vector cannot be rejected (Wald test); $z = 0.87$	Yes

Table 6.1: Overview of studies on the intertemporal model of the current account

Studies	Data	Test results	Sustainable according to the benchmark?
Callen and Cashin (1999)	India/ 1952/53-1998/99; r is 4%	C_t and $NO_t + rB_{t-1}$ are $CI(1,1)$ (Phillips and Hansen (1990) fully modified method); $v = 0.967$ (FMOLS); H_0 that CAB_t does not Granger-cause ΔNO_t cannot be rejected; CA-surpluses and CA-deficits jointly Granger-cause the decreases and increases in NO_t (F-test); H_0 that $\mathbf{k}$ is a $(p+1)^{st}$ unit vector cannot be rejected (Wald test)	Yes if the asymmetric access to international financial markets is taken into account
Makrydakis (1999)	Greece/1950-1992; $r = 4\%$	C_t, NO_t, and $NO_t + rB_{t-1}$ are mainly $I(1)$ (ADF, DFGLS, ZA, and KPSS tests); C_t and $NO_t + rB_{t-1}$ are $CI(1,1)$ (EG/ADF and GH tests); $v = 0.946$ (FMOLS); H_0 of no Granger causality between CAB_t and ΔNO_t cannot be rejected (Wald-test); $z = 1.66$; $corr = 0.742$; $\mathbf{k}$ is not a $(p+1)^{st}$ unit vector (Wald test)	(Possibly) no
Adedeji (2001)	Nigeria/1960-1997	CAB_t and ΔNO_t are each $I(0)$ (ADF and PP tests); C_t and $NO_t + rB_{t-1}$ are $CI(1,1)$ (Johansen trace and ME tests); $v = 0.96$ (FMOLS); CAB_t Granger-causes ΔNO_t; CA-surpluses Granger-cause the decreases in NO_t, yet H_0 that CA-deficits Granger-cause the increases in NO_t cannot be rejected (F-test); Γ is not orthogonal to past information (F-test); $corr = 0.97$; $z = 3.83$	No

Table 6.1: Overview of studies on the intertemporal model of the current account

Studies	Data	Test results	Sustainable according to the benchmark?
Cashin and McDermott (2002)	Australia/1984.Q1-1999.Q1; r is 4%	C_t and NO_t are $CI(1,1)$ (GH test); v is sign. less than 1 before and after the structural break in 1990.Q4; CAB_t Granger-causes ΔNO_t only before 1990.Q4; H_0 that $\mathbf{l}$ is a $(p+1)^{st}$ unit vector is rejected only before 1990.Q4 (linear Wald test); z is close to 1 before 1990.Q4 and is larger than 1 afterwards; $corr$ is 0.60 before 1990.Q4 and 0.65 afterwards	No before 1990.Q4, possibly yes afterwards
Kim et al. (2002)	New Zealand/1982.Q2-1999.Q3	TB_t, and CAB_t are each $I(0)$, C_t and $TB_t + rB_{t-1}$ are each $I(1)$ (ADF test) and together $CI(1,1)$ (EG/ADF test); v is sign. different from 1; CAB_t Granger-causes ΔNO_t (F-test); H_0 that Γ is orthogonal to past information cannot be rejected (F-test); H_0 that $\mathbf{k}$ is a $(p+1)^{st}$ unit vector cannot be rejected (Wald test)	Yes
Hudson and Stennett (2003)	Jamaica/1961-2002	CAB_t and ΔNO_t are each $I(0)$ (ADF test); C_t and NO_t are $CI(1,1)$; $v = 1.02$; (Johansen trace and ME test); CAB_t Granger-causes ΔNO_t (F-test); the average deviation of the observed from the predicted CAB_t is 1.3; $corr = 0.98$; $\mathbf{k}$ is not a $(p+1)^{st}$ unit vector (Wald test)	Yes

Table 6.1: Overview of studies on the intertemporal model of the current account

Studies	**Data**	**Test results**	**Sustainable according to the benchmark?**
Ismail and Baharumshah (2008)	Malaysia/1960-2004; $r = 4\%$	CAB_t and ΔNO_t are each $I(0)$ (ADF, PP, NP, and KPSS tests); C_t and $(NO_t + rB_{t-1})$ are $CI(1,1)$ (Johansen ME and trace tests); v is not sign. different from 1; CAB_t Granger-causes ΔNO_t (F-test); H_0 that Γ is orthogonal to past information cannot be rejected (F-test); H_0 that **k** is a $(p+1)^{st}$ unit vector cannot be rejected (Wald test)	Possibly yes
Ogus and Sohrabji (2008)	Turkey/1992.Q1-2004.Q4; r is 2%, 3%, and 6%	CAB_t and NO_t are each $I(0)$ (ADF, PP, KPSS, and ZA tests); C_t and $(NO_t + rB_{t-1})$ are $CI(1,1)$; $v = 0.93$ (EG/ADF and EG/DW tests); CAB_t Granger-causes ΔNO_t (F-test); **k** is not a $(p+1)^{st}$ unit vector (Wald test); Γ is not orthogonal to past information (F-test)	No
Karunaratne (2010)	Australia/1959.Q3-2007.Q1	$NO_t + rB_{t-1}$ and C_t are each $I(1)$ (ADF, PP, KPSS, and ZA tests) and are $CI(1,1)$ (EG/ADF test, Johansen (1988) trace and maximum eigenvalue test, and GH test for the full sample period); v is less than 1; CAB_t Granger-causes ΔNO_t for the full sample period and the subperiods 1959.Q3-1983.Q4 and 1984.Q1-2007.Q1 (F-test); H_0 that **k** is a $(p+1)^{st}$ unit vector is rejected for 1959.Q3-2007.Q1 and 1959.Q3-1983.Q4 (Wald test)	Yes

Table 6.1: Overview of studies on the intertemporal model of the current account

Studies	Data	Test results	Sustainable according to the benchmark?
Consumption-smoothing and consumption-tilting components of the current account under power utility			
Belkar et al. (2008)	Australia/1949-2005; $r = 4\%$; σ ranges from 0.35 to 0.75	CAB_t and NO_t are each $I(1)$ (ADF test); v^P is sign. less than 0 (DOLS); CAB_t Granger-causes ΔNO_t during 1949-2005 and the subperiod 1984-2005 (F-test); **k** is not a $(p+1)^{st}$ unit vector during 1949-2005 and the subperiod 1949-1983 (Wald-test)	Yes during 1984-2005 and possibly no during 1949-1983
Habit formation			
Gruber (2004)	Canada, Japan, the UK, and the US/1958.Q2-2002.Q3, France, Italy, and Spain/1971.Q2-2002.Q3, the Netherlands/1978.Q2-2002.Q2 (dem., ratios of GDP), $r = 4\%$	Without habits ($\delta = 0$): Γ is not orthogonal to past information in Italy, Japan, the Netherlands, and Spain, in the UK only for I_{t-2}, in the US only for I_{t-1} (F-test); H_0 that **k** is a $(p+1)^{st}$ unit vector cannot be rejected in France, Japan, and the US (Wald-test); with habits: δ is on average 0.873, δ is sign. different from 0 in Canada, Italy, Japan, the Netherlands, Spain, and the US (GMM); Γ^h is not orthogonal to past information only in Canada (F-test); H_0 that **k** is a $(p+1)^{st}$ unit vector cannot be rejected in all countries but Canada (Wald test); $z^h > 1$ in France and the UK; $z^h < 1$ in Japan and the US	No in Italy, Japan, the Netherlands, Spain, the UK, and the US when habit formation is not considered; no only in Canada and possibly yes in the rest of the sample when habit formation is taken into account

Table 6.1: Overview of studies on the intertemporal model of the current account

Studies	Data	Test results	Sustainable according to the benchmark?
		Durable goods and/or non-traded goods	
Işcan (2002)	Canada/1926-1995 and 1961.Q1-1997.Q2; r is 4% or 14%; $\delta = 0.18$	CAB_t, ΔNO_t, and ΔNO_t^T are each $I(0)$ (ADF, PP, and KPSS tests); Γ is predictable given past information both for the baseline model without durables and for the model with durables; H_0 that Γ is orthogonal to past information cannot be rejected only for annual models in the model with durables and non-traded goods (F-test)	Possibly yes only for annual data when the model allows for durable and non-traded goods
		Traded goods	
Bergin and Sheffrin (2000)	Canada, Australia, and the UK/1961.Q4-1996.Q2 (s.); $\beta = 0.94$; α is 0.5 or 0.75; γ is 0.5, or 1.0, or the level which minimizes χ^2, or the level which matches the variance	cab_t, Δno_t, and r_t^* are each $I(0)$ (ADF and PP tests); in Australia and Canada, H_0 that $\mathbf{k}^T$ is a $(p+1)^{st}$ unit vector cannot be rejected when exchange rate and real interest rate changes are included and can be rejected when there are only changes in the real interest rate or no changes in the exchange rate and the real interest rate; in the UK, H_0 is rejected in the UK disregarding whether there are changes in the exchange rate and/or the interest rate (Wald test)	Possibly yes in Australia and Canada only when changes in the real interest rate and the real exchange rate are considered; possibly no in the UK

Table 6.1. Overview of studies on the intertemporal model of the current account

Studies	Data	Test results	Sustainable according to the benchmark?
Landeau (2002)	Chile/1960.Q1-1999.Q4; $\beta = 0.95$; α is 0.5 or 0.75; γ is 0.5 or chosen as to match the variance	H_0 that $\mathbf{k}^T$ is a $(p+1)^{st}$ unit vector cannot be rejected when (i) there are no changes in the interest and exchange rates, (ii) when there are only exchange rate changes, (iii) when there are only interest rate changes, and (iv) there are both exchange rate and interest changes (Wald test); z is 0.28 in (i), 0.14 in (ii), 0.78 in (iii), and 1 in (iv)	Possibly yes
Saksonovs (2006)	10 crisis countries (Spain/1975.Q1-2005.Q4, France/1978.Q1-2004.Q4, Italy/1981.Q1-2005.Q4, South Korea/1975.Q1-2002.Q4, Mexico/1980.Q1-2005.Q4, Norway/1978.Q1.2005.Q4, Philippines/1981.Q1-2002.Q4, South Africa/1975.Q1-2003.Q4, Sweden/1980.Q1-2004.Q4, the UK/1975.Q1-2001.Q4) and 7 no-crisis countries (Australia/1975.Q1-2004.Q4, Canada, Japan, Germany/1975.Q1-2005.Q4, the Netherlands/1977.Q1-2003.Q4, Switzerland/1981.Q1-2005.Q4, the US/1975.Q1-2005.Q4) (dem.); $\beta = 0.98$, $\alpha = 0.5$, $\gamma = 0.1$	no_t and r^* are each $I(0)$ in all countries (ADF and PP tests), cab_t is $I(0)$ only in Japan (ADF and PP tests), Spain (only PP test), and Switzerland (ADF and PP tests); H_0 that $\mathbf{k}^T$ is a $(p+1)^{st}$ unit vector can be rejected in 6 non-crisis countries (Canada, Germany, Japan, the Netherlands, Switzerland, the US) and in 5 crisis countries (Korea, Mexico, Norway, Philippines, Sweden) (Wald test)	Possibly no in Canada, Germany, Japan, Korea, Mexico, the Netherlands, Norway, the Philippines, Sweden, Switzerland, and the US; possibly yes for the rest of the sample

Table 6.1: Overview of studies on the intertemporal model of the current account

Studies	Data	Test results	Sustainable according to the benchmark?
Kano (2008)	Canada, the UK/1960.Q1-1997.Q4 (s.); γ is 0.001 for Canada and 0.08 for the UK	cab_t, no_t, and r_t are each $I(0)$ (ADF test); $\mathbf{k}^T$ is not a $(p+1)^{st}$ unit vector in both countries when only changes in the real interest rate are considered (Wald-test)	Possibly no
Moccero (2008)	Argentina/1885-2002 (dem.); $\beta = 0.98$, $\alpha = 0.5$; γ is 0.2, 0.5, 0.9 or chosen to match the variance; $b = 0.5$	cab_t and no_t are each $I(0)$ (DFGLS and PP tests); $\mathbf{k}^E$ is not a $(p+1)^{st}$ unit vector (Wald-test) when there are (i) no real interest rate and real exchange rate changes, (ii) only real interest rate changes, and (iii) both real interest rate and real exchange rate changes (both for the full sample and for 1885-1930)	Possibly no

Table 6.1: Overview of studies on the intertemporal model of the current account

Studies	Data	Test results	Sustainable according to the benchmark?
Darku (2010)	Ghana/1960-2002; $\gamma = 0.45$, $\alpha = 0.85$; $\beta = 0.96$	cab_t, no_t, and r_t^* are each $I(0)$ (ADF and PP tests); baseline model with no changes in r_t^*: $\mathbf{k}^E$ is not a $(p+1)^{st}$ unit vector (Wald test); model with changes in r_t^*, both with free and constrained capital mobility: H_0 that $\mathbf{k}^E$ is a $(p+1)^{st}$ unit vector can be rejected for the full sample period and during 1960-1982, but not during 1983-2002 (Wald test); *ca*-surpluses Granger-cause future *no*-declines during the whole sample period and the two subperiods; H_0 that *ca*-deficits Granger-cause future *no*-increases cannot be rejected for the full sample period and during 1960-1982, but it can be rejected during 1983-2002 (F-test)	Possibly no when there are no changes in the consumption-based real interest rate and free capital mobility; yes when changes in the consumption-based real interest rate and the asymmetric access to international financial markets are taken into account

Table 6.1: Overview of studies on the intertemporal model of the current account

Studies	Data	Test results	Sustainable according to the benchmark?
Campa and Gavilan (2011)	Belgium/ 980.Q1-2005.Q3/ $\alpha = 0.26$/ $\beta = 0.9907$; France/1977.Q1-2005.Q4/ $\alpha = 0.38$/ $\beta = 0.9926$; Italy/1980.Q1-2005.Q3/ $\alpha = 0.40$/ $\beta = 0.9909$; the Netherlands/1977.Q1-2005.Q3/ $\alpha = 0.26$/ $\beta = 0.9929$; Portugal/1977.Q1-2005.Q4/ $\alpha = 0.42$/ $\beta = 0.9979$; Spain/1977.Q1-2005.Q4/ $\alpha = 0.35$/ $\beta = 0.9929$; Austria/1977.Q1-2005.Q4/ $\alpha = 0.33$/ $\beta = 0.9937$; Finland/1977.Q1-2005.Q4/ $\alpha = 0.26$/ $\beta = 0.9905$; Germany/1991.Q1-2005.Q4/ $\alpha = 0.36$/ $\beta = 0.9950$; Ireland/1997.Q1-2005.Q4/$\alpha = 0.41$/ $\beta = 0.9990$; γ is 0.1, 0.25, 0.5, 0.75, or 0.9; s.	H_0 of unit root in *cab* cannot be rejected in Germany, Ireland, Spain, and Portugal; no_t and r_t^* are $I(0)$ in all countries (ADF and PP tests); H_0 that Γ is orthogonal to past information is rejected for Austria, Finland, Germany, and Ireland, but cannot be rejected for Belgium, France, Italy, the Netherlands, Portugal, and Spain for values of γ below 0.75 (F-test); H_0 that $\mathbf{k}^E$ is a $(p+1)^{st}$ unit vector can be rejected for Portugal, Austria, Germany, Finland, and Ireland for all γ-values, for Belgium (only for $\gamma = 0.75$), Italy (only for γ above 0.5), Spain (only for $\gamma = 0.1$, 0.25, and 0.75) (Wald test); *cab* Granger-causes Δno in Belgium (except for $\gamma = 0.9$), Italy (only for $\gamma = 0.9$), Portugal, Spain (only for $\gamma > 0.25$), Austria (only for $\gamma = 0.1$ and $\gamma = 0.25$), and Ireland (except for $\gamma = 0.9$)	No in Austria, Finland, Germany, and Ireland; yes in Belgium (except for $\gamma =$ 0.9), Italy (only for $\gamma =$ 0.9), Portugal, Spain (only for $\gamma > 0.25$), Austria (only for $\gamma = 0.1$ and $\gamma =$ 0.25); possibly no for Italy (only for $\gamma = 0.75$), Spain (only for $\gamma = 0.1$ and $\gamma =$ 0.25); possibly no in the remaining countries

Table 6.1: Overview of studies on the intertemporal model of the current account

Studies	Data	Test results	Sustainable according to the benchmark?

Abbreviations and symbols:

- Data and variables:
  α: share of traded goods over private consumption, B_t: real net international investment position; β: discount factor, CAB_t: real current account balance; $cab_t \equiv \ln(CAB_t)$; C_t: real (private) consumption; *corr*: correlation between the observed and the estimated current account; δ: the habit parameter; dem.: demeaned; det.: detrended; G_t: real government spending; Γ is defined as $CAB_t - \Delta NO_t - R^{-1}CAB_{t-1}$; γ: intertemporal elasticity of substitution; ε: coefficient of appreciation of real exchange rates; H_0: null hypothesis; I_t: real investment; I_{t-1} and I_{t-2} are the public information sets conditional on information available up to period $t-1$ and $t-2$, respectively; $\mathbf{k}$ is a $2p$-column vector defined as $\mathbf{k} \equiv -\mathbf{e}_1{}'\mathbf{RA}(\mathbf{I}-\mathbf{RA})^{-1}$; $\mathbf{k}^E \equiv -\left(\mathbf{e}_1' - \gamma\mathbf{e}_{2p+1}' - (1-\gamma)(1-\alpha)\mathbf{m}'\right)\beta\mathbf{A}^E\left(\mathbf{I}-\beta\mathbf{A}^E\right)^{-1}$ is a $5p$-column vector; $\mathbf{k}^T \equiv -\left(\mathbf{e}_1' - \theta\mathbf{e}_{2p+1}'\right)\beta\mathbf{A}\left(\mathbf{I}-\beta\mathbf{A}\right)^{-1}$ is a $3p$-column vector; NO_t: real net output; NO^T: real net output from traded goods; $no_t \equiv \ln(no_t)$; ν: the consumption-tilting parameter under linear-quadratic utility; ν^P: the consumption-tilting parameter under power utility; r: real interest rate; r_t^*: consumption-based real interest rate, s: seasonal adjustment; sign: significantly; TB_t: real trade balance; θ: the fraction of net output consumed by the consumers which have no access to international financial markets; the UK: the United Kingdom; the US: the United States; Y_t: real Gross Domestic Product (GDP); z: the ratio of the variance of the actual current account to the variance of the predicted current account; z^h: the ratio of the variance of the actual current account to the variance of the predicted current account under habit formation.

- Tests and models:
  ADF test: Augmented Dickey-Fuller test (Said and Dickey, 1984); DFGLS test: Dickey-Fuller Generalized Least Squares test (Elliott et al., 1996); DW: Durbin-Watson test; EG test: Engle-Granger test (Engle and Granger, 1987); FMOLS estimator: Fully Modified Ordinary Least Squares estimator (Phillips and Hansen, 1990); GH test: Gregory-Hansen test (Gregory and Hansen, 1996); GMM estimator: Generalized Method of Moments estimator; Johansen ME and trace tests: Johansen Maximum Eigenvalue and trace tests (Johansen, 1988; Johansen and Juselius, 1990), KPSS test: Kwiatkowski-Phillips-Schmidt-Shin test (Kwiatkowski et al., 1992); LR test: Likelihood Ratio test; L_c test: L_c test (Hansen, 1992); OLS: Ordinary Least Squares estimator; PP test: Phillips-Perron test (Phillips, 1987; Phillips and Perron, 1988); NP test: Ng and Perron (2001) unit root test; ZA test: Zivot and Andrews (2002) test.

7

Indicators of external sustainability

There exists a large number of indicators on which both policy makers and economists rely in their assessment of external sustainability. The general consensus is that no single indicator is capable of fully capturing external sustainability (IMF, 2002). This chapter focuses on the most widely used indicators; many of them involve the notion of solvency, that is, require that the economy meets its intertemporal budget constraint.

Section 7.1 examines the resource gap, which measures the resource transfer required to prevent the ratio of net foreign debts to the respective economy's repayment ability from rising. The resource gap is based on the notion that a continually increasing ratio of net foreign debts is unsustainable even if the respective economy remains solvent. As there exist numerous ways to calculate the resource gap, section 7.1 will occupy significantly more space than the other sections of this chapter.

The stricter sustainability notion suggested by Milesi-Ferretti and Razin (1996a) considers those cases in which the adjustment required for preserving solvency leads to an abrupt policy shift causing a recession or precipitates a financial crisis to be unsustainable. The indicators of "unsustainability", i.e., of drastic policy shifts and financial crises are discussed in section 7.2. The reversal in the trade balance required to satisfy the intertemporal budget constraint is often accompanied by an adjustment or a reversal in the current account balance. Indicators of current account reversals are reviewed in section 7.3.

Section 7.4 analyzes indicative thresholds implemented in the sustainability assessment conducted by the International Monetary Fund and the World Bank. Section 7.5 discusses indicative thresholds recently proposed by the European Commission to identify excessive macroeconomic imbalances. Finally, section 7.6 concludes.

7.1 Resource gap as a sustainability indicator

7.1.1 Non-increasing ratio of net foreign debts as a sustainability criterion

The popular sustainability concept discussed in this section amplifies the notion of solvency by requiring that the economy's net foreign debts should be non-increasing in proportion to its capacity to generate external revenues (e.g., Milesi-Ferretti and Razin, 1996a; Roubini and Wachtel, 1998; Roubini, 2001). The rationale behind this concept is that the economy's repayment capacity—which is usually approximated by the respective economy's GDP— is bounded. Net foreign debts which indefinitely grow as a fraction of output (even if they are consistent with the IBC) might lead[1] to a situation in which net interest payments outstrip GDP and, thus, exceed the economy's capacity to generate net exports. When this happens, an economy cannot finance consumption and debt service entirely on its own even if it manages to generate a trade surplus. To satisfy the IBC, it requires either a debt default/restructuring or it can increase, if possible, new borrowing (which is equivalent to a Ponzi scheme). In any case, solvency is violated.

The unsustainable situation in which net interest payments exceed GDP in some future period $t+N$, even though at present time t they do not, can be prevented by requiring that output should grow at least at the same rate as net foreign debts.[2] Hence, external imbalances are considered sustainable when net foreign debts are non-increasing in proportion to output while being consistent with economy's solvency. The relevant literature (e.g., Milesi-Ferretti and Razin, 1996a) typically formalizes solvency by requiring the real interest rate to exceed the real GDP growth rate. This requirement is sufficient to ensure that the "specific" intertemporal budget constraint in proportion to output (3.32) will be meaningful for a large class of future economic scenarios (in particular all those where the paths of the trade balance-to-output ratio and the net foreign debts-to-output ratio are bounded). Under the simplifying assumption that the real interest rate r, the real GDP growth rate γ, and the growth rate of net foreign debts g_B are constant, one obtains the following sustainability criterion:

$$r > \gamma \geq g_B. \tag{7.4}$$

The criterion (7.4) in particular rules out the unsustainable situation in which $r < \gamma$ and Ponzi games are forever feasible ($g_B \geq r$) because net foreign debts are constant or falling as a fraction

[1] In fact, they *will* lead there unless they asymptotically approach a certain fraction of output.

[2] This can be illustrated by means of the following simple example: Let net foreign debts and GDP grow exponentially at constant rates g_B and γ, respectively. Further, the very mild assumptions that the real interest rate r is constant with $r \geq 0$, the stock of net foreign debts is positive or zero ($B_{t-1} \geq 0$), output is strictly positive ($Y_t > 0$), and the growth rate of net foreign debts is larger than -1 ($g_B > -1$) are imposed. Then, even if net interest payments are smaller than output in the initial period t, i.e.,

$$rB_{t-1} < Y_t, \tag{7.1}$$

the net interest payments will exceed output in period N, i.e,

$$rB_{t-1}(1+g_B)^N > Y_t(1+\gamma)^N \tag{7.2}$$

whenever $\gamma < g_B$. In contrast, inequality (7.2) fails for all sufficiently large N if $\gamma \geq g_B$. The reason is that, under the said assumptions, inequality (7.2) is equivalent to

$$\sqrt[N]{\frac{rB_{t-1}}{Y_t}} > \frac{1+\gamma}{1+g_B}. \tag{7.3}$$

The left-hand side of inequality (7.3) is always less than one due to inequality (7.1), but is monotonically increasing in N and converges to one as N goes to infinity. Hence, inequality (7.3) and thus inequality (7.2) will never hold if $\gamma \geq g_B$ (whence the right-hand side of inequality (7.3) is larger than one). However, if $\gamma < g_B$ (whence the right-hand side of inequality (7.3) is less than one), inequality (7.3) and thus inequality (7.2) holds for all sufficiently large N (that is, for all N that are $> \log(rB_{t-1}/Y_t) / \log\left(\frac{1+\gamma}{1+g_B}\right)$). Hence, regardless of the value of r, net interest payments will never exceed GDP if $\gamma \geq g_B$, but will inevitably do so in the long run if $\gamma < g_B$.

of output ($\gamma \geq g_B$). The sustainability criterion (7.4) is stronger than the intertemporal budget constraint and the transversality condition (both in absolute terms and in proportion to output) because the latter are fully consistent with increasing foreign debts (in proportion to output or in absolute terms) as long as they are growing at a lesser rate than the appropriate discount rate.

In the standard intertemporal approach to the current account, the interest rate is the risk-free interest rate, which is the same for borrowing and lending. Thus, the requirement of $r > \gamma$ implies that the respective economy is dynamically efficient in a deterministic environment. For this reason, it has been argued that $r < \gamma$ is not likely to occur anyway (e.g., Romer, 2006, p. 564). However, as already mentioned in chapter 3, in the more realistic case of a stochastic environment, dynamic efficiency depends on the relationship between the real output growth rate and the return on the "risky capital" (Abel et al., 1989; Zilcha, 1992). In other words, the GDP growth rate may exceed the risk-free interest rate for a long period of time, as was for example observed in the United States (Bohn, 1995b, p. 257).

However, the violation of the criterion (7.4) does not necessarily imply unsustainability mainly for two reasons: Firstly, $r > \gamma$ is merely sufficient for the intertemporal budget constraint (3.32) to be satisfied. One can, at least hypothetically, imagine a situation in which $0 < r < \gamma$ and the economy under consideration does not engage in Ponzi finance ($r > g_B$), so that net foreign debts are declining in proportion to output ($\gamma > g_B$). Then, the ratio of net foreign debts to output is sustainable according to our sustainability definition, yet it violates the sustainability criterion (7.4) because of $r < \gamma$. Nevertheless, this situation is rather improbable: Because the "specific" intertemporal budget constraint is satisfied for $r < \gamma$ even if no net interest payments have ever been made, the economy in question has—under our assumptions—no incentives to voluntarily abstain from Ponzi games.

Secondly, as Bohn (1995b) shows, the "specific" transversality condition and intertemporal budget constraint make Ponzi finance impossible only in certain special cases such as the absence of uncertainty (see section 3.2 of chapter 3 for details). The "general" transversality condition and intertemporal budget constraint (both in proportion to output) depend on the relationship between the GDP growth rate and the stochastic discount rate as opposed to the interest rate. Thus, a sufficient condition for infeasibility of Ponzi games under uncertainty is that the stochastic discount rate exceeds the average GDP growth rate.

The criterion (7.4) is typically employed in assessing the sustainability of net foreign debts to output. Naturally the question arises whether it can also be applied to net foreign assets. For net creditor economies, the first inequality in the criterion (7.4), i.e., $r > \gamma$, is sufficient to secure the infeasibility of Ponzi games in all those cases in which the interest rate is the appropriate discounting rate for the intertemporal budget constraint. Regarding the second half of the criterion (7.4), it is more difficult to justify why the unbounded growth of net foreign assets in proportion to output is unsustainable. On the one hand, when the numbers of both lenders and borrowers are finite, one could have the following situation: that there is an economy whose net foreign assets increase in proportion to its output, and that this increase forces the net foreign debts of at least one other net borrower economy to exceed that country's output. Such a situation is clearly unsustainable for both the net creditor and the net debtor country. On the other hand, such an instance of unsustainability might also occur even when net foreign assets remain constant in proportion to the net creditor economy's output.[3] However, even if a continually increasing ratio of net foreign assets to output may be technically feasible, it might nevertheless be desirable for such an economy to reduce lending to foreigners and instead increase consumption and investment (Kool, 2010, p. 78). In sum, there are good, even though perhaps not universally compelling, reasons for equating sustainability with a non-increasing ratio of net foreign assets to output. Therefore, we shall apply the sustainability criterion (7.4) to net foreign assets as well in the subsequent sections. However, it should be borne in mind that even a continually increasing ratio of net foreign assets to GDP might be sustainable in certain cases.

The criterion of the non-increasing ratio of the NIIP to output indicates either that the NIIP-to-GDP ratio is on the sustainable path (when it is non-increasing) or on the unsustainable path (when it is rising). In the latter case, the question arises how to return to the sustainable path, that is, how to prevent the NIIP-to-GDP ratio from increasing. However, this question cannot be answered on the basis of the criterion (7.4) only. The reason is that the inequality (7.4) only stipulates the sustainable relationship between the *rates* of the real interest, the real GDP growth, and the NIIP growth. Thus, virtually any *level* of the NIIP-to-GDP ratio which satisfies the criterion (7.4) is regarded as sustainable as long as the NIIP-to-GDP ratio is constant or falling and $r > \gamma$. Suppose that the net borrower economy faces rising net foreign debts in proportion to output. This situation is unsustainable because our sustainability criterion (7.4) is violated. The unsustainable debt dynamics can be halted when this economy generates trade surpluses which are sufficiently large to prevent the ratio of net foreign debts to output from rising. Because the size of the trade surplus required to achieve sustainability depends on the level of the NIIP-to-GDP ratio, the question arises at which level net foreign debts in proportion to output should be stabilized or from which level on they should be falling.

7.1.2 Stabilizing the NIIP-to-output ratio at the current or recently observed average level

One-period resource gap

One approach to achieve sustainability is to stabilize the ratio of net foreign debts to output at its *current* level and to keep it constant or falling afterwards (Roubini, 2001, p. 8). The so called "resource (balance) gap" indicates the size of the resource transfer required to prevent the current NIIP-to-GDP ratio from rising. The concept of the "resource gap" is motivated by the "primary gap" which was suggested by Buiter et al. (1985) and Blanchard (1990) to measure the adjustment in the government's primary deficit required to keep the fiscal debt-to-GDP ratio constant.

The starting point for defining the resource gap is the single-period budget constraint derived in section 3.1 of chapter 3. For convenience, the following considerations focus on the budget

[3] This can be most easily demonstrated by means of the following example: Consider a world which consists of two countries only, the domestic net creditor economy and the foreign net debtor economy. Then, of course, domestic net foreign assets must grow at the same rate g_B as the foreign country's net foreign debts. A ratio of domestic net foreign assets to output that is non-increasing ($g_B \leq \gamma$) may then be perfectly consistent with a continually increasing ratio of the foreign country's net foreign debts to output ($g_B > \gamma^f$), thus implying that $\gamma^f < \gamma$. In other words, the net lender economy engages in Ponzi finance even while the ratio of net foreign assets to output is non-increasing.

constraint in real terms and can be analogously applied to the budget constraint in nominal terms (3.14). The single-period budget constraint in real terms (3.10) is given by

$$b_t - b_{t-1} = tb_t + \left(\frac{r_t - \gamma_t}{1+\gamma_t}\right) b_{t-1}. \tag{7.5}$$

Stabilizing the NIIP-to-GDP ratio at the current level b_{t-1} implies $b_{t-1} = b_t \equiv \overline{b_{t-1}}$ so that the left-hand side of equation (7.5) is zero. Solving equation (7.5) for tb_t and using the asterisk to denote the trade balance-to-GDP ratio which allows maintaining $\overline{b_{t-1}}$ yields

$$tb_t^* = -\left(\frac{r_t - \gamma_t}{1+\gamma_t}\right) \overline{b_{t-1}} \tag{7.6}$$

where $r_t > \gamma_t$ by assumption. The ratio of net foreign debts (assets) b_{t-1} is non-increasing if the economy generates at least the trade surplus (deficit) tb_t^* in period t. Provided that $r_t > \gamma_t$, equation (7.6) implies that the stabilization of net foreign debts to output ($b_{t-1} < 0$) requires a trade surplus ($tb^* > 0$), and the non-increasing ratio of net foreign assets to output ($b_{t-1} > 0$) is consistent only with a trade deficit ($tb^* < 0$). The higher *ceteris paribus* the real interest rate, the lower the real GDP growth rate, and the higher the ratio of net foreign debts (assets) to output, the higher must be the trade surplus (deficit) in proportion to GDP required to prevent the NIIP-to-GDP ratio from increasing.

Using equation (7.6), the resource gap can be defined as the difference between the trade balance required to maintain the constant NIIP-to-GDP ratio in period t (tb_t^*) and the trade balance which is expected or planned to be realized in period t (tb_t):

$$tb_t^* - tb_t = -\left(\frac{r_t - \gamma_t}{1+\gamma_t}\right) \overline{b_{t-1}} - tb_t \tag{7.7}$$

provided that $r_t > \gamma_t$. Equation (7.13) shows that the one-period resource gap simply equals the change in the current NIIP-to-GDP ratio (Blanchard, 1990, p. 14). For the net debtor economy, the positive resource gap (i.e., the stabilizing trade surplus is higher than the current trade balance) indicates the need for adjustment in the trade balance in order to achieve sustainability. In contrast, the resource gap which is zero or negative implies that the ratio of net foreign debts to output is non-increasing and, therefore, sustainable. For the net creditor economy, it is the opposite way around: The negative resource gap (i.e., the stabilizing trade deficit is smaller than the current trade balance) implies the need for adjustment in order to prevent the ratio of net foreign assets to output from rising, and the positive or zero resource gap indicates sustainability. Note that the stable NIIP-to-GDP ratio does not necessarily require the constant one-period resource gap. The latter may change from period to period when the real interest rate and the real GDP growth rate are also time-varying.

When the current values of r, γ, and tb are unusually high or low in comparison to their historical values, the one-period resource gap might be misleading. For example, when growth is temporarily low, the real interest rate is high, and the trade balance temporarily improves due to the decline in the GDP growth rate, the cyclical component in the relevant variables can be reduced by using the medium-term or long-term values of r, γ, and tb (Roubini, 2001, pp. 7-8). Besides, the one-period resource gap does not take into account predictable changes in the economy or in economic policy affecting the real interest rate, real GDP growth, and the trade balance as a share of output (Blanchard, 1990, p. 14).

Medium-term resource gap

Inspired by the medium-term fiscal indicators suggested by Blanchard (1990), the medium-term resource gap measures the average resource transfer required for debt stabilization over the medium-term horizon. The medium-term resource gap can be defined as

$$\sum_{i=t}^{n} tb_i^* - \sum_{i=t}^{n} tb_i = -\left(\frac{\sum_{i=t}^{n} r_i - \sum_{i=t}^{n} \gamma_i}{1+\sum_{i=t}^{n} \gamma_i}\right)\overline{b_{t-1}} - \sum_{i=t}^{n} tb_i. \tag{7.8}$$

Denoting the average values by the superscript ϕ, equation (7.8) can be written more compactly as

$$tb^{*\phi} - tb^{\phi} = -\left(\frac{r^{\phi} - \gamma^{\phi}}{1+\gamma^{\phi}}\right)\overline{b_{t-1}} - tb^{\phi}. \tag{7.9}$$

An alternative to stabilizing at the current level of the ratio of net foreign debts to output $(\overline{b_{t-1}})$ is the stabilization of that ratio at the average level $(\sum_{k=t-m}^{t} b_k \equiv \overline{b^{\phi}})$ observed over the last, say, three years (e.g., Zanghieri, 2004; Aristovnik, 2006). This approach is particularly suited to situations where the current value of net foreign debts to output is disproportionately high in comparison to previous years.

There is no consensus, however, on how long the time-horizon n defining the medium-term time horizon should be. Blanchard (1990, p. 15) originally suggests the current and the next two years (i.e., $n = 3$), yet points out that the ultimate choice of n is rather arbitrary and should be primarily motivated by the availability of data.

Permanent resource gap

A related approach is the permanent resource gap which—following Buiter (1997), Milesi-Ferretti and Razin (1996a), and Roubini (2001)—is defined as the difference between the trade balance (tb^*) required to maintain the current NIIP-to-GDP ratio indefinitely and the projected long-run trade balance (tb). The stabilizing long-run trade balance is given by

$$tb^* = -\left(\frac{r-\gamma}{1+\gamma}\right)\overline{b_{t-1}} \tag{7.10}$$

where $r > \gamma$ by assumption and the absence of the time index indicates the long-run values. For the net borrower economy, the ratio in brackets on the right-hand side of equation (7.10) can also be interpreted as the burden that the net foreign debt imposes on the economy. The higher the debt burden the greater—all other things being the same—the likelihood that a country will not be able to repay its net foreign debts (Obstfeld and Rogoff, 1996, p. 68).

Equation (7.10) is the single-period budget constraint when it is assumed, in addition, that the economy is in the steady-state equilibrium. Herein, the steady state is defined as the situation in which all variables remain constant in proportion to output and all growth rates are constant, too (Milesi-Ferretti and Razin, 1996a, p. 10).[4] An important implication of the steady state is that

[4] The steady-state budget constraint (7.10) follows directly from the "specific" intertemporal budget constraint in proportion to output (3.32) when the additional assumption of the steady state is imposed. For constant tb and $\overline{b_{t-1}}$ as well as a constant long-run real interest rate r and GDP growth rate γ, the "specific" IBC (3.32) becomes

the "specific" transversality condition and intertemporal budget constraint equal their "general" counterparts when the economy remains in the steady-state equilibrium indefinitely.[5] Thus, in this case, the stochastic discount rate equals the real market interest rate so that discounting by the real interest rate is sufficient to ensure solvency under uncertainty.

Another important implication of the steady-state approach is that it provides a justification for the sustainability criterion of a constant ratio of net foreign assets to output. Following the analysis of fiscal sustainability in Zee (1988, p. 666) and Horne (1991, p. 3), external imbalances can be defined as sustainable if the economy converges to or is in the steady state in the long run provided that there are no unanticipated shocks. By this definition, the ratio of net foreign assets which remains constant to output is sustainable.

Using equation (7.10), the permanent resource gap is given by

$$tb^* - tb = -\left(\frac{r-\gamma}{1+\gamma}\right)\overline{b_{t-1}} - tb \tag{7.13}$$

where $r > \gamma$. The resource gap indicates the need for a long-run adjustment in the trade balance if it is positive for the net debtor economy and negative for the net creditor economy. In practice, however, calculating the permanent resource gap "is likely to be something of a nightmare" (Buiter, 1997, p. 19) as it requires inferences of the long-run rates of the real interest and the real GDP growth as well as projections of the trade balance-to-GDP ratio under plausible scenarios over a long time horizon, say, at least 50 years.

In the following, we show two main modifications of the resource gap. For simplicity, we do not specify the time horizon by omitting time indices or superscripts except in $\overline{b_{t-1}}$. Our following considerations can be equally applied to the one-period, medium-term, or permanent resource gap.

Resource gap augmented for changes in the real exchange rate

Following Milesi-Ferretti and Razin (1996a, pp. 9-11), the resource gap (7.13) can be augmented by incorporating real exchange rate changes. This allows explicitly taking into account the effect of changes in the respective economy's competitiveness on external sustainability.

$$\overline{b_{t-1}} = -tb\sum_{n=t}^{\infty}\left(\frac{1+\gamma}{1+r}\right)^{n-t+1}. \tag{7.11}$$

Assuming $r > \gamma$ and exploiting the formula for the infinite geometric series, equation (7.11) simplifies to

$$\overline{b_{t-1}} = -tb\left(\frac{1+\gamma}{r-\gamma}\right). \tag{7.12}$$

Solving equation (7.12) for tb and using the asterisk finally leads to equation (7.10).

[5] In the steady state, the trade balance in proportion to output is a constant tb, whence for all $n \geq t$,

$$TB_n = Y_n tb = Y_t(1+\gamma)^{n-t+1} tb.$$

This expression is deterministic given the information available at time t, and in particular, $E_t[TB_n] = TB_n$ for all $n \geq t$. Therefore, the conditional covariance between TB_n and the stochastic discount factor in the "general" intertemporal budget constraint (3.54) is zero. Analogous considerations apply to the "general" transversality condition (3.50). Hence, in the steady state, the "general" IBC is indistinguishable from the "specific" IBC, and the "general" TC from the "specific" TC.

The real exchange rate in indirect quotation is defined as the ratio of the domestic price index (p_t) to the foreign price index (p_t^f) multiplied by the reciprocal nominal exchange rate in price quotation (s_t): $q_t = p_t/(s_t p_t^f)$. The rate of real exchange rate changes is defined as $1+\varepsilon_t = q_t/q_{t-1}$. Dividing each term by q_t, one can put the single-period budget constraint (3.10) in terms of foreign goods:

$$\frac{b_t}{q_t} - \frac{b_{t-1}}{q_t} = \frac{tb_t}{q_t} + \left(\frac{r_t - \gamma_t}{1+\gamma_t}\right)\frac{b_{t-1}}{q_t}. \tag{7.14}$$

Defining $tb_t/q_t \equiv tb_t$, $b_{t-1}/q_{t-1} \equiv b_{t-1}$, and $b_t/q_t \equiv b_t$ and making use of $(1+\varepsilon_t) = q_t/q_{t-1}$, the budget constraint (7.14) can be rewritten as

$$b_t - b_{t-1} = tb_t + \frac{(1+r_t)-(1+\gamma_t)(1+\varepsilon_t)}{(1+\gamma_t)(1+\varepsilon_t)} b_{t-1}. \tag{7.15}$$

When the NIIP-to-GDP ratio remains unchanged at $\overline{b_{t-1}}$ and the real interest rate and the GDP growth rate are constant, the constant trade balance-to-GDP ratio tb^* required to maintain $\overline{b_{t-1}}$ is given by

$$tb^* = -\left\{\frac{(1+r)-(1+\gamma)(1+\varepsilon)}{(1+\gamma)(1+\varepsilon)}\right\}\overline{b_{t-1}} \tag{7.16}$$

provided that $r > \gamma$. For small values of r, γ, and ε, tb^* in equation (7.16) can be linearly approximated by[6]

$$tb^* = -(r-\gamma-\varepsilon)\overline{b_{t-1}} \tag{7.17}$$

where $r > \gamma$. All things being equal, real depreciation ($\varepsilon < 0$) raises the real value of an economy's liabilities, as they are typically denominated in a foreign currency, and increases, therefore, the real value of net foreign debts in proportion to output. Hence, a higher trade balance-to-GDP ratio is needed for debt stabilization (Roubini, 2001, p. 6). In contrast, real appreciation ($\varepsilon > 0$) reduces *ceteris paribus* the real value of net foreign debts to output and, thus, the stabilizing trade surplus. The higher the long-run real appreciation rate, the higher is—all things the same—the decline in the stabilizing trade balance-to-GDP ratio. When the rate of real appreciation ($\varepsilon > 0$) raises to a level that entails $r-\gamma-\varepsilon < 0$, the stabilization of net foreign debts in proportion to output can be achieved even if the economy under consideration runs a trade deficit. For $\varepsilon = 0$ and $r > \gamma$, the net debtor economy only needs to pay out the excess of the real interest rate over the real GDP growth rate in order to maintain a steady-state ratio of net foreign debts to GDP (Obstfeld and Rogoff, 1996, p. 68). In an economy with positive real interest rates, but zero growth and zero real appreciation ($\gamma = \varepsilon = 0$), the stabilizing trade balance-to-GDP ratio simply equals the net interest payments (receipts) on the NIIP in proportion to GDP.

The augmented resource gap can be defined using equation (7.17) as

$$tb^* - tb = -(r-\gamma-\varepsilon)\overline{b_{t-1}} - tb \tag{7.18}$$

where $r > \gamma$. As before, the positive (negative) resource gap indicates unsustainability for the net debtor economy (net creditor economy). Real depreciation *ceteris paribus* increases the

[6] Equation (7.16) can be linearly approximated by $tb^* = -(r-\gamma-\varepsilon)\overline{b_{t-1}}$ because the difference between $(r-\gamma-\varepsilon)$ and $\frac{(1+r)-(1+\gamma)(1+\varepsilon)}{(1+\gamma)(1+\varepsilon)}$ is zero for small values of γ, r, and ε.

stabilizing trade balance ratio (tb^*) and thus the size of the adjustment required to achieve sustainability. However, the increase in the absolute value of the resource gap might be, at least partly, offset if real depreciation improves the observed long-run trade balance ratio (tb) in case of the validity of the Marshall-Lerner condition. In the short run, the trade balance may temporarily deteriorate due to the J-curve effect. However, as already mentioned in section 3.3 of chapter 3, the empirical literature provides only weak support both for the validity of the Marshall-Lerner condition and the J-curve phenomenon.

Resource gap augmented for changes in the net foreign direct investment

Hitherto it was assumed that net lending and borrowing occurs only through international trade in bonds. Thus, other asset categories such as foreign direct investment[7] and reserve assets have been ignored so far. Doisy and Hervé (2003) suggest to include foreign direct investment (FDI) in the calculation of the resource gap because current account deficits in many countries (in particular in transition countries) are to a large extent financed through direct investment inflows. For this purpose, the overall current account can be split into two components:

$$CAB_t = \Delta B_t - NFDI_t \tag{7.19}$$

where ΔB_t is, as before, the change in net foreign assets or debts resulting from trade in bonds. $NFDI_t$ denotes an increase in net direct investment outflows (i.e., an increase in net claims towards the rest of the world) or a decrease in net direct investment inflows (i.e., a decrease in net foreign liabilities) if $NFDI < 0$, and a decline in net direct investment outflows or a rise in net direct investment inflows if $NFDI > 0$.

Only the non-interest part of the current account balance can be allocated to repay foreign debts. Thus, subtracting $r_t B_{t-1}$ on both sides of equation (7.19) yields

$$PB_t = \Delta B_t - r_t B_{t-1} - NFDI_t. \tag{7.20}$$

The left-hand side is the non-interest current account balance or primary balance (PB_t): $PB_t = CAB_t - r_t B_{t-1}$. Dividing equation (7.20) by $q_t Y_t$ results in

$$\begin{aligned}\frac{PB_t}{q_tY_t} &= \frac{B_t}{q_tY_t} - \frac{B_{t-1}}{q_tY_t} - \frac{rB_{t-1}}{q_tY_t} - \frac{NFDI}{q_tY_t} \\ &= \frac{B_t}{q_tY_t} - \frac{B_{t-1}}{(1+\gamma_t)(1+\varepsilon_t)q_{t-1}Y_{t-1}} - \frac{rB_{t-1}}{(1+\gamma_t)(1+\varepsilon_t)q_{t-1}Y_{t-1}} - \frac{NFDI}{q_tY_t}.\end{aligned} \tag{7.21}$$

The lower-case notation allows rewriting equation (7.21) in the form

$$pb_t = b_t - \frac{(1+r)}{(1+\gamma_t)(1+\varepsilon_t)} b_{t-1} - nfdi_t \tag{7.22}$$

where pb_t denotes $pb_t/(q_tY_t)$ and $nfdi_t \equiv NFDI_t/(q_tY_q)$. Using equation (7.22), the primary balance-to-GDP ratio required to stabilize the NIIP-to-GDP ratio at $\overline{b_{t-1}}$ becomes

[7] Foreign direct investment denotes "cross-border investment associated with a resident in one economy having control or a significant degree of influence on the management of an enterprise that is resident in another economy" (IMF, 2008, p. 144), for details see the classification by IMF (2008, pp. 144-158).

$$pb^* = \left\{ \frac{(1+r)-(1+\gamma)(1+\varepsilon)}{(1+\gamma)(1+\varepsilon)} \right\} \overline{b_{t-1}} - nfdi \tag{7.23}$$

provided that $r > \gamma$. Analogously to equation (7.17), the linear approximation of equation (7.23) can be obtained as[8]

$$pb^* = -(r-\gamma-\varepsilon)\overline{b_{t-1}} - nfdi. \tag{7.26}$$

The larger the increase in net direct investment inflows ($nfdi > 0$) or the smaller the decrease in net direct investment outflows ($nfdi < 0$), the smaller is—all other things being the same—the ratio of the primary balance to output which prevents the NIIP-to-GDP ratio from rising. The increase in net FDI might be even so large that the ratio of net foreign debts to output may remain stable when the trade balance is permanently in deficit.

The resource gap can be calculated as the difference between the stabilizing ratio of the primary balance to output—given by equation (7.26)—and the projected primary balance ratio:

$$pb^* - pb = -(r-\gamma-\varepsilon)\overline{b_{t-1}} - nfdi - pb. \tag{7.27}$$

The positive (negative) sign of the resource gap indicates the need for adjustment in order to achieve sustainability in net debtor (net creditor) economies. The larger the increase in net FDI inflows or the decrease in FDI outflows, the smaller in absolute terms is *ceteris paribus* the required reversal in the primary balance. In contrast, the larger the current stock of net foreign debts to output, the larger *ceteris paribus* the need for the adjustment. Thus, the resource gap (7.27) indirectly shows that primary deficits which are financed by inflows of direct investment rather than by issuing bonds are more likely to be sustainable because direct investment is a more stable form of investment than (short-term) bonds (Roubini and Wachtel, 1998, pp. 7-8).

However, the version of the resource gap given by (7.27) is weaker as a concept than the resource gap without net FDI. To see this, consider the net borrower economy which runs a primary deficit. According to the resource gap (7.27), the stabilization of net foreign debts in proportion to output can be achieved by a sufficiently high and stable increase in net FDI inflows. For constant values of the real interest rate, the real GDP growth rate, and the real appreciation rate, this situation is sustainable as long as the increase in net FDI inflows remains unchanged. Though direct investment is less prone to shifts in investors' sentiments than other

[8] The change in net foreign direct investment can be alternatively rewritten as

$$\frac{NFDI_t}{q_t Y_t} = \frac{FDI_t - FDI_{t-1}}{q_t Y_t} = \frac{FDI_t}{q_t Y_t} - \left(\frac{1}{(1+\gamma_t)(1+\varepsilon_t)} \right) \frac{FDI_{t-1}}{q_{t-1} Y_{t-1}}$$

where FDI_t denotes net foreign direct investment inflows ($FDI_t > 0$) or outflows ($FDI_t < 0$) at the end of period t. Using the lower-case notation and setting $fdi_t = fdi_{t-1} \equiv fdi$ one obtains in the steady-state equilibrium

$$\frac{NFDI}{qY} = -\left(\frac{(1+\gamma)(1+\varepsilon)-1}{(1+\gamma)(1+\varepsilon)} \right) fdi. \tag{7.24}$$

Using the linear approximation of equation (7.24), equation (7.26) can be alternatively written as

$$pb = -(r-\gamma-\varepsilon)b - (\gamma+\varepsilon)fdi. \tag{7.25}$$

The higher the GDP growth rate and the higher the real appreciation rate, the more a given of net FDI inflows ($fdi > 0$) *ceteris paribus* reduces the stabilizing primary balance.

forms of financing, foreign investors might withdraw their funds, for example, due to the emergence of political upheavals. In this situation, the non-increasing ratio of net foreign debts to output can only be maintained when the economy brings about a sufficiently high reversal in the trade balance—which is difficult to achieve in the short run. Thus, the economy in question is more vulnerable to unfavorable shocks as if it had initially relied on the "internal financing" through primary surpluses.

Further, equation (7.27) does not take into account possible "maturity mismatch" problems. Direct investment is rather illiquid because it is tied to physical investment (McGettigan, 2000, p. 25). In contrast, the debt repayment requires liquid financing. Thus, the economy might become illiquid even if the resource gap does not indicate violations of solvency.

Finally, the resource gap (7.27) ignores direct investment income such as dividends and interest.[9] Theoretically, host countries can engage in a kind of Ponzi scheme by attracting new FDI to pay the return on the cumulated FDI stock (Liang, 2007, p. 115; Kregel, 2004, p. 587). Similarly to debt-creating instruments, one could require that the growth rate of net FDI inflows must be less than the rate of return on the FDI stock in order to rule out Ponzi games. Aside from difficulties associated with the measurement of the rate of return on FDI (Bosworth et al., 2007; Higgins et al., 2007), the question is whether such a requirement is sufficient to avoid Ponzi financing under uncertainty. So far, there has been no published research on sustainability of net foreign direct investment flows. In view of all these limitations, we conclude with the words of Reisen (1998, pp. 119) that sustainability considerations in the spirit of equation (7.26) "do not make sense for FDI flows, as long as there is no widely held notion about the sustainability of net foreign liabilities for the stock of FDI invested in a country."

Even if net FDI inflows are to be included in the calculation of the resource gap, equation (7.27) has still further drawbacks. Firstly, it is assumed that there exist no feedback effects from net FDI flows to GDP growth. However, there is some—though not unambiguous—empirical evidence that FDI inflows do promote economic growth in host countries by producing positive externalities in the form of technology transfers and knowledge spillovers for the entire economy (see Balasubramanyam et al., 1996 for economies with an export-substituting trade strategy; Borensztein et al., 1998 for economies with a minimum threshold stock of human capital; Hermes and Lensink, 2003 and Alfaro et al., 2004 for economies with well-developed financial markets).[10]

Secondly, Fry (1996) reports for a group of six Pacific Basin economies and a control group of eleven other developing economies that FDI inflows increase national saving directly and indirectly (through accelerated growth) and, therefore, improve—all other things being the same—the current account balance, and *ceteris paribus* the primary balance in the long run. If this result were shown to apply also for industrialized economies, the increase in net FDI inflows should be incorporated with a positive sign into equation (7.26).

---

[9] Details on different types of direct investment income can be found in IMF (2006a, pp. 299-306).

[10] In contrast, empirical studies by Harrison (1995), Aitken and Harrison (1999), and Carkovic and Levine (2005) do not find a positive (causal) relationship between FDI and growth. A summary of the empirical literature on the relationship between FDI flows and economic growth is provided by Mello (1997) and Lim (2001).

Empirical studies

Resource gaps are a popular tool for assessing fiscal sustainability. They are, however, less widely used in the analysis of external sustainability. First of all, resource gaps are an integral part of the International Monetary Fund's debt sustainability analysis (DSA) for market-access countries (i.e., countries which have a significant access to international markets)— which was introduced in 2002 and refined in 2003 and 2005. The DSA contains two main elements: (i) a baseline medium-term scenario which shows the historical and the projected evolution of the external debt-to-exports ratio, the external debt-to-GDP ratio, and the public debt-to-revenues ratio; (ii) a series of sensitivity tests around the baseline medium-term scenario. The resource gap is computed under the assumption that all the relevant variables remain at the level reported in the last year of projection both in the baseline scenario and the sensitivity tests (IMF, 2008, pp. 11-12). The debt stabilizing primary balance is calculated on the basis of equation (7.16) which is expressed in nominal terms and which takes into account that a portion of total external debt is denominated in domestic currency:

$$pb^{*n} = \left(\frac{(1+\hat{i}_N) - (1+\gamma_N)(1+\pi_N) + \varepsilon^n \alpha (1+\hat{i}_N)}{(1+\gamma_N)(1+\pi_N)} \right) \overline{b_{N-1}^{nG}} \tag{7.28}$$

where N refers to the last year of the medium-term projection and the superscript n denotes nominal variables. The nominal interest rate which is calculated as the weighted average of domestic and foreign nominal interest rates is denoted by $\hat{i}$, γ is, as before, the real GDP growth rate, ε^n is the nominal exchange rate appreciation, π is the change in the domestic GDP deflator expressed in US dollars, α denotes the share of domestic-currency debt in total external debt, and b^{nG} is gross foreign debt in US dollars in proportion to nominal GDP. Equation (7.28) typically contains a residual due to a change in gross foreign liabilities because the DSA uses the gross external debt, and not the net external debt. The main reason for the use of the gross external debt is that entities in the economy which possess external assets may be different from entities which have external liabilities. Therefore, the rollover and the non-repayment risk is likely to be related to gross (rather than net) financing needs (IMF, 2002, p. 26).

However, the assumptions underlying medium-term scenarios have been the subject of substantial critique. A large body of empirical literature finds that projections of economic growth have a systematic bias towards "over-optimism" (Musso and Phillips, 2002; Baqir et al., 2005; Atoian et al., 2006; Leo, 2009; Frankel, 2011). One explanation is that the IMF programs which are based on higher growth projections underestimate the adjustment required to achieve sustainability and, therefore, facilitate the negotiations between the IMF and the authorities of the countries seeking the financial assistance (Bird, 2005). However, Dreher et al. (2008) arrive at the contrary conclusion: The IMF's forecasts of GDP growth are unduly pessimistic for non-OECD countries in their data set. This result might be explained by the attempt on the part of the IMF to increase its lending to the countries in debt distress by overestimating the adjustment needed to correct external imbalances.

Apart from the IMF's debt sustainability framework, resource gaps are widely used to examine the hypothetical adjustment in the trade balance under different scenarios (e.g., Callen and Cashin, 1999, Harms, 2008, pp. 228-229). To our knowledge, there exist only five studies which rely on "real" data: Obstfeld and Rogoff (1996, pp. 68-70) estimate the burden imposed by the net foreign debt in selected, mainly developing countries. Powell (2002) investigates whether the Argentinian currency crisis was caused by a lack of external sustainability. Doisy and Hervé (2003), Zanghieri (2004), and Aristovnik (2006) compute the debt-stabilizing primary surplus in transition economies. Due to space limitations, we concentrate on the latter three studies; details on the analysis performed in Obstfeld and Rogoff (1996, pp. 68-70) and Powell (2002) can be found in appendix 7.A. The said three studies on transition economies can be compared easily because they are based on similar data sets. Such a comparative investigation also permits a more in-depth evaluation of the resource gap as a concept of its own.

Doisy and Hervé (2003) investigate external sustainability in six Central and Eastern European (CEE) countries prior to their entry into the European Union.[11] Table 7.1 shows the countries in the sample (column 1), the data provided by Doisy and Hervé (2003), and the resource gap. Following Doisy and Hervé (2003), the stabilization of net foreign debts as a fraction of GDP is to be achieved at the 1998 level (column 4). The projected values of the real interest rate, the real GDP growth rate, and the real appreciation rate are approximated by the average rates during the reference period 1993-1998 for Bulgaria, Hungary, and Slovakia and 1992-1998 for the rest of the sample (columns 2, 3, 5, and 6). The rather short reference period of six or seven years represents more the medium-term, rather than the long-term perspective.

We calculate the primary balance-to-GDP ratio which stabilizes the 1998 ratio of net foreign debts to output over the medium term under two scenarios: (i) FDI inflows are not included; (ii) the increase in net FDI inflows (in proportion to GDP) remains stable at the average value during the respective reference period (see column 6).[12] The stabilizing primary balance-to-GDP ratio under the first scenario can be found in column 7 and the one under the second scenario in column 10.

In line with the data provided by Doisy and Hervé (2003), we take the "myopic" approach suggested by Buiter (1997, p. 19)[13] which approximates the projected primary balance by its latest available level. Thus, the medium-term resource gap is calculated as the difference between the stabilizing primary balance-to-GDP ratio and the 1998 primary balance-to-GDP ratio (pb_{1998}):

$$pb^{*\phi} - pb_{1998} = -(r^{\phi} - \gamma^{\phi} - \varepsilon^{\phi})\overline{b_{1998}} - nfdi^{\phi} - pb_{1998}, \quad r^{\phi} > \gamma^{\phi} \tag{7.29}$$

where $nfdi^{\phi} = 0$ under the first scenario. Column 8 shows the 1998 value of primary deficits in proportion to GDP. Columns 9 and 11 specify the "myopic" medium-term resource gap under the first and the second scenario, respectively.

Table 7.1 shows that all countries in the sample experience real appreciation ($\varepsilon^{\phi} > 0$) which can be explained by the Balassa-Samuelson effect. According to the Balassa-Samuelson theo-

[11] Czech Republic, Hungary, Poland, and Slovakia joined the EU in 2004 whereas Bulgaria and Romania became EU members in 2007.

[12] For reasons unknown to us, our calculations of the stabilizing primary balance as a fraction of GDP shown in columns 7 and 10 of table 7.1 differ from those in Doisy and Hervé (2003); we were unable to reproduce the findings of Doisy and Hervé (2003).

[13] Originally, Buiter (1997, p. 19) coins the term "myopic" in connection with the government's primary gap which is calculated as the difference between the stabilizing primary surplus and the current—rather than the projected long-run—primary balance.

rem,[14] relative growth leads to real exchange rate appreciation largely driven by international productivity differences between traded and non-traded goods.

The requirement $r^{\phi} > \gamma^{\phi}$ is not satisfied in Hungary and Slovakia. However, as already discussed in subsection 7.1.1 of this chapter, $r^{\phi} < \gamma^{\phi}$ does not necessarily mean that the economy is not able and/or willing to repay its foreign debts. In the remaining four countries in the sample, the real interest rate exceeds the real GDP growth rate, thus implying that these countries are at least able to pay (denoted by the dark grey color).

[14] The observation of the Balassa-Samuelson effect has precursors in the work of Ricardo (1821) and Viner (1937). Prior to the prominent works of Balassa (1964) and Samuelson (1964), the early analysis was also given by Harrod (1933). Related independent research was done in the so called "Penn" studies (Kravis et al., 1975, 1978) and by Bhagwati (1984). For this reason, the Balassa-Samuelson effect might be more precisely referred to as "Ricardo-Viner-Harrod-Balassa-Samuelson-Penn-Bhagwati" effect (Samuelson, 1994, p. 201).

Table 7.1: Medium-term resource gap in six Central and Eastern European countries during the reference period 1992-1998

(1)	(2)	(3)	(4)	(5)	(6)	(7)	(8)	(9)	(10)	(11)
Country	γ^{ϕ} (average)* in %	r^{ϕ} (average)* in %	b_{1998} 1998 in %	ε^{ϕ} (average)* in %	$nfdi^{\phi}$ (average)* in %	$pb^{*\phi}$ $(nfdi = 0)$ in %	pb_{1998} 1998 in %	$pb^{*\phi} - pb_{1998}$ $(nfdi = 0)$	$pb^{*\phi}$ $(nfdi = (6))$ in %	$pb^{*\phi} - pb_{1998}$ $(nfdi = (6))$
Bulgaria	-2.0	1.9	-80.8	6.3	2.2	-1.9	-0.5	-1.4	-4.1	-3.6
Czech R.	1.6	3.0	-44.9	6.4	3.0	-2.2	-1.9	-0.3	-5.2	-3.3
Hungary	3.0	4.0	-59.8	0.1	5.1	0.5	-4.9	5.4	-4.6	0.3
Poland	5.2	0.8	-30.1	4.4	1.2	-2.6	-4.3	1.7	-3.8	0.5
Romania	0.2	2.6	-24.9	12.0	1.8	-2.4	-7.8	5.4	-4.2	3.6
Slovakia	5.9	4.2	-48.6	3.6	1.1	-2.6	-10.1	7.5	-3.7	6.4

Source: Doisy and Hervé (2003) and author's own calculations

Notes: * The average values refer to the reference period 1993-1998 for Bulgaria, Hungary, and Slovakia and 1992-1998 for Czech Republic, Poland, and Romania.

In addition to the requirement $r^{\phi} > \gamma^{\phi}$, Bulgaria and Czech Republic meet the second sustainability criterion: The resource gap is negative, disregarding of whether net FDI inflows are taken into account. Thus, net foreign debts and primary deficits in those countries can be perceived as sustainable (denoted by the light grey color). In Hungary, Poland, Romania, and Slovakia, the positive resource gap indicates an increase in the ratio of net foreign debts to output over the medium-term horizon. As expected, considering net FDI inflows implies a smaller adjustment in the primary balance. The difference between the two measures of the resource gap is the largest in case of Hungary: Whereas the resource gap is almost zero when the increase in net FDI inflows of 5.1% of GDP is taken into account, the resource gap without FDI flows requires a primary balance reversal of more than 5 percentage points.

Zanghieri (2004) also analyzes external sustainability in CEE countries using a sample of ten countries based on the reference period during 2000-2002. For the reference period from 2000 to 2003, Aristovnik (2006) in addition considers two further CEE countries and five countries which belong to the Commonwealth of Independent States (CIS). Column 1 in tables 7.2 and 7.3 specifies the countries under investigation. The real GDP growth rate (column 2 in both tables) is the projected average value during the period from 2003 to 2008 in Zanghieri (2004) and from 2000 to 2008 in Aristovnik (2006). The real interest rate is approximated by the latest available level (column 3 in both tables). Both studies assume that net foreign debts in proportion to GDP should be stabilized at the average value ($\overline{b^{\phi}}$) observed over the particular reference period (column 4 in both tables). Further, Aristovnik (2006) simplifies the analysis by ignoring the effects of real exchange rate changes ($\varepsilon^{\phi} = 0$). In contrast, Zanghieri (2004) assumes that the real exchange rate is fully flexible and that central banks do not attempt to prevent real appreciation due to the Balassa-Samuelson effect. When calculating the real appreciation rate (column 5 of table 7.2), Zanghieri (2004) computes the inflation differences of the transition countries *vis-á-vis* the European Union and assumes that the share of non-traded goods remains constant at 70 percent for both transition and then EU-member countries (the time period is not reported). Regarding changes in net foreign direct investment inflows, both studies examine three scenarios: (i) no change in net foreign direct investment inflows ($nfdi = 0$); (ii) stable net FDI inflows of 4 percent of GDP per year ($nfdi = 4.0$); (iii) the change in net FDI inflows stabilizes in proportion to output at the average value $nfdi^{\phi}$ during the particular reference period. The average value of changes in net FDI inflows is shown in column 6 of table 7.2 and column 5 of table 7.3.

Overall, the data depict the medium-term rather than the long-term perspective. We again take the "myopic" approach and use the average value of the primary balance to GDP (pb^{ϕ}) provided by Zanghieri (2004) and Aristovnik (2006) for the particular reference period (column 7 in table 7.2 and column 6 in table 7.3). The "myopic" medium-term resource gap (7.27) is calculated as follows:

$$pb^{*\phi} - pb^{\phi} = -(r_t - \gamma^{\phi} - \varepsilon^{\phi})\overline{b^{\phi}} - nfdi^{\phi} - pb^{\phi} \tag{7.30}$$

provided that $r_t > \gamma^{\phi}$. The computed resource gap under the three scenarios for net FDI inflows can be found in the last three columns of tables 7.2 and 7.3.

Table 7.2: Medium-term resource gap in ten transition economies during the reference period 2000-2002

(1) Country	(2) γ^{ϕ} (average 2003-2008) in %	(3) r_{2002} in %	(4) b^{ϕ} (average 2000-2002) in %	(5) ε^{ϕ} in %	(6) $nfdi^{\phi}$ (average 2000-2002) in %	(7) pb^{ϕ} (average 2000-2002) in %	(8) $pb^{*\phi} - pb^{\phi}$ $(nfdi = 0)$	(9) $pb^{*\phi} - pb^{\phi}$ $(nfdi = 4.0)$	(10) $pb^{*\phi} - pb^{\phi}$ $(nfdi^{\phi} = (6))$
Bulgaria	5.2	5.4	-76.6	7.2	5.6	-5.5	-0.2	-4.2	-5.8
Czech Rep.	3.8	4.4	-37.1	4.4	13.7	-5.5	3.6	-0.4	-10.1
Estonia	5.5	4.9	-63.7	4.4	9.0	-8.0	5.6	1.6	-3.4
Hungary	3.3	4.2	-66.5	3.5	5.3	-3.0	0.1	-3.9	-5.2
Latvia	6.1	8.7	-73.7	4.2	6.5	-5.1	0.1	-3.9	-6.3
Lithuania	6.2	8.0	-44.4	4.0	6.0	-8.1	5.6	1.6	-0.4
Poland	4.4	11.0	-40.8	4.0	6.4	-4.3	0	-4.0	- 6.4
Romania	5.1	6.1	-31.1	6.8	3.9	-4.3	1.9	-2.1	-2.1
Slovakia	4.8	6.6	-55.3	3.5	15.7	-7.0	4.1	0.1	-11.6
Slovenia	3.5	6.4	-36.2	4.4	6.2	-0.4	-2.3	-6.3	-8.4

Source: Zanghieri (2004) author's and own calculations

Table 7.3: Medium-term resource gap in 17 transition economies based on the average primary balance from 2000 to 2003

(1) Country	(2) γ^{ϕ} (average 2000-2008) in %	(3) r_{2003} in %	(4) b^{ϕ} (average 2000-2003) in %	(5) $nfdi^{\phi}$ (average 2000-2003) in %	(6) pb^{ϕ} (average 2000-2003) in %	(7) $pb^{*\phi} - pb^{\phi}$ ($nfdi = 0$)	(8) $pb^{*\phi} - pb^{\phi}$ ($nfdi = 4.0$)	(9) $pb^{*\phi} - pb^{\phi}$ ($nfdi^{\phi} = (5)$)
Bulgaria	4.3	1.9	-70.2	6.3	-4.4	2.7	-1.3	-3.5
Croatia	4.0	1.7	-66.1	5.7	-2.7	1.1	-2.9	-4.6
Czech R.	3.5	2.4	-36.7	8.5	-1.4	1.0	-3.0	-7.5
Estonia	6.4	3.6	-59.7	5.7	-4.0	2.4	-1.6	-3.4
Hungary	3.8	1.7	-55.8	1.4	-2.2	1.0	-3.0	-0.4
Kazakhstan	8.6	2.2	-69.3	9.1	-4.3	-0.2	-4.2	-9.3
Latvia	6.7	6.4	-70.0	3.8	-8.4	8.2	4.2	4.4
Lithuania	6.6	4.1	-34.7	3.6	-3.9	3.1	-0.9	-0.6
Macedonia	3.7	7.8	-42.0	5.2	-4.9	6.6	2.6	1.4
Moldova	5.4	3.0	-84.1	7.3	-17.2	15.2	11.2	7.8
Poland	3.6	1.0	-37.5	3.1	-2.3	1.3	-2.7	-1.8
Romania	4.6	2.8	-31.3	2.7	-3.7	3.1	-0.9	0.6
Russia	5.7	2.9	-48.5	0.0	13.7	-15.1	-19.1	-15.0
Slovakia	4.2	2.3	-55.9	8.8	-3.8	2.7	-1.3	-6.1
Slovenia	3.2	4.6	-36.4	2.4	-0.2	0.7	-3.3	-1.7
Ukraine	6.9	5.2	-35.3	2.1	7.3	-7.9	-11.9	-10.0
Uzbekistan	2.8	4.8	-42.7	0.9	4.3	-3.4	-7.4	-4.3

Source: Aristovnik (2006) and author's own calculations

As in table 7.1, all cases in which the real interest rate is higher than the real GDP growth rate are marked by the dark grey color. In table 7.2, this requirement is satisfied for all countries except Estonia. In contrast, in 14 out of 17 countries in table 7.6, this requirement is violated, and evidence in favor of economy's ability to repay its net foreign debts is obtained only for Macedonia, Slovenia, and Uzbekistan.

The light grey color denotes all—potentially sustainable—cases in which the resource gap is zero or negative. In table 7.2, only three out of ten countries (Bulgaria, Poland, and Slovenia) exhibit the non-rising ratio of net foreign debts to GDP under the first scenario in which FDI inflows are not included. These are the only countries in table 7.2 which have a non-increasing net foreign debt-to-GDP ratio under all three scenarios. Moreover, these countries could even run higher primary deficits and still remain sustainable. Among countries with a positive resource gap, the adjustment in the trade balance required to achieve sustainability is the highest in Estonia and Lithuania with 5.6 percentage points each and in Slovakia with 4.1 percentage points. In table 7.3, only four out of 17 countries (Kazakhstan, Russia, Ukraine, and Uzbekistan) do not need to adjust the primary balance in order to restore sustainability in the first scenario. The resource gap remains negative in those countries under the second and the third scenario as well. However, evidence in favor of ability to pay is found only for Kazakhstan which meets the requirement $r_t > \gamma^\phi$. The resource gap for Estonia, Lithuania, and Slovakia is smaller than it was in table 7.2 (2.4, 3.1, and 2.7 percentage points, respectively). In table 7.6, the largest positive resource gap is found in Moldova with 15.2 percentage points.

As expected, the inclusion of net FDI inflows in the second and the third scenarios reduces the resource gap. In table 7.2, seven out of ten countries exhibit sustainability due to the stable increase in net FDI inflows of 4 percent of GDP in the second scenario. The need for the adjustment is smaller than in the first scenario: 1.6 percentage points in Estonia and Lithuania as well as the—almost negligible—0.1 percentage points in Slovakia. In table 7.6, the resource gap indicates unsustainability only in Latvia (4.2), Macedonia (2.6), and Moldova (11.2).

Finally, when net FDI inflows are assumed to stabilize at the recently observed average value in the third scenario, all countries in table 7.2 are sustainable. In table 7.6, unsustainability is found in Latvia, Macedonia, and Moldova—as in the last two scenarios—and in addition in Romania. Thus, empirical results show once again that the resource gap which takes into account net FDI inflows is a weaker concept than the resource gap with no net FDI flows.

Since tables 7.2 and 7.3 refer to similar reference periods, the results can be compared for the intersection between the two samples (i.e., for all ten countries in table 7.2). Tables 7.2 and 7.3 show no agreement in the sign of the resource gap only for three out of ten countries (Bulgaria, Poland, and Slovenia) under the first scenario, for five out of ten countries (Estonia, Latvia, Lithuania, Romania, and Slovakia) under the second scenario, and for two out of ten countries (Latvia and Romania) under the third scenario. However, the size of the adjustment required to prevent the ratio of net foreign debts to output from rising differs in many cases. For instance, the resource gap under the first scenario for the Czech Republic equals 3.6 in table 7.2 and only 1.0 in table 7.3. The difference in the results can be explained by slightly different reference periods, differing sources of data, and varying treatment of real appreciation. However, it also demonstrates that the concept of the resource gap is quite sensitive towards differences in estimations of the relevant variables.

Further, the "myopic" approach to the medium-term resource gap might be a poor approximation when the current primary balance-to-GDP ratio is untypically high or low. Similarly, the approximation of the medium-term real interest rate by the current level might be misleading. Using the past average value as the projection of the average future value is a rather simple way of forecasting which does not take into account any predictable changes in the future.

Finally, the ratio of net foreign debts to output at which the stabilization is to be achieved appears to be rather high in some countries (e.g., Bulgaria and Moldova). In case of exogenous shocks (such as the exogenous decline in demand for domestic exports), foreign investors are more likely to get concerned about ability and willingness to pay of the economy in question when the ratio of net foreign debts is, say, 80 percent of GDP than when it is 30 percent of GDP. Thus, in order to reduce the economy's vulnerability towards unfavorable shocks, it might be more appropriate to stabilize the ratio of net foreign debts to output at a lower level than the current one.

7.1.3 Stabilizing the foreign debt-to-exports ratio at the current level

The implicit assumption behind seeking to stabilize the ratio of net foreign debts to GDP or GNP is that resources can be easily transferred from the rest of the economy to the sector of traded goods in order to earn foreign exchange. However, this assumption may not apply to many developing economies—in particular those which have a history of import substitution—because they might only have a small sector of traded goods (Goldstein, 2003, p. 9). Thus, output earned in the sector of traded goods might be a better proxy for an economy's foreign exchange revenues than GDP or GNP. Due to problems with availability of data, output from the tradables sector will often have to be approximated, for example, by the figure of export revenues. For this reason, Cohen (1985) calculates the primary balance in proportion to *exports* which is required to stabilize the ratio of net foreign debts to *exports* at the current level. Cohen (1985) calls the stabilizing ratio of the primary balance to exports "solvency index"; for convenience, we adopt this terminology (although the stabilizing ratio of net foreign debts to output could, strictly speaking, also be referred to as a solvency index).

The solvency index ζ is defined as the factor by which the present value of future export revenues must be multiplied if one wishes to obtain the initial stock of net foreign debts at the beginning of period t:

$$-B_{t-1} = \zeta \sum_{n=t}^{\infty} X_n \left(\frac{1}{1+r}\right)^{n-t+1} \tag{7.31}$$

where X denotes export revenues and the real interest rate is assumed to be constant. Exports are assumed to grow at the same constant rate as output, i.e.: $X_n = X_{t-1}(1+\gamma)^{n-t+1}$ for all $n \leq t$. Thus, one obtains

$$-B_{t-1} = \zeta X_{t-1} \sum_{n=t}^{\infty} \left(\frac{1+\gamma}{1+r}\right)^{n-t+1}. \tag{7.32}$$

The requirement $r > \gamma$ is sufficient to ensure that equation (7.32) is well-defined. Provided that $r > \gamma$, the discount factor in equation (7.32) is in absolute terms less than one. In this case, equation (7.32) can be simplified using the formula for the infinite geometric series:[15]

[15] In detail, one obtains for $r > \gamma$

$$-B_{t-1} = \zeta X_{t-1}\left(\frac{1+\gamma}{r-\gamma}\right). \tag{7.33}$$

Solving equation (7.33) for ζ finally yields the solvency index

$$\zeta = -\frac{B_{t-1}}{X_{t-1}}\left(\frac{r-\gamma}{1+\gamma}\right) \tag{7.34}$$

where $r > \gamma$ by assumption. Equation (7.36) shows that the solvency index is the minimum amount of repayment needed to stabilize the ratio of net foreign debts to exports at $\overline{B_{t-1}/X_{t-1}}$ (let alone to make it falling). For variable real interest rates and GDP growth rates, the solvency index becomes

$$\zeta = -\frac{B_{t-1}}{X_{t-1}}\sum_{n=t}^{\infty}\prod_{v=t}^{n}\left(\frac{1}{1+\phi_v}\right), \quad \phi_v = \frac{r_v-\gamma_v}{1+\gamma_v} \tag{7.35}$$

where $r_n > \gamma_n$ for all $n \geq t$ by assumption. The index ζ can be compared to the primary balance-to-exports ratio because the primary surplus can be used to reduce the stock of net foreign debts. The alternative "myopic" resource gap can be represented as

$$\zeta - \frac{PB_t}{X_t} = -\left(\frac{r-\gamma}{1+\gamma}\right)\overline{\frac{B_{t-1}}{X_{t-1}}} - \frac{PB_t}{X_t}. \tag{7.36}$$

Cohen (1985) calculates the solvency index for 75 countries and deals with the infinite horizon by dividing the infinite repayment period starting by the end of 1982 into two subperiods: The first subperiod spans the years from 1983 to 1995, the second subperiod starts in 1996 and lasts indefinitely. For the first subperiod, it is assumed that the world real interest rate is 12% during 1983-1985 and 9% during 1986-1995. The growth of exports is assumed to be 3.4% during 1983-1985 and 5.0% during 1986-1995 for Latin American countries (regarding the growth rates for other regions see Cohen, 1985, p. 165). For all countries in the sample, the real interest rate exceeds the growth rate of exports. For the second subperiod, Cohen (1985) makes the "practical" assumption that r and γ are constant with $(r-\gamma)/(1+\gamma) = 5\%$; this is a rather pessimistic estimate relative to historical data. The initial ratio of net foreign debts (exclusive of concessional loans) to exports refers to the end of 1982 (see Cohen, 1985, p. 166 for details of the calculation).

Latin America and the Caribbean is the region with the highest solvency index: 16.4% of exports should be devoted to the repayment of foreign debts. The lowest index is found in Middle Income Asia with 2.9% of exports. The four countries with the highest index are Sudan (22.7%), Argentina (16.4%), Brazil (15.0%), and Ivory Coast (15.0%). Those are all countries which underwent a debt restructuring prior 1983. For the rest of the sample, the need for adjustment required for solvency does not exceed 13% of exports. For the region with the highest solvency index, Cohen (1985) also reports the primary balance in 1983 and 1984. This allows us to calculate the resource gap in proportion to exports. The results can be found in table 7.4. Column 1 shows the country and column 2 specifies the solvency index ζ calculated by Cohen

---

$$\sum_{n=t}^{\infty}\left(\frac{1+\gamma}{1+r}\right)^{n-t+1} = \left(1-\frac{1+\gamma}{1+r}\right)^{-1} - 1 = \frac{1+\gamma}{r-\gamma}.$$

(1985). The primary balance in proportion to exports for years 1983 and 1984 can be found in columns 3 and 4, respectively. Finally, columns 5 and 6 contain the resulting resource gaps. The light grey color denotes all sustainable cases in which the resource gap is negative (or zero) provided that the economy's real interest rate exceeds the real GDP growth rate (which is the case for the whole sample).

Table 7.4: Resource gap (on the basis of exports) in selected Latin American countries in 1983 and 1984

(1)	(2)	(3)	(4)	(5)	(6)
Country	ζ in %	$\frac{PB_{83}}{X_{83}}$ in %	$\frac{PB_{84}}{X_{84}}$ in %	$\left(\zeta - \frac{PB_{83}}{X_{83}}\right)$	$\left(\zeta - \frac{PB_{84}}{X_{84}}\right)$
Latin America	16.40	28.80	35.40	-12.40	-19.00
Oil Exporters					
Ecuador	9.73	25.00	26.10	-15.27	-16.37
Mexico	12.11	62.80	61.80	-50.69	-49.69
Peru	11.17	1.30	12.60	9.87	-1.43
Venezuela	5.31	41.60	44.70	-36.29	-39.39
Oil Importers					
Bolivia	12.67	17.70	16.40	-5.03	-3.73
Argentina	16.40	37.70	37.70	-21.30	-21.30
Brazil	15.00	18.60	39.70	-3.60	-24.70
Colombia	4.95	-127.50	-59.00	132.45	63.95
Costa Rica	12.36	-5.60	-22.90	17.96	35.26
Chile	12.01	14.10	-3.50	-2.09	15.51
Dominican Republic	7.07	-44.70	-11.2	51.77	18.27
Paraguay	3.10	-61.70	-55.30	64.80	58.40
Uruguay	6.31	18.80	27.00	-12.49	-20.69

Source: Cohen (1985) and author's own calculations

Table 7.4 shows that eight out of 13 Latin American countries adjusted sufficiently to the debt crisis in the early 1980s. In Mexico, the primary surplus in 1984 exceeds the stabilizing primary surplus by almost 50 percentage points. In contrast, Colombia and Paraguay which still run a primary deficit should raise the primary balance in proportion to exports by 64 and 58 percentage points in order to achieve sustainability.

By definition, net foreign debts will be higher in proportion to exports in countries with greater intra-regional (as opposed to international) trade than in more open countries (Roubini, 2001, p. 15). When uniform ad-hoc thresholds are used to assess sustainability, high debt-to-exports ratios might be interpreted as evidence in favor of unsustainability even if primary surpluses as a fraction of exports are sufficiently high to achieve debt stabilization. This shows once again that the resource gap is the more superior sustainability indicator than country-unspecific sustainability thresholds.

This point can be illustrated by means of a simple example devised by Roubini (2001, p. 15). Consider two identical countries which both have GDP of 100, net foreign debts of 50, and exports of 20, of which one half is exported to each other and the other half is exported to the rest of the world. Then the ratio of net foreign debts to output equals 50 percent, and the ratio of net foreign debts to exports is 250 percent. Both ratios are assumed to be sustainable. Suppose now that these two economies are merged so that total GDP equals 200, total net foreign debts are 100, total exports are only 20 (because the previous exports between each other are now intra-regional trade). Then, net foreign debts constitute 50 percent of output and 500 percent of exports. If certain uniform thresholds —such as that net foreign debts in exceed of, say, 60 percent of output and 300 percent of exports are unsustainable—are applied for sustainability analysis, the "combined" economy is considered as insolvent on the basis of the debt-to-exports ratio and solvent on the basis of the debt-to-output ratio. Note that the resource gap correctly indicates no need for the adjustment neither before nor after the merger of the two countries. This can be seen by adopting two additional assumptions: Both economies receive no imports from the rest of the world, and the (long-run) real interest rate and the (long-run) real growth rate of GDP and exports are constant with $(r-\gamma)/(1+\gamma) = 0.2$ in both countries. Since each country's imports equal 10, the resource gap before the merger can be calculated as follows: $0.2 \cdot 2.5 - (20-10)/20 = 0$. Thus, the debt-to-export ratio of 250 percent will remain stable and is, therefore, sustainable. After the merger, the trade surplus in proportion to exports equals 100 percent because the "combined" economy receives no imports from the rest of the world (imports of 10 are now inter-regional trade). The resource gap is, as before, zero: $0.2 \cdot 5.0 - 1.0 = 0$. Thus, trade surpluses are sufficiently high to stabilize net foreign debts at the current level of 500 percent of output.

In addition to exports and output, net foreign debts might be scaled to fiscal revenues (Roubini, 2001, p. 16). This approach is in particular insightful when a large portion of net foreign debt is a sovereign, rather than private debt.

7.1.4 Stabilizing the NIIP-to-output ratio at the level desired by investors

The current level of net foreign debts in proportion to GDP, GNP, or exports might be so high and the interest to be paid on it so large that the primary surplus required to prevent the net foreign debts ratio from rising might not be economically feasible—as it would, for example, require a large cut in domestic private or government consumption or even imply zero consumption (Roubini, 2001, p. 8). Even if the stabilizing primary surplus is economically feasible, it might be politically infeasible—as it was the case during the Argentinian currency and debt crisis in 1999-2002 when the Argentinian government could not even agree on generating a primary surplus of one to two percent of GDP (Goldstein, 2003, p. 11). Besides, as already mentioned above, higher levels of net foreign debt-to-output ratios produce higher vulnerabilities towards exogenous shocks (Goldstein, 2003, p. 14). An alternative to stabilizing the NIIP ratio at the current level is stabilizing it at the level that would rationally be desired by international investors. The appropriate theoretical framework for determining the stabilizing primary balance ratio is the portfolio or stock equilibrium approach which was already discussed in section 6.2 of chapter 6.

Deriving the resource gap

Following Sasin (2001, p. 16), the starting point here is the long-run relationship between the economy's net international investment position and domestic and foreign wealth (see equation (7.1.4)):

$$B_t = (1-\alpha) W_t - \alpha^f W_t^f.$$

Although this equation refers to the long-run equilibrium, it will now be insightful to include time indices in our notation. Under the assumption that the wealth W_t of the country under consideration is a δ-proportion of total world's wealth (i.e., $W_t = \delta(W_t + W_t^f)$), foreign wealth W_t^f can be cancelled out in equation (7.1.4). This yields

$$B_t = \left[(1-\alpha) - \alpha^f \left(\frac{1-\delta}{\delta}\right)\right] W_t.$$

Following Edwards et al. (1996, p. 89), it is assumed that the economy's wealth is proportional to its GDP with the proportionality factor θ (i.e., $W = \theta Y$), whence one obtains

$$B_t = \theta \left[(1-\alpha) - \alpha^f \left(\frac{1-\delta}{\delta}\right)\right] Y \equiv \lambda Y_t. \tag{7.37}$$

The factor λ represents the portfolio share of domestic assets in proportion to GDP desired by foreign investors and is, by assumption, constant. Taking the first difference of the second equality in equation (7.37) and substituting $CAB_t = \Delta B_t$ results in

$$CAB_t = \lambda \Delta Y_t \tag{7.38}$$

Following Edwards et al. (1996) and Reisen (1998), the ratio of net foreign debt is stabilized in proportion to output, analogous considerations apply to the stabilization in proportion to exports. Dividing equation (7.38) by Y_t and assuming that output grows at a constant rate of γ, one obtains

$$cab_t = \lambda \left(\frac{\gamma}{1+\gamma}\right) \tag{7.39}$$

where $CAB_t/Y_t \equiv cab_t$. Equation (7.39) can be linearly approximated by

$$cab_t = \lambda \gamma. \tag{7.40}$$

Equation (7.40) shows that in the long-run equilibrium, the current account deficit in proportion to output equals the ratio of net foreign liabilities to GDP desired by international investors multiplied by the domestic GDP growth rate (Edwards et al., 1996, p. 90).

Edwards et al. (1996) and Reisen (1998) augment equation (7.40) by including net accumulation of international reserve assets (ΔFX) in proportion to output:

$$cab_t = \lambda \gamma + \frac{\Delta FX_t}{Y_t}. \tag{7.41}$$

The net purchase of international reserve assets ($\Delta FX_t > 0$) in proportion to output *ceteris paribus* reduces the current account deficit for a given equilibrium ratio of net foreign debts to output ($\lambda < 0$). One of the important determinants of international reserves is the volume of imports (Heller, 1966; Grubel, 1971; Frenkel, 1974; Aizenman and Marion, 2003; Prabheesh et al., 2007). A possible explanation is that growing imports must be "covered" by a corresponding growth in international reserves in order to cushion external shocks. Frenkel (1974, p. 21) finds that the "precautionary motive" is stronger in developing countries than in developed countries: The former increase foreign exchange reserves at the same rate at which their imports are growing whereas the ratio of reserves to imports tends to be declining in developed economies (which have a better access to international financial markets and, therefore, more facilities to hedge against external shocks).

Therefore, for the sample of developing economies, Reisen (1998, pp. 116-117) assumes that the target level of international reserves to imports is constant. In other words, international reserves grow at the same rate η as imports: $FX_t = (1+\eta)FX_{t-1}$. Reisen (1998, p. 115) seems to interpret $\Delta FX_t/Y_t$ as $FX_t/Y_t - FX_{t-1}/Y_{t-1}$. However, according to Reisen's (1998) and our previous notation, $\Delta FX_t/Y_t$ should be understood as $(FX_t - FX_{t-1})/Y_t$. Nevertheless, in order to illustrate Reisen's (1998) methodology, we adopt this—otherwise inconsistent—notation by assuming, for the moment, that $\Delta FX_t/Y_t \approx FX_t/Y_t - FX_{t-1}/Y_{t-1}$, which is a good approximation when t-period's output does not significantly differs from $t-1$-period's output. Accordingly, one obtains

$$\frac{FX_t}{Y_t} - \frac{FX_{t-1}}{Y_{t-1}} = \frac{(1+\eta)FX_{t-1}}{(1+\gamma)Y_{t-1}} - \frac{FX_{t-1}}{Y_{t-1}} \tag{7.42}$$

$$= \left(\frac{\eta-\gamma}{1+\gamma}\right)\frac{FX_{t-1}}{Y_{t-1}}. \tag{7.43}$$

Taking into account equation (7.43) and using the lower-case notation, equation (7.41) can be rewritten as

$$cab_t = \lambda\gamma + \left(\frac{\eta-\gamma}{1+\gamma}\right)fx_{t-1}. \tag{7.44}$$

Provided that the growth rate of imports exceeds the GDP growth rate, the higher the stock of international reserves ($fx_{t-1} > 0$) and the higher the rate of import growth, the lower is the current account deficit for a given equilibrium level λ of domestic assets in investors' portfolios.

Further, GDP growth affects the current account via the Balassa-Samuelson effect. Real appreciation per unit of GDP growth (denoted, as before, by ε) reduces both the ratio of international reserves to GDP fx and the "equilibrium portfolio share" λ. Following Reisen (1998, p. 116), real appreciation can be incorporated into equation (7.44) as follows:

$$cab_t = \lambda(\gamma+\varepsilon) + \left(\frac{\eta+\varepsilon-\gamma}{1+\gamma}\right)fx_{t-1}. \tag{7.45}$$

Strictly speaking, ε should also enter the denominator of the last-term on the right-hand side of equation (7.45):[16]

$$cab_t = \lambda(\gamma+\varepsilon) + \left(\frac{\eta+\varepsilon-\gamma}{1+\gamma+\varepsilon}\right)fx_{t-1}. \tag{7.49}$$

[16] This can be illustrated by introducing the real exchange rate into equation (7.42):

However, the difference between equations (7.45) and (7.49) is small for small values of ε. Omitting eventually the time indices, equation (7.49) becomes

$$cab^* = \lambda(\gamma+\varepsilon) + \left(\frac{\eta+\varepsilon-\gamma}{1+\gamma+\varepsilon}\right) fx. \tag{7.50}$$

The asterisk denotes the level of the current account balance to output which is consistent with the sustainable level of net foreign debts to output, i.e., with the level desired by international investors. In this sense, cab^* can be interpreted as the sustainable current account-to-output ratio. The question is, however, how to interpret positive or negative deviations of the observed current account balance from cab^*. When λ is the optimal share of domestic assets in foreign investors' portfolios, higher or lower values of the current account balance and net foreign debts than cab^* and λ should be regarded as unsustainable. However, when λ is interpreted as the maximum level of domestic assets desired by foreign investors, investors can be equally comfortable with lower levels for λ, and the current account balance can be considered as sustainable when it does not exceed cab^*. Based on this interpretation, one can calculate the resource gap by subtracting net interest payments on both sides of equation (7.50) and comparing the stabilizing primary balance against the long-run primary balance. This yields

$$pb^* - pb = -\lambda(r-\gamma-\varepsilon) + \left(\frac{\eta+\varepsilon-\gamma}{1+\gamma+\varepsilon}\right) fx_{t-1} - pb. \tag{7.51}$$

When the resource gap is positive, equation (7.51) permits the calculation of the long-run transfer required to prevent the portfolio share of domestic assets in proportion to domestic output from increasing.

Empirical studies

Reisen (1998) estimates the sustainable current account balance for four Latin American and four Asian countries in 1996. It is assumed that investors tolerate a ratio of net foreign debts to GDP of 50 percent in all countries (i.e., $\lambda = 50$) and that the target level of international reserves fx equals half the import ratio (six months of imports). The projected long-run real GDP growth rate is computed by identifying the peak of actual GDP in each cycle during the period from

---

$$\frac{FX_t}{q_tY_t} - \frac{FX_{t-1}}{q_{t-1}Y_{t-1}} = \frac{(1+\eta)FX_{t-1}}{(1+\gamma)(1+\varepsilon)q_{t-1}Y_{t-1}} - \frac{FX_{t-1}}{q_{t-1}Y_{t-1}}$$
$$= \left(\frac{(1+\eta)-(1-\gamma)(1+\varepsilon)}{(1+\gamma)(1+\varepsilon)}\right)\frac{FX_{t-1}}{Y_{t-1}} \tag{7.46}$$

For small γ and ε, equation (7.46) can be linearly approximated by

$$\frac{FX_t}{q_tY_t} - \frac{FX_{t-1}}{q_{t-1}Y_{t-1}} = \left(\frac{\eta-\gamma-\varepsilon}{1+\gamma+\varepsilon}\right)\frac{FX_{t-1}}{Y_{t-1}}. \tag{7.47}$$

Using equation (7.47), equation (7.45) can be rewritten as

$$cab_t = \lambda(\gamma+\varepsilon) + \left(\frac{\eta+\varepsilon-\gamma}{1+\gamma+\varepsilon}\right) fx_{t-1}. \tag{7.48}$$

1960s to the mid-1990s and connecting these data points by interpolation. Estimates of the real exchange rate appreciation effect of GDP growth relative to the United States are calculated for the period from 1960 to 1990. Finally, estimates of the long-run real import growth rate are extrapolated from the period after the "openness" reform for each country (e.g., since 1991 for Argentina and Peru or 1986 for Mexico). Details on data and data sources can be found in Reisen (1998, pp. 128-129).

Table 7.5 shows the country (column 1), the real GDP growth rate (column 2), the real appreciation rate (column 3), and the rate of import growth (column 4). Columns 5 and 6 show the target level of international reserves *fx* and the ratio of net foreign debts to output which is desired by international investors, respectively. The sustainable current account balance is calculated according to equation (7.45):

$$cab^* = -50.0\%(\gamma + \varepsilon) + \left(\frac{\eta + \varepsilon - \gamma}{1 + \gamma}\right) fx.$$

Column 8, 9, and 10 contain the 1996 estimate of the total external debt to GDP ratio, the 1996 estimate of international reserves as a fraction GDP, and the 1996 current account balance in percent of GDP, respectively.

Table 7.5: Sustainable current account balance in proportion to GDP in eight selected developing economies

(1)	(2)	(3)	(4)	(5)	(6)	(7)	(8)	(9)	(10)
Country	γ in %	ε in %	η in %	fx in %	λ in %	cab^* in %	λ_{1996} in %	fx_{1996} in %	cab_{1996} in %
Argentina	4.3	0.7	31.8	3.5	-50.0	-1.6	-34.0	6.1	-2.5
Chile	4.2	0.6	6.9	11.4	-50.0	-2.0	-30.0	20.2	-3.9
Indonesia	6.1	0.4	7.3	9.9	-50.0	-3.0	-45.0	8.7	-3.2
Malaysia	6.5	0.1	11.1	39.6	-50.0	-1.7	-38.0	28.3	-4.4
Mexico	5.2	0.8	12.6	14.0	-50.0	-1.9	-51.0	5.4	-0.6
Peru	7.8	0.9	15.2	6.5	-50.0	-3.8	-51.0	13.6	-6.5
Philippines	5.7	0.4	11.2	16.6	-50.0	-2.1	-56.0	13.5	-4.2
Thailand	7.2	1.0	13.3	19.7	-50.0	-2.8	-50.0	20.0	-7.9

Source: Reisen (1998); World Economic Outlook Database (April, 2013)

The estimated sustainable ratios of the current account to GDP are relatively small—ranging from 1.6 percent of GDP in Argentina to 3.8 percent in Peru. The actual ratios of net foreign debts to output are much lower than the assumed equilibrium level of 50 percent of GDP in Argentina, Chile, and Malaysia. Thus, these countries could run even higher current account deficits. The target level of international reserves in proportion to output also deviates from the observed long-run level in many countries (exceptions being Indonesia and Thailand).

Reisen (1998) does not report the projected long-run current account to GDP ratios for the countries in his data set. In order to obtain at least a rough picture of how much the observed current account deficit deviates from its sustainable level, we take the "myopic" approach and compare cab^* with the 1996 ratios of the current account to GDP from the World Economic Outlook Database (April, 2013). Table 7.5 shows that the observed current account deficit does not exceed the "sustainable" level only in Mexico (denoted by the light grey color) and exceeds cab^* in in Indonesia only by 0.2 percentage points—which can, actually, be neglected since the calculated cab^* should itself be viewed as an approximation. In contrast, the current account deficits in Malaysia, Philippines, and Thailand are at least twice as high as their respective sustainable levels and are, therefore, clearly unsustainable provided that investors' desired portfolio share of domestic assets equals 50 percent of domestic GDP and the target level of international reserves equals six months of imports.

Aristovnik (2006) adopts Reisen's (1998) methodology and estimates equation (7.45) for 16 transition economies. It is assumed that foreign investors tolerate the net foreign debt ratio of 45 percent ($\lambda^{*\phi}$) and that the domestic economy has its target level of foreign exchange reserves ($fx^{*\phi}$) at half the import ratio (six months of imports) of the 2000-2003 period. Aristovnik (2006) considers three scenarios: no change in net foreign direct investment ($nfdi = 0$); (ii) the change in net FDI inflows remains constant at 4.0 percent; (iii) the average change in net FDI inflows is kept constant in the medium term. The long-run value of the real effective appreciation rate is approximated by its historical drift. The real import growth rate is the 2000-2003 period average ratio. Table 7.6 is organized similarly to tables 7.5 and 7.3.

Table 7.6: Sustainable current account-to-GDP ratio in 16 transition economies

(1)	(2)	(3)	(4)	(5)	(6)	(7)	(8)	(9)	(10)	(11)	(12)
Country	γ^{ϕ} (average 2000-2008)	r_{2003}	$\lambda^{*\phi}$ (average 2000-2003)	ε^{ϕ}	η^{ϕ} (average 2000-2003	$fx^{*\phi}$ (average 2000-2003)	$cab^{*\phi}$ ($nfdi = 0$)	$cab^{*\phi}$ ($nfdi = 4.0$)	$nfdi^{\phi}$ (average 2000-2003)	$cab^{*\phi}$ ($nfdi^{\phi} = (10)$)	cab^{ϕ} (average 2000-2003)
in %	in %	in %	in %	in %	in %	in %	in %	in %	in %	in %	in %
Bulgaria	4.3	1.9	-45.0	0.26	13.3	42.8	1.8	-2.2	6.3	-4.5	-6.6
Croatia	4.0	1.7	-45.0	0.08	10.2	27.8	-0.2	-4.2	5.7	-5.9	-5.5
Czech R.	3.5	2.4	-45.0	0.45	9.7	47.6	1.3	-2.7	8.5	-7.2	-5.9
Estonia	6.4	3.6	-45.0	0.07	14.8	59.4	1.9	-2.1	5.7	-3.9	-4.0
Hungary	3.8	1.7	-45.0	0.36	10.2	41.1	0.8	-3.2	1.4	-0.7	-7.7
Kazakhstan	8.6	2.2	-45.0	-0.02	6.1	19.4	-4.3	-8.3	9.1	-13.4	-1.1
Latvia	6.7	6.4	-45.0	-0.05	11.5	31.8	-1.6	-5.6	3.8	-5.4	-8.4
Lithuania	6.6	4.1	-45.0	0.26	14.1	44.3	-0.1	-3.9	3.6	-3.5	-5.6
Macedonia	3.7	7.8	-45.0	0.82	4.4	27.6	-1.6	-5.6	5.2	-6.8	-5.9
Moldova	5.4	3.0	-45.0	-0.06	61.4	61.4	4.5	0.5	7.3	-2.8	-7.4
Poland	3.6	1.0	-45.0	0.10	7.4	17.6	-1.0	-5.0	3.1	-4.1	-3.4
Romania	4.6	2.8	-45.0	0.21	18.2	32.2	2.1	-1.9	2.7	-0.6	-4.6
Russia	5.7	2.9	-45.0	0.18	20.8	12.6	-0.8	-4.8	0.0	-0.8	11.4
Slovakia	4.2	2.3	-45.0	0.11	10.1	41.4	0.5	-3.5	8.8	-8.3	-5.2
Slovenia	3.2	4.6	-45.0	0.04	5.3	34.2	-0.7	-4.7	2.4	-3.2	-0.2
Ukraine	6.9	5.2	-45.0	-0.02	-3.0	30.5	-5.9	-9.9	2.1	-8.0	5.5

Source: Aristovnik (2006)

All sustainable cases in which the observed current account balance equals at least the sustainable current account balance are denoted by the light grey color. The dark grey color denotes all cases in which the real interest rate exceeds the real GDP growth rate. The observed current account balance is sustainable in Kazachstan, Russia, Slovenia, and Ukraine under all three scenarios and in Croatia, Czech Republic, Macedonia, and Poland under the second and the third scenario. There is no evidence in favor of sustainability in Estonia, Moldova, Romania, and Slovakia under any scenario. For the rest of the sample, the current account balance is sustainable either under second or the third scenario. Comparing the analysis in table 7.6 with table 7.3 shows that the results are the same for six out of 17 countries (Kazachstan, Russia, Ukraine, Croatia, Poland, and Moldova).

Based on the data used by Aristovnik (2006), we in addition calculate the myopic medium-term resource gap in order to determine the size of the possibly necessary adjustment in the primary balance:

$$pb^{*\phi} - pb^{\phi} = -45\%(r_{2003} - \gamma^{\phi} - \varepsilon^{\phi}) + \left(\frac{\eta^{\phi} + \varepsilon^{\phi} - \gamma^{\phi}}{1 + \gamma^{\phi}}\right) fx^{*\phi} - nfdi^{\phi} - pb^{\phi}. \qquad (7.52)$$

Table 7.7 shows the countries in the sample (column 1) and the corresponding ratios of the primary balance to GDP which stabilize net foreign debts at 45 percent of output under three scenarios for net FDI inflows (columns 2, 3, and 4). Column 5 specifies the primary balance as a fraction of GDP which is calculated as the average over the period 2000-2003. Finally, columns 6, 7, and 8 show the "myopic" medium-term resource gap under the three scenarios. Under the first scenario with no net FDI inflows, the resource gap indicates sustainability only in Romania and Ukraine. Under the second and the third scenarios, half of the sample exhibits sustainability. Under all three scenarios, the highest adjustment in the primary balance required to achieve sustainability has to be managed by Moldova.

In comparison to table 7.3, table 7.7 indicates sustainability for substantially fewer countries. For example, under the second and the third scenario, only three countries have an unsustainable dynamics as regards the ratio of net foreign debts to output in table 7.3—compared with eight countries in table 7.7.

Table 7.7: Medium-term resource gap in 16 transition countries based on Reisen's (1998) methodology

(1)	(2)	(3)	(4)	(5)	(6)	(7)	(8)
Country	$pb^{*\phi}$ $(nfdi = 0)$	$pb^{*\phi}$ $(nfdi = 4.0)$	$pb^{*\phi}$ $(nfdi^{\phi})$	pb^{ϕ} (2000-2003)	$pb^{*\phi} - pb^{\phi}$ $(nfdi = 0)$	$pb^{*\phi} - pb^{\phi}$ $(nfdi = 4.0)$	$pb^{*\phi} - pb^{\phi}$ $(nfdi^{\phi})$
Bulgaria	2.7	-1.3	-3.6	-4.4	7.1	3.1	0.8
Croatia	0.6	-3.4	-5.1	-2.7	3.3	-0.7	-2.4
Czech R.	2.4	-1.6	-6.1	-1.4	3.8	-0.2	-4.7
Estonia	3.5	-0.5	-2.3	-4.0	7.5	3.5	1.7
Hungary	1.6	-2.4	0.1	-2.2	3.8	-0.2	2.3
Kazakhstan	-3.3	-7.3	-12.4	-4.3	1.0	-3.0	-8.1
Latvia	1.3	-2.7	-2.5	-8.4	9.7	5.7	5.9
Lithuania	1.7	-2.1	-1.7	-3.9	5.6	1.8	2.2
Macedonia	1.9	-2.1	-3.3	-4.9	6.8	2.8	1.6
Moldova	5.9	1.9	-1.5	-17.2	23.1	19.1	15.8
Poland	-0.6	-4.6	-3.7	-2.3	1.8	-2.3	-1.4
Romania	3.4	-0.6	0.7	-3.7	7.1	3.1	4.4
Russia	0.5	-3.5	0.5	13.7	-13.2	-17.2	-13.2
Slovakia	1.5	-2.5	-7.3	-3.8	6 5.3	1.3	-3.5
Slovenia	1.4	-2.6	-1.1	-0.2	1.6	-2.4	-0.9
Ukraine	-3.6	-7.6	-5.7	7.3	-10.9	-14.9	-13.0

Source: Aristovnik (2006) and author's own calculations

However, simply assuming that foreign lenders are willing to hold a certain portion of an economy's assets does not fully exploit the portfolio-balance framework. A more sophisticated approach would be first to estimate the equilibrium share of an economy's assets in lenders' portfolio (for example, as it is done in the study by Calderon et al. (2000) discussed in section 6.2 of chapter 6) and then to estimate the resource gap.

7.1.5 Conclusion

Provided that the real interest rate exceeds the real GDP growth rate, the criterion of a non-increasing NIIP—in proportion to GDP, exports, or government revenues— ensures the respective economy's ability to pay while in addition taking into account the boundedness of the economy's repayment ability. When the economy's ratio of net foreign debts or assets (to output, exports, or goverment revenues) is rising, it can be stabilized at some target level—typically either at the current level, at the recently observed average level, or at the level which is supposed to be desired by international investors. The transfer of resources required for stabilizing NIIP-to-output/exports/revenues ratio is measured by the resource gap.

There are several approaches to the calculation of the resource gap. The resource gap can refer to one period, to the medium-term or the long-run horizon. It can be calculated taking into account movements in the real exchange rate, the foreign exchange reserves, and/or flows of net foreign direct investment. As the empirical results discussed above show, different calculations largely do affect the sustainability assessment.

The concept of the resource gap abstracts from potential feedback effects among the variables involved. For example, if the reversal in the trade balance required to restore sustainability is achieved by a cut in private investment, the economy's capital stock declines. This might result in a decrease in the GDP growth rate which, in turn, worsens sustainability prospects (Roubini, 2001, p. 9). Moreover, if there is some positive probability that external debt might exceed the economy's repayment ability at some point in future, expected debt service cost might discourage further investment, reduce growth, and exacerbate the economy's ability to pay (Pattillo et al., 2002, p. 5). In this situation—known as "debt overhang" (Krugman, 1988)—the reduction, rather than the stabilization of the net foreign debt ratio might be needed in order to promote growth (Krugman, 1988). Using a large panel set of 93 developing countries during 1969-1998, Pattillo et al. (2002) find that external debt on average negatively affects growth when external debt exceeds 160–170 % of exports or 30–40 % of GDP. These are relatively low values—at least compared to the values at which the stabilization of net foreign debts was to be achieved in many countries in tables 7.1, 7.2, 7.3, 7.5, and 7.6.

Besides, the above definition of a resource gap is based on the assumption that debts can be rolled over indefinitely. However, in practice, the interest and principal must be repaid on fixed dates (Smeets, 2010, 2011). Further, exogenous changes in interest rates during the reference period might undermine an economy's solvency even if the ratio of net foreign debts to exports, output, or government revenues remains constant: Contagion effects—e.g., due to a financial crisis in another country—might lead investors to increase their assessment of the probability of a (partial) default. Higher default probability might be reflected in higher risk premia which *ceteris paribus* make it difficult to service the economy's debts. This situation might give rise to multiple equilibria. The increase in borrowing costs might lead to a self-fulfilling default even if it is not justified by underlying fundamentals of the economy (Roubini, 2001, pp. 17-18).

However, this criterion does not impose any restrictions on the *level* of the NIIP-to-GDP ratio. In other words, any NIIP-to-GDP ratio is sustainable as long as it is non-increasing. The primary balance-to-GDP ratio which stabilizes the particular NIIP-to-GDP ratio and the resulting current account-to-GDP ratio are sometimes called "sustainable" in the literature (e.g., Aristovnik, 2006; Reisen, 1998). However, they are sustainable only under the assumption that the stabilized NIIP-to-GDP ratio is sustainable. Yet a debt ratio which modestly increases from a "low" initial level might entail less risks for sustainability than a stabilization at a "high" level of debt—although the latter is clearly preferable to a debt ratio which increases from a "high" initial level (IMF, 2002, p. 42). Finally, even though the resource gap gives an indication about the size of the adjustment required to achieve sustainability, it provides no further information—neither on the time frame within which the adjustment is to take place in order to ensure sustainability nor on the manner in which it has to occur ("smooth" or "hard" landing).

7.2 "Unsustainability" indicators in a nonstructural approach

Neither the resource gap nor the intertemporal budget constraint provide further information on the manner in which the adjustment in the trade balance required to restore/ maintain solvency will take place. However, Milesi-Ferretti and Razin (1996a,b) suggest to regard those trade balance reversals which are accompanied by a drastic policy shift (such as a sudden fiscal tightening causing a recession) and/or a financial crisis[17] (which might force a country to default on its external obligations) as unsustainable—even if solvency is not violated and the NIIP ratio is non-increasing. Accordingly, external imbalances should be considered sustainable if a continuation of the current policy stance does not entail an abrupt shift in monetary and financial policies and does not lead to a financial crisis.

Based on this definition, episodes of prolonged external imbalances—which *ex post* proved to be either sustainable or not sustainable—can be used to identify empirical regularities that will help to differentiate between sustainability and no sustainability. Milesi-Ferretti and Razin (1996a) are, in particular, interested in indicators which discriminate between sustainable episodes and unsustainable episodes that are characterized by a financial crisis. Their data set contains seven countries and nine episodes which can be grouped into three categories. The first category comprises two sustainable episodes: Australia (1981-1994) and Malaysia (1991-1994) which ran prolonged current account deficits, yet without drastic policy shifts or external crises. The second category contains four unsustainable episodes where an abrupt policy reversal was required to prevent a potential external crisis: Ireland (1979-1986), Israel (1982-1984),

[17] There exists no uniform definition of financial crises and types of financial crises. The IMF (1998, pp. 74-75) categorizes financial crises as falling into three groups: currency, banking, and external debt crises. A *currency crisis* refers to a situation in which a speculative attack on the currency leads to a devaluation or a sharp depreciation of the currency, or forces the monetary authorities to defend the currency by selling large volumes of international reserves or by sharply raising interest rates. A *banking crisis* occurs when actual or potential bank runs lead banks to default on their obligations or result in a large-scale government assistance for the bank "in trouble." An *external debt crisis* arises from a situation in which a country cannot service its foreign (public or private) debt. Finally, a *sovereign debt crisis* may be defined as a situation in which the sovereign is in (large) arrears on principal or interest obligations or arranges a rescheduling agreement with its foreign private creditors (Paoli et al., 2006, p. 7). However, some authors (e.g., Reinhart et al., 2003b; Detragiache and Spilimbergo, 2001) operate with a definition of sovereign debt that also includes private external debt.

Malaysia (1979-1984), and South Korea (1977-1982). Finally, the last group consists of three unsustainable episodes which were accompanied by an external crisis: Chile (1979-1981) and Mexico (1977-1981 and 1991-1994).

The set of potential sustainability indicators covers structural features, macroeconomic policy stance, market expectations as well as political instability, uncertainty, and credibility. Because a policy shift or a crisis might also be triggered by an external shock—possibly in combination with unfavorable fundamentals such as a high ratio of net foreign debt to exports—Milesi-Ferretti and Razin (1996a) include, in addition, indicators which are supposed to capture the intensity of external shocks and examine vulnerability of countries to various types of external shocks. The intensity of external shocks can be measured on the basis of two criteria: the evolution of the terms of trade and the dynamics of the real interest rate on external debt. Milesi-Ferretti and Razin (1996a) compute the measure of external shocks for two possible breakdowns of the relevant period in order to control for the differences in the length of the episodes under investigation since those differences might affect the intensity of shocks.

Large increases in the real interest rate and large deteriorations of the terms of trade were observed in Chile, Malaysia, Mexico, and South Korea at the time of the debt crisis in 1982. The impact of the shocks, however, was different in these countries: Malaysia and South Korea were able to resist the shock without an external crisis—in contrast to Chile and Mexico which did suffer an external crisis. Thus, the intensity of external shocks does not clearly indicate future external crises. This finding is consistent with other studies reviewed, e.g., in Cline (1995). In order to evaluate the contribution of further potential sustainability indicators, it is assumed that the variety of country experiences does not primarily result from the differences in the intensity of external shocks.

Milesi-Ferretti and Razin (1996a) find that the sustainability analysis should involve a combination of indicators rather than a single variable. Persistent trade and current account deficits are likely to result in an external crisis when external debt and the interest burden are high in proportion to exports, the ratio of exports to GDP is small, the real exchange rate (in a price quotation) is appreciated relative to the historical average, and national savings are low. In contrast, both external debt and the interest burden do not warrant a differentiation between sustainable and non-sustainable episodes when they are expressed as fractions of GDP. Further, while the absence of fiscal imbalances does not indicate sustainability, large fiscal deficits do indicate future policy shifts. The composition of capital flows also seems to be important; however, the limited number of episodes in the sample studied by Milesi-Ferretti and Razin (1996a) precludes drawing inferences. Further, weaknesses in the financial system were observed during all "crisis episodes." Finally, Milesi-Ferretti and Razin (1996a) find that the level of current account balances relative to GDP does not help to predict unsustainability! This result, however, is at odds with the related literature on current account reversals and indicators of currency crises (see below).

We apply the findings obtained by Milesi-Ferretti and Razin (1996a) to the United States; figure 7.1 plots the main "unsustainability" indicators: the ratio of exports to GDP, gross national savings relative to GDP, the ratio of external debt to exports, and the real effective exchange rate (REER) based on the consumer price index (CPI).

It follows from figure 7.1 that exports are low in proportion to GDP in the mid 1980s, around 2002, and 2009. Similarly, the external debt relative to exports is high around 1986, in 2004 and

2006, as well as in 2010. Gross national savings do not fluctuate much over the sample period and basically display two lows (in 2003 and around 2009). Finally, the CPI-based REER series exhibits three main peaks: in 1985, in 2002, and in 2009. In sum, these indicators imply three unsustainability periods (in the mid-1980s, in the early/mid-2000s, and in the late 2000s) which are likely to result in an external crisis. *Ex post*, we know that no external debt or currency crisis has occurred in the aftermath of these unsustainability periods and that only the latter episode has been accompanied by the US subprime crisis and the subsequent financial crisis. However, this does not necessarily imply that prolonged trade and current account deficits in the United States have caused the US subprime crisis (see section 1.1 of chapter 1 for a short discussion).

The main difficulty in applying the unsustainability indicators lies in the nature of the nonstructural approach. Firstly, it gives little information on "worrisome" levels or changes in the indicator variables (e.g., how low must national savings be to indicate unsustainability?). Secondly, the relative predictive power of the indicators cannot be quantified. Finally, the indicator variables can only signal a high probability of an external crisis in the near future, but they do not foretell the date when a crisis will occur. A more formal analysis based on the approach suggested by Milesi-Ferretti and Razin (1996a) would be desirable.

The approach taken by Milesi-Ferretti and Razin (1996a) is related to the large body of literature on early warning indicators of financial crises.[18] Currency crises are likely to occur when the real exchange rate is appreciated, current account deficits are high, and the stock of international reserves is low (Kaminsky et al., 1998; Abiad, 2003; Frankel and Saravelos, 2012). Further, high public (both domestic and external) debt helps to predict external debt crises, and high foreign (public and private) debt precedes banking crises—which, in turn, accompany sovereign debt crises (Reinhart and Rogoff, 2011). Finally, the probability of sovereign debt crises rises when external debt is high in proportion to a measure of the repayment ability (such as GDP or exports), when short-term debt is high relative to foreign reserves, and when public debt is high as a fraction of government revenues (Schimmelpfennig et al., 2003).

However, indicators of financial crises cannot be used directly to detect unsustainability as not every financial crisis is caused by unsustainable external imbalances. Currency crises, for example, might result from unsustainable domestic policies such as the combination of exchange rate pegs and monetized fiscal deficits (Krugman, 1979; Flood and Garber, 1984; Flood et al., 1996). Even if a country adopts macroeconomic policies that are consistent with the fixed exchange rate, a speculative attack can lead to an unfavorable equilibrium outcome and trigger a currency crisis (Obstfeld, 1986, 1994; Jeanne and Masson, 2000). Further, banking crises might be precipitated by maturity and capital structure mismatches in the balance sheets of domestic banks which are not necessarily linked to external imbalances (Chang and Velasco, 1999; Schneider and Tornell, 2000; Allen et al., 2002).[19]

[18] The indicators identified by Milesi-Ferretti and Razin (1996a) are also to a certain extent supported by the literature on medium-term determinants of current account. In both developed and developing countries, current account deficits are positively correlated with fiscal deficits and net foreign debt position; in developing countries, they are also positively correlated with terms of trade and indicators of financial deepening (Calderon et al., 2002; Chinn and Prasad, 2003; Yang, 2011; Morsy, 2012).

[19] A survey of the theoretical and empirical literature on financial crises can be found in Kaminsky (2003), Breuer (2004), and Glick and Hutchison (2011).

7.3 Indicators of current account reversals

The results obtained by Milesi-Ferretti and Razin (1996a) are also in large part consistent with the literature on indicators of (large) current account reversals. The link between sustainability and current account reversals is illustrated by the following example: Consider a net debtor economy which runs persistent trade and current account deficits. A stabilization of net foreign debts in proportion to a measure of the country's repayment ability requires an improvement in the trade balance or even a reversal from a trade deficit to a trade surplus. Because the current account balance equals the trade balance plus net interest payments (receipts) on the NIIP, a reversal in the trade balance leads to a reversal in the current account balance unless it is offset by a sufficiently large decline in the real interest rate, which *ceteris paribus* decreases net interest payments. However, in a situation in which net foreign debts as well as trade and current account deficits are so high that an adjustment is needed, interest rates are, if anything, more likely to rise in order to raise the attractiveness of domestic assets for foreign investors. Thus, reversals in the trade balance are in many cases accompanied by reversals in the current account balance.

Current account reversals are typically defined either using *ad hoc* criteria (which stipulate the size and the speed of a reversal as well as the time period within which a reversal takes place)[20] or statistical tests for structural breaks. Reversals of current account *deficits* are likely to occur when current account and trade deficits are high relative to GDP, the deterioration of the terms of trade is large, the accumulation of international reserves is slow, openness to trade (measured by the average share of exports and imports to GDP) is high, national savings are low as a fraction of GDP, and fiscal deficits are high (Milesi-Ferretti and Razin, 1998a,b; Freund, 2000; Eichengreen and Adalet, 2005; Freund and Warnock, 2005; Edwards, 2006; Debelle and Galati, 2007). The probability of reversals of current account *surpluses* in advanced economies and emerging markets increases when there is an increase in domestic demand, an acceleration of GDP growth, and a strong real appreciation. Surplus reversals in oil-exporting countries are primarily associated with a substantial decline in GDP growth, yet also with a large deterioration in the terms of trade due to a decline in commodity prices (IMF, 2007). In contrast to reversals of current account deficits, reversals of current account surpluses are less persistent and tend to take place smoothly (Edwards, 2007).

Cross-country experiences of current account reversals can be used to estimate the thresholds at which the current account balance starts reverting. Thresholds of current account reversal are summarized in table 7.8. Typical reversals of current account *deficits* begin in industrial countries and/or high-income countries when deficits are about four to five percent of GDP (Croke et al., 2005; Freund, 2005; Freund and Warnock, 2005; Hoffmann, 2007). This result

[20] The *ad hoc* criteria which have to be satisfied by reversals of current account *deficits* can be illustrated using the example of the study by Milesi-Ferretti and Razin (1998a): The average reduction in the current account deficit should at least equal three (five) percentage points of GDP over the period of three years after the current account trough compared to the three years before the event. The average current account deficit must be reduced by at least one third. Further, the maximum current account deficit after reversal must be no larger than the minimum deficit in the three years before the reversal. Finally, adjacent reversals occurring within the two years of the previous reversal should be excluded. The IMF (2007) defines large and sustained reversals of current account *surpluses* as changes in the current account balance of at least 2.5 percent of GDP and at least 50 percent of the initial current account imbalance that are sustained for at least five years.

is in line with Clarida et al. (2006) who test a threshold autoregressive model and find that the adjustment in the US current account deficit starts at 4.19 percent of net output. The threshold of five percent of GDP or GNP also corresponds to the *ad hoc* rule suggested by the former Chief Economist at the World Bank Lawrence Summers (Summers, 1995, 2005, 2004). Middle- and low-income countries have higher deficit reversal thresholds than industrial countries: ten to eleven percent of GDP and 17 percent of GDP, respectively (Hoffmann, 2007).

Reversals of current account *surpluses* typically occur when the current account balance is about two percent of GDP in advanced economies, three percent of GDP in emerging markets, and 12 percent of GDP in oil exporting countries (IMF, 2007). For Germany, the TAR model tested by Clarida et al. (2006) also implies a reversal threshold of 1.19 percent of net output.

Comparing the estimated reversal thresholds to the observed global imbalances (depicted in figure 1.1 on page 2) implies that the US current account deficit has been unsustainable from 2004 to 2008, before returning to the sustainable path in 2009. The Japanese current account surplus exceeded the threshold of 1.9 percent for advanced countries over the periods 1984-1989, 1991-1995, and 1997-2011 (see figure 1.1). Similarly, the Chinese current account surplus was higher than the threshold of 3.9 percent for emerging markets between 2004 and 2010 (see figure 1.1). The total current account surplus in the oil-exporting countries have been remaining below the threshold of 12.3 percent since 1980.

Table 7.9 shows current account balances in percent of GDP for the euro area from 2000 to 2013. Several surplus countries have been violating the respective threshold of 1.9 percent: Austria over 2004-2010, Belgium before 2005, Finland before 2008, Germany since 2004, Luxembourg and the Netherlands over the whole sample period. Among the deficit countries, Greece, and Portugal, for example, have been running from 2000 to 2011 current account deficits which were significantly higher than the threshold of 5.3 percent of GDP for high-income countries.

According to the literature on current account reversals, one would expect the reduction in current account imbalances to take place within at most four years after crossing the respective threshold (Aristovnik, 2005; Freund, 2005; Hoffmann, 2007). In practice, however, our data (figure 1.1 and table 7.9) show that many countries have been running imbalances above the respective thresholds for a prolonged period of time. One could argue that group-specific thresholds might not be applicable to individual countries. In fact, column 3 of table 7.8 shows a large cross-country variation in the reversal thresholds. For exposition, we single out, at least for the moment, the reversal thresholds estimated by Hoffmann (2007) for Greece (-7.98%), Spain (-4.1%), and Portugal (-11.76%).[21] Using the country-specific threshold for Portugal leads to almost contrary results: The Portuguese current account deficit is sustainable over the whole sample period except in 2008. For Spain, the individual threshold is lower in absolute value than the group-specific threshold so that its period of current account unsustainability ranges from 2004 to 2010 and thus exceeds the duration of the group-specific period. In the case of Greece, the period of unsustainability reduces by six years to the period over 2006-2011, yet the current account deficit starts reverting after reaching 15 percent of GDP (i.e., twice as large as the estimated threshold). Thus, the question still remains why Greece and Spain have been displaying deficits far above the estimated thresholds for five and six years, respectively.

The above considerations warrant the conclusion that the indicative thresholds of current account reversals are only of limited use for the sustainability assessment. While they can be

[21] To our knowledge, country-specific thresholds are not available for surplus countries.

utilized as rough indicators of a possible adjustment in the current account imbalances, they seem to yield only imprecise forecasts regarding the timing of the adjustment and the level at which the adjustment starts. Besides, not every (large) trade and current account reversal is accompanied by an abrupt policy shift and/or a financial crisis and is, therefore, unsustainable in the sense of the definition suggested by Milesi-Ferretti and Razin (1996a). Trade and current account reversals which restore solvency might take place smoothly without losses in GDP growth or a financial crisis—there is no objective justification for regarding those reversals as unsustainable. This implies that the above reversal indicators should be applied with a caution in the sustainability analysis.

Fig. 7.1: Exports (in percent of GDP), gross national savings (in percent of GDP), external debt (in percent of exports), and REER in the United States

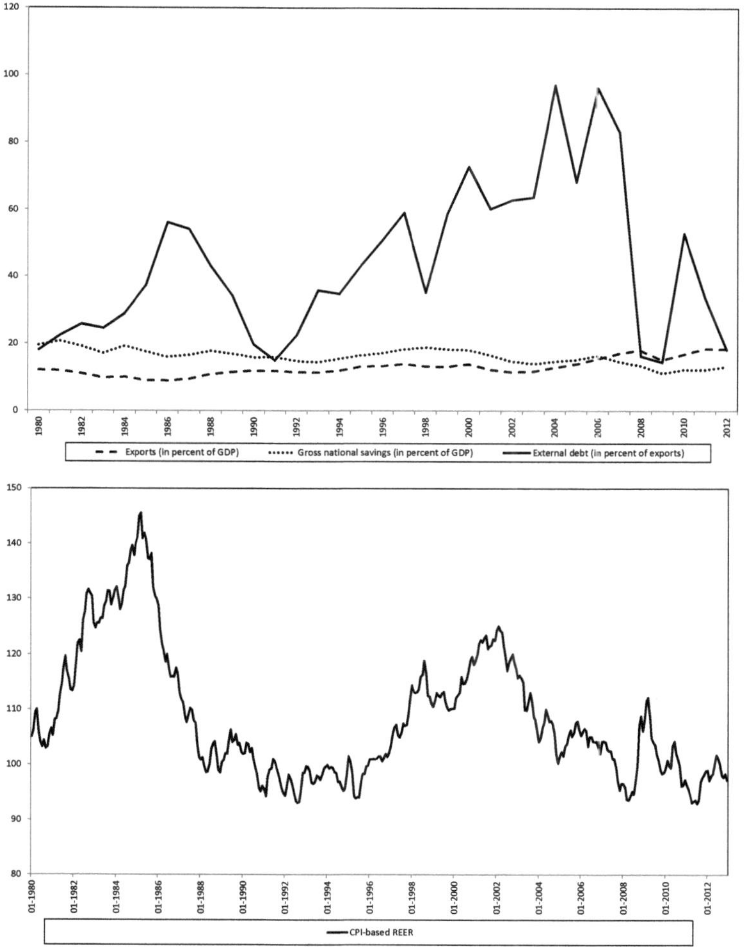

Source: International Monetary Fund, World Economic Outlook Database, April 2013; US Bureau of Economic Analysis; Bank of International Settlements

Notes: Exports, gross national savings, external debt, and GDP are measured in nominal values. External debt is approximated by foreign-owned assets in the United States, excluding financial derivatives. The real effective exchange rate (REER) is based on the Consumer Price Index (CPI); the data are monthly averages (2010=100).

Table 7.8: Indicative thresholds of current account reversals

Study	Data	Range of the thresholds in % of GDP	Median threshold in % of GDP	Mean threshold in % of GDP
Reversals of current account deficits				
Milesi-Ferretti and Razin (1998a)	low-and middle-income c.	n.s.	−10.3	n.s.
Aristovnik (2005)	transition c.	from −2.9 to −27.0	−11.6	−11.8
Croke et al. (2005)	industrial c.	from −13.1 to −1.9	−3.9	−5.0
Freund (2005)	industrial c.	from −2.2 to −16.8	−4.9	−6.3
Freund and Warnock (2005)	industrial c.	from −2.1 to −16.1	−4.2	−5.6
Hoffmann (2007)	high-income c.	from −2.4 to −19.7	−5.3	−7.2
	middle-income c.	from −4.2 to −41.3	−11.0	−12.5
	low-income c.	from −6.8 to −52.7	−17.0	−19.8
IMF (2007)	advanced c.	from −0.15 to −15.13	−3.5	−4.1
Reversals of current account surpluses				
IMF (2007)	advanced c.	from 0.1 to 7.6	1.9	2.4
	emerging c.	from 0.1 to 21.2	3.2	4.7
	oil-exporting c.	from 1.4 to 68.1	12.3	18.9

Abbreviations: c.: countries; n.s.: not specified

Table 7.9: Current account balances in the euro area (in percent of GDP)

Country	2000	2001	2002	2003	2004	2005	2006	2007	2008	2009	2010	2011	2012	2013
Austria	-0.73	-0.82	2.66	1.68	2.20	2.17	2.80	3.51	4.87	2.71	3.40	0.58	1.99	2.22
Belgium	4.03	3.39	4.47	3.42	3.18	1.98	1.86	1.89	-1.32	-1.41	1.91	-1.42	-0.49	-0.13
Cyprus	-5.32	-3.29	-3.76	-2.26	-5.03	-5.88	-6.97	-11.78	-15.62	-10.73	-9.83	-4.72	-4.89	n/a
Estonia	-5.36	-5.17	-10.58	-11.28	-11.30	-9.96	-15.32	-15.95	-9.15	3.42	2.93	2.13	-1.20	0.04
Finland	7.78	8.35	8.46	4.83	6.20	3.35	4.16	4.27	2.63	1.75	1.52	-1.61	-1.71	-1.7
France	1.45	1.76	1.25	0.72	0.54	-0.49	-0.58	-1.00	-1.74	-1.33	-1.56	-1.95	-2.41	-1.28
Germany	-1.73	-0.00	2.00	1.89	4.66	5.06	6.26	7.45	6.21	5.96	6.25	6.22	7.01	6.09
Greece	-7.79	-7.23	-6.52	-6.53	-5.79	-7.64	-11.39	-14.61	-14.92	-11.17	-10.13	-9.90	-2.88	-0.29
Ireland	-0.36	-0.64	-0.99	-0.00	-0.58	-3.49	-3.55	-5.364	-5.69	-2.33	1.14	1.12	4.95	3.39
Italy	-0.20	0.27	-0.43	-0.78	-0.33	-0.88	-1.50	-1.28	-2.85	-1.99	-3.52	-3.07	-0.53	0.32
Luxembourg	13.22	8.76	10.53	8.14	11.86	11.55	10.37	10.09	5.36	7.17	8.23	7.11	6.00	6.64
Malta	-12.07	-3.68	2.36	-2.96	-5.72	-8.51	-9.68	-4.00	-4.87	-7.82	-4.57	-0.51	0.29	0.51
Netherlands	2.04	2.6	2.64	5.54	7.63	7.4	9.34	6.72	4.29	5.18	7.67	9.74	8.35	8.67
Portugal	-10.34	-10.32	-8.23	-6.43	-8.33	-10.32	-10.69	-10.10	-12.64	-10.92	-10.57	-7.01	-1.55	0.14
Slovak Republic	-3.45	-8.27	-7.87	-5.93	-7.82	-8.49	-7.85	-5.27	-6.63	-2.60	-3.72	-2.06	2.28	2.16
Slovenia	-3.14	0.18	1.07	-0.78	-2.65	-1.73	-2.48	-4.76	-6.16	-0.70	-0.60	0.00	2.28	2.66
Spain	-3.96	-3.94	-3.26	-3.51	-5.25	-7.35	-8.96	-10.00	-9.62	-4.82	-4.48	-3.74	-1.07	1.10

Source: International Monetary Fund, World Economic Outlook Database, April 2013

Notes: Estimates start after 2010 for Malta, after 2011 for Austria, Belgium, Ireland, Luxembourg, the Netherlands, Slovenia, and after 2012 for the remaining countries. “n/a” indicates “not available”.

7.4 Indicative thresholds in the IMF's debt sustainability analysis

The International Monetary Fund's debt sustainability analysis for public[22] and external debt aims to help detecting, preventing, and resolving potential debt crises. A review of the sustainability analysis for *total* public (domestic and external) debt is beyond the scope of the present study; the following considerations consequently focus on *external* public debt.[23] Similarly to Milesi-Ferretti and Razin (1996a), the IMF defines external debt sustainability as a situation in which a borrower is expected to be able to continue servicing its debts, that is, to remain solvent without an unrealistically large future correction to the balance of income and expenditure (IMF, 2002). In other words, sustainability rules out any situations in which an economy has to resort to debt default, relief, or restructuring, or to an accumulation of arrears (Boote and Thugge, 1997, p. 17). The IMF distinguishes between market-access countries (i.e., countries which have significant access to international capital markets) and low-income countries (for which grants and concessional loans are the main source of external finance). Debt sustainability analysis is also performed for heavily indebted poor countries (HIPC) under the joint HIPC initiative of the IMF and the World Bank.

7.4.1 Debt sustainability analysis for market-access countries

The debt sustainability analysis for market-access countries, already mentioned in section 7.1, does not rely on definitive thresholds. It is rather intended as a flexible approach where country teams at the IMF may exercise judgment in interpreting a country's actual and projected debt evolution and employ alternative methods, as long as the main standards of the sustainability template are met (IMF, 2005, pp. 44, 52).

However, the ratio of gross external (public and publicly guaranteed) debt to GDP of about 40 percent serves as a rough benchmark, as the study conducted by the IMF (2002) for all the IMF member countries (except the advanced industrialized countries) and transition countries shows. Using two techniques—relative frequency distributions and binary recursive trees[24]—the IMF (2002) finds that the conditional probability of a debt crisis or a correction[25] is about two to five percent for countries with an external debt ratio below 40 percent of GDP and around 15-20 percent for countries with an external debt ratio above 40 percent of GDP. This does not mean that an external debt ratio which exceeds 40 percent of GDP necessarily implies

[22] Herein, the term "public sector" refers to the consolidated non-financial public sector, except for countries in which sub-national governments and public enterprises do not borrow (IMF, 2002, p. 27).

[23] The analysis of sovereign debt crises and the indicative thresholds of overall public debt can be found in Schimmelpfennig et al. (2003); IMF (2005); Caner et al. (2010); Reinhart and Rogoff (2010b,a); Herndon et al. (2013).

[24] In case of a single explanatory variable, a binary recursive tree identifies a threshold value of debt—which best discriminates between a crisis and a non-crisis—that minimizes the sum of type I and type II errors (IMF, 2002, p. 43).

[25] When defining a "debt crisis", the IMF (2002) uses the classification suggested by Detragiache and Spilimbergo (2001): A "debt crisis" is an event in which an economy is in arrears (above some *de minimis* threshold) with principal or interest on external obligations towards commercial creditors (banks or bondholders) or reschedules or restructures its commercial debt. A "debt correction" is a broader term which includes all situations with a sharp decline or "correction" of the debt ratio—disregarding of whether this correction results from debt default, debt restructuring, or an adjustment through primary surplus. The data set analyzed by the IMF (2002) contains 43 debt crises and 53 debt corrections .

unsustainability of external public debt since the probability of not having a crisis or correction for those countries is about 80-85 percent. A further finding is that more open countries may sustain higher external debt-to-GDP ratios since they can more easily generate higher primary surpluses. When less open countries with export-to-GDP ratios below 10 percent are excluded from the sample, the threshold for a debt crisis amounts to 53 percent of GDP and the threshold for a debt correction is almost 50 percent of GDP.

7.4.2 Debt sustainability analysis for low-income countries

The IMF's debt sustainability analysis for low-income countries[26] is conducted under the debt sustainability framework (DSF) which was jointly designed by the IMF and the Word Bank in 2004 and reviewed in 2006, 2009, and more recently in 2012. The framework explicitly relies on indicative policy-dependent thresholds against which projections of external (public and publicly guaranteed) debt over the next 20 years are compared.

A country's policy and institutional capacity is measured by the World Bank's Country Policy and Institutional Assessment (CPIA) index which consists of 16 indicators grouped into four categories: (1) economic management, (2) structural policies, (3) policies for social inclusion and equity, and (4) public sector management and institutions (IMF, 2012b). The CPIA index ranges from a score of 1 (the lowest level of policy) to a score of 6 (the highest level of policy).

The DSA for low-income countries applies two indicators—the stock of gross external debt and the service of gross external debt —which are set in proportion to different measures of an economy's repayment capacity (GDP, exports, and fiscal revenues). The debt service is measured by its face value which reflects the immediate cash flow impact of external debt and largely depends on the maturity structure of the external debt stock (IMF, 1999). In contrast, the debt stock is measured by its net present value (rather than the face value) in order to capture the cross-country differences in the repayment structure and in the contractual structure of debt (IMF, 2004; Dias et al., 2011). The discount rate is the currency-specific commercial interest reference rate (CIRR) which corresponds to secondary-market yields on government bonds in advanced economies with maturities of at least five years and is a proxy for a risk-free, forward-looking world market interest rate. The idea is that discounting by a risk-free interest rate yields a "commercial equivalent" of the debt stock, that is, the amount that a country must invest at a risk-free interest rate today in order to cover its future debt obligations. The discount rate is set initially at the (rounded) current level of the US-dollar CIRR of five percent, but is adjusted by 100 basis points whenever the US-dollar CIRR (6-month average) deviates from it by at least this amount for a consecutive period of six months (IMF, 2004, p. 15).

The thresholds for the present value of debt to GDP, exports, and revenues rely on the analysis conducted by the IMF (2004) whereas thresholds for the debt service in proportion to exports and revenues are calibrated using the study by Kraay and Nehru (2004). Using probit regressions for all low- and middle-income countries, Kraay and Nehru (2004) find that a substantial fraction of the cross-country and time series variation in the incidence of debt distress can be explained by the following three factors: the debt burden (measured by the debt service), the

[26] The DSAs for low-income countries are prepared only for those countries which are eligible both for funds under the IMF's Poverty Reduction and Growth Trust (PRGT) and/or for lending by the International Development Association (IDA) (IMF, 2012b, p. 6).

quality of policies and institutions (measured by the CPIA index), and shocks. The unconditional probability of a debt distress in their sample (i.e., the frequency of debt distress episodes observed in the sample) is about 22 percent for the debt service in proportion to revenues and 18 percent for the debt service in proportion to exports. The study by the IMF (2004) applies the methodology utilized by Kraay and Nehru (2004) to low-income countries.[27] The unconditional probability of a debt distress in their sample is about 20 percent.

The resulting indicative thresholds are shown in table 7.10. Countries with strong policy (corresponding to a CPIA score of at least 3.75) are able to sustain much higher debt and debt service ratios than countries with medium policy (corresponding to a CPIA score between 3.25 and 3.75) and weak policy (i.e., with a CPIA score of at most 3.25).

Table 7.10: Indicative thresholds for public and publicly guaranteed gross external debt in the IMF-World Bank debt sustainability framework for low-income countries

	Present value of debt in % of			Debt service in % of	
	GDP	exports	revenues	revenues	exports
Weak policy ($CPIA \leq 3.25$)	30 (28)	100 (131)	200 (184)	25 (18)	15 (17)
Medium policy ($3.25 < CPIA < 3.75$)	40 (36)	150 (179)	250 (217)	30 (20)	20 (20)
Strong policy ($CPIA \geq 3.75$)	50 (44)	200 (226)	300 (250)	35 (22)	25 (24)

Source: IMF (2004, 2012b). Thresholds in round brackets are the values re-estimated by the IMF (2012b).

The indicative thresholds in round brackets in table 7.10 are values re-estimated by the IMF (2012b) based on more recent data and the single methodology for both debt stock and debt service thresholds. The thresholds are determined using three different concepts of probability of a debt distress: (i) the unconditional probability of a debt distress, (ii) the probability of a debt distress corresponding to the median value of the relevant debt and debt service ratio immediately prior to an outbreak of a debt distress; and (3) the probability of a debt distress that minimizes the number of missed crises and false alarms. Distress probabilities under the first two methods range from 11 to 16 percent, and the last method yields distress probabilities ranging from 13 to 15 percent. The re-estimated thresholds for the present value of debt to exports are higher than the current thresholds whereas other re-estimated thresholds are lower than the

[27] Kraay and Nehru (2004) define episodes of a "debt distress" as periods of three years or longer in which an economy resorts to at least one of the three forms of exceptional financing: (i) arrears on interest and principal which are higher than five percent of the stock of external public and publicly guaranteed outstanding debt to all (official and private) creditors, (ii) a debt relief or rescheduling from the Paris Club of bilateral creditors, and (iii) a balance of payments support from the IMF under its non-concessional Standby Arrangements or Extended Fund Facilities which exceeds 50 percent of the country's IMF quota. The "non-distress" episodes are defined as non-overlapping periods of five consecutive years in which none of the three mentioned conditions are satisfied. The study by the IMF (2004) characterizes episodes of a debt distress solely on the basis of criterion (i).

current thresholds. In particular, the debt service-to-revenues thresholds deviate significantly from the current thresholds. When, in addition, remittances—which can improve an economy's repayment capacity—are included, the thresholds are, as expected, lower: The threshold for the present value of debt to the sum of GDP and remittances is approximately 10 percent lower than the corresponding threshold without consideration of remittances whereas export-based thresholds with remittances are roughly 20 percent lower than the thresholds without remittances. However, the IMF's Executive Board decided against the update of the DSF thresholds, yet allowed for more flexibility in "cases where remittances should be included" (IMF, 2012a).

Based on the comparison of the current and projected debt and debt service (both in the medium-term baseline scenario and sensitivity tests) with the indicative thresholds, one of four ratings for the risk of external public-debt distress can be assigned:

- Low risk: Observed and projected values are well below the thresholds.
- Moderate risk: Observed and projected values are below the thresholds in the baseline scenario, but stress tests indicate that thresholds could be breached if there are external shocks or abrupt changes in macroeconomic policies.
- High risk: Both the baseline scenario and stress tests indicate a protracted breach of thresholds, but the country currently does not face any repayment difficulties.
- In debt distress: A country is already having repayment difficulties.

7.4.3 Heavily Indebted Poor Countries Initiative

The main goal of the joint IMF-World Bank Heavily Indebted Poor Countries (HIPC) Initiative, which was launched in 1996 and modified in 1999, is the reduction of the external debt of heavily indebted poor countries[28] to more sustainable levels.

Key indicators for external sustainability are the debt service-to-exports ratio and the net present value of debt in proportion to exports or government revenue where debt is defined as gross external public and publicly guaranteed debt outstanding and disbursed (as opposed to debt committed) and includes arrears on principal and interest. As in the DSF for low-income countries, the debt service is measured by the face value and the debt stock by the net present value. The use of the net present value is in particular relevant for the HIPC countries which have a significant portion of concessional debt: Because the interest rate charged on concessional terms is lower than the prevailing market interest rate, the net present value—which is calculated by discounting at the market interest rate—is smaller than the face value of debt. The discount rate under the HIPC Initiative is the six-month average of the CIRR which corresponds to a maturity of approximately ten years. The net present value is calculated on a loan-by-loan basis so that payments are not converted into a single currency on the basis of exchange rate-projections—in contrast to the DSF for low-income countries (IMF, 2005, p. 12).

The indicative thresholds for external sustainability in the (enhanced) HIPC Initiative are (i) a ratio of debt service to exports of at most 15-20 percent and (ii) a ratio of the net present value of debt to exports of at most 150 percent. For economies with a large share of exports, scaling

[28] In order to be eligible for the debt relief under the HIPC initiative, a country must be eligible for the Enhanced Structural Adjustment Facility and only for concessional financing from the International Development Association and have unsustainable debt even after traditional debt relief mechanisms are applied fully. Such countries are also obliged to undertake adjustment programs supported by the IMF and the World Bank (IMF, 1999).

by exports results in lower debt ratios. Thus, for open economies with an export-to-GDP ratio of above 30 percent, sustainability is assessed on the basis of the net present value of debt in proportion to fiscal revenue: this value should not exceed 250 percent. Since countries might have incentives to lower the tax base in order to raise the amount of debt relief under the HIPC initiative (Cohen, 2001), open economies are in addition obliged to show a sufficiently high "revenue effort" objectively demonstrated by a revenue-to-GDP ratio of above 15 percent. A comparison with table 7.10 shows that the thresholds under the HIPC initiative correspond to the respective thresholds in the DSF for low-income countries with medium or weak policy. However, in contrast to the DSF, the thresholds have not been justified empirically specifically for the HIPC countries (see also Hjertholm (2003) for the review of the history of thresholds under the HIPC initiative).

7.4.4 Conclusion

The indicative thresholds applied in the IMF's debt sustainability analysis include only public and public guaranteed debt. However, the private sector (e.g., households, banks, and enterprises) might also hold a large portion of external liabilities which cannot be repaid. Besides, in case of the non-repayment, private sector's liabilities can become at least partly official sector's liabilities—as it was most recently observed in Ireland, Spain, Portugal, and Cyprus. For example, high external debt accumulated in particular by domestic banks was one of the major causes of the recent financial crisis in Ireland whereas external public debt expanded during, and not before, the crisis (Creedon et al., 2012).

The reliance on the net present value also has several drawbacks: (i) it does not consider countries' ability to grow (which is in particular relevant when maturity periods are long); it does not provide information on when possible future debt servicing difficulties might occur, (iii) it is sensitive to the choice of the discount rate and might be misleading when discount rates change due to developments in market conditions (IMF, 2004, p. 14), and finally (iv) it neglects the probability that the debt will indeed be honored (Cohen, 2001).

As an alternative to the face value, Dias et al. (2011) construct the zero-coupon equivalent face value measure that has the advantage of being invariant to the division of the cash flows of a debt contract into principal and interest. Dias et al. (2011) find that the zero-coupon equivalent face value of external public debt is almost 50 percent greater than the traditional face value of external debt—thus possibly requiring a revision of debt indicators measured at face value.

The use of the *gross* external debt is on the one hand justified because entities which have external debt might differ from those which have external assets and because netting of liabilities and assets might mask large cross-border positions (IMF, 2002; Borio and Disyatat, 2011; Obstfeld, 2012; Essl and Stiglbauer, 2012). On the other hand, this approach may underestimate the repayment capacity of a country because neither net interest receipts nor foreign assets themselves (which can be potentially liquidated) are taken into account. At least the external sustainability analysis of the public sector (which is less heterogeneous than the private sector) might be enhanced by an additional use of thresholds for *net* external debt. Catão and Milesi-Ferretti (2013) find that net external debt matters much more for the risk of an external crisis than gross external debt. Using the sample of 70 countries during the period from 1970 to 2011, they show that the risk of an external crisis[29] increases sharply as net foreign liabilities exceed 50 percent of GDP.

The indicative thresholds both in the DSA and under the HIPC initiative consider only the level of debt liabilities in proportion to an economy's repayment ability. However, the composition of the NIIP, i.e., debt liabilities in proportion to other components of the NIIP such as international reserves and foreign direct investment might also matter for the sustainability analysis. Catão and Milesi-Ferretti (2013) find that the risk of an external crisis increases with the share of debt liabilities and decreases with the share of FDI in the overall NIIP.

Further, country-specific thresholds may deviate largely from the thresholds which have been determined for a group of countries (such as low-income countries or countries with strong policy) since sustainability thresholds might be influenced by a country's default and inflation history. Reinhart et al. (2003a) find that indicative thresholds for external public debt might be as low as 15 percent of GNP in "debt intolerant" countries, i.e., countries which already experienced a series of defaults.

As already discussed above, the IMF projections of the debt evolution and in particular of GDP growth tend to be unduly optimistic, thus presenting the envisaged adjustment under the IMF programs in a more favorable light. The IMF lending might also be associated with moral hazard problems which might, in turn, contribute to a financial crisis (Dell'Ariccia et al., 2002; Dreher, 2004; Akyüz, 2007; Lee and Shin, 2008, for the counter-arguments see Jeanne and Zettelmeyer, 2005; Phillips and Lane, 2000).[30]

Finally, the thresholds in the IMF's framework are only of limited use for the assessment of sustainability of recent global imbalances. The indicative threshold for the external debt-to-GDP ratio in the framework for market-access countries has been derived excluding the advanced industrialized countries. Thus, it might not be applicable to the United States, Japan, Germany and other advanced economies which play an important role in global imbalances. The debt sustainability analysis for low-income and heavily-indebted countries can also be hardly applied to those Asian low-income countries which are involved in global imbalances as they have been mostly displaying current account surpluses and positive net international investment positions since the mid 1990s. For the derivation of sustainability indicators for high-income countries, it might prove fruitful to apply the methodology of Kraay and Nehru (2004) and the IMF (2004) to this set of countries.

7.5 Scoreboard of the Macroeconomic Imbalances Procedure in the EU

The Macroeconomic Imbalances Procedure (MIP) was set up in December 2011 in order to prevent and to correct macroeconomic imbalances in the European Union. The early warning system of the MIP is based on an indicator based scoreboard which is published annually in the Alert Mechanism Report and is complemented by an economic reading thereof. The violation of the indicative thresholds does not automatically lead to the conclusion that this country has a macroeconomic imbalance. Over the course of the economic reading, additional indicators

[29] An external crisis is defined as including external defaults, rescheduling events, and the recourse to large multilateral/the IMF's financial support (Catão and Milesi-Ferretti, 2013).

[30] A survey of the theory and empirical evidence regarding the IMF's operations is provided by Bird (2007).

and any other country-specific information can be drawn on (European Commission, 2012b). In case that—based on the scoreboard—the European Commission arrives at the conclusion that significant imbalances do exist, detailed country-specific in-depth studies are conducted in order to determine whether the imbalances are benign or are going to threaten financial stability in the EU (European Commission, 2012b). In the latter case, the Excessive Imbalances Procedure (EIP) can be opened for the affected EU-member state.

The scoreboard consists of eleven indicators with indicative thresholds which can be found in appendix 7.B. The indicators can be grouped into two categories: (i) external imbalances and competitiveness and (ii) internal imbalances. The first group includes the current account balance and the NIIP which should capture potential external imbalances. Competitiveness is measured on the basis of the real effective exchange rate, export market shares, and nominal unit labor costs. The second group contains indicators for changes in deflated house prices, private sector credit flow, unemployment rate, private sector debt, general government debt, and more recently changes in total financial sector liabilities.

The indicative thresholds have been derived in a simple statistical distribution analysis for the data set starting in 1970 for most of the old EU member states and in early/mid 1990s for the new EU member states and ending in 2007 (details concerning the data source and the determination of the threshold values can be found in appendix 7.B). The threshold for general government debt of 60 percent based on GDP is the same as in the Stability and Growth Pact. However, as the present study deals with external sustainability, we shall henceforth focus on the indicators for external imbalances.

The current account balance in percent of GDP is calculated as the three-year backward moving average which helps to control for short-term fluctuations of the annual data and to provide indications of the persistence of a current account imbalance (European Commission, 2012c). The indicative threshold for current account deficits of four percent of GDP corresponds to the first quartile of the distribution of the three-year backward average of current account balances. This value is roughly in line with the threshold for reversals of current account deficits in industrial countries reported in table 7.8.

The threshold for current account surpluses which equals six percent of GDP has been computed as the sum of the upper quartile of the distribution (two percent) and an additional *ad-hoc* margin of four percentage points. As already discussed in section 7.1.1 of this chapter, net creditor economies can run large and growing current account surpluses as a fraction of GDP, without compromising sustainability. However, the composition and the maturity structure of net foreign assets do affect external sustainability. When extensive lending is coupled with imprudent investment behavior, as it was the case with European banks prior the European sovereign debt crisis, limits on the overall lending could reduce the risk of a financial crisis or at least mitigate the consequences of a crisis for both lenders and borrowers (Turner, 2013).

The second indicator is the ratio of the NIIP to GDP at −35 percent which is a first quartile of the NIIP distribution. The scoreboard does not contain a threshold for the positive NIIP because net external assets are not considered to be problematic. However, the accumulation of net external assets is, in fact, constrained by the threshold for current account surpluses of six percent since an increase in net foreign assets implies a current account surplus.

It bears emphasizing that the indicative thresholds for external imbalances are neither designed nor intended as sustainability thresholds. Whether external *im*balances (i.e., current account balances in the lower and in the upper quartile) should be regarded as benign or as unsustainable is to be analyzed on a case-by-case basis in the in-depth studies carried out by the European Commission. The in-depth reviews, in turn, do not rely on definitive indicators or thresholds and are not based on a pre-specified template (e.g., the in-depth reviews for Cyprus (European Commission, 2012a) and Italy (European Commission, 2013)).

Nevertheless, there is some evidence that the scoreboard could have predicted the recent European sovereign debt crisis. Using the signals approach introduced by Kaminsky et al. (1998), Knedlik and Schweinitz (2012) find for 12 euro-area countries that the ten scoreboard indicators in use in 2011 (the indicator of changes in total financial sector liabilities was added to the scoreboard in 2012) could have foretold the European financial crisis. Analyzing the ten scoreboard indicators for eight selected European countries during 2005-2007, Essl and Stiglbauer (2011) also conclude that the scoreboard could have predicted a crisis in Greece, Ireland, Portugal, and Spain. More concretely, current account deficits and net foreign liabilities are above their threshold values in Greece, Portugal, and Spain. Competitiveness indicators (export shares and nominal unit labor costs) are in a "danger zone" in Ireland. The indicators for internal imbalances (in particular the private sector debt and government debt indicators) exceed their thresholds in Ireland, Portugal, and Spain. However, in the case of Italy, only two indicators imply any problems: export market shares and government debt.

Further, almost all scoreboard indicators for Cyprus exceeded their thresholds immediately prior to the crisis of 2012: current account deficits, net foreign liabilities, export market shares, private sector credit flow, private sector debt, and government debt (see the 2011 MIP scoreboard for Cyprus in appendix 7.B).

Additional indicators which are taken into account in the economic reading of the Alert Mechanism Report include more detailed data on external liabilities (such as FDI inflows in percent of GDP), net lending/borrowing in percent of GDP), key figures associated with economic activity and investment (such as real GDP growth rate and gross fixed capital formation as a fraction of GDP), trade performance, and nominal and real convergence inside and outside the euro area (European Commission, 2012b). A list of additional indicators can be found in appendix 7.B. Notably, current account balances and the NIIP are only scaled to GDP. Other measurements of a country's repayment ability such as exports and fiscal revenue which might in some cases be better than GDP at capturing the risk of unsustainability (as discussed above) are not taken into account.

Finally, a reverse qualified-majority voting rule—that is, a voting rule according to which the European Commission can recommend corrective measures or impose sanctions that are automatically adopted unless opposed by the qualified majority in the European Council—might hamper the enforceability and the effectiveness of the EIP. Although this semi-automatic procedure is stricter than the simple qualified majority voting, it nevertheless does not fully eliminate the risk that the members of the European Council—which are potential candidates for the EIP—absolve each other by voting against the corrective measures recommended by the European Commission or the sanctions.

7.6 Conclusion

This chapter has focused on the most widely used external sustainability indicators. Further indicators, which due to limited space have not been discussed in the present study, include (among others) the liquidity gap ratio, the solvency ratio, and the share of domestic assets in the global investors' portfolio.

The liquidity gap ratio is defined as the ratio of short-term debt (i.e., debt with a maturity of up to one year) minus current account balance to the sum of export receipts and unilateral transfers (UNCTAD, 2009, p. 2). This ratio is a proxy for the illiquidity risk in so far as it shows the liquidity gap which needs to be covered by short-term borrowing. Ucal and Oksay (2011) suggest the "solvency ratio" as an indicator of external debt crises. The solvency ratio is defined as the sum of the current and capital account balances in proportion to the debt service and is inspired by the solvency ratio used to measure a firm's ability to pay long-term debts. If the solvency ratio is close to one or even greater than one, the respective economy is able to service its foreign debt obligations. A value of less than one indicates a shortage of foreign currency and a possible external debt crisis.[31]

Many indicators capture a net borrower economy's ability to pay without explicitly considering how much international investors are willing to invest in the domestic economy. Foreign investors' willingness to lend can be gauged by the share of domestic assets in the global investors' portfolio. As this ratio might be difficult to estimate due to the lack of sufficient data, an alternative is the ratio of an economy's net capital inflows relative to global savings. Since many investment portfolios are subject to a home bias (French and Poterba, 1991; Tesar and Werner, 1995; Warnock, 2002), scaling by global savings might, however, overestimate investors' wealth available for investments (Mann, 2002).

Most indicators are only to a certain extent applicable to the observed global imbalances. The resource gap is a useful concept to calculate the adjustment required to stabilize a particular ratio of net foreign debts. However, it requires assumptions about the sustainable level of net foreign debts. The application of the "unsustainability" indicators derived by Milesi-Ferretti and Razin (1996a) is limited as the relative predictive power of the indicators and the possible timing of the external crisis cannot be assessed. Indicative group- or country-specific thresholds largely facilitate the sustainability assessment. However, they might be self-fulfilling in certain equilibria. As investors perceive that some macroeconomic variables exceed their indicative thresholds, they might cease lending to the country in the anticipation of an external crisis, thus contributing to a financial crisis.

[31] Ucal and Oksay (2011) define a debt crisis as an economy's inability to repay its external debts to non-resident lenders provided that the respective economy's expenditure levels are not altered radically and the terms of quittance are not re-discussed. Ucal and Oksay (2011) calculate the solvency ratio for Turkey for the period spanning 1980-2009 and find that Turkey's solvency was severely disrupted in the periods 1980-1984, 1991, 1994, and 2000-2001. The OIC (2012) computes the solvency ratio for the member states of the Organisation of Islamic Cooperation (OIC) for the years 2005-2009. They find that Benin, Burkina-Faso, Guinea-Bissau, and Senegal—which have already qualified for HIPC initiative—have the largest negative solvency ratios among the OIC members and, therefore, face the highest risk of an external crisis.

Appendix to Chapter 7

7.A Appendix to subsubsection 7.1.2.6

On the basis of equation (7.10), Obstfeld and Rogoff (1996, pp. 68-70) calculate the foreign debt burden for nine selected countries at three points of time (1970, 1983, 1991). They choose $r = 8\%$ as a proxy for the real rate of return on equities. The real GDP growth rate is calculated individually for each country as an average value during 1970-1980 for the 1970 debt burden, during 1980-1991 for the 1983 debt burden, and during 1970-1991 for the 1991 debt burden. The results are summarized in table 7.11. Column 1 specifies the countries; the ratios of net external debt burden to real GDP for the years 1970, 1983, and 1991 can be found in columns 2, 3, and 4.

Table 7.11: Real net foreign debt burden in percent of real GDP in nine selected countries

Country	**Foreign debt burden in % of GDP**		
	1970	**1983**	**1991**
Argentina	0.5	2.9	3.9
Australia	1.7	1.3	2.4
Brazil	0.0	1.3	0.8
Canada	1.2	1.6	1.6
Chile	1.7	1.5	3.1
Hungary	0.0	2.3	3.8
Mexico	0.1	3.1	1.5
Nigeria	0.1	1.1	4.8
Thailand	0.0	0.0	0.2

Source: Obstfeld and Rogoff (1996, pp. 68-70)

The 1991 debt burden is the highest in Nigeria and the lowest in Thailand. According to Obstfeld and Rogoff (1996, p. 69), trade surpluses in Thailand are much higher than required to finance both the external debt burden and the net foreign debt itself, thus implying sustainability. In neither country in the sample, the debt burden exceeds 5 percent of GDP. The debt burden in Latin American countries increases between 1970 and 1983. This, however, does not necessarily indicate unsustainability because trade surpluses might still be sufficiently high.

The absence of information on the observed ratio of net foreign debt to output as well as on the observed trade balance as a fraction of output makes it difficult to evaluate sustainability solely on the basis of the net foreign debt burden. Further, the varying lengths of the reference periods—based on which the particular GDP growth rate is calculated—hamper the comparison of the debt burdens. Finally, Obstfeld and Rogoff (1996) do not report whether the requirement $r > \gamma$ is satisfied in their sample.

Powell (2002) estimates the stabilizing ratio of the primary balance to GDP in Argentina for each quarter in 1999-2001 under the assumption that the change in net FDI inflows remains fixed at the average level over the period 1998-2001. Powell (2002) then plots the stabilizing primary balance ratio and the actual primary balance ratio, however, without reporting his data in detail. The stabilizing primary balance slightly exceeds the actual primary balance in 1999, roughly equals it in 2000 and is significantly below the actual primary balance in 2001. Thus, on the basis of this analysis, there is evidence in favor of external sustainability in 2000 and 2001 in Argentina.

7.B Appendix to section 7.5

Table 7.12: Scoreboard indicators and their indicative thresholds in the Macroeconomic Imbalances Procedure

	% y-o-y growth of real GDP	Gross fixed capital formati on as % GDP	Gross domestic expenditure on R&D as % GDP	Current Account balance as % of GDP, BoP data	Net lending / borrowing % GDP, BoP data	Net external debt as % GDP	foreign direct invest ment Inflows as % GDP	Net Trade Balance of energy products as % GDP	% Change (3 years) in real effective exchange rate vs. EA (17)	% y-o-y change in Export Market Shares, volumes	% y-o-y growth of Labour Produc- tivity	% y-o-y growth of Employ- ment	% Change (10 years) in Nominal unit labour cost	% Change (10 years) in Effective unit labour cost vs. EA (17)	% Change (3 years) in Nominal house Prices	Resi- dential Constru ction as % GDP
Year	2011	2011	2011	2011	2011	2011	2011	2011	2011	2011	2011	2011	2011	2011	2011	2011
BE	1.8	20.7	2.0	-1.4	-1.7	-127.6	20.1	-3.7	1.4	-1.6	0.4	1.3	20.3	3.7	5.1	na
BG	1.7	20.9	0.6	0.3	1.6	33.9	4.5	-0.6		5.2	6.1	-4.2	69.5		-32.4	na
CZ	1.9	23.9	1.8	-2.8	-2.5	1.1	2.5	-1.4		5.2	1.6	0.6	23.2		-5.0	3.8
DK	0.8	17.2	3.1	5.6	5.9	18.0	3.8	0.7		1.2	1.2	-0.5	29.3		-11.9	4.7
DE	3.0	18.1	2.8	5.7	5.7	-2.9	1.1	-19.8	-0.9	2.5	1.6	1.4	5.5	-14.1	5.4	5.6
EE	8.3	21.7	2.4	2.1	6.3	6.5	1.2	na	3.2	25.7	1.2	6.7	64.4	44.8	-28.0	3.5
IE	1.4	10.1	1.7	1.1	1.0	-339.2	5.2	na	-6.5	-1.7	3.6	-2.1	15.4	0.1	-38.7	2.6
EL	-7.1	15.1	na	-9.9	-8.6	-98.0	0.4	-2.7	4.6	-6.0	-1.6	-5.6	31.1	11.5	-3.5	4.7
ES	0.4	21.1	1.3	-3.5	-3.0	93.5	2.0	-8.5	0.4	3.2	2.2	-1.6	25.3	4.3	-15.3	6.4
FR	1.7	20.1	2.3	-2.0	-2.0	36.1	1.5	-12.7	-0.4	-0.8	1.2	0.5	22.3	5.1	3.5	6.1
IT	0.4	19.6	1.3	-3.1	-3.0	49.0	1.6	-13.9	0.9	-0.2	0.3	0.3	28.3	11.1	0.4	5.5
CY	0.5	16.3	0.5	-4.7	-4.5	37.9	5.5	na	0.7	-2.3	0.0	0.4	34.6	12.4	-16.7	5.0
LV	5.5	21.3	0.7	-2.2	0.0	46.4	5.1	-0.2		6.8	14.8	-8.4	94.4		-38.7	1.5
LT	5.9	17.8	0.9	-3.7	-1.3	32.3	3.4	-0.5		7.9	3.8	2.0	33.6		-30.8	1.8
LU	1.7	19.0	1.4	7.1	6.8	-3022.2	645.3	na	2.0	-2.2	-1.2	2.6	35.7	14.0	6.5	3.4
HU	1.6	17.9	1.2	0.9	3.3	52.6	3.7	-1.4		2.7	1.2	0.8	44.3		-8.5	1.8
MT	1.9	14.8	0.7	-0.3	0.7	-158.3	4.7	0.0	1.8	-4.8	-0.5	2.5	23.7	7.0	-4.6	2.5
NL	1.0	17.7	2.0	9.7	9.7	36.8	1.6	-4.6	0.0	-1.9	0.5	0.6	20.0	3.2	-7.5	4.9
AT	2.7	21.4	2.8	0.6	0.4	24.4	3.5	-2.8	1.2	0.9	1.3	1.7	13.2	-1.6	-2.9	4.4
PL	4.3	20.3	0.8	-4.9	-2.9	35.8	3.7	na		1.5	3.3	1.1	5.7		-7.6	2.6
PT	-1.7	18.1	na	-6.5	-5.3	83.4	4.4	na	-0.5	2.7	-0.1	-1.9	19.4	1.4	2.0	3.4
RO	2.5	24.6	0.5	-4.4	-3.9	38.0	1.3	-0.7		4.1	2.0	-1.3	154.9		-39.5	na
SI	0.6	18.5	2.5	0.0	-0.3	37.5	2.0	-0.5	0.4	1.0	2.2	-1.4	38.9	21.0	-6.8	3.0
SK	3.2	23.1	0.7	0.1	1.3	21.7	2.2	-1.0	5.0	5.0	1.4	1.5	28.8	12.6	-17.8	2.3
FI	2.7	19.6	3.8	-1.6	-1.5	30.9	1.0	-1.4	2.2	-6.6	1.6	1.1	21.9	3.8	11.1	6.8
SE	3.9	18.4	3.4	6.4	6.3	62.4	2.7	-1.6		0.6	1.6	2.2	8.1		13.8	3.7
UK	0.9	14.2	1.8	-1.9	-1.7	45.2	2.3	-2.2		-1.2	0.4	0.5	26.2		-2.0	3.2

Source: European Commission (2012c)

Notes: (a) for EU trading partners, the Harmonised Index of Consumer Prices (HICP) is used while for non-EU trading partners, the deflator is based on a consumer price index (CPI) close to the HICP in methodology; (b) index providing ratio of nominal compensation per employee to real GDP per person employed; (c) changes in house prices relative to the consumption deflator of EUROSTAT; (d) private sector is defined as non-financial corporations, households, and non-profit institutions serving households; (e) sum of loan and securities other than shares; non-consolidated liabilities; (f) the sustainability of public finances is not assessed in the context of the Macroeconomic Imbalances Procedure since this issue is already covered by the Stability and Growth Pact. However, this indicator is part of the scoreboard because public indebtedness contributes to total indebtedness of the country and therefore to the overall vulnerability of the economy (European Commission, 2012c).

Table 7.13: The Macroeconomic Imbalances Procedure scoreboard with values for 2011

	External imbalances and competitiveness					Internal imbalances					
Year 2011	3 year average of Current Account Balance as % of GDP	Net International Investment Position as % of GDP	% Change (3 years) of Real Effective Exchange Rate with HICP deflators	% Change (5 years) in Export Market Shares	% Change (3 years) in Nominal unit labour cost	% year-over-year change in deflated House Prices	Private Sector Credit Flow as % of GDP	Private Sector Debt as % of GDP	General Government Debt as % of GDP	Unemployment rate - 3-year average	year-over-year % change in Total Financial Sector Liabilities, non-consolidated data
Thresholds	-4/+6%	-35%	±5% & ±11%	-6%	+9% & +12%	+6%	15%	160%	60%	10%	16.5%
BE	-0.3	65.7	-0.5	-10.2	6.2	-0.1	11.6		98.0	7.8	4.7
BG	-3.4	-85.6	3.1	17.2	20.3	-9.0	-6.7	146.0	16.0	9.4	5.6
CZ	-3.0	-49.3	0.3	8.4	3.3	0.0	2.5	78.0	41.0	6.9	3.8
DK	5.0	24.5	-1.7	-16.9	4.7	-4.9	-2.2		47.0	7.0	4.7
DE	5.9	32.6	-3.9	-8.4	5.9	1.4	4.8	128.0	81.0	6.9	2.1
EE	2.8	-57.8	0.8	11.1	-6.2	3.3	6.8	133.0	6.0	14.4	-4.4
IE	0.0	-96.0	-9.1	-12.2	-12.8	-15.2	4.0		106.0	13.3	-0.6
EL	-10.4	-86.1	3.1	-18.7	4.1	-5.1	-5.5	125.0	171.0	13.2	-3.4
ES	-4.3	-91.7	-1.3	-7.6	-2.1	-10.0	-4.1		69.0	19.9	3.7
FR	-1.6	-15.9	-3.2	-11.2	6.0	3.8	4.0		86.0	9.6	7.3
IT	-2.9	-20.6	-2.1	-18.4	4.4	-2.0	2.6	129.0	121.0	8.2	3.8
CY	-8.4	-71.3	-0.9	-16.4	8.8	-8.5	16.1		71.0	6.6	-0.2
LV	3.1	-73.3	-0.6	23.6	-15.0	4.9	-2.5	125.0	42.0	18.1	-4.5
LT	0.0	-52.6	3.6	25.2	-8.4	2.4	-0.8	70.0	39.0	15.6	8.9
LU	7.5	107.8	0.8	-10.1	12.5	1.5	2.5		18.0	4.8	11.3
HU	0.6	-105.9	-3.3	-2.8	3.7	-4.1	6.4		81.0	10.7	-2.6
MT	-4.3	5.7	-3.0	11.7	5.8	-2.3	2.2		71.0	6.8	1.4
NL	7.5	35.5	-1.6	-8.2	5.8	-4.0	0.7		66.0	4.2	7.2
AT	2.2	-2.3	-1.0	-12.7	5.9	-8.0	4.1		72.0	4.4	-0.3
PL	-4.6	-63.5	-10.9	12.8	4.3	-5.7	7.1	80.0	56.0	9.2	4.4
PT	-9.1	-105.0	-1.9	-9.5	0.9	-3.6	-3.2		108.0	11.9	-0.7
RO	-4.3	-62.5	-2.4	22.8	12.9	-18.9	1.8	72.0	33.0	7.2	4.3
SI	-0.4	-41.2	-0.3	-6.1	8.3	1.0	1.9	128.0	47.0	7.1	-1.3
SK	-2.1	-64.4	4.3	20.9	4.4	-5.6	3.3	76.0	43.0	13.4	1.2
FI	0.6	13.1	-1.3	-22.9	9.1	-0.3	4.6		49.0	8.1	30.8
SE	6.6	-8.3	3.9	-11.6	1.2	1.0	6.3		38.0	8.1	3.6
UK	-2.2	-17.3	-7.1	-24.2	8.1	-5.4	1.0		85.0	7.8	8.5

Note: Cut-off date: November 1, 2012

Table 7.14: Additional indicators used in the economic reading of the MIP scoreboard, 2011

	% y-o-y growth of real GDP	Gross fixed capital formation as % GDP	Gross domestic expenditure on R&D as % GDP	Current Account balance as % of GDP, BoP data	Net lending / borrowing % GDP, BoP data	Net external debt as % GDP	foreign direct invest ment Inflows as % GDP	Net Trade Balance of energy products as % GDP	% Change (3 years) in real effective exchange rate vs. EA (17)	% y-o-y change in Export Market Shares, volumes	% y-o-y growth of Labour Productivity	% y-o-y growth of Employment	% Change (10 years) in Nominal unit labour cost	% Change (10 years) in Effective unit labour cost vs. EA (17)	% Change (3 years) in Nominal house Prices	Residential Construction as % GDP	Private Sector Debt as % GDP, consolidated data	Financial sector leverage (debt to equity)
Year	2011	2011	2011	2011	2011	2011	2011	2011	2011	2011	2011	2011	2011	2011	2011	2011	2011	2011
BE	1.8	20.7	2.0	-1.4	-1.7	-127.6	20.1	-3.7	1.4	-1.6	0.4	1.3	20.3	3.7	5.1	na	143	641
BG	1.7	20.9	0.6	0.3	1.6	33.9	4.5	-0.6		5.2	6.1	-4.2	69.5		-32.4	na	136	414
CZ	1.9	23.9	1.8	-2.8	-2.5	1.1	2.5	-1.4		5.2	1.6	0.6	23.2		-5.0	3.8	73	624
DK	0.8	17.2	3.1	5.6	5.9	18.0	3.8	0.7		1.2	1.2	-0.5	29.3		-11.9	4.7	238	377
DE	3.0	18.1	2.8	5.7	5.7	-2.9	1.1	-19.8	-0.9	2.5	1.6	1.4	5.5	-14.1	5.4	5.6	109	524
EE	8.3	21.7	2.4	2.1	6.3	6.5	1.2	na	3.2	25.7	1.2	6.7	64.4	44.8	-28.0	3.5	132	373
IE	1.4	10.1	1.7	1.1	1.0	-339.2	5.2	na	-6.5	-1.7	3.6	-2.1	15.4	0.1	-38.7	2.6	281	158
EL	-7.1	15.1	na	-9.9	-8.6	-98.0	0.4	-2.7	4.6	-6.0	-1.6	-5.6	31.1	11.5	-3.5	4.7	125	2728
ES	0.4	21.1	1.3	-3.5	-3.0	93.5	2.0	-8.5	0.4	3.2	2.2	-1.6	25.3	4.3	-15.3	6.4	204	941
FR	1.7	20.1	2.3	-2.0	-2.0	36.1	1.5	-12.7	-0.4	-0.8	1.2	0.5	22.3	5.1	3.5	6.1	139	461
IT	0.4	19.6	1.3	-3.1	-3.0	49.0	1.6	-13.9	0.9	-0.2	0.3	0.3	28.3	11.1	0.4	5.5	126	1172
CY	0.5	16.3	0.5	-4.7	-4.5	37.9	5.5	na	0.7	-2.3	0.0	0.4	34.6	12.4	-16.7	5.0	281	2539
LV	5.5	21.3	0.7	-2.2	0.0	46.4	5.1	-0.2		6.8	14.8	-8.4	94.4		-38.7	1.5	118	704
LT	5.9	17.8	0.9	-3.7	-1.3	32.3	3.4	-0.5		7.9	3.8	2.0	33.6		-30.8	1.8	67	633
LU	1.7	19.0	1.4	7.1	6.8	-3022.2	645.3	na	2.0	-2.2	-1.2	2.6	35.7	14.0	6.5	3.4	267	50
HU	1.6	17.9	1.2	0.9	3.3	52.6	3.7	-1.4		2.7	1.2	0.8	44.3		-8.5	1.8	147	562
MT	1.9	14.8	0.7	-0.3	0.7	-158.3	4.7	0.0	1.8	-4.8	-0.5	2.5	23.7	7.0	-4.6	2.5	169	362
NL	1.0	17.7	2.0	9.7	9.7	36.8	1.6	-4.6	0.0	-1.9	0.5	0.6	20.0	3.2	-7.5	4.9	224	231
AT	2.7	21.4	2.8	0.6	0.4	24.4	3.5	-2.8	1.2	0.9	1.3	1.7	13.2	-1.6	-2.9	4.4	146	378
PL	4.3	20.3	0.8	-4.9	-2.9	35.8	3.7	na		1.5	3.3	1.1	5.7		-7.6	2.6	77	377
PT	-1.7	18.1	na	-6.5	-5.3	83.4	4.4	na	-0.5	2.7	-0.1	-1.9	19.4	1.4	2.0	3.4	223	542
RO	2.5	24.6	0.5	-4.4	-3.9	38.0	1.3	-0.7		4.1	2.0	-1.3	154.9		-39.5	na	71	662
SI	0.6	18.5	2.5	0.0	-0.3	37.5	2.0	-0.5	0.4	1.0	2.2	-1.4	38.9	21.0	-6.8	3.0	116	639
SK	3.2	23.1	0.7	0.1	1.3	21.7	2.2	-1.0	5.0	5.0	1.4	1.5	28.8	12.6	-17.8	2.3	76	1079
FI	2.7	19.6	3.8	-1.6	-1.5	30.9	1.0	-1.4	2.2	-6.6	1.6	1.1	21.9	3.8	11.1	6.8	153	616
SE	3.9	18.4	3.4	6.4	6.3	62.4	2.7	-1.6		0.6	1.6	2.2	8.1		13.8	3.7	216	305
UK	0.9	14.2	1.8	-1.9	-1.7	45.2	2.3	-2.2		-1.2	0.4	0.5	26.2		-2.0	3.2	na	1187

Source: EUROSTAT except for deflated House Prices (Eurostat data completed with the European Central Bank), Export Market Shares volumes (World Economic Outlook, IMF), Real Effective Exchange Rate with HICP deflators (Directorate General for Economic and Financial Affairs), Effective unit labour cost versus euro area (Directorate General for Economic and Financial Affairs)

Notes: Cut-off date: November,1 2012. Abbreviations: BoP: Balance of Payments, EA: Euro Area, GDP: Gross Domestic Product, R&D: Research & Development, y-o-y: year-over-year.

8

Concluding discussion

The present dissertation has evaluated the existing methods and studies for the assessment of external sustainability. Sustainability measures can be roughly grouped into two categories: empirical tests and indicators. The first category includes tests on the validity of an economy's intertemporal budget constraint as well as tests of the "dynamic" sustainability benchmarks implied by the intertemporal and portfolio approaches to the current account. The second category comprises a variety of sustainability indicators, either based on a theoretical model or on some *ad-hoc* rules of thumb. We have focused on the resource gap which is a widely used indicator and on the "unsustainability" indicators constructed by Milesi-Ferretti and Razin (1996a). We have also examined whether indicators of current account reversals can be exploited for the sustainability analysis. Finally, we have analyzed sustainability indicators applied in the International Monetary Fund's debt sustainability analyses and the Scoreboard of the European Macroeconomic Imbalances Procedure.

Despite its theoretical limitations, the most popular criterion for assessing sustainability is the intertemporal budget constraint. There exist mainly three possibilities to test the validity of the IBC in the data: (i) unit root tests, (ii) cointegration tests combined with the estimation of a cointegrating vector, and (ii) tests for a sufficiently large negative feedback from the NIIP to the trade balance. The large majority of unit root and cointegration tests cautiously points to weak sustainability in the United States. Alongside with the United States, there is also evidence for sustainability of other countries which experience large external imbalances: strong sustainability in Saudi Arabia, in GIIPS, and the Netherlands; weak sustainability in China and Germany. The evidence on the form of sustainability (strong or weak) is, however, mixed in the cases of Japan and France. Overall, these findings rather suggest that the recently observed global and euro-area imbalances have been sustainable.

For a large panel data set, Durdu et al. (2010) obtain evidence in favor of a negative feedback from the NIIP to the trade balance. This result implies strong sustainability provided that the interest rate does not exceed seven percent and weak sustainability otherwise. Since the panel approach by Durdu et al. (2010) provides little information on external sustainability specifically in the United States, we use time series analysis and find a positive relationship between the NIIP and the trade balance—this yields no support for sustainability. In contrast, a series of unit root tests unanimously indicates strong sustainability in the United States. To resolve this disagreement, further research such as tests for fractional integration, nonlinear time series techniques, or right-sided unit root tests (in order to detect any explosive patterns in the time series) would be needed. If further research verified explosive behavior in the both series, we could conclude that testing for feedback effects from the NIIP to the trade balance exhibits greater precision as a method of assessing sustainability than unit root tests.

However, the tests on the validity of the IBC failed to predict the occurrence of a European sovereign debt crisis. Even if the root of the European sovereign debt crisis had not been primarily in external imbalances, external debt played an important role at least in Portugal and Greece (Gros, 2011). One explanation for this lack of predictive power is that statistical tests, by their nature, are based on historical data and are inherently backward-looking. Even if the IBC is found to be satisfied for a particular historical data set, sudden changes in the economic environment might undermine investors' confidence in an economy's solvency, lead to a sudden stop in capital flows, and possibly result in an external debt crisis. Finally, international investors might base their lending decisions on additional criteria which go beyond the IBC. One option for arriving at a stronger sustainability notion than mere satisfaction of the IBC would be to equate sustainability with the strong form of sustainability.

Another possibility is to require, for sustainability, any external imbalances to be consistent with the agents' optimal balances (e.g., Edwards, 2007; Blanchard and Milesi-Ferretti, 2009, 2011). In this approach to external sustainability, one compares the observed path of external imbalances with an optimal (or equilibrium) "dynamic" benchmark path that previously has been derived for that purpose within some economic model. We have evaluated two "dynamic" benchmarks: the intertemporal approach to the current account and the portfolio approach to the current account.

Notably, a finding of sustainability according to the intertemporal approach to the current account also implies that the IBC is satisfied (yet not vice versa). We have discussed both the "workhorse" model under certainty equivalence as well as its extensions (such as the presence of consumption tilting, precautionary saving, or habit formation). However, the most widely used test in this literature—the "nonlinear" Wald test—yields imprecise estimations when the current account series is persistent (Mercereau and Miniane, 2004, 2008). In contrast to the tests on the validity of the IBC, only few studies examine the United States since this methodology, strictly speaking, is applicable only to small economies. These studies provide some (although not unanimous) support for the validity of the intertemporal model of the current account in the United States, Japan, Italy, Spain, and Portugal, yet no support for Germany. This also shows that the tests do not predict a future financial crisis in Portugal and Spain. The recent data for Asian economies or oil-exporting economies have not been examined so far.

In contrast to the intertemporal approach to the current account, the portfolio or stock equilibrium approach to the current account explicitly takes into account the determinants of investors' portfolio decisions. Although a large theoretical literature on the portfolio approach to the current account has emerged, there exists, to our knowledge, only one study which examines external sustainability both theoretically and empirically: For a large panel data set, Calderon et al. (2000) find that the "dynamic" sustainability benchmark based on the portfolio approach is satisfied in countries with low capital controls and/or high and upper-middle income, but not in countries with high capital controls and/or low income. One explanation is that external imbalances are not sustainable in those countries. Another, and more likely, explanation is that capital controls lessen the importance of risk and return for portfolio decisions and that the NIIP positions in low-income countries are largely determined by non-market forces (such as political interests or humanitarian reasons) rather than by investors' optimal diversification decisions (Calderon et al., 2000). However, panel data do not allow to draw inferences about the sustainability for individual countries. Exploiting the recent theoretical literature on the portfolio approach for the sustainability analysis also might prove to be a promising avenue. Finally, a violation of a "dynamic" sustainability benchmark (disregarding of the underlying theoretical model) involves an identification problem: It can be interpreted either as evidence against sustainability or as evidence against some assumptions used to derive the benchmark (such as agents' preferences). Generalizations of the theoretical and empirical framework used to derive a "dynamic" benchmark help to mitigate this identification problem, even though they cannot eliminate it.

Aside from statistical tests, we have also examined the most widespread indicators of external sustainability. The resource gap is based on the idea that an economy's net foreign debts are sustainable when they are constant or falling in proportion to the economy's repayment ability, provided that Ponzi games are not feasible. This indicator applies primarily to net foreign debts; however, as a continually growing ratio of net foreign assets to GDP might be undesirable, it can also be used to assess sustainability of net foreign assets. The resource gap indicates the size of the resource transfer required to prevent an economy's net foreign debts (assets) in proportion to the economy's repayment ability from rising. We have reviewed all empirical studies that estimate the resource gap and/or the trade or primary surplus required to prevent the debt ratio from increasing, calculating the resource gap on our own when it has not been reported in the respective study. Comparing different methods of calculating the resource gap for transition countries, we find that the size of the resource gap (rather than the sign) is quite sensitive towards differences in estimations. However, a major limitation of the resource gap is that it does not impose any restrictions on the level of the NIIP-to-GDP ratio: Any NIIP-to-GDP ratio is sustainable as long as it is non-increasing. Yet a debt ratio which is the result of a moderate rise from a "low" initial level might constitute a smaller risk for sustainability than a stabilization at a "high" level of debt.

Neither the intertemporal budget constraint, nor the dynamic benchmarks, nor the resource gap provide further information on the manner in which the adjustment in the trade balance required to restore/maintain solvency will take place. Milesi-Ferretti and Razin (1996a,b) derive indicators which help to discriminate between unsustainable episodes—which are accompanied by a drastic policy shift (such as a sudden fiscal tightening causing a recession) and/or a financial crisis (which might force a country to default on its external obligations)—and sustainable episodes. The main results are that persistent trade and current account deficits are likely to result in an external crisis when external debt and the interest burden are high in proportion to exports, the ratio of exports to GDP is small, the real exchange rate (in a price quotation) is appreciated relative to the historical average, and national savings are low. Overall, these findings are to a large extent supported by the literature on medium-term determinants of the current account and the literature on early warning indicators of financial crises. Applying the main "unsustainability" indicators to the United States, we have identified three unsustainability periods: in the mid-1980s, in the early/mid-2000s, and in the late 2000s. However, the nonstructural approach does not allow to quantify the problematic levels of the indicator variables, the relative predictive power of the indicators, and the possible timing of the external crisis. A more formal analysis based on the approach suggested by Milesi-Ferretti and Razin (1996a) would be desirable.

We have also compared the thresholds for current account reversals, identified by the empirical literature, with the observed current account positions in the United States, Japan, China, the oil-exporting countries (as a group), and in the euro area. We have found that many countries have been running imbalances which exceed by far the respective thresholds for prolonged periods of time. This warrants the conclusion that the (country-specific) reversal thresholds yield only imprecise forecasts regarding the level and the timing at which the reduction of a current account imbalance starts.

Further, we have also reviewed the indicators used in the IMF's framework for conducting debt sustainability analysis for market-access countries and low-income countries as well as for heavily indebted poor countries. Key indicators are the stock of gross public external debt and the service of gross public external debt—which are set in proportion to different measures of the respective economy's repayment capacity (GDP, exports, and fiscal revenues). The debt service is measured by its face value whereas the debt stock is meausured by its net present value.

The indicative thresholds applied in the IMF's debt sustainability analysis and under the HIPC initiative only include public and publicly guaranteed debt. However, the private sector (e.g., households, banks, and enterprises) might also hold a large portion of external liabilities which cannot be repaid. Besides, in the case of non-repayment, private sector liabilities can become at least in part official sector liabilities—as has most recently been observed in Ireland, Spain, Portugal, and Cyprus. The use of the *gross* external debt may underestimate the repayment capacity of a country because neither the interest to be received on external assets nor external assets themselves (which can be liquidated) are taken into account. At least the external sustainability analysis of the public sector (which is less heterogeneous than the private sector) might be enhanced by an additional use of thresholds for *net* external debt. Further, the indicative thresholds in the DSAs for market-access countries have been derived excluding the advanced industrialized countries and might, therefore, not be applicable to the United States, Japan, Germany and other advanced economies which play an important role in global imbalances. Also, the debt sustainability analysis for low-income and heavily-indebted countries can hardly be applied to many of the low-income countries involved in recent global imbalances as they have typically displayed current account surpluses and positive net international investment positions since the mid-1990s.

At the end, we have discussed the indicators used to identify external imbalances in the Macroeconomic Imbalances Procedure (MIP) introduced in 2011 in the European Union. It bears emphasizing that these indicative thresholds are neither designed nor intended as sustainability thresholds: They are devised merely to detect the presence of external *im*balances and do not indicate whether those imbalances should be regarded as sustainable or unsustainable. Finally, even if indicative group- or country-specific thresholds largely facilitate the sustainability assessment, they might be self-fulfilling in certain equilibria. As investors perceive that some macroeconomic variables exceed their indicative thresholds, they might cease lending to the country in anticipation of an external crisis, thus contributing to a financial crisis.

Most indicators focus on current account deficits (rather than current account surpluses) and foreign liabilities (rather than foreign assets). The main reason is—as discussed above—that in relation to GDP, increasing current account surpluses and foreign assets have been considered to be less worrisome than growing current account deficits. This view is backed by the study conducted by Edwards (2007) who finds that episodes of large current account surpluses have been less persistent in the past than current account deficits and have been typically resolved smoothly. In contrast, the tests on the validity of the IBC and on the dynamic sustainability benchmarks are fully applicable to both external deficits and surpluses. In particular in connection with recent global and euro-area imbalances, claims have been increasingly made that both deficit and surplus countries should bear the cost of the adjustment of external imbalances (e.g., Goldstein, 2010; Williamson, 2011; Gros, 2012).[1] In avoidance of (more or less) arbitrary thresholds for excessive and/or unsustainable current account surpluses—such as the threshold of six percent in the MIP or four percent suggested by then-US Treasury Secretary Timothy Geithner prior to the G20 meeting in 2010—, more research should be devoted to determining indicators for sustainability of current account surpluses and foreign asset positions.

Finally, the general consensus is that no single indicator is capable of fully capturing external sustainability. We have pointed out that many indicators are only to a limited extent or not at all applicable in the analysis of actually observed global imbalances and that modifications of the existing indicators are therefore desirable. Nevertheless, in particular in those cases in which various sustainability tests provide conflicting information, the existing indicators can complement the econometric tests on external sustainability. For the United States, for example, we have found a positive feedback from the NIIP to the trade balance. The "unsustainability" indicators derived by Milesi-Ferretti and Razin (1996a) have shown three unsustainability episodes, but have signaled some recovery after 2010. Further, the US current account deficit has remained below the reversal threshold of four percent of GDP since 2009. Thus, one might expect the trade balance to respond negatively to changes in the NIIP at last. In general, the joint use of tests and indicators is a fruitful approach to enhance the analysis of external sustainability.

[1] Such claims are not at all new. For example, during the pre-Bretton Woods negotiations, John Maynard Keynes suggested that countries should finance their external imbalances by accumulating and spending balances in a synthetic currency called "bancor" and that both deficits and surpluses should be penalized through interest payments (Williamson, 2011).

References

Abbas, S. M. A., Bouhga-Hagbe, J., Fataás, A., Mauro, P., and Velloso, R. C. (2011). Fiscal policy and the current account. *IMF Economic Review*, 59(4):603–629.

Abel, A. B. (1979). *Investment and the Value of Capital (Outstanding Dissertations in Economics)*. New York, NY: Garland Publishing, 1st edition.

Abel, A. B., Mankiw, N. G., Summers, L. H., and Zeckhauser, R. J. (1989). Assessing dynamic efficiency: Theory and evidence. *Review of Economic Studies*, 56(1):1–19.

Abiad, A. (2003). Early warning systems: A survey and a regime-switching approach. IMF Working Papers 03/32, International Monetary Fund.

Abiad, A., Leigh, D., and Mody, A. (2007). International finance and income convergence: Europe is different. IMF Working Papers 07/64, International Monetary Fund.

Acemoglu, D. (2008). *Introduction to Modern Economic Growth*. Princeton, NJ: Princeton University Press.

Acharya, V. V. and Schnabl, P. (2010). Do global banks spread global imbalances? The case of asset-backed commercial paper during the financial crisis of 2007-09. NBER Working Papers 16079, National Bureau of Economic Research.

Adedeji, O. (2001). The size and sustainability of the Nigerian current account deficits. IMF Working Papers 01/87, International Monetary Fund.

Afonso, A. and Rault, C. (2010). What do we really know about fiscal sustainability in the EU? A panel data diagnostic. *Review of World Economics*, 145(4):731–755.

Agénor, P.-R., Bismut, C., Cashin, P., and McDermott, C. (1999). Consumption smoothing and the current account: Evidence for France, 1970–1996. *Journal of International Money and Finance*, 18(1):1–12.

Aguiar, M. and Gopinath, G. (2007). Emerging market business cycles: The cycle is the trend. *Journal of Political Economy*, 115(1):69–102.

Ahearne, A., Schmitz, B., and Hagen, J. (2007). Current account imbalances in the euro area (draft version). Technical Report 345, CASE Network Studies and Analyses.

Aitken, B. J. and Harrison, A. E. (1999). Do domestic firms benefit from direct foreign investment? Evidence from Venezuela. *American Economic Review*, 89(3):605–618.

Aizenman, J. (2008). Large hoarding of international reserves and the emerging global economic architecture. *Manchester School*, 76(5):487–503.

Aizenman, J. and Lee, J. (2007). International reserves: Precautionary versus mercantilist views, theory and evidence. *Open Economies Review*, 18(2):191–214.

Aizenman, J. and Marion, N. (2003). The high demand for international reserves in the Far East: What is going on? *Journal of the Japanese and International Economies*, 17(3):370–400.

Akaike, H. (1974). A new look at the statistical model identification. *Automatic Control, IEEE Transactions on*, 19(6):716–723.

Akyüz, Y. (2007). Debt sustainability in emerging markets: A critical appraisal. Working Papers 61, United Nations, Department of Economics and Social Affairs.

Alessie, R. and Lusardi, A. (1997). Consumption, saving and habit formation. *Economics Letters*, 55(1):103–108.

Alessie, R. and Teppa, F. (2010). Saving and habit formation: Evidence from Dutch panel data. *Empirical Economics*, 38(2):385–407.

Alfaro, L., Chanda, A., Kalemli-Ozcan, S., and Sayek, S. (2004). FDI and economic growth: The role of local financial markets. *Journal of International Economics*, 64(1):89–112.

Allais, M. (1947). *Economie et Intérêt*. Paris: Imprimerie Nationale et Librairie des Publications Officielles, 1st edition.

Allen, M., Rosenberg, C. B., Keller, C., Setser, B., and Roubini, N. (2002). A balance sheet approach to financial crisis. IMF Working Papers 02/210, International Monetary Fund.

Amano, R. A. and van Norden, S. (1995). Unit root tests and the burden of proof. Econometrics 9502005, EconWPA.

Amemiya, T. (1994). *Introduction to Statistics and Econometrics*. Cambridge, MA: Harvard University Press.

Andrews, D. W. K. (1991). Heteroskedasticity and autocorrelation consistent covariance matrix estimation. *Econometrica*, 59(3):817–858.

Ang, J. (2007). Are saving and investment cointegrated? The case of Malaysia (1965–2003). *Applied Economics*, 39(17):2167–2174.

Anoruo, E. (2001). Saving-investment connection: Evidence from the ASEAN countries. *The American Economist*, 45(1):46–53.

Apergis, N., Katrakilidis, K. P., and Tabakis, N. M. (2000). Current account deficit sustainability: The case of Greece. *Applied Economics Letters*, 7(9):599–603.

Apergis, N. and Tsoumas, C. (2009). A survey of the Feldstein-Horioka puzzle: What has been done and where we stand. *Research in Economics*, 63(2):64–76.

Arai, Y. (2004). Testing for linearity in regressions with I(1) processes. CIRJE F-Series 303, CIRJE, Faculty of Economics, University of Tokyo.

Arai, Y. and Kurozumi, E. (2007). Testing for the null hypothesis of cointegration with a structural break. *Econometric Reviews*, 26(6):705–739.

Arezki, R. and Hasanov, F. (2013). Global imbalances and petrodollars. *The World Economy*, 36(2):213–232.

Argimón, I. and Roldán, J. M. (1994). Saving, investment and international capital mobility in EC countries. *European Economic Review*, 38(1):59–67.

Aristovnik, A. (2005). Current account reversals in selected transition countries. International Finance 0510021, EconWPA.

Aristovnik, A. (2006). How sustainable are current account deficits in selected transition economies? MPRA Paper 485, University Library of Munich, Germany.

Arize, A. C. (2002). Imports and exports in 50 countries: Tests of cointegration and structural breaks. *International Review of Economics & Finance*, 11(1):101–115.

Arrow, K. J. (1964). The role of securities in the optimal allocation of risk-bearing. *The Review of Economic Studies*, 31(2):91–96.

Arrow, K. J. (1970). *Essays in the Theory of Risk-Bearing*. Amsterdam, etc.: North-Holland.

Atoian, R., Conway, P., Selowsky, M., and Tsikata, T. (2006). Macroeconomic adjustment in IMF-supported programs: projections and reality. In Mody, A. and Rebucci, A., editors, *IMF-supported Programs: Recent Staff Research*. Washington, DC: International Monetary Fund, September.

Backus, D., Henriksen, E., Lambert, F., and Telmer, C. (2009). Current account fact and fiction. NBER Working Papers 15525, National Bureau of Economic Research.

Backus, D. and Kehoe, P. J. (1992). International evidence on the historical properties of business cycles. *American Economic Review*, 82(4):864–888.

Bagnai, A. (2004). Keynesian and neoclassical fiscal sustainability indicators, with applications to EMU member countries. Public Economics 0411005, EconWPA.

Baharumshah, A. Z., Lau, E., and Fountas, S. (2003). On the sustainability of current account deficits: Evidence from four ASEAN countries. *Journal of Asian Economics*, 14(3):465–487.

Bahmani-Oskooee, M. and Ratha, A. (2004). The J-curve: A literature review. *Applied Economics*, 36(13):1377–1398.

Bahmani-Oskooee, M. and Rhee, H.-J. (1997). Are imports and exports of Korea cointegrated? *International Economic Journal*, 11(1):109–114.

Baillie, R. T. (1996). Long memory processes and fractional integration in econometrics. *Journal of Econometrics*, 73(1):5–59.

Bajo-Rubio, O. (1998). The saving-investment correlation revisited: The case of Spain, 1964–1994. *Applied Economics Letters*, 5:769–772.

Balassa, B. (1964). The purchasing-power parity doctrine: A reappraisal. *Journal of Political Economy*, 72(6):584–596.

Balasubramanyam, V. N., Salisu, M., and Sapsford, D. (1996). Foreign direct investment and growth in EP and IS countries. *The Economic Journal*, 106(434):92–105.

Banerjee, A. (1999). Panel data unit roots and cointegration: An overview. *Oxford Bulletin of Economics and Statistics*, 61(S1):607–629.

Banerjee, A. and Hendry, D. F. (1992). Testing integration and cointegration: An overview. *Oxford Bulletin of Economics and Statistics*, 54(3):225–255.

Banerjee, A., Marcellino, M., and Osbat, C. (2005). Testing for PPP: Should we use panel methods? *Empirical Economics*, 30(1):77–91.

Baqir, R., Ramcharan, R., and Sahay, R. (2005). IMF programs and growth: Is optimism defensible? *IMF Staff Papers*, 52(2):260–286.

Barkoulas, J., Filizetkin, A., and Murphy, R. (1996). Time series evidence on the saving-investment relationship. *Applied Economics Letters*, 3(2):77–80.

Barnichon, R. (2009). The optimal level of reserves for low-income countries: Self-insurance against external shocks. *IMF Staff Papers*, 56(4):852–875.

Barro, R. J. (1974). Are government bonds net wealth? *Journal of Political Economy*, 82(6):1095–1117.

Barro, R. J. (1976). Reply to "Perceived wealth in bonds and social security" and "Barro on the Ricardian equivalence theorem.". *Journal of Political Economy*, 84(2):343–349.

Barro, R. J. (1979). On the determination of the public debt. *Journal of Political Economy*, 87(5):940–971.

Barro, R. J. and Sala-i-Martin, X. (1990). World real interest rates. In *NBER Macroeconomics Annual 1990*, volume 5 of *NBER Chapters*, pages 15–74. National Bureau of Economic Research.

Bartolini, L. and Lahiri, A. (2006). Twin deficits, twenty years later. *Current Issues in Economics and Finance*, 12(7).

Baxter, M. (2005). International trade and business cycles. In Grossman, G. and Rogoff, K., editors, *Handbook of International Economics*, volume 3, pages 1801–1864. Amsterdam, NL: North-Holland.

Baxter, M. and Crucini, M. J. (1993). Explaining saving-investment correlations. *American Economic Review*, 83(3):416–436.

Bayoumi, T. (1990). Saving-investment correlations: Immobile capital, government policy, or endogenous behavior? *IMF Staff Papers*, 37(2):360–387.

Belkar, R., Cockerell, L., and Kent, C. (2008). Current account deficits: The Australian debate. In Cowan, K., Edwards, S., Valdés, R. O., Loayza, N., and Schmidt-Hebbel, K., editors, *Current Account and External Financing*, volume 12 of *Central Banking, Analysis, and Economic Policies Book Series*, chapter 13, pages 491–535. Central Bank of Chile.

Belke, A. and Dreger, C. (2013). Current account imbalances in the euro area: Does catching up explain the development? *Review of International Economics*, 21(1):6–17.

Belke, A. and Schnabl, G. (2013). Four generations of global imbalances. *Review of International Economics*, 21(1):1–5.

Ben-David, D., Lumsdaine, R. L., and Papell, D. (1996). The unit root hypothesis in long-term output: Evidence from two structural breaks for 16 countries. CEPR Discussion Papers 1336, C.E.P.R. Discussion Papers.

Berenguer-Rico, V. and Carrion-i-Silvestre, J. L. (2011). Regime shifts in stock-flow I(2)-I(1) systems: The case of US fiscal sustainability. *Journal of Applied Econometrics*, 26(2):298–321.

Bergheim, S. (2008). *Long-Run Growth Forecasting*. Berlin, Heidelberg: Springer.

Bergin, P. R. and Sheffrin, S. M. (2000). Interest rates, exchange rates and present value models of the current account. *Economic Journal*, 110(463):535–558.

Bergman, M. (2001). Testing government solvency and the No Ponzi game condition. *Applied Economics Letters*, 8(1):27–29.

Bernanke, B. S. (2005). The global saving glut and the U.S. current account deficit. Homer Jones Lecture, St. Louis, MO, April 14, 2005, http://www.federalreserve.gov/boarddocs/speeches/2005/20050414/default.htm.

Bernanke, B. S. (2009). Financial reform to address systemic risk. Speech at the Council on Foreign Relations, Washington, DC, March 10, 2009, http://www.federalreserve.gov/newsevents/speech/bernanke20090310a.htm.

Bertola, G., Driffill, J., James, H., Sinn, H.-W., Sturm, J.-E., and Valentinyi, A. (2013). European imbalances. In EEAG, editor, *The EEAG Report on the European Economy*, pages 55–72. Munich, DE: CESIFO.

Bertola, G., Foellmi, R., and Zweimuller, J. (2005). *Income Distribution in Macroeconomic Models*. Princeton, NJ: Princeton University Press.

Bewley, T. F. (1972). Existence of equilibria in economies with infinitely many commodities. *Journal of Economic Theory*, 4(3):514–540.

Bhagwati, J. N. (1984). Why are services cheaper in the poor countries? *Economic Journal*, 94(374):279–286.

Bhattacharya, R. N. and Waymire, E. C. (2009). *Stochastic Processes with Applications*. New York, NY [etc.]: Wiley & Sons.

Bickerdike, C. F. (1920). The instability of foreign exchange. *Economic Journal*, 30(117):118–122.

Bierens, H. J. (2005). *Introduction to the Mathematical and Statistical Foundations of Econometrics*. New York, NY: Cambridge University Press.

Binmore, K. and Shaked, A. (2010). Experimental economics: Where next? *Journal of Economic Behavior & Organization*, 73(1):87–100.

Bird, G. (2005). Over-optimism and the IMF. *World Economy*, 28(9):1355–1373.

Bird, G. (2007). The IMF: A bird's eye view of its role and operations. *Journal of Economic Surveys*, 21(4):683–745.

Blanchard, O. (1985). Debt, deficits, and finite horizons. *Journal of Political Economy*, 93(2):223–247.

Blanchard, O. (1990). Suggestions for a new set of fiscal indicators. OECD Economics Department Working Papers 79, OECD Publishing.

Blanchard, O. and Fischer, S. (1989). *Lectures on Macroeconomics*. Cambridge, MA: MIT Press.

Blanchard, O. and Giavazzi, F. (2002). Current account deficits in the euro area: The end of the Feldstein Horioka puzzle? *Brookings Papers on Economic Activity*, 33(2):147–210.

Blanchard, O. and Mankiw, N. G. (1989). Consumption: Beyond certainty equivalence. NBER Working Papers 2496, National Bureau of Economic Research.

Blanchard, O. and Milesi-Ferretti, G. M. (2009). Global imbalances: In midstream? IMF Staff Position Note 09/29, International Monetary Fund.

Blanchard, O. and Milesi-Ferretti, G. M. (2010). Global imbalances: In midstream? CEPR Discussion Papers 7693, C.E.P.R. Discussion Papers.

Blanchard, O. and Milesi-Ferretti, G. M. (2011). (Why) should current account balances be reduced? IMF Staff Discussion Note 11/03, International Monetary Fund.

Bodman, P. M. (1995). National savings and domestic investment in the long term: Some time series evidence from the OECD. *International Economic Journal*, 9(2):37–60.

Bodman, P. M. (1997). The Australian trade balance and current account: A time series perspective. *International Economic Journal*, 11(2):39–57.

Bohn, H. (1991). On testing the sustainability of government deficits in a stochastic environment. Rodney L. White Center for Financial Research Working Papers 17–91, The Wharton School, University of Pennsylvania.

Bohn, H. (1995a). On testing the sustainability of government deficits in a stochastic environment. Working papers, Department of Economics, University of California at Santa Barbara.

Bohn, H. (1995b). The sustainability of budget deficits in a stochastic economy. *Journal of Money, Credit and Banking*, 27(1):257–271.

Bohn, H. (1998). The behavior of U.S. public debt and deficits. *The Quarterly Journal of Economics*, 113(3):949–963.

Bohn, H. (2007). Are stationarity and cointegration restrictions really necessary for the intertemporal budget constraint? *Journal of Monetary Economics*, 54(7):1837–1847.

Bonatti, L. and Fracasso, A. (2013). Origins and prospects of the Euro existential crisis. DEM Discussion Papers 2013/03, Department of Economics and Management.

Boote, A. R. and Thugge, K. (1997). Debt-relief for low-income countries and the HIPC initiative. IMF Working Papers 97/24, International Monetary Fund.

Borensztein, E., Gregorio, J. D., and Lee, J.-W. (1998). How does foreign direct investment affect economic growth? *Journal of International Economics*, 45(1):115–135.

Borio, C. and Disyatat, P. (2011). Global imbalances and the financial crisis: Link or no link? BIS Working Papers 346, Bank for International Settlements.

Bosworth, B., Collins, S. M., and Chodorow-Reich, G. (2007). Returns on FDI: Does the U.S. really do better? NBER Working Papers 13313, National Bureau of Economic Research.

Bouakez, H. and Kano, T. (2009). Tests of the present-value model of the current account: A note. *Applied Economics Letters*, 16:1215–1219.

Bracke, T., Bussière, M., Fidora, M., and Straub, R. (2008). A framework for assessing global imbalances. Occasional papers 78, European Central Bank.

Bracke, T. and Fidora, M. (2008). Global liquidity glut or global savings glut? A structural VAR approach. ECB Working Papers 911, European Central Bank.

Braeu, R. (2010). Consumption tilting and the current account: Evidence from Canada. *International Review of Economics & Finance*, 19(2):304–312.

Brainard, W. C. and Tobin, J. (1968). Pitfalls in financial model building. *American Economic Review*, 58(2):99–122.

Braun, P. A., Constantinides, G. M., and Ferson, W. E. (1993). Time nonseparability in aggregate consumption: International evidence. *European Economic Review*, 37(5):897–920.

Breitung, J. (2000). The local power of some unit root tests for panel data. In Baltagi, B. H., Fomby, T. B., and Hill, C. R., editors, *Nonstationary Panels, Panel Cointegration, and Dynamic Panels (Advances in Econometrics)*, volume 15, pages 161–178. New York, NY: Elsevier Science Inc.

Breitung, J. (2002). Nonparametric tests for unit roots and cointegration. *Journal of Econometrics*, 108(2):343–363.

Breitung, J. and Das, S. (2005). Panel unit root tests under cross-sectional dependence. *Statistica Neerlandica*, 59(4):414–433.

Breitung, J. and Taylor, A. M. R. (2003). Corrigendum to nonparametric tests for unit roots and cointegration. *Journal of Econometrics*, 117(2):401–404.

Breuer, J. B. (2004). An exegesis on currency and banking crises. *Journal of Economic Surveys*, 18(7):293–320.

Breuer, J. B., McNown, R., and Wallace, M. (2002). Series-specific unit root tests with panel data. *Oxford Bulletin of Economics and Statistics*, 64(5):527–546.

Brooks, C. (2008). *Introductory Econometrics for Finance*. Cambridge, UK: Cambridge University Press, 2nd edition.

Buiter, W. H. (1997). Aspects of fiscal performance in some transition economies under fund-supported programs. IMF Working Papers 97/31, International Monetary Fund.

Buiter, W. H. and Patel, U. R. (1992). Debt, deficits, and inflation: An application to the public finances of India. *Journal of Public Economics*, 47(2):171–205.

Buiter, W. H., Persson, T., and Minford, P. (1985). A guide to public sector debt and deficits. *Economic Policy*, 1(1):13–79.

Buiter, W. H. and Sibert, A. C. (2004). Deflationary bubbles. NBER Working Papers 10642, National Bureau of Economic Research.

Burnside, C. (2005). Some tools for fiscal sustainability analysis. In Burnside, C., editor, *Fiscal Sustainability in Theory and Practice — A Handbook*, pages 35–80. Washington, DC: The International Bank for Reconstruction and Development / The World Bank.

Bussiére, M., Fratzscher, M., and Müller, G. J. (2010). Productivity shocks, budget deficits and the current account. *Journal of International Money and Finance*, 29(8):1562–1579.

Caballero, R. J. (1990). Consumption puzzles and precautionary savings. *Journal of Monetary Economics*, 25(1):113–136.

Caballero, R. J., Farhi, E., and Gourinchas, P.-O. (2008a). An equilibrium model of "global imbalances" and low interest rates. *American Economic Review*, 98(1):358–393.

Caballero, R. J., Farhi, E., and Gourinchas, P.-O. (2008b). Financial crash, commodity prices and global imbalances. NBER Working Papers 14521, National Bureau of Economic Research.

Caballero, R. J. and Krishnamurthy, A. (2001). International liquidity illusion: On the risks of sterilization. NBER Working Papers 8141, National Bureau of Economic Research.

Calderon, C., Chong, A., and Loayza, N. (2002). Determinants of current account deficits in developing countries. *The B.E. Journal of Macroeconomics*, 2(1).

Calderon, C., Loayza, N., and Serven, L. (2000). External sustainability: A stock equilibrium perspective. Policy Research Working Papers 2281, The World Bank.

Callen, T. and Cashin, P. (1999). Assessing external sustainability in India. IMF Working Papers 99/181, International Monetary Fund.

Camarero, M., Carrion-i-Silvestre, J. L., and Tamarit, C. (2013). Global imbalances and the intertemporal external budget constraint: A multicointegration approach. *Journal of Banking & Finance*, In press.

Campa, J. M. and Gavilan, A. (2011). Current accounts in the Euro Area: An intertemporal approach. *Journal of International Money and Finance*, 30(1):205–228.

Campbell, J. Y. (1987). Does saving anticipate declining labor income? An alternative test of the permanent income hypothesis. *Econometrica*, 55(6):1249–1273.

Campbell, J. Y., Lo, A. W., and MacKinlay, A. C. (1997). *The econometrics of financial markets*. Princeton, NJ: Princeton University Press.

Campbell, J. Y. and Mankiw, N. G. (1990). Consumption, income, and interest rates: Reinterpreting the time series evidence. NBER Working Papers 2924, National Bureau of Economic Research.

Campbell, J. Y. and Perron, P. (1991). Pitfalls and opportunities: What macroeconomists should know about unit roots. NBER Technical Working Papers 0100, National Bureau of Economic Research.

Campbell, J. Y. and Shiller, R. J. (1987). Cointegration and tests of present value models. *Journal of Political Economy*, 95(5):1062–1088.

Campbell, J. Y. and Shiller, R. J. (1988). The dividend-price ratio and expectations of future dividends and discount factors. *Review of Financial Studies*, 1(3):195–228.

Campbell, J. Y. and Shiller, R. J. (1989). The dividend ratio model and small sample bias: A Monte Carlo study. *Economics Letters*, 29(4):325–331.

Caner, M., Grennes, T., and Koehler-Geib, F. (2010). Finding the tipping point — When sovereign debt turns bad. Policy Research Working Papers 5391, The World Bank.

Caner, M. and Hansen, B. E. (2001). Threshold autoregression with a unit root. *Econometrica*, 69(6):1555–1596.

Caner, M. and Kilian, L. (2001). Size distortions of tests of the null hypothesis of stationarity: Evidence and implications for the PPP debate. *Journal of International Money and Finance*, 20(5):639–657.

Canzoneri, M. B., Cumby, R. E., and Diba, B. T. (2001). Is the price level determined by the needs of fiscal solvency? *American Economic Review*, 91(5):1221–1238.

Carkovic, M. and Levine, R. (2005). Does foreign direct investment accelerate economic growth? In Moran, T. H., Graham, E. M., and Blomström, M., editors, *Does Foreign Direct Investment Promote Development? New Methods, Outcomes and Policy Approaches*, pages 195–220. Washington, DC: Peterson Institute for International Economics, Center for Global Development.

Carranza, L. (2002). Current account sustainability. In Mohsin S. Khan, Saleh M. Nsouli, C.-H. W., editor, *Macroeconomic management: Programs and policies*, pages 98–138. Washington, DC: IMF Institute.

Carrion-i-Silvestre, J. L. and Sansó, A. (2006). Testing the null of cointegration with structural breaks. *Oxford Bulletin of Economics and Statistics*, 68(5):623–646.

Cashin, P. and McDermott, C. J. (1998). Are Australia's current account deficits excessive? *The Economic Record*, 74(227):346–361.

Cashin, P. and McDermott, C. J. (2002). Intertemporal consumption smoothing and capital mobility: Evidence from Australia. *Australian Economic Papers*, 41(1):82–98.

Cass, D. (1965). Optimum growth in an aggregative model of capital accumulation. *The Review of Economic Studies*, 32(3):pp. 233–240.

Cass, D. (1972). On capital overaccumulation in the aggregative, neoclassical model of economic growth: A complete characterization. *Journal of Economic Theory*, 4(2):200–223.

Catão, L. A. V. and Milesi-Ferretti, G. M. (2013). External liabilities and crises. IMF Working Papers 13/113, International Monetary Fund.

Cavaliere, G. (2005). Limited time series with a unit root. *Econometric Theory*, 21(05):907–945.

Cavaliere, G. and Xu, F. (2012). Testing for unit roots in bounded time series. *Journal of Econometrics*, forthcoming.

Çelik, Ş. (2012). Theoretical and empirical review of asset pricing models: A structural synthesis. *International Journal of Economics and Financial Issues*, 2(2):141–178.

Cerrato, M., de Peretti, C., Larsson, R., and Sarantis, N. (2011). A nonlinear panel unit root test under cross section dependence. Working Papers 2011_08, Business School — Economics, University of Glasgow.

Chambers, M. J. (1996). Fractional integration, trend stationarity and difference stationarity: Evidence from some U.K. macroeconomic time series. *Economics Letters*, 50(1):19–24.

Chang, R. and Velasco, A. (1999). Liquidity crises in emerging markets: Theory and policy. NBER Working Papers 7272, National Bureau of Economic Research.

Cheung, Y.-W. and Lai, K. S. (1993). Finite-sample sizes of Johansen's likelihood ratio tests for conintegration. *Oxford Bulletin of Economics and Statistics*, 55(3):313–328.

Cheung, Y.-W. and Lai, K. S. (1997). Bandwidth selection, prewhitening, and the power of the Phillips-Perron test. *Econometric Theory*, 13:679–691.

Chiappori, P. and Paiella, M. (2011). Relative risk aversion is constant: Evidence from panel data. *Journal of the European Economic Association*, 9(6):1021–1052.

Chinn, M. D. and Ito, H. (2007). Current account balances, financial development and institutions: Assaying the world of "saving glut". *Journal of International Money and Finance*, 26(4):546–569.

Chinn, M. D. and Prasad, E. S. (2003). Medium-term determinants of current accounts in industrial and developing countries: An empirical exploration. *Journal of International Economics*, 59(1):47–76.

Choi, I. (1992). Effects of data aggregation on the power of tests for a unit root: A simulation study. *Economics Letters*, 40(4):397–401.

Choi, I. (2001). Unit root tests for panel data. *Journal of International Money and Finance*, 20(2):249–272.

Choi, I. and Chung, B. S. (1995). Sampling frequency and the power of tests for a unit root: A simulation study. *Economics Letters*, 49(2):131–136.

Chortareas, G. and Kapetanios, G. (2009). Getting PPP right: Identifying mean-reverting real exchange rates in panels. *Journal of Banking & Finance*, 33(2):390–404.

Chortareas, G., Kapetanios, G., and Uctum, M. (2004). An investigation of current account solvency in Latin America using non linear nonstationarity tests. *Studies in Nonlinear Dynamics & Econometrics*, 8(1):1–17.

Chow, G. (1988). Rational versus adaptive expectations in present value models. Papers 328, Princeton, Department of Economics, Econometric Research Program.

Chow, G. (2011). Usefulness of adaptive and rational expectations in economics. Working Papers 1334, Princeton University, Department of Economics, Center for Economic Policy Studies.

Christiano, L. J. (1992). Searching for a break in GNP. *Journal of Business & Economic Statistics*, 10(3):237–250.

Christopoulos, D. and León-Ledesma, M. (2004). Current account sustainability in the US: What do we really know about it? Studies in Economics 0412, Department of Economics, University of Kent.

Christopoulos, D. and León-Ledesma, M. (2010). Current account sustainability in the US: What did we really know about it? *Journal of International Money and Finance*, 29(3):442–459.

Chu, H.-P., Chang, T., Chang, H.-L., Su, C.-W., and Yuan, Y. (2007). Mean reversion in the current account of forty-eight African countries: Evidence from the panel SURADF test. *Physica A*, 384(2007):485–492.

Clarida, R. H., Goretti, M., and Taylor, M. P. (2006). Are there thresholds of current account adjustment in the G7? NBER Working Papers 12193, National Bureau of Economic Research.

Cline, W. R. (1995). *International debt reexamined.* Number 46. Washington, DC: Institute for International Economics.

Coakley, J. and Kulasi, F. (1997). Cointegration of long span saving and investment. *Economics Letters*, 54(1):1–6.

Coakley, J., Kulasi, F., and Smith, R. (1998). The Feldstein-Horioka puzzle and capital mobility: A review. *International Journal of Finance & Economics*, 3(2):169–188.

Cochrane, J. H. (1991). A critique of the application of unit root tests. *Journal of Economic Dynamics and Control*, 15(2):275–284.

Cohen, D. (1985). How to evaluate the solvency of an indebted nation. *Economic Policy*, 1(1):139–167.

Cohen, D. (2001). The HIPC initiative: True and false promises. *International Finance*, 4(3):363–380.

Conlisk, J. (1996). Why bounded rationality? *Journal of Economic Literature*, 34(2):669–700.

Copeland, T. E., Weston, J. F., and Shastri, K. (2005). *Financial Theory and Corporate Policy.* Boston, MA [etc.]: Pearson Addison Wesley, 4th edition.

Corbin, A. (2004). Capital mobility and adjustment of the current account imbalances: A bounds testing approach to cointegration in 12 countries (1880–2001). *International Journal of Finance & Economics*, 9(3):257–276.

Corsetti, G., Pesenti, P., and Roubini, N. (1999). What caused the Asian currency and financial crisis? *Japan and the World Economy*, 11(3):305–373.

Corsetti, G. and Roubini, N. (1991). Fiscal deficits, public debt, and government solvency: Evidence from OECD countries. *Journal of the Japanese and International Economies*, 5(4):354–380.

Coudert, V., Couharde, C., and Mignon, V. (2013). On currency misalignments within the euro area. *Review of International Economics*, 21(1):35–48.

Creedon, C., Fitzpatrick, T., and Gaffney, E. (2012). Ireland's external debt: Economic and statistical realities. Economic Letters 12/EL/12, Central Bank of Ireland.

Croke, H., Kamin, S. B., and Leduc, S. (2005). Financial market developments and economic activity during current account adjustments in industrial economies. International Finance Discussion Papers 827, Board of Governors of the Federal Reserve System (U.S.).

Cuestas, J. C. (2013). The current account sustainability of European transition economies. *Journal of Common Market Studies*, 51(2):232–245.

Damodaran, A. (2007). *Strategic Risk Taking: A Framework for Risk Management (paperback).* Upper Saddle River, NJ: Pearson Prentice Hall, 1st edition.

Darku, A. B. (2010). Consumption smoothing, capital controls and the current account in Ghana. *Applied Economics*, 42(20):2601–2616.

Davies, R. B. (1987). Hypothesis testing when a nuisance parameter is present only under the alternative. *Biometrika*, 74(1):33–43.

De Vita, G. and Abbott, A. (2002). Are saving and investment cointegrated? An ARDL bounds testing approach. *Economics Letters*, 77(2):293–299.

Debelle, G. and Galati, G. (2007). Current account adjustment and capital flows. *Review of International Economics*, 15(5):989–1013.

Debreu, G. (1959). *Theory of value: an axiomatic analysis of economic equilibrium.* New Haven, CT: Yale University Press.

Dell'Ariccia, G., Zettelmeyer, J., and Schnabel, I. (2002). Moral hazard and international crisis lending: A test. IMF Working Papers 02/181, International Monetary Fund.

Demetrescu, M., Hassler, U., and Tarcolea, A.-I. (2006). Combining significance of correlated statistics with application to panel data. *Oxford Bulletin of Economics and Statistics*, 68(5):647–663.

Detragiache, E. and Spilimbergo, A. (2001). Crises and liquidity — evidence and interpretation. IMF Working Papers 01/2, International Monetary Fund.

Devereux, M. B. and Sutherland, A. (2007). Solving for country portfolios in open economy macro models. IMF Working Papers 07/284, International Monetary Fund.

Devereux, M. B. and Sutherland, A. (2010). Country portfolio dynamics. *Journal of Economic Dynamics and Control*, 34(7):1325–1342.

Diamond, P. A. (1965). National debt in a neoclassical growth model. *American Economic Review*, 55(5):1126–1150.

Dias, D. A., Richmond, C. J., and Wright, M. L. (2011). The stock of external sovereign debt: Can we take the data at "face value"? NBER Working Papers 17551, National Bureau of Economic Research.

Diba, B. T. and Grossman, H. I. (1984). Rational bubbles in the price of gold. NBER Working Papers 1300, National Bureau of Economic Research.

Dickey, D. A., Bell, W. R., and Miller, R. B. (1986). Unit roots in time series models: Tests and implications. *The American Statistician*, 40(1):pp. 12–26.

Dickey, D. A. and Fuller, W. A. (1979). Distribution of the estimators for autoregressive time series with a unit root. *Journal of the American Statistical Association*, 74(366):427–431.

Didier, T. and Lowenkron, A. (2009). The current account as a dynamic portfolio choice problem. Policy Research Working Papers 4861, The World Bank.

Doisy, N. and Hervé, K. (2003). Les déficits courants des PECO: Quelles implications pour leur entrée dans l'union Européenne et la zone euro? *Économie internationale*, 93:59–88.

Dooley, M. P., Folkerts-Landau, D., and Garber, P. (2003). An essay on the revived Bretton Woods system. NBER Working Papers 9971, National Bureau of Economic Research.

Dooley, M. P., Folkerts-Landau, D., and Garber, P. (2004a). Direct investment, rising real wages and the absorption of excess labor in the periphery. NBER Working Papers 10626, National Bureau of Economic Research.

Dooley, M. P., Folkerts-Landau, D., and Garber, P. (2004b). The US current account deficit and economic development: Collateral for a total return swap. NBER Working Papers 10727, National Bureau of Economic Research.

Dreher, A. (2004). Does the IMF cause moral hazard? A critical review of the evidence. International Finance 0402003, EconWPA.

Dreher, A., Marchesi, S., and Vreeland, J. R. (2008). The political economy of IMF forecasts. *Public Choice*, 137(1-2):145–171.

Drèze, J. H. and Modigliani, F. (1972). Consumption decisions under uncertainty. *Journal of Economic Theory*, 5(3):308–335.

Duesenberry, J. (1952). *Income, Saving, and the Theory of Consumer Behavior.* Cambridge, MA: Harvard Univ. Press.

Duffie, D. (2003). Intertemporal asset pricing theory. In Constantinides, G., Harris, M., and Stulz, R. M., editors, *Handbook of the Economics of Finance*, volume 1 of *Handbook of the Economics of Finance*, chapter 11, pages 639–742. Amsterdam, NL: Elsevier Science.

Dülger, F. and Özdemir, Z. A. (2005). Current account sustainability in seven developed countries. *Journal of Economic and Social Research*, 7(2):47–80.

Dunaway, S. (2009). *Global Imbalances and the Financial Crisis (Council Special Report No. 44).* New York, NY: Council on Foreign Relations.

Dunn, K. B. and Singleton, K. J. (1986). Modeling the term structure of interest rates under non-separable utility and durability of goods. *Journal of Financial Economics*, 17(1):27–55.

Durdu, C. B., Mendoza, E. G., and Terrones, M. E. (2010). On the solvency of nations: Are global imbalances consistent with intertemporal budget constraints? IMF Working Papers 10/50, International Monetary Fund.

Dynan, K. E. (2000). Habit formation in consumer preferences: Evidence from panel data. *American Economic Review*, 90(3):391–406.

ECB (2007). Adjustment of global imbalances in a financially integrating world. *European Central Bank Monthly Bulletin*, August:61–74.

Edwards, S. (2006). The U.S. current account deficit: Gradual correction or abrupt adjustment? *Journal of Policy Modeling*, 28(6):629–643.

Edwards, S. (2007). On current account surpluses and the correction of global imbalances. NBER Working Papers 12904, National Bureau of Economic Research.

Edwards, S., Steiner, R., and Losada, F. (1996). Capital inflows, the real exchange rate and the Mexican crisis of 1994. In Sautter, H. and Schinke, R., editors, *Stabilization and reforms in Latin America: Where do we stand? (Göttinger Studien zur Entwicklungsokonomik)*, pages 69–118. Frankfurt am Main: Vervuert/Iberamericana.

Eichengreen, B. (2004). Global imbalances and the lessons of Bretton Woods. NBER Working Papers 10497, National Bureau of Economic Research.

Eichengreen, B. and Adalet, M. (2005). Current account reversals: Always a problem? NBER Working Papers 11634, National Bureau of Economic Research.

Eickmeier, S., Gambacorta, L., and Hofmann, B. (2013). Understanding global liquidity. BIS Working Papers 402, Bank for International Settlements.

Elliott, G. (1998). On the robustness of cointegration methods when regressors almost have unit roots. *Econometrica*, 66(1):149–158.

Elliott, G., Rothenberg, T. J., and Stock, J. H. (1996). Efficient tests for an autoregressive unit root. *Econometrica*, 64(4):813–836.

ELSTAT (2013). Annual National Accounts. The Hellenic Statistical Authority (ELSTAT). http://www.statistics.gr/portal/page/portal/ESYE/PAGE-themes?p_param=A0702, retrieved on 2013-05-31.

Enders, W. (2004). *Applied Econometric Time Series*. Hoboken, NJ: John Wiley & Sons, 2nd edition.

Enders, W. and Granger, C. W. J. (1998). Unit-root tests and asymmetric adjustment with an example using the term structure of interest rates. *Journal of Business & Economic Statistics*, 16(3):304–311.

Engle, R. F. and Granger, C. W. J. (1987). Co-integration and error correction: Representation, estimation, and testing. *Econometrica*, 55(2):251–76.

Engle, R. F. and Yoo, B. S. (1987). Forecasting and testing in co-integrated systems. *Journal of Econometrics*, 35(1):143–159.

Engsted, T., Gonzalo, J., and Haldrup, N. (1997). Testing for multicointegration. *Economics Letters*, 56(3):259–266.

Essl, S. and Stiglbauer, A. (2011). Prevention and correction of macroeconomic imbalances: The Excessive Imbalances Procedure. *Monetary Policy & the Economy*, Q4/11:99–113.

Essl, S. and Stiglbauer, A. (2012). Global banking glut and loan risk premium. *IMF Economic Review*, 60(2):155–192.

European Commission (2012a). Macroeconomic imbalances — Cyprus. Occasional Papers 101, European Commission.

European Commission (2012b). Report from the Commission to the European Parliament, the Council, the European Central Bank, the European Economic and Social Committee, the Committee of the Regions and the European Investment Bank on the Alert Mechanism Report 2013. Prepared in accordance with Articles 3 and 4 of the Regulation on the prevention and correction of macroeconomic imbalances COM(2012) 751 final, European Commission.

European Commission (2012c). Scoreboard for the surveillance of macroeconomic imbalances. Occasional Papers 92, European Commission.

European Commission (2013). Macroeconomic imbalances — Italy 2013. Occasional Papers 138, European Commission.

Evans, G. W. (1991). Pitfalls in testing for explosive bubbles in asset prices. *American Economic Review*, 81(4):922–930.

Fair, R. C. and Jaffee, D. M. (1972). Methods of estimation for markets in disequilibrium. *Econometrica*, 40(3):497–514.

Fattouh, B. (2005). Capital mobility and sustainability: Evidence from U.S. current account data. *Empirical Economics*, 30(1):245–253.

Feenstra, R. C. and Taylor, A. M. (2008). *International Macroeconomics*. New York, NY: Worth Publishers.

Feige, E. L. and Pearce, D. K. (1976). Economically rational expectations: Are innovations in the rate of inflation independent of innovations in measures of monetary and fiscal policy? *Journal of Political Economy*, 84(3):499–522.

Feldstein, M. and Horioka, C. (1980). Domestic saving and international capital flows. *Economic Journal*, 90(358):314–329.

Feroli, M. (2003). Capital flows among the G-7 nations: A demographic perspective. Finance and Economics Discussion Series 2003-54, Board of Governors of the Federal Reserve System (U.S.).

Ferrero, A. (2010). A structural decomposition of the U.S. trade balance: Productivity, demographics and fiscal policy. *Journal of Monetary Economics*, 57(4):478–490.

Ferson, W. E. and Constantinides, G. M. (1991). Habit persistence and durability in aggregate consumption: Empirical tests. *Journal of Financial Economics*, 29(2):199–240.

Fiebig, D. G. (2003). Seemingly unrelated regression. In Baltagi, B. H., editor, *A companion to theoretical econometrics*, pages 101–121. Oxford, UK: Blackwell Publishing.

Fischer, S. and Easterly, W. (1990). The economics of the government budget constraint. *World Bank Research Observer*, 5(2):127–142.

Fisher, S. (1980). On activist monetary policy with rational expectations. In Fisher, S., editor, *Rational Expectations and Economic Policy*, chapter 7. Chicago, Il: The University of Chicago Press.

Fisher, S. R. A. (1930). *The Theory of Interest*. New York, NY: Macmillan.

Fisher, S. R. A. (1932). *Statistical Methods for Research Workers*. Edinburgh, UK: Oliver & Boyd.

Fleming, M. J. and Garbade, K. D. (2004). Repurchase agreements with negative interest rates. *Federal Reserve Bank of New York: Current Issues in Economics and Finance*, 10(5):1–7.

Flood, M. D. (1991). An introduction to complete markets. *Federal Reserve Bank of St. Louis. Review*, Mar:32–57.

Flood, R. P. and Garber, P. M. (1980). Market fundamentals versus price-level bubbles: The first tests. *Journal of Political Economy*, 88(4):745–770.

Flood, R. P. and Garber, P. M. (1984). Collapsing exchange-rate regimes: Some linear examples. *Journal of International Economics*, 17(1-2):1–13.

Flood, R. P., Garber, P. M., and Kramer, C. (1996). Collapsing exchange rate regimes: Another linear example. *Journal of International Economics*, 41(3–4):223–234.

Forbes, K. J. (2010). Why do foreigners invest in the United States? *Journal of International Economics*, 80(1):3–21.

Ford, G. S., Jackson, J. D., and Kline, A. D. (2006). Misleading inferences from panel unit root tests: a comment. *Review of International Economics*, 14(3):508–511.

Fountas, S. and Wu, J.-L. (1999). Are the U.S. current account deficits really sustainable? *International Economic Journal*, 13(3):51–58.

Fox, R. and Taqqu, M. S. (1986). Large-sample properties of parameter estimates for strongly dependent stationary Gaussian time series. *The Annals of Statistics*, 14:517–532.

Frankel, J. (1992). Measuring international capital mobility: A review. *American Economic Review*, 82(2):197–202.

Frankel, J. (2011). Over-optimism in forecasts by official budget agencies and its implications. *Oxford Review of Economic Policy*, 27(4):536–562.

Frankel, J. and Saravelos, G. (2012). Can leading indicators assess country vulnerability? Evidence from the 2008–09 global financial crisis. *Journal of International Economics*, 87(2):216–231.

Frederick, S., Loewenstein, G., and O'Donoghue, T. (2002). Time discounting and time preference: A critical review. *Journal of Economic Literature*, 40(2):351–401.

French, K. R. and Poterba, J. M. (1991). Investor diversification and international equity markets. *American Economic Review*, 81(2):222–226.

Frenkel, J. A. (1974). The demand for international reserves by developed and less-developed countries. *Economica, New Series*, 41(161):14–24.

Freund, C. (2000). Current account adjustment in industrialized countries. International Finance Discussion Paper 692, Board of Governors of the Federal Reserve System (U.S.).

Freund, C. (2005). Current account adjustment in industrial countries. *Journal of International Money and Finance*, 24(8):1278–1298.

Freund, C. and Warnock, F. (2005). Current account deficits in industrial countries: The bigger they are, the harder they fall? NBER Working Papers 11823, National Bureau of Economic Research.

Friedman, M. (1957). *A theory of the consumption function*. General series / National Bureau of Economic Research. Princeton, NJ: Princeton University Press.

Friend, I. and Blume, M. E. (1975). The demand for risky assets. *American Economic Review*, 65(5):900–922.

Fry, M. J. (1996). How foreign direct investment in Pacific Asia improves the current account. *Journal of Asian Economics*, 7(3):459–486.

Fudenberg, D. (2006). Advancing beyond "advances in behavioral economics". *Journal of Economic Literature*, 44(3):694–711.

Fuller, W. A. (1976). *Introduction to statistical time series*. New York, NY: John Wiley & Sons.

Gammeltoft, P. (2003). Remittances and other financial flows to developing countries. In Hear, N. V. and Sörensen, N. N., editors, *The Migration-Development Nexus*, pages 101–132. Genf: International Organization for Migration and New York, NY: United Nations.

Gandolfo, G. (2001). *International Finance and Open-Economy Macroeconomics*. Berlin [etc.]: Springer.

Gaspard, M. (2004). Individual behaviors and collective welfare: Ramsey's microfoundations of macroequilibrium. The Eighth Annual Conference of the European Society for the History of Economic Thought, University of Treviso, Italy, 26–29 February 2004.

Gaulier, G. and Vicard, V. (2012). Current account imbalances in the euro area: Competitiveness or demand shock? *Quarterly selection of articles — Bulletin de la Banque de France*, 27:5–26.

Geanakoplos, J. (1990). An introduction to general equilibrium with incomplete asset markets. *Journal of Mathematical Economics*, 19(1–2):1–38.

Ghosh, A. R. (1995). International capital mobility amongst the major industrialised countries: Too little or too much? *Economic Journal*, 105(428):107–128.

Ghosh, A. R. and Ostry, J. D. (1995). The current account in developing countries: A perspective from the consumption-smoothing approach. *World Bank Economic Review*, 9(2):305–33 3.

Ghysels, E. and Perron, P. (1993). The effect of seasonal adjustment filters on tests for a unit root. *Journal of Econometrics*, 55(1–2):57–98.

Ginsburgh, V. and Keyzer, M. (2002). *The Structure of Applied General Equilibrium Models*. Cambidge, MA: MIT Press.

Giraitis, L., Kokoszka, P., Leipus, R., and Teyssiere, G. (2003). Rescaled variance and related tests for long memory in volatility and levels. *Journal of Econometrics*, 112(2):265–294.

Glick, R. and Hutchison, M. (2011). Currency crises. Working Papers 2011–22, Federal Reserve Bank of San Francisco.

Glick, R. and Rogoff, K. (1995). Global versus country-specific productivity shocks and the current account. *Journal of Monetary Economics*, 35(1):159–192.

Goldstein, M. (2003). Debt sustainability, Brazil, and the IMF. Working Papers WP03–1, Peterson Institute for International Economics.

Goldstein, M. (2010). Confronting asset bubbles, too big to fail, and beggar-thy-neighbor exchange rate policies. Policy Briefs PB10–3, Peterson Institute for International Economics.

Gourinchas, P.-O. and Parker, J. A. (2001). The empirical importance of precautionary saving. *American Economic Review*, 91(2):406–412.

Gourinchas, P.-O. and Rey, H. (2007a). From world banker to world venture capitalist: U.S. external adjustment and the exorbitant privilege. In Clarida, R., editor, *G7 Current Account Imbalances: Sustainability and Adjustment*, pages 11–55. Chicago, IL: University of Chicago Press.

Gourinchas, P.-O. and Rey, H. (2007b). International financial adjustment. *Journal of Political Economy*, 115(4):665–703.

Granger, C. W. J. (1969). Investigating causal relations by econometric models and cross-spectral methods. *Econometrica*, 37(3):424–438.

Granger, C. W. J. and Joyeux, R. (1980). An introduction to long-memory time series models and fractional differencing. *Journal of Time Series Analysis*, 1(1):15–29.

Granger, C. W. J. and Lee, T. H. (1989). Investigation of production, sales and inventory relationships using multicointegration and non-symmetric error correction models. *Journal of Applied Econometrics*, 4(S1):S145–S159.

Granger, C. W. J. and Newbold, P. (1974). Spurious regressions in econometrics. *Journal of Econometrics*, 2(2):111–120.

Granger, C. W. J. and Teräsvirta, T. (1993). *Modelling Nonlinear Economic Relationships — Advanced Texts in Econometrics*. Oxford, UK: Oxford University Press.

Gregory, A. W. (1994). Testing for cointegration in linear quadratic models. *Journal of Business & Economic Statistics*, 12(3):347–360.

Gregory, A. W. and Hansen, B. E. (1996). Residual-based tests for cointegration in models with regime shifts. *Journal of Econometrics*, 70(1):99–126.

Gregory, A. W., Nason, J. M., and Watt, D. G. (1996). Testing for structural breaks in cointegrated relationships. *Journal of Econometrics*, 71(1–2):321–341.

Gros, D. (2011). External versus domestic debt in the euro crisis? CEPS Policy Briefs 243, Centre for European Policy Studies.

Gros, D. (2012). Macroeconomic imbalances in the euro area: Symptom or cause of the crisis? CEPS Policy Briefs 266, Centre for European Policy Studies.

Grossman, S. J. and Hart, O. D. (1979). A theory of competitive equilibrium in stock market economies. *Econometrica*, 47(2):293–329.

Grubel, H. G. (1971). The demand for international reserves: A critical review of the literature. *Journal of Economic Literature*, 9(4):1148–1166.

Gruber, J. W. (2002). Productivity shocks, habits, and the current account. International Finance Discussion Papers 733, Board of Governors of the Federal Reserve System (U.S.).

Gruber, J. W. (2004). A present value test of habits and the current account. *Journal of Monetary Economics*, 51(7):1495–1507.

Guariglia, A. and Rossi, M. (2002). Consumption, habit formation, and precautionary saving: Evidence from the British Household Panel Survey. *Oxford Economic Papers*, 54(1):1–19.

Gulley, O. D. (1992). Are saving and investment cointegrated?: Another look at the data. *Economics Letters*, 39(1):55–58.

Gundlach, E. and Sinn, S. (1992). Unit root tests of the current account balance: Implications for international capital mobility. *Applied Economics*, 24(6):617–625.

Guo, K. and Jin, K. (2009). Composition and growth effects of the current account: A synthesized portfolio view. *Journal of International Economics*, 79(1):31–41.

Haan, J. and Siermann, C. (1994). Saving, investment, and capital mobility: A comment on Leachman. *Open Economies Review*, 5(1):5–17.

Hadri, K. (2000). Testing for stationarity in heterogeneous panel data. *Econometrics Journal*, 3(2):148–161.

Hakkio, C. S. and Rush, M. (1991a). Cointegration: How short is the long run? *Journal of International Money and Finance*, 10(4):571–581.

Hakkio, C. S. and Rush, M. (1991b). Is the budget deficit "too large?". *Economic Inquiry*, 29(3):429–445.

Hall, A. (1994). Testing for a unit root in time series with pretest data-based model selection. *Journal of Business & Economic Statistics*, 12(4):461–470.

Hall, R. E. (1978). Stochastic implications of the life cycle-permanent income hypothesis: Theory and evidence. *Journal of Political Economy*, 86(6):971–987.

Hall, S. G., Psaradakis, Z., and Sola, M. (1999). Detecting periodically collapsing bubbles: A Markov-Switching unit root test. *Journal of Applied Econometrics*, 14(2):143–154.

Hamilton, J. D. (1989). A new approach to the economic analysis of nonstationary time series and the business cycle. *Econometrica*, 57(2):357–384.

Hamilton, J. D. (1994). *Time Series Analysis*. Princeton, NJ: Princeton University Press.

Hamilton, J. D. and Flavin, M. A. (1986). On the limitations of government borrowing: A framework for empirical testing. *American Economic Review*, 76(4):808–819.

Hamilton, J. D. and Whiteman, C. H. (1985). The observable implications of self-fulfilling expectations. *Journal of Monetary Economics*, 16(3):353–373.

Hamori, S. (2009). The sustainability of trade accounts of the G-7 countries. *Applied Economics Letters*, 16(17):1691–1694.

Hansen, B. E. (1992). Tests for parameter instability in regressions with I(1) processes. *Journal of Business & Economic Statistics*, 10(3):321–335.

Hansen, B. E. (1996). Inference when a nuisance parameter is not identified under the null hypothesis. *Econometrica*, 64(2):413–430.

Hansen, B. E. (1997). Inference in TAR Models. *Studies in Nonlinear Dynamics & Econometrics*, 2(1):1–14.

Hansen, B. E. (1999). Threshold effects in non-dynamic panels: Estimation, testing, and inference. *Journal of Econometrics*, 93(2):345–368.

Hansen, H. and Johansen, S. (1999). Some tests for parameter constancy in cointegrated VAR-models. *Econometrics Journal*, 2(2):306–333.

Hansen, L. P. and Sargent, T. J. (1980). Formulating and estimating dynamic linear rational expectations models. *Journal of Economic Dynamics and Control*, 2(2):7–46.

Hansen, L. P. and Sargent, T. J. (1991). Two difficulties in interpreting vector autoregressions. In Hansen, L. P. and Sargent, T. J., editors, *Rational Expectations Econometrics*, pages 77–119. Boulder, CO: Westview Press.

Harms, P. (2008). *Internationale Makroökonomik*. Tübingen: Mohr Siebeck.

Harris, R. D. F. and Tzavalis, E. (1999). Inference for unit roots in dynamic panels where the time dimension is fixed. *Journal of Econometrics*, 91(2):201–226.

Harrison, A. (1995). Determinants and effects of direct foreign investment in Cote d'Ivoire, Morocco, and Venezuela. MPRA Paper 36594, University Library of Munich, Germany.

Harrod, R. F. (1933). *International economics*. New York, NY: Cambridge University Press. Cambridge Economics Handbooks.

Hartog, J., Ferrer-i-Carbonell, A., and Jonker, N. (2002). Linking measured risk aversion to individual characteristics. *Kyklos*, 55(1):3–26.

Hartung, J. (1999). A note on combining dependent tests of significance. *Biometrical Journal*, 41(7):849–855.

Hassler, U. and Wolters, J. (1994). On the power of unit root tests against fractional alternatives. *Economics Letters*, 45(1):1–5.

Haug, A. A. (1991). Cointegration and government borrowing constraints: Evidence for the United States. *Journal of Business & Economic Statistics*, 9(1):97–101.

Haug, A. A. (2002). Temporal aggregation and the power of cointegration tests: A Monte Carlo study. *Oxford Bulletin of Economics and Statistics*, 64(4):399–412.

Hausman, J. A. (1978). Specification tests in econometrics. *Econometrica*, 46(6):1251–1271.

Hausmann, R. and Sturzenegger, F. (2006). Why the US current account deficit is sustainable. *International Finance*, 9(2):223–240.

Hausmann, R. and Sturzenegger, F. (2007). The missing dark matter in the wealth of nations and its implications for global imbalances. *Economic Policy*, 22:469–518.

Hayashi, F. (1982). Tobin's marginal q and average q: A neoclassical interpretation. *Econometrica*, 50(1):213–224.

Hegerty, S. W., Harvey, H., and Bahmani-Oskooee, M. (2013). Empirical tests of the Marshall-Lerner condition: A literature review. *Journal of Economic Studies*, 40(3).

Heien, D. and Durham, C. (1991). A test of the habit formation hypothesis using household data. *The Review of Economics and Statistics*, 73(2):189–199.

Heller, H. R. (1966). Optimal international reserves. *The Economic Journal*, 76(302):296–311.

Hendry, D. F. (1995). *Dynamic econometrics*. Oxford, UK: Oxford University Press.

Hermes, N. and Lensink, R. (2003). Foreign direct investment, financial development and economic growth. *Journal of Development Studies*, 40(1):142–163.

Herndon, T., Ash, M., and Pollin, R. (2013). Does high public debt consistently stifle economic growth? A critique of Reinhart and Rogoff. Working papers, Political Economy Research Institute of Massachusetts Amherst.

Herwartz, H. and Xu, F. (2008). Reviewing the sustainability & stationarity of current account imbalances with tests for bounded integration. *Manchester School*, 76(3):267–278.

Herzberg, F. and Herzberg, A. (2013). Testing fiscal sustainability via strong convergence of Gaussian random variables. *Communications in Statistics – Theory and Methods*, 42(18):2535–2542.

Herzer, D. and Nowak-Lehmann, F. (2006). Is there a long-run relationship between exports and imports in Chile? *Applied Economics Letters*, 13(15):981–986.

Higgins, M. and Klitgaard, T. (2004). Reserve accumulation: Implications for global capital flows and financial markets. *Current Issues in Economics and Finance*, 10(10):1–8.

Higgins, M., Klitgaard, T., and Lerman, R. (2006). Reserve accumulation: Implications for global capital flows and financial markets. *Current Issues in Economics and Finance*, 12(9):1–7.

Higgins, M., Klitgaard, T., and Tille, C. (2007). Borrowing without debt? Understanding the U.S. international investment position. *Business Economics*, 42(1):17–27.

Hjertholm, P. (2003). Theoretical and empirical foundations of HIPC debt sustainability targets. *Journal of Development Studies*, 39(6):67–100.

Hlouskova, J. and Wagner, M. (2006). The performance of panel unit root and stationarity tests: Results from a large scale simulation study. *Econometric Reviews*, 25(1):85–116.

Hoffmann, J. (2007). *Bestimmungsfaktoren, Tragfähigkeit und Dynamik internationaler Leistungsbilanzungleichgewichte.* Hamburg: Verlag Dr. Kovač.

Hoffmann, M. (1999). The Feldstein-Horioka puzzle and a new measure of international capital mobility. Discussion Papers in Economics and Econometrics 9916, Economics Division, School of Social Sciences, University of Southampton.

Hoffmann, M. (2001). The relative dynamics of investment and the current acccunt in the G7-economies. *The Economic Journal*, 111(471):C148–C163.

Holman, J. A. (2001). Is the large U.S. current account deficit sustainable? *Economic Review*, Q I:5–23.

Holmes, M. J. (2003). Are the trade deficits of less developed countries stationary? Evidence for African countries. *Applied Econometrics and International Development*, 3(3):7–24.

Holmes, M. J. (2006). How sustainable are OECD current account balances in the long run? *Manchester School*, 74(5):626–643.

Holmes, M. J. and Panagiotidis, T. (2009). Cointegration and asymmetric adjustment: Some new evidence concerning the behavior of the U.S. current account. *The B.E. Journal of Macroeconomics*, 9(1):1–25.

Holmes, M. J., Panagiotidis, T., and Sharma, A. (2007). The sustainability of India's current account (1950–2003): Evidence from parametric and non-parametric unit root and cointegration tests. Working Papers 41–07, Rimini Centre for Economic Analysis.

Honkapohja, S. (1993). Adaptive learning and bounded rationality: An introduction to basic concepts. *European Economic Review*, 37(2–3):587–594.

Hooker, M. A. (1993). Testing for cointegration: Power versus frequency of observations. *Economics Letters*, 41(4):359–362.

Horne, J. (1991). Indicators of fiscal sustainability. IMF Working Papers 91/5, International Monetary Fund.

Hosking, J. R. M. (1981). Fractional differencing. *Biometrika*, 68(1):165–176.

Hu, W. (1996). Time aggregation and skip sampling in cointegration tests. *Statistical Papers*, 37:225–234.

Huang, C.-H. (1993). An empirical study on Taiwan's current account: 1961–90. *Applied Economics*, 25(7):927.

Huang, C.-H. and Lin, K. S. (1993). Deficits, government expenditures, and tax smoothing in the United States: 1929–1988. *Journal of Monetary Economics*, 31(3):317–339.

Hudson, S. and Stennett, R. (2003). Current account sustainability in Jamaica. Working Papers 02/11, Bank of Jamaica.

Hurst, H. E. (1951). Long-term storage capacity of reservoirs. *Transactions of the American Society of Civil Engineers*, 116:770–808.

Hussein, K. A. (1998). International capital mobility in OECD countries: The Feldstein-Horioka 'puzzle' revisited. *Economics Letters*, 59(2):237–242.

Husted, S. (1992). The emerging U.S. current account deficit in the 1980s: A cointegration analysis. *The Review of Economics and Statistics*, 74(1):159–166.

Ibarra, R. (2009). Perron unit root test EViews source code. http://http://forums.eviews.com/viewtopic.php?f=23&t=6054.

Işcan, T. B. (2002). Present value tests of the current account with durables consumption. *Journal of International Money and Finance*, 21(3):385–412.

Im, K. S., Pesaran, M. H., and Shin, Y. (2003). Testing for unit roots in heterogeneous panels. *Journal of Econometrics*, 115(1):53–74.

IMF (1998). Financial crises: Characteristics and indicators of vulnerability. In *World Economic Outlook*. Washington, DC: International Monetary Fund, September.

IMF (1999). Debt relief for low-income countries. The Enhanced HIPC Initiative. IMF Pamphlet Series. Prepared by David Andrews and Anthony R. Boote and Syed S. Rizavi and Sukhwinder Sing 97/51, Washington, DC: International Monetary Fund.

IMF (2002). Assessing sustainability. Prepared by the Policy Development and Review Department, in consultation with the Fiscal Affairs, International Capital Markets, Monetary and Exchange Affairs, and Research Departments, approved by Timothy Geithner, Washington, DC: International Monetary Fund.

IMF (2004). Debt sustainability in low-income countries — Proposal for an operational framework and policy implications. Prepared by the staffs of the IMF and the World Bank, approved by Mark Allen and Gobind Nankani, Washington, DC: International Monetary Fund.

IMF (2005). Information note on modifications to the Fund's debt sustainability assessment framework for market access countries. Prepared by the Policy Development and Review Department, approved by Mark Allen, Washington, DC: International Monetary Fund.

IMF (2006a). Annual report. In *IMF Committee on balance of payments statistics*. Washington, DC: International Monetary Fund, September.

IMF (2006b). Oil prices and global imbalances. In *World Economic Outlook*. Washington, DC: International Monetary Fund, September.

IMF (2007). Exchange rates and the adjustment of external imbalances. In *World Economic Outlook*. Washington, DC: International Monetary Fund, April.

IMF (2008). *Balance of Payments Manual*. Washington, DC: International Monetary Fund, 6th edition.

IMF (2008). Staff guidance note on debt sustainability analysis for market access countries. Prepared by the Policy Development and Review Department, approved by Mark Allen, Washington, DC: International Monetary Fund.

IMF (2012a). IMF Executive Board reviews the joint IMF — World Bank debt sustainability framework for low-income countries. Public information notice no. 12/17, Washington, DC: International Monetary Fund.

IMF (2012b). Revisiting the debt sustainability framework for low-income countries. Prepared by staffs of the IMF and World Bank, approved by Siddharth Tiwari and Otaviano Canuto, Washington, DC: International Monetary Fund.

Inada, K.-I. (1964). Some structural characteristics of Turnpike theorems. *The Review of Economic Studies*, 31(1):43–58.

Irandoust, M. and Ericsson, J. (2004). Are imports and exports cointegrated? An international comparison. *Metroeconomica*, 55(1):49–64.

Isard, P., Faruqee, H., Kincaid, G. R., and Fetherston, M. (2001). Methodology for current account and exchange rate assessments. IMF Occasional Papers 209, International Monetary Fund.

Ishii, S. and Habermeier, K. F. (2003). *Exchange arrangements and foreign exchange markets: Developments and issues*. Washington, DC: International Monetary Fund.

Ismail, H. and Baharumshah, A. (2008). Malaysia's current account deficits: An intertemporal optimization perspective. *Empirical Economics*, 35(3):569–590.

Jansen, W. J. (1996). Estimating saving-investment correlations: Evidence for OECD countries based on an error correction model. *Journal of International Money and Finance*, 15(5):749–781.

Jeanne, O. (2007). International reserves in emerging market countries: Too much of a good thing? *Brookings Papers on Economic Activity*, 38(1):1–80.

Jeanne, O. and Masson, P. (2000). Currency crises, sunspots and Markov-switching regimes. *Journal of International Economics*, 50(2):327–350.

Jeanne, O. and Zettelmeyer, J. (2005). The Mussa theorem (and other results on IMF-induced moral hazard). *IMF Staff Papers*, 52(Special Issue):64–84.

Johansen, S. (1988). Statistical analysis of cointegration vectors. *Journal of Economic Dynamics and Control*, 12(2–3):231–254.

Johansen, S. (1992). Determination of cointegration rank in the presence of a linear trend. *Oxford Bulletin of Economics and Statistics*, 54(3):383–397.

Johansen, S. (1995). *Likelihood-Based Inference in Cointegrated Vector Autoregressive Models*. Oxford University Press.

Johansen, S. and Juselius, K. (1990). Maximum likelihood estimation and inference on cointegration — With applications to the demand for money. *Oxford Bulletin of Economics & Statistics*, 52(2):169–210.

Johansen, S., Mosconi, R., and Nielsen, B. (2000). Cointegration analysis in the presence of structural breaks in the deterministic trend. *Econometrics Journal*, 3:216–249.

Kahneman, D. and Tversky, A. (1973). On the psychology of prediction. *Psychological Review*, 80(4):237–251.

Kahneman, D. and Tversky, A. (1979). Prospect theory: An analysis of decision under risk. *Econometrica*, 47(2):263–291.

Kalyoncu, H. (2006). International intertemporal solvency in OECD countries: Evidence from panel unit root. MPRA Paper 855, University Library of Munich, Germany.

Kamihigashi, T. (2000). A simple proof of Ekeland and Scheinkman's result on the necessity of a transversality condition. *Economic Theory*, 15(2):463–468.

Kamihigashi, T. (2005). Necessity of the transversality condition for stochastic models with bounded or CRRA utility. *Journal of Economic Dynamics and Control*, 29(8):1313–1329.

Kamihigashi, T. (2006). Transversality conditions and dynamic economic behavior. Discussion Paper Series 180, Research Institute for Economics & Business Administration, Kobe University.

Kaminsky, G. (2003). Varieties of currency crises. NBER Working Papers 10193, National Bureau of Economic Research.

Kaminsky, G., Lizondo, S., and Reinhart, C. M. (1998). Leading indicators of currency crises. *IMF Staff Papers*, 45(1):1–48.

Kano, T. (2008). A structural VAR approach to the intertemporal model of the current account. *Journal of International Money and Finance*, 27(5):757–779.

Kano, T. (2009). Habit formation and the present-value model of the current account: Yet another suspect. *Journal of International Economics*, 78(1):72–85.

Kao, C. (1999). Spurious regression and residual-based tests for cointegration in panel data. *Journal of Econometrics*, 90(1):1–44.

Kao, C. and Chiang, M.-H. (1999). On the estimation and inference of a cointegrated regression in panel data. CEPR working papers, Center for Policy Research.

Kapetanios, G. and Shin, Y. (2002). Unit root tests in three-regime SETAR models. Working Papers 465, Queen Mary, University of London, School of Economics and Finance.

Kapetanios, G., Shin, Y., and Snell, A. (2003). Testing for a unit root in the nonlinear STAR framework. *Journal of Econometrics*, 112(2):359–379.

Karunaratne, N. D. (2010). The sustainability of Australia's current account deficits — A reappraisal after the global financial crisis. *Journal of Policy Modeling*, 32(1):81–97.

Kasa, K. (2003). Testing present value models of the current account: A cautionary note. *Journal of International Money and Finance*, 22(4):557–569.

Kejriwal, M. (2008). Cointegration with structural breaks: An application to the Feldstein-Horioka puzzle. *Studies in Nonlinear Dynamics & Econometrics*, 12(1):3.

Kennedy, D. P. (1976). The distribution of the Maximum Brownian Excursion. *Journal of Applied Probability*, 13(2):371–376.

Khan, A. and Thomas, J. K. (2008). Adjustment costs. In Durlauf, S. N. and Blume, L. E., editors, *The New Palgrave Dictionary of Economics*. Basingstoke, UK: Palgrave Macmillan.

Kilian, L. and Taylor, M. P. (2003). Why is it so difficult to beat the random walk forecast of exchange rates? *Journal of International Economics*, 60(1):85–107.

Kilic, R. (2003). Testing procedure for unit root in the STAR model. *Unpublished manuscript, Georgia Institute of Technology*.

Kim, K., Hall, V. B., and Buckle, R. A. (2002). New Zealand's current account deficit: Analysis based on the intertemporal optimisation approach. New Zealand Treasury Working Papers 01/02, New Zealand Treasury.

Kim, K. and Schmidt, P. (1990). Some evidence on the accuracy of Phillips-Perron tests using alternative estimates of nuisance parameters. *Economics Letters*, 34(4):345–350.

Kimball, M. S. (1990). Precautionary saving in the small and in the large. *Econometrica*, 58(1):53–73.

Kimbrough, K. P. (1988). Optimal tax policy for balance of payments objectives. In Frenkel, J. A., editor, *International Aspects of Fiscal Policies*, pages 309–348. Chicago, IL: University of Chicago Press.

Kirman, A. (1992). Whom or what does the representative individual represent? *Journal of Economic Perspectives*, 6(2):117–136.

Kirman, A. (2006). Heterogeneity in economics. *Journal of Economic Interaction and Coordination*, 1(1):89–117.

Klein, M. (2001). *Mathematical Methods for Economics*. Addison Wesley, 2nd edition.

Knedlik, T. and Schweinitz, G. V. (2012). Macroeconomic imbalances as indicators for debt crises in Europe. *Journal of Common Market Studies*, 50(5):726–745.

Kolb, R. W., editor (2011). *Sovereign Debt: From Safety to Default (Robert W. Kolb Series)*. Hoboken, NJ: John Wiley & Sons.

Kool, C. (2010). The sustainability of global financial imbalances. In Balling, M., Berk, J., and Strauss-Kahn, M.-O., editors, *The Quest for Stability: the Macro View. SUERF Study 2010/2*, pages 61–86. Vienna, Austria: SUERF — The European Money and Finance Forum.

Koopmans, T. C. (1963). On the concept of optimal economic growth. Cowles Foundation Discussion Papers 163, Cowles Foundation for Research in Economics, Yale University.

Körner, F. M. and Zemanek, H. (2013). On the brink? Intra-euro area imbalances and the sustainability of foreign debt. *Review of International Economics*, 21(1):18–34.

Kraay, A., Loayza, N., Serven, L., and Ventura, J. (2000). Country portfolios. NBER Working Papers 7795, National Bureau of Economic Research.

Kraay, A. and Nehru, V. (2004). When is external debt sustainable? Policy Research Working Papers 3200, The World Bank.

Kraay, A. and Ventura, J. (2000). Current accounts in debtor and creditor countries. *The Quarterly Journal of Economics*, 115(4):1137–1166.

Kraay, A. and Ventura, J. (2002). Current accounts in the long and short run. NBER Working Papers 9030, National Bureau of Economic Research.

Kraay, A. and Ventura, J. (2005). The dot-com bubble, the Bush deficits, and the U.S. current account. NBER Working Papers 11543, National Bureau of Economic Research.

Kravis, I. B., Heston, A., and Summers, R. (1978). *World Product and Income: International Comparisons of Real Gross Product*. Baltimore, MD: Johns Hopkins University Press.

Kravis, I. B., Heston, A., and Summers, R. (1982). *World Product and Income: International Comparisons and Real GDP*. Baltimore, MD: Johns Hopkins University Press.

Kravis, I. B., Kenessey, Z., Heston, A., and Summers, R. (1975). *A System of International Comparisons of Gross Product and Purchasing Power*. Baltimore, MD: Johns Hopkins University Press.

Kregel, J. (2004). Can we create a stable international financial environment that ensures net resource transfers to developing countries? *Journal of Post Keynesian Economics*, 26(4):573–590.

Kremers, J. J. M. (1988). Long-run limits on the US Federal debt. *Economics Letters*, 28(3):259–262.

Kremers, J. J. M. (1989). U.S. federal indebtedness and the conduct of fiscal policy. *Journal of Monetary Economics*, 23(2):219–238.

Kremers, J. J. M., Ericsson, N. R., and Dolado, J. J. (1992). The power of cointegration tests. *Oxford Bulletin of Economics and Statistics*, 54(3):325–348.

Krugman, P. (1979). A model of balance-of-payments crises. *Journal of Money, Credit and Banking*, 11(3):311–325.

Krugman, P. (1988). Financing vs. forgiving a debt overhang. *Journal of Development Economics*, 29(3):253–268.

Krugman, P. and Obstfeld, M. (2003). *International economics. Theory and policy*. Boston etc.: Addison-Wesley.

Kwiatkowski, D., Phillips, P. C. B., Schmidt, P., and Shin, Y. (1992). Testing the null hypothesis of stationarity against the alternative of a unit root: How sure are we that economic time series have a unit root? *Journal of Econometrics*, 54(1–3):159–178.

Lahiri, K. and Mamingi, N. (1995). Testing for cointegration: Power versus frequency of observation — Another view. *Economics Letters*, 49(2):121–124.

Laibson, D. (1997). Golden eggs and hyperbolic discounting. *The Quarterly Journal of Economics*, 112(2):443–477.

Landeau, S. A. S. (2002). The intertemporal approach to the current account: Evidence for Chile. *Revista de Análisis Económico*, 17(2):95–121.

Lane, P. R. and Milesi-Ferretti, G. M. (2007). Europe and global imbalances. *Economic Policy*, 22(51):519–573.

Lanne, M., Lütkepohl, H., and Saikkonen, P. (2002). Comparison of unit root tests for time series with level shifts. *Journal of Time Series Analysis*, 23(6):667–685.

Lanzafame, M. (2012). Current account sustainability in advanced economies. MPRA Papers 42384, University Library of Munich, Germany.

Lau, E. and Baharumshah, A. Z. (2003). Sustainability of external imbalances: The case of Malaysia. *Singapore Economic Review*, 48(1):61–80.

Lau, E. and Baharumshah, A. Z. (2005). Mean-reverting behavior of current account in Asian countries. *Economics Letters*, 87(3):367–371.

Lau, E., Baharumshah, A. Z., and Haw, C. T. (2006). Current account: Mean-reverting or random walk behavior? *Japan and the World Economy*, 18(1):90–107.

Leachman, L. (1991). Saving, investment, and capital mobility among OECD countries. *Open Economies Review*, 2(2):137–163.

Lee, J. (2008). The effect of the background risk in a simple chance improving decision model. *Journal of Risk and Uncertainty*, 36(1):19–41.

Lee, J., Huang, C. J., and Shin, Y. (1997). On stationary tests in the presence of structural breaks. *Economics Letters*, 55(2):165–172.

Lee, J.-W. and Shin, K. (2008). IMF bailouts and moral hazard. *Journal of International Money and Finance*, 27(5):816–830.

Leiderman, L. and Razin, A. (1992). Determinants of external imbalances: The role taxes, government spending and productivity. NBER Working Papers 3738, National Bureau of Economic Research.

Leland, H. E. (1968). Saving and uncertainty: The precautionary demand for saving. *The Quarterly Journal of Economics*, 82(3):465–473.

Leo, B. (2009). Will World Bank and IMF lending lead to HIPC IV? Debt déjà-vu all over again. Working Papers 193, Center for Global Development.

Lerner, A. P. (1944). *The Economics of Control*. New York, NY: Macmillan.

LeRoy, S. F. and Werner, J. (2001). *Principles of financial economics*. Cambridge, MA: Cambridge University Press.

Levin, A., Lin, C.-F., and Chu, C.-S. J. (2002). Unit root tests in panel data: Asymptotic and finite-sample properties. *Journal of Econometrics*, 108(1):1–24.

Levy, D. (2004). Is the Feldstein-Horioka puzzle really a puzzle? International Finance 0402002, EconWPA.

Levy, H. (1994). Absolute and relative risk aversion: An experimental study. *Journal of Risk and Uncertainty*, 8(3):289–307.

Leybourne, S. J. and McCabe, B. P. M. (1994). A consistent test for a unit root. *Journal of Business & Economic Statistics*, 12(2):157–166.

Liang, Y. (2007). Does foreign direct investment provide desirable development finance? The case of China. *China & World Economy*, 15(2):104–120.

Lim, E.-G. (2001). Determinants of, and the relation between, foreign direct investment and growth: A summary of the recent literature. IMF Working Papers 01/175, International Monetary Fund.

Lima, L. R. and Xiao, Z. (2010). Is there long memory in financial time series? *Applied Financial Economics*, 20(6):487–500.

Liu, P. C. and Tanner, E. (1996). International intertemporal solvency in industrialized countries: Evidence and implications. *Southern Economic Journal*, 62(3):739–749.

Ljungqvist, L. and Sargent, T. J. (2004). *Recursive Macroeconomic Theory*. Cambidge, MA: MIT Press, 2nd edition.

Lo, A. W. (1991). Long-term memory in stock market prices. *Econometrica*, 59(5):1279–1313.

Lopes, S. R. C., Olbermann, B. P., and Reisen, V. A. (2004). A comparison of estimation methods in non-stationary ARFIMA processes. *Journal of Statistical Computation and Simulation*, 74(5):339–347.

Lovell, M. C. (1986). Tests of the rational expectations hypothesis. *American Economic Review*, 76(1):110–124.

Lucas, R. (1978). Asset prices in an exchange economy. *Econometrica*, 46:1429–1445.

Lucas, R. (1982). Interest rates and currency prices in a two-country world. *Journal of Monetary Economics*, 10(3):335–359.

Ludlow, J. and Enders, W. (2000). Estimating non-linear ARMA models using Fourier coefficients. *International Journal of Forecasting*, 16(3):333–347.

Lumsdaine, R. L. and Papell, D. H. (1997). Multiple trend breaks and the unit-root hypothesis. *The Review of Economics and Statistics*, 79(2):212–218.

Lütkepohl, H. (1985). Comparison of criteria for estimating the order of a vector autoregressive process. *Journal of Time Series Analysis*, 6(1):35–52.

Lütkepohl, H. (2004). Univariate time series analysis. In Lütkepohl, H. and Krätzig, M., editors, *Applied Time Series Econometrics*, pages 8–85. New York, NY: Cambridge University Press.

Lütkepohl, H. (2007). *New Introduction to Multiple Time Series Analysis*. Berlin, Heidelberg: Springer.

Luukkonen, R., Saikkonen, P., and Teräsvirta, T. (1988). Testing linearity against smooth transition autoregressive models. *Biometrika*, 75(3):491–499.

Mackey, G. W. (1946). On convex topological linear spaces. *Transactions of the American Mathematical Society*, 60:519–537.

Maddala, G. S. and Kim, I.-M. (1999). *Unit Roots, Cointegration, and Structural Change (Themes in Modern Econometrics)*. Cambridge, UK: Cambridge University Press.

Maddala, G. S. and Wu, S. (1999). A comparative study of unit root tests with panel data and a new simple test. *Oxford Bulletin of Economics and Statistics*, 61(0):631–652.

Magill, M. and Quinzii, M. (1994). Infinite horizon incomplete markets. *Econometrica*, 62(4):853–880.

Magill, M. and Quinzii, M. (1996). Incomplete markets over an infinite horizon: Long-lived securities and speculative bubbles. *Journal of Mathematical Economics*, 26(1):133–170.

Makrydakis, S. (1999). Consumption-smoothing and the excessiveness of Greece's current account deficits. *Empirical Economics*, 24:183–209.

Mamingi, N. (1997). Saving-investment correlations and capital mobility: The experience of developing countries. *Journal of Policy Modeling*, 19(6):605–626.

Mandelbrot, B. (1972). Statistical methodology for nonperiodic cycles: From the covariance to R/S analysis. In Berg, S. V., editor, *Annals of Economic and Social Measurement*, number 1(3), pages 259–290. National Bureau of Economic Research.

Mann, C. L. (1999). *Is the U.S. Trade Deficit Sustainable?* Washington, DC: Institute for International Economics, U.S.

Mann, C. L. (2002). Perspectives on the U.S. current account deficit and sustainability. *Journal of Economic Perspectives*, 16(3):131–152.

Mark, N. (2001). *International Macroeconomics and Finance: Theory and Econometric Methods*. Malden, MA: Blackwell Publishers Ltd.

Markowitz, H. M. (1952). Portfolio selection. *The Journal of Finance*, 7(1):77–91.

Marshall, A. (1923). *Money, Credit and Commerce*. London, UK: Macmillan.

Mastroyiannis, A. (2007). Current account dynamics and the Feldstein and Horioka puzzle: The case of Greece. *European Journal of Comparative Economics*, 4(1):91–99.

Matsubayashi, Y. (2005). Are US current account deficits unsustainable? Testing for the private and government intertemporal budget constraints. *Japan and the World Economy*, 17(2):223–237.

McCallum, B. T. (1984). Are Bond-Financed Deficits Inflationary? A Ricardian Analysis. *Journal of Political Economy*, 92(1):123–135.

McGettigan, D. (2000). Current account and external sustainability in the Baltics, Russia, and other countries of the former Soviet Union. IMF Occasional Papers 189, International Monetary Fund.

Mehra, R. and Prescott, E. C. (1985). The equity premium: A puzzle. *Journal of Monetary Economics*, 15(2):145–161.

Mello, L. R. D. (1997). Foreign direct investment in developing countries and growth: A selective survey. *Journal of Development Studies*, 34(1):1–34.

Mendoza, E. G., Quadrini, V., and Rios-Rull, J.-V. (2007). Financial integration, financial deepness and global imbalances. NBER Working Papers 12909, National Bureau of Economic Research.

Mendoza, E. G., Quadrini, V., and Ríos-Rull, J.-V. (2009). Financial integration, financial development, and global imbalances. *Journal of Political Economy*, 117(3):371–416.

Mercereau, B. and Miniane, J. (2004). Challenging the empirical evidence from present value models of the current account. IMF Working Papers 04/106, International Monetary Fund.

Mercereau, B. and Miniane, J. (2008). Should we trust the empirical evidence from present value models of the current account? *Economics — The Open-Access, Open-Assessment E-Journal*, 2(34):1–36.

Michel, P., Thibault, E., and Vidal, J.-P. (2006). Intergenerational altruism and neoclassical growth models. In Kolm, S.-C. and Ythier, J. M., editors, *Handbook of the Economics of Giving, Altruism and Reciprocity: Applications*, pages 1055–1106. Amsterdam, Oxford: North-Holland.

Milbourne, R. and Otto, G. (1992). Consumption smoothing and the current account. *Australian Economic Papers*, 31(59):369–384.

Milesi-Ferretti, G. M. and Lane, P. R. (2006). The external wealth of nations mark II: Revised and extended estimates of foreign assets and liabilities, 1970–2004. IMF Working Papers 06/69, International Monetary Fund.

Milesi-Ferretti, G. M. and Razin, A. (1996a). Current-account sustainability. Princeton Studies in International Economics 81, International Economics Section, Department of Economics, Princeton University.

Milesi-Ferretti, G. M. and Razin, A. (1996b). Current account sustainability: Selected East Asian and Latin American experiences. NBER Working Papers 5791, National Bureau of Economic Research.

Milesi-Ferretti, G. M. and Razin, A. (1998a). Current account reversals and currency crises: Empirical regularities. NBER Working Papers 6620, National Bureau of Economic Research.

Milesi-Ferretti, G. M. and Razin, A. (1998b). Sharp reductions in current account deficits: An empirical analysis. *European Economic Review*, 42(3–5):897–908.

Miller, S. M. (1988). Are saving and investment co-integrated? *Economics Letters*, 27(1):31–34.

Mills, J. A. and Prasad, K. (1992). A comparison of model selection criteria. *Econometric Reviews*, 11(2):201–234.

Mills, T. C. (1999). *The Econometric Modelling of Financial Time Series*. New York, NY: Cambridge University Press, 2nd edition.

Moccero, D. N. (2008). The intertemporal approach to the current account: Evidence for Argentina. *Journal of Applied Economics*, pages 327–353.

Moon, H. R. and Perron, B. (2008). Seemingly unrelated regressions. In Durlauf, S. N. and Blume, L. E., editors, *The New Palgrave Dictionary of Economics*. Basingstoke, UK: Palgrave Macmillan.

Moreno, R. (1997). Saving-investment dynamics and capital mobility in the US and Japan. *Journal of International Money and Finance*, 16(6):837–863.

Morin, R. A. and Fernandez Suarez, A. (1983). Risk aversion revisited. *Journal of Finance*, 38(4):1201–1216.

Morsy, H. (2012). Current account determinants for oil-exporting countries. *Emerging Markets Finance and Trade*, 48(3):122–133.

Müller, U. K. (2005). Size and power of tests of stationarity in highly autocorrelated time series. *Journal of Econometrics*, 128(2):195–213.

Musso, A. and Phillips, S. (2002). Comparing projections and outcomes of IMF-supported programs. *IMF Staff Papers*, 49(1):3.

Muth, J. F. (1961). Rational expectations and the theory of price movements. *Econometrica*, 3(29):315–335.

Naik, N. Y. and Moore, M. J. (1996). Habit formation and intertemporal substitution in individual food consumption. *The Review of Economics and Statistics*, 78(2):321–328.

Nankervis, J. C., Savin, N. E., DeJong, D. N., and Whiteman, C. H. (1992). Integration versus trend stationarity in time series. *Econometrica*, 60(2):423–433.

Naqvi, K. and Morimune, K. (2005). An empirical analysis of sustainability of trade deficits. Discussion Paper 072, Interfaces for Advanced Economic Analysis, Kyoto University.

Narayan, P. K. (2005). The saving and investment nexus for China: Evidence from cointegration tests. *Applied Economics*, 37(17):1979–1990.

Narayan, P. K. and Narayan, S. (2005). Are exports and imports cointegrated? Evidence from 22 least developed countries. *Applied Economics Letters*, 12(6):375–378.

Nason, J. M. and Rogers, J. H. (2006). The present-value model of the current account has been rejected: Round up the usual suspects. *Journal of International Economics*, 68(1):159–187.

Neely, C. J. and Rapach, D. E. (2008). Real interest rate persistence: Evidence and implications. *Review*, Nov:609–642.

Neumeyer, P. A. and Perri, F. (2005). Business cycles in emerging economies: The role of interest rates. *Journal of Monetary Economics*, 52(2):345–380.

Newey, W. K. and West, K. D. (1987). A simple, positive semi-definite, heteroskedasticity and autocorrelation consistent covariance matrix. *Econometrica*, 55(3):703–708.

Ng, S. (1995). Testing for unit roots in flow data sampled at different frequencies. *Economics Letters*, 47(3–4):237–242.

Ng, S. and Perron, P. (1995). Unit root tests in ARMA models with data-dependent methods for the selection of the truncation lag. *Journal of the American Statistical Association*, 90(429):268–281.

Ng, S. and Perron, P. (1997). Estimation and inference in nearly unbalanced nearly cointegrated systems. *Journal of Econometrics*, 79(1):53–81.

Ng, S. and Perron, P. (2001). Lag length selection and the construction of unit root tests with good size and power. *Econometrica*, 69(6):1519–1554.

Nyberg, P. (2010). 21st century economics: A reference handbook. In Free, R. C., editor, *Asset Pricing Models*, pages 203–214. Thousand Oaks, CA: Sage Publications, Inc.

Obstfeld, M. (1986). Rational and self-fulfilling balance-of-payments crises. *American Economic Review*, 76(1):72–81.

Obstfeld, M. (1994). The logic of currency crises. NBER Working Papers 4640, National Bureau of Economic Research.

Obstfeld, M. (1996). International capital mobility in the 1990s. NBER Working Papers 4534, National Bureau of Economic Research.

Obstfeld, M. (2012). Financial flows, financial crises, and global imbalances. *Journal of International Money and Finance*, 31(3):469–480.

Obstfeld, M. and Rogoff, K. (1994). The intertemporal approach to the current account. NBER Working Papers 4893, National Bureau of Economic Research.

Obstfeld, M. and Rogoff, K. (1996). *Foundations of International Macroeconomics*. Cambridge, MA: MIT Press.

Obstfeld, M. and Rogoff, K. (2009). Global imbalances and the financial crisis: Products of common causes. CEPR Discussion Papers 7606, C.E.P.R. Discussion Papers.

Ocakverdi, E. and Tang, C. (2009). Gregory-Hansen cointegration test EViews source code. http://forums.eviews.com/viewtopic.php?f=15&t=976#p3427.

O'Connell, S. A. and Zeldes, S. P. (1988). Rational Ponzi games. *International Economic Review*, 29(3):431–450.

Ogus, A. and Sohrabji, N. (2008). On the optimality and sustainability of Turkey's current account. *Empirical Economics*, 35(3):543–568.

OIC (2012). Assessment of sustainability and insolvency of the external debt. OIC Outlook Series. Prepared by the Statistical, Economic and Social Research and Training Centre for Islamic countries (SESRIC), Ankara, TR: Organisation of Islamic Cooperation (OIC).

Olekalns, N. (1994). Testing for unit roots in seasonally adjusted data. *Economics Letters*, 45(3):273–279.

Onafowara, O. A., Owoye, O., and Huart, F. (2011). The temporal relationship between saving and investment: Evidence from advanced EU countries. *International Journal of Business and Social Science*, 2(2):1–12.

Önel, G. and Utkulu, U. (2006). Modeling the long-run sustainability of Turkish external debt with structural changes. *Economic Modelling*, 23(4):669–682.

Osterwald-Lenum, M. (1992). A note with quantiles of the asymptotic distribution of the maximum likelihood cointegration rank test statistics. *Oxford Bulletin of Economics and Statistics*, 54(3):461–472.

Ostry, J. D. (1997). Current account imbalances in ASEAN countries: Are they a problem? IMF Working Papers 91/51, International Monetary Fund.

Otto, G. (1992). Testing a present-value model of the current account: Evidence from US and Canadian time series. *Journal of International Money and Finance*, 11(5):414–430.

Ozcicek, O. and McMillin, W. D. (1999). Lag length selection in vector autoregressive models: Symmetric and asymmetric lags. *Applied Economics*, 31(4):517–524.

Özmen, E. (2007). Financial development, exchange rate regimes and the Feldstein-Horioka puzzle: Evidence from the MENA region. *Applied Economics*, 39(9):1133–1138.

Özmen, E. and Parmaksiz, K. (2003). Policy regime change and the Feldstein-Horioka puzzle: The UK evidence. *Journal of Policy Modeling*, 25(2):137–149.

Paoli, B. D., Hoggarth, G., and Saporta, V. (2006). Costs of sovereign default. Financial Stability Paper 01, Bank of England.

Papapetrou, E. (2006). The saving-investment relationship in periods of structural change: The case of Greece. *Journal of Economic Studies*, 33(2):121–129.

Paravisini, D., Rappoport, V., and Ravina, E. (2010). Risk aversion and wealth: Evidence from person-to-person lending portfolios. NBER Working Papers 16063, National Bureau of Economic Research.

Pattillo, C., Poirson, H., and Ricci, L. (2002). External debt and growth. IMF Working Papers 02/69, International Monetary Fund.

Pavlova, A. and Rigobon, R. (2010a). An asset-pricing view of external adjustment. *Journal of International Economics*, 80(1):144–156.

Pavlova, A. and Rigobon, R. (2010b). International macro-finance. NBER Working Papers 16630, National Bureau of Economic Research.

Pedroni, P. (1999). Critical values for cointegration tests in heterogeneous panels with multiple regressors. *Oxford Bulletin of Economics and Statistics*, 61:653–670.

Pedroni, P. (2000). Fully modified OLS for heterogeneous cointegrated panels. Department of Economics Working Papers 2000–03, Department of Economics, Williams College.

Pedroni, P. (2001). Purchasing power parity tests in cointegrated panels. *The Review of Economics and Statistics*, 83(4):727–731.

Pelagidis, T. and Mastroyiannis, T. (2003). The saving-investment correlation in Greece, 1960–1997: Implications for capital mobility. *Journal of Policy Modeling*, 25(6–7):609–616.

Perron, P. (1989). The great crush, the oil price shock and the unit root hypothesis. *Econometrica*, 57(6):1361–1401.

Perron, P. (1997). Further evidence on breaking trend functions in macroeconomic variables. *Journal of Econometrics*, 80(2):355–385.

Perron, P. and Campbell, J. Y. (1993). A note on Johansen's cointegration procedure when trends are present. *Empirical Economics*, 18(4):777–789.

Perron, P. and Ng, S. (1996). Useful modifications to some unit root tests with dependent errors and their local asymptotic properties. *The Review of Economic Studies*, 63(3):435–463.

Pesaran, M. (2004). General diagnostic tests for cross section dependence in panels. Cambridge Working Papers in Economics 0435, Faculty of Economics, University of Cambridge.

Pesaran, M. H. (2006). Estimation and inference in large heterogeneous panels with a multifactor error structure. *Econometrica*, 74(4):967–1012.

Pesaran, M. H. (2007). A simple panel unit root test in the presence of cross-section dependence. *Journal of Applied Econometrics*, 22(2):265–312.

Pesaran, M. H. (2011). On the interpretation of panel unit root tests. Working Papers September 2011, Trinity College, Cambridge, UK.

Pesaran, M. H. and Shin, Y. (1995). An autoregressive distributed lag modelling approach to cointegration analysis. Cambridge Working Papers in Economics 9514, Faculty of Economics, University of Cambridge.

Pesaran, M. H. and Shin, Y. (1997). An autoregressive distributed lag modelling approach to cointegration analysis. Cambridge Working Papers in Economics 9514, Faculty of Economics, University of Cambridge.

Pesaran, M. H., Shin, Y., and Smith, R. (1999). Pooled mean group estimation of dynamic heterogeneous panels. *Journal of the American Statistical Association*, 94(446):621–634.

Pesaran, M. H., Shin, Y., and Smith, R. (2001). Bounds testing approaches to the analysis of level relationships. *Journal of Applied Econometrics*, 16(3):289–326.

Pesaran, M. H. and Smith, R. (1995). Estimating long-run relationships from dynamic heterogeneous panels. *Journal of Econometrics*, 68(1):79–113.

Pestman, W. R. and Alberink, I. B. (1998). *Mathematical Statistics: Problems and Detailed Solutions.* Berlin: Walter De Gruyter Inc.

Phelps, E. (1961). The golden rule of accumulation: A fable for growthmen. *American Economic Review*, 51(4):638–643.

Phillips, P. C. B. (1987). Time series regression with a unit root. *Econometrica*, 55(2):277–301.

Phillips, P. C. B. and Hansen, B. E. (1990). Statistical inference in instrumental variables regression with I(1) processes. *Review of Economic Studies*, 57(1):99–125.

Phillips, P. C. B. and Loretan, M. (1991). Estimating long-run economic equilibria. *Review of Economic Studies*, 58(3):407–436.

Phillips, P. C. B. and Ouliaris, S. (1990). Asymptotic properties of residual based tests for cointegration. *Econometrica*, 58(1):165–193.

Phillips, P. C. B. and Perron, P. (1988). Testing for a unit root in time series regression. *Biometrika*, 75(2):335–346.

Phillips, S. and Lane, T. D. (2000). Does IMF financing result in moral hazard? IMF Working Papers 00/168, International Monetary Fund.

Pitchford, J. (1995). *The current account and foreign debt.* London, UK: Routledge.

Plott, C. R. and Zeiler, K. (2005). The willingness to pay—willingness to accept gap, the "endowment effect," subject misconceptions, and experimental procedures for eliciting valuations. *American Economic Review*, 95(3):530–545.

Polat, O. (2011). Sustainability of the current account deficit in Turkey. *African Journal of Business Management*, 5(2):577–581.

Pollak, R. A. (1970). Habit formation and dynamic demand functions. *Journal of Political Economy*, 78(4):745–763.

Ponthière, G. (2003). Should we discount future generations' welfare? A survey on the "pure" discount rate debate. CREPP Working Papers 0302, Centre de Recherche en Economie Publique et de la Population (CREPP) (Research Center on Public and Population Economics) HEC-Management School, University of Liège.

Powell, A. (2002). Argentina's avoidable crisis: Bad luck, bad economics, bad politics, bad advice. *Brookings Trade Forum*, pages 1–58.

Prabheesh, K. P., Malathy, D., and Madhumathi, R. (2007). Demand for foreign exchange reserves in India: A co-integration approach. MPRA Paper 13969, University Library of Munich, Germany.

Pratt, J. W. (1964). Risk aversion in the small and in the large. *Econometrica*, 32(1/2):122–136.

Quintos, C. E. (1995). Sustainability of the deficit process with structural shifts. *Journal of Business & Economic Statistics*, 13(4):409–417.

Raffalovich, L. E., Deane, G. D., Armstrong, D., and Tsao, H.-S. (2008). Model selection procedures in social research: Monte-Carlo simulation results. *Journal of Applied Statistics*, 35(10):1093–1114.

Ramsey, F. P. (1928). A mathematical theory of saving. *Economic Journal*, 38(152):543–559.

Ramsey, J. B. (1969). Tests for specification errors in classical linear least-squares regression analysis. *Journal of the Royal Statistical Society. Series B (Methodological)*, 31(2):350–371.

Raybaudi, M., Sola, M., and Spagnolo, F. (2004). Red signals: Current account deficits and sustainability. *Economics Letters*, 84(2):217–223.

Razin, A. (1995). The dynamic-optimizing approach to the current account: Theory and evidence. NBER Working Papers 4334, National Bureau of Economic Research.

Reinhart, C. M. and Rogoff, K. S. (2010a). From financial crash to debt crisis. NBER Working Papers 15795, National Bureau of Economic Research.

Reinhart, C. M. and Rogoff, K. S. (2010b). Growth in a time of debt. *American Economic Review*, 100(2):573–578.

Reinhart, C. M. and Rogoff, K. S. (2011). From financial crash to debt crisis. *American Economic Review*, 101(5):1676–1706.

Reinhart, C. M., Rogoff, K. S., and Savastano, M. A. (2003a). Addicted to dollars. NBER Working Papers 10015, National Bureau of Economic Research.

Reinhart, C. M., Rogoff, K. S., and Savastano, M. A. (2003b). Debt intolerance. *Brookings Papers on Economic Activity*, 34(1):1–74.

Reisen, H. (1998). Sustainable and excessive current account deficits. *Empirica*, 25(2):111–131.

Reitz, S. and Taylor, M. P. (2008). The coordination channel of foreign exchange intervention: A non-linear microstructural analysis. *European Economic Review*, 52(1):55–76.

Ricardo, D. (1821). *On the principles of political economy and taxation*. London, UK: John Murray.

Ricciuti, R. (2003). Assessing Ricardian equivalence. *Journal of Economic Surveys*, 17(1):55–78.

Riedel, F. and Wichardt, P. (2007). *Mathematik für Ökonomen*. Berlin: Springer.

Rivera-Batiz, F. L. and Rivera-Batiz, L. (1994). *International finance and open economy macroeconomics*. New York, NY: Macmillan Publishing Company, 2nd edition.

Robinson, J. (1949). The foreign exchanges. In Ellis, H. S. and Metzler, L. A., editors, *Readings in the Theory of International Trade*, pages 83–103. Philadelphia, PA: Blakiston,.

Robinson, P. M. (1994). Efficient tests of nonstationary hypotheses. *Journal of the American Statistical Association*, 89(428):1420–1437.

Robinson, P. M. (1995). Log-periodogram regression of time series with long range dependence. *The Annals of Statistics*, 23(3):1048–1072.

Romer, D. (2006). *Advanced Macroeconomics*. New York, NY: McGraw-Hill/Irwin, 3rd edition.

Roubini, N. (2001). Debt sustainability: How to assess whether a country is insolvent. Technical report, Stern School of Business, New York University.

Roubini, N. and Wachtel, P. (1998). Current account sustainability in transition economies. NBER Working Papers 6468, National Bureau of Economic Research.

Rubinstein, A. (2001). A theorist's view of experiments. *European Economic Review*, 45(4–6):615–628.

Rubinstein, A. (2003). "Economics and Psychology"? The Case of Hyperbolic Discounting. *International Economic Review*, 44(4):1207–1216.

Ryder, Harl E., J. and Heal, G. M. (1973). Optimal growth with intertemporally dependent preferences. *The Review of Economic Studies*, 40(1):1–31.

Sachs, J. (1982). The current account in the macroeconomic adjustment process. *Scandinavian Journal of Economics*, 84(2):147–159.

Said, S. E. and Dickey, D. A. (1984). Testing for unit roots in autoregressive-moving average models of unknown order. *Biometrika*, 71(3):599–607.

Saikkonen, P. (1991). Asymptotically efficient estimation of cointegration regressions. *Econometric Theory*, 7(01):1–21.

Saikkonen, P. and Lütkepohl, H. (2000a). Testing for the cointegrating rank of a VAR process with an intercept. *Econometric Theory*, 16(03):373–406.

Saikkonen, P. and Lütkepohl, H. (2000b). Trend adjustment prior to testing for the cointegrating rank of a vector autoregressive process. *Journal of Time Series Analysis*, 21(4):435–456.

Saikkonen, P. and Lütkepohl, H. (2002). Testing for a unit root in a time series with a level shift at unknown time. *Econometric Theory*, 18(2):313–348.

Saksonovs, S. (2006). The intertemporal approach to the current account and currency crises. Darwin College Research Report DCR-005, Darwin College, Cambridge University, UK.

Salvatore, D. (2007). *International Economics*. Hoboken, NJ: John Wiley & Sons, 9th edition.

Samuelson, P. A. (1937). A note on measurement of utility. *The Review of Economic Studies*, 4(2):155–161.

Samuelson, P. A. (1958). An exact consumption-loan model of interest with or without the social contrivance of money. *Journal of Political Economy*, 66:467.

Samuelson, P. A. (1964). Theoretical notes on trade problems. *The Review of Economics and Statistics*, 46(2):145–54.

Samuelson, P. A. (1994). Facets of Balassa-Samuelson thirty years later. *Review of International Economics*, 2(3):201–226.

Sandmo, A. (1970). The effect of uncertainty on saving decisions. *The Review of Economic Studies*, 37(3):353–360.

Sarafidis, V. and Wansbeek, T. (2012). Cross-sectional dependence in panel data analysis. *Econometric Reviews*, 31(5):483–531.

Sargent, T. J. (1993). *Bounded Rationality in Macroeconomics: The Arne Ryde Memorial Lectures*. OUP Catalogue. Oxford, UK: Oxford University Press.

Sarno, L. and Taylor, M. P. (1998). Savings-investment correlations: Transitory versus permanent. *The Manchester School of Economic & Social Studies*, 66(0):17–38.

Sasin, M. (2001). The importance of the real exchange rate overvaluation and the current account deficit in the emergence of financial crises. In Dabrowski, M., editor, *Currency crises in emerging markets — Selected comparative studies*, pages 9–28. Warsaw: Center for Social and Economic Research (CASE).

Sawada, Y. (1994). Are the heavily indebted countries solvent?: Tests of intertemporal borrowing constraints. *Journal of Development Economics*, 45(2):325–337.

Schimmelpfennig, A., Roubini, N., and Manasse, P. (2003). Predicting sovereign debt crises. IMF Working Papers 03/221, International Monetary Fund.

Schlitzer, G. (1995). Testing the stationarity of economic time series: Further Monte Carlo evidence. *Ricerche Economiche*, 49(2):125–144.

Schmidt, K. and Trenkler, G. (2006). *Einführung in die moderne Matrix-Algebra, mit Anwendungen in der Statistik*. Berlin [etc.]: Springer.

Schmidt, M. B. (2001). Savings and investment: Some international perspectives. *Southern Economic Journal*, 68(2):446–456.

Schneider, M. and Tornell, A. (2000). Balance sheet effects, bailout guarantees and financial crises. NBER Working Papers 8060, National Bureau of Economic Research.

Schwarz, G. (1978). Estimating the dimension of a model. *The Annals of Statistics*, 6(2):461–464.

Schwert, G. W. (1989). Tests for unit roots: A Monte Carlo investigation. *Journal of Business & Economic Statistics*, 7(2):147–159.

Servén, L. and Nguyen, H. (2010). Global imbalances before and after the global crisis. Policy Research Working Papers 5354, The World Bank.

Sheffrin, S. M. and Woo, W. T. (1990). Present value tests of an intertemporal model of the current account. *Journal of International Economics*, 29(3-4):237–253.

Shiller, R. J. and Perron, P. (1985). Testing the random walk hypothesis: Power versus frequency of observation. *Economics Letters*, 18(4):381–386.

Shin, D. W. and Lee, O. (2001). Tests for asymmetry in possibly nonstationary time series data. *Journal of Business & Economic Statistics*, 19(2):233–244.

Shittu, O. and Asemota, M. (2009). Comparison of criteria for estimating the order of autoregressive process: A Monte Carlo approach. *European Journal of Scientific Research*, 30(3):409–416.

Simon, H. A. (1955). A behavioral model of rational choice. *The Quarterly Journal of Economics*, 69(1):99–118.

Simon, H. A. (1956). Dynamic programming under uncertainty with a quadratic criterion function. *Econometrica*, 24(1):74–81.

Simon, H. A. (1957). *Models of Man*. New York, NY: Wiley & Sons.

Singh, T. (2008). Testing the saving-investment correlations in India: An evidence from single-equation and system estimators. *Economic Modelling*, 25(5):1064–1079.

Sinha, D. (2002). Saving-investment relationships for Japan and other Asian countries. *Japan and the World Economy*, 14(1):1–23.

Sinha, D. and Sinha, T. (1998). An exploration of the long-run relationship between saving and investment in the developing economies: A tale of Latin American countries. *Journal of Post Keynesian Economics*, 20(3):435–443.

Sinn, H.-W. and Wollmershäuser, T. (2012). Target loans, current account balances and capital flows: The ECB's rescue facility. *International Tax and Public Finance*, 19(4):468–508.

Smeets, H.-D. (2010). Ist Griechenland noch zu retten? *Wirtschaftsdienst*, 90(5):309–313.

Smeets, H.-D. (2011). Staatsschuldenkrise in Europa — Ist die Finanzierung der Schuldnerländer alternativlos? *Ordnungspolitische Perspektiven*, 20:1–70.

Smith, G. W. and Zin, S. E. (1991). Persistent deficits and the market value of government debt. *Journal of Applied Econometrics*, 6(1):31–44.

Sollis, R. (2009). A simple unit root test against asymmetric STAR nonlinearity with an application to real exchange rates in Nordic countries. *Economic Modelling*, 26(1):118–125.

Sowell, F. (1990). The fractional unit root distribution. *Econometrica*, 58(2):495–505.

Srivastava, V. and Dwivedi, T. (1979). Estimation of seemingly unrelated regression equations: A brief survey. *Journal of Econometrics*, 10(1):15–32.

Srivastava, V. and Giles, D. E. (1987). *Seemingly Unrelated Regression Equations Models (Statistics: A Series of Textbooks and Monographs)*. New York, NY: Marcel Dekker, Inc.

Stein, H. (1997). Herb Stein's unfamiliar quotations. Slate (web magazine). http://www.slate.com/articles/business/it_seems_to_me/1997/05/herb_steins_unfamiliar_quotations.3.html.

Stock, J. H. (1987). Asymptotic properties of least squares estimators of cointegrating vectors. *Econometrica*, 55(5):1035–1056.

Stock, J. H. and Watson, M. W. (1993). A simple estimator of cointegrating vectors in higher order integrated systems. *Econometrica*, 61(4):783–820.

Stockman, A. C. and Tesar, L. L. (1995). Tastes and technology in a two-country model of the business cycle: Explaining international comovements. *American Economic Review*, 85(1):168–185.

Stokey, N. L., Lucas, R. E., and Prescott, E. C. (1989). *Recursive Methods in Economic Dynamics*. Cambridge, MA: Harvard University Press.

Summers, L. H. (1995). Ten lessons to learn. *The Economist*, December 23, 1995:62–64.

Summers, L. H. (2004). The United States and the global adjustment process. Speech, Speech at the Third Annual Stavros S. Niarchos Lecture, March 23, Washington, DC: Institute for International Economics. http://www.iie.com/publications/papers/paper.cfm?&researchid=200.

Summers, L. H. (2005). Commentary. In Hausmann, R. and Rojas-Suárez, L., editors, *Volatile capital flows: Taming their impact on Latin America*, pages 53–57. Washington, DC: Inter-American Development Bank; Baltimore, MD: John Hopkins University Press.

Tang, C. F. and Lean, H. H. (2011). Revisit Feldstein-Horioka puzzle: Evidence from Malaysia. *Economics Bulletin*, 31(3):2237–2249.

Tang, T. C. (2006). A new approach to examining the sustainability of external imbalances: The case of Japan. *Applied Economics Letters*, 13(5):287–292.

Taylor, A. M. (1996). International capital mobility in history: The saving-investment relationship. NBER Working Papers 5743, National Bureau of Economic Research.

Taylor, A. M. (1998). Argentina and the world capital market: Saving, investment, and international capital mobility in the twentieth century. *Journal of Development Economics*, 57(1):147–184.

Taylor, A. M. (2002). A century of current account dynamics. *Journal of International Money and Finance*, 21(6):725–748.

Taylor, J. F. (2010). Getting back on track: Macroeconomic policy lessons from the financial crisis. *Federal Reserve Bank of St. Louis Review*, 92(3):165–176.

Taylor, M. P. and Peel, D. A. (2000). Nonlinear adjustment, long-run equilibrium and exchange rate fundamentals. *Journal of International Money and Finance*, 19(1):33–53.

Taylor, M. P. and Sarno, L. (2001). Official intervention in the foreign exchange market: Is it effective and, if so, how does it work? *Journal of Economic Literature*, 39(3):839–868.

Teräsvirta, T. (1994). Specification, estimation, and evaluation of smooth transition autoregressive models. *Journal of the American Statistical Association*, 89(425):208–218.

Teräsvirta, T. (2004). Smooth transition regression modeling. In Lütkepohl, H. and Krätzig, M., editors, *Applied Time Series Econometrics*, pages 222–242. New York, NY: Cambridge University Press.

Tesar, L. L. (1991). Savings, investment and international capital flows. *Journal of International Economics*, 31(1-2):55–78.

Tesar, L. L. and Werner, I. M. (1995). Home bias and high turnover. *Journal of International Money and Finance*, 14(4):467–492.

Teverovsky, V., Taqqua, M. S., and Willinger, W. (1999). A critical look at Lo's modified R/S statistic. *Journal of Statistic Planning and Inference*, 80:211–227.

Theil, H. (1957). A note on certainty equivalence in dynamic planning. *Econometrica*, 25(2):346–349.

Tille, C. (2003). The impact of exchange rate movements on U.S. foreign debt. *Current Issues in Economics and Finance*, 9(1):1–7.

Tille, C. and van Wincoop, E. (2010). International capital flows. *Journal of International Economics*, 80(2):157–175.

Tirole, J. (1982). On the possibility of speculation under rational expectations. *Econometrica*, 50(5):1163–1181.

Tirole, J. (1985). Asset bubbles and overlapping generations. *Econometrica*, 53(5):1071–1100.

Tobin, J. (1958). Liquidity preference as behavior towards risk. *The Review of Economic Studies*, 25(67):65–86.

Tobin, J. (1969). A general equilibrium approach to monetary theory. *Journal of Money, Credit and Banking*, 1(1):15–29.

Tong, H. (1978). On a threshold model. In Chen, C. H., editor, *Pattern recognition and signal processing. NATO ASI Series E: Applied Sciences (29)*, pages 575–586. Amsterdam, NE: Sijthoff & Noordhoff.

Tong, H. (2011). Threshold models in time series analysis — 30 years on. *Statistics & Its Interface*, 4:107–118.

Tong, H. and Lim, K. S. (1980). Threshold autoregression, limit cycles and cyclical data. *Journal of the Royal Statistical Society. Series B (Methodological)*, 42(3):245–292.

Trachanas, E. and Katrakilidis, C. (2013). Fiscal deficits under financial pressure and insolvency: Evidence for Italy, Greece and Spain. *Journal of Policy Modeling*, in press.

Trehan, B. and Walsh, C. E. (1991). Testing intertemporal budget constraints: Theory and applications to U.S. federal budget and current account deficits. *Journal of Money, Credit and Banking*, 23(2):206–223.

Tsay, R. S. (1984). Order selection in nonstationary autoregressive models. *The Annals of Statistics*, 12(4):1425–1433.

Tsay, R. S. (2005). *Analysis of Financial Time Series*. Hoboken, NJ: John Wiley & Sons, 2nd edition.

Tsoukis, C. and Alyousha, A. (2001). The Feldstein-Horioka puzzle, saving-investment causality and international financial market integration. *Journal of Economic Integration*, 16:262–277.

Turner, P. (2013). Caveat creditor. BIS Working Papers 419, Bank for International Settlements.

Ucal, M. and Oksay, S. (2011). The solvency ratio of external debt (SRED) as an indicator of debt crisis: The case of Turkey. *International Journal of Economic Research*, 2(1):166–172.

Uctum, M. and Wickens, M. (2000). Debt and deficit ceilings, and sustainability of fiscal policies: An intertemporal analysis. *Oxford Bulletin of Economics and Statistics*, 62(2):197–222.

UNCTAD (2009). *Compendium on Debt Sustainability and Development. United Nations Conference on Trade and Development (UNCTAD)*. New York, NY and Geneva, CH: United Nations.

Ventura, J. (2001). A portfolio view of the U.S. current account deficit. *Brookings Papers on Economic Activity*, 32(2001-1):241–258.

Viner, J. (1937). *Studies in the theory of international trade*. New York, NY: Harper & Sons.

Warnock, F. E. (2002). Home bias and high turnover reconsidered. *Journal of International Money and Finance*, 21(6):795–805.

Waysand, C., Ross, K., and de Guzman, J. (2010). European financial linkages: A new look at imbalances. IMF Working Papers 10/295, International Monetary Fund.

Weber, A. (1994). Foreign exchange intervention and international policy coordination: Comparing the G-3 and EMS experience. CEPR Discussion Papers 1038, Center for Policy Research.

Weber, E. J. (2007). The role of the real interest rate in US macroeconomic history. Economics Discussion / Working Papers 07-01, The University of Western Australia, Department of Economics.

Whittle, P. (1953). Estimation and information in stationary time series. *Arkiv för Matematik*, 2:423–434.

Wickens, M. (2008). *Macroeconomic Theory: A Dynamic General Equilibrium Approach*. Princeton University Press.

Wickens, M. and Uctum, M. (1993). The sustainability of current account deficits: A test of the US intertemporal budget constraint. *Journal of Economic Dynamics and Control*, 17(3):423–441.

Wilcox, D. W. (1989). The sustainability of government deficits: Applications of the present-value borrowing constraint. *Journal of Money, Credit and Banking*, 21(3):291–306.

Williamson, J. (2011). Getting surplus countries to adjust. Policy Briefs PB11-1, Peterson Institute for International Economics.

World Bank (2013). How we classify countries. http://data.worldbank.org/about/country-classifications, retreived on August 14, 2013.

Wu, J. (2000). Mean reversion of the current account: Evidence from the panel data unit-root test. *Economics Letters*, 66(2):215–222.

Wu, J., Chen, S., and Lee, H. (2001). Are current account deficits sustainable?: Evidence from panel cointegration. *Economics Letters*, 72(2):219–224.

Wu, J., Fountas, S., and Show-lin, C. (1996). Testing for the sustainability of the current account deficit in two industrial countries. *Economics Letters*, 52(2):193–198.

Yaari, M. E. (1965). Uncertain lifetime, life insurance and the theory of the consumer. *The Review of Economic Studies*, 32(2):137–150.

Yan, H.-D. (1999). Intertemporal current account balance and the East Asian currency crises. *International Advances in Economic Research*, 5(3):277–288.

Yang, L. (2011). An empirical analysis of current account determinants in emerging Asian economies. Cardiff Economics Working Papers E2011/10, Cardiff University, Cardiff Business School, Economics Section.

Yule, G. U. (1926). Why do we sometimes get nonsense-correlations between time-series? — A study in sampling and the nature of time-series. *Journal of the Royal Statistical Society*, 89(1):1–63.

Zanghieri, P. (2004). Current accounts dynamics in new EU members: Sustainability and policy issues. Working Papers 2004-07, CEPII research center.

Zee, H. H. (1988). The sustainability and optimality of government debt. *IMF Staff Papers*, 35(4):658–685.

Zeldes, S. P. (1989). Optimal consumption with stochastic income: Deviations from certainty equivalence. *The Quarterly Journal of Economics*, 104(2):275–298.

Zhou, S. (2001). The power of cointegration tests versus data frequency and time spans. *Southern Economic Journal*, 67(4):906–921.

Zilcha, I. (1992). Efficiency in economic growth models under uncertainty. *Journal of Economic Dynamics and Control*, 16(1):27–38.

Zivot, E. and Andrews, D. W. K. (2002). Further evidence on the great crash, the oil-price shock, and the unit-root hypothesis. *Journal of Business & Economic Statistics*, 20(1):25–44.

MIX
Papier aus verantwortungsvollen Quellen
Paper from responsible sources
FSC® C105338

If you have any concerns about our products,
you can contact us on
ProductSafety@springernature.com

In case Publisher is established outside the EU,
the EU authorized representative is:
Springer Nature Customer Service Center GmbH
Europaplatz 3, 69115 Heidelberg, Germany

Printed by Libri Plureos GmbH
in Hamburg, Germany

Sustainability of External Imbalances